D1714765

HISTORY

OF THE EARLY SETTLEMENT

OF

BRIDGEWATER,

IN PLYMOUTH COUNTY,

MASSACHUSETTS,

INCLUDING AN EXTENSIVE

FAMILY REGISTER.

———◆———

By NAHUM MITCHELL.

———◆———

BOSTON:
PRINTED FOR THE AUTHOR.
BY KIDDER & WRIGHT, 32 CONGRESS STREET.
1840.

PREFACE.

More than twenty years ago I wrote a short account of the origin and first settlement of Bridgewater, which was published in the 7th vol. 2d series of the Collections of the Massachusetts Historical Society. In course of the requisite enquiries and researches it came in my way to acquire some distinct knowledge of the names and families of the original proprietors and early residents. To the stock of information thus obtained I subsequently, from time to time, as opportunity presented, made considerable accessions till my manuscripts became numerous and somewhat particular. This becoming generally known to my friends in the town and vicinity, applications were frequently made to me for information as to the genealogy of particular families; and at length desires were strongly expressed that what I had collected in this way should be published. These solicitations have been repeated and multiplied for several years past, and have sometimes been met on my part with partial promises of compliance. Many causes have concurred to delay a final determination, and it is not without much hesitation, and some reluctance, that I have come at last to the conclusion to publish.

While many seem to care but little, and think less, about their own descent, or from whom they are sprung: there is, nevertheless, in most of us a strong desire to know something of those who have preceded us on the same stage, and of the manner in which they have performed their respective parts. There is also an increasing attention to the biography of our fathers and the first planters of New England. Each one finds a pleasure in knowing something of his own particular ancestor, who first left the old world and set his foot on the new; and in being able to

trace accurately his own descent from him. But the elements of
such knowledge are fast fading away, and the difficulties of acquir-
ing it, already great, are constantly increasing.

The principal purpose of the present publication is to afford
the inhabitants of Bridgewater, and those who were born or early
resided there, wherever they may now live, some knowledge of
those from whom they are descended, and if possible to enable
them to see every link of the chain connecting them with their
first American ancestor.   There are but few instances where it
has been practicable to go beyond our own shores in search of
European ancestry ; and in many cases it has been difficult, and
often impossible, to ascertain the first ancestor even in our own
country.   This has been the case especially where new families
in later times came into the town from other distant places. And
where any individual, with or without his family, has removed
from the town, it has not generally been attempted to trace the
descent any further.   It would be not only difficult, but liable to
much error.   It must be observed also, that as most of this work
was prepared many years ago, the descent is not generally brought
down much within the present century, and that therefore the
younger families born since, and most of the numerous families, who have come into town within the last twenty or thirty
years, will not appear at all in the account here presented.   It
would have swelled the book, already large, to an unwieldy size.
Having brought it down within the knowledge and memories of
the present generation, they can continue it, each one for himself,
if disposed.   In giving dates, months and days are generally
omitted, but can be supplied when necessary by a recurrence to
the records.   The insertion of them would have occupied much
room without any adequate advantage.

Great as has been the labor of research and the care in com-
piling this publication, there will still appear in it great deficiencies.
No notice will be found of many individual members, and even
whole branches of many of the families. Some parents neglected altogether to have their children recorded.   Others had it
done partially, their younger children not being found on the
record.   These defects were to be supplied only, if at all, by
resorting to other sources, many of which were not always to be
relied on, and family traditions and recollections least of any.

All, who have been most conversant with investigations of this kind, have had frequent opportunity to test the truth of this last remark. These defects are much to be regretted as they often occasion an apparent breach in the line of descent.

The first part of this work contains a short history of the original purchases, locations, and early settlement of the town, embracing much of the former account, with such additions as were thought to be generally interesting. There is a great similarity in the general history and internal management of public affairs, in all our New England towns, the recital of which therefore, to most readers, would be but dull repetitions, and uninteresting details. Very little of this nature is here inserted; and individual biography also, always a delicate subject, and often leading to invidious distinctions, has been for the most part avoided. Facts have been principally regarded, and the most sedulously sought, both in the historical and genealogical department of the work.

The plan here adopted in presenting the genealogy of families may be objectionable; but after a full examination of all the methods, which have fallen under my notice, and after much consideration of the subject, this appeared the most simple and easy of comprehension. Every head of a family is numbered, the common ancestor being number one, expressed or understood, and after disposing of the daughters by showing who they married or otherwise, and such of the sons as had no families, or removed from town, then the first son who had a family is taken and numbered two, and then the next son, numbered three, and so on, proceeding with the family of each, as with that of the father; and this course is pursued through each generation. It will not therefore be expected always to find the son next in place immediately after the father, but he must be looked for often several numbers further on, and sometimes at a considerable distance. So in tracing back a descent the inner numbers within the parenthesis will direct where the father may be found, and being found the parenthesis there will direct where the grandfather will be found, and so on quite back to the common ancestor. A little use will render it familiar, and it is believed to be the simplest method, on the whole, which could have been adopted, especially in such numerous and extended familes as sometimes occur. It will often be

found that some of the children named are not afterwards noticed, which happens in cases only where no knowledge of them
could be obtained. Female ancestors, if inhabitants of the town,
will be ascertained generally by a recurrence to the respective
families to which they belong.

Much labor and care have been bestowed to render the work
correct, but after all it cannot be but many mistakes have been
made. The genealogy in particular is peculiarly liable to them.
In large families there are often the same christian names to be
found in the different branches, and one may be often mistaken
for another, and in this way, among others, no doubt much confusion may have happened. Probable as it is, however, that
many errors will be detected, it is still hoped those partial friends
who have been most solicitous for its publication, and who anti-
cipate both pleasure and profit from its perusal, may not be
wholly disappointed. Having labored for their gratification, it
will be gratifying in turn to find the labor has not been in vain.

In preparing the work the records of the town of Bridgewater,
and of its several parishes and churches, have been the first and
principal sources, whence the materials have been derived. The
old Colony and Plymouth county records have furnished also
valuable information. Judge Davis' improved edition of Morton's
New England Memorial, Farmer's Register, the Collections of
the Mass. Hist. Society, and various local histories have also been
advantageously consulted. But so many and so various have
been the sources, both public and private, from which information
and facts have been obtained, that it would be difficult, if recol-
lected, to enumerate them. The loss of all the early records of
Duxbury previous to 1654, which are said to have been burnt, is
greatly to be regretted, as it was the parent town of Bridgewater,
the first home and residence in this country of most of our fathers
and original settlers in this then Plantation. It may well be
supposed those records would have furnished us with much valuable information. The Colony records of births and deaths previous to 1647 are also lost, some of the first leaves by time or
accident having been destroyed, which to the antiquarian is a
deprivation much to be deplored.

Some remarks on the old and new style with regard to time
are here subjoined as not perhaps inappropriate.

There was formerly among all nations, as well christian as pagan, a great diversity not only with regard to the commencement of the year, some adopting the autumnal and some the vernal equinox, some the winter and some the summer solstice, and others other periods of the year; but also as to the epochs of the different eras, as the creation of the world, the deluge, the call of Abraham, and the departure of the Israelites out of Egypt, in sacred chronology, and the destruction of Troy, the building of Rome and other events, adopted among the ancient and eastern nations. There seemed to be no specific common standard.

When the computation of time by the Christian era commenced, which was about the year 527, the year was made to commence on the 25th of March, supposed to be the day of the Annunciation of the Incarnation of Christ. This, known now by the name of the Old Style, continued in England and throughout all her dominions till 1752, when by an Act of Parliament eleven days were stricken from the month of September, calling the 3d the 14th, and one day added to February every 4th year, herein conforming to other nations, several of whom on the continent had about 1582 adopted this computation, for the purpose of correcting the error occasioned by the precession of the equinoxes; and by the same act the 1st day of January instead of the 25th of March was also established as the commencement of the year. In the interim, between the time of its adoption by other nations and 1752, when England adopted it, double dating from January 1st to March 25th was frequently practised in England and her Colonies in order to correspond with the computation on the continent. Thus, for instance, February 8th 1720–21, or 1720–1 was substituted for simply February 8, 1721, the last number being the true date, and if omitted might occasion an error of a year. This has been called the Gregorian year (Pope Gregory 13th having established it in 1582), or New Style, and is very necessary to be known and observed by all when consulting ancient dates and records. In this work ancient dates are generally made to conform to the New Style, double dating being rejected.   **NAHUM MITCHELL.**

Boston, May 7th, 1840.

CORRECTIONS.

Page 37. To the Senators there mentioned may be added the names of Hon. William Baylies, Aaron Hobart, Abel Kingman, and John A. Shaw.

Page 73. 1702, last line but one, for Ensign Mitchell's, read Ensign Mitchell's *land*.

Page 93. James Alger (s. of Thomas 12.) m. Olive, D. of Joseph Snell, 1781, and not Mehitabel Briggs of Norton: this last was copied by mistake from Thomas 12, page 92.

Page 114. Joseph Beal 1752, finally removed to Plainfield, where he was Deacon, and the subject of the "Mountain Miller"; and Azariah was son of Jonathan 5, and not (of Samuel 1.).

Page 152. 8. Benjamin m. 1715, not 1755.

Page 157. Erskin, 2d line, Gain, not Gaius.

Page 161, *No.* 12. The title of *Judge* prefixed to Abner Fobes should be *General* in both instances; and Edward of Buckland had William, Sarah, and Abner who gra. Williams College 1820, and is preceptor of the Smith School in Boston, and writes his name *Forbes*. Also under No. 19, for *Phrez* read Perez.

Page 162. Susanna, D. of Eliab Fobes, m. a King, partner of Thomas Fobes in Boston, and afterwards a Lamphear, who afterwards m. Lucinda, D. of David Ames of Springfield; and Hannah m. a Tucker. Susanna who m. a Hooper, and Hannah who m. a Macomber, belonged to some other family probably.

Page 163, *No.* 2. Polly Ford m. Abner Fobes, son of Benjamin, and not *Judge* (or *General*) Abner.

Page 167. 10. Simeon of—the *of* should be within the parenthesis (s. of &c.

Page 169. James H. Gurney m. Delpha Stetson 1813, not Deborah Reed 1816.

Page 228. 7. Line 9, for New Bedford read Newport.

The reader is informed that besides the abbreviations noticed at the head of the Register, the initials only of the neighboring and adjoining towns are often used; as A. for Abington, C. for Canton, E. for Easton, H. for Halifax, M. for Middleborough, P. for Pembroke, R. for Raynham, S. or St. for Stoughton, T. for Taunton, &c.

HISTORY

OF THE

EARLY SETTLEMENT OF BRIDGEWATER.

ORIGINAL GRANTS, ADDITIONS, AND BOUNDARIES.

BRIDGEWATER was originally a plantation granted to Duxbury. When the township of Marshfield became a separate and distinct corporation, Duxbury, from which Marshfield had been principally taken, applied to the Old Colony court, at Plymouth, for a grant of common land, or, as they expressed it, "an extension to the westward," as a compensation for the great loss of territory they had thus sustained. We find in the records the following order of court relating to it:—

"March, 1642. It is concluded upon by the court, that the northerly bounds of Marshfield shall be, from the rock that is flat on the top, to the North River, by a north-west line from Green's Harbor Fresh, to the tree called Poole's, and to take in Edward Bonpass' land; provided that Duxbury have enlargement beyond Massachusetts' path, when they have viewed it."

Two years afterwards the court passed the following more explicit and definite order:—

"August, 1644. Upon the petition of Duxbury men it is

2

thought good by the court, that there be a view taken of the lands described by them, namely, twelve miles up into the woods from Plymouth bounds at Jones' River; and if it prove not prejudicial to the plantation to be erected at Teightaquid, (Titicut,) nor to the meadows of Plymouth at Winnytuckquett, (Winnetuxet,) it may be confirmed unto them; provided, also, the herring or alewife river at Namassachusett shall be equally between the two towns of Duxbury and Marshfield."

The next year the grant was made and confirmed to them as follows :—

" 1645. The inhabitants of the town of Duxbury are granted a competent proportion of lands about Saughtuchquett, (Satucket,) towards the west, for a plantation for them, and to have it four miles every way from the place where they shall set up their centre; provided it intrench not upon Winnytuckquett, formerly granted to Plymouth. And we have nominated Capt. Miles Standish, Mr. John Alden, George Soule, Constant Southworth, John Rogers, and William Brett, to be feofees in trust for the equal dividing and laying forth the said lands to the inhabitants."

How the town proceeded in dividing these lands among the inhabitants, or how, by whom, or when it was determined what residence or other circumstance should entitle any one to a share, no record informs us; we are only told in subsequent writings, and particularly in Gov. Hinckley's confirmation, that the inhabitants settled this matter "by an agreement among themselves." They were at first but fifty-four, each of whom had one share, and were denominated original proprietors. Their names are thus given on the town records :—

WILLIAM BRADFORD,	EDWARD HALL,
WILLIAM MERRICK,	NICHOLAS ROBBINS,
JOHN BRADFORD,	THOMAS HAYWARD,
ABRAHAM PIERCE,	Mr. RALPH PARTRIDGE,
JOHN ROGERS,	NATHANIEL WILLIS,
GEORGE PARTRIDGE,	JOHN WILLIS,
JOHN STARR,	THOMAS BONNEY,
Mr. WILLIAM COLLIER,	Mr. MILES STANDISH,
CHRISTOPHER WADSWORTH,	LOVE BREWSTER,

John Paybody,
William Paybody,
Francis Sprague,
William Bassett,
John Washburn,
John Washburn, Jr.,
John Ames,
Thomas Gannett,
William Brett,
Edmund Hunt,
William Clarke,
William Ford,
Mr. Constant Southwort ,
John Cary,
Edmund Weston,
Samuel Tompkins,
Edmund Chandler,
Moses Simmons,

John Irish,
Philip Delano,
Arthur Harris,
Mr. John Alden,
John Fobes,
Samuel Nash,
Abraham Sampson,
George Soule,
Experience Mitchell,
Henry Howland,
Henry Sampson,
John Brown,
John Haward,
Francis West,
William Tubbs,
James Lendall,
Samuel Eaton,
Solomon Leonard.

To these fifty-four shares the proprietors afterwards added two more, and granted one to the Rev. James Keith, of Scotland, their first minister, and the other to Deacon Samuel Edson, of Salem, who erected the first mill in the town, making in all fifty-six shares.

The grant of this plantation was considered by the court as preemptive merely, and as little more than an authority or right to purchase it of the natives: and accordingly Capt. Miles Standish, Samuel Nash, and Constant Southworth, were appointed to make the purchase, which service they performed as will appear by the following deed.

"Witness these presents, that I Ousamequin, Sachem of the country of Poconocket, have given, granted, enfeofed, and sold unto Miles Standish of Duxbury, Samuel Nash and Constant Southworth of Duxbury aforesaid, in behalf of all the townsmen of Duxbury aforesaid, a tract of land usually called Satucket, extending in the length and breadth thereof as followeth, that is to say, from the wear at Satucket seven miles due east, and from the said wear seven miles due west, and from the said wear seven miles due north, and from the said wear seven miles due south; the which tract the said Ousamequin hath given, granted, enfeofed, and sold unto the said Miles Standish, Samuel Nash, and Constant Southworth in the behalf of all the townsmen of Duxbury as aforesaid, with all the immunities, privileges, and profits whatsoever belonging to the said tract of land, with all and singular all woods, underwoods, lands, meadows, rivers, brooks, rivulets, &c., to have and to hold to the said Miles Standish, Samuel Nash, and Constant Southworth in behalf of all the townsmen of the town of Duxbury, to them and their heirs forever. In witness whereof I the said Ousamequin have hereunto set my hand this 23d of March, 1649.

JOHN BRADFORD,   ⎰ Witness the

WM. OTWAY (alias) PARKER. ⎱   mark of   OUSAMEQUIN.

———

In consideration of the aforesaid bargain and sale, we the said Miles Standish, Samuel Nash, and Constant Southworth do bind ourselves to pay unto the said Ousamequin for and in consideration of the said tract of land as followeth :—

  7 Coats, a yard and a half
      in a coat,
  9 Hatchets,   MILES STANDISH,
  8 Hoes,   SAMUEL NASH,
 20 Knives,   CONSTANT SOUTHWORTH.
  4 Moose Skins,
 10 Yards and a half of Cot-
      ton.

It appears the worthy old Sachem, when called on to execute his deed, endeavored to verify the testification he had offered, by affixing his mark or signature to the instrument as near as he could in the rude form and shape of his *hand.* The grantor, Ousamequin, or Ossamequin, sometimes also written Woosemequin, was the good old Massasoit himself, who in the latter part of his life had adopted that name. It was no uncommon occurrence for these Chiefs or Sachems to assume new names, which were probably appropriate and expressive of the principal exploits or events, which had occasioned the change.

This purchase and contract were said to have been made and executed on a small rocky hill, anciently called Sachem's Rock, a little south of Whitman's Mills, where the East Bridgewater manufacturing establishment now is, and near the house where

Seth Latham formerly lived, now owned and occupied by David Kingman. The Indian name of the place was Wonnocooto. The wear, which was made the central point of the purchase, was some distance above the present mills, directly back of the late Deacon William Harris' house on the south side, and of the late Deacon Barzillai Allen's house, on the north side of the river, near the ancient fording place and where the first mill on the river was erected. Traces of the old road are still visible on both sides of the river, and particularly on the south side. The mill was subsequently taken down, and a new one erected further down stream, near where the works now stand. The old wear was entirely overflowed by the new mill pond, and of course discontinued as a fishing place.

This river, and the pond from which it proceeds, now called Robins' Pond, as well as the whole neighborhood in which they are situated, still retain the name of Satucket, a contraction of Saughtuckquett, Saughquatuckquett, or Massaquatuckquett, as it was sometimes written. While the grant from the court was only four miles every way from the wear, equal to eight miles square, this purchase from the Indians was seven miles every way, equal to fourteen miles square. The reason of this difference is not very obvious, but probably the purchase was made thus extensive, with a view to additional contemplated grants, or perhaps to give themselves room to locate their four miles every way more advantageously, as they had the express privilege of setting up their centre, wherever they should deem it most conducive to their interest. For some reasons, however, now inexplicable, they neglected to fix and establish their centre, notwithstanding the frequent and pressing admonitions of the court. In 1656, eleven years after the grant of the plantation, and the same year in which Bridgewater was incorporated into a distinct township, a grant of three hundred acres had been made to Capt. Miles Standish, "with a competency of meadow to such a proportion of upland, lying and being at Satucket Pond; provided it came not within the court's grant of Bridgewater." Hence it became necessary that the centre of Bridgewater should be fixed, in order to ascertain its limits and extent. It was with this view, and for the purpose of running out and

locating Capt. Standish's grant, that the court had so urgently
called on Bridgewater to fix and "set up" their centre. In the
spring of 1658 the court ordered, "that the centre of the town
of Bridgewater should be set sometime this summer before
October court." Still it was not done. Again in 1660, Mr.
(William) Bradford, Constant Southworth and William Paybody
were "requested and appointed by court to lay out the land
granted to Capt. Standish, at Satucket Pond;" and at the same
time "Mr. Josiah Standish was appointed by the court to join
with any two, whom the town of Bridgewater should appoint,
to set out the bounds of their town, betwixt that time and the
last of July then next on the penalty of fifty shillings, which, if
forfeited, should be paid to those appointed to lay out Capt.
Standish's land, who were ordered to lay out their line." It
seems, however, the town still neglected it, as we find no record
of any committee appointed for the purpose, nor any other
movement or agency of the town concerning it. The only
record relating to the subject appears altogether historical,
without date, and quite out of place in the book where it is
inserted. It is as follows:—

"The town, receiving an order from the court at New Plymouth to fix and set up the centre of their town in order to the
laying out of Mr. *Alexander* Standish's land, joining to the
outside of said Bridgewater four mile line from the said centre;
which being, according to said order, done about the year 1659;
the centre being a small white oak tree of low stature about a
foot over, standing on high ground, on the westerly side of a
stony swamp and brook, about ten rods to the westerly side of
said brook on the southerly side of the highway; the said tree
being marked on the easterly side with an S, and on the westerly
side with a C, it being a mile and a quarter to the eastward of
said Bridgewater meeting house." This entry, without date, by
the place it occupies in the records, and the dates of entries
immediately before and after it, appears not to have been made
before 1695, thirty years or more after the work was performed;
and it is moreover incorrect as to the year in which it was done,
as the court's committee was not appointed till 1660, and Standish's land was not laid out till 1663. It is very evident also that

the court's committee at last, and not the town, fixed the centre, as the monumental tree bore the initials of Constant Southworth, (C. S.,) who no doubt was the efficient member of the court's committee in performing the work. Capt. Miles Standish had in the mean time deceased, and the land was laid out to his son Alexander. It cannot be doubted that Bridgewater was assenting to, if not aiding in this result, as there is neither record or tradition that any dissatisfaction was ever manifested by them. This centre is about a mile and a half west of the old *wear* at Satucket, and the place has ever since been called the *Centre*, and is near the house of Thomas Hayward, now aged eighty-six, whose father *Thomas*, and grandfather *Thomas* lived on the same spot, which will probably also descend to his son *Thomas* now living with him. They have successively owned and occupied it from its first settlement; about 140 years.

In 1658 the town petitioned the court for a grant of a large and valuable tract of swamp and meadow lands, called by the Indians *Hockomock*, lying on the west side of the town towards Taunton, (now Easton and Raynham,) as appears, as well as the reasons assigned for it, in the following order of court :—

" It is agreed by the court that there shall be chosen such as the town of Bridgewater shall think meet, that are no ways engaged in the new plantation of Duxbury, to view out the land and meadow desired by Bridgewater, and to consider of the reasonableness of their desire, in reference to the accommodating of some useful men in church and commonwealth, and make true report of the same to the court."—The same was afterwards granted, and confirmed to them as follows :—

" 1662. In answer to a petition preferred to the court by Bridgewater it is agreed, that the meadow land lying northward and westward from the *Centre* within the *seven* miles is granted them."

The centre here, as well as the seven miles, refers no doubt to the original purchase of the Indians, the new centre tree not having been then fixed and established. This will appear from the deposition of Constant Southworth and Samuel Nash, two of the purchasers, which had been taken about this time in consequence of some doubts entertained by the court probably, whether the purchase would include the lands prayed for by the town. It is here subjoined :—

"The town (Duxbury) appointed me with others to purchase of Ossamequin a tract of land about a place known to our town by the name of Satucket, which we did from the centre six miles, which *centre* is the *wear* in the river above expressed, and we paid him for it; the writing or deed expressed, under Ossamequin's own hand, was *seven* miles.—The oath of Constant Southworth, Lieut. Nash being also deposing to the same; in court held at Plymouth, June 10th, 1662."

A few years afterwards, July 5, 1667, the town made application to the court for a more general and extensive grant, whereupon "Capt. Bradford, (William) and the Treasurer, (Constant Southworth) were appointed to view the land desired by Bridgewater in reference to their enlargement according to their petition." The following grant was accordingly made :—

"An additional grant made by the court of New Plymouth to the town of Bridgewater, AD., 1688. In reference to a former grant upon a petition presented to the court by Bridgewater, desiring their enlargement may extend to where the *six* miles extends that they purchased of the Indians by order from the court; the court having granted unto the township of Bridgewater that they shall have six miles from the centre on the north side, if the line of the Colony hindereth not, and on the west side up to Taunton bounds, (now Raynham and Easton,) and on the south and south-easterly sides unto Titicut River, as far as the six miles extends; and so likewise on the east side; that is to say, the whole six miles from the centre east, west, north and south; always provided that grants of lands formerly made by the court be not molested. It is also ordered, that as to those lands that are between Bridgewater and Namasket, (Middleborough,) already granted, it shall be determined by the court unto what town they shall belong; and that the Indians be not molested, notwithstanding this enlargement; and that all these grants that are within the six miles shall belong to the township of Bridgewater; and that the said town of Bridgewater be careful to accommodate Mr. Keith, (their minister,) with a competency of land within the said grant of six miles."

This has been commonly called the "two miles additional grant," and the first one, the "old four mile grant." It would seem by this grant, as well as by Constant Southworth's deposition, as if it were understood by the court, that the original purchase of the Indians had been only *six* miles each way, and not *seven* as the fact was. This, however, was so expressed in conformity with the new centre, which had been established a mile or more farther west, leaving them not more than six miles on the west side, and on the east six miles would extend to, and even beyond the Major's purchase, so called, of which the great cedar swamp in Hanson constitutes a principal part, and which, being an earlier grant, was the utmost limit of their purchase on that side of the town. By this additional grant, therefore, they obtained their two miles on the north towards the Massachusetts Colony line, and a part on the south, but little, if any, on the east and west. On the south, the six miles would extend into the Indian settlement at Titicut, which the court reserved in all their subsequent adjacent grants. This reserve had been early made to the Titicut Indians, extending three miles on each side of the river. In the former account of Bridgewater, it is stated that the Indian plantation of Titicut was granted by Chickatabut, a Sachem of Massachusetts living at Neponsit. This is probably incorrect, as he died in 1633, of the small pox; and Titicut, as we have already seen, was not established till after 1644, when it was spoken of as "being about to be erected." If granted at all, therefore, it must have been done by his son Josias Chickatabut or Wampatuck, who lived at Mattakeset, or Pembroke, and who went to the Mohawk country after 1666, and there died, and whose son Josiah gave a deed of confirmation of the Titicut purchase to Bridgewater in 1686, who had a son Jeremy, whose son, Charles Josiah, was the last of the race. If it was ever granted, or was anything more than a reserve, the limits were probably not very accurately defined; as the court in their grants round about it required the grantees not to encroach or locate their lands "too near to Titicut," or to "molest the Indians." There seems to have been some uncertainty as to the precise limits of the respective jurisdictions of Massasoit and Chickatabut. We find on record the

3

deposition of five Indians taken before Increase Nowell, John
Eliot, and John Hoaré in 1650, as follows :—" We do all affirm,
that Chickatabut's bounds did extend from Nishamagoguanett,
near Duxbury mill, to Titicut, near Taunton, and to Nunckata-
teset, (a pond in Bridgewater,) and from thence in a straight
line to Wanamampuke, (Whiting's Pond in Wrentham,) which
is the head of Charles River, this they do all solemnly affirm."
Notwithstanding this, Massasoit as we have seen, sold and conveyed the whole of the eight mile square, containing the principal part of Bridgewater, and a part of Abington and Pembroke,
all within the above limits, to Duxbury ; which corroborates a
remark of Prince in his chronology, that "these Massachusetts
Sachems were not completely independent, but acknowledged a
degree of subjection to Massasoit."   This Indian testimony
favors the plea of Massachusetts, in the case pending between
us and Rhode Island with regard to the line of jurisdiction, in
which the great Wrentham Pond is claimed to be the southernmost part of Charles River, which claim is contested by Rhode
Island.   All the land on the north side of Titicut River was
within the six miles, and Bridgewater were allowed afterwards
to purchase it, and Nicholas Byram, Samuel Edson, and William
Brett were appointed by the court for that purpose ; and the
deed they procured is as follows :—

"This deed, made November 20th, AD. 1672, witnesseth, that
I, Pomponoho, alias Peter, an Indian, living at Titicut, in the
colony of New Plymouth, in New England, have sold for the
full sum of sixteen pounds, viz., six pounds of current money
of New England, and ten pounds in good merchantable corn,
as by bill appeareth, all the lands lying on the north side of
Titicut River within the bounds of Bridgewater, what lands
were mine, or were either my father's or grandfather's, or any
otherwise conferred on me, excepting those lands expressed as
follows, viz:—one hundred acres of land lying up the river to
the eastward of small brook, given to an Indian called Charles,
my brother-in-law, and a certain parcel of land lying against
the wear, and bounded by the landing place, running to the
head of my field, containing about ten acres at the utmost, I
say, I, the abovesaid Pomponoho, alias Peter, have bargained,

sold, and by these presents do bargain, and sell for myself, my heirs and assigns forever, unto Nicholas Byram, sen., Samuel Edson, sen., and William Brett, sen., in and for the use of the townsmen of Bridgewater, joint purchasers with them, which persons above mentioned were ordered by the court to make purchase of those lands, as by court record appears, I say I have sold all these lands, with every part thereof, and all the immunities and privileges belonging thereunto to them, their heirs and assigns forever, the same quietly and peaceably to possess, without the lawful let, interruption, or molestation of me, the abovesaid Pomponoho, alias Peter, or other persons whatsoever lawfully claiming by, from, or under me, them, or any of them. In witness whereof I have here set to my hand and seal.   his

Read, sealed, and delivered   POMPONOHO,   (P.)   ••
in presence of us,   mark.   ••
JOSEPH HAYWARD,
JOHN CARY, Sen."

Acknowledged before JOSIAH WINSLOW, Gov., Feb. 20, 1676.

Recorded by NATHANIEL CLARK, Secretary, March, 1685.

The two reserved lots, in the above grant, were afterwards purchased by individuals in the town. Thus all the lands within the most extensive limits of the town appear to have been justly and fairly purchased of the Indians; and we have the above named Governor Winslow's attestation on record, that this was the case in all the towns in the Old Colony of Plymouth.

In the year 1685, the court of assistants were empowered to examine, allow, and confirm from time to time all claims and titles to land formerly granted either to towns or individuals by the general court, and, when allowed, they were to "pass the seal of the Government for confirmation." In pursuance of this order, all the grants made to Bridgewater as above stated and described, were confirmed by the following deed under the hand of Governor Hinckley, and the seal of the Government.

" At his Majesty's Court of Assistants, held at Plymouth, the 6th of March, AD. 1685–6.

To all to whom these presents shall come, Thomas Hinckley,

Esq., Governor of his Majesty's Colony of New Plymouth, in New England, sendeth greeting.—Whereas, at his Majesty's general court held at Plymouth the 4th of June 1685, it was ordered and enacted, that the court of assistants be from time to time a committee empowered to examine, allow, and confirm all such claims and titles to lands, which were formerly granted or allowed by the general court, either to townships or particular persons; which being allowed by the said committee, shall pass the seal of the Government for further confirmation thereof; and forasmuch as it hath been made to appear to the said court of assistants now sitting at Plymouth, the first Tuesday in March, 1685–6, that a certain tract of land was granted by William Bradford, Esq., and his associates assembled in court in the year of our Lord 1645, unto the inhabitants of the town of Duxbury, (a competent proportion of lands,) about a place called by the Indians Massaquatucket, for a plantation for them the inhabitants of Duxbury, and that they shall have it four miles every way from the centre; the inhabitants of Duxbury being fifty-six in number, by agreement among themselves, every one were to have equal shares, who, by the approbation and appointment of his Majesty's honored court in New Plymouth 1645, did employ Mr. Constant Southworth, with some others, to purchase the above mentioned tract of land of Ossamequin, chief Sachem of the Poconocket country, which being done, and now inhabited by many of the proprietors, is now called Bridgewater, and all such privileges allowed to them as the court allows or grants to other townships; and having set up their centre, his Majesty's court held at Plymouth 1668, did grant to Bridgewater six miles from the centre on all four sides, where former grants made by the court hindereth not, as appears in court records, and is bounded out by the agents of each respective town adjoining, as appears by their hands to their agreement, and assented to and acknowledged before the Governor and his associates, sitting in his Majesty's court held at Plymouth, the 2d of March 1685–6, the bounds of the whole township being settled between them and other towns adjoining, are as followeth:—The bounds betwixt Bridgewater and Taunton being a heap of stones lying four miles west from

the centre, and running north from station to station, till it meet
with the line of the colonies; and from said heap of stones
south, to a heap of stones lying to the west of Unketest Pond,
and from thence south-east unto a great white oak being marked
with a T for Taunton, and on the north side with a B for
Bridgewater; and so from station to station till it come to the
great river on the westward side of a spot of meadow, according to the agreement of the agents of both towns. And the
bounds between Middleborough and Bridgewater is the great
river, until it come to the north side of Mr. Standish's land,
lying on the mouth of Winnetuxit river, and so from the north
side of said Standish's land until it meet with the eastermost
line of Bridgewater, being a heap of stones four miles from the
centre, which is the bounds between them and the Major's
purchase, running from said heap of stones south and by west
half a point westerly, until it meet with said Standish's land,
&c., and from the aforesaid heap of stones running north north-
east from station to station to four white oaks, the easternmost
marked on all four sides, and so from station to station until it
meet with the north line. The north bounds being six miles
from the centre, to a company of small trees marked, being to
the northward of a great rock, and from the aforesaid marked
trees running east until it meet with the abovesaid north-east
line, and from the aforementioned marked trees running west
till it meet with the line of the colonies, and with the line of the
colonies till it meet with the westerly line and Taunton (now
Easton) bounds. All which lands, both upland and meadow,
swamps, cedar swamps, ponds, rivers, brooks, springs, wood,
underwood, and all herbage, feedings, minerals, with all rights,
liberties, privileges, and appurtenances thereto belonging, unto
the appropriated inhabitants and other proprietors, though not
inhabitants of the said town of Bridgewater, according to each
person's several and respective title or interest therein, excepting two-fifth parts of the royal mine, one fifth part to his royal
Majesty, and the other fifth part to the President and Council.
To have and to hold unto the said town and proprietors respectively, to their and every of their heirs and assigns forever,
according to the tenor of our charter or letters patent granted

by the honorable council at Plymouth, in the county of Devon, for the planting, ordering, and governing of New England, derivatory from his Majesty King James the first of happy memory; and in testimony hereof, doth allow the public seal of the Government to be affixed thereunto for the further confirmation thereof.   THOMAS HINCKLEY, Governor.   ●●
                                                                                                     ●●
Attest NATHANIEL CLARK, Secretary.

A confirmation of the original purchase made of Ossamequin was also obtained about the same time, as follows :—

"To all christian people to whom these presents shall come, Josiah Wampatuck sendeth, greeting.—Know ye, that I Josiah aforesaid, for and in consideration of ten pounds in money to me in hand paid, and one hundred acres of land lying on the upper end of Poor Meadow, on the lower side of a foot path that goeth to Scituate, lying on both sides of the river, doth confirm, establish, and ratify unto Samuel Edson, sen., Ensign John Haward, and John Willis, sen., in behalf of the purchasers and town of Bridgewater in New Plymouth Colony in New England, and to their heirs, executors, administrators, and assigns forever, all that whole tract of land lying northward of the south four mile line of Bridgewater, which Ossamequin, Sachem of the Poconocket country, by the consent and approbation of his Majesty's general court held at Plymouth, in New England, in the year 1645, sold to the inhabitants of Duxbury, as appears by deed under Ossamequin's hand to Capt. Miles Standish, Mr. Constant Southworth, and Samuel Nash, as agents for the town of Duxbury. I, the abovesaid Josiah do ratify and confirm the above said sale of Ossamequin's, and bargain of lands belonging to Bridgewater, as uplands, swamps, meadows, brooks, rivers, ponds, timber, underwood, herbage, mines, with all commodities, benefits, privileges, immunities and appurtenances whatever therein contained. I the abovesaid Josiah also do ratify, establish, and confirm, and forever make over all my right, title, and interest in the above mentioned land from me, my heirs, executors and assigns, unto the abovesaid Samuel Edson, John Haward, and John Willis, agents for the town of Bridgewater, their heirs, executors, administrators and assigns forever; to have and to hold, occupy and enjoy, as their proper right, forever, without any claim, title, interest or molestation to be made by me, my heirs, executors, or assigns, or any other person or persons to any part or parcel thereof, in, by, or under me any way appertaining, and do by these presents bind myself, and heirs, and executors, and assigns, to maintain and defend the above mentioned sale of lands against any other Indian or Indians, that shall make any claim or title to any part or parcel thereof. In witness whereof, I have set to my hand and seal this twenty-third day of December, and in the second year of the reign of our Sovereign Lord King James II, AD. one thousand six hundred and eighty-six.

The mark of JOSIAH WAMPATUCK. ∧

Signed, sealed, and delivered
   in presence of us :
      JOHN SOULE,
      JOSEPH BARSTOW,
      SAMUEL TINSLEY.

Acknowledged before
    WILLIAM BRADFORD,
      Deputy Governor.
  December 23d, 1686.

Recorded p. 425, Great Book of Records.
          Pr. SAMUEL SPRAGUE, Recorder.

The one hundred acres mentioned in the above confirmation were afterwards re-purchased by individuals in the town. From this deed it appears the greatest part of the town was twice purchased of the Indians, once of Massasoit, and again of Wampatuck, and a valuable consideration paid each time.

By the boundaries of the town, as described in Governor Hinckley's deed of confirmation, it is evident a gore of land was still left on the north between Bridgewater and the line of the colonies, commencing at the point where the six mile line met the colony line towards the north-west corner of the town, and thence extending easterly to the north-east corner of the town, where the distance to the colony line is considerable. The westerly and narrow end of this gore, having been purchased of the Government after the union of the colonies, by Daniel Howard and Robert Howard, was on the petition of the selectmen of the town, annexed to Bridgewater October 15th, 1730.

These several grants and additions constituted all the territory ever belonging to Bridgewater in its greatest extent. The greatest part of Abington, and what is now Hanson, at that period, belonged to Bridgewater, which must then have contained about ninety-six square miles. In this situation, and with these extensive territorial dimensions the town remained, without change or diminution, till June 10, 1712, when Abington was incorporated.

When the Abington petitioners first applied for an act of incorporation, July 4, 1706, they denominated themselves "certain inhabitants of the east part of the town of Bridgewater, and proprietors of a certain tract of land between the towns of Weymouth, Hingham, Scituate, and Bridgewater;" and when the act was finally passed in 1712, the boundaries were thus described. "On the north with the line of the colonies of the Massachusetts Bay and Plymouth,—on the east upon the town of Scituate,—on the south with the line that is the southerly bounds of land of John Cushing, Esq., and of John Cushing, Jr., Esq.,—thence on the south-westerly side by certain bounds, which the town of Bridgewater have set and prefixed, to Beaver Brook,—and on the west with the said brook, until it comes to the extent of Bridgewater northward: together with a small gore of land lying between the said town of Bridgewater and the said line of the colonies: the town of Bridgewater having signified their consent thereto." By the plain and express language of the statute, the whole gore is included in Abington; but for some reasons now unknown, the "Howard Farms" seem, as the selectmen of Bridgewater in their petition stated, to have been considered as "belonging to no town," till they were annexed to Bridgewater in 1730.

Another considerable tract on the east part of the town was annexed to Pembroke June 7, 1754, and now constitutes the greater part of Hanson. The old Bridgewater line was as far east as the west line of the farm formerly owned and occupied by the late Rev. Dr. Hitchcock. These two are the only instances in which any considerable portions of the town have been annexed to other corporations. Questions and disputes as to boundaries were formerly frequently arising between this and neighboring towns. The latest occurred with Middleborough, which was finally settled by court June 8, 1716, when the great river was constituted the boundary between them. This seems to have been done in pursuance of the express power which the court had reserved to itself in the "two mile additional grant."

The boundaries of the town as finally settled, may be thus described :—On the east it is bounded by Halifax and Hanson ; on the north by Abington, Randolph, and Stoughton ; on the west by Easton and Raynham ; and on the south by Middleborough, Titicut river there constituting the boundary. It is the north-west town in the county of Plymouth, adjoining the county of Norfolk, or Old Colony line on the north, and the county of Bristol on the west. Its dimensions may be estimated at about twelve miles by six, and as containing at least seventy square miles. The centre of the town is about twenty-six miles from Boston, twenty from Plymouth, and ten from Taunton.

SETTLEMENT, DIVISIONS, AND PROPRIETORS.

BRIDGEWATER was the first interior settlement in the Old Colony. The grant of the plantation, as we have seen, was made in 1645, but the actual settlement was not commenced till after 1650. Each settler had at first a grant of a house lot of six acres on the town river, then called Nuckatest or Nuncketetest, an Indian name in close affinity with that of the pond from which it flows, now called Nippenicket, formerly written Neapnucket or Neapnuncket. The first lots were taken up in West Bridgewater, and the first houses built, and first improvements made there ; and the settlement was called after the name of the river, Nuncketest, or Nunckety, sometimes Unkety. These Indian names were variously written in the early records and documents. We have seen that in Governor Hinckley's deed of confirmation, the pond itself is called Unketest. The plantation bore the more general appellation of Satucket. These house lots were contiguous, and the settlement compact, with a view to mutual aid when common protection and defence against the Indians should be required, and extended on each side of

4

the river, from where Seth Lothrop lately lived, down to Johnson's four corners, a little easterly of where Capt. Rider now lives. The proprietors or original purchasers, whose names have already been given were fifty-four in number, and were all inhabitants of Duxbury, excepting William Bradford, about whom there are some doubts. He is supposed to have been the son of the Governor and afterwards Deputy Governor. He lived in Kingston, near the line of Duxbury, and owned land in Duxbury, and, as it is said, attended meeting there. He was about twenty years old when the grant was made, but before the actual settlement of it, he was over twenty-six, and when the town was incorporated was over thirty. These were probably house holders, or heads of families; many of them were so certainly, and probably all. Deacon Samuel Edson, from Salem, was an early settler in the new plantation, and built the first mill in the place; and the Rev. James Keith, from Scotland, was their first minister; and the proprietors gave to each of them one share, making the whole number of shares fifty-six, as has been before stated. Of these proprietors, not more than one-third actually removed and became inhabitants of the new plantation. The rest from time to time conveyed their shares to their sons, or sold them to others, who became residents there. The following original purchasers became permanent settlers, viz:—

THOMAS HAYWARD,	JOHN CARY,
NATHANIEL WILLIS,	SAMUEL TOMPKINS,
JOHN WILLIS,	ARTHUR HARRIS,
WILLIAM BASSETT,	JOHN FOBES,
JOHN WASHBURN,	EXPERIENCE MITCHELL,
JOHN WASHBURN, Jr.,	JOHN HAWARD,
JOHN AMES,	SOLOMON LEONARD,
THOMAS GANNETT,	Mr. JAMES KEITH,
WILLIAM BRETT,	Dea. SAMUEL EDSON.

None of these, except Bassett and Mitchell, were among the Plymouth "Old Comers" or Forefathers, who arrived in the three first ships, viz:—the May Flower, the Fortune, and the Ann; nor is it ascertained at what time they came over; but it is certain they were here very early. The names of most of them appear on the colony records soon after 1630. In 1629 thirty-five of the Leyden people, with their families, arrived at Plymouth: and in 1630, sixty more came. Many of the Bridgewater proprietors were doubtless among these.

The plantation was incorporated into a separate and distinct town in June 1656, by the following concise and laconic order of court, agreeably to the usage of those early times:—

"Ordered, that henceforth Duxbury New Plantation be allowed to be a township of itself, distinct from Duxbury, and to be called by the name of Bridgewater; provided that all public rates be borne by them in equal proportions:" and the same year this proportion was settled by the court, by the following order:—"The court have agreed that for the present year the town of Bridgewater is to bear one part of three with Duxbury, of their proportion of the country rates for the officers' wages and other public charges." And by a tax assessed about that time, it appears that Duxbury accordingly paid £6, 0, 9, and Bridgewater £2, 0, 3. The plantation in some early records had been called Bridgewater before its incorporation. The name was probably adopted from fancy, as many of the names of towns in the vicinity were, none of the settlers here, as we can ascertain, having come from Bridgewater, in England. From this period the town took its place with others in the public records, while its own have also been generally well preserved, which will render its subsequent history more authentic. John Cary was chosen Constable 1656, the first officer ever chosen in town, and the only one in that year, as it was not incorporated in season for the spring elections. In May, 1657, the town officers were John Willis, Deputy; Lawrence Willis, Grand Juror; Samuel Tompkins, Constable; Arthur Harris and John Haward, Surveyors of highways. The first freemen were

WILLIAM BRETT,	Ens. JOSIAH STANDISH,
WILLIAM BASSETT,	JOHN CARY,
THOMAS HAYWARD,	LAWRENCE WILLIS,-
JOHN WILLIS,	THOMAS HAYWARD, Jr.,
SAMUEL TOMPKINS,	ARTHUR HARRIS.

These had taken the Freeman's oath probably before the incorporation of the plantation. In 1657 we find among the freemen of Bridgewater, these additional names, viz :—

SAMUEL EDSON,   MARK LATHROP,
FRANCIS GODFREY,   WILLIAM SNOW,
JOHN AMES,   JOHN HAWARD.
GUIDO BAYLEY,

These names assist us in ascertaining who were the first settlers in the place. Some of them, as Standish, Lawrence Willis, Godfrey, Bayley, Lathrop, and Snow, were not original proprietors, but most of them came from Duxbury, and had afterwards probably became purchasers. Josiah Standish was the second son of Capt. Miles Standish, and had his father's share perhaps; he married Sarah, daughter of Samuel Allen, of Braintree, and settled here, but after a few years returned again to Duxbury. Besides these and a few others from Duxbury, as Mitchell, Alden, and Leonard; there soon came in several families from the adjoining towns in Massachusetts, as Packard, Byram, Allen, Whitman, Shaw, Bacon, Kingman, Conant, Hooper, Hudson, Lazell, Dunbar, Hill, Perkins, Johnson, Leach, and others, as also Field from Providence, Alger from Taunton, Snell from England, Latham from Marshfield, and others from different parts of the country. We have been told that, before the two colonies of Plymouth and Massachusetts were united into one Province in 1691, and long after, a distinction was kept up in the town between the old Duxbury settlers and the Massachusetts settlers, each viewing the other, in some measure, as a separate race or clan. We never learnt, however, that it produced any unkindness or even unsocial habits, feelings of friendship and mutual courtesy having been generally observed and cherished among them.

From the west the settlements extended first into the south part of the town, towards the great pond on the road to Taunton, with which place they held their principal intercourse, where was the nearest corn mill, and whither also they were accustomed to go frequently on foot, with their grists on their backs.

Their proprietary concerns were managed in town meetings in the same way their other town affairs were conducted, and all the records and votes respecting their lands were entered by the town clerk in the town books. This was owing no doubt to the fact, that every inhabitant was at first a purchaser or proprietor. The first separate or distinct meeting held by the proprietors, of which we find any account, was July 9, 1672, at which they chose a large committee "to consider the manner to be adopted in future for laying out lands, and to report in October next;" and the same year application was made to court stating, that "some of the committee formerly appointed for laying out their lands, were dead, and others taken off by other occasions, and praying that they might depute some among themselves for that purpose," and the court "declared their willingness that they might so do, and in case the proprietors shall agree upon any thing respecting their lands, that the clerk of the town shall commit such their conclusions to the records of the town;" and consequently the clerk of the town was also generally clerk of the proprietors. The *town* also in 1674 " ordered that a new book for the *recording of lands* should be procured, and a committee appointed to see that the records were made and transcribed correctly, and on good evidence." Again in June 14, 1695. They "agreed that the town clerk should record all, that was of general concern to the purchasers, in their new book, namely, the preface, table, list of their names, court grants, several divisions of lands granted to be laid out by them, their general deeds of the Indians, and confirmations from the court, and lists of the names of the proprietors of all their land within their township, and to page said book. Chose also Lieut. Hayward and John Field to have some oversight of the recording of lands for the purchasers and proprietors." Hence it is that the same records sometimes appear on different books, having been transcribed agreeably to the aforesaid orders.

The outermost mile of the " old original four mile grant," that is, one mile in width all round on the outside of the purchase, was laid out in 1683 into four great divisions, one on each side of the town, and the shares in each were drawn by lot, by the original fifty-six proprietors, namely seventeen on the north, fifteen on the east, fourteen on the west, and ten on the south; and the proprietors in each division were authorised to lay out their lands among themselves in such manner as they saw fit. The following extract with regard to this proceeding are taken from the town records :—

"The purchasers being generally met together upon this 24th of December, 1683, it was then proposed to them the laying out of great divisions of land to every purchaser round the outside of the town in the four miles, or fourth mile from the centre; and it was to be done by casting of lots for them. After some agitation about it silence was desired, and this proposition was publicly and openly there propounded twice, and after proposal they were desired to declare their assent to it by their usual way of holding up their hands, which was done, and the major part by many, did declare their assent to it. The order of this division of land is, that it should be laid out a mile inward in breadth from the four miles square from the centre, and whatsoever purchaser in Bridgewater having any former lots of land laid out within this fourth mile should not be molested by this great division. Further, the order of this great division is, that there should be ten on the south side of the town, and fourteen on the west, and seventeen on the north, and fifteen on the east side; and every purchaser was to have his division of land as it fell to him by lot, the lots being drawn. Their names and lots are in order as followeth.

Those, whose lots fell out on the north, were to begin at the west at the line betwixt Taunton (now Easton) and Bridgewater, and to run seven miles east in length, and one mile in breadth from the north line southward.

Names of the Men of the North.

ROBERT LATHAM,	Mr. NATHANIEL WILLIS,
NICHOLAS BYRAM, } 2 lots. NICHOLAS BYRAM,	SAMUEL PACKARD,
	MARK LATHROP,
JOSEPH ALDEN,	GUIDO BAYLEY,
WILLIAM BASSETT,	SAMUEL EDSON, JR.,
JOHN CARY,	GILES LEACH,
JOSEPH HAYWARD,	JOSEPH WADSWORTH,

Widow (of Sam'l.) Wads-   Widow (of John) Robbins,
  worth,   —17 lots.———"
John Willis, Jr.,

"And from the extent of this seven miles of those on the
north, those on the east are to begin on the north line, and to
run a line due south till it meets with Mr. Alexander Standish's
land, or Middleborough (now Halifax) bounds. All the lands
lying easterly betwixt the above said line so run, and the line
that was run by the agents of Bridgewater and Middleborough,
(now Halifax,) and the Major's purchase, (now Hanson,) be-
longeth to these fifteen men whose names and lots as they fell
out are in order as followeth :—

The names of the Men on the East.

Nicholas Byram, Jr.,   John Ames,
John Hayward,   Nathaniel Hayward,
Ens. (John) Haward,   John Washburn, ⎱ 2 lots.
George Turner,   John Washburn, ⎰
Mr. (James) Keith,   Widow (Samuel,) Wads-
Samuel Packard,   worth,
Benjamin Willis,   Nathaniel Packard.
Josiah Edson,   —15 lots.———"
Edward Fobes,

"And those fourteen on the west are to begin at the end of
the mile in breadth at the north end, and to run along in the
line betwixt Taunton, (now Easton and Raynham,) and Bridgewater, till it meet with a cove in the pond that cuts the line
betwixt Taunton, (now Raynham,) and Bridgewater ; and are to
have a mile in breadth inward from the west line, as those have
upon the north line, except it be against the great meadow.

Their Lots and Names are as followeth :—

Thomas Whitman,   Dea. John Willis,
Samuel Allen,   John Washburn,
William Brett,   Joseph Wadswoth,
Jonathan Hill,   Widow Faxon, (formerly w.
Thomas Snell,   of Thomas Gannett,)

WILLIAM SNOW,   ELISHA HAYWARD,
WILLIAM ORCUTT,   Dea. SAMUEL EDSON."
JOSEPH BASSETT,

"And the ten on the south are to begin at Taunton, (now Raynham,) line, and to run east till it meet with the great river for length, and is to be a mile in breadth inward, as it is on the north.

Their Names and Lots, as they were drawn forth, are as followeth :—

ISAAC HARRIS,   JOHN WASHBURN,
JOHN WHITMAN,   JOSEPH EDSON,
Lt. (THOMAS) HAYWARD,   JAMES CARY,
SAMUEL TOMPKINS,   JOHN FIELD.
SAMUEL LEONARD,   —ten in all.——"
LAWRENCE WILLIS,

Of these persons, whose names are contained in these four divisions, it appears, that John Washburn at this time owned four lots, and of course, four proprietary shares, Nicholas Byram two, Joseph Wadsworth two, Widow Wadsworth two, and Samuel Packard two; and all the rest one share each. They were all inhabitants of the town except the Wadsworths, who retained their shares much longer than any of the non-residents, and were the last of the Duxbury proprietors to relinquish them. At this period forty-nine persons owned the entire original grant.

The inner three miles were never allotted, but still remained in common, as the whole had done before, to be occasionally laid out as their interest or necessities might require. When any of the common lands were appropriated and allowed to be taken up by individuals, it was done by what they called a division or grant. These grants were from time to time made of a certain number of acres to a share, which each proprietor was entitled to pitch and to have laid out to him by the locating committee; which, being done and recorded on the proprietors' books, created a perfect title in such proprietor. Any person, not a proprietor, finding common land, might purchase a right of any proprietor, who had not taken up his full quantity upon any of the existing grants, and procure to himself a title to it in the same way. Instances of common land having been found and thus taken up, have occurred even down to the present time. The following is a table of these grants in the order of time in which they were made, next after the house lots of six acres already mentioned :—

1651—20 acres,		1693—10 acres,
1654—20 "		Februa- ry 19th, 1695—10 "
" —2½ 1st div. of meadow,		March 27th, 1699—10 "
1657—50 acres,		
" — 2d. div. of meadow,		1700—the share land,
1665—3d division of meadow,		1712—10 " 1717—10 " 1724—20 "
1665—10 acres,		Februa- ry 7th, 1726—20 "
1666—20 "		
1672—50 "		May 31, 1731—10 "
1683—10 "		Mar. 14, 1739—10 "
1683—cedar swamp,		Jan. 28, 1745—10 "
1686—10, swamp or meadow land,		May 12, 1746—10 "
		Apl. 11, 1748—10 "
1686—40 wood land,		Apl. 17, 1749—10 "
March 23d. 1687—50 "		Februa- ry 11th, 1751—10 "
Februa- ry 11th, 1690—10 "		Apl. 14, 1755—10 "

All the lands obtained by the additional two mile grant, or six miles from the centre every way, including the lands at Titicut, contained in the deed from Pomponoho, were divided into lots and drawn by the proprietors in 1783. They were subdivided in the first place into four parcels or tracts, three on the north and one on the south. That on the south was called "the Titicut purchase." Those on the north were variously designated: the three miles at the west end were called the "West Shares;" the next, or middle division, was called the "easterly three miles;" and the most easterly one was called the "young men's shares." These divisions all appear on the proprietors' records, with the names of those to whom the lots respectively fell. The Titicut purchase was shared and divided agreeably to the following vote 1675. "All the householders and male children twenty years old and upwards, now found to

5

be sixty-four in number, shall be proprietors and full purchasers in the lands at Titicut, which had been bought of the Indians;" but the division was not actually made, and the lots drawn, till some years afterwards, viz: 1685, and consisted of two divisions of lots called the great lots and the little lots. Those who had the young men's shares above mentioned, were such as were twenty-one years of age and upward, and had no interest in any other lands, who were Samuel Lathrop, Mark Lathrop, Jr., Edward Lathrop, James Haward, Jonathan Haward, Nathaniel Brett, Jonathan Cary, Isaac Alden, John Whitman, John Aldridge, Jonathan Hill, Samuel Shiverick, William Snow, Jr., Benjamin Willis, Richard Holt, Solomon Leonard, James Latham, Samuel Leach, Joseph Snow, Samuel Allen, Jr.—The following is an early list of the proprietors, with the number of shares each owned, viz:—

	No. of Shares.		No. of Shares.
NICHOLAS BYRAM,	5	MARK LATHROP,	1
JOHN WASHBURN,	4	PETER THATCHER,	1
SAMUEL EDSON,	3	GEORGE PARTRIDGE,	1
SAMUEL PACKARD,	2	NATHANIEL WILLIS,	1
THOMAS HAYWARD,	2	Mr. JAMES KEITH,	1
THOMAS WHITMAN,	2	GEORGE TURNER,	1
SAMUEL WADSWORTH,	2	JOHN FIELD,	1
JOSEPH WADSWORTH,	2	MICHAEL BACON,	1
JOHN CARY,	1	MATTHEW GANNETT,	1
JOHN HAWARD,	1	SAMUEL TOMPKINS,	1
JOHN HAYWARD,	1	THOMAS HAYWARD, Jr.,	1
WILLIAM BRETT,	1	WILLIAM BASSETT,	1
JOHN WILLIS,	1	JOSEPH BASSETT,	1
NATHANIEL HAYWARD,	1	SOLOMON LEONARD,	1
LAWRENCE WILLIS, } JOHN WILLIS, Jr., }	1	JOHN ROBBINS,	1
		JOSEPH ALDEN,	1
GILES LEACH,	1	THOMAS SNELL,	1
JOHN AMES,	1	SAMUEL ALLEN,	1
JOHN CARY, Jr.,	1	ROBERT LATHAM,	1
EDWARD FOBES,	1	WILLIAM ORCUTT,	1
WILLIAM SNOW,	1	BENJAMIN WILLIS,	1
GUIDO BAILEY,	1	Total, 56 shares.	

All these, except the Wadsworths, Thatcher, Gannett, and Partridge, were residents in the town at this period, which was as early at least as 1680. But shares were frequently bought and sold, and the proprietors of course often changing.

The Town Clerks have been
John Cary from   1656 to 1681.
Thomas Hayward, Esq., appears
   to have made the entries in   1682 & 1683.
Samuel Allen was Clerk from   1783 to 1702.
Nathaniel Brett   "   "   1702 to 1736.
Nathaniel Brett, Jr. "   "   1736 to 1779, excepting that
Col. Josiah Edson was Clerk a
   few years previous to   1745.
Capt. Eliakim Howard   "   "   1779 to 1822, when the town
   was divided.

The first military officers were Josiah Standish, Lieutenant, 1660, who soon after returned to Duxbury, and Thomas Hayward, Jr., Lieutenant; and John Haward, Ensign, appointed 1664. And in 1689 they were promoted, and Samuel Packard appointed Ensign.—Deacon John Willis was appointed to administer oaths, &c., in 1660, but Captain Thomas Hayward, Jr., was the first Magistrate in town, and one of the Governor's Council or Assistants 1690, and also a Judge of the courts: he was killed by a fall from his horse, August 15, 1698, while on a journey to Marshfield on business.—Elihu Brett was the next Magistrate, and he was also appointed a Judge of the courts 1700; he died suddenly in his chair January 12th, 1712.

The first House of Representatives or Deputies in the Old Plymouth Colony convened in 1639. From June 3, 1656, the date of the incorporation of the town, to the year 1691 inclusive, when the two colonies were united into one province, the Representatives from Bridgewater to the general court at Plymouth, appear in the following order :—

1657 JOHN WILLIS,   to 1681 THOMAS HAYWARD,
to 1661 WILLIAM BRETT,   to 1683 THOMAS HAYWARD & JOHN HAWARD,
to 1666 JOHN WILLIS,
to 1676 JOHN WILLIS and SAMUEL EDSON,   1684 THOMAS HAYWARD,
1677 JOHN WILLIS,   1687 & 1688 None. Andros' Administration.

1689 THOMAS HAYWARD & }   1690 WILLIAM BRETT,
      WILLIAM BRETT, 2d. }   1691 JOSIAH EDSON.

From 1691 the Representatives to the General Court of Massachusetts, are as follows :—

1692 JOSIAH EDSON and }
      DAVID PERKINS, }
1693 SAMUEL ALLEN,
1694 DAVID PERKINS,
1695 ELIHU BRETT,
1696 DAVID PERKINS,
1697 SAMUEL EDSON,
1698 JOSIAH EDSON,
to 1700 ELIHU BRETT,
1701 None.—
1702 EDWARD FOBES,
to 1704 DAVID PERKINS,
to 1707 WILLIAM BRETT,
1708 EDWARD FOBES,
to 1710 JOSEPH HAYWARD,
1711 EDWARD FOBES,
to 1713 SAMUEL EDSON,
1714 JOSIAH EDSON,
1715 EDWARD FOBES,
1716 JOHN FIELD,
to 1719 RICHARD DAVENPORT,
to 1721 RICHARD DAVENPORT }
      & BENJAMIN SNOW, }
1722 EDWARD FOBES,
1723 EPHRAIM HAWARD,
1724 RICHARD DAVENPORT,
1725 THOMAS AMES,
1726 JOSEPH KEITH,
1727 ISAAC JOHNSON,
to 1729 ISAAC JOHNSON and }
      JOHN ALDEN, }
1730 ISAAC JOHNSON and }
      NEHEM'H. WASHBURN, }

1731 ISAAC JOHNSON,
to 1734 JOHN HOLMAN,
1735 JOSIAH EDSON, 2d.,
to 1737 JOHN HOLMAN,
1738 EBENEZER BYRAM,
1739 JOSIAH EDSON,
to 1741 EBENEZER BYRAM,
1742 NEHEMIAH WASHBURN,
1743 JOSIAH EDSON,
1744 JOHN HOLMAN,
1745 JOSIAH EDSON,
1746 JOSIAH EDSON, 3d,
to 1748 DANIEL HOWARD,
to 1750 JOSIAH EDSON,
to 1755 DANIEL HOWARD,
to 1766 JOSIAH EDSON,
to 1769 EDWARD MITCHELL,
to 1771 JOSIAH EDSON,
1772 DANIEL HOWARD,
1773 JOSIAH EDSON,
1774 } EDWARD MITCHELL &
1775 } RICHARD PERKINS were
      delegates to the Provincial
      Congress at Salem, Con-
      cord, and Cambridge.
1776 EDWARD MITCHELL,
      HUGH ORR,
      ELIPHALET CARY,
      NATH'L. REYNOLDS,
      OAKES ANGIER and
      THOMAS HOOPER.
1777 EDWARD MITCHELL &
      NATH'L. REYNOLDS,

1778 NATHAN MITCHELL &   1809 NAHUM MITCHELL,
     OAKES ANGIER,   1810 DANIEL MITCHELL,
1779 OAKES ANGIER &   to 1812 NAHUM MITCHELL,
     JOSIAH HAYDEN,   WILLIAM BAYLIES,
1780 NATHAN MITCHELL &   EZRA KINGMAN,
     DAVID KINGMAN,   GIDEON HOWARD,
1781 NATHAN MITCHELL,   DANIEL CRANE,
1782 HUGH ORR,   CALEB CARY.
1783 NATHAN MITCHELL,   1813 DANIEL HOWARD,
to 1785 NATHAN MITCHELL &   GIDEON HOWARD,
     ELISHA MITCHELL,   DANIEL CRANE,
1786 DANIEL HOWARD, 2d,   NATHAN MITCHELL, 2d.,
1787 ELISHA MITCHELL,   ABIEZER ALGER.
to 1790 JAMES THOMAS,   1814 DANIEL HOWARD,
1791 SIMEON DUNBAR,   to 1816 DANIEL HOWARD,
1792 BEZA HAYWARD,   BARTHOLOMEW BROWN,
1793 DANIEL SNOW,   EZRA KINGMAN,
to 1795 BEZA HAYWARD,   ABIEZER ALGER,
1796 DANIEL SNOW,   NOAH FEARING,
to 1798 NAHUM MITCHELL,   CALEB HOWARD.
to 1803 DANIEL SNOW,   1817 DANIEL HOWARD,
to 1806 DANIEL MITCHELL,   to 1820 WILLIAM BAYLIES,
to 1808 WILLIAM BAYLIES,   1821 HECTOR ORR.

Benjamin Willis and Nathan Mitchell were delegates to the convention at Cambridge for forming the Constitution of this Commonwealth, in September, 1779.—Daniel Howard, Elisha Mitchell, Hezekiah Hooper and Daniel Howard 2d, were the delegates to the convention of this State, at Boston, for adopting the constitution of the United States in 1788.

The counties in the Old Colony of Plymouth were formed and established in 1685. The Senators for the county of Plymouth, elected from Bridgewater, were for 1785 and 1786, Hugh Orr; for 1787, Nathan Mitchell; from 1788 to 1794, inclusive, Daniel Howard; from 1796 to 1805, Beza Hayward; for 1813 and 1814, Nahum Mitchell.

The members of Congress from Bridgewater have been the Rev. Dr. John Reed, Nahum Mitchell, William Baylies, and Aaron Hobart.

NOTE.—When 2d or 3d is affixed above to any name it means only that it is the 2d or 3d person of that name, who has represented the town.

PHILIP'S WAR.

MANY of the early settlers of Bridgewater were young men, born in this country, well acquainted with the Indian character, and therefore well calculated to encounter the troubles and dangers of the savage warfare they were soon to experience. In Philip's war, so called, which commenced early in 1675, they displayed great courage and intrepidity. Being wholly an interior settlement, remote from their friends on the sea-board, "they were strongly urged to desert their dwellings, and repair to the towns by the sea-side." They however resolutely kept their ground, and defended their settlement, and encouraged and assisted other towns to do the same. They erected a stockade or garrison on the south side of the river, and also fortified many of their dwelling houses. At the commencement of hostilities, June 21, 1675, seventeen of their number, " well armed and furnished with horses, the first that were on the march in all the country," went to Metapoiset, a small settlement about twelve miles from Swansey, "to strengthen the garrison at that place." They were met by people from Swansey, driven from their habitations and filled with terror, who advised them to return; but they fearlessly pursued their course and accomplished their object. They were in many perils while there, but returned safe after the greatest part of the garrison, consisting of seventy persons, most of whom were women and children, were safely conducted on to Rhode Island. Six persons of that vicinity, who were killed at that time, while they were with their teams conveying their corn into the garrison, were the first that fell in that war.

April 9, 1676, the enemy burnt a house and barn in the east part of the town. The following extract from a letter of the Rev. Mr. Keith to Thomas Hinckley thus alludes to it :—

"April 17, 1676. God hath now begun to pour out upon us the cup of trembling; yet the Lord doth remember us still with mercy, yea very great mercy. The 9th of this instant, being the Lord's Day, as we were assembling in the forenoon, we were

alarmed by the shooting of some guns from some of our garrisons upon discovery of a house being on fire, which was Robert
Latham's; his dwelling house and barn are wholly consumed.
The house was deserted but a few days before. He had considerable loss in lumber. The corn and chief of his goods were
saved. There were divers other out-houses rifled at the same
time, but no more burnt. There was a horse, or two, killed ;
three or four carried away ; and some few swine killed. We
sent out a party of men on the Lord's Day night upon discovery,
who found their trackings. Our men judged there might be
about ten of them. They followed them by their tracks several
miles, but having no provision, they were forced to leave the
pursuit. We are in expectation every day of an assault here.
The Lord prepare us for our trial."

May 8th, about three hundred Indians with Tispaquin for
their leader, made another assault on the east end of the village
on the south side of the river, and set fire to many of the
houses ; but the inhabitants issuing from their garrison houses,
fell upon them so resolutely, that the enemy were soon repelled ;
and a heavy shower of rain falling at the same time, the fires
were soon extinguished. The attack was then renewed on the
north side of the river, but it was soon defeated, and the next
morning the enemy entirely disappeared, after having burnt two
houses and one barn. On these several occasions thirteen
houses and four barns only were burnt, and but five of these
were in the village ; the rest were on the borders of the settlement and deserted at the time. Excepting the garrison houses,
it is said, every house but one in town was burnt. These were
probably the out dwellings only on the skirts, and not in the
village, where the houses were all in some measure fortified.
The house excepted is said to have been Nicholas Byram's,
which was in the east, where Capt. Isaac Whitman lately lived,
and quite remote from the principal settlement.

The following is an extract from an ancient manuscript, of
which Comfort Willis, who then held the office of "Town
Trooper," is supposed to have been the author :—

"On Saturday, Capt. (Thomas) Hayward, Sergeant (Samuel
Jr.) Packard, John Willis, and Isaac Harris, went out to see if

the Indians were coming down upon them, and they saw an
Indian, which made them think the enemy was at hand; and
they immediately pressed Comfort Willis and Joseph Edson to
go post to the Governor the same day at night to tell him of it.
And he went to Plymouth with them the next day, to send Capt.
Church with his company. And Capt. Church came with them
to Monponset on the Sabbath, and came no further that day;
and he told them he would meet them the next day. And Comfort Willis and Joseph Edson came home at night and told their
friends of it, and Ensign (John) Haward, Samuel Edson, Josiah
Edson, Joseph Edson, John Washburn, Samuel Washburn,
Thomas Washburn, John Field, Nicholas Byram, Samuel Allen,
Samuel Allen, Jr., John Gordon, John Hayward, John Packard, John Ames, Comfort Willis, Guido Bailey, Nathaniel
Hayward, John Whitman, John Packard and Samuel Leach
went out on Monday, supposing to meet with Captain Church;
but they came upon the enemy, and fought with them, and took
seventeen of them alive and also much plunder. And they all
returned, and not one of them fell by the enemy, and received
no help from Church."

The following extract of a letter from Gov. Josiah Winslow
to Thomas Hinckley was written about the same time :—

"May 23, 1676. Last Saturday, 4 o'clock P. M., a second
post came from Bridgewater, and informed they had discovered
about one hundred of the enemy at Titicut, very busy killing
cattle and horses, as if they intended some stay there; and
Taunton and Bridgewater had agreed in the night to advance
towards them in the morning; and requested a few men from us
if possible. The warning was very short, yet we obtained from
Plymouth, Duxbury, and Marshfield about forty smart lads and
sent to Bridgewater that night, but have not as yet heard of, or
from them. They knew of your intended march, and if they
miss of those Indians they may very probably meet with yours
to range toward Seconet. Mr. Church will inform you what I
have written to Rhode Island." There was also a skirmish
with the enemy near the great river in the south part of the
town, July 31, 1676, when some of Philip's "special friends"

were killed, and among others his uncle, who fell by his side.
Had the soldier known "which had been the right bird," as
Hubbard says in his narrative, Philip himself might have fallen,
and the war thus have been brought to a more speedy and less
disastrous result; but "the cunning fox escaped them for that
time." John Ames and Nicholas Byram are said to have distinguished themselves on that occasion.

Capt. Church joined them the next day and pursued the
enemy till the 3d of August, when, "having no provision but
what they took from the enemy, they hastened to Bridgewater,
sending an express before to provide for them, their company
being now very numerous, having killed and taken one hundred
and seventy-three. The gentlemen of Bridgewater met Capt.
Church with great expressions of honor and thanks, and received
him and his army with all due respect and kind treatment."
The prisoners were conveyed into the town pound at night, and
an Indian guard set over them. "They were well treated with
victuals and drink, and had a merry night; and the prisoners
laughed as loud as the soldiers, not having been so well treated
before for a long time." The next day Capt. Church arrived
safe at Plymouth with all his prisoners.

Amidst danger, and often actually assaulted in their dwellings,
it is remarkable that during the whole of that war, in which
from time to time great numbers were engaged, not one of the
inhabitants of Bridgewater were killed. All the narratives of
that conflict speak of the town as fortunate and highly favored
in this respect, while they unite in ascribing to the inhabitants
high praise for their courage and activity in the service. John
Snell, who was killed at the Isle aux Noix on Lake Champlain
in the French war in 1760, was the first inhabitant of the town
that ever fell in battle; and Capt. Jacob Allen and Abner Robinson, who were killed at Saratoga at the capture of Burgoyne
during the war of the American Revolution, in 1777, were the
next. Gideon Washburn was killed at sea about the same time.

Hubbard informs us that "in June, 1676, (it was 1675) a man
and woman were slain by the Indians at Dartmouth; and that
another woman was taken; but, because she had kept an Indian

6

child before, so much kindness was shewn her as that she was
sent back, after they had dressed her wounds; and the Indians
guarded her till she came within sight of the English." The
man and woman alluded to were probably Jacob Mitchell and
his wife; and Dorothy Hayward, who afterwards gave the following deposition, was probably the woman who was made a
prisoner, and treated with such exemplary humanity;—

"Dorothy Hayward, aged 30 years or thereabouts, being
engaged upon oath testifieth, that she being taken by the Indians
in June, in the year 1675,·in Dartmouth, in Plymouth Colony
saith, William Palmer was slain· by the Indians, and *Jacob
Mitchell* and *his wife*, and John Pope. This deponent saw these
Indians, Ponoho, Watanom, John Bryant, Nenpos, Potak, Tosa-
nem. These be the names of them that we know to be in being.
No further this deponent saith.—Taken before me upon oath,
                    JOSEPH CLARK, Assistant.
NEWPORT, R. I., June 25, 1677."

During the American Revolution, Bridgewater was firm and
patriotic, entering heartily into the struggle, and bearing her
full proportion of its burdens. Those who fell in battle were
not numerous, and some of the principal names have been
already given.

ECCLESIASTICAL HISTORY.

THE first settlements having been in the west parish, the first
church was of course formed there, and although social worship
on the Sabbath had not probably been omitted or at all neglected, yet having been few in number and feeble in substance,
they were at first unable to maintain a minister, and, by thus
forming themselves into a regular church, enjoy the full benefit
of the christian institutions. In this situation they remained
from 1651 to 1664, a period of a little more than twelve years.
They had in the mean time employed a Mr. Bunker, to preach
as a candidate, and made him an offer of settlement, which

however for some reason not appearing on the records did not take place. They also as early as 1661, agreed and voted to build a house for a minister, who should be called to settle among them, and to give him also an entire purchase right in the township.

Feb. 18, 1664, the settlement of the Rev. James Keith, their first ordained minister, is recorded, and the terms of it particularly expressed. He is there called " a student in divinity, having some competent time improved his gifts amongst them in the work of the ministry, and having also due approbation by the testimony of the Rev. Elders of other churches of Christ, to whom he was known." He was a Scotchman, educated at Aberdeen, and probably came to Boston about the year 1662, and was introduced to the church at Bridgewater by Dr. Increase Mather, whom he always esteemed as his patron and best friend. In the second preface to the " Bridgewater's Monitor," the first having been written by Increase and Cotton Mather, it is said, Bridgewater had not an ordained minister till 1663. This had reference to the old style, probably, when the year commenced on the 25th of March. The terms of his settlement were liberal; a double house lot of twelve acres with a house built thereon, and a purchase right, so called, being a fifty-sixth part of the original grant; £40 annual salary, £20 to be paid at Boston in money, and the other half at home. In 1667 they gave him an additional grant of thirty cords of wood annually, "the cutters of the wood to have five groats, and the drawers seven groats a cord." In 1681 they raised it from £40 to £50, £20 to be paid at Boston in money, and £30 at home in corn and provisions. In 1689 they agreed to allow him £10 in corn in lieu of his thirty cords of wood. He died July 23, 1719, æ. 76, of course was about 21 when he was ordained.

Mather, in the Magnalia, places him in the third class, " who were all such ministers as came over after the re-establishment of the Episcopal church government in England, and the consequent persecution of the non-conformists." This must have been a mistake, as Mr. Keith was from Scotland, and besides could not have been a minister before he came over, being very young and but a student when he arrived. The text he selected

for his first sermon was from Jeremiah 1, 6. "Behold I cannot
speak ; for I am a child." The Lord however indeed encouraged him, "and put his words into his mouth," and he proved
a worthy man and faithful shepherd over his infant and feeble
flock. His advice and influence with the civil authorities of the
colony were also considerable. In the case of the capture of
Philip's wife and son, when the question as to what should be
done with the son was in agitation, and the opinion of grave
divines desired, Mr. Keith's opinion, stated in a letter to the
Rev. Mr. Cotton, in favor of mercy, and differing from most
others, had great weight, if indeed it was not decisive on the
occasion. The boy's life was spared, and with his mother he
was sent out of the country, and probably to the Bermudas.
The letter follows, and is well worthy of a place here.

"October 30, 1676. I long to hear what becomes of Philip's
wife and his son. I know there is some difficulty in that Psalm
137, 8. 9, though I think it may be considered, whether there
be not some speciality and somewhat extraordinary in it. That
law, Deut. 24. 16, compared with the commended example of
Amazias, 2d Chron., 25. 4, doth sway much with me in the case
under consideration. I hope God will direct those whom it doth
concern to a good issue. Let us join our prayers at the throne
of grace with all our might, that the Lord would so dispose of
all public motions and affairs, that his Jerusalem in this wilderness may be the habitation of justice, and the mountain of
holiness, that so it may be also a quiet habitation, a tabernacle
that shall not be taken down." He preached the sermon at the
dedication of the new meeting house in South Bridgewater in
1717, two years only before his death, which was printed in the
"Bridgewater's Monitor," and which contains some pertinent
and impressive remarks on the subject of intemperance even at
that early period. "Besides other evils," said he, "which might
be mentioned, I would refer particularly to that of intemperance,
the excessive and prodigious expense upon strong drink, above
all, that of rum ; I say, the scandalous and horrible abuse of
rum, which threatens ruin unto this land and to this place ; a
ruin to all our dearest interests, both civil and religious. If
there be any such houses among you, as I fear there are, that

vend that strong drink contrary to the law of God and the wholesome law of this province, let such of you as are vested with civil power and stand obliged unto the oath of God; see that such grievous profanation be suppressed, lest that iniquity, the abuse of rum, be our ruin."

His posterity have been, and still are, very numerous. The names of two hundred of them in Bridgewater, alone appear on a late census; and there are a great many also in Middleborough, Easton, Mendon, Maine, and other parts of the United States. Israel Keith formerly Adjutant General of the Commonwealth was one of his descendants.

William Brett, among the first planters of the town, was a ruling elder in the church, ordained soon after Mr. Keith, and probably aided and assisted them in their public worship from the commencement of their settlement, and even after the ordination of Mr. Keith. He was a well educated and intelligent man as is manifest from his letters to Gov. Winslow, still extant, and was much esteemed by his brethren, and often employed in their secular affairs.—The following extract, bearing testimony to the worth and good character of the church and its officers, is taken from the early church records of Plymouth. " The worthy church of Christ at Bridgewater have for their pastor Mr. James Keith, who came by the wise disposing hand of Providence out of Scotland. William Brett, a grave and godly man, is their ruling elder; and John Willis, their deacon, a good man and one that hath proved himself faithful. They carry on in a way of peace, holiness, and good gospel order."

The Rev. Daniel Perkins, successor of Mr. Keith, was ordained October 4, 1721. He was a native of Topsfield, in the county of Essex, and graduated at Harvard University 1717. He died September 29, 1782, æ. 86th, and in the 62d year of his ministry, which was not long only, but peaceful and efficacious.

The Rev. John Reed, S. T. D., successor of Mr. Perkins, was ordained as his colleague June 7, 1780. He graduated at Yale College, 1772, and was son of the Rev. Solomon Reed, of Titicut, who was a native of Abington.—Dr. Reed died Feb. 17, 1831, æ. 79. He was an able and sound divine, and much

employed on ecclesiastical councils ; and although deprived of
his sight for many years previous to his death, he continued to
preach till the last, and with his psalm book open in his hand
would recite the psalm at length.—Many of his occasional sermons are in print, and also a work of his on infant baptism.

South Parish.

A second precinct was incorporated June 1, 1716. This did
not take place without some opposition. The original application was made in 1715, the petitioners calling themselves inhabitants of the easterly part of the town of Bridgewater. A
viewing committee was appointed consisting of John Cushing
and Edmund Quincy of the council, and George Leonard,
Henry Hodges and Jacob Thomson of the House. They made
a favorable report April 18, 1716, which was accepted, and an
act of incorporation passed with this condition, "that the whole
town stand obliged to an honorable maintenance of the Rev.
Mr. Keith, their present aged minister, if he should outlive his
powers and capacities of discharging the office and duty of their
minister." The dividing line began "at the brook, called the
mile brook, where the road from Boston to Taunton crosseth
the said brook, and from thence by a line running west and by
south to the uttermost extent of the said township, and from the
station first mentioned by a line running easterly in the midway
between the dwelling house of Wm. Hudson, and the dwelling
house of David Perkins, Jr., and from thence the said line to be
continued in the midst between the dwelling house of Edward
Mitchell and the dwelling house of Nathaniel Hayward, and
from thence the said line to be continued easterly in the midst
betwixt the dwelling house of James Latham, and the dwelling
house of Joseph Washburn, Jr., and from thence by a line due
east to the extent of the said township." The new parish
was called the south, and the old one the north precinct. Much
the largest part of the town remained with the north, as it was
suggested, "that there might soon be need of a third meeting-
house." They recommended that the new meeting-house be
erected " on the high or rising ground on the southerly side of
the highway, going by John Washburn's house, being the easterly

part of his field," and "that the old house remain where it was, for five years, and then be removed down to Isaac Johnson's field, where divers roads meet convenient for that purpose." The new meeting-house was dedicated June 14, 1717, and Mr. Keith delivered the sermon as has been already stated. Before the time arrived for removing the old house in the north, (now west,) the east began to think of being incorporated into a parish, and therefore they assisted in repairing the old house where it stood, and were to have the money refunded to them when they came to build their own, and so the house was never moved.

The Rev. Benjamin Allen, their first pastor, was a native of Tisbury, of Martha's Vineyard, graduated at Yale 1708, and ordained July 9, 1718. He continued with them about thirteen years, but being an unsuccessful manager of his private secular concerns, he fell into debt, and his parish after often relieving him, became at last weary of it, and he was dismissed by an ecclesiastical council. He preached his first sermon in the meeting-house August 18, 1717, and his last October 11, 1730. He was soon afterwards installed at Cape Elizabeth, and was the first minister of that place, where he died May 6, 1754, æ. 65. A grand-daughter of his by the name of Jourdan, married the Rev. Enos Hitchcock, D. D., of Providence.

The Rev. John Shaw, his successor, was a native of the east parish of Bridgewater, and son of Joseph Shaw : graduated at Harvard University 1729, and ordained November 17, 1731. He died April 29, 1791, æ. 82, and in the 60th year of his ministry, much beloved and respected by his people. He delivered the sermon at the ordination of the Rev. Mr. Taft, of Randolph, which is in print.

His successor, the Rev. Zedekiah Sanger, S. T. D., was born at Sherburne, and graduated at Harvard University 1771 : was first settled at Duxbury, and afterwards installed as colleague with the Rev. Mr. Shaw, December 17, 1788. He died November 17, 1820, æ. 73, after a life of usefulness and great activity. He was a scholar and a learned divine. His house was a seminary, in which he prepared young men for college, and instructed young students in divinity. Amidst his ministerial and pastoral labors, he was also for several years preceptor of the academy in his neighborhood. He enjoyed in a high degree the affections and respect of his people.—His successor was Richard M. Hodges, from Salem; graduated at Harvard University 1815, who after performing his pastoral duties there for many years, was peaceably dismissed at his own desire; and the present Rev. Theophilus P. Doggett, who graduated at Brown's University 1819, was settled as his successor.

There is a small ministerial fund in this parish, the trustees of which were incorporated Feb. 7, 1803. It was then nearly one thousand dollars, and has been augmented since.

The south was settled very soon after the west parish. Among those who came in from other towns and resided there before and soon after 1700, were Samuel Kinsley, Thomas Mitchell, William Orcutt, William Hudson, Daniel Hudson, John Washburn, John Washburn, Jr., Richard Jennings, David Perkins, John Aldrich, Eleazar Carver, Nathaniel Conant, Richard Davenport and Joseph Pratt.

East Parish.

December 14, 1723, the east end of the north parish, then so called, ever since called the west parish, together with nine persons of the south parish, namely, Barnabas Seabury, Thomas Latham, Charles Latham, Nicholas Wade, Nathaniel Harden, Thomas Hooper, William Conant, Isaac Lazell, and Joseph Washburn, with their families and estates, were constituted a precinct, called the east parish. This was done also in pursuance of a viewing committee of court, consisting of Isaac Winslow, Samuel Thaxter, Josiah Cotton, Isaac Little and John Quincy. The boundaries were on the west, a due north line from the south parish, through the centre tree: and on the southeasterly side the Old Plymouth Road to Halifax. The first meeting house was raised March 14, 1720.

The Rev. John Angier, graduated at Harvard University 1720, was their first Minister, ordained October 28, 1724. He was son of the Rev. Samuel Angier, of Rehoboth, and afterwards of Watertown. He died April 14, 1787, æ. 86th, and in the 63d of his ministry.

His son, the Rev. Samuel Angier, graduated at Harvard University 1763, was ordained colleague with him December 23, 1767, and died January 18, 1805, æ. 62d, and in the 38th of his ministry. The father, the Rev. John Angier, preached the ordination sermon, which appears bound with the last edition of the "Bridgewater's Monitor."

The successor of the Rev. Samuel Angier was the Rev. James Flint, D. D., a native of Reading, Mass., and graduated at Harvard University 1802, and ordained October 29, 1806; and after officiating among them in his pastoral office for twelve or fifteen years, he was dismissed at his own desire, and afterwards installed at Salem. The Rev. Benjamin Fessenden, from Sandwich, who graduated at Harvard University 1817, was then settled as his successor; who was dismissed November 7, 1825, at his own request, and removed to Rhode Island, and has retired from the ministry; and the Rev. John Adams Williams, of Roxbury, who graduated at Harvard University 1820, was settled as his successor, October 18th, 1826; who remained in his office but a short time, having been dismissed by his own solicitation, August 4, 1828; and was succeeded by the Rev. Eliphalet P. Crafts, who graduated at Brown University 1821, and ordained November 19, 1828, and who after a few years asked a dismission, which was granted him, March 28, 1836, and he is now installed at Sandwich.—And the parish is now vacant.

The first settlers in the east parish before 1700, who came in from abroad, were Robert Latham, Nicholas Byram, Jonathan Hill, Edward Mitchell, Thomas Whitman, Samuel Allen, and Joseph Shaw. Some of these were there about 1666.—Some of the sons of the first settlers in West Bridgewater were also among the early settlers in the East, as John Howard, Jr., William Brett, Jr., Elisha Hayward, Nathaniel Hayward, Jr., Isaac Alden, Francis Cary, Jonathan Cary, James Cary, Joseph Edson, Isaac Harris, and Samuel Harris.

7

North Parish.

January 3, 1738, the north part of the west parish and a small part of the north-west corner of the east parish were incorporated into a precinct, and called the north parish. It was bounded by a due east line from Easton, half a mile north of " the white oak tree at Jonathan Packard's corner" to the east parish line : and thence north-easterly to Beaver Brook, together with three families and their estates, on the east side of the river.

Their first pastor was the Rev. John Porter, a native of Abington, graduated at Harvard University 1736; ordained October 15, 1740; died March 12, 1802, æ. 87th, and in the 62d of his ministry.

His successor, the Rev. Asa Meach, was ordained October 15, 1800, and dismissed by a mutual council 1811, and afterwards installed at Canterbury, Connecticut. He was a native of that state.

His successor, the Rev. Daniel Huntington, a native of Norwich, Connecticut, graduated at Yale College 1816, was ordained October 28, 1812. He was brother of the late Rev. Mr. Huntington, of Boston, and son of General Jedediah Huntington, of New London. His salary was $700, the highest then of any in the town.—He remained with his parish many years, but by his own solicitation was at length dismissed, and returned to Connecticut. The Rev. Mr. Thompson was his successor, who continued but a short time, and the Rev. Paul Couch is now their pastor.

The north was the last settled part of the town. There were no settlements north of the old powder house in West Bridgewater, till after 1700. Among the first settlers were Daniel and Robert Howard, David, Solomon, John, James, Zaccheus and Abiel Packard, Henry Kingman, and Timothy Keith : all of whom came from West Bridgewater.

Titicut Parish.

February 4, 1743, the south-west part of the south parish, with a part of Middleborough, was incorporated into a precinct, called Titicut Parish. It lies south of the old four mile line, so called. The Rev. Solomon Reed before mentioned, a native of Abington, graduated at Harvard University 1739, was their first minister. The Rev. David Gurney, son of Perkins Gurney, of East Bridgewater, graduated at Harvard University 1785, was his successor. Their third minister is the present Rev. Philip Colby. The meeting-house is in Middleborough, and all their ministers have resided there, the largest part of the parish belonging to that town.

Besides these territorial precincts there is an Episcopal church in the south parish, incorporated June 14, 1815, by the name of Trinity Church. It is of much longer standing, having originated in a grant of about fourteen acres of land, made January 23, 1747, by Samuel Edson, of Bridgewater, to the society in England for the propagation of the gospel in foreign parts, on condition that the income be applied to the support of public worship according to the usage of the Church of England. Their house was erected in 1648 by individual subscription. In April, 1812, they conveyed the glebe to the trustees of donations at Boston, and it is leased for nine hundred and ninety-nine years to John Edson, one of the members, for twenty-one dollars a year. June 12, 1816, having repaired their house and laid an assessment for the support of public worship, it was solemnly consecrated by Bishop Griswold, and the Rev. Messrs. Blake and Crocker. The Rev. Henry Blackaller is now their pastor.

There is also a Baptist meeting-house in the west part of the west parish. The society consists of members partly from Easton and partly from Bridgewater. It was formed about the time Dr. Reed was ordained, but not incorporated till March 9, 1804.—Their ministers have been Mr. Robertson, Mr. Rathburn, Mr. Smith, Mr. Shurtliff, and the Rev. Bartlett Pease is now their pastor.

There is also a Congregational society in South Bridgewater, over which the Rev. Ebenezer Gay, who graduated at Harvard University 1814, is now settled, and another, over which the Rev. Mr. Raymond is pastor; and a Universalist society, in which the Rev. Lewis G. Brown sometimes officiates; and a New Jerusalem church, over which the Rev. Samuel Worcester is pastor.

There is also in North Bridgewater another Congregational society, over which the Rev. John Goldsbury, who graduated at Brown University, 1820, was pastor, but is now vacant; and there is another, of which the Rev. John Dwight was pastor, but in which the Rev. Mr. Huntington above named is now preaching; and a New Jerusalem church, over which the Rev. Warren Goddard is settled; and a Methodist society, of which the Rev. Charles Hayward is pastor.

There is also a 2d Congregational society in East Bridge-water, over which the Rev. Baalis Sanford, who graduated at Brown University 1823, is pastor.—There are also some of the New Jerusalem church there, and also some Universalists, who have regular meetings but no settled ministers.

The general longevity of the early ministers of Bridgewater is worthy of notice. Four of them, namely, Mr. Perkins, Mr. J. Angier, Mr. Shaw, and Mr. Porter, who were cotemporaries, and pastors of the four principal parishes, lived to the great ages respectively of 86, 86, 83 and 87, and died in the 62d, 63d, 60th and 62d year of their ministry, and all officiated occasionally, and some of them regularly, till their deaths.—Dr. Reed died also in his 80th year, and Dr. Sanger in his 74th. These with Mr. Keith, who was 76, and Mr. Samuel Angier, who was 62, are the only ministers who ever died in the town.

SCHOOLS AND EDUCATION.

THE town has been remarkable for its attention to education, both public and private. Mr. Keith and Elder Brett, in the very infancy of the settlement, procured a subscription of about £12 to be paid in Indian corn, for the use of the college at Cambridge. Assessments were also formerly made very liberally, both in the town and the parishes, for the maintenance of common schools. The interest of learning has always been cherished here, and its importance duly appreciated.

There is in the south parish an academy, established, and the trustees of it incorporated, February 28, 1799. The half township of land granted by the general court as an endowment, was sold for $5,000. The building was erected by individuals who subscribed $3,000 for that purpose. It has always had the reputation of a good seminary of instruction, and is still well patronised and in a flourishing condition. The Hon. John A. Shaw is the present preceptor.

The following are the names of those who have had collegiate education, arranged under the parishes to which they respectively belonged, with the years and colleges annexed, in which they received their degrees :—

West Parish.

ABIEL HOWARD,	1729	BEZER SNELL,	1789
EPHRAIM KEITH,	1729	CHARLES ANGIER,	1793
JOSEPH SNELL,	1735	FRANCIS HOWARD,	1797 B
NATHANIEL SNELL,	1740	GEORGE W. PERKINS,	1801 B
RICHARD PERKINS,	1748	JOHN REED,	1803 B
Elijah Packard,	1750	Daniel Johnson,	1806 B
Simeon Howard, S. T. D.,	1758	BARZILLAI HAYWARD,	1807 B
Daniel Johnson,	1767	JOHN WILLIS,	1807 B
Asa Dunbar,	1767	JOHN E. HOWARD,	1815 B
SILVANUS AMES,	1767	GEORGE COPELAND,	1815 B
SIMEON DUNBAR,	1772	CALEB REED,	1817
Bezaliel Howard, S. T. D.	1781	SAMPSON REED,	1818
Jonathan Burr,	1784	ELLIS AMES,	1830 B
Jonas Hartwell,	1787 D		

South Parish.

JOSIAH EDSON,	1730	Oakes Shaw,	1758
BENJAMIN WILLIS,	1740	Bezaliel Shaw,	1762
Silvanus Conant,	1740	William Shaw, S. T. D.,	1762

Timothy Alden,	1762	SETH FOBES,	1804 B
Perez Fobes, L. L. D.,	1762	NOAH WHITMAN,	1806 B
John Shaw,	1772	CYRUS ALDEN,	1807 B
BEZA HAYWARD,	1772	Zedekiah Sanger,	1807
JONAS WHITMAN,	1772 Y	Ralph Sanger,	1808
MARTIN KINSLEY,	1778	JOHN A. SHAW,	1811
Zephaniah Willis,	1778	Seth Alden,	1814 B
THOMAS PERKINS,	1779	Levi W. Leonard,	1815
JAMES ALLEN,	1785	Zebulon L. Shaw,	1815
SETH PRATT,	1785	Theodore Edson,	1822
NATHAN HAYWARD,	1785	ZEPHANIAH A. BATES,	1824
Kilborn Whitman,	1785	BENJAMIN WILLIS,	1825 B
JONATHAN LEONARD,	1786	Horatio Alger,	1825
BENJAMIN WHITMAN,	1788 B	Daniel Leach,	1830 B
Hezekiah Hooper,	1789	Nehemiah G. Lovell,	1833 B
DAVID LEONARD,	1792 B	Lorenzo O. Lovell,	1833 B
Zenas L. Leonard,	1794 B	DAVID PERKINS,	1834 B
RICHARD SANGER,	1800	GILES LEACH,	—— B
Gaius Conant,	1800 B	EPHRAIM FOBES,	—— B
NATHAN FOBES,	1803 B		

East Parish.

John Shaw,	1729	NAHUM MITCHELL,	1789
Eliab Byram,	1740	HECTOR ORR,	1792
Samuel Angier,	1763	EZEKIEL WHITMAN,	1795 B
THOMAS GANNETT,	1763	ASA MITCHELL,	1802
Caleb Gannett,	1763	JACOB HILL,	1807 B
OAKES ANGIER,	1764	ELIAB WHITMAN,	1807 B
William Conant,	1770 Y	Nathaniel Whitman,	1809
JAMES THOMAS,	1778	DANIEL WHITMAN,	1809 B
Levi Whitman,	1779	WILLARD PHILLIPS,	1810
Ebenezer Dawes,	1785	WELCOME YOUNG,	1814 B
BARZILLAI GANNETT,	1785	SILVANUS L. MITCHELL,	1817
Allen Pratt,	1785	Lucius Alden,	1821 B
David Gurney,	1785	Bernard Whitman,	1823*
Ebenezer Lazell,	1788 B	Jason Whitman,	1825

---

* He with many others in the class of this year, owing to a disturbance in college, failed to take his degree.

Joseph W. Cross,	1827	William Allen,	1837
Williams Latham,	1828 B	Edmund B. Whitman,	1838

North Parish.

James Thompson,	1761 N	*Naphtali Shaw,*	1790 D
John Porter,	1770 Y	Daniel Howard,	1797
Huntington Porter,	1777	Issachar Snell,	1797
Jonathan Porter,	1777	Lucius Cary,	1798 B
Eliphalet Porter, S. T. D.	1777	Daniel Noyes,	1813 Y
Thomas Crafts,	1783	*Jonas Perkins,*	1813 B
Asa Packard,	1783	Jonathan P. Crafts,	1817 B
Zechariah Howard,	1784	Austin Packard,	1821 B
Hezekiah Packard, S. T.		*Levi Packard,*	1821
D.,	1787	Lucius Kingman,	1830 B
Joshua Cushman,	1787		

Titicut.

Ephraim Keith,	1762	*Oliver Hayward,*	1804
Adam Edson,	1775 Y	*Jonathan Keith,*	1805 B
Jael Edson,	1784 Y	Calvin Pratt,	—— B
Daniel Crane,	1796 B		

D affixed to the year, stands for Dartmouth College—B for Brown University—Y for Yale College—N for Nassau or New Jersey College. Where no letter is affixed, Cambridge or Harvard University is to be understood. Those in italics are clergymen.

By comparing this list with the catalogue of Harvard, it appears that one quarter of the graduates in the class of 1785, were from Bridgewater.

———

PONDS AND RIVERS.

There are but two ponds of any considerable dimensions in the town. The largest lies on the south-west part of the town, adjoining Raynham, and was anciently called by the Indians

Nuncketest or Neapnuncket, and afterwards and now called Nippenicket. The other lies in the easterly part of the town, adjoining Halifax, and was anciently called by the Indians Satucket; but afterwards and now called Robins' Pond, after an Indian family of that name, who came from Mattakeeset, now Pembroke, and lived on the margin of it. Several families of Indians formerly settled and owned land on the shores of this pond; but are now nearly extinct.' There is a river issuing from the pond first abovementioned, which anciently bore the same name, Nuncketest; but after the erection of the first mill, was called Mill River, and for a long time, and perhaps ever since the incorporation of the town, has been called Town River. It first runs in a north-easterly course through the middle of the west parish, and then by a more south-easterly direction passes through the south parish. On this stream is the principal mill seat in the west, and two of the principal water privileges in the south parish. There are several tributary streams which augment this river in its course, as Cowesit and West Meadow Brook in the west, and South Brook in the south parish, and other smaller streams.

There is another river, which rises in Stoughton, south of the Blue Hills, and passes through the north parish, and is there called Salisbury River, from the circumstance of its running on the easterly side of Salisbury Plain, so called, and thence continues its course into the east parish, where it unites with Beaver Brook, and is then called Matfield River, from an Indian of that name, who is said to have lived on the banks of it, and lower down it unites with Byram's Brook, anciently called Spring Brook, now called Forge Brook, and is then called John's River, from *John* Howard, an early settler near it, where Dea. Samuel Keen now lives. It soon unites with the Poor Meadow river, and thence passes into the south parish and there unites with the Town River. There are, in the north parish, five or six mill seats on this river and Beaver Brook, and seven in the east, including those on Beaver and Byram's Brook. This river passes the whole length of the town, and may well be called Middle River, as it is the middle one of the three principal streams composing the Great River.

Poor Meadow River, above mentioned, passes through Abington and the north-west corner of Hanson, entering the east parish on the easterly side; and, uniting with the river coming from Halifax, through Monponset Pond and Robin's Pond, is then called Satucket River, and after receiving a small increase from Black Brook unites with John's River, as before stated. Hobart's works in Abington, and Cushing's in Hanson, formerly called Moor's Forge, stand on the Poor Meadow stream; and the extensive works at Halifax are on the other branch of the Satucket River. Whitman's Mills in the east, now called the East Bridgewater Manufacturing Establishment, are on this river; and just below the confluence of these three rivers, in the south parish, stand the new mills, so called, and the paper mill, owned by Hooker and Warren. The Great River, after receiving the waters of the Winnetuxet from Plympton, and of the Namasket from Middleborough, is commonly called Titicut River, but from Titicut to the sea is called Taunton Great River. There are several other small mill seats in various parts of the town, on the minor brooks and rivulets, which afford sufficient water for them in many instances during the winter and spring seasons.

Taunton River is called great only in comparison with its branches and tributaries, but is nevertheless large enough, even so high up as the south parish of Bridgewater, as to admit of ship building. Vessels of near one hundred and fifty tons were formerly built there, and carried down in time of freshets.

SOIL, AGRICULTURE, AND MANUFACTURES.

BRIDGEWATER is a very level township, having few or no great hills. The only one, which may be properly so called, is Sprague's Hill, anciently called the Great Hill, situated between the east and south parishes, and this is but small. The westerly part of the north parish, commonly called the "West Shares," is perhaps the highest land in the town.

The soil, as might well be supposed in so large an extent of territory, is various. In some parts, and particularly in those

8

adjoining the rivers and brooks, it is of a good quality and very productive. In other parts, as on the plains, it is suitable for tillage, being of a light mould, and produces good crops of grain with a moderate quantity of manure and little labor. Owing to the numerous water courses and large tracts of swampy grounds, the town, and particularly West Bridgewater, abounds with low meadow lands, producing a great supply of coarse hay, which formerly was held in great estimation, but since the great improvements in agriculture, and increased attention to the cultivation of English and other approved foreign grasses, it is considered of less value. These extensive meadows are still, however, of vast importance, and constitute one of its peculiar privileges as an agricultural town.

It has always had the reputation of a good farming town, and might therefore be supposed to be almost wholly engaged in husbandry, yet it abounds in mechanics and manufacturers. Iron manufactures of almost every description have always been largely carried on here. The making of small arms in New England, if not in the United States, commenced here. Many stand of arms were made here before the Revolution. Cannon were here cast solid and bored, at the commencement of that war, the first, perhaps, that were manufactured in this manner in the country. There were more edged tools and wrought nails formerly made here than in any other town in the State. Bar iron, anchors, cotton gins, sugar mills, shovels, edged tools, hoops, nails, tacks, and castings of every description are still made here, and some of these branches are carried on very extensively. There are here also a paper mill, cotton mills, and other manufacturing and mechanic establishments of various kinds. Chaise making has for many years been a considerable branch of business; but at present the shoe business exceeds all others; two thousand dollars a week being paid at one establishment alone to the laborers for the making only of shoes.

The Hon. Hugh Orr, himself a Scotchman, who manufactured the small arms and cannon as above stated, invited Robert Barr and Alexander Barr, brothers, from Scotland, to construct carding, spinning, and roping machines at his works in East

Bridgewater. And the General Court on the 16th of November, 1786, Mr. Orr himself then being one of the Senate, by a resolve of that date allowed them two hundred pounds for their ingenuity, and afterwards granted them a further compensation of six tickets in the land lottery of that period. These machines remained in the possession of Mr. Orr for the inspection of all disposed to see them, and he was requested by the General Court to exhibit the same and give all explanation and information in his power respecting them. These were the first machines of the kind ever made in the country. Mr. Slater, with the late Mr. Moses Brown, of Providence, came to examine them on Mr. Slater's first arrival in the country, and before he had commenced any establishment of the kind. The circumstances of this visit were communicated to the writer by Mr. Brown himself, who at the same time added, that these were the first machines of the kind ever made in the United States. Thomas Somers, another Scotchman, under the direction of Mr. Orr, constructed other machines for carding, roping, and spinning cotton, and on the 8th of March, 1787, the General Court placed in Mr. Orr's hands twenty pounds to encourage the artist. Mr. Orr also about the same time employed another foreigner by the name of McClure, to weave jeans and corduroys by hand with a fly shuttle, much in the same manner as it is now done by water power. It may therefore with truth be said, perhaps, that the first small arms, the first solid cannon cast and bored, the first cotton thread ever spun by modern machinery, in America, were made in Bridgewater. The first nails manufactured by machinery in the United States were made here; probably the first nail completely cut and headed by machinery at one operation in the world, was made in East Bridgewater, by the late Mr. Samuel Rogers. In laying the shingles on the present meeting house in East Bridgewater, which was erected in 1794, nails made by hand in a small machine invented by him, were principally used. The writer well recollects the circumstance, and often saw the machine in operation. It had been invented and constructed long before, and was supposed to be the first method ever discovered of making a perfect nail at one operation.

Some of the present manufactures carried on here, such as

cotton gins and others, are probably the first ever made in New
England.—Few places therefore have done more towards the
introduction and promotion of the manufacturing and mechanic
arts, than this ancient town of Bridgewater.

CENSUS.

	West.	South & Titicut.	East.	North.	Total.
1764,	880	1,318	959	833	3,990
1790,	——	——	——	——	4,975
1800,	——	——	——	——	5,200
1810,	1,065	1,552	1,195	1,354	5,166
1820,	1,055	1,692	1,435	1,480	5,662
1830,	1,042	1,855	1,653	1,953	6,503
1837,	1,145	2,092	1,927	2,701	7,865
Families in 1764,	121	221	157	131	630
Dwelling houses in 1764,	106	203	142	120	571

Families in 1790, - - - - - - 830
Houses in 1800, - - - - - - 740

Families in Titicut 1764 were   48 ⎫
Houses   "   "   "   "   41 ⎪ All included
Inhabitants "   "   "   "   262 ⎬ above with
  "   "   "   1810 "   318 ⎭ the South.

The last United States land tax was in the West, $505,47;
South, $552,99; East, $579,82; North, $598,52; Titicut,
$150,54. Total, $2,387,34.

Emigration from the town was formerly very great, and of
course the increase of population in it was small. They first
went to the western part of the State, and into New Hampshire
and Vermont. Afterwards principally into Maine. Emigration
of late has been less frequent, and of course population has
increased.

Bridgewater with Abington constitutes the 3d Regiment in
the first Brigade, and 5th Division of the Massachusetts militia.

MISCELLANEOUS EXTRACTS FROM EARLY RECORDS IN A
CHRONOLOGICAL ORDER.

1656.　June.—The town was incorporated.

"　November 3.—It is agreed upon by the town that all who
neglect to attend a town meeting after lawful warning
shall pay 1s. 6d.; and for tardiness, and not answering
when their names are called, 9d.—and the same for
going away before the meeting is closed.

"　Nathaniel Willis and Lawrence Willis bind themselves
to free the town from any charge in keeping their
brother Jonathan Willis.

"　About the holsters bought of Goodman Hill. Goodman
Hayward, Sen., and Goodman Harris, having engaged
for the payment of them, being 12s., the town is
willing to pay it them again in their rate in the best of
their pay, which they shall be amerced to pay out of
their rates.

"　It is agreed that there shall be five wolf-traps made.

1660.—It is ordered and agreed upon freely and willingly to
give to Mr. Bunker, if he shall come hither to supply
the place of a minister, the sum of £30, or £20 and
his diet.

1661.—It is agreed upon to build a house for a minister who
shall be called to settle with them, and to give him a
purchase right.

"　It is agreed upon that those things that are agitated by
the town for the good of the whole, shall be carried
on by a major vote, and the vote be called for by the
town clerk.

1663.—Constant Southworth and William Paybody laid out to
Miles Standish three hundred acres at Satucket Pond,
on the north side of Winnetuxet River, and butting
upon Satucket River, one hundred and sixty rods in
length from Satucket River.

1664.—The town make their agreement with Mr. Keith, student
in divinity, for settling him in the ministry, and give
him a purchase right and other lands, with a house
built thereon, on condition that he continues with
them.

1665.—Land granted to John Ames on both sides of a brook,
called Hullet's Brook, down at the end of Hullet's
Plain.

1666.—Samuel Edson, Nicholas Byram, and John Willis, appointed by the court Counsellors of War with the
military officers of the town.

1667.—A jury was named by the court to be empannelled to lay
out all ways requisite in the town of Bridgewater,
viz :—Nicholas Byram, Samuel Edson, Thomas Hayward, Samuel Packard, Nathaniel Willis, Lieutenant
Thomas Hayward, Jr., Arthur Harris, John Cary,
Ensign John Haward, Mark Lathrop, Robert Latham,
Joseph Alden, and if by Providence any of these be
hindered, that then Samuel Allen and John Ames do
supply.

1669.—Arthur Harris and John Ames chosen troopers this year.

1671.—Comfort Willis chosen trooper for five years, to find
horse and furniture, only the town to find a pair of
pistols and holsters, and if they were out of kelter at
any time, he to repair them ; and if he went to Yarmouth, he was to have 20s.; if to Plymouth, 15s.; and
if to Taunton, 10s.; and Israel Packard to be trooper
also on the same terms.

  "   John Hayward of the plain, and Nathaniel Willis to
enquire who drink strong liquors in ordinaries.

  "   Voted to build a new meeting-house, and granted four
score pounds and no more for falling, squaring, fram-
ing, enclosing, covering, flooring, glazing, and seating,
and whatsoever belongs to the finishing of the same,
excepting the galleries and ceiling : the dimensions to
be forty by twenty-six feet, and fourteen feet studs.

1672.—At a meeting of the purchasers or proprietors, a committee was appointed "to consider the manner to be adopted in future for laying out their lands. This was the first meeting held separately by the proprietors.

" The town being met the 17th of June, and Mr. Constant Southworth, assistant, coming through the town, and having been appointed by court to choose and give oath to a jury for laying out highways convenient in the town, did accordingly perform the service, and appointed Samuel Edson, (foreman,) Lieutenant Hayward, Ensign Haward, Mark Lathrop, Joseph Bassett, Samuel Tompkins, John Ames, Thomas Snell, John Washburn, John Hayward, John Willis, Jr., and John Cary.

1673.—It was voted that Mr. Keith, having been some competent time with them, should have the house and lands where he lived, twelve acres, and a whole purchase right.

1674.—The town ordered that a new book for the recording of lands should be procured, and a committee was chosen to see that the records were made and transcribed correctly, and on good evidence.

" The young men were allowed to build galleries to the meeting house, and to have the front seats to themselves.

1675.—The meeting-house and minister's house ordered to be fortified, powder and ball to be procured, and pay for soldiers provided.

" It was agreed there should be two wears to catch fish; and the parties for Satucket should be from the elder's, (William Brett's,) and so all the families along to Satucket, with John Washburn, Guido Bailey, John Leonard, Samuel Leonard, and Nathaniel Hayward: and all the rest of the town for Mill River.

" All the householders and male children twenty years old and upwards, now found to be sixty-four in number, shall be proprietors in the lands at Titicut, just bought of the Indians.

1675.—The fortification about the meeting house to be made with half trees seven feet high above the ground, six rods long and four rods wide, besides the flankers; and every quarter or squadron to do, each of them, a side or an end; and they that do the ends must make each of them a door, and each of them a flanker; to be done by the 6th of November.

" Provision made for soldiers that should be pressed into the service, and such necessaries procured and money raised as they might need.

1676.—A vote was called to see what should be done with the money that was made of the Indians, that were sold last, and it was voted, that the soldiers that took them should have it.

" Elder Brett, Deacon Willis, and Mr. Samuel Edson were appointed to distribute the contributions made by divers christians in Ireland for the distresses of the Indian wars.

" Deacon Willis and John Cary were chosen to take in the charges of the late war since June last, and the expenses of the scouts that were sent out before and since June.

1678.—Mr. Keith being sick, Elder Brett was chosen to assist him in carrying on the work of the ministry between this and May next.

1683.—The purchasers agreed that the old field to the northward of the highway, by Goodman Bailey's, be reserved for a training-field.

1685.—The Selectmen to take bond of Joseph Washburn for the maintenance of his uncle, Philip Washburn.

1686.—It was agreed by the town and purchasers that the four rods to lay out lands by, should be thirteen inches over by the box rule.

" It was agreed that the layers out of lands, when they leave lands for highways, shall leave four rods, or one line, in breadth for allowance for highways; and the highways through such lands where allowance is so made, shall not be less than forty feet.

1686.—Ten acres of wood land to be laid out to each purchaser nearest to their habitations, as the land will afford it to be laid out, viz :—

Lots on the south side of Town River, below Goodman Alden's, namely, to William Snow, Samuel Edson, Edward Fobes, John Ames, Elihu Brett, Samuel Edson, Jr., Josiah Edson, Matthew Gannett, (of Scituate,) Solomon Leonard, Giles Leach, Benjamin Willis.

North side of the Town River, viz :—John Willis, Nathaniel Hayward, John Willis, Jr., Captain Wadsworth, (Samuel, of Duxbury,) Lieutenant (Thomas) Hayward, Joseph Bassett, William Bassett, Joseph Alden, John Robbins, Goodman, (William) Orcutt, Joseph Wadsworth, (of Duxbury,) Thomas Washburn.

On the west end of the town, towards West Meadow Brook, viz :—Goodman, (Guido) Bayley, Goodman, (Mark) Lathrop, Ensign (John) Haward, Goodman, (Samuel) Packard, Elkanah Willis, Mr. Keith, Goodman, (George) Turner, John Field, John Hayward of the plain, Thomas Snell, Arthur Harris.

South side of South Brook, viz :—Goodman (John) Washburn, Goodman, (Thomas) Washburn, Goodman, (Samuel) Washburn, John Porter, Captain Wadsworth.

John Kingman, at the end of his land where his house is.

Joseph Cary, in the swamp below John Kingman's and John Hayward's.

Easterly side of Stony Brook at the Centre Tree, viz : Elisha Hayward, John Cary, Jonathan Hill, William Brett, Joseph Edson.

Easterly side of Satucket River, near Jonathan's plain, and down the river, viz :—Goodman (Robert) Latham, Samuel Allen, Thomas Whitman.

9

At the head of Spring Brook, viz ;—Nicholas Byram, Nicholas Byram, Jr., John Whitman, Thomas Whitman.

NOTE.—Gannett and the Wadsworths were not inhabitants of the town,—all the rest were, and these locations will give some idea of the places of their residence.

1687.—John Usher's warrant sent to the constable of Bridge-water for choosing commissioners for taking a list of males from sixteen years old and upward, and valuing estates, was received by me, Joseph Edson, constable, August 22. Samuel Allen chosen commissioner.

1688.—Division of highways third Monday of May, for repairs, viz :—

For John's Bridge. Goodman Bayley, Guido Bayley, Jr., Goodman Orcutt, William Orcutt, Jr., Richard Jennings ; John Packard, to make a horse bridge there.

NOTE.—This was formerly called Jennings' Bridge, then Packard's Bridge, and now Pope's Bridge. It was first called *John's* Bridge, after *John* Packard, who lived there, but was not long known by that name. Joppa Bridge was more usually called John's Bridge, after *John* Haward, who lived near it.

For the bridge at Satucket River, at Isaac Harris' house ; Joseph Washburn, James Latham, Joseph Latham, Thomas Whitman.

For the highway at Goodman Alden's swamp. Thomas Washburn, Goodman (Joseph) Alden, Comfort Willis.

For the ways over at Joseph Hayward's. Elihu Brett, Nathaniel Brett, John Bolton, Zaccheus Packard, John Kingman.

For South Brook to Comfort Willis'. Samuel Washburn, John Washburn, Goodman (Nathaniel) Conant, John Leonard, Benjamin Washburn.

For the bridge at Ensign Haward's.—Samuel Edson, Ensign Haward, Edward Fobes, John Ames.

For Salisbury Plain.—John Hayward on the plain, and Thomas Snell.

For Mile Brook.—John Willis, Benjamin Willis, John Aldrich.

1689.—Lieutenant Hayward and Samuel Allen chosen agents to go to Plymouth about settling the *Gournet.*

"   John Willis appointed by court to solemnize marriages, to summon witnesses before grand jurors, and to administer oaths, &c.

"   Josiah Edson, Nicholas Byram, and Edward Mitchell to issue the difference between the town and John Soul and Joseph Brastraw, (Barstow,) about the four mile line.

"   David Perkins, John Ames, and Samuel Washburn, to get in Mr. Keith's salary by all loving persuasions and legal means.

1690.—It was voted to be at charges for procuring a charter and to bear their proportion of the expense in case it may be obtained, and but one, Giles Leach, voted against it, and two appeared afterwards and spoke by word of mouth; voted also that Mr. Wiswall should be their agent to act for them.

1691.—It was voted the constables should not pay any more money towards the Canada expedition, till their own charges on that account be paid, and the rest of the towns in the colony had gathered and paid their proportion, as they themselves had done : and until further order of court at New Plymouth.

1694.—It was granted that Mr. David Perkins should have liberty to make a dam across the river below his house, against his own land, provided he damnifies none of his neighbors by overflowing their lands. And Thomas Washburn, by deed 1697, gave Perkins the right of joining the dam to his land.

"   Captain Thomas Hayward, Lieutenant John Haward, Deacon Brett, Thomas Snell, and Samuel Allen, to order the seats to each person in the meeting-house ; and Ensign Packard, Sergeant Josiah Edson, Sergeant Samuel Washburn, Sergeant Edward Mitchell, and Sergeant Nicholas Byram to seat the above committee.

"   Edward Mitchell and Jonathan Haward to inspect and
       take notice of any disorder among the young persons
       in the galleries on the Lord's day, and declare them
       by name after the exercise is done.

1694.—Thomas Snell, according to former agreement, bought a
       new book to record the purchasers' lands in, and they
       gave him for it eighteen acres of land.

1696.—Thomas Randall, William Manly, and their neighbors
       allowed to come here to meeting, and to make a horse
       bridge over Cutting Cove River.

1697.—The town agreed that for the time to come at every
       town meeting they would choose a moderator for said
       meeting.

1699.—The town agreed to choose town officers annually on the
       first Monday in March, beginning at 10 o'clock, and
       also to divide the town for constables into two parts.
       All on the south side of the town river, and from
       Lieutenant Haward's on the west side of the highway
       going to Braintree, to one constable. And from Lieu-
       tenant Haward's all on the east side of the highway
       going to Braintree, on the north side of the town
       river, to the other constable.

1703.—Voted to divide the town into three constablericks, as
       follows, viz :—All on the easterly side of Matfield and
       Satucket rivers to be one constablerick ; and the other
       two to be divided by the town river.

1708.—The town passed a clear vote to petetion the General
       Court for the continuance of the country road where
       it was laid out when removed from the place where
       the great bridge was at Jones' River, (at Kingston.)

1717.—The town gave Mr. Allen (minister) liberty to make use
       of the pine trees on the stated common on Bayley's
       Plain for drawing of turpentine.

1737.—The town voted their consent that the north should be-
       come a distinct town, agreeably to their petition ; and
       on November 29, 1738, they also voted their consent

that the south and east precincts might also each become distinct towns; but these votes were never attempted to be carried into effect only as it regarded the north, who, although they petitioned originally to become a *town*, were indulged so far only as to be incorporated into a *precinct*.

1757.—Voted to choose five selectmen : hitherto they had chosen but three, one from the west, one from the south, and one from the east; ever after they chose one from each of the five parishes, east, west, north, south, and Titicut.

1767.—Several of the neutral French were supported and provided for in this town for several years previous; and this year Joseph Latham was paid 21s. 4d., for carrying them to Plymouth; (for transportation probably.)

EARLY LOCATION OF HIGHWAYS.

1664.—It is ordered by the feofees, and agreed upon by the town, that every man shall have a convenient highway to his meadow lands.

"   They whom it doth concern may have a way through the spruce swamp.

1667.—There was a highway left by individuals between Nathaniel Hayward's six acre lot, and Thomas Snell's ten acre lot, upon the east side of Goodman Bacon's, on the plain, and a piece of common land between the lots in form like a gussett.

1668.—A way towards Plymouth, viz :—from the meeting-house to Arthur Harris' range, to the common—through the swamp to Sandy Hill—up the hill and over to John Hayward, Jr.'s range—and across his lot to Daniel Bacon's house—and in the old way to widow Bassett's lot to the wolf-trap—over the same lot to Thomas Hayward, Jr.'s lot, and across to Goodman John

Tompkin's lot—and so to a piece of land left for a road betwixt him and Thomas Snell—over a corner of Snell's lot, near the river to the bridge—through Nicholas Byram's land to his house—over a little river and over the plain to a narrow place in the swamp, and so to Arthur Harris' fifty acre lot, and on the hard ground to his son Samuel Harris' house—and in a straight line to a bridge on Satucket River, as the rocks will permit—and straight to the highway near Robert Latham's barn—then to the usual road to Plymouth, as far as the bounds of our town extends— only in the way we fetch a little compass to avoid a steep hill, a little way from Latham's lot.

1668.—2d.—A way towards Boston, viz ;—from the meeting-house on the same road above mentioned, to John Hayward's range—then to the usual road reaching into the bay as far as our bounds extend.

"   3d.—A way to Taunton, viz :—from the meeting-house to John Haward's—then over the river and between the lots that were Mr. Love Brewster's and John Fobes'— and so into the usual way that leads to Taunton.

"   4th.—A way to the great meadows, viz :—to come from out of Taunton way at the head of Edward Fobes' six acre lot—so to the head of Samuel Edson's six acre lots to William Snow's—then between said Edson's and Snow's lands to the common—then to the river.

These four were laid out by a jury in 1667 and 1668.

1673.—Thomas Snell was to make and maintain two horse bridges, one at the hither end of Salisbury plain, over the brook, and another at the further end over the river.

1677.—A piece of a highway granted to John Willis, through his lands, to the river.

1680.—Ten men were appointed to build and maintain a horse bridge over the river, near where the three rivers meet in the road way laid out by a jury for the Plymouth road to Pimpkin bridge. (At Pope's bridge.)

1684.—Lieutenant Thomas Hayward, Nathaniel Willis, Joseph Hayward and Francis Cary to maintain the bridge and causey at Lieutenant T. Hayward's house, fit for cart, horse, and foot : and are to be freed from all other highway work. And John Field, John Washburn, Jr., and Nathaniel Packard are to maintain a like bridge and causey towards Thomas Snell's house, at Sandy Hill, on the same conditions.

1685.—Samuel Allen, Samuel Allen, Jr., William Brett, Isaac Harris, John Haward, Jr., Jonathan Hill, and Thomas Whitman, pray for a road and bridge over Matfield River, (at Joppa.)

1690.—A way laid out from John Aldrich's to the corner of Goodman Edson's field, where it meets with the way that comes from the town : the way is to be where it's beaten.

" A way to Isaac Alden's ; beginning at the road leading from John Kingman's towards Nicholas Byram's—thence by the edge of *Huckleberry* plain to the old cow path and to the river—thence upon the plain commonly called Jonathan Cary's plain—thence by a slough and across a swamp to the northward of Jonathan Cary's house—thence to Beaver Brook, at the cartway between Isaac Alden's and James Cary's—thence to Isaac Alden's house—and thence to Snell's plain.—" The jury ordered to lay out such highways as are needful for the inhabitants to come to meeting and to mill, and to their meadows, especially the way to Indian Field and the meadows at Coasters' Kitchen."

" A way to the meadows called Coasters' Kitchen ; from the road at the corner of the land that was Mark Lathrop's—thence keeping the easterly side of the ridge to the meadows.

" A road laid out by a jury from Isaac Harris' house to Goodman Whitman's house on the east side,—thence

to the river, and over the river and between Edward
Mitchell's and John Haward's—so across Haward's
land where the way is above his barn, or between his
house and barn—so along the way to town.

1690.—A way from Goodman Bayley's farm and South Brook
agreed upon, viz :—the way now goes from South
Brook to Samuel Washburn's, where the way now is,
it runs on the north side of the barn to a tree where
it meets with a way that comes from South Brook
below Goodman Ames' meadow, where the way goes
over the brook to the said tree—and thence to a white
oak—thence in the way over a small run—thence to
John Leonard's house—thence with the way to Samuel
Edson's land, and down on Comfort Willis' land, and
across Samuel Edson's land to John Willis' land—
then to a wild cherry tree—then to a rock near the
outside of John Willis' land—then through Samuel
Edson's land to marked trees—and then to town.

"   A way from the north end of Samuel Lathrop's land in
town over the Spruce Swamp where the bridge is—
so straight up through Jonathan Haward's land and
Elkanah Willis' land to Ensign Packard's land—
thence to a tree on the east side of the way in Lieutenant Hayward's land—then to the way that comes
from the west meadow, where there is a rock on the
easterly side—then as the way is to West Meadow,
till it comes to Samuel Tompkin's land—then between
Mr. Keith's and Samuel Tompkin's land, till it meets
the west meadow path.

"   Road from (Sproats) or the meeting-house in Middleborough, over Thompson's bridges, to the road leading from Bridgewater to Plymouth, (at Thomas Drews)
then following Bridgewater road by James Latham's
to Byram's plain, to the road leading to Weymouth—
then as the road goes on the westerly side of Andrew
Ford's house, and so to the patent line.

1697.—A way ordered to be laid out to and over Satucket

River at the great Gall at Thomas Mitchell's and Nathaniel Allen's, and so to Plymouth road.

1698.—The town agreed to make a cart bridge over the town river at Lieutenant Haward's, and the owners of the saw mill, viz :—Josiah Edson, Edward Fobes, Ephraim Haward, Thomas Snell, and Joseph Hayward agreed to do their parts to it over and above what the rest of the town did, because their mill pond made a necessity for the bridge.

" The selectmen ordered to lay out a highway from John Whitman's to the commons.

1701.—The selectmen authorised to lay out a road from Taunton road, at the other side of Four Mile Brook, to John Leach's house, and so to Taunton (now Raynham) line.

1702.—A road laid out from Ensign Mitchell's, along the lane where the way is now trodden, and across Nathaniel Hayward's land, and crossing Samuel Hayward's land, and so along the beaten way, and passing on the easterly side of a great rock with a cleft in it, straight down to Plymouth road, and along the old way that went to John Packard's, till it comes to Ensign Mitchell's, and keeping the beaten cartway to his farm in the neck.

" A way determined on at the westerly end of Samuel Hayward's land, next Israel Alger's to John Bolton's lower lot.

" A way laid out from Taunton road by Samuel Keith's house to Edward Fobes' land and Thomas Wade's land, and over the brook and south side of Wade's house to William Bassett's house, and over Nathan Packard's and Samuel Leach's lands, and by Leach's barn across the brook to the north side of Ebenezer Leach's house, to the corner of the pond at the mouth of the brook, across the neck, and over the corner of the pond to Taunton (now Raynham) line.

10

1702.—A road laid out from Jonathan Haward's, at the rocky
gutter, running out of Cranberry Meadow, directly to
the bridge over Lathrop's swamp—then turning on the
westerly side of the swamp, and in the trodden path
to the next swamp—so onward to the south side of
Mr. Keith's land—so over the river where the bridge
is, and across John Turner's land to the line of the
north purchase, (now Easton.)

1703.—A way laid out from Taunton road between Captain
Edson's and Edward Fobes' land, to the brow of the
hill, near Captain Edson's, and turning along the
beaten way to John Willis' land, and over Joseph
Leonard's land, and turning between the land of John
Washburn and said Leonard, and by Leonard's house,
and so to the way formerly laid out. And beginning
again at Jonathan Washburn's, a way was laid out on
the west side of his house and barn, and by the west
end of old Goodman Conant's house, and crossing
South Brook at Captain Edson's meadow, and so to
Amos Snell's land.

"   A way from the bay road on Little Plain, south of Richard Field's house, easterly to Matfield River, and
crossing the river at the cart way, and across Thomas
Snell's land, and turning up the side of pine swamp,
and warping about again to the south-east corner of
Samuel Kingman's field.

"   A way beginning a little to the west of Zaccheus Packard's land, so as to run square over Daniel Field's land
to the south-west corner of John Snell's orchard, and
by his house to the common.

1706.—A road laid out from the old way between South Brook
and Ebenezer Whitman's house, and running across
his land to the river—so over on to Benjamin Hayward's land—so to the range between said Hayward
and John Hooper—so near said Hayward's house and
barn—and over the plain to Plymouth Road.

1710.—John Haward and John Field were permitted to stop up the old road across their house lots, and turn it down the mill lane, and so before John Field's door, and along by the river.

1713.—A way from the bridge, over South Brook, at William Orcutt's—then up the hill by Orcutt's door—so near the corner of a swamp, and into the beaten way—so over the causey at bear swamp, and up the hill, and as near the ridge as may be, to Josiah Washburn's fence—then turning on the northerly side of his house to the plain, and down the plain to the south end of it—then more westerly across a little swamp, and along the beaten foot-path to the burnt swamp, and through it to the plain not far from Nathaniel Woodward's field—then easterly, by the north side of his house, to Nathaniel Allen's land.

" A way from Josiah Washburn's to Josiah Leonard's, running by Widow Willis' fifty acres, and a little northerly from the fence of Josiah Washburn, Jr., and over the causey by Noah Washburn's—so running before his door, and across the swamp, to the south side of Josiah Leonard's land.

1714.—A way new marked and settled, from the north-west corner of William Ripley's land, over a little swamp, on a corner of Joseph Keith's land, to the range of James Haward's land—then turning by the southerly side of the swamp to a rock—so straight into the old way, to the east end of said Haward's barn—and then again from the rock in the range of said Keith's and Haward's land, till it meet the way that was laid out to Daniel Packard's.

1715.—Allowed thirty hands to build a bridge at William Conant's, they to be freed from all other highway work so long as they should keep said bridge in good repair.

" A way from where the road was laid, from James Keith's, toward the neck, at Joseph Hayward's—running over the bridge to the east end of Hayward's house—

turning on the east side of a pond to the range between
Jonathan Haward and Joseph Hayward—turning westerly in the range of said lots, till it passes the second
valley, to a corner of Joseph Hayward's fifty acres—so
to the bridge—so over the bridge and Joseph Hayward's land, to the north purchase line, (now Easton.)

1716.—A way laid out toward Poor meadow : beginning on the
east side of the river, and running across the meadow
and river, and by a bound of John Whitman's meadow
—and so between John Whitman's and John Read's
lands westerly crossing a poison bottom, by John
Whitman's corner bounds and a pond hole—so straight
into the old beaten path on the north-east side of a
great rock—and so keeping the beaten way, to the
swamp at Ebenezer Allen's where the way was formerly laid out.

"   A road from where the old way over Spruce Swamp
ended, running first northerly and then westerly, and
so into the old saw mill way, crossing the swamp to
the north-west, and keeping the old way till it crosses
James Haward's land, and comes to the land left for
a way from the old saw mill to West Meadow.

1717.—A way laid out, beginning where the three ways part to
the eastward of Ensign Johnson's, and so along the
southernmost beaten path by John Willis' house—
then over a corner of Willis' field, and running down
by Thomas Washburn's door, and a little beyond his
barn—then turning eastward across a steep ridge, and
on the southerly side of a pond hole, and so into the
old beaten path that goes to Joseph Alden's.

"   A way towards Titicut from Benjamin Washburn's land,
and so on the south side of the four mile line on
Nehemiah Washburn's land to Joseph Hayward's land,
and across his land to the common land ; and beginning again at John Keith's house, and running northward to Samuel Edson's land, and so over South
Brook, and into the way formerly laid out.

1721.—A private way from the country road on Byram's plain, at the northwest corner of Elisha Allen's land—then southerly by his house across the trodden path, to John Haward's land, and across his land and over the westerly side of Elisha Allen's land, to the north-west corner of John Haward's twenty acre lot, and so on said lot in or near the beaten path to the westerly side of Josiah Allen's land, and then across the bridge at burnt hill gutter over Josiah Allen's land to his northwest corner—then over a poison bottom in Ebenezer Byram's land, and by his barn, and over Black Brook as far as John Haward's land—so easterly to the outside of Byram's land.

"   A private way from the road between Joseph Latham's and the ridge—so across James Latham's and Whitman's lands, near to the corner of Jonathan Washburn's land—then on the westerly side of a swamp over Washburn's land, and running above the head of Joseph Washburn's home land, and by the head of Isaac Lazell's land, and over a corner of it, and along over William Conant's land, and by the easterly end of his house to the highway.

"   A way from Deacon Alden's to Mr. Perkin's, keeping the beaten way to John Bolton's lane, and through Jonathan Sprague's field, to the range between him and John Bolton, Jr., and then to come into and keep the beaten way to Mr. David Perkins'.

"   A way from the old road, over Flaggy Meadow Brook. to the top of the hill—then turning and going near by the house of Israel Alger, Jr., so down over the swamp on the side of a pond hole, and into the way to the bridge over the cove—so westerly near Joseph Alger's house, and by the mile line to Cutting Cove fence. And from the bridge a way was laid over the slough by the west side of Israel Alger's meadow fence, and so by the east side of Thomas Alger's fence to John Field's land.

1721.—A way from West Meadow, at a corner of Joseph Snell's fence, near Josiah William's, across Snell's land and Benoni Hayward's land, to Seth Brett's land, and so by Brett's land to the country road. Hayward and Snell leave to set up gates.

"   A way from Thomas Wade's to Jonathan Cary's : from near Wade's house to where Joseph Bassett, Jr., was going to build—so turning into and keeping the cartway to Cary's land—so over the swamp and Cary's land, and by his house in a drift way, to the old road leading to the great meadow over Bassett's plain.

1722.—A way from Edmund Hobart's orchard to Lieutenant Davenport's house—then between Davenport's and Joseph Pratt's land out to the common. And Davenport and Thomas Hayward agreed Hayward should have a way to pass with horse or cart across said Davenport's land, on a stony ridge out into the above way, Hayward keeping sufficient gates.

"   A way from Plymouth old road towards Weymouth road, viz :—from the ridge through and over the swamp, and not far from Isaac Harris' fence, and so by his barn in the old way to the river where the bridge is, and up the hill, and turning more easterly, and coming into the way from Josiah Allen's, and keeping said way towards Elisha Allen's—then on the east side of John Haward's and west side of Elisha Allen's land, northerly over the plain to the east side of a tree in Elisha Allen's other lot, and across the road leading to Ebenezer Allen's—so over the corner of Captain Byram's lot, and on the west side of Ebenezer Allen's corner, and across the east corner of Samuel Allen's land, and by the side of this lot into the road leading to Weymouth.

1724.—A way beginning twenty rods westerly of the house of Jonathan Haward, Jr.—then northerly over said Haward's land, and on the westerly side of Lathrop's swamp, over Joshua Haward's and Thomas Hayward's lands, to the range between Elihu Brett and John

Lathrop's lands—so to the extent of Brett's land, and to the top of the hill—still northerly to Samuel Cary's land, and so across Cary's, Brett's, and Joseph Hayward's lands, keeping the beaten way to the saw mill.

1724.—A way from the head of the lane by Samuel Kingman's, northerly by the swamp to John Kingman's house, and by John Wormell's house, across Benjamin Edson's land, and on the easterly side of a little pond hole, and still northerly over John Kingman's land, to a small run of water, and across Henry Kingman's land, and down to James Packard's land, to the south-eastward of a ridge, and so on the ridge by the easterly side of James Packard's land to the saw mill.

1725.—A way from the easterly side of Captain Edson's meadow, near South Brook, first southerly, and then easterly to land of Ruth and Hannah Field—so near to Benjamin Pratt's, and still easterly across Joseph Pratt's land, to the way leading by Lieutenant Davenport's.

"   A way from the road on the northerly side of Benjamin Willis' land—then easterly to and over Samuel Lathrop's land, to John Benson's house.—Also from the road leading by William Orcutt's to the causey, and over a brook and so to Amos Snell's land.—Also from the road north side Benjamin Willis' house, to run between his house and barn south to Amos Snell's land.

1726.—A way from William Orcutt's land easterly towards Amos Snell's, and over a corner of his orchard, and by his house, and southerly by William Washburn's land to the road leading from Josiah Washburn's to William Washburn's.

"   A road from the old way, leading by the easterly end of Josiah William's house to West Meadow—southerly to Joseph Packard's house, and thence to the new saw mill on West Meadow Brook.

"   A way from widow Bolton's to Mr. David Perkins', between land of John Willis and land he sold Jonathan Washburn, to said Perkin's land—so westerly and down the hill, and over the bridge above **Mr. Perkin's** mill, and by the coal house till it comes into the road near Mr. Perkin's house.

" The way by Chilton Latham's turned westerly on the northerly side of his land to the new saw mill, and over the river just above the mill dam—then to extend northerly to the way leading to Byram's Plain.

1727.—A way from the old malt house of Ensign Mitchell, deceased, near his late dwelling house—then in the old range, formerly between him and John Haward, deceased, to Plymouth road—then westerly to land of Francis Cary, deceased, to Ebenezer Hill's land, to Nathaniel Hayward's land, to Ebenezer Hill's shop— so along the beaten way to the Centre Tree—so along to Ensign Johnson's, between his and Solomon Johnson's house, and so along the beaten way to the old meeting-house.

" A way from Samuel Edson's, by the house of Joseph Snow, and Joseph Snow, Jr., and Henry Kingman's— then turning southerly till it comes to Daniel Johnson's, and so between his house and barn to David Johnson's, where the three roads meet.

1728.—The way at Robinson's turned to go where the bridge now is.

1729.—A private way from the road by Ebenezer Alden's, to the country road by Josiah Byram's : beginning at a stake between Isaac Alden's and Ebenezer Alden's— thence south twenty-three deg., east thirty-six rods— thence south eleven deg., east forty-seven rods—thence south four deg., west fifty-eight rods—thence south twenty deg., west seventy-seven rods—thence south ten deg., east thirty-six rods to the country road aforesaid.

" A way from where two roads part, about twenty rods east of Black Brook—one leading to Moses Bisbee's, and the other to Samuel Pratt's—thence to Samuel Pratt's house—so on to Mr. Moore's house—thence to the saw mill, and over the bridge below the mill—then over rocks and mire, and leaving the old way, about two rods to the left hand, and going through the swamp to William Gould's land, where his house stands.

1730.—The bridge below Moses Bisbee's to be moved further down where the old bridge was, if the selectmen find it convenient.

" The way leading from Isaac Harris' to Abington, turned to the eastward of widow Allen's land.

" A way from the road between John Keith's and Francis Wood's easterly to a small brook—then turning up a hill—and so northerly to the range between Keith and Wood, and easterly to a corner bound of Wood's land.

" A road from Ephraim Jennings' over Joseph Jennings' land, and by his house, and over land of John Brett, and over a small brook—so to land formerly William Brett's, and by Nathaniel Hayward's house to land of Zechariah Standish, and so to Middleborough (now Halifax) line.

" A road over Comfort's Bridge to the house of John Willis, Jr., and to the road leading from Thomas Washburn's to David Johnson's.

1731.—A way from Benjamin Hayward's, over John Hayward's land, and the said Benjamin's land to Josiah Hayward's land, and between his house and barn, and over Jennings' bridge, and on John Packard's and Joseph Packard's land, and so over Samuel Jennings' and Richard Jennings' land, and over a small brook, and so between Jennings' house and barn, and up the hill, and by Ephraim Jennings' house and barn, and over Joseph Jennings' land, up a hill, and so to a small slough by Plymouth road.

" A way from Taunton road to Moses Washburn's land—thence a drift way through gates and bars to the island in the great meadow, to run between the field of Samuel Packard, Jr., and the pond, and on the west side of Packard's house, and so to the great meadow.

11

1732.—A way from Titicut River, at the road over the brook
    below the saw mill—then over Nehemiah Washburn's
    land, and by Nathaniel Hooper's house and orchard,
    and so by William Hooper's house—then turning
    easterly to the brook, and keeping the beaten way by
    Nehemiah Washburn's house to the road already laid
    out.

"   A way from Taunton road on the hill south of Ebenezer
    Willis' to the southerly side of the plain, and along
    by a rock south-west of Samuel Alden's house, and
    along to the west side of Joshua Fobes' house, and to
    the arm of the saw mill pond, and so between the land
    of Captain Edson and Nehemiah Washburn, and so
    east to the great river at Titicut.

"   An open road from Nicholas Wade's to the Plymouth
    road, at Sandy Hill, viz:—from Wade's land at the
    bank of the pond westerly over the mouth of the
    river, and south of David Robin's house, and to a tree
    within the gate, and so along by a pond hole, and so
    along eight rods south of the house of Benjamin Hay-
    ward, Jr., and along the old road to the top of the
    hill, and along by the corner of Chilton Latham's
    land to the Plymouth road at Sandy Hill.

1733.—Nathaniel Woodward and Solomon Leonard agree upon
    a road by their houses, and across their lands.

"   A way from John Lathrop's across the swamp to Joseph
    Cary's land, and between Cary's and Lieutenant Haw-
    ard's land, and by Thomas Hayward's bars at West
    Meadow across a swamp and over the brook, and over
    a corner of a swamp in Samuel Packard's land, and
    so to the beaten path leading to West Meadow, and
    so to the road leading to Josiah Williams' and Joseph
    Packard's, on the east side of Williams' house.

1734.—A way from Captain Edson's house northwesterly to
    Benjamin Snow's house—then westerly to Samuel Ed-
    son's land, and so to Taunton road.

"   A way from Joseph Washburn's, on the side of the hill

between his house and causey, as it goes to Thomas
Conant's—so over the causey and the beaten way from
said Conant's to Nathaniel Conant's, and into the lane
by Nathaniel Conant's, and up along to the bounds
between Nathaniel Ames and Bethiah Ames, and so
before Lindsay's door and by Richard Davenport's
land to the bounds between John Washburn and Ichabod Orcutt to said Orcutt's house and the old road.

" A way laid out anew or turned, at the request and free
consent of John Johnson, Isaac Lazell, David Conant,
and John Holman, between Major Holman's and William Conant's, from the corner of Holman's pasture,
turning out of the old way, and into the pasture
southwesterly to a flat rock near Johnson's fence, and
so over his field, and between his house and shop,
straight to the east end of Lazell's house, and so by
his orchard fence to an old coal pit—then turning
more easterly to David Conant's range, and gradually
entering on said Conant's land, till it has the whole
way on it, and so keeping Conant's line ten or twelve
rods—then across Conant's field to the highway.

1741.—A way turned on the further end of Byram's plain, out
of the old road, at the south-west end of Josiah Kingman's field, straight to the westerly end of Captain
Byram's barn, and so between the house and barn, and
thence straight to the north-east corner of the old
orchard on the plain, that was formerly Jeremiah
Newland's.

" A drift way for David Kingman and his near neighbors
to go to meeting, viz :—from the south-west corner of
Cornet Beals' ten acre lot, where John Hanmer lives,
straight to Dr. Byram's house—thence to the north
end of the forge dam, and so to the Little House, and
thence by the fence to the waste way that runs before
the door.

" A way from Ames' land by Downey's house, and so on
between Abiel Packard's and Daniel Richards' land to
the country road.

1746.—A way from Abington, to the road near Captain Bass'
house, viz:—from the line between Bridgewater and
Abington, south of Thomas White's house, in the lane
between his house and barn—thence to Samuel Porter's barn, and by his house to land of Thomas Whitmarsh and James Lovell, and between their lands to
Woodbridge Brown's land, and keeping the beaten
path or near it over the said Brown's land to Snell's
meadows, and over the meadows where the causey is
made, and by Eleazar Whitman's house, and so to
James Latham's field, and by his house, and between
his house and barn in the beaten way to Lieutenant
Beals' land—then turning westerly till it comes even
with Ensign Kingman's house, and then turning down
by his house straight to Joseph Byram's barn, and so
to the bridge across the Forge Pond, and over the
bridge and by the pond in the trodden way, till it
comes to the country road a little northward of Capt.
Bass' house : laid out at the request of the neighbors.

" A way laid out on William Gould's land from a great
rock, and running south eleven deg. east twenty rods
against his house—thence south twenty-three deg. east
twenty-five rods to Pembroke line. (This road is now
in Hanson.)

1756.—The way turned from Ephraim Cary's straight to Edward
Mitchell's, by his request, and thence straight to Timothy Hayward's and into the old way.

1757.—The road turned from a stake standing on the south side
of the road, by Moses Bisbee's, south nine deg. east
from the south-west corner of Charles Bisbee's house,
and running ninety rods on the same point to Job
Chamberlin's land, where it meets the road;—this was
done at the request of Moses Bisbee, Nathaniel Chamberlin, Isaac Lazell, Jr., Job Chamberlin, and Simeon
Whitman.

FAMILY REGISTER.

EXPLANATIONS.

—a. before a date, stands for about—b. for born—d. for death or died—m. for married—s. for son—ss. for sons—w. for wife—gra. for graduate or graduated—B. U. for Brown University—D. for daughter—Ds. for Daughters—H. U. for Harvard University · ✳ added to a name or date of a birth, signifies that the person died in youth or without issue—W. B. for West Bridgewater—S. P. for South Parish of Bridgewater, now Bridgewater—E. B. for East Bridgewater—N. B. for North Bridgewater—Tit. for Titicut. Other abbreviations will occur, which being usual and common, need no explanation.

ALDEN.—Hon. John Alden arrived with the Pilgrims at Plymouth in the May Flower, 1620 ; was about 21 years old, and was one of the Governor's Assistants' many years, and otherwise much employed and greatly distinguished in·the infant colony ; he removed early to Duxbury, and was one of the original proprietors of Bridgewater, as we have already seen ; he d. at Duxbury Sept. 12, 1687, æ. 88, of course was born 1599 : he m. Priscilla, D. of Wm. Mullens, 1623, and had John, Joseph, David, Jonathan, Elizabeth, Sarah, Ruth and Mary.— John was a captain, a mariner and master of a vessel, removed to Boston, m. Elizabeth, widow of Abiel Ewrill, and D. of Maj. Wm. Phillips, 1660, and had John 1663, William 1669, Nathaniel 1670, Zechariah 1673, gra. H. U. 1692, Nathan 1677, and Henry, and also several Ds.; he d. 1702, she 1719 ; his will dated 1701. He was accused of witchcraft.—David and Jonathan remained at Duxbury, and had families there.—Elizabeth m. Wm. Paybody.— Sarah m. Alexander Standish.—Ruth m. John Bass, 1657.— Mary m. Thomas Delano.

2. Joseph, (2d son of Hon. John 1.) had his father's proprietary share in Bridgewater, and was an early settler here ; he m. Mary, D. of Moses Simmons, sometimes written Symonson ; and had Isaac, Joseph, John, and probably Elizabeth, who m. Benjamin Snow, 1691, and Mary who m. Samuel Allen, 1700 ; he d. 1697, æ. a. 73.

3. Isaac, (s. of Joseph 2.) settled in E. B., and m. Mehitabel, D. of Samuel Allen, 1685, and had Mehitabel 1687, Sarah 1688, Mary 1691, Isaac 1692, Ebenezer 1693, Mercy 1696, Abigail 1699, Jemima 1702, and John.—Mehitabel m. Benjamin Richards, 1711.—Sarah m. Seth Brett, 1712, and afterwards Dea.

Recompence Cary, 1727.—Mary m. John Webb, of Braintree, 1720, and d. 1772, æ. 82.—Isaac lived a bachelor, and left a large real estate.—Mercy m. Zaccheus Packard, 1725.—Jemima m. Dea. Thomas Whitman, 1727.

4. Dea. Joseph, (s. of Joseph 2.) lived in S. B., and m. Hannah, D. of Daniel Dunham, of Plymouth, 1690; and had Daniel 1690, Joseph 1693*, Eleazar 1694, Hannah 1696, Mary 1699, Joseph 1700*, Jonathan 1703*, Samuel 1705, Mehitabel 1707, Seth 1710; he and she both d. 1747, he æ. 80, she 78.—Hannah m. Mark Lathrop, 1722; Mary m. Timothy Edson, 1719; Mehitabel m. Barnabas Eaton, and d. æ. 30.

5. John (s. of Joseph 2.) had his father's homestead in W. B., and sold it to Isaac Johnson a. 1700, and removed to Titicut in Middleborough; m. Hannah, D. of Captain Ebenezer White, of Weymouth; she was born 1683; he had David, who m. Judith Padelford, and was father of Solomon; Priscilla, w. of Abraham Borden; Thankful, w. of Francis Eaton; Hannah, w. of Thomas Wood; Lydia, w. of Samuel Eddy, and afterwards of John Fuller; Mary, w. of Noah Thomas; Abigail, w. of Nathan Thomas; Joseph, who m. Hannah Hall; John, who first m. Lydia Lazell, and had Capt. John, of Fairhaven, and Nathan, and then m. Rebecca Weston, and d. April, 1821, æ. 102; Ebenezer, who at the age of 20 went to Cuba, and was taken prisoner and suffered hardships for 10 years, m. Anna Whitaker, and afterwards Rebecca Smith, and settled in Ashfield; Noah born 1725, a Baptist minister, settled at Stafford 1755, and afterwards installed at Bellingham 1766, a member of the convention for forming the Constitution of Massachusetts in 1780, and also of the convention for adopting the Constitution of the United States in 1788, m. Joanna Vaughn, and had 3 ss. and several Ds., and d. 1797, æ. 71.

6. Capt. Ebenezer (s. of Isaac 3.) lived in E. B., and m. Anna, D. of Joseph Keith, 1717, and had Anna 1718, Susanna 1719, Abigail 1721, Nathan 1727, Ezra 1732.—Anna m. Eleazai Washburn, Susanna m. Ephraim Cary, Abigail m. Ebenezer Byram, Jr., Esq., all three m. together, at the same time, viz :— Nov. 22, 1738.—The mother d. 1775, æ. 79, the father 1776, æ. 83, and was the last surviving member of the first church in East Bridgewater, gathered in 1724.

7. John (s. of Isaac 3.) lived in E. B., and m. Hannah, D. of Henry Kingman, 1727, and had John* and James*, twins, 1729; Isaac 1731, Jonathan 1733, Hannah 1736, Adam 1738*, Abigail 1742*, Keziah 1743; his w. d. 1744, and he m. Rebecca Nightingale 1745, and had Rebecca 1745, John 1747, Esther 1749*, James 1751, Adam 1754, Joseph 1755, Benjamin 1757; the father d. 1762, æ. a. 67; Rebecca m. John Sprague 1767, and they with the mother and John went to Warwick; James, Adam, Joseph and Benjamin went to Claremont, N. H.

8. Daniel, Esq., (s. of Dea. Joseph 4.) m. Abigail, D, of Joseph Shaw 1717, and had Joseph 1718, Daniel 1720, Abigail 1722, Zephaniah 1724, Hannah 1726*, Hannah 1727, Mehitabel 1729*, Barnabas 1732, Ebenezer 1734, Mary 1737 ; he removed to Stafford with his family, where he d. æ. 80.—Joseph m. Susanna, D. of Solomon Packard, 1742, and had Zenas 1745*, and Martha 1747*, and d. at Worcester, æ. 50.—Daniel, Esq., m. Jane Turner 1747, and d. at Lebanon, near Dartmouth College, æ. 70, and was father of the late Dr. Ebenezer Alden, of Randolph, born at, Stafford 1755.—Abigail m. Dea. Eleazar Whitman, sen., 1742.—Zephaniah m. Hopestill, D. of Thomas Wade, 1748, and d. at Stafford, æ. 80.—Hannah m. Joshua Blodget, at Stafford, and there d., æ. 70.—Barnabas d. at Ashfield, æ. 60.—Ebenezer d. at Stafford, æ. 21.—Mary m. Isaac Fuller 1764.

9. Eleazar (s. of Dea. Joseph 4.) lived in S. B., and m. Martha, D. of Joseph Shaw, 1720 ; she d. 1769, æ. 69, he 1773, æ. 79 ; he had Jonathan 1721, Eleazar 1723, Abraham 1725*, David 1727, Joshua 1729, Caleb 1731*, Ezra 1734, Timothy 1736.—Jonathan m. Experience, D. of Nathaniel Hayward, 1743, and went to Greenwich where he d., æ. 80, and she d. there 1809, æ. 90.—David m. Lucy, D. of Noah Thomas, of Mid'o., and went to Ashfield, and d. there, æ. 80.—Ezra went to Greenwich, was a Deacon there, and d. æ. 84.—Rev. Timothy gra. H. U. 1762, settled at Yarmouth Dec. 13, 1769, and d. 1828, æ. 92 ; he m. Sarah, D. of Rev. Habijah Weld, of Attleboro'; she d. 1796, æ. 58; he had Timothy, Isaiah, Martin, Oliver, Sarah Weld, Martha Shaw.

10. Samuel, (s. of Dea. Joseph 4.) lived in Titicut ; m. Abiah, D. of Capt. Josiah Edson, a. 1728, and had Abiah 1729, Mehitable 1732, Sarah 1734, Samuel 1736, Josiah 1738, Simeon 1740, and Silas.—Samuel, the father, m. Rebecca, D. of Josiah Washburn, 1752, and d. æ. 80.—Abiah m. Seth Harris 1751.—Mehitabel m. Joshua Packard, 1755.—Silas d. æ. 21.

11. Capt. Seth (s. of Dea. Joseph 4.) lived in S. B., and m. Mehitabel, D. of Eleazar Carver, 1740, and had Oliver 1740, Seth 1741, Caleb 1744* and Joseph 1747 ; she d. 1757, and he m. Jael, wid. of Timothy Hayward, 1758, she was wid. Peterson when she m. Hayward ; he d. 1784, æ. 75.

12. Dea. Nathan (s. of Capt. Ebenezer, 6.) m. Mary, D. of Daniel Hudson, 1750, and had Nathan 1751 ; she d. 1755, and he m. Lydia, D. of Benjamin Richards, 1757, and had Isaac 1758* ; he d. 1807, æ. 80, she 1823, æ. 90.

13. Ezra (s. of Capt. Ebenezer, 6.) m. Rebecca, D. of Josiah Keith, of Easton, 1756, and had a son 1757*, Abby 1759*, Abigail 1761, Isaac 1763, Susanna 1766 ; he d., and his wid. m. John Bisbee 1771, and d. 1777, æ. 41.—Abigail m. George Vining 1778, and Susanna m. Jacob Allen 1784, and both went to Plainfield.

14. Isaac (s. of John 7.) m. Martha, D. of Solomon Packard,

1755, and had Nabby 1757, Isaac 1758; he d., and the wid. m.
Israel Bailey, 1760.—Nabby m. Joseph Whiting 1778.

15. Jonathan (s. of John 7.) m. Experience, D. of Cornelius
Washburn, 1766, and had Mehitabel 1767, Isaac, John, Ezra,
Daniel; she d. 1775, and he m. Hannah, wid. of Thomas White,
1777, her maiden name Green, and had Cyrus, Samuel Green,
Jonathan and Polly; she, the mother, d. 1811, æ. 63; she m.
White 1772; Jonathan, the father, d. 1825, æ. 93.—Mehitabel
m. Henry Jackson 1786, and went to Minot.—Isaac m. Ruth, D.
of Josiah Byram, 1794, and had Joanna, w. of Wm. Bird, m.
1818, Nabby and Lewis; he d. 1832, æ. 60, and his wid. m.
Alpheus Fobes.—John m. Deborah, D. of Benjamin Robinson,
1798, and had Benjamin, Mary, Alvina, Charles, and went to
Minot.—Ezra m. Nabby, D. of Wm. Vinton, 1798, and had Edward V., who d. young at the south, and William V., who lives
in Boston.—Capt. Cyrus m. Nabby K., Daughter of Capt. Daniel
Kinsley, 1808, and had Mary K. 1809, Hannah G. 1811, and
Nabby Vinton 1813, and then went to Minot.—Samuel G. m.
Rhoda, D. of Benjamin Richards, 1804, and had Benjamin,
Samuel G., and Bartlett R., and d. 1814, æ. 36, was killed by
the bursting of a cannon at Eastport in the last war.—Daniel
and Jonathan went to the westward.—Polly m. Abel Barrell 1810.

16. Eleazar (s. of Eleazar 9.) m. Sarah, D. of Nicholas
Whitman, 1748, and had Martha, 1752, Mary 1754, Abigail
1756, Sarah 1759, Hannah 1762, Eleazar 1767; the father d.
1803, æ. 80, the mother 1819, æ. 93.—Martha m. Silvanus Blossom 1774, and d. 1802.—Mary d. single.—Abigail m. Wm. Snell
1774.—Sarah d. 1778.—Hannah m. Levi Latham 1782.—Eleazar
m. Deborah, sister of Eleazar Churchill 1794; she d. 1804, and
he m. Abigail Pierce, of Mid'o., 1819, and had Lewis, Isaac,
Rebecca.   Isaac m. Minerva Waterman 1821.

17. Lt. Joshua (s. of Eleazar 6.) m. Mary, Widow of Seth
Alden, Jr., and D. of Eleazar Carver 1781; had no children;
d. 1809, æ. 80, she 1811, æ. 63; he gave legacies to the church,
parish, and singing choir, in S. B.

18. Samuel (s. of Samuel 10.) m. a Williams, and lived in a
corner of Abington included in the north parish of Bridgewater;
had Daniel, Silas, Joseph, Samuel, Williams, Seth, Hosea, and
Hannah w. of James Cary, m. 1798; d. 1816, æ. 81.—Daniel
m. Sarah, D. of Jon'a. Cary, 1786, and had Otis, Daniel, Alpheus, and Sally, who m. Jon'a. Burr, of Worthington.   Otis
m. an Adams, Daniel m. Eunice, D. of Perez Southworth, 1815;
he and Alpheus went to Randolph.—Silas and Joseph went to
Jay.—Samuel m. Sally, D. of Mark Ford, 1799, and had Sanford, Mehitabel, Hannah, and Sally, w. of Sidney Howard, m.
1815.—Williams m. a Lynfield, and had Mary, Lavinia, and
Clarissa.—Dea. Seth m. Harmony, D. of Perez Southworth,
1802, and removed to Stoughton.—Hosea m. Milly, D. of Wm.
Edson, 1817.—Wid. Sarah Alden m. Lazarus Beal, of Weymouth, 1809.

19. Josiah (s. of Samuel 10.) m. Bathsheba Jones, of Raynham, 1761, and had Elijah 1763, Hazael, Josiah.—Elijah m. Rebecca Fuller, of Kingston, 1783.—Josiah, and Elijah his son, went to Brimfield, now Wales.—Hazael m. Bethany Wilbor 1791. It appears also on record that Bethany Alden m. Eliphalet White, of Raynham, 1791.

20. Simeon (s. of Samuel 10.) m. Mary, D. of Seth Packard, 1764, and had Simeon, Alpheus, Silas, Solomon, David, Jonathan, Isaac and Lot.

21. Oliver (s. of Capt. Seth 11.) m. Experience, D. of Capt. Solomon Leonard, 1765, and had Caleb 1766, Peddy, (Experience,) Oliver 1770*, Cromwell 1773*. He d. æ. over 80.— Peddy m. Silvanus Pratt 1803.

22. Seth (s. of Capt. Seth 11.) m. Mary, D. of Eleazar Carver, 1767, and had Seth 1769, Mehitabel 1771; he had three other children, who d. 1775. Seth, the father, d. 1775, and his wid. m. Lt. Joshua Alden 1781.—Seth m. Sally, D. of Wm. Snell, 1800, and removed to Maine, and had a s. William S., now living in S. B.

23. Capt. Joseph (s. of Capt. Seth 11.) m. Bethiah, D. of Eleazar Carver, and had Mehitabel 1775, Joseph 1777, Daniel 1780, Thomas 1782, Cyrus 1785, Eunice 1788, Seth, Bethiah, and Betsy; he d. 1803, æ. 55.—Mehitabel m. Thomas Mitchell 1797.—Capt. Joseph, Jr., m. Polly, D. of Amos Hayward, 1800.—Daniel m. Joanna Tilson 1804, and went to Belchertown.—Thomas m. Matilda, D. of Daniel Copeland, 1815.— Cyrus and Seth were gra. B. U.; the former an attorney in Boston, now in Bristol co., the latter a minister at Marlboro'.— Eunice d. single.—Bethiah m. Alfred Arnold, of Greenwich, 1813.—Betsy m. Joseph Hooper, Jr.

24.—Nathan, Esq., (s. of Dea. Nathan 12.) m. Sarah, D. of William Barrell, 1776, and had Mary 1777, Lydia 1779, Marcus 1782, Isaac 1786, Sarah 1792, Lucius 1796. The mother d. 1816, æ. 61, and he then m. wid. Joanna Soule, of M., 1819.— Mary m. Capt. Wm. Vinton 1797, and d. 1799.—Lydia m. David Keith, Jr., 1801.—Marcus m. Salome, D. of Col. Aaron Hobart, of A., 1807, and had Aaron Hobart 1809, Susanna Hobart 1815, and went to N. Y.—Isaac, Esq., m. Clarissa, D. of Ephraim Whitman, of A., 1811, and had Wm. Barrell 1813, and Henry 1817.—Sarah m. James P. Tolman, of St., 1818.— Rev. Lucius was gra. B. U. 1821, and is settled in E. Abington.

25. Isaac (s. of Ezra 13.) m. Mary, D. of Thomas Russell, 1781, and had Ezra, Thomas Russell, both baptized 1800. James Sullivan 1804, one other*, and the mother d. 1814, æ. 47; he m. Betsy, wid. of Benjamin Palmer, and D. of Daniel Willis, 1814, and had several children, and d. 1827, æ. 64.—Ezra m. Susan Dyer 1813, and went to Abington.—Thomas R. m. Jane, D. of Matthew Allen, 1813, and afterwards Dorothy, D. of Stephen Hearsey, and d. 1835, æ. 45.—James S. went to Weymouth.

26. Solomon (s. of David, and grandson of John 5.) m. Sarah
Hall 1755, and had Sarah 1756, Solomon 1757, Noah, Alexander, Amasa, and three other Ds.—Solomon m. Patty King 1786,
and had 2 ss., Solomon (a bachelor) and Lewis.—Noah m.
Elizabeth Miller, of M., 1793, and had 2 ss., Noah and Hiram,
and went to Illinois.—Alexander m. Lucy Leonard 1792, and
went to Me.—Amasa m. Sally Hathaway, of M., 1799, and had
2 Ds.—Of the 4 Ds., one m. Elijah Alden; one, Sarah m. Azel
Shaw; one, Hannah, m. Seth Miller, Esq., 1796; and one m.
Eliphalet White.—Noah Alden m. Vodicia Hayford 1804.—
Elizabeth m. Soranus Shaw 1816.
27. Caleb (s. of Oliver 21.) m. Sally, D. of Benjamin Hayward, 1790, and had Oliver, Cromwell, Susan, Sally, Mehitabel,
and Mary.—Oliver m. Melinda, D. of Edward Mitchell.—
Cromwell m. Mary, D. of Joseph Hall.—Susan m. Samuel
Sanger.—Sally m. Sidney Howard.—Mehitabel m. in Lancaster
where she lives.
Ebenezer Alden of M., m. Ruth Fobes 1763.—Anthony Alden
joined the church in W. B. 1742.—Ruth m. Daniel Faunce, of
P., 1777.—Rosanda, of M., m. Joseph Fobes, 2d, 1781.—Silence
of M., m. Zephaniah Hathaway, of T., 1792.—Andrew, of M.,
m. Silence (or Selina) Fobes 1797.—Caleb, of M., m. Susanna
Dunbar 1787.—Lucy of M. m. Eleazar Cary 1794.—Daniel m.
Deborah Fullerton, of A., 1798.—Caleb 2d. m. Polly Alden
1814.—Daniel m. Olive Tucker 1819.—Sally m. Jonathan Burr,
of Worthington, 1820.
ALDRIDGE or ALDRICH.—1. George and Catharine Aldrich, of Braintree, had John 1644, Sarah 1645, Peter 1648,
Mercy 1650, Jacob 1652, Mattathias 1656.
2. Henry and Mary Aldridge, at Dedham, had Mary 1643,
Samuel 1644. Henry, the father, d. 1645.
3. Josiah and his wife Mary settled in Bridgewater, and had
William 1719, Henry 1721, Josiah 1723.
4. John m. Sarah, D. of Giles Leach, and settled in S. B.,
and had a D. Sarah, who m. Benjamin Hayward a. 1700.
5. John m. Elizabeth Cooper 1722, and had Timothy 1723.
6. Joseph, of Braintree, m. Patience Osbourne 1661, and had
Joseph 1663.—John Aldridge, of Bridgewater, was a soldier at
Roxbury, and d. there Feb. 1776.—There were also Nathan and
Lydia Aldridge, in Bridgewater.—Josiah m. Sarah Baker 1753.—
Joseph m. Elizabeth Andros, of T., 1754.—Benjamin m. Mary
Shaw 1721.—Catharine m. Jacob Bump 1716.—Peter Aldridge
was on the jury 1707.—Mary m. Joseph Newcomb 1768.—Daniel, of M., m. Keziah Pratt 1797.—Phebe m. David Vaughn, of
M., 1802.—Polly m. Lot Pratt 1787.—Eaton Aldridge m. Nabby,
wid. of Otis Holmes, of T., and D. of Ezra Fobes, 1807; she
m. O. Holmes 1796.

ALGER.—Thomas Alger, from Taunton, (perhaps Easton now) settled in W. B. and m. Elizabeth, D. of Samuel Packard, 1665, and had Israel and Deliverance, and perhaps other children.

2. Israel, (s. of Thomes 1.) m. Patience, D. of Nathaniel Hayward, and had Israel 1689, Joseph 1694, Thomas 1697, Nathaniel 1700, John 1704.—Nathaniel went to Easton, was there in 1727 and 1729.—John d. 1730, and his brother Israel settled his estate.

3. Israel (s. of Israel 2.) m. Alice, D. of Joseph Hayward, and had Patience 1713; the mother d. 1716, and Patience was then called Alice to bear up her mother's name; he then m. Su sanna, D. of William Snow, 1717, and had Israel, Daniel 1727, James 1729; the mother d. and he m. Rachel, D. of Thomas Wade, 1731, but had no children by her.—Alice, Israel, and Daniel were all baptized 1727.—Alice m. Shepard Fiske 1732.

4. Joseph (s. of Israel 2.) m. Mary, D. of Wm. Ames, 1719, and had Mary 1720, Joseph 1723, Patience 1726, Bethiah 1729, John 1732, Susanna 1734, Nathan 1737*, Edmund 1739.—Mary m. Abner Hayward 1739.—Patience m. Isaac Lathrop 1743.— Bethiah m. Isaac Lazell 1748.—Susanna m. Ephraim Burr 1755.

5. Thomas (s. of Israel 2.) m. Sarah, D. of Peter Dunbar, 1724, and had a s. Thomas, and perhaps other children.

6. Israel (s. of Israel 3.) m. Abial, D. of Samuel Lathrop, 1747, and had Sarah 1754*; he d. 1755, and the wid. m. Jon'a. Bozworth, 1756.

7. James (s. of Israel 3) m. Martha, D. of Jon'a. Kingman, 1750, and had Anna 1752, Alice 1755, Abiezer 1757, Martha 1760, Phebe 1763, James 1765*, and James 1770, and 3 others who d. in infancy; he d. 1800, she 1813.—Anna m. Jesse Fuller Sturtevant 1771, and Amos Keith 1774.—Alice m. Peter Dunbar 1773.—Martha m. Calvin Keith 1779.—Phebe m. Thaxter Dunbar 1779.

8. Daniel (s. of Israel 3.) m. Susanna, D. of Benjamin Fobes, and had Daniel 1751, Susanna 1753, Israel 1755, Kezia 1757, Benjamin 1760, Chloe and Silvia 1761, Nathan 1763, Martha 1766, David 1768, Abiel 1772.—Susanna m. Mark Packard.— Kezia m. John Dickerman 1786.—Benjamin m. Hannah, D. of Daniel Snow, Esq., 1785, and lived in Easton.—Chloe m. Tisdale Howard 1791.—Silvia m. Col. Caleb Howard.—Martha m. Mark Howard 1788.—David m. Sarah, D. of Jon'a. Lathrop 1790.—Abiel m. Rhoda Drake 1789, and David and Abiel went to Winchendon.

9. Joseph (s. of Joseph 4.) m. Naomi, D. of Elisha Hayward 1747, and had Edward 1750*, Bethiah 1752, Mary 1754, Hannah 1757, Silence 1759, Joseph 1762, Susanna 1767, Ebenezer 1769.—Bethiah m. Joseph Johnson 1771.—Mary m. Nathaniel Perkins 1775.—Hannah m. Jacob Hewins 1776.—Silence m. Barnabas Dunbar 1780.

10. John (s. of Joseph 4) m. Abihail (or Abial,) D. of Maj.

John Johnson 1754, and had John 1755.—The father d., and
the wid. and her father Johnson settled the estate 1756.—The
wid. m. Ebenezer Pratt 1758.
  11. Edmund (s. of Joseph 4.) m. Ruth, D. of Dea. Isaac
Willis, 1761, and had Edmund 1762, Isaac 1764, Nathan 1768,
Ruth 1770, Willis 1773.—Edmund m. Huldah, D of Josiah
Lathrop, 1786, and had William 1787, and Huldah 1791, and
went to Canada.—Isaac m. Susanna, D. of Joseph Johnson, 1788,
and went to Attleboro'.—Ruth m. Dea. Nathan Alger 1792.—
Edmund Alger m. Molly Thompson 1796.
  12. Thomas (s. of Thomas 5.) m. Mehitabel Briggs, of Norton, and had James and Daniel both baptised 1766.—Daniel d.
soon after the revolutionary war.—Thomas Alger d. 1793.—
Wid. Alger d. 1795, æ. 67.
  13. Abiezer, Esq., (s. of James 7.) m. Hepsibah, D. of Ebenezer Keith, 1778, and had Jesse 1781*, Cyrus 1782, Olive 1785,
Abiezer 1788, Hepzibah 1792, Cornelia 1799*.—Cyrus, Esq., m.
Lucy, D. of Nathan Willis, 1804, and lives in Boston, and has
Olivia, Francis, Lucy, Mary Ann, Eliza, Martha, Cyrus.—Olive
m. the Hon. John Reed, of Yarmouth, 1809.—Abiezer m. Anna
Cushing 1812.
  14. Dea. James, (s. of James 7.) m. Hannah, D. of Joseph
Bassett, 1791, and had Adin 1791, Nahum 1794, Phebe Cushman 1798, Zenas 1802, Horatio 1806.—Adin m. Clarissa, D. of
Jason Fobes, 1814.—Phebe C. m. Cyrus Copeland 1716.—Horatio gra. H. U. 1825, and settled in the ministry at Chelsea.
  15. Daniel (s. of Daniel 8.) m. Sarah, D. of Theophilus Howard, 1781, and had Sukey 1782, Parnel 1783, Daniel 1786,
Sally 1788, Minerva 1790, Howard 1793, Silvia 1796, and Ruth
1802.—Daniel m. Lydia Wilkes 1807.—Sally m. Martin Dunbar
1812.—Minerva m. Libeus Packard 1812.
  16. Israel, Esq., (s. of Daniel 8.) lived within the limits of
Easton; m. Rachel, D. of George Howard, 1785, and had
George, Israel, Barnard, Roland, Rachel, and several other
Ds.—George m. Sally Lathrop 1814.—Israel gra. B. U. 1811,
and settled in the ministry.—Barnard m. Betsy Lathrop 1810.
  17. Dea. Nathan (s. of Daniel 8.) m. Ruth, D. of Edmund
Alger, 1792, and had Martin 1793, Abigail 1795, Nathan 1798,
Lyman 1800, Benjamin 1803, Edmund 1806*, Emily 1809*.—
The mother d. 1826, æ. 55.—Abigail m. Albe Howard 1814.
  18. Joseph (s. of Joseph 9.) m. Olive, D. of Joseph Ames,
1785, and had Tiley 1786, Ansel 1788, Lucinda 1790, Joseph
1792, Olive 1795, Betsey 1798, Henriette 1801, Mary 1803,
Caroline 1807, Jane 1810, Elijah Ames 1813.
  19. Ebenezer (s. of Joseph 9.) m. Polly Capen, of Sharon,
1792, and had Otis 1793, Polly 1795, Lucy 1797, Ebenezer
1799, Nancy 1801, Eliza 1803, Sanford 1805, William 1808.—
Polly m. Waldo Hayward, Jr., 1816, and d. 1817.—Otis m.
Susanna Perkins 1817.—Nancy m. Waldo Hayward, Jr., 1818.

20. Nathan (s. of Edmund 11.) m. Rachel Smith 1809, and had Rhoda 1811, Edmund 1813, Bathsheba 1815.

21. Willis (s. of Edmund 11.) m. Susanna Capen, of Sharon, 1795, and had Anna C. 1797, Leonard 1799, Stillman 1801, Isaac 1802, Ward 1805, Davis 1807, Susan 1809, Semantha 1814.—Anna C. m. Nathan Hewins 1818.—Leonard m. Hannah R. Lathrop 1821.

22. James (s. of Thomas 12.) m. Mehitabel Briggs, of Norton, and had Daniel, James, and several Ds., one, Olive, m. Daniel Tyler, of Pittsfield, 1811.—Daniel m. Salome, D. of Joseph Keith, 1806, and had Emily Williams 1807, Daniel Francis 1810, James Newton 1812, Joseph Allen 1815, Eliza Sherman 1816, Merton, and George.

The name of Alger has been variously written; sometimes Aulgar, Augur, Augre, Auger, Agur, Ager, Eager, and Agar, and were, perhaps, originally the same name. And although the family in Bridgewater have generally written it Alger, yet it was formerly invariably pronounced Auger. In Willis' History of Portland we find the names of Arthur and Andrew Alger, of Scarborough, in 1650; the latter is found on the court records as early as 1640. Both of these were killed in Philip's war 1675. It is remarkable that they were written often in the same variable manner, Alger and Auger. There was also a Sampson Alger, written Auger, in Old York, made freeman at Kittery 1652. These three last have been mistaken by Farmer, in his Register, for Angier, and so was Thomas, ancestor of the Bridgewater family, on the Old Colony records as copied by Nichols, in consequence of being there written Auger, the u as generally written not being easily distinguishable from an n.—In Winthrop's Journal, p. 23d, we find "a vessel arrived from Bristol in 1631, and among the passengers the name of *Augre* appears. We find also the name of a Mr. Augur, at New Haven, 1667." The families of John and Hannah Aulgar, of John and Sarah Aulgar, and of Matthew and Martha Aulgar, appear from 1652 to 1682, on Boston records; where also it appears John Alger m. Sarah Seely 1721.—Farmer's Register also gives the name of Nicholas Auger, a learned physician of New Haven, 1638, and his brothers, John and Robert; taken from Dodd's East Haven Register. William Auger, or Agar, also was admitted freeman in Mass. 1631, and lived in Salem 1637, and d. 1654. Jonathan Ager or Auger was also of Salem in 1665. Jacob Auger was at Braintree 1689.

ALLEN.—Samuel Allen, of Braintree and his wife Ann, had Samuel 1632, Joseph, James, Sarah 1639, Mary and Abigail. His w. Ann d. 1641, and he had a 2d. w. Margaret; whether she was mother of any of the children is not known; his will 1669, wherein the children are named in the above order.— Sarah m. Lieut. Josiah Standish.—Mary m. Nathaniel Greenwood 1655.—Abigail probably m. John Cary 1670.

1. Samuel Allen, a Deacon, and son of Samuel Allen above named, settled in E. B. as early as 1660, and was the second town clerk, to whom we are much indebted for the fulness and perfection of the records; he m. Sarah, D. of George Partridge of Duxbury; she was born 1639; they had Samuel 1660, Essiel 1663, Mehitabel 1665, Sarah 1667, Bethiah 1669, Nath'l. 1672, Ebenezer 1674, Josiah 1677, Elisha 1679, Nehemiah 1681. His will 1703; he d. 1703, æ. 71.—Mehitabel m. Isaac Alden 1685.—Sarah m. Jonathan Cary, who d. about 1695, and she afterwards m. Benjamin Snow 1705.—Bethiah m. John Pryor.

2. Samuel (s. of Samuel 1.) m. Rebeckah, D. of John Cary, 1685, and had Samuel 1686, Ephraim 1689, Timothy 1691, Joseph 1693*, Mehitabel 1695. The mother d. 1697, and he m. Mary (D. perhaps of Joseph Alden,) 1700; and had Joseph 1701, Benjamin 1702, Mary 1704, Rebecca 1706, Matthew 1708, Seth 1710, and Abigail. His will 1736.—Timothy, Joseph and Benjamin perhaps, went to N. J. or elsewhere; Mehitabel m. a Bushnell.—Mary m. Henry Kingman 1726.—Rebeckah m. John Kingman.—Abigail m. Shubael Waldo, of Windham, 1730. (There was a Samuel Allen who m. Jane Turner, of Weymouth, 1728, and d. 1750, and called Jr., probably the son; there is no further record of him.)—Ephraim went to Berkley, and was a blacksmith.

3. Nathaniel (s. of Samuel 1.) m. Bethiah, D. probably of Nathaniel Conant, 1696, and lived at Conant's Bridge, and afterwards in S. B., and had Andrew 1698, Hannah 1700, James 1704. The mother d., and he had a 2d. wife Abigail, (it is Mary on the town records,) and had Abigail 1711, David 1713.—Andrew, Hannah and David, no account of, perhaps they went to the Cape.—Abigail m. Nathaniel Carver 1736.—Perhaps there was another D. Mercy, who m. Moses Orcut 1739.

4. Ebenezer (s. of Samuel 1.) m. Rebeckah Scate 1698, and had Sarah 1699, Rebeckah 1701, Jacob 1702, Joanna 1704, Abigail 1706, John 1708, Ebenezer 1709*, Ephraim 1711, Isaac 1719, Joshua*, James, Jemima*, Deborah*.—The father d. 1730.—Sarah m. Jon'a. Crooker.—Joanna m. David Pratt 1722.—Abigail m. Samuel Smith.—Ephraim d. 1734, and Jacob settled his estate.—Rebecca was baptized 1725, and died single.

5. Josiah (s. of Samuel 1.) m. Mary Read 1707, perhaps D. of Micah Read; had Micah 1708, Josiah, Mary, Esther, Sarah, Nathan 1722, Betty 1724, William 1726. Her will 1751, proved 1759.—Mary m. Benjamin Vickery 1737.—Esther m. James Edson 1749.—Sarah m. Japhet Byram 1742. The father was dead in 1736.—Micah, Nathan, and Betty sold to Benjamin Whitman 1761.

6. Elisha (s. of Samuel 1.) m. Mehitabel, D. of Nicholas Byram 1701, and had Elisha 1704, Japhet 1705, Matthew 1708, Samuel 1710, Mehitabel, Susanna, Mary, Silence.—Mehitabel m. Jonathan Alden, of Duxbury, 1731.—Susanna m. John Cary 1733.—Silence m. Edmund Jackson 1741.—(Quere if it was

not Elisha's D. Mary that m. Benjamin Vickery 1737, and not Josiah's above.)—Samuel probably m. Susanna, D. of David Perkins, 1733, and died 1737.

7. Nehemiah (s. of Samuel 1.) m. Sarah Wormel 1707, and had Alice 1707, Sarah 1710, Martha 1713, Nehemiah 1715*, Bethiah, Lydia.—Alice m. Arthur Latham 1733, and then Jonathan Allen, of Braintree, 1739.—Sarah m. Nath'l. Pratt, of Bridgewater, 1734.—Martha m. Dea. Jacob Hayward 1736.— Bethiah m. Micah Turner, of Weymouth.—Lydia m. Richard Vining, of Weymouth.—Jonathan Allen, of Braintree, m. Mary, D. of Capt. Chilton Latham, 1742, and had several Ds. m. here; 2 m. Ramsdell's, and one m. Seth Hobart.

8. Benjamin (s. of Samuel 2.) m. Mehitabel, D. of Ephraim Cary, 1730, and had Benjamin, Ephraim, Hannah, Mehitabel 1737.—The father died, and his estate was settled among the children 1754.—Hannah m. John Edson 1751.—Mehitabel, the daughter, m. Benanuel Leach.—Mehitabel Allen, the widow, m. Caleb Washburn 1756.—Benjamin went to Kingston and m. a Delano, and was a Sergeant with Gen. Winslow, 1755, in seizing the neutral French at Nova Scotia, where he died; he enlisted from Plymouth, where he was a tanner.—This family lived where Dexter Pratt now lives.

9. Capt. Matthew (s. of Samuel 2.) m. Sarah, D. of Seth Brett, 1735, and had Nehemiah 1736*, Ezra 1739, Nehemiah 1741*, Sarah 1747, Mary 1750*, Simeon 1753.—He d. 1787, æ. 79; she 1794, æ. 76.—Sarah d. single 1812, æ. 65.—Simeon m. Huldah, D. of Ephraim Cary, 1785, and had Susanna 1786*, Simeon 1788*, and Alpheus 1792, who m. 2. Ds. in succession of Maj. Nath'l. Wilder, of Middleborough, and removed to Boston, and there d. 1828, without children.—Simeon, the father, d. 1805, æ. 52, and Huldah, the mother, d. 1802, æ. 50.

10. Dea. Seth (s. of Samuel 2.) m. Rebeckah Rickard, of Plympton, 1735, and had Betty 1739, Mary* and Rebecca*, twins, 1743*. He d., and the wid. m. Deacon Thomas Whitman 1767.—Betty m. Nathan Whitman 1761.

11. James (s. of Nathaniel 3.) there is no record, or tradition, rendering it certain that this man was the son of Nathaniel, but the age and birth make it probable, and leave but little doubt of it; he m. Mary, D. of Daniel Packard, 1732, and had Nehemiah 1733, James 1735, Ruth 1738, Bethiah 1740*, Susanna 1742, Jesse 1744, Bethiah 1749, Caleb 1751, Silas 1754, Hannah 1756.—The father d. 1778, æ. 74.—Nehemiah went to Oakham.— Ruth m. Ichabod Packard 1757, and went to Oakham.—Susanna m. Capt. Jonathan Willis 1764.—Jesse m. Abigail, D. of Stoughton Willis, 1768, and went to Oakham, and had James and Chloe.—Bethiah m. George Black.—Caleb went to Conway.— Silas went to Heath.—Hannah m. Ebenezer Keith 1773.—Chloe Allen, of Oakham, m. Jonas Leonard 1804, and afterwards Gaius Conant.—Salome Allen m. Calvin Waterman 1793.

12. Jacob (s. of Ebenezer 4.) m. Abigail, D. of Henry Kingman 1730, and had Abigail 1730, Jonathan 1732, Jemima 1735,
Jacob 1739, Ephraim 1743*, Josiah 1746, Ephraim 1747.—The
father was killed by a cart wheel running over him.—Abigail m.
Jonathan Randall 1749.—Jemima also m. a Randall.—Josiah
and Ephraim left no sons.—The mother d. a widow 1770, æ.
65.—Josiah m. a Nightingale, and had several Ds., and d. 1816,
æ. 70; his wid. d. 1722, æ. 74.

13. John (s. of Ebenezer 4.) lived where Isaac Hobart
lived, m. Lydia Kingman, 1733, and had Lydia, Deborah, John,
Bethia*, Joshua*, all baptized in E. B 1748.—Lydia m. David
Hatch.—John went to Maine.—Deborah m. John Hatch.—John
Allen had a wife Alice, of Marshfield.—John Allen m. Sarah
Campbell 1753.

14. Isaac (s. of Ebenezer 4.) m. Joanna, D. of Solomon
Packard, 1745, and had Phebe 1745, Martha 1748, Isaac 1752,
Molly 1755, James 1757, Jennet 1759, Huldah 1761, David
1763, Eunice 1766, Sarah 1769.—The mother d. 1787, æ. 62,
and he then m. wid. Susanna, late wife of William Allen, and
D. of Joseph Packard, but had no children by her.—He d. 1791,
æ. 71; she 1818, æ. 87.—Phebe m. Wm. Bonney 1766.—Martha
m. Benaiah Niles 1770.—Isaac m. Silvia, D. of Seth Brett, 1776,
and afterwards Matilda, D. of Thomas Pratt, 1796, and d. 1822,
æ. 72, leaving one D. Sophronia, an only child, who m. Joseph
Dunbar 1812.—Molly m. Capt. Levi Washburn 1774.—Capt.
James m. Polly, D. of Wm. Whitman, 1778, and went to
Maine.—Jennet m. Capt. John Thompson 1778, and went to
Maine.—Huldah m. Isaac Washburn 1781, who went to Maine.—
Eunice m. Josiah Johnson 1784.—David m. Rachel, D. of Jesse
Dunbar, 1796, and had several children, viz: Melinda 1796,
Zebina 1798, Nahum 1800, Galen 1802, Sidney 1806, and
Joanna.—Sarah m. Zenas Whitman 1791, who went to Maine.

15. James (s. of Ebenezer 4.) m. Bethiah, D. of John Kingman, 1736, and had Ebenezer 1737, Bethiah.—His wife died,
and he m. wid. Ann, late wife of Joseph Pryor, 1742, her maiden
name Moore, and had Hannah 1742*, James 1743*, Thankful
1746*.—Ebenezer Allen m. Mary Bradley, of Abington, 1757,
and had James 1760, Mary 1763. The parents both died 1763.—
Bethiah m. Thomas Snell, Jr., 1755, who went to Maine.—Mary
Allen m. Isaac Mehurin 1781.

16. Micah (s. of Josiah 5.) m. Hannah, D. of Timothy Edson
1737, and had Mary 1737, Micah 1740, Joseph 1742, Daniel
1743.—He d., and the wid. m. Thomas Phillips 1747.—Mary d.
single 1820, æ. 82.—Micah and Daniel went to Easton, and
Daniel afterwards went to Brookfield.

17. Josiah (s. of Josiah 5.) m. Sarah Orcut 1741, and they
had only one child, Josiah 1742, who d. 1785, æ. 43, a bachelor.—The father d. 1745, æ. a. 35. The mother d. 1806, æ. 100.

18. Nathan (s. of Josiah 5.) m. Rebeckah, D. of Stephen

Read, 1743, and had Abigail 1743, Nathan 1747*, Nathan 1749, Rebeckah 1751, Esther 1753, Philip 1757, Hannah 1760, Philemon 1762.—Abigail m. James Thompson, of Halifax, 1765.— Rebeckah m. Levi Gilbert, of Brookfield, whither the family removed.—Esther m. Amasa Ross, of Brookfield.—Hannah m. John Bacheldor.—Sally Allen, of Brookfield, m. Daniel Snow, 3d, 1792.—There was a Mehitabel Allen, who d. 1776, æ. 13.

19. William (s. of Josiah 5.) m. Susanna, D. of Joseph Packard, 1748, and had Susanna 1750, William 1752, Rhoda 1754, Edward 1756, Elijah 1758, Abel 1760, Robert, Betty 1767.— He died, and the wid. Susanna m. Isaac Allen, and afterwards Dea. Othniel Gilbert, of Brookfield.—This family went to Brookfield, and afterwards further westward.

20. Elisha (s. of Elisha 6.) m. Rebecca, D. of David Pratt, 1745, and had Mehitabel 1752, Huldah 1753, David 1755, Abijah 1758.

21. Matthew (s. of Elisha 6.) m. Sarah Harden 1734, and had Susanna 1735, Samuel 1737, Japhet 1739, Sarah 1743, Mary 1745, Matthew 1747*.—The mother d. 1793, æ. 77.—Susanna m. Seth Gannett 1754.—Sarah m. Lot Dwelly 1763; Mary m. John Hobart 1765, father of John Hobart, Esq., of Leicester, and afterwards a Bearce.—The father, Matthew, d. 1784, æ. 76.

22. Ephraim (s. of Benjamin 8.) m. Betty, D. of Jonathan Wood, 1758, and had Seth 1759, Susanna 1761, Hannah 1764, Betty 1766, Sarah 1769.—Susanna m. Nathan Edson 1778.

23. Ezra (s. of Capt. Matthew 9.) m. Phebe, D. of Ephraim Cary, 1761, and had Molly 1762, Zenas 1763, Phebe 1765, Ezra 1767, Asahel 1770, Samuel 1772, Bezaliel 1774, Alice 1776, Waldo 1778, Ethan 1780, Ambrose 1784.—The father d. 1795, æ. 55.—Molly m. William Brett 1782.—Zenas went to the westward.—Phebe d. single 1803.—Ezra went to the westward.— Asahel m. Rhoda Tilson 1794, and had several children, viz : Jason 1795*, Ethan 1797, Marven 1798, Alice 1802*, and then went to Benson, Vt. His son Ethan, gra. of Middlebury College, was an Episcopalian Clergyman at the city of Washington.—Samuel went westward.—Bezaliel m. Pamela Hall, of Raynham, and had several children, viz : Harriet*, d. 1807, æ. 10 ; Almira*, d. 1829, æ. 28 ; Bezaliel Cary, who was a physician, and went to the southward ; Pamela Hall d. 1834 ; Henry Clinton, who was educated at Brunswick, but did not graduate, began to preach, and d. 1831, æ. 24 ; Evelina Augusta, m. a Hall, and lives in Boston ; Harriet Amanda, m. a Rainsford, and d. 1837, æ. 24.—Alice m. Capt. Abisha Stetson 1796, and d. 1821, æ. 45.— Waldo and Ambrose went to the eastward.—Ethan d. 1802, æ. 22.—The mother, wife of Bezaliel, d. 1831, æ. 62.

24. Maj. James (s. of James 11.) m. Martha, D. of Dea. Jacob Hayward, 1761, and had Nehemiah 1763*, Oliver 1765, James 1766, Galen 1769, Benjamin 1772.—The father d. of the

13

small pox 1789, æ. 54.—Oliver m. Susanna, D. of Samuel Whitman, 1790, and had several children, viz: James Seymour, Oliver, and a D. James S., s. of Oliver, m. Mary, D. of Nathan Mitchell, Esq., 1816, and died young, leaving only one child, a D. Mary; Oliver m. Rachel Wood, 1819.—James gra. H. U. 1785, and died young and unmarried.—Benjamin m. Rebecca Clark 1795.—Galen (named of N. H.) m. Hannah Copeland 1797.

25. Jonathan (s. of Jacob 12.) m. Sarah, D. of Capt. Jonathan Bass, 1755, and had Bathsheba 1759, Barzillai 1769.—The father d. 1780, æ. 47, the mother 1777, æ. 41.—Bathsheba m. Capt. Isaac Whitman 1785, and d. 1829, æ. 70.—Dea. Barzillai m. Joanna, D. of William Bonney, 1796, and had a D. Clara 1797, who m. Freedom Whitman, and lived in Boston, and d. young.—The mother Joanna d. 1799, æ. 25, and he m. Lucy, D. of the Rev. Samuel Baldwin, of Hanover, 1802, and had Sarah Bass 1804, Samuel Baldwin 1807, Lucy 1810, Abigail 1812*, William 1815, gra. H. U. 1837.—The father Barzillai d. 1826, æ. 56.—Sarah Bass m. the said Freedom Whitman for his 2d wife.

26. Capt. Jacob (s. of Jacob 12.) m. Abigail, D. of Israel Bailey, 1762, and had Jacob 1763, Timothy 1764, Bailey 1766, Betty 1768, Jemima 1770, Jonathan 1773, Ward 1775*.—He commanded a company in the revolutionary war, and was killed at Saratoga, at the capture of Burgoyne, in 1777, æ. 38.—The wid. Abigail m. Isaac Lazell.—Jacob m. Susanna, D. of Ezra Alden, 1784, and went to Cummington.—Timothy m. Celia, D. of Nathan Whitman, 1788, and had twins, who both d. in infancy, and the mother d. also 1789, and then he m. wid. Betty, late wife of Joseph Keith, and D. of Anthony Sherman, 1791, and had several children, viz: Joseph 1792, Jennett 1794, Bailey 1796, Orra 1798*, Anthony Sherman 1800, Timothy Wales 1801, Betsy Rogers 1803, Orra 1804, Dicy Hill 1807. He removed to Plymouth where his wife d., and he m. a 3d w., and d. 1827.—Bailey (s. of Capt. Jacob) removed to the westward.— Betty m. Samuel Rogers 1790.—Jemima m. Elisha Bisbee, his 2d. wife.—Jonathan removed from town.

27. Joseph (s. of Micah 16.) m. Mehitabel, D. of Zebulon Cary, 1771, and had Zebulon, Josiah*, Joseph 1785, Daniel, Susanna, Mehitabel.—Joseph, the father, d. 1826, æ. 84; the mother d. 1799, æ. 48.—Zebulon m. Priscilla Atwood 1795, and removed to the westward.—Joseph d. 1828, æ. 43. He m. Diana, D. of Lot Phillips, 1814, and has left children; his wid. m. Thos. Whitmarsh.—Susanna m. Thomas Snell 1792.—Mehitabel m. Ezra Phillips 1809, and d. young.—Daniel m. Priscilla Smith, of Middleborough, 1815, and d. young.—The whole family d. of consumption.

28. Samuel (s. of Matthew 21.) m. Hannah, D. of Joshua Pratt, 1758, and had Matthew 1759, Hannah 1761, Byram 1763, Molly 1765, Huldah 1767, d. 1795, Eunice 1770, Samuel 1772,

Pratt 1775.—The father d. 1787, æ. 49.—The wid. m. Nehemiah Latham 1801.—Matthew m. Jane, D. of Lemuel Keen, 1786, and had several children, viz: Mehitabel, Bethiah, Jane, Huldah, Electa, Eliza, and d. 1803, æ. 44.—Hannah m. John Ramsdell 1784, father of Martin Ramsdell.—Molly m. Nathaniel Damon 1786.—Eunice m. Ezra Whitman 1795.—Samuel went to Boston, and afterwards to N. B.—Pratt m. Ann Stockbridge, and had several children, viz: Samuel Barker, Patience Barker, Pratt 1801, and removed to the Cape.—Byram m. Elizabeth Childs 1786, and had Capt. Seth, of Halifax, Byram, Robert, Samuel, and both d. 1833, he æ. 70, she 69.—Jane m. Thomas R. Alden 1813.—Huldah m. Thomas Barrell 1815.—Betsey (or Eliza) m. Noah Ramsdell 1818.—Electa m. a Slocum.—Mehitabel Allen m. John Clapp, of Roxbury, 1804.

29. Japhet (s. of Matthew 21.) m. Betty Thomas of Marshfield, 1761, (she was sister of Nathan Kingman's wife,) and had Sarah 1765, Laban 1766, Phebe 1768, Japhet 1771, Betty 1773, Jenny 1775, Lydia 1778*, and Isaac born at Tamworth, N. H., whither the family all removed.

30. William Allen (or Allan) m. Catharine Demsel 1756; their child d. 1757, and the mother d. 1757.—He then m. Hannah Copeland 1758, and had William 1759, Catharine 1760, David 1765.—He sold his estate to Hugh Orr, Esq., 1760.—This family lived in W. B., and had no connexion with the Allen family in this town. It was probably a Scotch family.

31. Eleazar Allen, of Rochester, m. Mary, D. of Anthony Sherman, and had Elisha, Zephaniah, Betty, and other Ds.—He d. and the wid. and children came to E. B.—Elisha settled in Maine.—Zephaniah never m.—Betty m. Nathan Bates, 1789.

East Bridgewater is principally indebted to the Allen family for the burying ground, meeting-house lot, and common or training-field, which were given by them.

AMES.—John and William Ames were sons of Richard Ames, of Bruton, Somersetshire, England; the former settled in W. B., and the latter in Braintree, here in New England, as early as 1640.

1. John Ames above came from Duxbury to this town; was an original proprietor here, and m. Elizabeth Hayward 1645; she was probably sister of Thomas Hayward; they had no children, but he had a large estate which he gave by deeds in 1697 to his nephew John, son of his brother William, of Braintree, and to the sons of his said nephew. He d. a. 1698.— (William, of Braintree, d. 1654; his wife Hannah; his children, according to Boston records, were Hannah 1641, Rebecca 1642, Lydia 1645, John 1647, Sarah 1650, Deliverence 1653.—Hannah m. John Hayden 1660, m. by Gov. Endicot.)

2. John (s. of William, of Braintree, and nephew of John 1.) m. Sarah, D. of John Willis, and came to W. B. as early as

1672, and probably earlier, and had John 1672, William 1673, Nathaniel 1677, Elizabeth 1680, Thomas 1682, Sarah 1685, David 1688, and Hannah.—His estate settled a. 1723.—Elizabeth m. Capt. John Field 1697.—Sarah m. Daniel Field 1706.— Hannah m. David Packard 1712.

3. John (s. of John 2.) m. Sarah, D. of John Washburn, 1697, and had Elizabeth 1697, John 1700, Sarah 1702, Abigail 1705, Jonathan 1707, Deborah 1710, Daniel 1712, Benjamin 1715, Joshua 1718*.—His will 1755, p. 1756.—Elizabeth m. Joseph Bassett, at Boston, 1724.—Sarah m. Abiel Packard 1723.—Abigail m. Thomas Wade (his 2d or 3d wife) 1752, and d. 1789, æ. 84.—Deborah was never m.; Jonathan was to take care of her.—John m. Mehitabel, D. of Israel Packard, 1725, and had children, but left none; Mehitabel, the wid., m. Samuel West 1727, and was dead 1752.—Benjamin refused executorship, and dates his refusal at Scituate. Jonathan executor alone.

4. William (s. of John 2.) m. Mary, D. of John Hayward, 1698, and had Mary 1699, William 1701, Martha 1704, Bethiah 1706, Sarah 1708, Hannah 1710.—He d. a. 1712.—David Packard guardian to Bethiah, and Nathaniel Ames to the rest.—Mary m. Joseph Alger 1719.—Martha m. Thomas Conant.—Bethiah m. Timothy Keith 1737.—Hannah m. Samuel Keith 1734.

5. Capt. Nathaniel (s. of John 2.) m. Susanna, D. of John Howard 1702, and had Nathaniel 1708, Susanna 1711, Seth 1713, Sarah 1716, Ann, Mary*.—Susanna m. a Tripp of Providence.—Sarah m. a Spaulding, of Killingsly.—Ann m. a Payne, an attorney.—Seth d. æ. 25, at Guinea, supposed to have been poisoned by the negroes.—Seth Ames m. Elizabeth, D. of John Prince, of Rochester, 1734. She afterwards m. Joshua Lazell, of M., 1742.—Nathaniel Ames m. Mary Lindsay 1734.

6. Thomas, (s. of John 2.) m. Mary, D. of Joseph Hayward, 1706, and had Thomas 1707, Solomon 1709, Joseph 1711, Ebenezer 1715, Mary 1717, Susanna 1720, Nathan 1722, Sarah 1724, Betty 1727.—Mary m. Seth Howard 1735.—Susanna m. Thomas Willis 1741.—Sarah m. Capt. Josiah Packard 1747.— Betty m. James Ames 1748.—Mary Ames m. John Buck 1739, perhaps the mother, then a widow.

7. David (s. of John 2.) m. wid. Mary, late wife of Nathaniel Reynolds, and D. of Thomas Snell, 1722, and had David and Mary 1723, James 1725.—He d. 1726, she 1757.—Mary m. Zechariah Gurney 1754.—David left no posterity.—Mary, the wid's. will, dated 1755, p. 1757, mentions David, James, Mary Gurney, and Betty Ames, (perhaps James' wife.) She also mentions her sons Nathaniel, and Thomas Reynolds, and grand daughter Mary Reynolds.—Nathaniel Reynolds executor.

8. Jonathan, (s. of John 3.) m. Keziah Tinkham 1757, and had Jonathan 1759, Keziah 1761, Susanna 1763, Molly 1765.— He d. 1775.—Keziah m. Thaddeus Howard 1785.—Susanna m. a Tinkham.—Molly m. Capt. David Gurney 1789.—Keziah, the mother, m. James Howard 1776.

9. Daniel (s. of John 3.) m. Hannah, D. of Timothy Keith, 1742, and had John 1742, Timothy 1744, Noah 1748, Daniel 1751, Job 1752, Sarah 1754, Hannah 1756, Phebe 1760.—He d. of the small pox 1778, æ. 60.—John was a physician, m. Martha Park 1771, and settled at Rehoboth; he left no children.— Sarah m. Benjamin Fuller 1777.—Hannah m. Israel Burr 1779.— Phebe d. single.

10. Benjamin (s. of John 3.) m. Dorcas, D. of Hezekiah Thayer, of Braintree, and had Joshua 1760.—Joshua m. Hannah, D. of Mark Ford, 1786, and had James 1787, David 1788, Hannah 1790, Betsy 1796.—Capt. David m. Lucinda, D. of Jonas Packard, 1815.—James a bachelor.—Betsy m. Zephaniah French 1816, and went to Albany.—Hannah m. John Talbot 1814, and went to N. Y.—(Benjamin Ames m. Hannah White 1793. Boston records.)

11. William (s. of William 4.) m. Elizabeth, D. probably of Richard Jennings, 1721, and had Mary 1722, William 1723, Barnabas 1725*, Silence 1727, Peace 1729, Anne 1730, Abraham 1731*, Amos 1732, Charity 1733, Elizabeth 1735, Sarah 1736.—It is said this family removed to Connecticut.

12. Dr. Nathaniel (s. of Nathaniel 5.) removed to Dedham, and m. two wives in succession by the name of Fisher, viz:— Mary, D. of Joshua Fisher, m. 1735, and Deborah, D. of Jeremiah Fisher, m. 1740.—By his first he had a son named Fisher, who died in infancy, but not till after his mother, upon which the famous law suit took place, in which it was determined, for the first time, that the estate ascended to the father, as next of kin to his son, by the Province law, contrary to the English common law. By the last wife he had several children, viz:— Nathaniel 1741, Seth, Fisher 1758, Deborah and William; the two last died young.—William was lost at sea.—Nathaniel gra. H. U. 1761, was a physician, lived to old age, but left no children.—Seth gra. H. U. probably 1764, and was a physician, and d. 1778.—Fisher was the late Hon. Fisher Ames, of distinguished talents, who gra. H. U. 1774, m. Frances, D. of Col. John Worthington, and had several children, viz: John Worthington, Nathaniel, Hannah, Jeremiah Fisher, William, Seth, and Richard.

Dr. Eliot, in his biographical dictionary, deduces the late Hon. Fisher Ames' descent from the Rev. William Ames, son of the famous Dr. William Ames of England, author of "Medulla Theologiæ," and this is repeated in the preface to Fisher Ames' works; but the account here given of the family, drawn from authentic sources, renders this supposition altogether improbable. Besides, William Ames of Braintree, the ancestor of this family, was married about 1640, and died at Braintree 1654, whereas the Rev. William Ames, son of the Franequar Professor, and who came to N. E. with his mother, was graduated at Cambridge, N. E., 1645, and returned to England and settled there at Wrentham in the ministry, and died there 1689, æ. 65. The

family record also, still preserved, deduces the Bridgewater
family, as here given, from Richard Ames, of Bruton; and
hence perhaps the name of *Richard* appears among those of the
Hon. Fisher Ames' children.

13. Thomas (s. of Thomas 6.) m. Keziah, D. of Jonathan
Howard, 1731, and had Keziah 1732, Susanna 1734, Thomas
1736, John 1738, Mehitabel 1740, Silvanus 1744.—The father
d. 1774, æ. 67.—Keziah m. David Howard 1751.—Susanna m.
Josiah Snell 1752.—Mehitabel m. Eliab Fobes 1759.

14. Solomon (s. of Thomas 6.) m. Susanna, D. of Samuel
Keith, 1737, and had Simeon 1739, Solomon 1741, Jotham
1743.—Simeon and Solomon under guardianship 1757.—The
mother, a wid., m. Isaac Swift 1749.—Solomon m. Eunice, wid.
of Benjamin Sprague, and D. of Ephraim Holmes 1781, and d.
1814, leaving no children.—Jotham m. Keziah, wid. of David
Howard, and d. of Thomas Ames, 1767. He afterwards m.
Sarah Bryant 1786, and d. at N. Y.

15. Joseph (s. of Thomas 6.) m. Susanna, D. of Nathaniel
Littlefield, of Braintree, probably 1736, and had Phebe 1737,
Ebenezer 1739, Nathaniel 1741, Elijah 1743, Susanna 1744,
Joseph 1747, Sarah, William 1752, Bethiah.—His w. d. and he
m. Ruth, wid. of Israel Packard, and D. of Richard Field 1754,
and had Zephaniah 1755. She d. and he m. Abihail, wid. of
Jonathan Bosworth, late wid. of Israel Alger, Jr., and D. of
Samuel Lathrop, 1768, and had Olive 1769, James 1771, and
Fiske 1773.—Phebe m. Capt. Jonathan Howard 1756.—Nath'l.
m. Mary, D. of Josiah Hill, 1783, and left no son.—Elijah m.
Betty, D. of Isaac Johnson, 1769, and went to Pennsylvania.—
Susanna m. Daniel Copeland 1764.—Sarah m. Josiah Williams
1778.—William went to Connecticut.—Bethiah m. Ephraim
Fobes 1769.—Zephaniah, a bachelor.—Olive m. Joseph Alger
1785.—James m. Jenny Fenno, of Boston, 1794, and had Leonard 1797*, Franklin 1799, James 1803. Leonard was killed by
the falling of a tree. Franklin m. Polly, D. of Benjamin Keith,
1821.

16. Ebenezer, (s. of Thomas 6.) m. Sarah, D. of Maj. Jona.
Howard, and had Rufus 1739, Sarah 1741, Parmenas 1743,
Mary 1747.—He d. and his wid. m. Thomas Hooper.—Parmenas m. a Kinsley, and then Mehitabel, D. of Simeon Ames, and
wid. of Daniel Harvey, 1804 ; and he and Rufus both lived in
Easton.—Ebenezer Ames and wife dis. fm. W. B. ch. to Easton
1748.—Sarah Ames m. Josiah Williams, of Easton, 1763.

17. Nathan (s. of Thomas 6.) m. Elizabeth, (or Betty) D. of
Eleazar Snow,' 1751, and had Sarah 1752, Nathan 1753*, d.
1776.—The father died, and the mother then m. Wm. Tolman
1757, and afterwards Micah White.—Sarah m. Aaron Bozworth.

18. James (s. of David 7.) m. Betty, D. of Thomas Ames,
1748, and had Mary 1756, Betty 1773.—He had a 2d wife
Dorcas, who d. 1816.—Mary m. John Snow 1784.

19. Jonathan (s. of Jonathan 8.) m. Deborah Pratt of Easton, 1780; she d. and he then m. Patience, D. of Caleb Sturtevant of Halifax, 1783, and had Jonathan 1784, Sarah 1786, Lewis 1788, Susanna 1790, William 1792, Charles 1794, Willard 1798. Jonathan and his w. Sally had Ellis 1809, gra. B. U. 1830, Sally Capen 1811, Mary Fobes 1820.—Lewis m. Hannah Loring 1815.

20. Timothy (s. of Daniel 9.) m. Abigail, D. of George Howard, 1778, and had Hannah 1779*, Seba 1781*. The mother d. 1784, and he m. Ruth Carver 1786, and had Abigail 1787, Sibil 1789, Theron 1792, Phebe 1975.—Abigail m. Oliver Bryant.— Sibil m. Capt. Jeremiah Beals.—Theron m. Patty, D. of Capt. Robert Packard, 1816.

21. Noah (s. of Daniel 9.) m. Ruhama, D. of John French, 1778, and had one son John 1779, an only child, who m. Hannah, D. of Perez Southworth, 1802, and he and his father both went to Winthrop, Me.—John's children were Noah 1803, Ruhama French 1805, Franklin 1806, Mary 1809, Thomas Thompson 1811.

22. Daniel (s. of Daniel 9.) m. Mehitable, D. of Josiah Perkins, 1780, and had Benjamin 1781, Josiah 1783.—Benjamin m. Zelopha, D. of John French, 1803, and had Damaris 1804, Nancy 1806, Daniel French 1809.—Josiah Ames m. Prudence, D. of Capt. William Thayer, of Braintree, and went to Dracut, and had George 1813, Sarah Jones 1815, Josiah 1817, Harriet 1819, and John 1823.

23. Job (s. of Daniel 9) m. Mary, D. of Samuel Dyke, 1782, and had Azel 1783, Hannah 1785, Joel 1787, Elijah 1789, Nathaniel 1795.—Capt. Azel and Elijah settled in Marshfield.— Hannah m. Zebedee Snell, Jr., 1804.—Joel, m. Reliance, D. of Josiah Edson, 1818.—Job Ames m. Abigail Carver, of Marshfield, 1814.

24. Thomas (s. of Thomas 13.) m. Deborah, D. of Nathaniel Brett, 1758, and had Parnel 1759, Abiel 1761, Thomas 1763, Olive 1765, Rebecca 1766*, Rebecca 1772, Betty 1775.—The father d. 1812, the mother 1819.—Parnel m. George Howard, Jr., 1777.—Capt. Abiel m. Alice Wetherell, of Norton, 1791, and d. 1838, æ 77, and had Charlotte 1793*, Charles 1795, Charlotte 1798, Thomas 1800, George 1804, Alice 1806, Fisher 1812.— Thomas m. Nancy Sturtevant, 1789, and went to Burlington.— Olive m. Elijah Burr, 1789.—Betty m. Calvin Burr, 1796, and both removed to Worthington, and Rebecca m. also in Worthington.

25. Capt. John (s. of Thomas 13.) m. Susanna, D. of Ephraim Howard, 1759, and had David 1760, Kezia, Susanna, Huldah 1768, Abigail 1769, Cynthia 1772*, John 1775, Oliver 1777. Kezia first m. Elijah Packard 1783, and afterwards Benjamin Robinson 1798.—Abigail m. Joseph Lazell, 1787.—Susanna m. Joseph Fobes, Esq.—Huldah m. Isaac Willis, 1786.

26. Silvanus (s. of Thomas 13.) m. Huldah, D. of Maj. Isaac

Johnson 1768, and had Bezer 1769, Silvanus 1771, Cyrus and Huldah.—Silvanus and Cyrus went to the westward.—Silvanus the father gra. at Cambridge 1767, was Rector of the Episcopal church at Taunton 1773, and d. young, and his wid. (Huldah) m. John Willis, Esq. 1784.—Silvanus m. Abigail D. of Thos. Johnson 1795.—Bezer m. Rebecca Joslyn, of Pembroke 1791, and had Bezer 1792, Nabby 1795, Diana 1796, Marcus 1798, Cyrus 1800, Philander 1803, Lydia 1805, Rebecca J. 1807, Charles H. 1812; he went to Mid'o. and afterwards to Milton, where he d.— Huldah m. Timo. Hayward 1792.

27. Simeon (s. of Solomon 14.) m. Experience Standish 1765, and had Barzillai 1766*, Alex'r. 1767, Mehitabel 1770, Solomon 1773, Simeon 1776, Susanna 1780, Jotham 1786.—Mehitabel m. Dan'l. Harvey 1795, and afterwards Parmenas Ames 1804. —Solomon m. Sally Harden 1794, and went to N. Y.—Simeon went to Ohio.—Susanna d. single.—Jotham went to Easton. Alex'r. m. Susanna Cole of M. 1789, and had Aaron 1791, Sarah 1793, Bethiah 1794, Sampson 1797, Priscilla Standish 1799, Simeon 1801*, Edwin 1803, Susanna 1805, Mary 1808.—Sarah m. Martin Swift 1806, Bethiah m. Squire Fuller of Vt., 1815, Sampson m. Betsy Richmond, of T. 1819.

28. Joseph (s. of Joseph 15.) m. Martha, D. of Josiah Williams 1770, and had Seth 1771, Bethiah 1773, Zeph'h. 1776, Joseph and Martha 1778, Anne 1781, Lucy 1784*, Jane 1787, Waldo 1789, Lucy 1795, Nath'l. Fisher 1795.—The father d. 1813.—Seth m. Elizabeth Bartlett 1798. and had Horace 1798. Virgil 1804.—Bethiah m. Joshua Bates 1796.—Joseph m. Hannah W. Shaw 1812, and d. 1813.—Martha m. Ezra Hyde 1805. Anne m. George W. Perkins 1802.—Jane m. Eph'm. Sprague Jr. 1813.—Lucy m. Benj. Sprague 1818.

29. Ebenezer (s. of Joseph 15.) m. Jane D. of Dr. Abiel Howard 1763, and had Ambrose 1765, Charles 1767, Walter 1773. Wm. 1777, and Eben'r.—Ambrose removed to Greenfield.— Charles m. Rhoda D. of Dea. Elijah Snell 1789.—Walter m. Mehitabel Packard 1796.—Most of the family removed to the westward.

30. Fiske (s. of Joseph 15.) m. Betsy Covington 1803, and had Betsy Covington 1805, Cyrus 1806*, Geo. Robinson 1808, Wm. 1810, Joseph Thomas 1813.—His w. d. and he m. Dinah D. of Benj. Leach 1819, and had Elbridge, Mary and John.

31. David (s. of Capt. John 25.) m. Rebeckah D. of Maj. Isaac Johnson 1781, and had Lucinda, Mary, Rebecca, Susanna, David, Abigail, Galen, Charlotte and John.—The first 6 bap. at W. B. May 5, 1795: he with his family removed to Springfield. Lucinda m. a Lamphear.—Mary, single.—Rebecca m. James Wells.—Susan m. Edw'd. Pynchon Esq.—David m. Mary O. D. of Nahum Mitchell.—Abigail m. Rob't. McDermot.—Galen m. Eliza Kent.—Charlotte m. Nathan Oakes.—John not married.

32. John (s. of Capt. John 25.) m. Deborah, D. of the Rev.
Dr. Sanger, 1799, and removed to Sangersfield N. Y., and had
Caroline Sanger 1800, Irene Freeman 1802, Christiana Sterling
1803.
33. Oliver (s. of Capt. John 25.) m. Susanna, D. of Oakes
Angier Esq., and went to Easton and had Horatio, Oakes A.,
Angier*, Oliver, Sarah, William, Harriet, and John.
34. Dea. Josiah Eames (from Marshfield, a descendant of
Anthony Eames probably), his wife was an Eames also: he came
to N. B. 1770, and had a son Elisha.—Elisha m. Sarah, D. of
Timothy Packard, and had Josiah 1787, and Isaac 1789.—The
mother d. 1790.—Josiah m. Rebecca, D. of Ephraim Noyes,
1808, and had Sarah 1812, Luther 1813.—Isaac m. Abby Hayward 1811.—This family went to Long Island.—Elisha m. Ann
Mann, of St. 1791.
N. B. In the early records some of the family of Ames were
sometimes written Eames ; but whether Anthony and others in
Marshfield of the name of Eames, were of the same family with
that of Ames in Bridgewater, is not ascertained. There was a
John and Martha Ames, of Boston, whose children were William 1656, Martha 1659 ; (Boston Records) ; he appears to have
been cotemporary with William of Braintree and John of Bridgewater. There was also a Thomas Eames at Dedham who had
John 1642, and Thomas Eames also of Sudbury 1676, and
Anthony, John and Mark Eames at Hingham and Marshfield
from 1637 to 1649.
ANGIER.—Edmund Angier, of Cambridge, 1636, freeman
1640, m. Ruth, D. of the Rev. Dr. William Ames, an English
divine of great celebrity, the famous Franequar professor, and
author of "Medulla Theologiæ," and had John 1645*, Ruth
1647, Ephraim, Samuel 1654, John 1656*. His w. d. 1656, and
he m. Ann Pratt 1657, and had Edmund 1659, Hannah 1660,
Mary 1663, John 1664, Nathaniel 1665, and Elizabeth.—There
was also a John Angier gra. H. U. 1653 ; and Mr. John Angier,
of Boston, bought a house of Wm. Aspinwall 1652 ; and John
and Hannah Angier, of Boston, had a son John born 1652.—
John Angier m. Elizabeth Worthylake 1713, and had John 1714,
Robert 1717, and Elizabeth 1719.—(Boston records.)
2. Rev. Samuel (s. of Edmund 1.) gra. H. U. 1673, and settled
in the ministry at Rehoboth 1679, m. Hannah, D. of the Rev.
Urian Oakes, Pres. of H. U. Sept. 2, 1680, and had Ames 1681,
Hannah 1682, Ruth 1684*, Edmund 1685, Urian, Oakes, Samuel, Dorothy, Sarah, Eunice 1698, John 1701, Elizabeth, and
Ruth 1705 ; he was dismissed on account of feeble health from
Rehoboth, and afterwards was installed at Watertown 1697,
and several of his youngest children were born there; he d.
1719, æ. 65, she d. 1714 at her son Ames' in Boston.—Ames
gra. H. U. 1701, and m. Margaret McCarty, in Boston 1708,
and had a s. William 1714, and d. in Eng. 1720.—Hannah d.
14

single, at Watertown, 1714.—Eunice d. single at E. Bridgewater 1771, æ. 73.—Ruth m. the Rev. John Shaw, of S. Bridgewater.

3. Rev. John (s. of Rev. Samuel 2.) gra. H. U. 1720, and settled in E. B., 1724; m. Mary, D. of Ezra Bourne, Esq., of Sandwich, (her mother was Martha, D. of Samuel Prince, and her (Martha's) mother was Mercy, D. of Gov. Thomas Hinckley, and her (Mercy's) mother was D. of Lawrence Smith;) he had Martha 1733*, John 1735*, Ezra 1738*, Mary 1740, Samuel 1743, Oakes 1745.—He d. 1787, æ. 85 years and 8 months.— Mary m. Rev. Ephraim Hyde, of Rehoboth, 1767.

4. Rev. Samuel (s. of Rev. John 3.) gra. H. U. 1763, and settled as colleague with his father 1767, m. late in life, Judith D. of Rev. Josiah Smith, of Pembroke, 1797, but had no children. She d. 1803, æ. 55; he Jan. 18, 1805, æ. 62.

5. Oakes, Esq., (s. of Rev. John 3.) gra. H. U. 1764, read law with the elder President Adams, and settled as an attorney in W. B., and was eminent in his profession; m. Susanna, D. of Col. Edward Howard 1774, and had Charles 1774, Mary 1776, John 1778, Sarah 1780, Susanna 1783, Oakes 1785.—He d. 1786, æ. 41, and his wid. m. Jesse Fobes, 1792.—Charles gra. H. U. 1793, and m. Frances McClench, 1796, was an attorney, and d. young, leaving an only child, Susanna McClench Howard, born 1797; his wid m. Archelaus Lewis, Esq., of Falmouth, Me, and the D. m. a Flinn, of Boston.—Mary m. Dr. Hector Orr 1795.— Sarah m. Josiah W. Mitchell, Esq., of Freeport, Me.—Susanna m. Oliver Ames, of Easton, 1803.—Oakes m. Frances, D. of John Hathaway, of Dighton, and was an attorney, first in Belfast, Me., and afterwards in Dighton, and d. leaving a s. John.

6. John (s. of Oakes 5.) m. Lavinia, D. of John Hathaway, of Dighton, and settled in Belfast, Me., as a merchant, and had Harriet Lavinia 1805*, John Francis Howard 1807, Charles Frederick 1810, George Christopher 1812, Harriet Lavinia 1814, who m. James H. Mitchell 1833, and Oakes 1816.—He d. Nov. 17, 1829, æ. 51.—John F. H. gra. Waterville College, and m. Jane, D. of Judge Wm. Crosby, and settled as an attorney in Belfast.—Charles F. and Oakes settled as merchants in Belfast.— George C. gra. Brunswick College, and settled as an attorney in Bangor.

Rev. Dr. Gad Hitchcock, of Pembroke, now Hanson, m. an Angier, cousin probably of the Rev. John Angier.

The name of *Alger*, often written and formerly pronounced *Auger*, has been sometimes mistaken for Angier. See Farmer's Register, where Arthur, Andrew, and Sampson Angier are mentioned, the name of each of whom was Alger or *Auger*, and not Angier.—(See *Alger*.)

BACON.—Daniel Bacon made free 1647 was an early settler in W. B., owned a purchase right, and the farm where Timothy Reed Esq. lately lived; all which he sold to his nephew Michael Bacon Jr. of Billerica, who sold it to John Kingman of Weymouth 1685, and Kingman and his descendants have ever since occupied it. It came into the possession of Reed by his marriage with Hannah the only child of the late Caleb Kingman deceased, the last of the name who owned it.—Daniel Bacon was one of the jury for laying out highways in 1664, and is mentioned again in 1668, but the family early left the town.

BAILEY or BAYLEY.—Guido Bayley was among the first settlers of the town: took the oath of fidelity here in 1657: purchased John Irish's proprietary right or share 1659, and was called of Bridgewater: he first lived in W. B. "near Goodman Lathrop's and the flaggy meadow," but afterwards appeared in S. B. near where the late Zechariah Whitman afterwards lived: he sold his place there to his nephew Manasseh Marston of Salem in 1696; the selectmen consenting to it, to whom he from age and infirmity had previously applied for assistance; Marston to maintain him and his D. Mary; he had in 1687 conveyed his whole estate "excepting what he had before given to the rest of his children" to his son Guido, who died immediately after, and it came again to the father. He d. a. 1700; his wife's name was Ruth: he had Guido, Mary, Ruth and Elizabeth.—Guido d. a. 1690 and Ebenezer Hill settled his estate.—Mary first m. a Randall and then Isaac Leonard perhaps 1701; she conveyed twenty acres of land to her cousin Marston 1697, who was to take care of her, and he conveyed it to Leonard 1702.—Ruth m. Ebenezer Hill 1684.—Elizabeth m. James Harris 1693; her father gave her his estate and farm in W. B. by Lathrop's.—In 1703 the town directed the selectmen "to take care of the wid. Bayley and keep her in possession of her just right in her late husband's estate as far as may be." This family is extinct here.

2. Adams Bailey b. 1722 (s. of Joseph who was s. of John of Scituate) m. Sarah D. of Jonathan Howard of W. B. 1746 and settled there; and had Seth 1747, Adams 1748, Joseph 1749, (all b. at Scituate), Sarah 1752, Charity 1754, Jonathan 1756, Caleb 1759, Ebenezer 1760, Charlotte 1763, Daniel 1765, Caleb 1768, Paul 1770, (the 9 last b. at Bridgewater).—Sarah m. Isaac Lathrop 1775.—Paul m. Betsy D. of Jeremiah Thayer 1798 and went to Sidney Me.

3. Seth (s. of Adams 2) m. Deborah D. of Capt. Jacob Packard 1770, and had Sally 1770, Deborah 1772, Jacob 1775.

4. Capt. Adams (s. of Adams 2) m. Catharine Little 1775; he was an officer in the revolutionary war and lived and died at Charlestown, where he was master or superintendant of the U. S. marine hospital: he had a s. Adams b. 1780, who lives in Boston.

5. Joseph (s. of Adams 2) m. Abigail D. probably of Capt. Jacob Packard, 1771, and had Charlotte 1772: he d. young probably.—Wid. Abigail Bailey d. 1775, æ 47, as appears on E. B. records.

6. Jonathan (s. of Adams 2) m. Catharine Nichols 1778, and had Mephibosheth 1778, Sarah 1780, Catharine 1782.—Sarah m. Caleb Snell 1799.

7. Ebenezer (s. of Adams 2) m. Silvia D. of Capt. Eliakim
Howard 1782, and had Mehitabel 1782, Adams 1784, and then
went westward.
Lydia Bailey d. 1794, æ 21.—Thankful Bailey m. Thos. Lindsay Jr. 1786.—Joseph Bailey of Freeport m. Patience Holmes
1796.

8. Capt. Israel, b. at Scituate 1708 (s. of John of Hanover,
who was son of John of Scituate) was cousin of Adams 2, and
uncle of Col. John of Hanover of revolutionary memory. He
m. Keziah Perry 1730, and settled in E. B.: his will 1749, proved
1750; his w. and brother John of Hanover ex'ors.; he had Rhoda
1731*, Israel 1732, Keziah 1734, Hannah 1736, Abigail 1738,
Rachel 1740, Ward 1742, Sarah 1744*, Elizabeth 1746*, (all b.
at Scituate before he came to E. B.); his widow m. Joseph
Keith 1763 and d. 1796, æ. 90.—Keziah m. John Richards 1751.—
Hannah m. Solomon Packard 1760.—Abigail m. Capt. Jacob
Allen 1762, and afterwards Isaac Lazell senr.—Rachel m. Benjamin Byram 1760.

9. Israel (s. of Capt. Israel 8.) m. Martha, wid. of Isaac Alden
and D. of Solomon Packard senr. 1760, and d. 1773, æ. 41; he
had Eliphalet 1760, Israel 1764, John 1766, and Timothy 1768.—
Eliphalet m. Martha, D. of John Robinson, 1782, and had Ward,
Eliphalet, Winslow Clift, Nahum, Ira, John, Melville, and several ds., and removed to Plymouth where he d.—Israel m. Lucy,
D. of William Whitman, 1789.—Timothy m. Anna Washburn,
D. of Amos Whitman, 1796.—Israel, John, and Timothy removed
to Minot, Me.

10. Ward (s. of Capt. Israel 8.) m. Polly, d. of Rev. Christopher Sergeant of Methuen, 1765, and had Christopher Sergeant
1767, Susanna 1768 : he then removed to Vermont.

11. Winslow Clift Bailey (s. of Eliphalet: see Israel 8.) and
his w. Nancy had Lucy E. 1808, Hope S. 1810, Eliphalet, b. in
Plymo. 1813, William E. 1815, Nancy 1819.

BARBER.—James Barber had Mary 1692, Hezekiah 1696,
b. here, and there is no further account of the family.—Patience
Barber m. John Cole of Plympton 1709.

BARRELL.—William Barrell (s. of William of Boston, who
d. in early life) settled in Scituate and m. Lydia, wid. of
John James, 1680, and had William 1683, Lydia 1684, who m.
Saml Stockbridge 1703, Mary 1686, James 1687.

2. William (s. of William 1.) m. Elizabeth, D. of John Bailey,
1706; lived in Scituate, and had Hannah 1706, Lydia 1709, who
m. Joseph Young 1726, William 1714 : his w. d. and he m. a 2d
w. and had James 1727, Colburn, John, and Elisha 1735 : the
family were remarkable for longevity.—James d. April 17, 1827,
having lived nearly to the age of 100, and left James, William,
Noah, and Bartlett.—Colburn was a soldier in the American,
and also the old French war, and a man of extraordinary strength
and activity, and d. a. 1782.—Elisha completed his 94th year and
d. 1829.

3. William (s. of William 2. and cousin of Capt. Israel Bailey) m. a Simmons and had a son Joshua in Scituate and then his w. dying, he came and settled in E. B. and m. Sarah, an only child of Dea. James Cary, 1751, and succeeded in her right to her father's estate, and had James 1753*, Sarah 1754, Lydia 1757, Hannah 1759, Ruth 1762, Content 1764, James 1766.—Sarah m. Nathan Alden, Esq. 1776.—Lydia m. Dea. Eliphalet Packard 1782.—Hannah d. single 1784, æ. 24.—Ruth m. Capt. Robert Packard 1782.—Content d. single 1823, æ. 57.—William, the father d. 1806, æ 91. his wid. Sarah d. the same year æ 84.

4. John (s. of William 2.) came also to E. B., and m. Judith D. of Isaac Snow, 1756, and had Molly 1757*, John 1760, Judith 1763 : he d. 1762, and the family afterwards removed westward.

5. Joshua (s. of William 3.) m. Olive, D. of Capt. Jonathan Bass, 1769, and had Susanna 1771, Jennet 1774, William 1776, Jona. Bass 1779*, Samuel 1781, Elijah 1784, Azor 1786, Charles 1789, Paschal 1796.—Susanna m. Oakes Whitman 1790.—Jennet m. John Loring Esq. 1794.—William m. Huldah, D. of John Bisbee, 1801, and parents and children all removed to Turner, Me.

6. Maj. James (s. of William 3.) m. Betsy, D. of Thomas Russell, 1785, and had James Cary*, Ruth, Hannah, Abigail, all baptized 1800, George Whitfield 1801.—Maj. Barrell d. 1810, æ 43 ; his w. still survives.—Ruth m. Dr. Caleb Swan of E. 1816.— Hannah m. Dr. Daniel Sawin 1810.—Abigail m. Hon. Jared Whitman of Abington 1813 : these Ds. all d. in early life.— George W. m. a D. of Dr. Samuel Guild Esq. of Easton.

7. James (s. of James and grandson of William 2.) lived in Scituate and had James, Abel, Thomas, Elias and Colburn, most of whom came to E. B.—James keeps the poor house there.— Abel m. Polly, D. of Jonathan Alden, 1810.—Thomas m. Huldah, D. of Matthew Allen, 1815.—Elias m. Deborah Tilden 1813.

George and John, brothers of the first William Barrell of Boston, lived in Boston : George d. there 1643, leaving John and James and perhaps other children.—John's will is on record there dated 1658.

BARRETT.—James Barrett and his w. Mary lived in E. B., and had Martha 1725, Solomon 1727, Stephen 1730, Mary 1732, John and Joseph 1734, Sarah 1736, James 1738.—This family soon removed from the town.

BARTLETT.—Wright Bartlett, from Hingham probably, m. Bethiah, D. of Samuel Packard, 1731, and settled in W. B., and had Samuel, Relief, Lydia, Phillis, and perhaps others.— Relief m. Ebenezer Hooper 1761.—Lydia m. Ebenezer Hinds 1751.—Phillis m. Edward Powers 1753.—John Bartlett and his wife and Catharine Williams were warned out of town 1739, and Wright Bartlett was "forewarned not to entertain them any longer."

2. Samuel (s. of Wright 1.) m. Susanna, D. of David Dunbar, 1757, and had Susanna 1758, Sarah 1760, Lucy 1762, Job Pack-

ard 1764*, Samuel 1766, Hannah 1769, Rachel 1772, Keziah
1775, David 1778.—Susanna m. David Gurney 1792.—Sarah m.
Isaiah Hayward 1777.—Lucy m. Waldo Hayward 1781.—Samuel m. Lucy Jenkins 1785 and went to Croydon, N. H.—Hannah
m. Simeon Howard 1794.—Rachel m. Barnabas Lathrop.—Keziah m. Abiel Howard 1798.
    3. David (s. of Samuel 2.) m. Polly, D. of George Howard, and
had Charlotte 1797*, Job 1799, Polly 1801, Jane 1804, Susanna
1807, David 1811 : his w. d. and he m. Susan Fish 1814, and had
Charlotte and Julia.
    4. Richard Bartlett, an Englishman, lived in Boston and had
a s. Richard, and a D. who m. Rev. Mr. Hinds of Middleborough.
    5. Richard (s. of the above) m. Mary, D. of Gain Robinson
of E. B. and had Lydia 1757, Mary 1759, Margaret 1761, Gain*,
Martha, Richard, Elizabeth, Robert, Edward, Jane, William.—
Lydia m. Capt. John Savage.—Mary m. Benjamin Richards
1782.—Margaret m. James Taylor.—Martha m. a McNeal.—
Elizabeth m. Andrew Mushero.—Jane m. Shadrach Holly.—
Richard, the father, was a soldier at Annapolis Royal with Gen.
John Winslow in 1755 in seizing and dispersing the neutral
French ; and all of the family except Mrs. Richards and Robert
resided in Nova Scotia, and most of them were born there.—
Robert is a mariner and shipmaster at N. York.
    Richard Bartlett m. Rebecca Holmes 1763.—Edward m. Zil-
phah, D. of Ephraim Cole, 1772.—Solomon m. Huldah Washburn 1781.—Elizabeth m. Seth Ames 1798.—Hannah Thomas
Bartlett m. John Cumner of Wayne 1813.—Sarah, D. of Andrew
of Plymo. m. David P. Reynolds 1818.—Lewis Bartlett's w. d.
in E. B. 1823, æ. 31.
    BASS.—Samuel Bass and his w. Anne settled in Roxbury a.
1630 : he was admitted freeman 1634, removed to Braintree, now
Quincy, 1640, and was the first Deacon of the Church there, and
represented the town 12 years : his w. d. 1693, he d. 1694, æ 94 :
they had John 1632, b. at Roxbury, Samuel, Hannah, Mary 1643,
Thomas, Joseph, Sarah.—The ss. settled in Braintree.—Hannah
m. Steph. Payne 1651.—Mary m. Capt. John Capen 1647.—Sarah
m. first Dea. John Stone of Watertown, and then Dea. Joseph
Penniman 1693, and she lived to be nearly 100 years old.
    2. John (s. of the above) m. Ruth, D. of Hon. John Alden of
Duxbury 1657, (m. by her father,) and had John 1658, Samuel
1660, Ruth 1662, Joseph 1665, Hannah 1667, Mary 1669, Sarah
1672 : his w. d. and he m. Anne, wid. of Saml. Sturtevant of
Plymo., 1675 : he d. 1716, æ. 84.—John and Joseph settled in
Braintree.—Ruth probably m. a Walesby and left an orphan D.
Hannah.—Hannah m. Joseph Adams, grandfather of the first
President Adams.—Mary m. Christopher Webb Jr. 1686, and
then Wm. Copeland 1694.—Sarah m. Ephraim Thayer 1792.
    3. Dea. Samuel (s. of John 2) m. Mary D. of Joseph Adams
(father of Joseph, above) and wid. of Saml. Webb 1696, and had
Jonathan and Abigail bap'd. 1697, Mary 1698, Samuel 1700,

Bethiah 1704; his w. d. 1706 and he m. probably Bethiah Night-ingale 1796, and had a child that d. 1708 and Bathsheba bapd. 1711 : he lived at Randolph, but in his old age removed to E. B. and lived with his son Capt. Jonathan, and d. there 1751 æ. 90.—Mary m. William Bowditch 1720.—Samuel settled at Randolph and was a Deacon there-—Bathsheba m. Naphthali Thayer 1732.

4. Capt. Jonathan (s. of Dea. Samuel 3.) settled in E. B. a. 1723, and m. Susanna, D. of Capt. Nicholas Byram, Oct. 18, 1717, and had Jonathan 1720, Susanna 1722, both b. at Braintree, now Randolph, Mary 1724, Mehitabel 1728, Bethiah 1730*, Bathsheba 1733, Sarah 1736, Eunice 1737 : he d. 1750, æ 55, she 1783, æ. 89.—Susanna m. Zechariah Cary 1742.—Mary m. the Hon. Hugh Orr 1742.—Mehitabel m. Dr. Isaac Otis 1742.— Bathsheba m. Ignatius Loring Esq. of Plympton 1750.—Sarah m. Jonathan Allen 1755.—Eunice m. John Young 1752.

5. Capt. Jonathan (s. of Capt. Jonathan 4.) m. Susanna, D. of Josiah Byram, 1741, and had Bethiah 1742*, Ruth 1745*, Mary 1747*, Susanna 1749, Olive 1751, Jonathan 1753, Ruth 1755, Eunice 1758, Sarah 1761 : he d. over 80 years of age.—Susanna m. Elijah Dean of Raynham 1768, and afterwards Thomas Dean, and d. 1829.—Olive m. Joshua Barrell 1769.—Jonathan went to Conn. and had a family there.—Ruth m. a Williams of Pomfret, Conn.—Eunice m. Seth Whitman 1781, and then Peter Salmon 1785.—Sarah m. Joseph Chamberlin 1784.

BASSETT.—William Bassett, one of the forefathers, came over in the ship Fortune 1621, and settled first in Plymouth, then in Duxbury, and finally in W. B.; was an original proprietor of the town, and d. 1667 ; was a large land holder in the colony, and left a large library : his w., Elizabeth, was probably a Tilden.— He had William, Nathaniel, Joseph, Sarah, Elizabeth, Jane and perhaps others.—William settled in Sandwich and his s. William had his grandfather's house and land in B by the will, which was nuncupative, and dated 1667 : this grandson was Marshal, and otherwise distinguished in the Colony.—Nathaniel settled in Marshfield and afterwards in 1684 appeared at Yarmouth.—Sarah m. Peregrine White.—Elizabeth m. William Hatch.—Jane m. Thomas Gilbert of T. 1639.

2. Joseph (s. of William 1.) settled in W. B. with his father and m. Martha, D. of Edmund Hobart of Hingham, 1677 : he d. 1712.—He had Joseph, William, Elnathan, Jeremiah, Lydia w. of Daniel Whittemore, Ruth w. of John Whittemore, m. 1692, both of Charlestown, and Elizabeth w. of Wm. Fenton.—Jeremiah had the homestead, near Isaac Johnson's, and sold it to Johnson 1713, and went to Norton.

3. Joseph (s. of Joseph 2.) and his w. Bethiah had Bethiah 1693, Mehitabel 1697, Lydia 1703 : he d. 1736.—Lydia m. Saml. Phillips of Norton 1726.—Mehitabel m. a Hollaway of M.— Bethiah, Executrix, m. William Coddington of Norton a. 1737.

4. William (s. of Joseph 2.) and Sarah his wife had William

1694, Joseph 1696, Ruth 1700, Nathan 1702: the mother d. 1703, and the father m. Mary Bump 1703, and had Sarah 1704, Elizabeth 1706, Thankful 1710, Benjamin 1712, Seth 1715.—William m. Mary Mehurin 1719.—Ruth m. Joseph Davis and d. 1730.

5. Elnathan (s. of Joseph 2.) m. Mary Hill 1702, and d. 1750, leaving Mary, who m. Samuel Beal 1725.

6. Joseph (s. of William 4.) m. Elizabeth, D. of John Ames, 1724, (m. in Boston), and had Dorothy 1726, Joseph 1731, Sarah 1734: he d. 1741, and the mother, who undertook to settle the estate, d. in 1744.—Dorothy m. David Packard 1767.—Sarah m. Christopher Dyer 1757.

7. Nathan (s. of William 4.) m. Hannah Washburn 1733, and had John 1734, Nathan 1737, Ruth 1740, David 1743, Hannah 1745, Joseph 1747, Jonathan 1750.—Jonathan went to Killingsly, Conn.

8. Benjamin (s. of William 4.) m. Hannah Macomber 1737, and had Daniel 1740, Benjamin 1742, Joshua 1745, Hannah, Zilphah, Phebe 1753.

9. Seth (s. of William 4.) and his wife Mary had Sarah and Mary 1738, and went to N. H.

10. Joseph (s. of Joseph 6) m. Phebe Cushman 1756, and had Caleb 1757, Phebe, Nathan 1763, Abigail, Joseph 1769, Hannah 1771, David and Cushman.—His w. d. 1796, æ. 59, and he m. Sarah, wid. of John Eaton, of Greenwich, former wid. of Josiah Fobes Jr., and D. of Joseph Prior, 1798: she d. 1839, æ. 100.— His will dated 1798, proved 1803.—Phebe m. Barna. Leonard 1780.—Nathan went to Genesee.—Abigail (or Abial) m. Seth Lathrop Jr. 1783.—Hannah m. Dea. James Alger 1791.—David m. Phebe Dean of R. 1796.—Cushman was a Preacher, and he and David went to Maine.

11. Joseph Esq. (s. of Nathan 7.) m. Hannah, D. of Josiah Lathrop 1776, and had William, Nathan, Jonathan, Josiah, Paschal, Joseph, George, Sarah and Hannah.—Nathan m. a Daniels or a Snow.—Jonathan m. Sarah, D. of David Leonard, 1813, and afterwards a D. of John Fobes.—Josiah m. Lucretia, D. of Bradford Mitchell, 1810.—Paschal m. Mary, D. of Winslow Hooper, 1811, and had Mary Winslow 1812, and Sarah Church 1814.—Joseph m. Hannah Williams 1816.—George m. Hannah, D. of Maj. Theodore Mitchell, 1819.—Sarah m. Hampden Keith 1799.—Hannah m. Ezra Fobes Jr. 1810.

12. Caleb (s. of Joseph 10.) m. Bethiah, D. of Benjamin Keith, 1782, then called of New Gloucester, and had Cyrus, Caleb Keith, Lewis*, Abigail, Bethiah, Eunice, and Sophronia: he removed to M.—Cyrus m. Cynthia Randall 1808, and Cyrus m. Urania Billings 1814.—Caleb m. Mary Holmes 1811.—Abigail m. Shepard Dunbar 1806.—Bethiah m. a Kennedy.

13. Joseph (s. of Joseph 10.) m. Ruth, D. of James Leach, 1792, and had Charles 1792, Mary 1795, Cushman 1799, Davis 1802*, Eliza Maria 1805, Emeline 1808, Jane 1810, Phebe Leonard 1813.—Charles m. Laura, D. of Jason Fobes 1816.—Mary

m. Hartwell Keith 1816.—Cushman m. a Newman and lives in
Boston.—Jane m. a Daniels.
14. William (s. of Joseph Esq. 11.) m. Abiah Williams 1800,
and had William Church 1803, Williams 1806, Hannah 1809,
Abial 1811, Henriette 1813, Harriet 1815, Josiah 1818, Cornenia
Abier 1820.
Wid. Abigail Bassett m. Benjamin Leach 1763.—Lydia Bassett of Norton m. Dea. David Edson 1786.—Sally Bassett m.
Abijah Thayer Jr. 1802.
BATES.—Joshua Bates (from Hanover) m. Bethiah, D. of
Joseph Ames, 1796, and settled in S. B., and had Joshua C.
1797, Zephaniah 1803, George W. 1805, Samuel W. 1808,
Bethiah W. 1813 : he d. 1839, æ. 72.—Saml. W. m. Helen, D.
of Z. Crooker.
2. Christopher Bates lived in E. B. and had Christopher, Moses, Nahum, Daniel and others.
3. Moses (s. of Christopher 2.) m. Deborah Dyer 1808, and
had Kitty Dyer 1809, Christopher 1813*, Moses 1815, Deborah
1819.
Obadiah Bates and- his w. Ruth.—Wm. R. Bates of Cummington m. Polly, D. of Dea. Isaac Lazell, 1803.—James of W.
m. Lucy, D. of Daniel Orcutt, 1805.—Daniel m. Jane Reed
1811.—Jacob m. Lucy Dyer of A. 1816.—Cotton of W. m.
Rhoda, D. of Josiah Johnson, 1817.—Rufus of Hanover m.
Huldah, D. of Eleazar Keith, 1821.—Christopher Jr. m. a Howland.
BATTLES.—John Battles (from Plymouth) settled in Stoughton Corner within the North Parish of Bridgewater, and m.
Hannah, D. of Edward Curtis, and had John*, Jonathan, Samuel, Asa, Uriah, Edward, Curtis, Hannah, Rebecca, and Susanna.—Hannah m. a Jordan.—Rebecca m. a Billings.—Susanna
m. a Lord.—Jonathan m. Hannah, D. of Joseph Porter, aud set-
tled in Stoughton.—Edward and Curtis went to Vt.—Susanna
Battles m. Benjamin Washburn 1742.
2. Samuel (s. of John 1.) settled in N. B. and m. Dorothy, D.
of Christopher Dyer, 1786, and had Sybil 1786, Lucinda 1788,
Daniel Dyer 1790*, David 1792, Dorothy 1796, Saml. 1798*, Jason
Dyer 1800, Nahum 1802, Mary Dyer 1806*, Anson 1810, Mary
Dyer 1814.—Sybil m. Ruel Fobes 1806.—Lucinda m. Luke
Packard 1806.—David m. Jerusha Adams 1816.—Dorothy m.
Ansel Perkins 1819.—Jason D. removed to Boston.
3. Asa (s. of John 1.) settled also in N. B. and m. Mary, D.
of John Pratt, and had Polly 1788, Ara 1790, John 1792, Betsy
1794, William 1796, Susanna 1798, Amelia 1800, Isabella, and
Hannah.—Polly m. a Cleaveland.—Ara m. Polly, D. of Samuel
Cheesman.—Jno. m. Milicent Porter 1816.—Betsy m. a Branch.—
Susanna m. a Reynolds.—Isabella m. a Miller.—Susanna Battles m. Nathl. Leeds 1806.
BEAL or BEALS.—Samuel Beal (probably from Pembroke)
settled in E. B., where Eleazer Keith lived, and m. Mary, only
14

child of Elnathan Bassett, 1725, and had Samuel 1726, Nathan 1727, Daniel 1729, Jonathan 1730, Joseph* and Benjamin 1733, Seth 1736*, Mary 1742, Joseph 1743*: the father d. 1750.

2. Samuel (s. of the above) m. Elizabeth Blackman 1745, and had David 1746*, Samuel 1748, after his father's death, and his mother, the wid., m. Theophilus Byram 1749.

3. Nathan (s. of Saml. 1.) and his w. Bathsheba had Mary 1750, Nathan 1752, Nehemiah 1755, John 1759.—Mary m. Nehemiah Shaw 1775.—(See David Hill).

4. Daniel (s. of Saml. 1.) m. Mehitabel, D. of Josiah Byram, 1750, and had Samuel 1750, Daniel 1753, Joshua 1755, Mehitabel 1758.—Joshua m. Susanna, D. of Dea. David Edson, 1768.

5. Jonathan (s. of Saml. 1.) m. Abigail Harlow 1751, and had Joseph 1752, Azariah 1753, Abigail 1755, Jonathan 1758, Hannah 1760*, Hannah 1762, Molly 1770: his w. d. 1779, æ. 50, and he m. Abigail, wid. of John Egerton and D. of James Snow, 1780: he d. 1813, æ. 83; she 1810, æ. 83.—Joseph went to Abington.—Abigail m. Josiah Hill 1779.—Hannah m. Noah Hill 1780.—Molly m. Bela Reed 1793.

6. Benjamin (s. of Saml. 1.) and his w. Sarah had Isaac 1753, Levi 1755.

7. Azariah (s. of Saml. 1.) m. Bathsheba Bisbee 1776, and had Danl. 1779, Ezra 1781.—Most of the above families removed to Cummington and Plainfield.

8. Jeremiah Beal (s. of Isaac of Weymouth) settled in N. B. 1760, and m. Mary, D. of Dependence French, 1768, and had Sarah 1768, Hannah 1771, Rachel 1774, Olive 1778, Mary 1782, Jeremiah 1786.—Sarah m. Asa Ford 1793.—Hannah m. Oliver Snell 1792.—Rachel m. Capt. Asa Jones 1792.—Olive m. Joseph Brett 1797.—Mary m. Elijah Smith 1803.—Capt. Jeremiah m. Sibil, D. of Timothy Ames, 1807, and had Rachel 1808, Seba Ames 1812.

. 9. Japhet Beal lived in N. B., m. Patience Keith 1770, and had Susanna 1771, Isaac 1774, Oliver 1776, Japhet 1781, Patience 1784.—Susanna m. Elijah Packard 1789.—Isaac m. Elizbeth Stevens 1797 and went to Me.—Japhet, the father, m. wid. Content Packard probably for a 2d w. 1803 and went to Minot.— Japhet, the son, m. Mehitabel, D. of Gideon Lincoln, 1803, and went to Augusta.

10. Jonathan Beal m. Polly; D. of Moses Cary, 1807, and had Bethiah Lewis 1808, Mary Cary 1810, Elizabeth 1813, Jonathan 1817.

Andrew Beal had a D. Lydia bapd. in E. B. 1782 : he had lived in Newton and had two ch. b. there.—Hannah m. Ezekiel Reed 1742.—Saml. from Hanson, and his w. Olive, had a D. Olive 1797.—Seth m. Thirza Hatch 1799.—Elijah of Hingham m. Betsy, D. of Wm. Pincin, 1804.—Levi of Hingham m. Ruth Whiting 1810.—Betsy of H. m. Allen Marshall Porter 1816.— Martin of Hingham m. Mehitabel Pincin 1816.—Lazarus of

Weymouth m. Sarah, wid. of Daniel Alden, and D. of Dea.
Jona. Cary, 1809.—Asaph had Phebe Howard 1818.
All of the name of Beal in this vicinity descended no doubt
from John Beal, who with his w. and 5 ss. and 3 Ds. and 2 ser-
vants, came from Hingham in Eng. and settled here in Hingham
1638. They came in the ship Diligent of Ipswich, John Martin,
master, in which were 133 passengers. The 5 ss. were probably
John, Jeremiah, Caleb, Nathaniel and Joshua.—John's children
were Rebecca 1641, Jacob 1642, Martha 1646, Nathaniel 1648,
John 1650, Mary 1657, who first m. a Stowell and then Nathaniel
Hobart : his wife died 1658 and he m. wid. Jacobs 1659.—John
Beal was Rep. from Hingham 1649.—Lt. Jeremiah m. Sarah
Ripley 1654 and d. 1716, æ. 86 : he had Jeremiah 1655, Eliza-
beth 1659*, Mary 1661*, Lazarus 1661, Mary 1662, Sarah 1662,
Phebe 1664.—Caleb died at Hingham 1716, æ. 80, born in
England.—Nathaniel had John who (was burnt and) d. 1655, Sa-
rah and John 1659.—Joshua had a D. 1661, and another, Eliz-
abeth 1663*.—Jacob and Joshua d. 1716.

BEARCE.—Austin Bearce was admitted freeman 1652, and
on the grand jury 1653 : he had Mary 1640, Priscilla 1643, Sarah 1646, Abigail 1647, Hannah 1649, Joseph 1651, Hester 1653,
Lydia 1655, Rebeckah 1657, James 1660 ; all b. at Barnstable.—
Austin Bearce was at Halifax, probably a descendant of the
above, and went to Cornwall.—Andrew Bearce of Halifax m.
Margaret Dawes of E. B. 1736.—Consider Bearce of Halifax m.
Elizabeth Perkins of E. B. 1761—Margaret, D. of Andrew
above, m. Arthur Latham of E. B.—Experience Bearce m.
Zadock Hayward 1768.—Ford, Jacob, Isaiah, Job and Thomas,
were brothers.—Ford was a schoolmaster and d. young in S. B.
of small pox 1778.—Jacob settled in Hanson, and Dea. Jacob is
his son.—Isaiah and Thomas d. young.—There were also two
Ds. Lydia and Hannah.

2. Job Bearce (above) m. Sarah, D. of Lt. James Keith, 1780,
and settled in E. B., and had Dexter 1781, Sally 1784, Hannah
1789*, Lydia 1791, Ford 1794, Charles 1796*, Susanna Keith
1798 : he d. 1828, æ. 79 ; she 1838, æ. 84.—Dexter moved to
New Gloucester and m. a Chandler.—Sally m. Martin Keith
1809, and afterwards Edward Hayward of W. B.—Lydia m.
Amory Leach 1817, and went to Jay, Me.—Susanna K. m. Silvanus Rogers and d. 1828.—Ford m. Harriet Shaw of M. 1820,
and d. 1838.

BELCHER.—Mayhew Belcher (from Boston) lived in E. B.
and d. unmarried 1778 : his sister Ann m. John Keith 1774.—
Deborah Belcher m. Seth Dunbar 1761.—Rebecca m. Jesse Edson 1764.—Hannah m. Capt. Moses Curtis 1769.—Amie m. Wm.
Tribou 1784.

BENSON.—John Benson (from Weymouth perhaps and s. of
John of Hull) settled in S. B., m. Elizabeth, D. probably of
Jonathan Washburn, 1710, and had Susanna, Benjamin, Eliza-
beth, Mary, Hannah and Jonathan : he d. 1770, his will dated

the same year, in which it appears Benjamin, Elizabeth, Mary and Hannah were then dead.—Susanna m. Jonathan Cushman 1736.—Hannah m. James Dunbar Jr. 1746 and d. a. 1757.

2. Benjamin (s. of John 1.) m. Keziah, D. of Amos Snell 1745, and had Benjamin, an only child, who m. Abigail, D. probably of Nathan Pratt 1770.—Benjamin the father d. 1749, and his w. Keziah 1750: his will 1748, hers 1749: the w. of Benjamin Jr. d. 1771.

3. Jonathan (s. of John 1.) m. Martha, D. of Amos Snell, 1740, and had John 1742, Eunice 1744, Mary 1745, Martha 1749, Lois 1751, Jonathan 1752, Ebenezer 1755, David 1756, Jonas 1759: he d. 1788 of small pox; she 1801, æ. 84: his will dated 1788, hers 1791.—Eunice m. John Harden 1766.—Mary m. Benjamin Hayward Jr. 1767.—Martha m. Elisha Waterman of Halifax 1774.—Lois m. Cornelius Washburn Jr.

4. Jonathan (s. of Jonathan 3.) m. Lydia, D. probably of Samuel Harden, 1774, and had John, Betsy, Cyrus, Jonathan and Abigail, and perhaps others: he d. 1802, æ. 50.—John d. 1805, æ. 27.—Cyrus m. Lydia, D. of Capt. Simeon Wood, 1806.—Jonathan m. Jane, D. of Jonah Benson, 1820.—Abigail m. Samuel Jones 1811.

5. Ebenezer (s. of Jonathan 3.) m. Silence, D. of Nehemiah Packard and wid. of Seth Leonard, 1777, and had a D. Olive, who m. Martin Conant 1797, and two ss., Asa and Hosea; and all went to Jay in Me.

6. David (s. of Jonathan 3.) m. Charity, D. of Seth Hayward, 1780, and had Tabitha 1781, Eunice 1782, Charity 1784, Sarah 1786, David 1788, Seth 1790, Bethiah 1793, Keziah 1796, Polly 1798.—Tabitha m. Wm. Fuller 1801.—Eunice m. Abner Keith 1803.—Charity m. Ebenezer Cushman of Kingston 1805.—Sarah m. James Pool Jr. a. 1808.—Bethiah m. Seth Thompson 1815.—Keziah m. John Atwood Jackson 1815.—Polly m. Ebenezer Chamberlin 1820.

7. Jonah (s. of Jonathan 3.) m. Martha Thompson of Halifax 1782, and had Jonah, Waitstill, Patty, Nahum, Lucia and Jane.—Jonah m. Chloe Hathaway 1819.—Waitstill m. Benjamin Holmes 1807.—Patty m. Philander Wood 1813.—Nahum m. Chloe Dunbar 1819.—Lucia m. a Drake.—Jane m. Jona. Benson 1820.

John Benson m. Sarah Williams 1765.—Keziah m. Ebenezer Cushman Jr. of Kingston 1805.—Hannah m. Jabez Waterman of H. 1785.

BESSEE.—Nehemiah Bessee, with his wife Sarah, came probably from Wareham, and settled in S. B.: had Abisha 1760, Lucy 1762, Jonah 1764, John 1766, Abraham 1768, Adam 1770, Sarah 1772, Polly 1774: they had also a D. Charity, and two ss., Nehemiah and Anthony, who went to Woodstock.—Charity m. Ebenezer Pratt 1780.—Abisha m. Sally, D. of Jona. Conant, 1782.—Lucy m. David Conant 1782.—Jonah m. Eunice, D. of Daniel Washburn, 1787, and went to Me.—Adam m. Joanna, D.

of Dea. Seth Pratt, 1791, and d. 1793, and she m. Isaac Keith
1797.—Mary Bessee m. Moses Snell 1736.—Mary Bessee m.
Simeon Hayward 1757.—Thankful Bessee of Wareham m. Nathan Leonard 1744.—Lydia m. Saml. Leonard 1750.—Joanna,
D. of Adam, m. Martin Leonard 1818.

2. Reuben Bessee, with his wife, came from Me. with their
children, viz. William, Mary, Keziah and Thomas.—He was b.
in Wareham.—Keziah m. Luther French 1831. They lived
awhile in E. B. and moved back to Me.

These families were probably descended from Anthony Bessee,
who first settled in Lynn and removed to Sandwich 1637.

BICKNELL.—John Bicknell, and his w. Rebecca, came probably from Abington, and had John 1772, Noah 1773, Simeon
1775.—Jacob Bicknell Jr. of Abington m. Mehitabel, D. of Micah White 1803.—John Bicknell m. Susanna, widow of Saml.
Sturtevant and D. of Capt. Josiah Packard.

BISBEE.—Moses Bisbee (s. of John of Marshfield) and his
w. Mary settled in E. B. and had Abigail* Miriam 1724, Charles
1726, Joanna 1729, Mary 1733*, Tabitha 1735.—Joanna m. John
Churchill 1756.—Tabitha never m.

2. Charles (s. of Moses above) m. Bulah, D. of Rowse Howland, and had Elisha 1757, Charles 1758, Mary 1760, Moses,
John, Solomon, Calvin, Rowse.—This family removed to Pembroke.

3. Samuel Bisbee, from Pembroke, (s. probably of Elisha
Bisbee Esq.) settled in B. a. 1750, and m. Martha, D. of Joseph
Snell, 1751, and had Sarah 1751, Martha 1753, Hannah 1755,
Samuel 1757, Benjamin 1759.—Elisha m. Martha, D. of Nathan
Keith, 1779, and afterwards Jemima Allen, and went to Me.

Ebenezer had two wives: his first, Bathsheba Whitmarsh, m.
1745 and d. 1777, æ. 50, by whom he had a D. Jennet 1771*: his
2d w. was Mehitabel, D. of Ebenezer Shaw, m. 1778. He and
Luther went to Cummington.—Hannah m. Zechariah Shaw
1777.—Bathsheba Bisbee m. Azariah Beal 1776.

4. John Bisbee m. widow Rebecca, widow of Isaac Alden,
1771, and D. of Josiah Keith of E., and had John 1774, Rebecca 1777: the mother d. 1777, æ. 41, and he m. Huldah, D. of
Ebenezer Shaw, 1779, and had Ira 1780, Ebenezer 1782, Huldah
1784, Patty 1788: he had a 3d w. Mary, D. of John Edson, by
whom he had Ziba, Chandler and others: he d. 1817; she 1833,
æ. 61.—John went to Me.—Huldah m. William Barrell Jr. 1801.
Ira m. Rebecca, D. of Samuel Dyke, 1805, and had Algernon
Sidney 1806.—Ziba m. Sirena, D. of Gideon Lincoln, 1814.—
Molly m. Emery Brown 1817, Chandler Bisbee m. Mary Byram
Whitmarsh 1818.—Olive m. Cyrus Warren 1814.—Lavinia Bis-
bee of St. m. Alfred Howard 1794. Elizabeth of P. m. John
Tomson 1762. These families all descended probably from
Thomas Bisbee, who was at Scituate 1634, and Deacon of the
Church at its first institution there.

BLANCHARD.—Eli Blanchard (from Weymouth) m. Deborah, D. of John Harden, and settled in E. B., and had Eli 1798, Noah 1800, Lydia 1802, Mehitabel 1806, Evelina 1808, Elias Paine 1810, George W. 1813, Mary Ann 1815, Almira 1817, Semantha 1819, and Daniel Thomas 1821.—Eli m. Eliza Wood 1817.— Noah m. Lydia Binney of Boston, where he lives.—Lydia m. a Drake of Quincy.—Mehitabel m. a Chubbuck of Quincy.—Evelina m. Luther Churchill —Elias P. m. Julia Bryant, and lives in Boston.—George W. m. Nancy, D. of Thomas White.—Mary Ann m. Daniel Gloyd.—Almira m. Orrin Wilkes.—Semantha m. a Gurney.

BLOSSOM.—Silvanus Blossom m. Charity, D. of Amos Snell 1738, and settled in South Bridgewater, and had a family : one s. Silvanus b. 1746, m. Martha, D. of Eleazar Alden, 1774, and had Alden, Leonard, Libeus, and others perhaps.—Barnabas Blossom m. Sarah Pratt 1778.—Ebenezer Blossom and his wife Hannah sold land to Elijah Washburn of Hardwick 1777.—Levi Blossom m. Abigail, D. of Cornelius Washburn, 1797.—Abigail Blossom d. 1800, æ. 22.—Levi Blossom m Sally, D. of Calvin Keith, 1801.—Charity Blossom m. James Howard of M. 1801.—Polly Blossom of Eaton, N. H., m. Rufus Keith 1804.—Libeus Blossom of E. m. Rebecca, D. of Samuel Leonard, 1804.—Alden Blossom went to Turner, Me., where he was a General and High Sheriff.—Thomas Blossom was one of the forefathers, and the first Deacon at Plymo., and d. a. 1633.

BOLTON.—John Bolton (said to have come from Stonington, Conn.) and his w. Sarah settled early in B.; was probably a descendant from Nicholas Bolton of Dorchester, a mem. of the Ch. there 1644 : he had John a. 1686, Samuel 1688, Sarah 1690, Elizabeth 1692, Nicholas 1695, Mary 1697, Elisha 1700, Joseph 1704, Nathaniel 1706, Abigail 1709.—Samuel m. Rebecca Simmons 1742.—Sarah m. Wm. Leonard.—Elizabeth m. Michael May.—Mary d. single 1730.—Elisha d. 1777, æ. 77 : his w. Mary : they had Seth 1739, Jabez, Elisha, and Meshech.   Seth m. Anne Wade 1761.—Joseph m. Deliverance Washburn 1740, and had Joseph and Phillip.—Nathaniel m. Deborah, wid. of John Ripley and D. of Israel Washburn, 1740 : she d. 1759, he 1770 : he had a s. Nathaniel, perhaps, who m. Jane, D. of Thomas Thompson, 1777.—Abigail m. Samuel Ripley 1736.

2. John (s. of John 1.) m. Ruth Hooper 1710, and had Susanna 1711, Ruth, Elizabeth, Hannah 1722, Martha 1725 : his will 1755 : he was an Ensign, and left a large estate, and gave a tankard to S. B. Church.—Susanna m. Jabez Cowing 1741.— Ruth m. Ephraim Leach 1734.—Elizabeth m. Joseph Thompson 1733.—Martha m. Joab Willis 1745.

3. John Jr. (whose s. uncertain) m. Elizabeth Hayward 1751, and had Mary 1752, Anne 1754, John 1756, Betty 1760 : Elizabeth Bolton d. 1801, æ. 76.—Mary m. Joseph Bolton 1773.—Ann m. Jeremiah Pratt 1777.—John m. Betsy Dana of Boston.

4. Joseph (s. of Joseph) m. Mary, D. of John Bolton, 1773,

and had Philip 1774, Joseph 1776, John 1778, Deliverance 1781,
Barzillai 1783, Zimri 1786, Betty 1788, Mary and Silence.
5. John (of Raynham) m. Mary, D. of Thomas Pratt, 1787,
and had Micah 1788 at T., Margery 1791, Alfred 1793, Mary
Ann 1795, Anne Wade 1799, George W. 1801, Thomas J. 1805
at Charlestown.—Philip Bolton m. Bethiah Hayward 1786.—
Rhoda m. Abijah Dyer 1764.—Jabez m. Bethiah, D. of Christo-
pher Ripley, 1765.—Daniel m. Alice Leach 1776.—Jonathan m.
Hannah Snow 1794.—David m. Zilpha Snow 1794.
BONNEY.—William Bonney (from Pembroke) m. Phebe, D.
of Isaac Allen, 1766, and lived in E. B., and had Allen*, Wil-
liam, Joanna and Gladden.—William m. Molly, D. of Jesse Dun-
bar, 1796, and had Allen 1796*, Vesta 1798*, Harriet 1802,
Thos. Jefferson 1803, Joanna 1805, Lucius 1808, Eliza 1811.—
Joanna senr. m. Dea. Barzillai Allen 1796.—Gladden m. Mercy
Randall 1806, and had Mary Beal 1806, Gladden 1808, Hannah
Kingsbury 1812, Lucy Randall 1815.—Cynthia Silvester Bonney
m. Ebenezer Cutler 1797.—Noah of Hanson m. Agnes Keith
1819.—Harriet m. Harmon Washburn 1821.
BOWDITCH.—John Bowditch of Braintree, and his wife
Temperance, had William, John and Mary: his will 1718.—
Mary m. Thomas White.—William m Mary, D. of Dea. Sam-
uel Bass, 1820, and had Mary, Elizabeth, Abigail, Susanna, Jona-
than, Samuel, Bethiah and Bathsheba: he d. a. 1748.—Jonathan
and Susanna were put under guardianship of their uncle Capt.
Jona. Bass of E. B., and most of the children lived in E. B. and
m. there.—Mary m. Joseph Byram 1745.—Elizabeth m. Isaac
Snow 1748.—Abigail m. David Pratt Jr. 1753.—Samuel m.
Rebecca, D. of Josiah Byram, 1755, and had Bethiah 1757, Mary
1760.—Bethiah m. Daniel Bass of Boston.—Bathsheba m.
Ephraim Groves 1762.
BOZWORTH.—Jonathan Bozworth was at Hingham before
1640 : his children were Rebeckah 1641, Bethiah 1644, Benjamin*, Mehitabel and Mary 1647, Nathaniel and Jeremiah 1649,
Hannah and Deliverance 1650, Bellamy 1654, Edward 1659,
Bridget 1660, Benjamin 1668.
2. Dea. Jonathan Bozworth of Halifax : (grandson perhaps of
the above): his estate settled and divided 1751 : his wid. Ruth :
his children were Jonathan of Bridgewater, Alice, wife of Eleazar Waterman; Zadock, Noah, Ichabod and Jabez.—The wid.
afterwards m. a Packard and d. 1786.—Aaron Bozworth m. Sarah, D. of Nathan Ames.
3. Jonathan (son of Dea. Jonathan of Halifax) settled in W.
B. about 1750, and m. Mary Pain 1752, and had a D. 1753*,
Mary 1754*: (the mother d. 1754) and he m. Abihail, wid. of
Israel Alger Jr., D. of Samuel Lathrop, 1756; and had Jonathan
1757, Molly 1759, Sarah 1761, Chloe 1764, Israel 1767*.—The
father d. 1767, and the wid. m. Joseph Ames 1768.—Jonathan m.
Abigail Williams 1780.—Sarah m. Barnabas Lathrop 1777, and
d. 1813.—Chloe m. Daniel Tolman 1784.—Wm. Bozworth of

H. m. Lucy Hayward 1807.—Susan m. Ephraim Sampson 1821.
BRADLEY.—James Bradley m. Catharine Moore 1759: he
came from Abington, and had a D. Mille born here 1760.—William and Joanna Bradley had a son John b. here 1767.—George
Bradley m. Susanna Pierce 1753.—Mary Bradley of A. m. Ebenezer Allen 1757.—James and George were both b. in Dorchester,
and were both in the French war in 1755 with Gen. Winslow,
taking and dispersing the neutral French.

BRETT.—William Brett (probably from Kent in Eng.) was
at Duxbury 1645, and one of the original proprietors and settlers
in W. B.: an Elder of the Church; a leading man both in the
Church and in the Town : was often a Representative to the Old
Colony Court; often preached when Mr. Keith was sick, or
otherwise prevented. He d. 1681: his w. Margaret: his children were William, Elihu, Nathaniel, Lydia, Alice and Hannah.—Alice m. Joseph Hayward.—Hannah m. Francis Cary.

2. William (s. of William 1.) was a respectable man and a
Deacon : he m. Elizabeth, D. of John Cary: he had one D. Bethiah, an only child, who m. Thomas Hayward 1706: he lived
within the limits of E. B.: he d. a. 1713, the date of his will.

3. Elihu Esq. (s. of William 1.) was a Magistrate and a Justice of the Court of Common Pleas and Sessions, appointed
1700: he d. suddenly in his chair 1712: his w. named Ann: his
children were Mary, w. of John Willis; and Margaret, w. of
Samuel Willis, m. 1706; and Elihu.

4. Nathaniel (s. of William 1.) was a Deacon and Town
Clerk : he m. Sarah, D. of John Hayward, 1683: she d. 1737;
he 1740 : and had Alice 1686*, Seth 1688, Mehitabel 1692, Sarah
1695, Hannah 1699, William 1702, Nathaniel 1704.—Mehitabel
m. Samuel Edson 1721.—Sarah d. 1774.—Hannah m. Joseph
Gannett 1732.

5. Elihu (s. of Elihu 3.) m. Susanna, wid. of John Hayward
Jr. and D. of Samuel Edson, and had John 1707, Anne 1710,
Bethiah 1714 : his will 1744 : he d. 1745.—Anne m. Joseph Cary
1732.—Bethiah m. Joseph Drake.—He had also another D. Elizabeth, who m. a Drake and left 2 ch., Freelove and Ann Drake.

6. Seth (s. of Nathaniel 4.) m. Sarah, D. of Isaac Alden, 1712,
and had Samuel 1714, Silas 1716, Sarah 1718, Simeon 1720,
Seth 1722, after the death of his father, who died of the small
pox.—The wid. then m. Dea. Recompence Cary 1727.—Sarah m.
Capt. Matthew Allen 1735.—Silas entered college, but left it and
became a Preacher, and was settled in Berkley.

7. William (s. of Nathaniel 4.) m. Bethiah, D. of Samuel
Kinsley, 1732, and had Ephraim 1733, Mary 1734, Silence 1738,
Daniel 1740. It is said this family removed to Easton.

8. Nathaniel (s. of Nathaniel 4.) was also a Deacon and Town
Clerk: his w. Rebeckah : they had Hannah 1733, Deborah 1736,
Uriah 1740 : she d. 1771, and he m. the wid. Mary Dyer of Plymouth 1774, and d. 1779, æ. 74.—Deborah m. Thomas Ames 3d
1758.—Hannah m. Ephraim Howard Jr. 1753.

9. John, (s. of Elihu 5.) and his w. Freelove, had Susanna 1736 : his w. d. and he m. a 2d w., Alice Cady of Pomfret 1774, and had Freelove 1746, John 1748*, Alice 1749*, Silence 1752, Hannah 1754, Alice and Amity 1756, John 1759.—Susannah m. Nathl. Tilden 1755.—Silence m. Thomas Buck 1774.—Amity m. William Pratt of E. 1797.—John had a s. Daniel and both removed from town.

10. Samuel (s. of Seth 6.) m. Hannah, D. of David Packard, 1737, and settled in N. B., and had Isaac, Samuel, William, Hannah, Sarah, Mehitabel, Molly, Eunice : he d. 1807, æ. 92.— Hannah m. Mark Ford 1764.—Sarah m. Benja. Ford 1773.— Mehitabel m. Jonas Packard 1777.—Molly and Eunice d. single.

11. Simeon (s. of Seth 6.) m. Mehitabel, D. of David Packard, 1748, and settled in N. B., and had Jennet 1749, Rufus 1751, Simeon 1753, Zibia 1755, Mehitabel 1757, Ruby 1759, Amzi 1762, Daniel 1764, Luther 1766, Calvin 1768: he d. 1792, æ. 72.—Jennet m. Nathaniel Southworth 1777, and afterwards Ephraim Groves 1789.—Zibia m. John Noyes 1776.—Mehitabel m. Maj. Daniel Cary 1778.—Ruby m. Ephraim Field.—Rufus m. Susanna, D. of Zechariah Cary, 1775, and had Jona. 1776, Ezra 1779, Cynthia 1781.—Amzi m. Phebe, D. of Abia Packard, 1788, and had Sophia 1789, Charlotte 1791, Martin 1794, Ira 1800. Sophia m. Apollos Packard 1811.—Luther m. Sally Dwelly 1794.—Calvin m. Esther Hollis 1788.—Rufus, Amzi, Daniel and Luther removed to Me.

12. Seth (s. of Seth 6.) m. Patience Curtis 1744, and had Seth 1746, Silvia, Sybil, Celia, Abigail 1760.—Silvia m. Isaac Allen 1776.—Celia m. a Scott of Winchester, N. H., and was grandmother of Elijah Scott late of E. B.

13. Uriah (s. of Nathaniel 8.) m. Charity, D. of Jona. Kingman, 1760 and had Daniel 1761, Nathaniel 1764*, Macey 1768 : the father d. 1768, and Macey was then called Uriah, to bear up his father's name : the wid. m. David Keith 1772.

14. Isaac (s of Samuel 10.) m. Priscilla Jackson, and had Isaac 1768, Joseph 1770, Ephraim 1772*, Eliphalet, Zibeon, Polly.—Isaac went to Me.—Polly m. Capt. Ichabod Reynolds 1796.

15. Samuel (s. of Samuel 10.) m. Molly, D. of Capt. Josiah Packard, 1778, and had Josiah, Samuel, Mehitabel, Hannah, Sally.—Josiah m. Eunice, D. of Jonas Packard, 1812.—Mehitabel m. Alpheus French of St. 1800.

16. William (s. of Samuel 10.) m. Molly, D. of Ezra Allen, of E. B. 1782, and had Susanna 1784, Zenas 1785, William 1787, Cyrus 1789, Sally 1792, Polly 1794, and Phebe.—The mother d. and he then m. Betty Phillips 1801, and had Asa, Polly, Betsy, and Almira.—Zenas m. Sibil, D. of Wm. French, 1813.—William and Cyrus live in Boston.—Susanna m. Saml. Shepard of St. 1806.—Phebe m. Jabez Kingman 1818.

17. Simeon (s. of Simeon 11.) m. Susanna, D. of Luke Perkins, 1777, and had Alpheus, Parmenas, and a D*.—Alpheus m. Betsy Holmes of Halifax 1807, and Betsy Hall of Raynham 1815.

16

Parmenas m. Avis, D. of Zenas French of Braintree, and had
Simeon 1805, Elizabeth F. 1807, Susanna Relief 1809, Lucinda
1813*.—Simeon m. Lodency Wallis and had Erastus W. 1829,
and Betsy Jane 1832.—Elizabeth F. m. Philander Holmes a.
1827.—Susanna R. m. Erastus Wales.
    18. Seth (s. of Seth 12.) m. Susanna, D. of James Latham,
1769, and had Cynthia 1770, Ephraim 1773, and removed to
Winchester.
    19. Daniel (s. of Uriah 13.) m. Huldah, D. of Dea. Elijah
Snell, 1784, and had Daniel Searl 1785, Charles 1788, and Susanna.—Daniel S. m. Sarah, D. of Silvanus Hayward, 1807, and
lives in New Bedford.—Charles m. a D. of Jirch Swift.
    20. Uriah (s. of Uriah 13.) m. Nabby, D. of Nathan Kingman,
1790, and lived in E. B., and had Uriah, Nabby, Charity: his w.
d. and he m. Anna, D. of Benjamin Robinson, 1799, and had
Diana, Algernon Sidney, Royal and Sarah.—Uriah m. an Allen
in Dover where he settled.—Nabby m. Albert Edson 1817.—
Charity m. Nathan Soule 1815.—Diana m. Samuel Perry of Hanover 1820.—A. Sidney m. Huldah, D. of Turner Phillips.—
Uriah, the father, d. 1839, æ. 71.
    21. Joseph (s. of Isaac 14.) m. Olive, D. of Jeremiah Beal,
1797; had Ephraim 1798, Polly 1800, Charles 1803, Jeremiah
1805, Sarah 1807, Joel 1809, David 1816.
    22. Zibeon (s. of Isaac 14.) m. Lavinia, D. of Capt. Zebedee
Snell, 1804, and had Patty 1805, Abigail 1806, Zibeon 1808,
Sanford 1810, Mary 1812, Harriet Newell 1814, Lucy 1816.
    There was a John Brett of Boston who m. Ann Barnsdale
1710: he was master of a ship in the London trade, and d. at
Kingston, Jamaica, leaving a wid. and had Hannah 1711, John
1713, James and William, and one other D.—John d. at Newburyport Dec. 12, 1797, æ. 84: his son John was living there
1829, æ. 73; and in a letter of that year says, " his grandfather
John came from the County of Kent, in England, and he has
heard his father (John Jr.) say that the Bretts in Bridgewater
were his relations: he d. Sept. 13, 1839, æ. 83, called a revolutionary patriot.—James and Abigail Brett of Boston had Ann
1756, Abigail 1760, Elizabeth 1765, James 1767.—Ebenezer
Brett, æ. 71, d. at Chesterfield 1833.—Phebe m. Abel Dunbar
1805.—Polly Brett m. David Bartlett 1796.—There was a Thomas
Brett, schoolmaster, d. in Boston 1767, his wid. Ann settled his
estate.—John Brett m. Martha Mortell 1796.—(Boston Records.)
    BROWN.—Bartholomew Brown Esq. (s. of John Brown of
Sterling) was b. at Danvers and gra. H. U. 1799, and m. Betsy,
D. of Genl. Silvanus Lazell, 1801, and settled first in Sterling,
then in E. B. as an attorney, and had James Tilden*; Lucy Ann,
w. of Dr. Adolphus K. Borden; George Henry, who m. Emily
Porter of Sterling; and Harriet Mitchell.
    2. Capt. Woodbridge Brown (s. of Rev. Samuel and Dorothy
Brown of Abington: she was a Woodbridge) and his wife Anna
had Samuel 1737, John 1739, Josiah 1740, Joseph 1745, Dorothy

1748, and Mary, and perhaps others.—Dorothy only b. in E. B.:
she m. Eleazer Bates and d. 1839, æ. 91.—Joseph d. in E. B.
1825, æ. 80.—Mary m. Dea. Eleazer Whitman.
3. John (s. of Capt. Woodbridge 2.) m. Lydia Hearsey, and
lived in E. B. where his father lived awhile, and had Isaac, John,
David, Polly and Anna*, and perhaps others.—Isaac, and his
w. Elizabeth, had Isaac 1790, Betsy 1792, Emery 1795, and Alvan 1798.—John m. a Jenkins and d. 1816, æ. 37, and had Alfred,
Mehitabel, w. of Ward Richards ; and Lydia, w. of Philip Pratt.—
David m. 2 Ds. of Joseph Ramsdell, first Nabby 1812, and then
Lydia 1818, and has a family.—Polly m. Christopher Bates.—
Isaac m. Eunice Thayer 1813.—Betsy m. Daniel Barker of Han-
son.—Emery m. Molly, D. of John Bisbee, 1817.—Alvan m.
Betsy Elms of Hanson 1821, and is d.
4. Knight Brown (from Scituate or Cohasset) and his w. Pris-
cilla settled in E. B.: he d. here 1832, æ. 82 : and had Andrew
1780, Sarah 1782, David 1785, Lewis 1788, Lydia 1790, Charles,
Priscilla, and others perhaps.—Andrew remained in Scituate.—
Sarah m. Oliver Leach 1803.—David died a bachelor, æ. 46.—
Lewis m. Betsy Harden 1806.—Lydia m. John Thayer 1811.—
Charles m. Asenath D. of Isaac Chamberlin 1719.—Priscilla m.
Henry Thornbury Smith 1792.
Elizabeth Brown m. Jonathan Holloway 1746.—Daniel Brown
m. Mehitable Porter 1797.—Samuel Brown's w. d. in E. B. 1780
æ. 20.—Susanna Brown m. John Winnett 1800.—Charles Brown
m. Mehitabel French 1809, and had Polly and Charles.—Polly
m. Jacob Harden.—Moses Brown m. Eunice Harris of St. 1818.
5. David Brown m. Jennet Miller (this is one of the Irish
families that settled in N. B. about 1740,) he had Ann, John,
James, and David, all of whom d. in infancy,—and John 1750,
and James 1752, both went to Harpersfield.—He d. in the prime
of life, about 1753, which was the date of his will.—Jennet
Brown, perhaps the wid. m. Simon Griffin 1758.
BRYANT.— Ichabod Bryant m. Ruth Staples, and they had
a dis. from Raynham Ch. to W. B. 1745.—He d. 1759 ; he came
from M. to N. B. and had Philip, Nathan, Seth, Job, Gamaliel,
Phebe, Ruth, Sarah, Anna, and Prudence.—Nathan d. single.—
Gamaliel settled in New Bedford.—Phebe m. Henry Howard.—
Ruth m. a Holmes.—Sarah m. Francis Cook 1750.—Anna m. a
Robinson.—Prudence d. single,
2. Doct. Philip (s. of Ichabod, 1st,) m. Silence D. of Dr. Abiel Howard 1757, and had Oliver 1758*, Ruth 1760*, Daniel
1763*, Bezaliel 1765, Peter 1767, Cyrus 1769, Anna 1771, Silence 1774, and Charity 1777.—His w. d. and he m. Hannah D.
of Benjamin Richards 1779.—He d. 1816 æ. 84 : she d. 1816 æ.
80.—Silence m. Ichabod Bryant 1792.—Anna m. Capt. Henry
Kingman 1795.—Bezaliel and Charity removed to the State of
N. York.—Peter was a physician, settled in Cummington, and
m. a D. of Ebenezer Snell Esq. of that place, and was father
of William Cullen Bryant the poet.—Cyrus m. Polly Noyes 1795,

and had Zibia 1795, Daniel 1798, who m. Lucy Skinner of Mansfield 1817.—Zibia m. Benjamin Dickerman 1817.—The parents Cyrus and Polly, both d. 1798.

3. Seth (s. of Ichabod 1.) m. Elizabeth D. of Dependence French of St. 1765, and had Elizabeth 1766, Ichabod 1768, Dependence French 1770, Mary 1772, Zibeah 1774, Seth 1778, Olive 1781, Ira 1783.—This family removed westward.—Elizabeth m. Josiah Manly 1789.—Ichabod m. Silence Bryant 1792.—Dependence F. m. Rebecca Blackman, 1791, he lived in Cummington, Easton, Pembroke, and d. in N. Bedford, and had 3 who d. in infancy, and then Dion, Rebecca, Austin, Emily, Elizabeth, and William.—Mary m. Samuel Holmes 1791.

4. Job (s. of Ichabod, 1,) m. Mary Turner 1764 ; their children Anna 1764, Nathan 1766, Calvin 1768, Job Staples 1772, Thirza 1774, Oliver, Clement, David, Samuel, Asa,and Harriet.—Anna m. Abiel Phillips of Easton 1787, and was mother of the Dwarf.—Thirza m. Manasseh Dickerman 1791.—Job Staples m. Lovicey Pratt 1793.—Oliver m. Nabby D. of Timothy Ames, 1804, and has Ziba Bass 1804, Danville Ames 1806, Theron Carver 1808, George W. 1810.—Harriet m. David Dunbar, Jr. of Easton 1801.—Asa m. Mehitabel Snow of Easton 1810 and Betsy Snow 1811.

5. Daniel Bryant (s. of Seth of Halifax,) m. Jennet D. of Cushing Mitchell 1789, and first resided at Watertown, afterwards at Stroudwater in Maine, and finally settled in E. B. and had Seth, Mary, Jennet, Alice, Abby M. and Dorcas.—Seth m. Maria D. of Charles Keen, and lives in Boston ; she d. 1839, æ. 35.—Jennet m. Jonah Edson 1819.—Alice m. Simeon H. Edson 1833, and d.1836.—Abby M. m. Robert Curtis, removed to Boston and d. there 1832.—Dorcas m. a Fellows, and d. 1834.—Jennet the mother d. 1808, æ. 37, and he m. Wid. Charity, late w. of Isaac Chamberlin, and sister of Maj. Nathaniel Tomson of Halifax 1809, and had George, Laura, Elizabeth, and Lucy, who d. 1832, æ. 14.—George m. Elizabeth Deblois.—Laura m. Isaac Packard.—Elizabeth m. a Dyer.—Ruth, sister of Daniel, m. Benj. Faxon 1787, and d. 1788 æ. 19.

6. Dion Bryant (s. of Dependence F.) m. Lucretia H. Briggs of Pembroke 1821, and had Merton Cassius 1823, and Lucretia Hall 1826.

7. Calvin (s. of Job 4.) m. Rebecca Morse 1791, and had Silvia 1792, Clarissa 1798, Luther 1799, Wealthy 1801, Melinda 1803, Eleanor 1806, Paul 1811.

8. Nathan (s. of Job 4) m. Sarah Jordan 1790, and had Sally 1791, who m. Jona. Snow 1810, Nathan 1793, Anna 1795, who m. Wm. Carr, Jr. 1821, Abigail 1797, Mira 1799, Olive 1801, Issachar Snell 1805, Sophia 1808, Benj. Turner 1812.

9. Samuel (s. of Job 4) and his w. Sally had Samuel 1801, Betsy 1805, Erin 1806, Mary 1808, Addison 1814.

Martha Bryant m. Thomas Conant a. 1730.—Lydia Bryant m. Alexander Tirrell 1788.—Ruth Bryant m. Edward Hayford

1709.—Mary Bryant m. John Wormal 1729.—Jerusha Bryant of Plympton m. Solomon Leach 1738.—Nehemiah Bryant m. Bethiah Washburn 1741.—Daniel Bryant m. Sarah Washburn 1767.—Zebulun Bryant m. Mary Conant 1767.—Agatha Bryant of M. m. Jeremiah Keith 1776.—Sarah m. Jotham Ames 1786.—Abigail Bryant m. Alvan Snell 1799.—Mercy Bryant m. Seth Packard a. 1727.—Jona. Bryant and w. came from Boston 1737 had Mary 1739, and returned again to Boston 1740.—All these perhaps are descendants of John Bryant, who settled in Scituate as early as 1639, and m. Mary D.of Geo. Lewis of Barnstable 1643, and had John 1644, Hannah 1645, Joseph 1646*, Sarah 1648, Mary 1649, Martha 1651, Samuel 1653; in 1657 he m. a 2d. w., Elizabeth, D. of Rev. Wm. Witherell; she died early, and he m. Mary D. of Thomas Hiland, and had by her 10 children viz., Elizabeth 1665, Benjamin 1669, Joseph 1671, Jabez 1672, Ruth 1673, Thomas 1675, Deborah 1677, Agatha 1678, Ann 1680, Elisha 1682. (See Deane's History of Scituate for a further account of the family.)

BUCK.—Thomas Buck was eldest son of Isaac and Frances Buck of Scituate, and settled in Bridgewater before 1712—He m. Elizabeth D. of James Howard 1712, and had Mary 1713, Thomas 1715, Elizabeth 1717, John 1721, Matthew 1724, Tabitha 1728; he d. 1755; she 1760.—Mary m. David Hill 1733.—Elizabeth m. Elias Monk 1744.—John m. Mary Ames 1739, Tabitha m. Thomas Kimber 1755.—Some of this family settled in Easton.

2. Matthew (s. of the above) lived also in Bridgewater: his wife Elizabeth : he had Isaac 1750, Thomas 1752, Hannah 1755, Keziah 1757, Joshua 1760, Daniel 1762, Eliphalet 1765, Elizabeth 1769, Matthew 1772.—Isaac m. Sarah Hayward 1773.—Thomas m. Silence Brett 1774.

Isaac Buck first above named and his brother John, both of Scituate, the former Town Clerk, and the latter commonly called *Cornet* John, "having been Cornet of the Troopers," were probably sons of James Buck, at Hingham 1638.—Isaac d. 1695, and John's will is dated 1697.—There was also a Roger Buck at Cambridge 1643, who had sons, John 1644, and Ephraim 1646.

BUKER or BOWCKER.—Nelson Buker and his wife Alice Austin m. 1795, and had George 1796, Melinda 1799, Elijah 1803, Thomas 1810, Louisa 1813, Pamela 1814.

Israel Bowcker m. Bathsheba Carver 1784.—Elijah Bowcker m. Mary Belcher of St. 1820.—Molly Bowcker m. David Snell 1783.—David Bowcker had a D. Rebecca born in E. B. 1783.

BURR.—Jonathan Burr, Minister of Dorchester, ord. 1640, and d. 1641, was born at Redgrave in Suffolk, England 1604: came to N. E. 1639 with his wife Frances and 3 children, Jonathan, John, and Simon.—Jonathan a Physician, settled in Hingham and d. in the Canada expedition of the small pox 1690.—Simon also settled in Hingham a. 1646, and d. 1691, and had a son John 1659, who had a son John 1695, who settled in Bridge-

water.—The first John settled in Fairfield Conn. whose s. Judge
Peter Burr, was father of the Rev. Isaac Burr, who was father
of the Rev. Aaron Burr, Press. of N. Jersey College, father of
Aaron, Ex-Vice Press. of U. S.

1. John Burr (s. of John and Mary of Hingham) was born
1695 : his father d. at Hingham a. 1716 : his mother Mary was
probably D. of John Lazell of Hingham ; he came to Bridgewater a. 1720 : was a Deacon in W. B. and m. Silence D. of
Ephraim Howard 1722, and had John 1724, Elijah 1726, Mary
1728, Jonathan 1731, Seth 1734, Ephraim 1737.—She d. 1773 :
he 1777.—Elijah went to Connecticut.

2. John (s. of John 1.) m. Sarah Powers and had Sarah 1746,
William, Silence, Polly, (N. B. there is some uncertainty in the
record.—Sarah is called D. of John and Sarah Burr born 1746:
and again John Burr m. Mary Powers 1748, 2 years after ; which
may be reconciled by supposing he m. two sisters, first Sarah
and afterwards Mary) ; he d. 1776.—William d. young leaving
one daughter.

3. Jonathan (s. of John 1.) m. Martha Cudworth 1754, (a descendant probably of Gen. James Cudworth of Scituate, who
came from London to Boston probably a. 1632), and had Israel
1755, Jonathan 1757, Elijah 1759, Martha 1761, Luther 1764,
Martin 1766, John 1769, Calvin 1771, Ruth 1777, David 1783:
he m. Lydia D. of Samuel Kinsley a 2d w. 1792 : his will dated
1797.—Israel m. Hannah D. of Daniel Ames 1779, and Israel,
Elijah, and Calvin went to Worthington.—Elijah m. Olive 1789,
and Calvin m. Betsy 1796, Ds. of Thomas Ames.—Luther m.
Jane D. of Nathan Howard, Esq. 1785 and went to Maine.—
Martha m. Solomon Howard.—Jonathan gra. H. U. 1784, and
settled in the ministry at Sandwich 1789, and m. there but had
no children.—Martin m. Mary D. of Nathan Snell.—Jonathan
of Worthington m. Sally D. of Samuel Alden 1820.

4. Seth (s. of John 1.) m. Charity D. of Samuel Packard 1753,
and had Silence 1754, Charity 1755, Seth 1757, Simeon 1759,
Huldah 1761, Susanna 1763, Silvanus 1765, Rufus 1767, Elijah
1769, Persis 1771.—Seth m. Susanna Mehurin of Easton 1781.
Susanna, called of Norton, m. Samuel Hartwell 1781.—Silvanus
m. Sarah Warren 1790 and lived in E.

5. Ephraim (s. of John 1.) m. Susanna D. of Joseph Alger
1755, and had Molly 1756, Phebe 1758.—He d. 1786.—Phebe
m. John Foster 1780, she is also said afterwards to have m. a
Copeland of E.

6. John (s. of Jonathan 3.) m. Mary D. of Jonathan Copeland
1792, and had Betsey 1792, John Jay 1795, Martin Cudworth
1798, Mary 1800, and removed westward.

Heman M. Burr m. Nella Tucker of Milton 1812.—Sarah Burr
m. Isaiah Keith 1773.—Laban Burr m. Mary Ann Storrs of Boston 1820—Silence Burr m. John Howard 1773.—Polly m. Wm.
Blakely 1773.—Joseph Burr m. Hannah Richardson of Leicester 1792.—Wm. Burr m. Nabby Bent 1798.

BUTTERFIELD.—Jonathan Butterfield and his wife Rachel (from Lexington) settled in S. B ; he d. there 1769 æ. 74 ; he left no children ; gave a tankard to the church ; and left his estate principally to Rachel D. of Simeon Leonard, afterwards w. of Wm. Swift, and her mother was niece to Butterfield.

BYRAM.—1. Nicholas Byram according to family tradition, was son of an English gentleman of the county of Kent, who removed to Ireland about the time this son was born.—His father sent him at the age of 16 to visit his friends in Eng. in charge of a man, who betrayed his trust, robbed him of his money, and sent him to the West Indies, where he was sold to service to pay his passage, and after his term expired he made his way to New-England and settled at Weymouth.—He m. Susanna, D. of Abraham Shaw of Dedham, and had Nicholas, Abigail, who m. Thomas Whitman 1656, Deliverance, who m. John Porter 1660, Experience, who m. John Willis, Susanna who m. Samuel Edson, and Mary, who m. Samuel Leach.—These were all born at Weymouth. In 1660 he bought three proprietary or original purchase rights in Bridgewater viz. Moses Simmons', Philip Delano's, and George Soule's, and settled here soon after. He d. 1688 ; she d. a. 1698.

2. Capt. Nicholas (s. of the above.) m. Mary D. of Samuel Edson 1676, and had Bethiah 1678*, Margaret 1680*, Mehitabel 1683, a. s. 1685*, Nicholas 1687, Mary 1690, Ebenezer 1692, Susanna 1695, Josiah 1698, Joseph 1791.—Mehitabel m. Elisha Allen.—Mary m. Maj. Edward Howard.—Susanna m. Capt. Jonathan Bass.—He and his wife were the eldest and first named members of the ch., first instituted in E. B. 1724.—Both d. 1727.

3. Nicholas (s. of Nicholas 2.) m. Ann D. of Thomas Snell 1708, and had Bethiah 1709, Nicholas 1711, Ann 1712, Thomas 1714*, Jesse 1716, Mary 1718, Obin 1720*, Benjamin 1721*, Paul 1723*, and George*—Bethiah m. Samuel Pratt 1729.—Ann m. a Pettingill, and afterwards John Kingman 1771.—Mary m. Thomas Carr.

3. Capt. Ebenezer (s. of Nicholas 2.) m. Hannah D. of Joseph Hayward 1714, and had Ebenezer 1716, Eliab, Japhet, Naphthali, Hannah 1725, Mary 1728, Abigail 1730, Jepthah 1732.—He with all his children went to Windham in the County of Morris N. Jersey a. 1744.—He there became a major of the militia and Judge of the County Court, and died 1753, æ. 61.—Ebenezer married Abigail daughter of Capt. Ebenezer Alden 1738, and had Huldah 1739*, Huldah 1740, her grandson Rev. Philip Lindley, was V. Pres. of N. Jersey College, Edward 1742, Ebenezer 1744, (born here) Napthali, Joseph, Abigail, Anne, Mary, and Phebe, (born there).—He and she both d. a. 1665 ; his D. Anna was mother of the present Dr. Lewis Condict late member of Congress.—Eliab m. Phebe D. of Ephraim Leonard 1741, gra. H. U. 1740, and was settled as a clergyman at Hopewell N. Jersey : he had a son Eliab born here 1643, whose D. m. Josiah Deane Esq. of Raynham.—Japhet m. Sarah D. of Josiah

Allen 1742, and had a D. Sarah born here 1744, and Japhet and Nicholas b. in N. J.—Naphthali m. Hannah Brett 1744, no children born here.—Jephthah m. Susanna D. of Eleazar Washburn 1761, and had Eleazar, Eliab, Jephthah, Susanna, Abigail.—He d. a. 1805; she d. 1815.—Hannah m. Elihu Baldwin.—Mary m. Aaron Thompson, and afterwards Isaac Harlow.—Abigail m. Daniel Thompson and afterwards Benj. Pitney.

5. Josiah (s. of Nicholas 2.) m. Hannah Rickard of Plymton 1720, and had Susanna 1721, Josiah 1723, Theopholus 1725, Mehitabel 1730, Rebecca 1732 —Susanna m. Capt. Jonathan Bass, Jr. 1741.—Josiah d. young.—Mehitabel m. Daniel Beal 1750.—Rebecca m. Samuel Bowditch of Braintree 1755.—Josiah the father removed to New Jersey, his wife Hannah d. here, a widow, 1771 æ. 78.

6. Joseph (s. of Nicholos 2.) was a physician, and m. Martha D. of David Perkins 1724, and had Joseph 1726, Martha 1728, Benjamin 1731, Mary 1734, Elizabeth 1738*, Susanna 1742.— He d. and his wid. m. Matthew Gannet 1750, and d. 1779 æ. 74. Martha m. Henry Cary 1749, and afterwards Abner Pratt 1764.— Mary m. John Lazell 1750.

7. Nicholas (s. of Nicholas 3.) m. Elizabeth D. of Matthew Gannett 1738, and had Seth 1739, Content 1740; the father d. and the wid. m. Thomas Hayward 1746.—Content m. David Harvey 1756.

8. Theophilus (s. of Josiah 5.) m. Elizabeth wid. of Samuel Beal Jr. 1749, she was a Blackman, and had Josiah 1750, Oliver 1751, David 1753, James 1756, Melzar 1759, and Susanna; and removed to North Yarmouth, Me.

9. Jesse (s. of Nicholas 3.) m. Abigail D. of David Thurston of Rehoboth 1742, and had Josiah 1743.—Mary Thurston her sister d. here 1776 æ. 53.—David Thurston of Rehoboth the father m. Mercy D. of James Cary 1713, and had John 1714, Abigail 1716, James 1718, David 1721, Mary 1723, James m. Phebe Perkins 1749 —Hannah Thurston of Rehoboth m. John Cary of Windham 1716.

10. Joseph (s. of Dr. Joseph 6.) m. Mary D. of Wm. Bowditch of Braintree 1745, and had Elizabeth 1747, Joseph 1748*, William 1750, Asa 1751, Susanna 1753, Ebenezer 1755, Mary 1756, Martha 1757.—Elizabeth m. Winslow Richardson 1768.— William removed to Raynham.—Asa went to New York.—Susanna m. Ebenezer Howard of Braintree 1773, and afterwards a Holbrook and went to Cummington.—Ebenezer went to Me.— Mary d. single.—Martha m. a Phillips.

11. Benjamin (s. of Dr. Joseph 6.) m. Anne D. of Capt. John Holman 1757, and had one child Anne 1757; his w. d. and he m. Rachel D. of Israel Bailey 1760, and had Jenny 1761, Kezia 1761, Ward 1763*, Rachel 1765, Susanna 1766, Ruth 1769, Mehitabel 1771, Benjamin 1774, George W. 1776, Nicholas 1778*.—Anne m. John Mitchell 1781.—Jenny m. Maj. Isaac Lazell 1779.—Kezia m. a Leonard of T.—Rachel m. Nathan

Mitchell, Esq. 1793.—The father then with all the rest of his family removed to Coos.

12. Seth (s. of Nicholas 7.) m. Sarah Vinal of Scituate 1762, and had Seth, Stephen, Sally, he d. 1781, and his wid. m. Capt. Simeon Whitman 1784.—Stephen went away and d. young.—Sally m. Caleb Copeland 1787.

13. Josiah (s. of Jesse 9.) m. Sarah D. of Reuben Hall 1766, and had George 1767, David 1768, Mercy 1770, Abigail 1775, Ruth 1777, Branch 1780, Mary 1788.—He d. 1806 æ. 63 ; she d. 1828 æ. 84.—George m. Phebe Randall 1788, and David m. Lucy Randall 1791, and had a D. Sally 1792, and both moved away westward.—Mercy m. Nathan Whitman 1788.—Abigail m. Nath'l. Clift, and afterwards a Turner.—Ruth m. Isaac Alden, 3d.—Mary m. Calvin Shepard 1807.

14. Seth (s. of Seth 12.) m. Matilda D. of Stephen Whitman 1791 : he was master of a fishing Vessel, and was lost on the Grand Banks ; she d. 1807 æ. 35.—He had Robert Jamieson, (named for a Scotch gentleman of that name, who lived with her grandfather, the Hon. Hugh Orr,) Sally, and Lucy.—Robert J. m. Mercy D. of Elisha Faxon 1814 and lives in Boston.

15. Capt. Branch (s. of Josiah 13.) m. Anne D. of Isaac Washburn 1802, and had Harrison Gray, Branch, Lewis, Lucia Anna, Asa Washburn, Josiah, George Henry, and Sarah.—Lucia Anna m. her cousin Marsena Whitman.

This is the only family, and Branch, of the name, remaining in B. Some of these are now writing their name Byron, but the name is unquestionably Byram : and has been uniformly so spelt and written by the family themselves from Nicholas the first, down to Branch. It is an old English name.

CARR.—1. Thomas Carr m. Mary D. of Nicholas Byram, and had two ss. Thomas and Hugh, and perhaps others : one, D. Elizabeth, m. Nathan Pettingill probably 1760.—Daniel Carr m. Martha Edson 1770.

2. Thomas (s. of the above) and his wife Mercy had Anne 1757, Thomas 1759, Mary 1762, John 1765, Reading 1767, Elizabeth 1770, William 1773, Ebenezer 1776, Mercy 1778, Simeon and Abigail 1781.—Reading m. Mercy West 1795.—Elizabeth m. Asa Pettingill 1789.—William m. Rhoda French of St. 1797. Mercy m. Daniel Carr 1799.—William Jr. m. Anna Bryant 1820.

CARVER.—1. Eleazer Carver and his w. Experience settled in S. B., and had Eleazer, Nathaniel, Joseph, Experience, Mehitable, and perhaps others.—Nathaniel m. Abigail D. of Nathaniel Allen 1736, and went to Taunton.—Experience m. Jonathan Cary 1719.—Mehitabel m. Capt. Seth Alden 1740.

2. Eleazer (s. of the above) and his w. Catharine of M. had Mary 1722, Eleazer 1724, Catharine 1726, Timothy 1728, Rhodolphus 1735, John 1738.—Mary m. Abraham Perkins 1743.—Catharine d. single.—Timothy removed and left no family here.—Mercy d. 1767.—Rhodolphus m. Abigail Bowman of Bedford 1763, and went to Oakham.

17

3. Joseph (s. of Eleazer 1.) m. Elizabeth D. of Benjamin Snow 1725, and had Joseph 1727, Benjamin 1729, Elizabeth 1731, Sarah 1737, Experience 1739, Robert 1742, Rebecca 1744.—Some of this family removed to Scituate R. Island.—Elizabeth m. Samuel Packard 1757.—Sarah m. Hezekiah Porter of Windsor 1757.—The mother Elizabeth d. 1755, Joseph Carver d. 1778, quite aged.

4. Eleazar (s. of Eleazar 2.) m. Hepzibah, D. of Thomas Perkins, 1746, and had Mary 1748, Eleazar 1749, Nathaniel 1752, Bethiah. 1754 : he d. and the wid. m. Ebenezer Keith 1759.— Mary m. Seth Alden 1767.—Nathl. learned a trade with Alden, and moved away.—Bethiah m. Capt. Joseph Alden.

5. John (s. of Eleazar 2.) m. Bathsheba Edson 1762 : he had a D. Bathsheba, who m. Israel Bowcker 1783 ; and a D. Eunice, who m. Joseph Knapp of Easton 1784.—His son John m. Huldah, D. of Abner Pratt, 1795.—John Carver d. 1803, æ. 65 : he had a large family, who removed westward.

6. Joseph (s. of Joseph 3.) m. Sarah Hartwell 1746, and had Hannah 1747, Rhoda 1749, Oliver 1751, Bernice 1753.—Oliver m. Mary Perkins 1774.—This family went to Providence.

7. Dr. Eleazar (s. of Eleazar 4.) was a physician ; m. Sarah, D. of Ephraim Keith Esq., 1776 ; and had Sarah 1777, Betsy 1779, Hepzibah 1781, Mary 1783, Eleazar 1785, Nathaniel 1787, Lucinda 1789.—Sally m. Benjamin Willis 1801, and afterwards Seth Washburn Esq. 1812.—Betsy m. Chilton Latham 1803, and afterwards Joseph Barrows, 1816.—Hepzibah m. Thomas Howard 1810.—Mary m. Capt. Abram Washburn 1804.—Eleazar is one of the firm of Carver, Washburn & Co. and m. Bathsheba Smith of Hanson 1821, and had Lucia 1822*, Joseph 1824, Mary 1826.—Nathaniel went away young.

Ruth Carver m. Timothy Ames 1786 —Ruth m. Beza Harvey 1795.—Jabez m. Sarah Perkins 1742.—Wid. Sarah m. Joseph Clapp 1746.—Clifford of R., son of John, m. Wid. Polly Leonard 1806.—Sally m. Solomon Washburn Jr. 1801, Abigail of Marshfield m. Job Ames 1814.—Eleazar 2d m. Nancy Jones 1787.—John Carver and Sukey (perhaps D. of Benj. Snell) had Grenville 1824, and Olive Snell 1826.—John Carver (or Cavener) m. Ann Jennings 1718.—Jonathan Carver was a Lieut. with Gen. John Winslow at Annapolis Royal, N. Scotia, 1755.—Jonathan m. Sarah Holmes 1746, and had John, father of Clifford.— Richard Carver at Watertown : his will 1638; his w. Grace : his Ds. Elizabeth and Susanna. William Carver d. at Marshfield Oct. 2, 1760, æ. 102 : (nephew of Gov. John Carver, being his brother's son): he left behind him the 5th generation of male issue.—Robert Carver, one of the train band in Marshfield 1643.

CARY.—John Cary (from Somersetshire, Eng.) settled in Duxbury as early as 1639 : he m. Elizabeth, D. of Francis Godfrey, 1644, and was an original proprietor, and among the first settlers of W. B., and the first Town Clerk : he d. 1681 ; his w. d. 1680 : he had John at Duxbury 1645, Francis 1647, Elizabeth

1649, James at Braintree 1652, Mary at Bridgewater 1654, Jonathan 1656, David 1658, Hannah 1661, Joseph 1663, Rebecca 1665, Sarah 1667, Mehitabel 1670.—Elizabeth m. Dea. William Brett Jr.—Rebecca m. Samuel Allen Jr. 1685.—David went to Bristol and Joseph to Windham, Ct.

2. John (s. of John 1.) m. Abigail, D. of Samuel Allen, 1670, and had John 1671*, Seth 1672, John 1674, Nathaniel 1676, Eleazar 1678, James 1680, and then went to Bristol, and afterwards, perhaps, to N. Jersey.—And Henry Cary, b. at Bristol 1710, grad. H. C. 1733, was one of this family.

3. Francis, (s. of John 1.) named after his grandfather Francis Godfrey, m. Hannah, D. of William Brett, and had Samuel, Ephraim, Mary, Lydia, Melatiah.—Mary m. Nicholas Whitman 1715 and d. 1719.—Lydia m. Joseph Edson 1704.—Melatiah m. Joseph Lucas 1727.—Samuel Tompkins gave his estate in E. B. to Francis Cary, who was brought up with him, and was to take care of him, hence Cary named his eldest son Samuel.

4. James (s. of John 1.) m. Mary, D. probably of John Shaw of Weymouth, 1682, and lived in E. B., and had Mercy 1686, Mary 1689, James 1692, Hannah 1696, Elizabeth 1700.—Mercy m. David Thurston of Rehoboth 1713.—Elizabeth m. John Whitman 1729.—James, the father, d. 1706: the mother, 1736.—Joseph Shaw to be overseer of James.

5. Jonathan (s. of John 1.) m. Sarah, D. of Samuel Allen, and had Recompence, John, Jonathan: he d. 1695, and his wid. m. Benjamin Snow 1705: the children chose their uncle Saml. Allen their guardian 1706—she settled the estate 1695.

6. Samuel (s. of Francis 3.) m. Mary Pool 1704, and had Joseph 1705, Lydia 1706, Alice 1707, Elizabeth 1709, Samuel 1711, David 1713, Nathan 1716, Eleazar 1718, Mary 1720.—This family probably removed to N. Jersey, Conn., or elsewhere.

7. Ephraim (s. of Francis 3.) m. Hannah Waldo 1709, and had Mehitabel 1709, Ezra 1710, Zechariah 1713, Ephraim 1714, Daniel 1716: he d. 1765; she 1777, æ. 90.—Mehitabel m. Benjamin Allen 1730.—Daniel m. Martha, D. of John Cary, 1742, and had a son Lewis 1742, and removed to N. Jersey.

8. Dea. James (s. of James 4.) m. Sarah, D. of Joseph Shaw, 1722, and had Sarah 1723, Joshua 1726 d. 1747: she d. 1730; he 1762, æ. 70. Sarah m. William Barrell 1751; his 2d wife.—Joshua was betrothed to Josiah Byram's D. Mehitabel, who afterwards m. Daniel Beals and named a s. Joshua, after her first lover.

9. Dea. Recompence (s. of Jonathan 5.) m. Mary, D. proba- of Seth Crossman, 1711: she was b. 1691: he had Seth 1714, d. 1742*; Ichabod 1715, Ebenezer 1717, d. 1744*; Sarah 1718, Simeon 1719, Zebulun 1721, Jonathan 1723, Josiah 1724, d. 1743*; Mary 1726: his w. d. 1726, and he m. Sarah, Wid. of Seth Brett, and D. of Isaac Alden, 1727: they had a D. Abigail 1729: the father d. 1759. Sarah m. Benjamin Hayward 1742.—Mary m. Joseph Crossman of Easton 1747.

10. John (s. of Jonathan 5.) and his w. Experience had John 1719, Martha 1721, Henry 1723, Susanna 1725, Beriah 1729: his w. d. 1729, and he m. a 2d wife Mary, and had Molly 1732: his 2d w. d. and he m. a 3d wife Susanna, D. of Elisha Allen, 1733: she d. 1734, and he m. a 4th wife, Sarah Drake 1734, and had Thankful 1745, Huldah 1750. John Cary Jr. m. Mary Harden 1741, and had Isaac 1742, Huldah 1744, and removed to N. Jersey.—Martha m. Daniel Cary 1742.—Thankful m. Jonathan Orcutt of Cohasset 1766 for his 2d wife.

This man owned the grist-mill at Orr's Works, and was called Old Miller Cary. The following distich was common in after times:—

Experience and Mary, Susanna and Sarah;
These were the wives of Old John Cary.

11. Jonathan (s. of Jonathan 5.) first m. Susanna, D. of Joseph Keith, 1717: she d. and he then m. Experience, D. of Eleazar Carver 1719, and had Seth 1721, Eleazar 1723, Susanna 1725, Anne 1728, Jonathan 1730, Eliphalet 1732, Experience 1734, Benjamin 1738, Jesse 1742. This family lived in S. B.— Susanna m. William Hooper 1759.—Anne m. the Hon. Nathan Mitchell 1754.—Eliphalet (Major) m. Hannah, Wid. of Josiah Edson and sister of Thos. Lawrence, 1782, and lived to a great age, but had no children.—Jonathan, the father, d. 1766; his widow, 1769.

12. Joseph (s. of Samuel 6.) m. Anne, D. of Elihu Brett, 1732, and had a son Barnabas 1733. He probably removed to Gloucester, R. I.

13. Ezra (s. of Ephraim 7.) m. Mary, D. of Col. John Holman, 1737, and had Sarah 1738, Shepard 1742. He removed to N. Jersey.

14. Zechariah (s. of Ephraim 7.) m. Susanna, D. of Captain Jonathan Bass, 1742, and settled in N. B., and d. 1788: he had Ezra 1749, Mehitabel 1752, Susanna 1755, Daniel 1758, Luther 1761. Mehitabel m. Zachariah Silvester of Duxbury.—Susanna m. Rufus Brett 1775.—Ezra m. Cynthia Tolman of Stoughton 1770, and had Thomas 1771, Zechariah 1773. Thomas m. Sally, D. of Lemuel Packard, 1798.—Daniel was a Major and m. Mehitabel, D. of Simeon Brett, and had Zibiah 1779, Eunice 1781, Olive 1783, Francis 1785, James, Zechariah 1791.—Luther, a Physician, m. a King of Raynham. These 3 brothers removed to Turner, Me.—Zibia m. Captain Roger Sumner of Stoughton 1801.—Olive m. Apollas Howard 1802, and afterwards had a 2d husband in Me.

15. Ephraim (s. of Ephraim 7.) m. Susanna, D. of Captain Ebenezer Alden, 1738, and had Anna 1739, Azubah 1741, Phebe 1742, Ephraim 1748, Susanna 1750, Huldah 1752, Daniel 1754: his w. d. 1783, æ. 64, and he m. Mary, wid. of Josiah Kingman of Easton, and D. of Josiah Williams, 1784.—Anna d. 1804 single.—Azuba m. Josiah Johnson.—Phebe m. Ezra Allen 1761.—

Susanna m. Asa Keith 1774, and afterwards Eleazar Keith 1795. Huldah m. Simeon Allen 1785.—Daniel m. Hannah, D. of Seth Thayer 1773, but had no children.—Ephraim, the father, d. 1791, æ. 77 ; his wid. d. 1803, æ. 85.

16. Ichabod (s. of Recompence 9.) m. Hannah, D. of Joseph Gannett, 1741, and had Seth 1747, Ichabod 1749, Aaron 1751, Joshua 1753, Zenas 1755, Hannah 1758, Mary 1761, Daniel 1762, Ebenezer 1765. This family went to Chesterfield, but returned, and most of them went into Bristol County. Hannah m. a Coloph of Sharon, one of Burgoyne's army.

17. Col. Simeon (s. of Recompence 9.) m. Mary, D. of Daniel Howard Esq. 1754, and had Molly 1755, Mehitabel 1757, Howard 1760, Martha 1765, Rhoda 1772.—Molly m. Simeon Keith 1775.—Mehitabel m. Bela Howard 1782, and afterwards Samuel Dyke 1793.—Martha m. Benjamin Keith 1788.—Rhoda m. Richard Wild 1794.—Col. Cary d. 1802, æ. 83.

18. Zebulun (s. of Recompence 9.) m. Mehitabel, D. of Matthew Gannett, 1747 : she d. 1748, and he then m. Lydia, D. of Thomas Phillips, 1749, and had Mehitabel 1751, Lydia 1753, Josiah 1754, Zebulun 1755, who d. young in Rochester ; Recompence 1757, Mary 1758.—Mehitabel m. Joseph Allen 1771. The rest of the family went to Brookfield and Ward, in Worcester County.

19. Dea. Jonathan (s. of Recompence 9.) m. Mary, D. of Captain Moses Curtis of Stoughton, 1747, and had Moses 1748, Dorothy 1752, Jonathan 1757, Alpheus 1761, Sarah 1763, James 1766.—Dorothy not m.—Alpheus m. Ruby, D. of Jonathan Perkins, 1786, and lived and died in Quincy, leaving a son Alpheus in Boston who m. Deborah Thayer and had Alpheus 1827.—Sarah m. Daniel Alden 1786, and afterwards Lazarus A. Beal 1809.

20. Henry (s. of John 10.) m. Martha, D. of Dr. Joseph Byram, 1749, and had Benjamin 1750*, killed under a water wheel ; Eunice 1758, Benjamin 1761   He died and she m. Abner Pratt 1764.—Eunice m. Wm. Snell of S. B. 1781.

21. Eleazar (son of Jonathan 11.) m. Betty, D. of Joshua Fobes, 1745, and had Caleb 1747 : she d. 1749, and he m. Mary, Wid. of Nathaniel Washburn, 1753 : she was a Pratt of M.: and had Betty 1754, Mary 1756, Sarah 1761.—Betty m. Wm. Perkins 1777, and afterwards Solomon Snow of Raynham.—Mary m. Nathl. Morton Esq. of Freetown 1782, and was mother of Judge Marcus Morton.—Sarah d. 1838 single.—Caleb m. Mary, D. of Abraham Perkins, 1778, and had a son Caleb, who died young and unmarried ; and a D. Betsy who m. Nathl. Gilbert 1802.—Eleazar Cary m. Lucy Alden of Mido. 1794. Eleazar Cary's w. d. 1790, æ. 73 : he d. 1806, æ. 82.

22. Jonathan (s. of Jonathan 11.) m. Lois, D. of Wm. Hooper, 1754, and had Jonathan 1754, Lois, Eunice 1760.—Jonathan d. of the camp ail 1775.—Lois m. Solomon Keith 1777.—Eunice m. Isaac Washburn of T.—William Cary d. 1775, probably his son.

23. Ephraim (s. of Ephraim 15.) m. Jane, D. of Capt. John Holman, 1771, and had Jane 1773, Salome 1774, Cyrus 1777, William Holman 1779, Ephraim 1782, Shepard 1784, Susanna 1787, Francis 1789, Jason 1791*, Asenath 1793, Harmony 1796. —Jane m. Zenas Keith 1792.—Salome m. Rodolphus Kinsley 1794.—Cyrus m. Nabby, D. of James Keith, 1802, and he and Wm. Holman both went westward.—Ephraim m. Anna, D. of *Jacob Hill, 1809, and had Lucius 1810, Horace 1811, Anne 1815, and Jane Holman; and then he, with his father and Aseneth, went to Minot. Shepard lived and d. at Dorchester. Ephraim, the father, d. at Minot 1828, æ. 80: she before at E. B. 1809, æ. 57.—Susanna m. John Eaton of Dorchester 1812.—Francis m. Harriet, D. of Thomas Hayward, 1816, and lives on the old family estate in E. B. and has a family.—Harmony m. James W. Watson 1821: he d. 1833, and she m. again at T.

24. Howard Esq. (s. of Col. Simeon 17.) m. Huldah, D. of Simeon Packard, 1785, and had Simeon, Daniel Howard, Zenas, William, Elbridge, Francis, Molly, Rhoda: his wife d. and he m. Wid. Hannah Brown 1810.—Simeon m. Roana, D. of Jonas Howard, 1806, and went to Me.—Daniel m. Martha, D. of Gideon Howard Esq. 1812.—Zenas went to Winthrop, Me.—Molly m. Ezra Dunham 1809.—Rhoda m. Maj. Nathan Hayward, 1818.

25. Moses (s. of Jonathan 19) m. Susanna D. of Jabez Field, 1773: he d. 1838, æ. 89: and had Lucius 1776, Barzillai 1780, Susanna 1783, Polly 1785, Cassandana 1788.—Lucius gra. B. U. 1798, was an attorney, and d. at Charleston, S. C., 1806, æ. 30.— Barzillai m. Vashty, D. of Nathan Snell, and had Susanna 1809, Betsy 1810, Almira 1812, Barzillai 1815.—Susanna m. Rev. John Shaw 1807.

26. Jonathan (s. of Jonathan 19.) m. Abigail, D. of Jonathan Perkins, 1784, and had Caleb, Jonathan, Luther, Martin, Huldah, Abigail, Sally, Mary. He m. Wid. Tiley Clark of Winslow, a 2d w., 1808. Caleb, Jonathan, and Luther went to Me.—Martin m. Bethiah, D. of Ichabod Howard.—Huldah m. Darius Howard 1808.—Abigail m. Isaac Dunham 1811.—Sally m. Ziba Keith 1813.

27. James (s. of Jonathan 19.) m. Hannah, D. of Samuel Alden, 1798, and had Lydia 1800: his w. d. and he m. Hannah, D. of Thomas Wales, 1803, and had Otis 1804, Nancy 1807, Austin 1809.—Lydia m. Ephraim Howard 1821.—Austin gra. Amherst 1837.—James Littlefield m. a Cary.

James Cary came from Bristol, Eng., and settled in Charlestown in 1639, the same year John came to Plymouth: they are supposed to have been brothers.

CASWELL.—Zephaniah Caswell m. Azubah, D. of James Hooper 1803, and had Zephaniah 1804, Harriet 1806, Winslow Wood 1809, Susanna Hooper 1814.—Jonathan Caswell m. Tabitha Leach 1769.

CHAMBERLIN.—Freedom Chamberlin of Pembroke (s. of William of Hull, who was s. of Henry, who was s. of Henry, who was s. of Henry, who with his wife, mother and 2 children, came from Hingham, Eng., and settled in Hingham here 1638) had several sons viz.: Capt. Freedom, who d. in Pembroke 1821, æ. 91; and Nathaniel, Job, Benjamin and John, who all settled in E. B.—John and his family soon moved away.—John Chamberlin of Westmoreland m. Eunice, D. of Samuel Edson, 1766.

2. Nathaniel (above) m. Sarah Foster, and had Nathaniel 1745, Sarah 1747, Ruth 1751, Mary 1754, Lydia 1756, Joseph and Benjamin 1761, Josiah 1764 : his w. d. 1765, and he m. Deliverance, D. of Thomas Snell, 1767.—Nathaniel, the father, d. 1814, æ. 91 : his last w., Deliverance, d. 1814, æ. 86.—Nathl., the son, m. Eleanor, D. of Zechariah Whitman, and had a son Nathaniel, and moved away.—Benjamin went into Maine.—Josiah m. Lucy Pratt, and afterwards had a 2d wife and lived in Pembroke.—Ruth m. Elisha Records of Pembroke 1774.—Mary m. Benjamin White of Hanover 1780.—Lydia m. Jona. Pratt.—Sarah m. Jabez Pratt.

3. Job (above) m. Rachel Bonney of Pembroke, and had Isaac 1749*, Elizabeth 1751, Job 1754, Nathan 1756, Thomas 1758, Rachel 1761, Celia 1765, Zerviah 1767, Isaac 1772 : he d. 1788, æ. 62 ; she 1825, æ. 97.—Celia m. Mark Phillips Jr. 1789.—Zerviah m. Daniel Cushing 1787.—The first Isaac d. 1769, æ. 20.—Rachel probably m. Ichabod Packard of Lebanon 1780.

4. Benjamin (above) m. Hannah, D. of Thomas Snell, 1756, and had Silvina 1757, Lewis 1758, Hannah 1760, Benjamin 1762, Aaron 1765, Chloe 1767, Deliverance 1773, Arza 1780; all but the two last b. in Pembroke : he d. 1803, æ. 78; she 1828, æ. 93.—Silvina d. 1829 single.—Lewis m. Rebecca, sister of Major Nathl. Tompson of H., 1793, and d. 1826, leaving one child, Lewis, b. 1796.—Hannah m. a Lamberton.—Benjamin and Aaron went westward.—Chloe d. 1828 single and gave a legacy of $100 to the first parish in E. B.—Deliverance d. 1826 single.—Arza is a bachelor.

5. Joseph (s. of Nathaniel 2.) m Sarah, D. of Capt. Jonathan Bass, 1784, and had Jonathan 1786, Susanna 1788, Joseph 1792. Jonathan was a Col. lives in West Stockbridge and has a family.—Susanna m. Thaxter Norton 1808, and lived in Sterling; now lives in Boston.—Joseph m. Alice, D. of Dea. William Harris, 1819 : she d. 1838, and he then m. Lusanna, wid. of Thomas Whitman and D. of Anthony W. Clift, and has William and Jennet, both by his 1st w.

6. Thomas (s. of Job 3.) m. Polly, D. of Nicholas Whitman, 1785, and had Job 1787, Molly 1792, Zerviah 1795, Jennet 1798, Calvin 1810, Luther, Rachel.—Rachel m. Asa Whitman 1820.

7. Isaac (s. of Job 3.) m. Charity, sister of Major Nathaniel Thompson of H., and had Ebenezer, Asenath, Wealthy, Nathan, Sophronia, and Josiah Holbrook : he d. 1806, and the wid. m. Daniel Bryant 1809.—Ebenezer m Polly, D. of David Benson, 1820, and removed to Barnstable County.—Asenath m. Charles Brown 1819.

7. Henry (no known connection with the above) m. Susanna Hinds 1740.—Joseph m. Mary Wethrell 1767, and had Joseph 1770, Polly 1776.

CHANDLER.—Samuel Chandler and his wife Mercy had Jonathan 1699, Mary 1702, Sarah 1703, Samuel 1709, Abraham 1711, Susanna 1715.—Mary m. Joseph Perry 1729. Jonathan Chandler m. Rebecca Packard, D. of George, before 1754.—Betty Chandler m. Israel Keith 1740 : perhaps she afterwards m. Joseph Harvey 3d 1749.—Jonathan Chandler m. Wid. Abthiah Wade 1745, and d. 1775; Abthiah Chandler d. 1792, æ. 85.

CHEESMAN.—Samuel Cheesman (s. of Sam'l Cheesman of Braintree,) came to N. B. 1772 ; m. Martha D. of Dependence French, and had Noah, Samuel, Olive, Naomi, Polly, and Betsy.—Capt. Noah m. Lucinda D. of Robert Howard 1799, and had Zechariah Howard 1801, Olive 1803, Noah 1810, Lucinda 1814,.—Samuel m. Mehitabel D. of Giles Leach 1806, and went to Merrimack.—Olive m. James Thompson 1798.—Naomi m. Josiah Orcutt 1806.—Polly m. Ara Battles.—Betsy m. Bazillai King 1812.—Olive 2nd. m. Reuben Drake 1819.—Ruth Cheesman m. Azor Howe 1791.

CHIPMAN.—George Chipman m. Huldah D. of James Leach 1803, and had Ann Waterman 1804, Hazadiah Keith 1807, Charlotte Lazell 1810*, Isabella 1814.—The mother d. 1835.

CHURCHILL.—1. Jabez Churchill and his w. Alice, had Alice 1753, Rachel 1754, who m. Thaddeus Pratt 1777.

2. Ephraim and Jemima had Ephraim 1753, Hannah 1755, Dorcas 1759, Jemima 1761, James 1764, Sarah 1767, Susanna 1770.—Ephraim m. Silence D. of Dependence French 1787.— Hannah m. Calvin Snow 1784.—Dorcas m. Eliab Snow 1787.— Jemima m. James Packard 1778.—James m. Mary D. of Zechariah Gurney 1794.—Susanna m. Elijah Drake 2nd. 1800.

3. Eleazar m. Lucy Otis of Scituate 1788, and lived in W. B. and had Sophia 1789, Charles 1791, Polly 1794, Rhoda, Harriet, Hannah Otis, and another.—He d. suddenly in his chair 1818.—One D. m. a Nash.—One m. a Pennyman.—One m. an Erskin.—Rhoda m. Sam'l Keen Jr.—Harriet m. John Reed Jr. of Ab. 1819.—Hannah O. m. a Douglas of N. Bedford.

4. Levi (from Plympton) m. Cynthia D. of Solomon Packard, and lives in E. B. and has Levi, Luther, Abisha, David, William, Cynthia, Azuba, Elizabeth*, Bethiah, and Lurania*.— His w. d. 1832 æ. 53, and he m. again.—Cynthia m. Joshua Bennet.—Azuba m. Lewis Keith 1819.—Wid. Sarah, mother of Levi sen. d. 1834, æ. 78.—Levi Jr. m. Lucretia D. of Charles Keen. Luther m. Evelina D. of Eli Blanchard.

Wid. Mercy of Plympton m. Joshua Fobes 1754.—John m. Joanna D. of Moses Bisbee 1756.—Ruth m. Jonathan Whitman 1776.—Josiah m. Sarah Rogers 1781.—Priscilla m. Benjamin Sprague 1785.—David Jr. m. Molly Hearsey 1797.—Fidelia m. Wm. Hunt 1798.—Deborah, sister of Eleazar, m. Eleazar

Alden 1794.—Ezra m. Bethiah Mehurin of Pem. 1799.—Silence m. Asa Randall 1821.

CLEAVELAND.—Ephraim Cleaveland m. Hannah Hayward 1747, and settled in W. B., and had Joseph 1749, Benjamin 1751, Elijah 1753, Lucy and Ebenezer 1755, Olive 1758, Persis 1760.

CLIFT.—Nathaniel Clift of Marshfield m. Deborah D. of Anthony Winslow, and had Anthony Winslow, Nathaniel, and Deborah.—They both d., he a. 1762, and their father Winslow came to E. B. before 1770 and brought these 3 gr. ch. with him.—Deborah m. George Keith 1768.—Nath'l. d. 1773 æ. 22.—Anthony W. m. Bethiah D. of the Hon. Hugh Orr 1777, and had Nathaniel, Margaret, Bethiah Orr, Lusanna Winslow, and Phidelma.—Margaret m. Dea. Sam'l Keen 1804.—Bethiah O. m. Charles Mitchell 1813.—Lusanna W. m. Thomas Whitman 1818, and Joseph Chamberlin 1839.—Phidelma m. George Keith 1815.—Nathaniel m. Nabby D. of Josiah Byram 1799, and d. leaving 2 ss. Angier Byram*, and Belus, and 2 Ds. ; and his wid. m. Job Turner and is again a wid.

COBB.—Ansel Cobb lived in W. B. m. Sarah D. of Ezra Hayward and had Hayward 1801, and Lucinda.—He d. and the s. and D. live in Mid'o.

Susanna Cobb m. John Sprague 1746.—Nath'l. Jr. of Plympton m. Penelope Standish 1763.—Penelope m. Ichabod Leach 1770.—Lydia m. Wm. Pettingill 1784.—Eleanor m. Obadiah Pettingill 1792.

COLE.—1. Joseph Cole (from Plympton) and his w. Mary settled in N. B. and had Samuel, Ephraim, Joseph, Molly, Susanna, Catherine, Eliza, Eleazar 1747, Sarah 1749, Silence 1755*.—Molly m. Col. Frederick Pope 1758.—Susanna m. a Niles.—Catherine m. Daniel Littlefield 1762.—Eliza m. Solomon Smith of E. 1761.—Sarah m. a Withington.—Eleazar m. Lucy Shurtliff 1769, and went to Me.

2. Samuel (s. of Joseph 1.) m. Sarah D. of Seth Packard 1752, and had William 1753, Rebecca 1755*, Samuel 1761, and removed westward.—William m. Molly Lazell 1773.—Rebecca m. Amaziah Cole 1775.

3. Ephraim (s. of Joseph 1.) m. Hannah Randall and had Zilpha 1754, Ephraim 1756, Hannah 1759, Molly 1764, Rachel 1768.—Zilpha m. Edward Bartlett 1772.—Hannah m. Isaac Keith 1775, and afterwards Capt. Seth Keith.—Molly m. John Drake 1782.—Rachel m. Ichabod Packard 1786.

4. Joseph (s. of Joseph 1.) m. Betty D. of Constant Southworth 1757, and had Desire 1758, and went westward.—Desire m. Noah Pratt 1777, and went to Vermont.

5. Ephraim (s. of Ephraim 3.) m. Silence Webb 1777, and had Ephraim, Thomas, Zibion, Ornan, Alvan, and Hannah.— Ephraim m. Susanna D. of Adin Packard 1808, and had Susanna 1808.—Thomas m. Silence Thayer 1810.—Zibion m. Mary D. of Barzillai Field 1819.—Ornan m. Lucy D. of Perez Southworth.—Alvan m. Eliza D. of David French 1823.—Hannah m. Silas Snow 1800.   18

John Cole of Plympton m. Patience Barber 1709.—Content
of Pem. m. Wm. Whitman 1778.—Molly of Mid'o. m. Rufus Edson 1783.—Susanna of Mid'o. m. Alex. Ames 1789.—Polly m.
Winslow Thomas 1780.—Caleb m. Lucy Hall 1792.—Joseph of
Plymouth m. Sarah Atwood 1793.—Patty m. Stephen Snell
1796.—Edward m. Phebe Alden of Mid. 1797.—Sally of Scituate m. Edwin Howard 1803.—Phebe m. Samuel Snell 1810.—
Ephraim of Plymouth m. Sarah D. of Francis Cook s. of Jacob.
   COLWELL.—Ebenezer Colwell m. Sarah D. of Benjamin
Price 1769, and settled in W. B., and had Brett 1771, Keziah
1775, Ebenezer 1779, Sally 1781, Melvin 1786, John 1791.—
The mother d. 1816.—Hannah Colwell d. 1815.—Ebenezer m.
Betsy Hayward 1804.—Sally m. Albertus Edson of Grafton, Vt.
1804.—Keziah m. Ebenezer Edson 1797.—John m. Hannah D.
of Silvanus Hayward 1813, and afterwards m. Tabitha another
D. of Silvanus Hayward 1816.
   CONANT.—1. Nathaniel Conant (from Beverly) with his w.
Hannah settled in S. B. before 1690 : he was a descendant of
Roger Conant, who came to N. E. 1623, and lived at Plymouth,
Nantasket, Cape Ann, and afterwards at Salem, where he built
the first house, about 1626, and died at Beverly 1679 in his 89th
year. Nathaniel's will 1712, proved 1732.—He had Nathaniel, Josiah, Lot, William, Bethiah, Hannah, Martha, Lydia, Rebecca; the births of Lot 1690, Lydia 1692, and Rebecca 1694,
are on Bridgewater Records, Bethiah married Nathaniel Allen
1696.—Hannah married Nathanial Hill 1710.—Lydia m. Andrew Lovell 1712.—Rebecca m. Shubael Ewers of Barnstable
1714. Roger (the first born child in Salem), Exercise, Lot, John,
and Joshua, were ss. of the pilgrim, Roger : Nathaniel was probably son of Lot.
   2. Nathaniel (s. of Nathaniel 1.) his first w. Mary, no children
probably ; 2d. w. Margaret, they had Thomas 1705, Bethiah
1709 ; 3d. w. Elizabeth Hains m. 1716, they had Jeremiah 1720,
Margaret 1722, John 1725, Elizabeth 1727; his will 1743; he
d. 1745; his last w.d. 1757.—Bethiah m. Elkanah Rickard 1733.
Margaret m. Abel Edson a.1739.—Elizabeth m. Dan'l Keith 1744.
   3. Josiah (s. of Nathaniel 1.) m. Elizabeth D. of John Washburn, Jr. 1701.—He d. a. 1721, and had Joseph, Josiah, Susanna,
and Prudence.
   4. Lot (s. of Nathaniel 1.) m. Deborah Goodspeed of Sandwich, and had Hannah 1712, Gershom 1714, Lot 1718, Silvanus
1720, Phinehas 1727, Deborah 1728, Timothy 1732.—Deborah
m. Isaac Washburn 1753.—Silvanus gra. H. U. 1740, and settled in the ministry at Middleborough, and d. of small pox 1777,
Dec. 7, æ. 58, in the 33d. year of his ministry, but left no posterity.—Lot, the father, d. 1774 æ. 84.—Hannah m. Nathaniel
Pratt 1745 probably.
   5. William (s. of Nathaniel 1.) m. Mary Trow of Beverly,
and lived in E. B.—They had Sarah 1708, Ruth 1711.—He had
other children : one, Mary, m. Nicholas Whitman 1719.—One,

William, died young,—Another, Elizabeth, m. Benjamin Hayward 1724.—Another, Hannah, d. 1773, and David.—Ruth d. 1780, æ. 69.—His will dated 1748, proved 1754.

6. Thomas (s. of Nathaniel 2.) m. Martha D. of Wm. Ames, and had Nathan 1731, Sarah 1733, Martha 1735, Rebecca 1737, Mary 1740, Zilphah 1742, he m. Mary D. of Elnathan Wood 1745, and had Abner 1746, Zenas 1748, Ezra 1750, Jedidah 1752, Abigail 1754*, Keturah 1756.—Sarah m. John Heiford of Mid'o. 1754.—Martha m. Seth Lathrop of E. 1755.—Rebecca m. Robert Randall of E. 1761.—Mary m. Zebulon Bryant 1767.—Zilphah m. Samuel Keith 1766.—Jedidah m. Roland Sears of Ashfield 1777.—Keturah m. Barnabas Washburn 1782.—Abner went to Hardwick and d. single.—Thomas the father d. 1787; Mary the mother d. 1802 æ. 83.

7. Jeremiah (s. of Nathaniel 2.) m. Martha D. of Daniel Packard 1739, and had Azubah 1739, Nathaniel 1743, Daniel, Betty, who m. Noah Phinney 1769, Roger 1749, Lydia 1752, Martha 1753, Chloe 1755, who m. a Walker.—Azubah m. Jesse Dunbar 1762.—Dan'l m. Joanna D. of Cornelius Washburn 1767, and went to Pelham.—Lydia m. Zephaniah Smith 1773.—Martha m. Josiah Mehurin 1779.—Martha, the mother, m. James Dunbar 1757.

8. John (s. of Nathaniel 2.) m. Abihail Pratt 1746, and had Abihail 1746, John 1749, Zenas 1751, Lucy 1753, Silvia 1755, Jeremiah 1758, Bethiah 1760, Thomas 1766.—Abihail m. John Willis 2d. 1774.—Lucy m. Ziba Hayward 1773.—Silvia m. Silvanus Conant 1773.—Jeremiah m. Mary D. of Solomon Leonard 1782, and Chloe D. of Dea. Seth Pratt 1793, and went to Pomfret Vt., and had John who m. Rebecca D. of Nath'l. Washburn and had a s. Chauncy and others probably.—Thomas m. Lydia D. of Calvin Edson 1789, and went to Oakham.

9. Gershom (s. of Lot. 4.) m. Anne D. of Henry Kingman 1738, and d. 1792, æ.78 : she D. 1791, æ. 81.—They had Anne 1740, Eunice 1743, Silvanus 1747.—Anne m. Joseph Muxam 1764.—Eunice m. Barnabas Snell 1783.—Silvanus m. Silvia D. of John Conant 1773, and went to Minot Me.

10. Lot (s. of Lot 4.) m. Betty Holmes of Halifax 1743 ; she d. 1773.—They had Sarah 1744*, Lydia 1746, Betty 1754, Benjamin 1756, and Rebecca.—Lydia m. Calvin Edson 1766.—Betty m. Zenas Conant 1774.—Benjamin m. Betty D. of Hezekiah Hooper 1783, and had Temperance 1783, Marcus 1785, Winslow 1788, Benjamin 1790, Hooper 1793, and went to Me.—Rebecca m. Benjamin Snell 1782.—Lot Conant's wife d. 1778, and he m. wid. Rhoda Perry 1780 ; she d. 1790.

11. Phinehas (s. of Lot 4.) m. Joanna D. of David Pratt 1749.—He d. 1798, æ 72 : she d. 1804. æ. 74.—They had Sarah 1752, Peter 1753, Joanna 1755, Phinehas 1759, David 1762 Jacob 1768.—Peter was a Deacon and m. Jane D. of Jona. Conant 1777, and had Peter, who m. Lucy Brewster 1809, Silvia who m. Joseph Hayward 2d. 1814, Ruth who m. Daniel Keith 1800, and Libeus, who was a minister at Northfield N. H. whither the

family removed.—Joanna m. Elias Conant 1774.—Phinehas m.
Joanna D. of Daniel Washburn 1785, and she d. 1829.—David
m. Silvia D. of Samuel Whitman 1783, and had Martha 1785,
Susanna 1787, and David 1790, and d. 1792, and she afterwards
m. Azariah Hayward Jr. 1798.

12. Timothy (s. of Lot 4.) m. Hannah Blackman 1754, and
had James 1755, Luther 1758, Susanna 1760, Lucy 1762, Deborah 1764, Timothy, Silvanus, Abigail, Sarah and Hannah*.—
Deborah m. Nathan Lazell Esq. 1783.—Timothy m. Nancy D.
of Solomon Pratt 1788.—The Mother Hannah, m. Hezekiah
Hooper for her 2d. husband.—Most [of this family removed to
Oakham and several of the children were born there.

13. David (s. of William 5.) m. Sarah D. of Benjamin Hayward 1723.—and had David 1726, Jonathan 1734, William 1742.
William gra. Yale College 1770, and settled in the ministry at
Lyme N. H.—He first m. a Cook, and afterwards wid. Patty Perkins, (Theodore's wid.) and D. of Nathan Conant.

14. Nathan(s. of Thomas 6.)m. Hannah D. of Isaac Lazell 1753,
and d. 1778, and had Hannah 1754, Lois 1756, Martha 1760, Caleb 1762, Rebecca 1764, and Mary 1768, who m. Isaac Smith
of Braintree 1785.—Lois m. Soloman Conant 1783.—Patty m.
Theodore Perkins 1783, and afterwards Wm. Conant.—Hannah
m. Jona. Washburn Jr. of M. 1778.—Caleb m. Olive Thrasher
1789, and moved to the westward.

15. Zenas (s. of Thomas 6.) m. Betty D. of Lot Conant 1774,
and had Betty, Oliver, Sarah, Olive.—Betty m. Levi Leach 1798.
Oliver m. Polly D. of Calvin Washburn 1796.—Sarah m. Ephraim
Leach 1805.—Olive m. Jacob Conant 1805, who went to Ohio,
and had Charles 1807, Jane 1809, William 1812, born here.

16. Ezra (s. of Thomas 6.)m. Mary D. of David Conant 1773;
she d. 1835 ; he had Gaius, gra. B. U. 1800, who m. Cassandra
D. of Zechariah Whitman 1802, and afterwards Chloe wid. of
Jonas Leonard, and D. of Jesse Allen, and settled in the ministry
at Paxton ; and Thomas who is a Baptist preacher.

17. Nathaniel (s. of Jeremiah 7.) m. Silence D. of Ephraim
Fobes 1772, and had Andrew 1774, Susanna 1777, Silence 1781.
Andrew m. Keziah D. of Benjamin Washburn 1795, and had
Jeremiah 1796, Olive 1801, Thomas Jefferson 1806, Andrew
1808.—Susanna Conant m. Wm. Durkey of Hampton, Conn
1812.

18. John (s. of John 8.) m. Deborah D. of Nathan Perkins
1772, and had Marlborough, Martin, Seth, Lucy, Deborah, who
m. Ansel Leonard 1807.—Marlborough m. Polly Dunbar 1796;
she d. 1796, æ. 21.—Lucy m. Jacob Pierce 1794, and afterwards
Andrew Tucker.—Martin m. Olive D. of Eben. Benson 1797.
Seth m. Hannah D. of Nathaniel Pratt 1801.—Martin Jr. m.
Lucy Mehurin 1806.

19. David (s. of David 13.) m. Rhoda D. of Thomas Latham
1748, and had Elias 1749, Mary 1752, Solomon 1756, Rufus
1757, David 1759.—David, the father, d. 1760.—Elias m. Joanna

D. of Phineas Cónant 1774,and had 2 ch. d. 1778, and William
and others.—Mary m. Ezra Conant 1773.—Solomon m. Lois
D. of Nathan Conant 1783.—Rufus m Thankful D. of Nathan
Leonard 1783.—David m. Lucy D. of Nehemiah Bessee 1782.
The 3 last named sons went to Lyme N. H.—David has a son,
John A. Conant now living in E. B.—William(s. of Elias) m. Mar-
tha Fobes 1803.—Rhoda, the mother, d. 1790 æ. 61: David d. 1792.
20. Jonathan (s. of David 13.) m. Jane D. of Arthur Latham
1759.—and had Jane 1760, Sally 1761, Josiah 1768, Lydia 1770,
Alice 1775, and removed to Greenwich.—Jane m. Dea. Peter
Conant 1777.—Sally m. Abisha Besse 1782.
Silvanus m. Mary Packard 1808.—Lucinda m. Seth Pratt
1816.—Ira Conant m. Lucy Leonard 1818.—Ziba or Liba m.
Deborah Leach 1820.—Polly m.Wm. Andrews 1818.—Patty
Conant m. Ellis Holmes Jr. 1803.—Mehitabel or Hitty m. Cornelius Holmes Jr. 1806.—Thomas m. Anne Leonard 1812.
COOK.—Francis Cook m. Sarah D. of Ichabod Bryant 1750,
and had Ruth 1751, Rhoda 1753, Sarah 1755, Phebe 1757, Ga-
maliel 1759 —Sarah m. John Lathrop 1780.—This man was a
descendant without doubt from Francis Cook who arrived at
Plymouth 1620 in the first ship, the *May Flower.*—John and his
wife Silence, had John 1782, Kingman 1786.—John Cook m.
Sally Lathrop 1790.—Kingman Cook m. Sarah Munro 1815,
and had Tiley Shurtliff 1817.—Hannah Cook from the Cape m.
Joseph Snell 1785.—Benjamin Cook of Br. (a soldier 1776) æ.
85, A. D. 1818.—Mr. Cook d. 1820 æ. 79.
COPELAND.—Lawrence Copeland of Braintree m. Lydia
Townsend 1651, and had Thomas 1654, William 1656, John 1658,
Ephraim 1665, and several Ds.—He d. 1699 said to be 110 years
old. Wm. (s. of Lawrence) m. Mary, wid. of Christopher Webb
Jr. and D. of John and Ruth Bass 1694, (Ruth was D. of the
Hon. John Alden, the Pilgrim;) and died at Braintree about
1716.—He had William 1695, Ephraim 1697, Ebenezer 1698,
Jonathan 1701, David 1704, Joseph 1706, Benjamin 1708, Moses
1710, and Mary 1713.—His son Joseph settled first in W. B. and
afterwards in Scituate, and had a numerous family remarkable
for their longevity.
1. Jonathan (s. of William, and grand. s. of Lawrence) m.
Betty D. of Thomas Snell Jr. 1723, and settled in W. B. and had
Abigail 1724, Betty 1726*, Jonathan 1728, Mary 1731, Joseph
1734, Hannah 1737, Elijah 1739, Daniel 1741, Sarah 1745, Ebenezer 1746, Betty 1750.—He d. 1790, æ. 90.—Abigail m. George
Howard 1745.—Mary m. Benjamin Gannett 1750.—Hannah m.
Jonathan Kingman 1759. Sarah m. David Keith of Easton 1769.
Betty m. Clifford Belcher of Sharon 1770.
2. Jonathan (s. of Jonathan 1.) m. Mehitabel D. of Samuel
Dunbar 1754, and had Jonathan 1755, Mehitabel, Sarah, Asa
1762, Caleb 1764, Ephraim 1767, Mary 1772, Martha 1774.—
Mehitabel m. Maj. Daniel Hartwell 1779.—Sarah (or Sally D.
of Caleb 9.) m. Stephen Fuller of Attleborough 1810.—Ephraim

m. Lucy D. of Eleazar Keith 1791, and had Ephraim 1792, Lucy 1794, and one other, and removed to Leicester.—Mary m. John Burr 1792.—Jonathan the father d. 1820 æ. 92.

3. Dea. Joseph (s. of Jona. 1.) m. Rebecca D. of John Hooper 1760 and had Rebecca, 1762, Joseph 1764, Salmon 1766, Hannah 1768, Polly 1771, Sarah 1773, Winslow 1775, Huldah 1777, Hezekiah 1780, and Lucy 1784: he d. 1811 æ. 77: she d. 1820.—Rebecca m. Eben'r. Dunbar 1785.—Joseph m. Sarah Swift Huxford of Chelsea 1808 and went to Me. and d. without issue.—Salmon m. Betty, D. of Nathan Snell 1799 and had Lyman 1800, Pardon 1803, Nathan 1805: he then m. his brother Joseph's wid. 1814.—Hannah m. Galen Allen perhaps 1797.—Polly m. Joseph Hall 1812.—Winslow m. Hannah Slader of Acworth N. H. 1804.—Huldah m. Howland Holmes 1804.—Hezekiah and his w. Lucy had Rowland Flagg 1805, and Willard Moore 1817, and he and Winslow went to N. H.—Lucy m. Ellis Holmes of Halifax 1806.

4. Elijah (s. of Jona. 1.) m. Rhoda D. of Josiah Snell, 1765, and went to E. and had Elijah 1766, Josiah 1768, Luther 1770, Rhoda, Abigail, Martin, Polly.—he d. æ. 78.—Elijah went to Weston.—Josiah m. Susanna Howard, and had Horatio 1796 Susanna, Hiram.—Luther went to Vt.—Josiah m. Phebe, D. of Ephraim Burr, 2d w. perhaps.

5. Daniel (s. of Jona. 1.) m. Susanna D. of Joseph Ames 1764, and had Azael 1764, Daniel 1766, Cyrus 1769, Susanna 1771, Martin 1774, Charlotte 1777, Matilda, Alfred, Betsy, Clara, Ralph —Azael m. Desire Lucas of Mid'o. 1791.—Daniel m. Abigail Shaw 1791.—Cyrus m. Abigail D. of Chistopher Dyer 1792, and had Cyrus 1793, Ward Cotton 1795, Christopher Dyer 1800, Jason 1803. Cyrus Jr. m. Phebe C. Alger 1816.—Martin m. Lucy Cowing 1802.—Charlotte m. Philip Bennet 1797.—Matilda m. Thomas Alden 1815.—Alfred m. a Williams.—Betsy m. Capt. Holmes Sprague 1808.—Ralph m. Anne Dunbar.

6. Ebenezar (s. of Jona. 1.) m. Abby Godfrey of Norton 1770, and had Ebenezer 1773, James 1775*, Betty, Lydia, Oakes 1793, Abby, Rachel*, Ruth*, Molly* ; he m. Bridget Wood of Norton 1801, a 2d. w.—Betty m. Calvin Williams 1799.—Lydia m. Nathan Howard 3d 1799.—Abby m. Elijah Snell Jr. 1796.—Ebenezer m. Mehitabel D. of Dea. Elijah Snell 1798, and had Mehitabel 1799; he then m. a 2d. w., Hannah Godfrey of Norton, 1801, and had James 1802, Rachel 1803, Mary Hodges 1804, Abby Godfrey 1806, Ruth 1808, Lawrence 1815.

7. Jonathan Esq. (s. of Jona. 2.) m. Deborah D. of Stephen Otis of Scituate, and had Mehitabel 1785 Jonathan 1787, Charles 1790, George 1793, Deborah Otis 1795, William 1798, Stephen Otis 1804.—He d. 1838.—Mehitabel m. Austin Keith 1813.—Jonathan m. Hannah D. of Dr. John Reed 1818, Charles m. Mehitabel D. of Oliver Howard 1816 and had Susan H. 1818, and Deborah Otis 1820, and d. 1821, and the. wid. m. Earl Thayer.—George gra. B. U. 1815 and is an Attorney on the Cape.—Deborah O. m. Ephraim Wales of Braintree.

8. Asa (s. of Jona. 2.) m. Persia D. of James Howard 1792 and had Albert 1793, Azel Howard 1795, Asa 1799, Francis 1803.—Albert m. Anna H. D. of ·George Williams 1819.
9. Caleb (s. of Jona. 2.) m. Sally D. of Seth Byram 1787, and had Lurany 1788, Tempe 1790, Caleb 1792, Sally 1794, Vesta 1796, Seth, Elizabeth, Almira, Ephraim, and Mary.—Lurany m. Silvanus Keith 1820.—Tempe m. Barzillai Keith 1819.—Caleb m. Olive D. of Maj. Cyrus Porter of St. 1821.—Sally (or Sarah D. of Jona. 2.) m. Stephen Fuller of Attleborough 1810. Vesta m. Nahum Perkins 1820.

CORTHRELL.—Daniel Corthrell and his wife Hannah had Daniel 1747, Elizabeth 1749, Abigail 1751, Phebe 1754.

COWING.—Jabez Cowing m. Susanna, D. of John Bolton, 1741, and had Jabez 1742, Abisha 1744, Reuben 1749, Benjamin 1754. Sarah Cowing m. John Hooper 1746.—Israel Cowing of Scituate m. Rebecca, D. of James Wade, 1788.

2. Joseph Cowing or Cowen (s. of Israel of Scituate, a Scotch family) m. Jane, D. of Samuel Keith, 1744: she d. 1794, æ. 65: they had Joseph 1745, Hannah 1747. Ward 1755.—Joseph m. Abigail, D. of Joshua Fobes 1772.—Hannah m. John Hooper 1777.—Lucy Cowing m. Martin Copeland 1802.—Betsy m. Silas Andrews 1803.

CRAFTS.—Dr. Thomas Staples Crafts, came from Newton; married a Park; settled in N. B. 1756: had Thomas, Samuel John, Moses, Edward, Zibeon, Patty and Polly. Patty married Rev. Zechariah Howard 1785.—Polly m. Rev. Naphthali Shaw 1798.—The Doctor, with his 4 ss. Samuel, Moses, Edward and Zibeon, went to Maine.

2. Rev. Thomas (s. of the above) gra. H. U. 1783; m. Polly, D. of Rev. John Porter, 1786; settled at Princeton 1786, and left there 1791, and was installed at Mid'o.: had Thomas*, Frederick, Eliphalet Porter, Mary, Betsy and Sophia, and d. 1819, æ. 60. Betsy m. Jesse Perkins 1815.—Sophia m. a Hartshorn.—Frederick gra. B. U. 1815.—Eliphalet P. gra. B. U. 1821, and settled in the ministry in E. B., and has been since installed at Sandwich, and m. Augusta Porter of Sterling.

3. John (s. of Thomas S. 1.) m. Olive, D. of Rev. John Porter, 1790, and had Jonathan Porter 1792, who gra. B. U. 1817, and d. 1822, æ. 30.

Samuel Crafts m. a Packard.—Moses m. Phebe, D. of Eleazar Snow 1799.—Zibeon m. Hannah Howard 1799.

CRANE.—Samuel Crane from Milton m. Sarah (wid. probably of Josiah) Washburn 1738, and had Samuel 1739, who d. a bachelor.

2. Dr. Jonathan Crane came from Berkley and settled in S. B., and m. Mary, D. of Col. Josiah Edson, 1770, and had Daniel 1771, (who gra. Brown U. 1796, and m. Anna Howard, D. of Jonathan, 1801, and left several children) Susanna 1776. Dr. Jona. m. Lydia Adams of Kingston, 2d wife, 1783, and d. Dec. 31, 1813, æ. 76.—Susanna m Oliver Eaton 1798, and afterwards

144 CROCKER.—CROOKER.—CROSS.—CURTIS.

a Dillingham of Troy. Benjamin Crane m. Eunice, D. of William Washburn, 1770.—Lydia Crane of Berkley m. Rodolphus Edson 1780.—John Crane m. Patience Pratt 1793.—Betsy Crane m. Lewis Packard 1808.—Spencer Crane of Canton m. Sally Pratt 1809.—Phebe Crane d. 1789.
CROCKER.—Perez Crocker (s. of Heman of Carver) m. a Thompson and came to N. B. 1802, and had Daniel, Henry, Edward, Charles, Frederick, Louisa, and Jane.—Louisa m. Capt. Charles Gurney.—Jane m. Cyrus Hooper.
CROOKER.—Zenas Crooker (s. of Jona. of Pem.) m. Content Stetson and settled in S. B., and had Zenas 1792, Ursula Barker 1794, Lucy 1796, Eliza 1799, Ralph 1801, Naomi Stetson 1804, Benjamin 1807, Helen 1809.—Zenas m. Hannah Richardson of Danvers.—Lucy m. Zephaniah Shaw.—Naomi S. m. a Hicks.—Helen m. Samuel W. Bates.
Jonathan m. Sarah D. of Ebenezer Allen.—John Crooker m. Polly D. of Joseph Smith 1798.—James d. in E. B. æ. over 80.
CROSS.—Capt. Nathaniel Cross (from Exeter N. H.) m. Margaret Bird of Dorchester and settled in E. B. and had Nathaniel Henry 1803, Joseph Warren 1808, Thaddeus William 1810, Margaret Granger 1813, Sarah Ann 1816, George Gilman. Nathaniel H. m. Lucy Vose of Boston and settled in N. B.— Joseph W. gra. H. U., m, a Hodges and afterwards Francis Vose of Boston and settled in the ministy at Boxborough.—Thaddeus W. m. a Brooks and settled in Quincy.—Margaret G. m. a Standart and is now a wid.—Sarah A. m. George Folsom.
CURTIS.—Edward Curtis, m. Abigail, D. of Joseph Pratt, 1759, and had Hannah 1760, Mercy 1762, Abigail 1764, Lydia 1766, and removed to Hardwick.
2. Barnabas (s. of Ashly of St.) lived in N. B. ; m. Esther D. of Pelatiah Phinney 1774, and had Olive 1776, Hannah 1780, Bela 1782, Isaac 1786, and Josiah Washburn 1794.—Hannah m. Alpheus Tribou 1804.—Bela m. Kezia D. of Nehemiah Lincoln 1803 and had Josiah 1803 Mira 1805, Beza 1806, Thomas Madison 1808, Barnabas 1810, Alanson 1812, Esther 1813, Patty Perkins 1816.—Isaac m. Mehitable D. of John Wales 1806, and had John 1806, Francis 1808*, Henry 1810, Hannah 1812*.
3. Capt. Simeon (s. of Simeon of Hanover) m. Bathsheba Silvester, and lived in E. B. and d. 1837 æ. 80: he had Bathsheba 1791, Silvester 1795, Simeon 1797, Robert 1799.—Bathsheba m. Capt. Isaac Keith 1815.—Silvester m. Heman Keith. Robert m. Abby M. D. of Daniel Bryant and lives in Boston.
Abigail Curtis m. Josiah Washburn 1746.—Rebecca m. William Washburn 1738.—Experience m. Ezekiel Washburn 1749.—Patience m. Seth Brett 1744.—Eunice D. of Theophilus m. Edmund Soper 1756.—Benjamin of Plymp. m. Experience D. of Elisha Hayward 1732.—Capt. Moses m. Hannah Belcher 1769, 2d. w.—wid. Curtis d. 1757.—Content d. 1763.—Aholibama m. Timothy Packard 1790.—Sally m. Nehemiah Howard 1791.— Samuel m. Sally Harris 1799.—Theresa (or Thirza) m. Benjamin

DANIELS.—DAVENPORT.—DAWES. 145

Munro of Hal. 1812.—Rebecca m. Enoch Thayer 1765.—Hannah m. John Battles.—Hannah m. Oliver Lathrop 1803.—Abigail m. George Briggs 1809.
DANIELS.—Charles Daniels m. Mehitabel Perkins 1814, and had Charles 1815, Elizabeth 1816, David 1820.—William Daniels' child d. in E. B. 1770.
DAVENPORT.—Richard Davenport (from Weymouth) settled in S. B. a. 1700 : was a Representative several years : had Richard, William, Abigail, Nathaniel, and Elizabeth : appears to have been at Shrewsbury 1731.—Abigail m. Zechariah Packard 1724.—Elizabeth m. Josiah Washburn 1723.—Nathaniel m. Lucy Wyman 1729.
2. Richard (s. of the above) m. Susanna D. of Amos Snell, and d. a. 1785 : had John, Elizabeth, Susanna, Eunice, and Abigail.—John m. Charity Pratt of Norton 1764.—Elizabeth m. Jacob Lazell of Mid'o.—Susanna m. Ichabod Orcutt Jr. 1757.—Eunice m. Wm. Lazell of Mid'o 1759.—Abigail m. Daniel Hayward and went to Greenwich.
3. William (s. of Richard 1.) m. Sarah Richards 1730, and had Abigail 1730, Anna 1732, Elizabeth 1735.
Eliphalet Davenport from Dorchester m. Jane Douglas, and lives in E. B.
DAWES.—1. Samuel Dawes m. Sarah Howland of Pembroke, where he lived and had Robert and Samuel ; he then removed to E. B. and had Abigail 1729, Content 1733, Ann 1735, Mary 1738, Jonathan 1745.—He d. a. 1755, and she m. Capt. Daniel Reed of Abington 1765. Abigail m. Josiah Vining 1751.—Ann m. Daniel Reed.—Mary m. Nathaniel Prior.—Jonathan m. Lydia Snell 1772, and went into the revolutionary war and never returned.
2. Jonathan (brother of Samuel perhaps) and his wife Lois who joined the church 1741, had Margaret, Mary, Jabez.—Margaret m. Andrew Bearce of Halifax 1736.—Mary joined the church 1742.
3. Robert (s. of Samuel 1.) m. Lydia D. of John Harden of Abington 1742, and had Robert 1747, Nathan 1751 ; the father d. 1755, and the wid. m. Isaac Tyrrell of Abington 1755 ; she d. in E. B. 1798, æ. 76.
4. Samuel (s. of Samuel 1.) m. Abigail D. of Isaac Kingman 1755, and had Ebenezer 1755, Betty and Sarah 1758*, Samuel 1760, John 1763, Howland 1766, Daniel 1768, Abby 1770, Mitchell 1772.—Ebenezer gra. H. U. 1785, and settled in the ministry at Scituate 1787 ; he m. Elizabeth, D. of Col. John Bailey of Hanover, and had William 1790, Ebenezer 1791, and d. the same year æ. 36.—All the rest of the family removed to Cummington.
5. Capt. Robert (s. of Robert 3.) m. Lydia D. of Isaac Tirrell of Abington, and had Susanna 1768, Lydia, and other Ds. and also 2 ss. Robert and Jonathan.—This family also removed to Cummington.—James Shaw, Beriah Shaw, and Eliphalet Packard, all of Cummington m. his Ds.—Maj. Robert and Jonathan
19

have both been Representatives from that town. Jonathan m. Huldah D. of Capt. Edmund Lazell.—Sabina Dawes of St. m. Joseph Randall Jr. 1820.

6. Nathan (s. of Robert 3.) m. Abigail D. of Jacob White 1772, and had Nathan 1775, Jacob 1778, Mary 1781, Abigail 1791.—Nathan went to Maine.—Jacob m. Martha Hearsey 1800 and lives in Abington, and has a D. Silvester Holmes born here. Mary m. Samuel Bicknell 1800.Abigail m. William Hearsey. Wm. Dawes at Boston 1640 : made free 1646 : d. 1703, æ. 86. had Ambrose at Braintree 1642, William and Robert at Boston a. 1645 and 1646.—John and Susanna had Hannah 1659*.—John and Mary had Samuel 1660, Elizabeth 1661.—Wm. and Susanna had Jonathan 1661.—James and Frances had James 1668.—Ambrose and Mary had Susanna 1668, William 1671, Susanna 1673, Joseph 1677, Thomas 1680 : his will 1705 mentions Ambrose, Thomas, Mary Webster, and Rebecca Moulton.—Jonathan and Hannah had Joanna 1687.—Thomas m. Mary Story 1702.—All the above from Boston records. Samuel of Weymouth d. "in his Majesty's service," and his wid. Experience m. Charles Clark before 1700.—Ambrose of Duxbury and his w. Mehitabel had Priscilla 1712, Ebenezer 1714, Gideon 1718.—Ebenezer m. Mary Chandler and had Ambrose 1740, Diana 1741, Gideon 1743.

DICKERMAN.—1. Manasseh Dickerman (from Stoughton) m. a Randall and settled in N. B. and had Samuel,* Benjamin, Daniel, Rebecca; he then m. Thirza D. of Job Bryant 1791, and had Oliver, Lyman, Manasseh, Ruth, Sally, Mary, Thirza, and Roana.—Daniel m. Ruth Tuel 1777.—Rebecca m. Lewis Dalie 1801.

Daniel married Rebecca Smith 1804.—Benjamin married Zibia D. of Cyrus Bryant 1817.—Ebenezer Jr. m. Mercy Stone 1768.—Abigail m. Hezekiah Mehurin 1760.—John of Roxbury m. Lydia Leach 1770.—John m. Keziah Alger 1786.—Nehemiah m. Ruth Clark 1800.—Joanna m. Wendell Sever 1813.—Ruth m. John Guinett 1814.—Polly m. Wm. Badger 1786.—Mary m. Eben. Shaw of Mid'o 1816.—Sally m. Nath'l Shepardson 1817.— Chloe m. Jona. Lathrop 1765.—Wm. Keith m. a Dickerman.

2. Samuel (s. of Manasseh 1. probably) m. Olive D. of Nathan Packard 1799 and had Vesta 1800, Oliver 1802, Abigail 1805, Samuel 1809, Julia Adeline 1814.—Samuel Dickerman m. Clara A. Packard 1822.

DIKE.—1. Samuel Dike (from Ipswich, now Hamilton, a. 1773) settled in N. B. : his w. was a Perkins : he had Samuel, Anthony, John, Nathaniel*, Veren, Mary, Sarah, Anna, and Abigail ; he d. 1800 æ. 79.—Capt. Anthony m. a Pool and went to Plymouth.—John went to Beverly.—Veren went to Southbury, Conn.—Mary m. Job Ames 1782.—Sarah m. Ephraim Noyes 1779.—Anna m. James Loud.

2. Samuel (s. of Samuel 1.) m. Lois D. of Isaac Fuller 1772, and had Lucinda 1773, Salmon 1775, Fuller 1778, Olive 1780, Rebecca 1782, Oliver 1785, Nathaniel 1787, Samuel 1790, ; he

m. a 2d. w. Mehitabel, wid. of Bela Howard and D. of Col. Simeon Cary 1793, and had Bela Cary 1798.—Fuller and Nath'l went to Me.—Olive m. Joseph Shaw 1805.—Rebecca m. a Bisbee.— Oliver m. Sibil D. of Bela Howard 1810 and had Lois Fuller 1812.—Samuel m. Betsy Burrill 1812, and had a s. Samuel, who gra. at B. U. 1838.

DOWNIE.—Walter Downie came from Scotland with his two children, William, and Isabel, about 1735, and settled in N. B. where Howard Cary Esq. lately lived.—William d. 1747 æ. 23, and Isabel m. Barnabas Pratt 1750.—He was so afflicted with the death of his son that he went back to Scotland.—His D. Pratt went to Me. and lived to be 102 years old or more.

DRAKE.—1. Richard Drake and his w. Mary had Rhoda 1770, Parnel 1773, and Mary 1776.

2. Robert Drake and his w. Rebecca had Bethuel 1776.

3. Ebenezer Drake had a son Isaac. These 3 families appear by the records to have lived in Bridgewater.—Sarah Drake m. John Cary 1734.—Francis m. Sarah Hayden 1775.—Ebenezer m. Martha D. of Zachariah Gurney 1781.—Hannah m. Caleb Dunbar 1782.—John m. Molly D. of Ephraim Cole 1782.—Rhoda m. Abiel Alger 1789.—Timothy m. Polly Dunbar 1789.— Polly of E. m. Asaph Hayward 1791.—Elijah 2d. m. Susanna Churchill 1800.—Polly m. Jacob Hearsey 1812.—Lydia m. John Packard 1817.—Reuben m. Olive Cheesman 1819.—Ira m. wid. Mary Pratt 1821.

DUMPHEY.—Elisha Dumphey and his w. Mary had Nathan 1782, Elijah 1785, Azel 1788, Jotham 1790, Elvin 1792.— Jotham m. a D. of John Harden.

DUNBAR.—1. James Dunbar (from Hingham) settled early in W. B., m. Jane D. of Isaac Harris, and had Robert 1689, who d. 1706, and was called "the only surviving son of James Dunbar, who came from Hingham;" the father d. 1690 ; and Jane, the wid. m. Pelatiah Smith.—Robert (of Hingham) his will 1693 : his w. Rose : had John, Joseph, Joshua, Peter, James, (above deceased) Mary, Sarah, and Hannah.—Mary m. Isaac Harris.

2. Peter (s. of Robert above perhaps) came from Hingham a. 1706 and settled in B. : his wife Sarah ; had Josiah 1706, John 1709, David 1711; bought a place of Jacob Leonard 1706; had other children before he came here, viz : Peter, Sarah, Abigail, and perhaps others.—Peter was guardian to John and David, who were called his brothers 1725.—Sarah m. Thomas Alger 1724.—Abigail m. Joshua Fobes 1711, she might have been sister to Peter, and not his D.

3. James (s. of James of Hingham perhaps) m. Experience D. of Samuel Hayward 1721, and had James 1721, Betty 1722, Josiah 1725, Jerusha 1727, Mary 1730, and Jesse 1742.—Betty m. Nathan Kingsley of Easton 1744.—Jerusha m. Nath'l Rickard 1751.—Mary m. Dan Leonard 1750.

4. Elisha (s. of James of Hingham) settled in N. B. ; m.

Mercy D. of Nathaniel Hayward 1727, and had Abigail 1728, Jacob 1730, Lemuel 1731, Elisha 1735, Seth 1737, Nathaniel 1739, Peter 1741, and Silas 1743.—Elisha, the father, d. 1773, æ. 74.—Lemuel was a captain in the French war, and d. 1762, æ. 31.—Abigail m. Andrew Gilmore 1752.—Elisha m. Rebecca Wade 1757, D. of Thomas Wade, and had Keziah 1762, Rebecca 1764, and went to Stoughton.—Seth m. Deborah Belcher 1761, and had Deborah 1766, Rebeckah 1768, Bethiah 1770, Joanna 1772, Seth 1775.—Nathaniel went into the war with his brother Lemuel, was taken prisoner and died —Peter m. Relief D. of Capt Theophilus Curtis 1764, settled in Easton, and had Simeon who m. a Bird and lives in N. B.—Bethiah m. Apollos Randall 1776.

5. Samuel (s. of James of Hingham) m. Melatiah D. of Joseph Hayward, and had Sarah 1733, Mehitabel 1735, Samuel 1737, Melatiah 1741, and Hannah 1743 ; he then married Mary D. of Dea. Thomas Hayward 1745, and had Asa 1745, Robert 1746, Daniel 1748, Peter 1750, Simeon 1752, Barnabas 1756, Thaxter 1758, and Caleb 1760—Sarah m. Elijah Snow 1767.—Mehitabel m. Jonathan Copeland 1754.—Melatiah m. Capt. Jesse Howard 1761.—Hannah m. Daniel Snow Esq. 1764.—Asa gra. H. U. 1767, and settled in the ministry at Salem 1772, and afterwards as a lawyer at Keene N. H. and d. 1788.—Robert m. Betty D. of Jona. Kingman 1770, and had Azel 1774, Oliver 1776, and removed to Belchertown.—Daniel m. Abigail D. of Henry Kingman 1771, and had Asa 1771, and went to George's River, Me.—Thaxter m. Phebe D. of James Alger 1779, and d. young leaving a D. Phebe, who m. David Harvey.—Caleb m. Hannah Drake 1782, and settled in Easton.

6. David (s. of Peter 2.) m. Susanna D. of Thomas Hayward 1738, and d. 1788,and had Susanna 1739, John 1742, David 1746, and Jemima 1747 ; his w. died 1749 ; he then m. Sarah Blake 1749 ; she d. and he then m. Mercy Soul 1763, and had Rhoda 1763, Abel 1767, Mercy 1769, Silvester 1772, and Walter 1775. Susanna m. Samuel Bartlett 1757.—John m. Mary Keith of Easton 1768.—Abel m. Sarah Howard 1784.—The wid. Mercy m. John Fann 1781.—Abel m. Phebe Brett 1805—Walter m. Lydia Rider of Mid'o 1796, and had Elizabeth 1796.

7. James (s. of James 3.) m. Hannah D. of John Benson 1746, and had Seth 1748, Benjamin 1749, Elizabeth 1752, Mary 1754, Benson 1757 ; she d. 1757, and he m. Martha wid. of Jeremiah Conant and D. of Daniel Packard 1757, and had Hannah 1760. Seth (called Seth Jr.) m. Lois Boyden of Walpole 1767.—Elizabeth m. Seth Washburn of Mid'o 1776.—Benjamin m. Wealthy Washburn of Mid'o 1773.—James the father d. 1778.

8. Capt. Josiah (s. of James 3.) and his w. Mary had Hannah 1755, Mary 1757 ; his w. d. 1757, and he m. Silence wid. of Nehemiah Packard and D. of Samuel Edson 1758, and had Josiah 1769 : his w. d., and he m. wid. Abigail Shurtliff 1798, and d. 1800

æ. 75.—Josiah m. Abia Goodspeed 1782.—Mary m. Oliver Packard 1785.
   9. Jesse (s. of James 3.) m. Azubah D. of Jeremiah Conant
1762, and had Susanna 1763, Jeremiah 1764, Martha 1768, Elias
1772, Lydia 1777, Dinah 1780, and Keziah 1782.—Susanna Dunbar m. Caleb Alden of Mid'o 1787.—Elias m. Roxilinia Leach
1799.—Keziah m. Simeon Wood of Boston 1809.
   10. Jacob (s. of Elisha 4.) m. Hannah Randall 1756, and had
Ebenezer 1757, Hannah 1758, Anna 1760, Mercy 1763, Jacob
1768, Lemuel 1771, and Thomas 1773.—The mother d. 1775.—
Lemuel m. Polly Morey 1795 and went to Maine.—Thomas went
to New York.—Jacob the father m. Thankful Thayer 1776.—
Hannah m. Eleazar Snow 1780.
   11. Silas (s. of Elisha 4.) m. Amy D. of Thomas Reynolds
1772, and had Patty 1773, Pamela 1775, Elisha 1777, Amy 1779,
Silas 1780, Reuel 1783, Josiah 1785, Oliver 1788, Thomas 1790,
Joseph 1792, and Perez 1794.—Capt. Silas m. Susanna D. of
Joseph Reynolds 1806, and went to Me.—Reuel m. Nancy D.
of John Willis 1805.—Josiah m. Sibil D. of Mark Perkins 1807,
and had Josiah, Lemuel, Mark, Francis and Daniel.—Thomas
m. Hannah D. of Seth Thayer 1810.—Joseph m. Sophronia D.
of Isaac Allen 1812, and had Sophronia Allen 1812, Matilda Allen 1814, Isaac Allen 1816, Franklin Dunbar 1830, Sibil Perkins
1833.—Perez m. his brother Reuel's wid. 1821.—Patty m. Joseph Reynolds 1798.—Pamela m. Thatcher Ewell 1800.—Amy
m. Levi Ramsdell 1801.—Oliver m. Sally D. of John Willis 1807.
   12. Samuel (s. of Samuel 5.) m. Mary D. of William Snow
1758, and had Elijah 1759, Oliver 1761, Lemuel 1763, Samuel
1765, and Alpheus 1769.—He removed to Mid'o.   Elijah settled
in Keene N. H. as a lawyer.—Samuel went to T. and m. an
Ingell.
   13. Peter (s. of Samuel 5.) m. Alice D. of James Alger 1773,
and settled in S. B., and had Polly 1775, Patty 1777, Shepard
1779, Lemuel 1781, Bethiah 1783, Peter 1785, Silas 1788, Martin 1791, Phebe 1794, William 1796.—Polly m. Marlboro' Conant 1796.—Lemuel m. Cordana D. of Ezra Fobes 1806.—Phebe m. Shepard Fobes 1814.—Shepard m. Abigail Bassett 1806.
Patty m. Calvin Edson 1797.—William m. Eunice Mitchell.—
Bethiah m. Levi H. Perkins 1804.—Martin m. Sally Alger 1812.
   14. Doct. Simeon (s. of Samuel 5.) m. Abigail D. of Rev.
Elijah Packard 1781, and had Sophia 1781, George 1783 went
away, William 1785, Asa 1787, Charles Frederick 1795; 2d. w,
Mary D. of Dr. Richard Perkins, m. 1804, no children.—He d.
1810.—William m. Sarah D. of John Snow 1807, and had Simeon
1808, William 1809, Mary 1811, Abigail 1813, John 1815, Sarah
Ann 1817.—Charles m. Susanna Willis D. of Zebulun 1717 and
had Irene Willis 1820.
   15. Barnabas (s. of Samuel 5.) m. Silence D. of Joseph Alger
1780; she d., and he m. Molly wid. of Daniel Howard and D.
of Edmund Hayward 1784 and had Daniel 1785, Samuel 1786,

Tiley (or Silence) 1788, Lavina 1790, Anna 1792, Dulcinia 1794.
Daniel m. Nicholas Wilbur 1809, and had Louisa 1809, Charles
Howard 1811 Barnabas 1813, Catherine 1815, George 1816—
Samuel m. Betsy D. of Mark Lathrop 1811.—Tiley m. John
Capen 1807.—Lavina m. Elijah Lathrop 1818.—Dulcinia m.
Capt. Parley Keith 1821.
16. Ebenezer (s. of Jacob 10.) m. Rebecca D. of Dea.
Joseph Copeland 1785, and had Martin 1787, Ebenezer 1788, Salmon
1791, Anna 1794, Charles Emanuel 1797, Vesta 1802, Nahum
1806.—Martin m. an Alger.
17. Jacob (s. of Jacob 10.) m. Hannah D. of Joseph Hayward
1794, and had Susanna 1795*, Avice 1797*, Hannah 1797, Olive
1801 ; he then m. Polly D. of Ephraim Willis 1803, and had
Stillman 1805, Jason 1809, Susanna or Sukey, 1803, Samantha
1807, and Polly 1812.—Hannah m. Avery Lathrop 1819.
18. Jesse and his w. Mary had Polly 1766, Molly 1769, Rachel and Sarah 1771, Persis 1773, Lydia 1775*, Lydia 1776, Mehitabel 1778, Cate 1780, Jesse 1782, and Olive 1785.—Rachel
m. David Allen, and Molly m. William Bonny, both at the same
time 1796.—Mehitabel m. Calvin Dunbar.—Olive m. David Harvey Jr. 1803.
19. Hosea Dubar of Halifax m. Jennet Henry (or Hendrey)
1767; and one of his Ds., Betty, m. William Mitchell 1793; and
another, Jennet, m. Allen Latham 1796 and afterwards Zephaniah Howard 1800.—Nanny Dunbar of H. m. Ebenezer Hall
1816.—Amie Dunbar m. Elias Sewall 1776.—Simeon Dunbar
2d. of H. m. Azubah D. of Thomas Pratt 1813.—Polly Dunbar m.
Timothy Drake 1789.—Bethia Dunbar m. Apollos Randall 1796.
Sibil m. Elijah Pratt 1798.—Lese m. Benjamin Ager 1801.—David Dunbar Jr. of Easton m. Harriet Bryant 1801. Samuel 3d.
m. Betsy Lathrop 1811.—Thomas Dunbar m. Hannan Thayer
1810.—Eliab Dunbar m. Lavina Hayford of M. 1793 and had
Chloe 1794, Seth 1796, Cyrus 1798, Betsy 1800, Eliab 1802.—
Sullivan Dunbar of Ab. m. Lydia Harden 1817.—Chloe m. Nahum Benson 1819.
DYER.—1. William Dyer was in Bridgewater 1699, a Sur-
veyor, Juror, and Constable 1708.
2. Christopher m. Sarah D. of Joseph Bassett 1757 and settled in S. B. and had Betty 1759, Sarah 1761, Ruth 1763, Dorothy 1765, Jason 1768, Abigail 1771, Chloe, and Polly ; he d.
1800 æ. 70, she 1805 æ. 71.—Dorothy m. Samuel Battles 1786.
Abigail m. Cyrus Copeland 1692.—Chloe m. Apollos Leach 1796.
3. John (brother of Chistopher) m. Bathsheba Monk 1768;
she d. 1777; he m. Susanna wid. of John Smith 1778; and had
John, Daniel, Celia, Ezekiel.—Ezekiel m. Clarissa D. of Joseph
Leach 1811.
4. Abijah (brother of the above perhaps) m. Rhoda Bolton
1764, and had Martha 1764, Amassa 1767, Abijah 1769, Rhoda
1771, and Olive 1774.—The family went to R. I.
5. John (of E. B.) m. Susanna D. of Jeremiah Thayer 1783,

and had Cynthia 1784, Tabitha 1786, and went to Leeds Me.—
Cynthia m. Benjamin Millett.— Ann Dyer m. Ebenezer Pratt 1717.—Roland Packard m. a
Dyer.—Freelove m. Abraham Packard 1774.—Wid. Mary of
Plymouth m. Nathaniel Brett 1774.—Bela of A. m. Lydia Cush-
ing White 1813.
EATON.—Benjamin Eaton and his w. Arabella had Benja-
min Howard (b. in Boston) 1806, Susanna Buxton 1808, John
Clark Howard 1810, Catherine 1813, Sally 1815.—He d. 1817;
she d. 1832.
EDDY.—1. Obadiah Eddy m. Sarah Lawrence 1750, and had
Mary 1751, Desire 1754, Azor 1759.—He d. 1789, æ. 69.—Mary
m Terry Owen 1776—Azor m. Hannh Fuller 1786.
2. Dea. Morton Eddy (s. of Capt. Joshua of Mid'o) m. Irene
D. of Maj. Isaac Lazell 1821, and settled in S. B.
Ebenezer of Norton m. Martha Leonard 1734.—Abigail of
Hal. m. Benjamin Hathaway 1743.—Joel Eddy joined the ch.
at W. B. 1741, and m. Rachel Force (or Vose) 1741, and went
to Halifax 1743, and had Hannah 1743, bap. at W. B. 1743—
Abigail m. Elisha Hayward 1747.—Jane m..Wm. Pierce of Sci.
1786.—Moses m. Keziah D. of Samuel Keith 1788.
EDSON.—Dea. Samuel Edson and his wife, Susanna Orcutt,
came from Salem. He was one of the first settlers in the town,
and owned the first mill, and probably built it : he d. 1692, æ. 80.
she 1699, æ. 81. He had Samuel, Joseph, Josiah, Susanna,
Elizabeth, Mary, Sarah, Bethiah. Susanna m. the Rev. James
Keith.—Elizabeth m. Richard Phillips of Weymouth.—Mary
m. Nicholas Byram Jr. 1676.—Sarah m. John Dean of Taunton
1663.—Bethiah m. Ezra Dean of Taunton 1678.—Benjamin Edson, who m. Sarah Hoskins at Plymouth 1660, was his son perhaps.
2. Samuel (son of Dea. Samuel 1.) m. Susanna, D. of Nicholas Byram : he d. 1719, she 1742 ; he had Susanna 1679, Elizabeth 1684, Samuel 1690. Susanna m. first John Hayward Jr.
and afterwards Elihu Brett Jr.—Elizabeth m. Samuel Packard
1705.
3. Joseph ; (s. of Samuel 1.); his first wife Experience: he
had Experience 1685 : 2d w. Mary m. 1686 : his estate was settled 1712: his children mentioned were Joseph, Josiah 1682,
Benjamin, Samuel 1687, by Mary 2d w. probably, Timothy,
Mary, Susanna.—Mary m. John Lathrop 1716.—Susanna m.
Solomon Johnson 1723.
4. Josiah Esq. (s. of Samuel 1.) m. Elizabeth, D. probably of
Nathaniel Hayward. They both d. 1734 : he æ. 83, she æ. 84 :
they left no children. His will proved 1734 ; Capt. Josiah Edson
Exor., Rev. John Angier and Joseph Pratt Trustees. He had a
large estate, and gave lands to the Town and to the South Parish,
where he lived, for the maintenance of schools, commonly called
the *school lands*: he made his nephew Capt. Josiah Edson, son of
his brother Joseph, his principal devisee, on whom also he

bestowed most of his estate before his death, viz., in 1704 : his nephew to maintain him and his wife during life.

5. Samuel (s. of Samuel 2.) and his wife Mary had Susanna 1708, Bethiah 1710, Mary 1712, Samuel 1714, Nathan 1716, Abel 1718, Obed 1720, Elizabeth 1722, Sarah 1724, Silence 1726, Ebenezer 1727, John 1729, Ezra 1730. The father d. 1771 : his will proved 1772. He gave the Church lands 1747 : the mother d. 1770. Mary m. Geo. Packard 1728.—Elizabeth m. Benanuel Leach 1745.—Silence m. Nehemiah Packard 1747.—Sarah m. John Cooper 1749.—Ebenezer m. Jane Griffin 1749, and wid. Hannah Leach 1758.—Susanna m. perhaps Samuel Hayward 1736.

6. Dea. Joseph, (s. of Joseph 3.) settled in E. B., and m. Lydia, D. of Francis Cary, 1704, and had Hannah 1709, Lydia 1711, Joseph 1712, Bethiah 1715, John 1717, Daniel 1720, David 1722, Jesse 1724, James 1726. She d. 1762, he 1768.—Hannah, (or Hannah, D. of Timothy 10.) m. Micah Allen 1737, and afterwards Thomas Phillips 1747.—Bethiah m. Jonathan Whitman 1753.—John m. Mary, D. of Matthew Gannett, 1744.

7. Captain Josiah (s. of Joseph 3.) settled in S. B., and had most of the estate of his uncle Josiah : was a Deacon, and often Representative of the town : m. Sarah, D. of Zaccheus Packard, 1704 : she d. 1754 ; he d. 1763, æ. 80: had Sarah 1705, Abiah 1706, Josiah Jan. 24, 1709 ; Huldah 1713, Abiezer 1715, Freelove 1718, Elijah 1720. Sarah m. Elisha Pierce of Scituate 1731, and had one D., Sarah, who m. a Holbrook, and afterwards a Park.—Huldah m. Hezekiah Hayward 1738.—Freelove m. Josiah Fobes 1740.—Abiah m. Samuel Alden a. 1728.

8. Benjamin (s. of Joseph 3.) m. Joanna, D. of William Orcutt, 1755, and d. 1758. He settled in N. B.; had Benjamin 1715, Nathan 1718, Peter 1720, Jacob 1722, William 1724, Seth 1726, Ichabod 1728, Ebenezer 1730, Joanna 1733, Abigail 1736. His will proved 1758, dated 1753, does not mention Nathan, Peter, Jacob, or Ichabod. Joanna m. Isaac Perkins 1754.—Abigail m. Josiah Perkins 1755.—Benjamin m. Ann Thayer 1739 ; m. at A.; and had one son Jacob, who m. Betty Packard 1759, and both removed to Pelham. Jacob's children born here were Benjamin 1759, Anna 1761, Betty 1764, Jacob 1765, Abiel 1768, Simeon 1770, Sarah 1772, Eurene 1775, Levi 1778. Nathan and Jacob probably d. young.—Seth settled in Stafford.—Abigail (perhaps Abiel above) m. Bezaliel Flagg of Petersham 1786.— Peter m. Sarah Southworth 1745, and had no children : his will dated 1750.

9. Samuel (s. of Joseph 3.) m. Mehitabel, D. of Dea. Nathl. Brett, 1721, and lived in E. B.; had Samuel 1722, Nathaniel 1728: she d. 1736, and he m. Mehitabel, D. of Joseph Hayward, 1738 : he d. 1750, she 1776. Samuel d. 1800 a bachelor.

10. Timothy (s. of Joseph 3.) m. Mary, D. of Joseph Alden, 1719, and lived in E. B.; had Hannah 1720, Timothy 1722, Anna, Abijah 1725, Jona. 1728, Mary 1730. Hannah (see Hannah

D. of Deacon Joseph 6.)—Abijah m. Susanna, D. of James Snow, 1747, and had Abijah 1748.—Mary m. James Snow Jr. 1758. This family all went to Stafford, and she d. there æ. 80, and Jonathan was in Ashfield 1770.—Timothy Jr. had 2 children, John and Huldah, b. here 1746 and 1748, and both d. in infancy.

11. Samuel (s. of Samuel 5.) m. Martha, D. of Nathan Perkins, 1738; had Martha 1740, Samuel 1742, Eunice, Lois, Jonah 1751, Betty, Sarah, Noah 1756, Huldah, Zilphah. Martha m. Daniel Carr 1770.—Eunice m. John Chamberlin of Westmoreland 1766.—Lois m. Jacob Staples Jr. of Taunton 1765.—Betty m. Rodolphus Borden of Middleborough 1774. (See Abel 13.)—Sarah m. Timothy Richards 1778.—Huldah m. Thomas Pope 1782.—Zilphah m. Daniel Willis Jr. 1778.—Jonah removed to Westmoreland.

12. Nathan (s. of Samuel 5.) m. Mary, D. of Jona. Sprague, 1738.—Mary Edson m. Joseph Pettingill 1745.

13. Abel (s. of Samuel 5.) m. Margaret, D. of Nathl. Conant; had Rachel 1744, Abel 1750, Levi 1754, Dan and Elizabeth 1756, Keziah 1758, Rufus 1765. Abel m. Betty, D. of William Trask, 1771.—Levi m. Sarah Hayward of Raynham 1774, and d. of small pox 1777.—Elizabeth m. Rodolphus Borden 1774. (See Samuel 11.)—Rufus m. Mary Cole of Mid'o. 1783.

14. Obed, (s. of Samuel 5.) and his wife Keturah, had Jesse 1744, Obed 1747, Lewis 1748: she d. 1750, and he m. a 2d wife, Martha, and had Keturah 1751, Thomas 1753, Lydia 1754, Silence 1756, Isaac 1758.—Jesse m. Susanna Hayward 1768, and had Caleb 1769*, and Hannah 1770.—Lewis m. Hepzibah Washburn 1770.

15. John (s. of Samuel 5.) m. Hannah, D. of Benjamin Allen, 1751; had John 1752, Benjamin 1754, Nehemiah 1758. John m. Tabitha Keen 1784.—Nehemiah m. Olive Perkins 1783, and both went to Vt.—The wid. Hannah m. Job Packard 1790.

16. Ezra (s. of Samuel 5.) m. Rebeckah, D. of David Johnson, 1756, and had Robert 1757, Ezra 1759, Molly 1760, Rebecca 1762, Vina 1765, Libeus 1769, Ebenezer, Hannah, Cyrus, Sarah. Robert m. Molly, D. of Josiah Hayward, 1782.—Ezra m. Sena Perkins 1782.—Molly m. Robert Wade 1780.—Rebecca m. Amos Fisher of Vt. 1787. (See Ebenezer 26.)—Vina m. Capt. Ephraim Sprague 1783.—Libeus m. Joanna Keen 1793, and had Ezra and Charles.—Hannah m. Simeon Packard 1796.—Cyrus m. Hannah Hudson 1797.—Sarah m. Jeremiah Washburn 1801.—Cyrus and Zidon live in Shrewsbury, Vt.—Ezra m. Anna White of Marshfield 1781.—Ezra Edson, s. of Libeus, m. Eliza Wentworth 1819.

17. Joseph (s. of Deacon Joseph 6.) m. Abigail Forrest 1739; had Daniel 1741, Mary, John 1748. The mother d. 1775.—Daniel had Isaiah and Reuben, twins (born 1769) by his w. Olive, D. of Isaac Fuller, m. 1765. He sold his farm, 45 acres, to Josiah Allen 1773, where Allen lived and died.

18. Dea. David (s. of Dea. Joseph 6.) m. Susanna, D. of Mat-
20

thew Gannett, 1746 ; had Susanna 1748, Mehitabel 1753, Huldah 1755. The mother d. 1755: he then m. Sarah, wid. of Peter Edson: she was a Southworth, and had David 1759. The father d. 1795, æ. 73. Susanna m. Joshua Beals of Windsor 1768.— Mehitabel m. Benja. Clark of Athol 1775.—Huldah m. Benja. Death of Montague.

19. Jesse (s. of Dea. Joseph 6.) m. Lydia Packard 1754, (wid. perhaps of Robert Packard: she was a Titus) and had Joseph 1755, John 1760: his w. died, and he then m. Rebecca Belcher 1764, and had Rebecca 1770. Rebecca m. Ezekiel Reed 1794. The estate divided 1784.—Jno. Edson 3d m. Susanna Orcutt 1785.

20. James (s. of Dea. Joseph 6.) m. Esther, D. of Josiah Allen, 1749, and had Josiah 1753, Barnabas 1757: she d. 1794; he 1808, æ. 82. Barnabas d. in the army young.—James Edson m. wid. Elizabeth Washburn 1796.

21. Col. Josiah (s. of Capt, Josiah 7.) gra. H. U. 1730; an amiable man, and very popular till the revolutionary troubles commenced, when being on the side of government, one of the 19 Rescinders so called, and a Mandamus Counsellor, he became a Refugee, and died very soon after on Long Island. The three Josiah Edsons commonly called in aftertimes "Old Justice Edson, Old Capt. Edson, and Old Col. Edson," were all distinguished men both in Church and State. They all represented the Town in succession, and sustained most of the public offices in the Town, and were deservedly highly esteemed and popular men. Col. Edson engaged in none of the learned professions, but was an agriculturalist, and hence Mrs. Warren in her Group designated him under the appellation of Crusty Crowbar.— He m. Ruth, D. of Joseph Bailey of Scituate, and sister of Capt. Adams Bailey, 1737; and had Josiah 1738, Ruth 1741: his wife d. 1743, and he then m. Mary, D. of Judge Daniel Parker of Barnstable, and sister of the Rev. Jonathan Parker of Plympton, where she was m. 1746, and had Mary 1749.—He must have had a 3d w. Abigail Dean, m. 1755.—Mary m. Doct. Jonathan Crane 1770.

22. Abiezer (s. of Capt. Josiah 7.) m. Sarah, D. of Samuel Lathrop, 1737: she d. and he m. Jael Bennett of Mid'o. 1740, and had Abiezer: she d. and he then m. Mary, D. of Samuel Packard, 1744, and had Abiel, Adam, Rodolphus, Pollycarpus 1756, Jael: he afterwards m. wid. Catharine Earl of Taunton 1781: she had before m. Dr. Lunt: her maiden name, Williams. Adam went to Albany, m. Mercy Hazard, and had Henry, George, and Eliza.—Abiezer went to Charlemont, and had one son.—Jael, a physician in Albany, never m.—Rodolphus m. Lydia Crane of Berkley 1780, and went to Oxford, and had Ephraim, Betsy, and Bradford, and d. 1833.

23. Dr. Elijah (s. of Capt. Josiah 7.) m. Anne, D. of Samuel Packard, 1741; had Elijah, Calvin, Daniel, Hosea, Caleb, Silvester, Ann, Olive, Susanna, Ruth. He died 1761, and she m. Jonathan Wood 1771. Elijah Edson m. Nancy Clark of Ply-

mouth 1818.—Eli Edson d. 1762.—Calvin Edson's wife d. 1778.—
Elijah Edson m. Martha Washburn 1766, and went to N. Braintree.—Olive m. Salmon Rickard 1786.—Calvin m. Lydia, D. of
Lot Conant, 1766, and went to Oakham. His D. Lydia m.
Thomas Conant 1789.
24. William (s. of Benjamin 8.) m. Martha, D. of Robert
Howard, 1754; had Keziah 1755, Seth 1761, Martha 1763, Abigail 1765, William 1767, Jennet 1769. He d. 1800, æ. 75.—Keziah m. a Harkness.—Martha m. Phillip Packard 1786.—Abigail
m. John Harris 1787.—Jennet m. Seth Kingman 1811.
25. Ichabod (s. of Benjamin 8.) m. Jemima, D. of Dea. James
Packard, 1759; had Relief 1761, Joanna 1765. He d. 1811, æ.
83. Relief m. Oliver Packard 1777.—Joanna m. Thomas
Packard 1788.
26. Ebenezer (s. of Benjamin 8.) m. Lucy, D. of Seth Packard, 1751 ; had Nathan 1753, Ebenezer 1755, Lucy 1757, Levina
1760, Peter, Zibia. Nathan m. Susanna, D. of Ephraim Allen,
1778. Ebenezer m. Mary Warren 1790, and they both went to
Rehoboth.—Lucy m. Alexander Thayer of Braintree 1788.—
Levina m. a Perkins.—Peter d. young in the army.—Zibia m.
Timo. West 1787.—Peter Edson m. Rebecca Manly 1784.—Rebecca m. Amos Fisher of Vt. 1787. (See Ezra 16.)
27. Dea. Nathaniel (s. of Samuel 9.) m. Joanna, D. of David
Snow, 1759, and had Mehitabel 1761, Joel 1763, Eunice 1765,
Joanna 1767, Lydia 1771, Nathaniel 1777. The father d. 1784,
æ. 56; she 1802, æ. 67.—Eunice m. Richard Thayer 1786.
28. Samuel (s. of Samuel 11.) m. Anna Hall of Raynham
1767, and had Abigail 1768, Chloe 1770, Anna 1772, Samuel
1775, Jane 1778, Alexander 1781, Oliver 1784, Hosea 1789.
Abigail Edson m. Azariah Willis of Oakham 1787.—Anna m.
John Winnett 1798.—Samuel 3d m. Hannah Ripley of Easton
1797.—Samuel m. Polly Barnes 1801.
29. Dea. Noah (s. of Samuel 11.) m. Elizabeth Rickard 1782;
had Zoroaster 1784, name now changed to Henry : she d., and
he then m. Mary, D. of Ebenezer Willis of Mid'o, 1787, and had
Eliphalet 1788, Noah 1790, Jonah 1792, Elijah 1794, Ephraim
1796, Jacob 1799. The mother d., and he then m. Keziah, D.
of Capt. Eliakim Howard, 1802, and had Simeon Howard 1804,
and Elizabeth Rickard 1808.—Zoroaster (now Henry) m. Betsy
Niles Little of Marshfield 1812.—Eliphalet m. Polly L. Johnson
1810.—Noah m. Huldah Kingman 1814, and lived in Hadley.—
Jonah m. Jennet Bryant 1819.—Elijah m. Nancy Clark of Plymouth 1818.—Simeon H. m. Alice Bryant 1833.
30. Benjamin (s. of John 15.) m. Deborah, D. of Thos. Perkins, 1782 ; had Hannah, John, Allen, Theodore ; he d. 1835.—
Hannah m. Increase Robinson 1812.—John m. a Bass of Quincy.—Allen m. Minerva Perkins 1815.—Theodore gra. H. U.
1822, m. Rebecca Jane, D. of Bishop Parker of Boston, and is
an Episcopal Clergyman in Lowell.
31. John (s. of Joseph 17.) m. Judith, D. of Dea. Zechariah

Shaw, 1770, and had Isaac 1770, Martha, Mary 1772, Sarah 1776, Ruth 1778, Isaiah 1781, Silvia 1783, Hannah 1784, Jacob 1786, Nehemiah Shaw 1789, Joseph 1792. Mary m. John Bisbee 1817.

32. Dea. David (s. of Dea. David 18.) m. Lydia Shaw, and had Hannah, Jonathan 1785 : he m. Lydia Bassett of Norton 1786, and had David 1789, Sarah 1791, Lydia 1793, Mehitabel 1795, Polly, Eliza, Rebecca.—Hannah m. John Smith of Canton 1805.—Sarah m. John Burrell Jr. 1816.—Polly m. Daniel Burrell 1817, both of Abington.

33. Joseph (s. of Jesse 19.) m. Mary Vinal of Scituate 1785, and had Jesse 1787, Sally 1791 : he d. 1791, she 1807. Sally m. Benjamin Keith 1811.

34. John (s. of Jesse 19.) m. Susanna, D. of Nathan Orcutt, 1785 ; their children, Fanny 1785, Orcutt 1787, Packard 1789, Osander 1792, Oris 1794, Oza 1797.

35. Josiah (s. of James 20.) m. Reliance, D. of Isaac Fuller, 1777 ; had Zilphah 1778, Susanna 1780, Sarah 1783, Barnabas 1786, Esther 1788, Reliance 1792, Olive 1795 : he d. 1820, æ. 67.—Zilphah m. Eliphalet Kingman 1801.—Susanna m. Israel Packard 1801.—Sarah m. Ira Hayward 1806.—Esther m. Ambrose Kingman of Reading 1810.—Reliance m. Joel Ames 1818.—Barnabas m. Betsy, D. of Zechariah Gurney 1815.—Olive m. Jacob Noyes 1818.

36. Capt. Josiah (s. of Col. Josiah 21.) m. Hannah, D. of Thomas Lawrence, 1760; had Caleb 1761, Josiah 1766. The father d. 1779, and she m. Maj. Eliphalet Cary 1782. Caleb m. Sally Dean of Taunton 1783.—Josiah m. Hannah Richards 1791.—Josiah m. Clarana C. Osborn 1820.

37. Capt. Pollycarpus (s. of Abiezer 22.) m. Lucy Eaton of Mid'o., and had Charles*, Sarah, Royal, Charlotte, Lucy : he d. 1796, she 1816. One D. m. Zechariah Eddy Esq., and one m. a Pratt.

38. Abiel (s. of Abiezer 22.) m. Hannah, D. of John Morton of Mid'o., 1774, where he settled, and had Abiel, Cyrus, Oliver, Mary, John, James, Daniel, Josiah, and Abiezer. He d. 1823, æ. a. 70.

39. Seth (s. of William 24.) m. Theodora Howard of Braintree 1784, had Sally 1787, Jacob 1789, Robert 1790, Polly 1794, Nancy 1796, Galen 1800, Phebe 1802, Melinda 1804. Sally m. Nathl. Shepardson of Dedham 1808.—Jacob removed to Dorchester.—Robert removed to Dedham.—Nancy m. Nathl. Shepardson of Dedham 1815.

40. William (s. of William 24.) m. Mary Randall 1790, and had David, Amzi, Milly, Ruby, Abigail, Abi, Patty, Mary, Mehitabel.—He m. Hannah, wid. of Zadock Perkins and D. of Abiah Packard, 1812, for a 2d wife.—Milly m. Hosea Alden of Abington 1817—Ruby m. Sam'l Spear of Randolph 1814.—Abigail m. Eben. Crocker of Easton 1816.—Abi m. Cyrus Howard.

41. Joel (s. of Dea. Nath'l 27.) m. Hannah, D. of Solomon

Packard 1789 ; had Albert 1789, Ard 1792, Pliny 1795.—
The mother d. 1818, æ. 56, and he m. Lurania Jones of Pembroke 1820 : he d. 1830, æ. 67.—Albert m. Abigail, D.
of Uriah Brett, 1817: she d. 1829, æ. 36.—Pliny m. Lucy Reed 1819.
42. Nathaniel (s. of Dea. Nathl. 27.) m. Betsy, D.
of Thomas Hayward, 1802 ; had Nathaniel 1805, Elizabeth Hayward 1807,
Cornelius Warren 1809, Joanna 1811, Newton 1814, Fidelia
1817, Horatio 1820.
43. Jesse (s. of Joseph 34.) m. Anne, D. of Josiah Williams,
1811 ; had Stillman Williams 1811, Alanson Sumner 1813,
George Francis 1816.
Joseph m. Bathsheba Proctor of Boston 1776.—Sarah m. Solo.
Perkins 1760.—Bathsheba m. John Carver 1762.—Olive m. Azel
Keith 1767.—Susanna m. Gershom Richmond 1773.—Alfred m.
Eunice Snow 1796.—Calvin m. Patty Dunbar 1797.—Ebenezer
m. Kezia Colwell 1797.—Orphah m. Marshall Harvey 1785.—
Albertus Edson of Grafton, Vt., m. Sally Colwell 1804.—Mary
Edson (or Etson) m. Capt. John Warner of Westport 1821.—
Sally Edson m. Jeremiah Washburn 1801.
EGERTON.—1. Dennis Egerton, and his wife Experience
lived in E. B ; he d. a. 1834 ; he had Hannah, John, Rebecca,
Experience, James, Hezekiah, Miriam, and Dennis.
2. John (s. of Dennis 1.) born 1721 ; m. Abigail D. of James
Snow, and had Ruth 1747, John 1750, Joseph 1756*, d. in the
army, Abigail 1760, Benjamin 1763, and Hannah 1765.—The
father d. 1779 æ. 58; his wid. m. Jona. Beal 1780.—Ruth m.
Nehemiah Washburn 1770, and removed to Williamsburgh.—
John and Benjamin removed to Shirley.—Hannah m. Samuel
Whitman and removed to Cummington.
3. Hezekiah (s. of Dennis 1.) m. Mary Hegebone (or Hitch
born) 1754, and had Molly 1755, Sarah 1757, Alice 1772, Han-
nah, Eunice and Jennet, b. probably at Nova Scotia where he
lived between 1757 and 1772, and whither he finally returned.—
He had no sons.—Molly m. John Willis 1781.—Sarah m. a Graves.
Hannah m. Wm. Robinson 1780.—Eunice m. Ephraim Willis
1779.—Jennet and Alice m. at Nova Scotia.
ERSKIN.—Christopher Erskin (from Ireland) m. Susanna
D. of Gaius Robinson 1729, and had Mary 1730, John 1732,
Christopher 1734, and Jeremiah 1736.—John had John 1752,
Elizabeth 1755, Christopher 1758, and James 1761.—Robert
Erskin had a D. Elizabeth in E. B. 1733.—These families finally
settled in Abington.
FAXON.—Elisha Faxon (from Braintree) lived in E. B. and
had Elisha, Samuel, Allen, Benjamin, and William.—Capt. Elisha
settled in Halifax.—Samuel m. Priscilla, sister of James Thomas
Esq. 1783, and had Charles, Luther, Piscilla and others, and went
to R. I.—Benjamin m. Ruth D. of Seth Bryant of Hal. and lived
and d. in Boston ; his w. d. in E. B. 1788 æ. 19.—Thomas Gannett's wid. Sarah m. a Faxon a. 1656.—Sarah m. Stephen Washburn 1770.—Lydia m. Benjamin Richards a. 1722.

FEARING.—Dr. Noah Fearing (s. of Gen. Israel Fearing of Wareham) gra. H. U. 1791, settled in S. B., and married Anne D. of Maj. Isaac Lazell 1799, and had Jane B. L. who married John Fuller of Boston 1819, Thomas, and George.—He d. and the wid. and children removed to Boston. This family is descended from John Fearing, who arrived at Hingham in 1638 from Cambridge in England.

FIELD.—1. John Field (from Providence) settled in W. B. a. 1677; his estate settled 1698; no widow mentioned: he had John 1671, Elizabeth 1673, Richard 1677, Lydia 1679, Daniel 1681, Ruth 1683 and Hannah.—Elizabeth m. Clement Briggs of Easton 1697.—Lydia m. Thomas Manly 1701.

2. Capt. John (s. of John 1.) m. Elizabeth D. of John Ames 1697, and had Elizabeth 1698, Sarah 1700, Susanna 1702, John 1704.—Sarah m. Jonathan Howard 1719.—Susanna m. Joseph Keith 1721.—Capt. John returned to Providence and was there 1749.

3. Richard (s. of John 1.) m. Susanna Waldo a. 1704, and had Zebulun 1707, Mary 1709, Richard 1711, Jabez 1713, Ruth 1715, Zobiah 1719, Mercy 1723, and Susanna 1725.—He d. 1725.— Zebulun m. Anna Williams and was in Taunton in 1749.—Ruth m. Israel Packard Jr. 1737.—Mercy m. Archibald Robinson 1747.—Susanna m. Nathan Hartwell 1746. Mary Field m. Samuel Noyes 1748.

4. Daniel (s. of John 1.) m. Sarah D. of John Ames 1706, and had Mehitabel 1706, Hannah 1709, Daniel 1712, Job 1714, Sarah 1718, Joseph, Abigail, and Susanna.—Mehitabel m. Edward Manton 1733.—Hannah m. Charles (or John) Beswick 1734. Abigail made her will and d. single 1750.—Susanna m. Israel Packard 1735.

5. John (s. of John 2.) m. Mary D. of Ephraim Howard 1726, and had John 1727, and James 1729.—He d. and the wid. settled his estate 1729; she afterwards m. Elisha Pierce of Scituate.

6. Jabez (s. of Richard 3.) m. Mary D. of Ephraim Fobes 1746, and had Jabez Fobes 1747, Susanna 1748, Richard 1751, William 1753, Ephraim 1755, Daniel 1758, Barzillai 1760, Bethuel 1763, and Waldo; he d. 1804, æ. 92.—Susanna m. Moses Cary 1773—Fobes and Bethuel lived single.—Waldo went to the westward.

7. Daniel (s. of Daniel 4.) m. Susanna Thayer 1733, and had Rachel, Anna, and Susanna.—He was a physician; made his will in 1757, and went into the French war, and d. probably at Crown Point.—Anna m. Eleazar Hill 1769.—Susanna m. Capt. Jesse Perkins 1769.

8. Joseph (s. of Daniel 4.) m. Rachel Pray 1748, and had John 1750, Abigail 1752, and Joseph 1753; his will and death 1754. Abigail m. Elkanah Palmer 1776.

9. John (s. of John 5.) m. Hannah Blackman 1760, and had Solomon 1760, and Bezaliel 1761.—John Field's w. d. 1757, first w. perhaps.

10. Richard (s. of Jabez 6.) m. Rebecca D. of Seth Harris a. 1778, and Polly 1779, Sally 1780, Belinda 1782, Cyrus 1784, Lois 1786, Susanna 1788, Zeruiah 1790, Hannah 1795, Eliza 1797, Rebecca 1800.—This family removed to Claremont N. H.

11. William (s. of Jabez 6.) m. Jemima D. of Levi Keith 1797, and had Ozias 1798, Jabez 1800, Zilpha, and Serena.—Widow Jemima d. 1839 æ. 72.

12. Ephraim (s. of Jabez 6.) m. Ruby D. of Simeon Brett, and had Mehitabel 1787, Galen 1788, Ansel 1790, Charlotte 1793, Jenny 1794, and Zibeon 1795.—This family removed to Paris Me.—Alson Field m. Orra Ripley 1820.

13. Daniel (s. of Jabez 6.) m. Hannah D. of Capt. Zebedee Snell 1786, and had Martha 1786, Zophar 1789, Waldo 1791.— Martha m. Gustavus Silvester 1811.—Zophar m. Bernice D. of Oliver Howard 1811.—Waldo m. Abigail Marshall 1816, and afterwards Sally D. of Mark Perkins 1820.

14. Barzillai (s. of Jabez 6.) m. Patty D. of David Packard 1794, and had John 1796, Chloe 1799, Mary 1802, Clarissa 1806, Lucius 1810.—He d. 1839 æ. 78.—John m. Olive D. of James Thompson.—Mary m. Zibeon Cole 1819.

15. Amassa Field (from Quincy) m. Clarissa D. of Simeon Gannett 1813, settled in E. B. and had Edward Gannett and others probably.—Capt. Edward Field d. there 1832 æ. 38.

FILLEBROWN.—James Fillebrown of W. B. and his wife Matilda had Luther Williams 1797, Jerusha 1799, Rodolphus Howard 1802, John 1804, James 1806.

FITZGERALD.—Michael Fitzgerald m. Margaret Matteson 1771, and had William 1772, and Thomas 1774.

FLINN.—Thomas Flinn and his wife Sarah, had Christopher 1764.—Christopher m. wid. Susanna Harlow 1806.

FOBES.—1. John Fobes (from Duxbury) was one of the original proprietors of Bridgewater, where he settled, and d. a. 1661; made his nuncupative will before William Brett and Arthur Harris ; his wid. Constant, sister of Experience Mitchell, m. John Briggs of Portsmouth R. I. 1662.—he had John, Edward, Mary, Caleb, William, Joshua, and Elizabeth.—John d. at George Allen's in Sandwich 1661.—William m. Elizabeth D. of Constant Southworth a. 1667, and settled finally at Little Compton, and was with Capt. Church in Phillip's war.—Joshua fell with Capt. Michael Pierce of Scituate in that disastrous battle with the Indians near Attleboro', in 1676.—Caleb went to Norwich.

2. Dea. Edward (s. of John 1.) m. Elizabeth D. of John Howard, and had Elizabeth 1677, John 1679, Mary 1681, Bethiah 1683, Hannah 1686, Ephraim 1688, Joshua 1689, Benjamin 1692, and William 1698.—Edward the father, d. a. 1732.—Elizabeth m. Joseph Keith.—Mary never m.—Bethiah m. Samuel Keith 1703. Hannah m. Timo. Keith, 1710.

3. John (s. of Edward 2.) m. Abigail Robinson 1704, and had Mary 1705, Edward 1707, Abigail 1709, Sarah 1711, John 1714, Josiah 1716, Nathan 1719, Silence 1722.—He d. a. 1725; she m.

160   FOBES.

Daniel Hudson 1739, and d. 1762.—Mary m. Daniel Hudson Jr.
1726.—Edward d. 1736.—Abigail m. Josiah Snell 1728.—Sarah
m. William Hudson 1737.—Nathan left no children.—Silence
m. Levi Chase of Sandwich 1771 who went to N. Y.
  4. Ephraim (s. of Edward 2.) m. Martha Snell 1714, and
had Ephraim 1716, Mercy 1722, Bethiah 1725, Martha 1728,
and Hannah 1731.—He d. 1755, she 1750.—Mary m. Jabez Field
1746.—Bethiah (or Betty) m. Edmund Soper 1754.—Martha m.
Jonathan Snell 1751.—Hannah m. Josiah Williams 1751.
  5. Joshua (s. of Edward 2.) m. Abigail D. of Peter Dunbar
1711, and had Bethiah 1712*, Hannah 1713, Joshua 1715, Mary
1717, Leah 1720, Betty 1724, and Abigail 1728.—He. m. perhaps Mercy Churchill of Plymton for a 2d. w. 1754.—He died
1767.—Mary m. Robert Washburn 1739.—Leah married Israel
Washburn 1740.—Abigail m. Daniel Snow of Tit. 1753.
  6. Benjamin (s. of Edward 2.) m. Martha Hunt 1721, and
went to Easton, and had Joseph, and Benjamin.—Jesse was son
of Benjamin Jr., and Abner was half brother of Jesse, and m.
Polly Ford 1791, and went westward.—Joseph Fobes of Easton
m. Olive Hayward 1780.—Anne Fobes of Easton m. Abijah
Packard 1767.—Jesse m. wid. Susanna Angier 1792.
  7. William (s. of Edward 2.) m. Thankful D. of John Dwelly
of Scituate 1725; she was b. 1706; they had Abner 1727, Lu-
cie 1732, (bap. Lusanna) William 1735, Edward 1738, Timothy
1740, Mercy 1744, and Mary 1746.—He d. 1764; she 1776.—
Lusanna m. Seth Williams 1750.—Mercy m. John Howard 2d.
1768.—William m. Hannah D. of Dea. Isaac Willis.—Edward
m. Orpha Leach 1761, and had John 1761, and Silvester 1764.
  8. John (s. of John 3.) m. Martha Pierce of Scituate 1738,
had Edward 1739, Martha 1741, and Libeus 1743.—He d. 1783;
she 1795, æ. 82.—Edward went to Lake Champlain.—Martha
m. Eliab Hayward 1762.
  9. Josiah (s. of John 3.) m. Freelove D. of Capt. Josiah Edson 1739, and had Josiah 1740, Perez 1742. Jason 1745, Abigail
1747, Silvia 1749, Ezra 1751, Freelove 1754, Alpheus 1756, Joseph and John 1758, and Nathan 1761.—The father d. 1794, æ.
78; she d. æ. 93.—Abigail m. Gideon Shaw of Raynham 1767.—
Silvia m. Abraham Gushe of Raynham 1773.—Nathan was a
physician and m. a Soule of Plymton and d. leaving a D. who
is also d.—Josiah Jr. m. Sarah D. of Joseph Pryor 1766, and d.
young, and she then m. John Eaton of Mid'o 1780, and afterwards Joseph Bassett 1798, and d. 1839 æ. 100.
  10. Ephraim (s. of Ephraim 4.) m. Susanna D. of Thomas
Willis, and had Eliab 1739, Silence 1745, Abigail 1746, Ephraim
1748, Thomas 1750, Susanna 1757, Lemuel 1761, Caleb 1773;
he d. 1802 æ. 85.—Silence m. Nath'l Conant 1772.—Abigail m.
John Morey of Norton 1776.—Susanna m. Wm. Morey 1780.—
Lemuel never m.
  11. Joshua (s. of Joshua 5.) m. Esther D. of Nicholas Porter
of Abington 1740, and had Azariah 1741*, Daniel 1742, Ruth

1744, Abigail 1747, Joshua 1749, Caleb 1750, Robert 1753, and Solomon 1756.—Ruth m. Ebenezer Alden of Mid'o 1763.—Abigail m. Joseph Cowen 1772.—Solomon had Laban, Martin and others.—Laban m. Hannah Richmond 1816, and remained here, the rest moved away.—Caleb m. Susanna D. of Ebenezer Keith 1776, and went to Lyme, Con.

12. Abner (s. of William 7.) m. Phebe D. of Benj. Leach, and had Absalom 1751, Hannah 1753, Edward 1755, Jotham 1758, and Molly 1761.—Absalom lived in Uxbridge and d. in the revolutionary war, and Judge Abner Fobes of Windsor Vt. is his son. Hannah m. Levi Leach 1771.—Edward went to Buckland.—Jotham went to the Genessee and his mother d. there.—Charles s. of Judge Abner, lives in Louisville Kentucky.

13. Timothy (s. of William 7.) m. Mary D. of William Dean of Mansfield, and had William 1767, Avery 1770, Dwelly 1774*, killed at the raising of the Baptist metting house, and Timothy 1783.—The father D. 1803; the mother 1814.

14. Libeus (s. of John 8.) m. Mehitabel D. of Ebenezer Howard 1775, and had Libeus and Mehitabel.—Libeus m. Mary D. of Benjamin Leach 1807.—Mehitabel m. a Leonard of Easton and went to Vermont.

15. Rev. Perez L. L. D. (s. of Josiah 9.) gra. H. U. 1762; m. Prudence D. of Rev. Samuel Wales of Raynham, and settled in the ministry at Raynham, and d. 1812 æ.70; he had 2 ss. who d. young, and 2 Ds. Anonima, who m. the Rev. Simeon Doggett, and Polly who m. Rev. Elijah Leonard of Marshfield.

16. Jason (s. of Josiah 9.) m. Leah D. of Israel Washburn Esq. of Raynham, and had Selina 1771, Philander 1773, Molly 1775, Salmon 1781, Davis 1783, Clarissa 1785, Shepard 1787, and Laura 1792.—Selina m. Andrew Alden 1797.—Philander went to Albany.—Molly m. Caleb Fobes 1799.—Clarissa m. Adin Alger 1814.—Laura m. Charles Bassett 1816.

17. Ezra (s. of Josiah 9.) m. Mary Shaw of Raynham 1776, and had Abigail 1777, Susanna 1779, Mary 1781, Cordana 1783, Ezra 1785, Sirena 1788, Celia 1793, Aremena 1796, and Eliza 1798.—Abigail m Otis Holmes of T. 1796, and Eaton Aldridge 1807.—Mary m. Calvin Hayward 1801.—Cordana m. Lemuel Dunbar 1806.—Sirene m. Gilbert Whitman 1813.—Celia m. Elijah Fobes of N. Y. 1819.

18. Alpheus (s. of Josiah 9.) m. Mehitabel D. of Seth Lathrop 1781, and had Seth 1783, Mehitabel 1786 ; his wife d. and he m. Lucy D. of Rev. Isaac Backus of Mid'o 1788, and had Isaac 1789, Sibil 1791, Josiah 1793, Alpheus 1795, and Aretas 1798—Mehitabel m. Alpheus M. Withington of Milton 1810.—Sibil m. Simeon Taylor 1816.—Isaac m. Mary D. of Timothy Hayward 1811, and then Olive D. of Edward Mitchell and wid. of Dr. Rufus Walker.—Alpheus went to N. Y.

19. Joseph Esq. (s. of Josiah 9.) m. Susanna D. of Capt. John Ames 1782, and had Phrez, and went to Oakham.

Joseph Fobes 2d. m. Rosanda Alden of Mid'o 1787,

20. John (s. of Josiah 9.) removed to Windsor and had Silas,
Enoch, John and Horatio: all now in N. York.—He had Ds.
also; one m. Jonathan Bassett in B.—Elijah m. Celia D. of Ezra
Fobes 1819.

21. Eliab (s.'of Ephraim 10.) m. Mehitabel D. of Thomas
Ames 1759, and had Kezia 1760, Martha 1762, Thomas 1764,
Chloe 1766, Mehitabel 1768, Eliab 1770, Hannah 1772, Susanna
1774.—Thomas and his w. Lydia lived in Boston, and left no
children; his wid. m. a Tucker.—Chloe m. Josiah Kingman of
Mid'o 1781.—Mehitabel m. Benjamin Packard 1784, and went
to Vermont.—Martha m. Oliver Washburn 1787.—Susanna m.
Thomas Hooper 1795.—Hannah Fobes m. Levi Macomber of
M. 1802.

22. Ephraim (s. of Ephraim 10.) m. Bethia D. of Joseph Ames
1769, and had Caleb, an only child.
Martin Fobes m. Betty Eaton of Plympton 1793.—Azariah
m. Olive Leach 1793.

23. William (s. of Timothy 13.) m. Freelove French 1796,
and had Mary Deane 1798, Dwelly 1801, Albert 1804, and Rhoda French 1807.—He d. 1812 and the wid. m. Jonah Willis 1816.

24. Robert (s. of Joshua 11.) and his w. Abiah had Zephaniah
1780, Reuel 1783, Bela 1786, Joshua 1789, and Abiah 1790.—
Zephaniah m. Lurania Wilbor 1810.—Bela m. Alice Washburn
1805.—Abiah m. a Knapp.—Joshua m. Chloe Keith 1809.

25. Avery Esq. (s. of Timothy 13.) m. Lois D. of Luther Hooper 1801; had Harriet 1802, Vesta 1804, Cornelia 1807, and Fanny 1810.

26. Jesse (s. or g. s. of Benj. 6.) m. Susanna, wid. of Oakes Angier Esq. and D. of Col. Edward Howard 1792, and had Henry
1792; she d. 1793; and he m. Polly D. of Rev. Elijah Packard
1795, and had Charles E. 1795, who is an Attorney at Northampton and writes his name Forbes.

27. Col. Salmon (s. of Jason 16.) m. Cloe D. of James Leach
1807, and had Sumner 1807, Lentha 1809, Justin 1811, Stella
Washburn 1813, Fidelia 1816.

28. Shepard (s. of Jason 16.)m. Phebe D. of Peter Dunbar 1814,
and had Alice Alger 1818, and Frederick Handel 1820.

29. Ezra (s. of Ezra 17.) m. Hannah D. of Joseph Bassett
Esq. 1810, and had Franklin Baylies 1811, and Joseph Bassett
1814.

30. Caleb (s. of Ephraim 22.) m. Molly D. of Jason Fobes
1799, and had Bethiah Ames 1800, Nancy Warner 1802, Ephraim
1805, Amelia Washburn 1808, Cassandra Angelina 1810, Mary
Wales 1812, Jason 1815, and Sarah Williams 1820.

31. Seth (s. of Alpheus 18.) and his w. Rachel had Elmira 1804,
Edwin 1806, Angeline 1810, Elbridge 1812, Hannah 1814, Daniel 1817.

32. Reuel.(s. of Robert 24.) m. Sibil D. of Samuel Battles
1806, and had Thomas Jefferson 1806, Henry Franklin 1809,
Reuel Battles 1812*, Willard Williams 1814, and Robert 1816.

33. Daniel (s. of Joshua 11.) m. Hannah D. of Miles Standish 1769, and had Azariah, Daniel and others.

Martha Fobes m. William Conant 1803.—Laban Fobes m. Hannah Richmond 1816.— Elizabeth Fobes m. Nathan Tompson 1802.

FORD.—1. Mark Ford (s. of Jacob of Abington) came to N. B. 1763, and m. Hannah D. of Samuel Brett 1764, and had Hannah 1765, Asa 1767, Samuel 1770, Sally 1772, and Mehitabel 1781.—Hannah m. Joshua Ames 1786.—Sally m. Samuel Alden Jr. 1799.—Mehitabel m. Isaac Reynolds 1805.—He d. 1821, æ. 80.—Asa m. Sarah D. of Jeremiah Beal 1793 and had Polly 1796, and Roxana 1797, Polly m. Wm. Tribou 1816.

2. Joseph Ford m. Betty D. of Seth Howard 1769, and had Polly 1770, Ephraim 1775, Joseph 1777, Charles 1779, Nicholas 1781, Walter 1783, Elizabeth 1785, Seth 1787, Sarah 1789, and George 1791.—Polly m. Judge Abner Fobes 1791.—Sarah m. Davis Packard 1813.

3. David (s. of Jacob, g. s. of Jacob above, and nephew of Mark) came from Abington to N. B. a. 1800, and m. Olive D. of Simeon Packard 1794, and had David, Olive, Rhoda, Packard, Daniel 1801, Noah 1804, Rachel 1806, Susan Margaret 1808, Richard 1811, Nancy Whitman 1814, Mary Alden 1816—David m. Polly Wild 1821.—Olive m. John Foster 1821.—Rhoda m. Elisha Belcher 1818.

4. Prince Ford m. Keziah D. of Edward Powers 1779, and had Packard 1783, Prince 1787, Martin 1790, Daniel 1793, Keziah 1795.—Packard m. Mary Kingman 1808.

Andrew m. Mercy Whitmarsh 1706, and d. 1750 æ. 69.—Lydia m. Richard Whitmarsh 1712.—Mary m. Zephaniah Perkins 1766. Amos of Marshfield m. wid. Sarah Pettingill 1766.—Benjamin m. Sarah Brett 1773.—Elizabeth m. George Keith 1780.—Hannah m. Joshua Ames 1786.—Sarah m. Barnabas Packard a. 1761. John had a son Abijah in E. B. 1741.—John m. Mehitabel Kingman 1794.—James m. Parna Howard 1800.—Bathsheba m. Lemuel Fuller of C. 1800.—Rebecca m. Oliver Pratt 1805.—Mercy of Marsh'd m. Nahum Packard 1817.—Simeon of Herkimer m. Sophia D. of David Kingman, and d. 1839, æ. 64.—Lauren m. her sister Mary Kingman 1816.—Hannah d. 1801 æ. 77.—Silence m. Anthony Sherman a. 1746.

FREELOVE.—John Freelove m. Abigail D. of William Washburn 1739: he d. about 1755, she d. in E. B. 1772, æ. 59; had Sarah, Abigail, John, and Thankful 1752.—John m. Sarah Fuller 1765 and had a child that d. 1773.—John Freelove m. Sarah Wood 1774.—Abigail Freelove m. Ebenezer Whitman 1760.— Thankful m. Ezra Whitman 1796.

FRENCH.—Dependence French (s. of John French of Randolph) lived in Stoughton corner, and was a member of the North Parish of Bridgewater, d. 1803, æ. 89; m. Mary Lynfield 1738, and had Dependence 1739, Levi 1740, Deliverance 1742, Mary 1744, John 1749, William 1751, Elizabeth, Silence 1756, Martha 1759, and Olive 1761.—Dependence m. Rebecca Hammond 1765, d. and left no children.—Elizabeth m. Seth Bryant 1765.— Mary m. Jeremiah Beals 1768.—Silence m. Ephraim Churchill 1787.—Martha m. Samuel Cheesman.

2. John (twin brother of Dependence above) m. Mary Fenno 1748, and wid. Christian Holbrook 1753, and had Rebecca 1754, Ruhama 1757, and John 1763.—Rebecca m. Jacob Packard 3d. 1774.—Ruhama m. Noah Ames 1778.

3. Levi (s. of Dependence 1.) m. Amy D. of William Packard 1764, and lived in N. B., and had Levi 1765, Samuel 1766, Ruhama 1768, Dependence and Rebecca 1771, Lemuel, Isaac, Silvanus, and Hannah.—Ruhama m. Barnabas Pratt 1787.—Rebecca m. Theophilus Curtis 1791.—Hannah m. Luther Swan 1796.—Samuel settled in Amherst.—Dependence m. Hannah D. of Seth Harris 1794.—Isaac m. Polly D. of Jonas Reynolds 1801, and lives in Stoughton.—Silvanus m. Silence D. of Jonathan Keith 1805.—Wid. Amy m. George Monk 1798.

4. Capt. John (s. of Dependence 1.) m. Damaris D. of Barnabas Howard Esq. 1779 and had Artemas, Daniel, Sidney, John, Zelopha, Olive, and Anna.—Zelopha m. Benjamin Ames 1804. Olive m. John Cobb.—Anna m. Isaac Keith 1810.

5. Capt. William (s. of Dependence 1.) m. Mary D. of Luke Perkins, and had Alpheus, Rhoda, Rebecca, Patty, Sibil, and Phebe.—Alpheus m. Mehitabel D. of Samuel Brett 1800.—Rhoda m. William Carr 1797.—Rebecca m. Col. Cyrus Porter 1800. —Patty m. John Packard 1803.—Sibil m. Zenas Brett 1813.— Phebe m. Capt. Nath'l Wales 1815.

6. Levi (s. of Levi 3.) m. Betsy Meritt 1799, and had Meritt 1800, Betsy 1806, and Levi 1808.—Levi French m. wid. Keziah Jenkins 1805.

7. Micah and his wife Ruth (s. of Thomas of Braintree, and nephew of Dependence 1.) settled in E. B. a. 1747, and had Micah 1747, Mary 1749, Bartholomew 1751, Ruth 1753, Prudence 1756, Anne (or Hannah) 1759, Barzillai 1762, and Alpheus 1767.—He removed to Stoughton.

8. David (brother of Micah above) m. Mehitabel D. of Samuel Pratt, and had Nathaniel 1756, Silas 1761, Joseph 1763, Barnabas, Daniel, Samuel Pratt, and David 1776, after his father's death.—The widow m. Benjamin Price 1782.—Nathaniel d. at N. York in the army, 1776 ; and Barnabas moved to Maine.— Joseph m. Hannah Mehuren 1784 ; he d. 1799 æ. 38 ; she d. 1788, æ. 36 ; she left a D. Mehitabel, who m. Charles Brown 1809.—Daniel m. Rhoda D. of Thomas Tribou 1792; had Daniel, who m. Sarah Standish 1817, and Rhoda who m. Joseph Keen 1815.—Samuel Pratt m. Olive Reed 1801, and had William*, Luther, Samuel, Lucy, and Polly ; Luther m. Keziah D. of Reuben Besse ; Polly m. Oliver Stark 1821 ; Lucy m. Marcus Packard 1821, and lives in Easton.—David m. Rachel Hanks 1797, and had several children, 2 only are living, viz : Abigail 1800, who m. Joseph Walton and Eliza 1803, who m. Alvan Cole

1823 ; his wife d. 1825, and he has a 2d. wife.—Silas m. a Brown and had Nathaniel.

9. William and his w. Alice D. of Ezekiel Washburn 1773, and had Mary 1777, Lydia 1778, Eli 1780, Jesse 1783, Ezekiel 1785, William 1787, and Sally 1791 —Lydia m. Isaac Keith 1801. William m. Anna Wales 1810.—Sally m. Asa Cushing 1813.— William French m. Lydia Kezer 1767.

10. Nathaniel (s. of Silas, see no. 8.) m. Eliza Waterman of H. 1811, and had Nathaniel Waterman 1813, Mary Brown 1815, Lucy Sampson 1818.

11. Ebenezer m. Elizabeth D. of William Orcutt 1717, and had Elizabeth, who m. Jonathan Pratt 1740.

Most of the above are descendants of John and Grace French of Braintree, who had John 1641, Thomas 1643*, Dependence 1648, Temperance 1651, William 1653, Elizabeth 1655, Thomas 1657, Samuel 1659 ; he d. 1692, æ. 80, she 1680.

David French m. Abigail Owen 1751.—Sarah m. Jedediah Jordan 1744.—Polly m. Abiah Packard Jr. 1788.—Warren m. Betsy Lathrop 1813.—Daniel of Quincy m. Hannah K. Haskell 1815. Capt. Zephaniah of St. m. Betsy Ames 1816.—Freelove m. William Fobes 1796.—Wid. Nabby m. Marlboro' Whiting 1796.— Mehitabel m. Joseph Pratt 1738.—Stephen French of Braintree m. Hannah D. of John Whitman-of Weymouth 1660, and had Mary 1662.

FULLER.—Isaac Fuller (from Halifax) settled in N. B. ; m. Sarah D. of Solomon Packard 1737, and had Isaac 1738, Olive 1740, Lemuel 1742, Isaiah 1744, Sarah 1746, Susanna 1748, Lois 1751, Benjamin 1754, Reliance 1756.—Isaac m. Mary D. of Daniel Alden 1764, and settled in Easton.—Lemuel d. in the army 1762.—Isaiah m. Mary Kezer 1768, and moved to Warwick.—Olive m. Daniel Edson 1765.—Sarah m. John Freelove 1764.—Susanna m. Ashly Curtis 1770.—Lois m. Samuel Dyke 1772.—Reliance m. Josiah Edson Jr. 1777.—Benjamin m. Sarah D. of Daniel Ames 1777, and he and his father Isaac removed to Winchester.

Jabez Fuller dis. from W. B. Ch. to Medfield Ch. 1747.—Elizabeth joined W. B. Ch. 1735.—Jabez Fuller d. of small pox 1788.

Jacob (s. of Isaiah above) m. Abigail Leonard 1800, and had Betsy 1801, Josiah 1803 ; she d. and he m. Hannah D. of Nath'l Orcutt 1806, and had Nabby 1807, Leonard Orcutt 1809, and Mary Flagg 1814.

Rebecca m. Elijah Alden 1783.—Lois m. Nathan Pratt 1786. Hannah m. Azor Eddy 1786.—Chloe of Attleborough m. Calvin Howard 1790.—Elizabeth m. Mason Johnson 1790.—Silence m. Samuel Harden 1792.—Lemuel Jr. of Canton m. Bathsheba Ford 1800.—William m. Tabatha Benson 1801.—Stephen of Att'o m. Sarah Copeland 1810.—Squire of Brookfield Vt. m. Bethiah Ames 1815.—John, of Boston, m. Jane B. L. Fearing 1819.

FULLERTON.—William Fullerton m. Mary Porter 1796, and had Mehitabel 1800, Harvey 1803, Almira 1805, Celestia

1807, William 1810, John 1813, James Porter 1815.—Ruth Ful
lerton (or Fullington) m. Samuel Pool 1759, and d. 1835, æ. 97.
GAGE.—Capt. Thomas E. and Mary Gage had Mercy E.
1802, Joshua E. 1804.

GANNETT.—Thomas Gannett was at Duxbury 1642, and
"able to bear arms" as early as 1643; was one of the original
proprietors and first settlers of Bridgewater; d. here 1655, the
first death in the town found on any record: he made a will, and
left a wid. Sarah, but no children. His estate went to his brother
Matthew of Scituate. His wid. afterwards m. a Faxon.—Matthew of Scituate was born in England 1618, and came early to
this country, and first settled in Hingham, and afterwards about
1651 removed to Scituate: he d. 1695, and had two sons Matthew and Joseph. Joseph m. a wid. Sharp (she had a s. Benoni
Sharp by her first husband) and d. before his father, leaving
Hannah 1684, Matthew 1688, Deborah 1690, Joseph 1693. These
2 ss. Matthew and Joseph, by their grandfather Matthew's will,
dated 1694, had the estate in Bridgewater, which came to their
grandfather by their great uncle Thomas above.—Hannah, wid.
of the first Matthew, made her will 1700, and it appears they
had other children, viz: Rehoboth, Elizabeth Leverett, Hannah
Adams, Abigail Dodson. Rehoboth d. at Morristown, N. J.,
without children.

2. Matthew (s. of Joseph, and g. s. of Matthew) m. Mary
Bacon 1718 in Scituate. He, with his brother Joseph, came to
E. B. a. 1713: he had Elizabeth, Mary 1721, Susanna 1723,
Mehitabel 1726, Sarah 1729. He m. Martha, wid. of Dr. Joseph
Byram, and D. of David Perkins, 1750, for his 2d wife: she d.
1779, æ. 74.—Elizabeth m. Nicholas Byram a. 1738, and Thos.
Hayward 1746.—Mary m. John Edson 1744.—Susanna m. Da-
vid Edson 1746.—Mehitabel m. Zebulun Cary 1747, and d. 1748.
Sarah m. Daniel Pettingill 1755, and afterwards Amos Ford of
Marshfield 1766.

3. Joseph (brother of Matthew next above) m. Hannah, D. of
Dea. Jonathan Hayward of Braintree; had Joseph 1722, Hannah 1724, Benjamin 1726*, Benjamin 1728, Jonathan 1730: she
d. 1731, and he m. Hannah, D. of Nathl. Brett 1732, and had
Seth 1734, Thomas 1736: he d. 1774, æ. 80; she 1777, æ. 78.—
Hannah m. Ichabod Cary 1741. She and Matthew's D. Susanna
were the first persons baptized by the Rev. John Angier, the first
minister of East Bridgewater.

4. Capt. Joseph (s. of Joseph 3.) m. Betty, D. of Charles
Latham, 1744; had Caleb Aug. 22, 1745, Betty 1749, Simeon
1752, Deborah 1755, Joseph 1760, Barzillai 1764: he d. 1789,
æ. 67; she 1813, æ. 86. Betty m. Nathan Hudson 1767.—Deborah m. Adam Porter, and removed to Cummington.

5. Benjamin (s. of Joseph 3.) m. Mary, D. of Jonathan Copeland, 1750, and removed to Stoughton: his son Benjamin m. the
famous female soldier, Deborah Sampson.

6. Jonathan (s. of Joseph 3.) m. Hannah Dyer of Abington,

and had Jacob 1753. He m. wid. Records for his 2d wife: he
m. a 3d wife from Weymouth. He m. Abigail 1785, wid. of
Silas Harris and D. of Ebenezer Shaw, and removed to Cummington.

7. Seth (s. of Joseph 3.) m. Susanna, D of Matthew Allen,
1754; had Matthew 1755, Hannah 1756, Mehitabel 1758, Susanna 1760, Sarah 1762, Seth 1764, Philena 1768, Nathl.
Brett 1770, Phebe 1773, Nabby 1775, Thomas 1778.—Hannah m. Oliver Washburn 1781.—Mehitabel m. Jacob Harden 1778.—Matthew m. Alice, D. of Nehemiah Latham, 1783.—Seth Jr. m.
Eliza Reed 1821.—The parents, and most of the family, removed
to Tamworth, N. H.

8. Thomas (s. of Joseph 3.) m. Susanna, D. of Dr. Pollycarpus
Loring of Plympton, where he lived and d. without children.
He grad. H. U. 1763: studied no profession: his wife d. 1801,
æ. 63; he 1810, æ. 74.

9. Caleb (s. of Capt. Joseph 4.) gra. H. U. 1763, and settled
in the ministry at Amherst and Cumberland, Nova Scotia, and
was ord. (at Hingham) 12th October, 1767; left Cumberland
1771, and returned to Mass., and was chosen a Tutor at H. U.
1773, and Steward 1780, in which office he remained till his
death, April 25, 1818. He was twice m.: by his first wife he had
John Mico and Thomas Brattle, (minister of Cambridgeport),
and by his last wife (D. of Pres. Styles) he had Ezra Styles,
minister in Boston.

10. Simeon of (s. Capt. Joseph 4.) m. a Reed of Abington
1775; had Clarissa 1789, and Charlotte: his w. d. 1808, æ. 50,
and he m. wid. Lydia Little of Scituate 1809. Clarissa m.
Amasa Field 1813.—Charlotte m. Thomas Whitmarsh 1811.

11.—Joseph (s. of Capt. Joseph 4.) m. Anna, D. of Thomas
Hobart of Hanson, 1783; had Luther 1784, Nancy 1787,
Christiana 1793, Joseph 1795, Susanna 1797, Mary 1804, and
Jane. Nancy d. 1817, æ. 30.—Christiana m. Marston Lazell.—
Joseph m. Lucy Stowell.—Susanna m. Ebenezer Noyes 1821;
she d. 1822: he then m. Mary, and she d. 1827.—Jane m. Luther
Faxon.—The mother d. 1826, æ. 62; he 1829, æ. 69.

12. Barzillai (s. of Capt. Joseph 4.) gra. H. U. 1785, studied
divinity and preached, but was never settled; removed to Gardner, Maine, and m. and had a family there; was Representative
of the Town, Clerk of the Sessions, and County Treasurer: he
went to Canada.

13. Capt. Luther (s. of Joseph 11.) m. Olive, D. of Capt. Levi
Washburn 1810; had Eliza Ann 1811, Luther 1814, George
1819: he removed to Belfast, Me.

Amelia Gannett m. Oliver Mitchell 1791.—Lucinda m. Lot
Ramsdell 1794.—Sally m. Zenas Harden 1815.

GAY.—Rev. Ebenezer Gay and Laura had Calvin 1725, Laura
1728.

GILBERT.—Nathaniel Gilbert m. Betsy, D. of Caleb Cary,
1802, and had Caleb C. 1803, Mary P. 1805, Grenville 1809,

Henry 1811, Nathaniel 1813, Marshall B. 1815, Betsy C. 1818, Charles 1820, George 1823.

Ebenezer Gilbert of the ch. W. B. after 1721.—Ruth Gilbert m. Reuben Hall 1741.

GILMORE.—James Gilmore m. Thankful Tyrrell of Ab. 1725; had Adam, Agnes, both bap. W. B. 1742, Thankful 1738, William 1740, Tyrrell 1744, Whitfield 1746.

2. Robert had a s. Robert bap. W. B. 1739.

3. Andrew m. Abigail, D. of Elisha Dunbar, 1752; had Andrew 1753.

William m. Mary Willis 1731.—Margaret m. John Cochran 1733.—Jane m. Thomas Kennedy 1735 —Jane m. Joseph Wesley 1739.—William m. Margaret Steward 1742.—David in B. 1744.—John m. Martha Smith 1764.—Joshua m. Hannah Lathrop 1789.—Sally m. Peleg Leach 1802.

GODFREY.—Francis Godfrey was an early settler in Bridgewater; was a Carpenter; d. between 1666, the date of his will, and 1669, when it was proved : mentions his D. Elizabeth Cary (wife of John) and grandson John Cary.

Abby Godfrey of Norton m. Ebenezer Copeland 1770.—Hannah Godfrey of Norton m. Ebenezer Copeland Jr. 1801.—Sally Godfrey m. Calvin Jackson 1810.

GOULD.—William Gould and his wife Grace had John 1721, Mary 1723, Hannah 1725.   He lived in what is now Hanson.

GROVES.—Ephraim Groves of N. B. m. Bathsheba, D. of William Bowditch, 1762; had Deborah 1762.—Susanna m. John Porter 2d 1790.—Ephraim Groves m. Jenny, wid. of Nathaniel Southworth, 1789, D. of Simeon Brett.

GURNEY.—Zechariah Gurney (s. probably of Zechariah, and g. s. of Richard of Braintree) and his wife Sarah, came from Abington and settled in N. B. a. 1746; had Zechariah 1729, Elisha 1731, Micah 1739, Mary 1747, Sarah 1750.   Mary m. a More.—Elisha m. Jane, D. of Henry Kingman, 1760, and had Betty 1761, and Jacob 1763, and went to Me.—Micah m. Hopestill Jackson 1765 and went to Me.

2. Zechariah (s. of Zechariah 1.) m. Mary, D. of David Ames, 1754; had John 1755, Mary 1757, Martha 1760, Zechariah 1762, David 1765, The father, a Lieut. in the revolutionary war, d. 1813, æ. 84; she 1800 æ. 77.—Mary m. James Churchill 1794.—Martha m. Ebenezer Drake 1781.—The father m. wid. Mary Southworth 1800.

3. John (s. of Zechariah 2.) m. Mehitabel, D. of Lemuel Southworth, 1777; had 'Mehitabel 1778, Patience 1780, Mille 1782, Martha 1784, John 1786, Sibil 1788, Anna 1790, Rhoda 1792, Lemuel 1794, Samuel 1797.   The father d. 1796.—Rhoda m. Baruck Morse of St. 1811.

4. Capt. Zechariah (s. of Zechariah 2.) m Matilda, D. of William Packard, 1783, and had Azel 1785, Olive 1786, Alpheus 1789, Betsy 1790, Ozen 1793, Matilda 1795, Zechariah 1797, Charles 1798, Thomas Jefferson 1803, Lucius 1804.—Olive m.

Capt. Oliver Jackson 1807.—Betsy m. Barnabas Edson 1814.—
Matilda m. Hezekiah Packard 1820.—Alpheus removed to Boston.—Ozen m. Melinda, D. of Ichabod Howard, 1820, and went
to Paris, Me.—Zechariah went to Mobile.—Azel m. Polly, D. of
Abijah Knapp, 1815, and had Mary 1816, and Alpheus 1818.—
Capt. Charles m. Louisa, D. of Perez Crocker, and had Charles*
and others.—Thomas J. m. Fidelia Wade of St.: she d. 1834,
æ. 31.
    5. Capt. David (s. of Zechariah 2.) m. Molly, D. of Jonathan
Ames, 1789; had Polly 1790: his wife d. 1791, and he m. Susanna, D. of Samuel Bartlett, 1792, and had David 1793, Austin
1795, Susanna 1796, Harris 1799, and went to Bath, Me.
    6. Perkins Gurney and his wife Jane (he was son of Joseph
and Mary of Abington, and was born 1723) settled in E. B.; had
David 1759, Thomas, Jonathan, Adam, Seth and Ruth. David
gra. H. U. 1785, and settled in the ministry at Titicut 1787.—
Thomas and Jonathan went to Me.—Adam d. in the army.
    7. Seth (s. of Perkins 11.) m. Rebeckah, D. of Edward
Packard, 1788, and had David 1791, Seth 1793, Jane 1795, Re-
becca 1801, Cyrus 1803, Almon 1805, Deborah 1807, Alva 1808.
David m. Lurana, D. of Ichabod Howland, 1815, and he is d.—
Seth m. Anna, D. of Christopher Bates, 1818.—Jane m. Abiah
Reed of Abington 1814.
    S. Benjamin and his w. Betty had Betty 1756, Asa 1758.
Ruth m. Peleg Stetson 1775.—Hannah m. Jo. Sampson
1780.—Molly m. Ephraim Tinkham 1787.—Silvia m. Solomon
Hearsey Jr. 1801.—James H. Gurney m. Deborah Reed 1816.—
Jona. R. Gurney m. Deborah Reed 1816.—Clarissa m. Peleg
Stetson 1819.—Daniel m. Mehitabel Harden 1819.—Sophronia
m. Gibeon Sharp 1820.
    HAINS or HINDS.—John Hains m. Hannah Shaw 1709;
had Hannah 1710, Elizabeth 1712, Abigail 1714, John 1717,
Ebenezer 1719, Susanna 1722. Abigail m. Stephen Cobb of Wal-
pole 1735.—John m. Hannah Lyon 1738.—Susanna m. a Cham-
berlin 1740.
    2. Ebenezer (s. of John above) and his w. Susanna had Ke-
ziah 1745, Salome 1747: his w. d. 1751, and he m. Lydia Bart-
lett 1751, and had Ebenezer 1753.—Elizabeth Hains m. Nath'l
Conant 1716.—Ebenezer Willis m. a Hinds.
    HALE.—Artemas Hale Esq. (s. of Moses of Winchendon) m.
Deborah Lincoln of Hingham 1815, and settled in S. B., and had
Caroline Augusta 1818, Deborah Lincoln 1820, Artemas 1822.
    HALL.—Reuben Hall m. Ruth Gilbert 1741, and lived in S.
B., and had Reuben 1742, Sarah 1744, Mercy 1745, Ruth 1747,
Gilbert 1748, Mehitabel 1752, Silvanus. He d. 1788, æ. 68.—Sa-
rah m. Josiah Byram 1766.—Mercy m. Abner Lewis, of M., 1763.
Silvanus m. and had a family.—Silvanus Jr. m. Almira, D. of
Jotham Cushman Esq. 1816.—Ebenezer m. Nanny Dunbar of
Hal. 1816.—Susanna m. Zion Swift 1718.—Wid. Sarah d. 1800,
æ. 44.
    22

Keziah m. Edward White 1739.—Abigail m. Captain David
Kingman 1752.—Sarah m. Solomon Alden 1755.—Philip m.
Hannah Keith 1760.—Mary m. Nathan Edson 1766.—Anne m.
Samuel Edson 1767.—Mary m. David Leonard 1769.—Luther
m. Abigail Mehuren 1781.—James m. Sarah Orcutt 1782.—Mason
of R. m. Hannah 'Willis 1789.—Samuel of T. m. Mercy (or
Mary) Willis 1718.—Nathan m. Ruth Waterman 1790.—Lucy
m. Caleb Cole 1792.—Vodisa m. Apollos Hooper 1799.—Jabez
m. Triphear Wilbor 1791.—Luther of R. m. wid. Mehitabel
Leach 1806.—Macey of R. m. Susanna Washburn 1807.—Joseph
m. Polly Copeland 1812.—Betsy R. m. Alpheus Brett 1815.—
Jemima m. Marcus Howard 1814.—Martha m. Peter Tribou
1817.—Wealthy of R. m. Earl Cushman 1820.

HANKS.—James Hanks resided in E. B., and had Joseph
1743, Hannah 1745.—Rachel Hanks m. David French 1797.

HAMLIN.—Isaac and Sarah Hamlin (she was a Shaw, D. of
Nicholas and Lydia of Abington, born 1726) had Isaac 1748,
David 1752, Molly 1754, Joseph 1756, Sarah 1760.

2. Eleazar and Lydia Hamlin (she was a Bonney, m. 1752)
had Asia 1753, Betty 1754. It is said this man had four sons
named Asia, Africa, Europe and America. They removed to
Harvard, and afterwards to Me.

3. Josiah and Mary Hamlin had Josiah 1779.—Mary Hamlin
m. Joseph Richards 1742.—Mary m. Thomas Moore 1746.—Elizabeth m. William Holmes 1750.—Mary m. Jonathan Perkins 3d
1765.

HANMER.—John Hanmer, sometimes written Handmore,
with his wife, came from Halifax and settled in B. 1739; wid.
Hanmer had Abigail, Jerusha and John all bap. in W. B. 1742.
Abigail m. Thomas Latham 1752.—Elizabeth m. Ebenezer Hay-
ward 1750.—Mary m. John Smith 1749.—Elizabeth m. Thomas
Wade 1743.—Jerusha m. John Orcutt Jr. 1752.

2. John (s. of the above) lived in E. B., m. Mary, D. of Joseph Prior, 1760, and had Nabby 1762, Lucinda 1763, Cynthia
1765, Zenas 1767, Peninnah 1770.—John Hanmer was at Plymouth 1638.

HARDEN.—John Harden (from Braintree) and his w. Hannah settled in S. B. a. 1707, and d. 1718; had Samuel, John,
Nathaniel, Peter, Sarah, (who m. perhaps John Hooper and
then Francis Wood), and others; Deborah who m. Thomas
Latham 1712, and Abigail who m. Samuel Harris 1710, might
have been his Ds. John perhaps settled in Abington.—Nath'l
m. Susanna, D. of James Latham, 1715, and had Nathaniel 1727,
Abraham, Seth 1731, and probably others.

2. Samuel (s. of John 1.) m. Elizabeth, D. of Nicholas Wade,
1739, and had John, Mary, Daniel, Samuel 1746, Lydia, Nathan
1749. The father d. before 1764; she, a wid., d. 1764. Lydia
m. Jonathan Benson Jr. 1774.—Daniel d. 1775 in the army.—
Nathan d. 1800, æ. 51.

3. John (s. of Samuel 2.) m. Eunice, D. of Jonathan Benson, 1766, and had John and Jonathan.
4. Samuel (s. of Samuel 1.) and his w. Phebe had Betsy, Silvia, Eunice, Stephen and Daniel all bap. in E. B. 1787, Rebeckah 1788. He d. 1799, æ. 53.
5. John (s. of Capt. John of Abington) m. Lydia Hearsey 1779, and lived in E. B., and had Deborah 1780, John 1782, Noah 1790, Lydia 1795, Charlotte 1800. Deborah m. Eli Blanchard 1798.—Lydia m. Sullivan Dunbar 1817.—Charlotte m. Oran Reed 1817.—Noah m. Alice Hearsey 1816.
6. John (s. of John 3.) m. Lucy Holmes of Plymouth 1792, and had John Constant, Ward, and others. One D. m. Jotham Dumphy.—John Constant m. Nancy Bates 1813.
7. Samuel (of S. B.) m. Silence, D. of Jabez Fuller probably, 1792, and had Lucia 1793, Jabez 1795, Thomas 1797, Harriet 1800, Rhoda 1802, Albert 1806. His w. d. 1816, and he m. Lydia Wade of Halifax 1819.—Lucia m. Benj. Hayward Keith 1819.—Harriet m. Carver Washburn.—Jabez m. Sarah, D. of Captain Simeon Pratt.
8. John (s. of John 5.) m. Jane, (or Jenny), D. of Peleg Stetson, 1803, and had Clarissa 1804, Salome 1806, Nahum 1808, Peleg Stetson 1810, Jane 1812, Maria 1814.
9. Thomas (s. of Samuel of A.) m. Mehitabel Harden 1811, and had Sarah 1812, Nancy White 1815.
Wid. Martha Harding d. 1633, leaving a son.—John Harding at Duxbury 1643.—Joseph Harding took the oath of fidelity at Eastham 1657.—Mary of Pem. (now Hanson) m. Jesse Hayward of Halifax 1763.—Sarah m. Matthew Allen 1734.—Hannah m. Christopher Sever 1771.—Reuben m. Rebecca Harden 1782, and had a son Seth.—Harlow m. Sarah Stetson 1795.—Mary Harden m. John Cary 1741.—Timo. Harding m. Sarah Stone 1793.—Sally m. Solomon Ames 2d 1794.—Willis m. Elizabeth Hobart 1802.—Nancy m. Thomas White 1803.—Betsy m. Lewis Brown 1806.—Wid. Betsy m. Enos Cox 1808.—Isabella m. Thos. White 1810.—Calvin m. Roxana Hatch 1813.—Zenas m. Sally Gannett 1815.—Mehitabel m. Daniel Harden Jr. 1819.—Abraham m. Ruth Perry 1740.
HARLOW.—Wm. Harlow was in Bridgewater 1742, and Capt. William Harlow's family are there now; he was from Plymouth.
HARRIS.—Arthur Harris, one of the original purchasers and proprietors of Bridgewater and among the first settlers in W. B. was at Duxbury as early as 1640.—He d. in Boston having made his will there in 1673. His wife's name was Martha (Lake perhaps, see Felt's History of Ipswich p. 160;) had two sons Isaac and Samuel and two Ds. Martha and Mary, and perhaps other children.—Samuel lived in E. B. but there is no account of his family.—Martha m. Thomas Snell.—Mary m. John Winchcomb of Boston, and she made her will in 1717, and mentions her cousins, (nephews,) Thomas Harris and Isaac Harris, her sister

Martha Snell, and cousin, (niece,) Jane Smith.—No certain account of Thomas.

Thomas Harris of Boston made his will 1714, mentioning his wife Giles, and ss. Thomas and John, and D. Elizabeth, and his sister Dorothy Skelton of London. There was also a Thomas there, who was d. in 1715, leaving a wid. Rebecca and a s. Benjamin, and Ds. Jane, Rebecca, and Mehitabel.—Thomas Harris there m. Susanna Cornish 1713, whether either of these was son or g. s. of Arthur is not ascertained.—Abner Harris there m. Elizabeth Lawrence 1709.—Sir Arthur Harris of Stowford, Devonshire, Eng. 1673.—Daniel and William Harris "said to be from Boston," were among the first settlers of Middletown Conn. 1670. Among the letters remaining in the Post Office at Montgomery (Ala.) 1821, were one to Wm. Harris, one to Joshua Harris, and another to Arthur Harris Esq.—James Harris, who m. Elizabeth D. of Guido Bailey 1693 and afterwards Elizabeth Irish 1696, may have been Arthur's son; he appears at Scituate and then at Taunton, now Easton 1696.

2. Isaac (s. of Arthur 1.) m. Mercy D. of Robert Latham, and had Arthur, Isaac, Samuel, Desire, Jane 1671, Susanna, Mary, Mercy 1680, Benjamin, and Martha; the 2 last were by Mary, a 2d. wife D. of Robert Dunbar of Hingham and sister of Peter Dunbar.—He and his w. both d. a. 1707.—Desire m. John Kingman.—Jane m. first James Dunbar, who d. 1690, and afterwards Pelatiah Smith.—Susanna m. Jeremiah Newland 1696.—Mary m. Daniel Packard 1713.—Arthur probably d. at sea; he wrote to his brother Isaac from an Eng. ship 1703, which is the last time he was heard of.—Mercy m. Josiah Sears probably and d. 1720, æ. 40.

3. Isaac (s. of Isaac 2.) m. Jane D. of Caleb Cook of Plymouth, (now Kingston probably) 1707; they were m. at Scituate; he had Arthur 1708, Abner 1710, Anne 1712, Elizabeth 1714, Jane 1716; his wife d. and he m. Elizabeth D. of Joseph Shaw, and wid. of Noah Washburn 1719, and had Isaac 1820.—Anne m. John Holman 1734.—Jane m. James Johnson, who removed to Middleton Con.—In the division of the estate among the heirs in 1740, Elizabeth and Isaac are not mentioned and therefore it is probable they d. young.

4. Samuel (s. of Isaac 2.) m. Abigail Harden 1710, and had Susanna, Abigail, Mary 1725, Seth 1726, Samuel 1728, the father then died.—The wid. warned out 1732.—Susanna m. Joseph Wilbur 1741.—Abigail m. Thomas Drew 1739.—Perhaps Joseph also was his son.—George Harris of B. who m. Hannah Lyon of Mid'o 1763, was probably Joseph's son.

5. Benjamin (s. of Isaac 2.) sold to Isaac, in 1722, 21 acres of land laid out to Isaac deceased, and lying to the westward of the road leading to Weymouth. He had then removed to Hingham; in 1724 he sold his lands on the North and West side of the river to his brother Isaac; he was then of Bridgewater, but removed again, perhaps to Taunton.

6. Arthur (s. of Isaac 3.) m. Mehitabel D. of Samuel Rickard of Plympton 1730, and had Benjamin 1731, Silas 1735, Lucy 1739; his wife d. and he m. Bethiah D. of Dea. Thomas Hayward 1741, and had Mehitabel 1747.—He d. and the wid. m. Robert Latham.—Lucy m. Nehemiah Latham 1757.—Silas m. Abigail D. of Ebenezer Shaw, and d. in the revolutionary war 1777, and she m. Jonathan Gannett of Cummington 1785.

7. Abner (s. of Isaac 3.) was at Taunton and enlisted into the French War 1755 under Gen. Winslow at the seizing of the Neutral French, m. Mary D. of Micah Pratt of Taunton 1735, and had Betty 1737, who m. Elijah Smith.

8. Seth (s. of Samuel 4.) went to M. and m. Abiah D. of Samuel Alden 1751, and then went to Abington and had Seth, Abiel, Oliver, John, and Rebecca; he afterwards m. Mary, wid. of Eliphalet Phillips D. of David Howard, and had Hannah.—He d. 1797 æ. 73 ; she 1816, æ. 74.

9. Samuel (s. of Samuel 4.) we have no certain account of. Samuel of Plymouth, coaster, 1759, and Samuel whose wife was Sarah, and who sold land to Dr. LeBaron at Plympton 1761, might have been this man.

10. Benjamin (s. of Arthur 6.) m. Sarah D. of James Snow 1751, and had Arthur 1753, Sarah 1755, William 1762, Benjamin 1765, Samuel 1768, John 1770.—Sarah m. Francis Gray of Boston 1777 and d. young leaving an only child, a D. who d. 1782.—He d. 1803, æ. 71 ; she 1807 æ. 75.—Samuel m. a Williams and lives in Boston.

11. Arthur (s. of Benjamin 10.) m. Celia D. of Col. Edward Mitchell 1781, and had Sarah 1784, Deborah 1787, Azor 1789, Celia 1796.—He d. 1813, æ. 60, she 1836, æ. 79.—Sarah m. Levi Washburn 1807.—Deborah m. Bezer Hall of Dorchester 1811. —Celia m. Daniel Whitman 1815.

12. Dea. William (s. of Benjamin 10.) m. Alice D. of Cushing Mitchell 1788, and had Jennet Orr 1790, William and Alice 1794 (born at Charlestown).—He d. 1831 æ. 69.—Jennet Orr m. Welcome Young, Esq. 1816, and d. 1821, æ. 31.—Alice m. Joseph Chamberlin Jr. 1819, and d. 1838.

13. Maj. Benjamin (s. of Benjamin 10.) m. Sarah D. of Col. Edward Mitchell 1791, and lived in Boston; he d. at E. B. 1828, æ. 63 ; she d. 1839, æ. 80.—They had no children.

14. John (s. of Benjamin 10.) m. Eunice D. of John Young 1795, and had Lucy, Lydia 1802, Samuel 1810; she d. 1811, æ. 36 : and he m. Rebecca Wood of Halifax 1811 ; he died 1829, æ. 58.

15. Azor Esq. (s. of Arthur 11.) m. Sarah Shaw of M. 1813, and had Esther, and Arthur.—Esther m. Galen Latham, Jr.

16. Dea. William (s. of Deacon William 12.) m. Mary W. D. of Winslow Thomas 1819, and had Benjamin Winslow 1823, Lucia, and William.

17. Joseph Harris (probably s. of Samuel 4.) and his wife Hannah ; she was bap. in East Bridgewater 1736 ; had Hannah,

bap. 1737, and Abigail bap. 1739.—He probably went to M. as
Joseph Harris appeared there in 1743 and 1770.
John Harris m. Mary Torrey 1743, both of M.—Sarah m.
James Hayward Jr. 1750.—Anne m. Joseph Leach 1736.—Alice
m. James Powell 1742.   Most of these may have been descendants of the first or 2d. Samuel, who probably went to Plympton
with the Newland family, and thence they spread into M.—Lucy
m. Samuel Boyden 1806.

HARTWELL.—Samuel Hartwell d. 1760, leaving Nathan,
Jonas, and Sarah perhaps, who m. Joseph Carver 1746, Hannah,
Silence and perhaps others.—Hannah m. Nath'l Reynolds Esq.
1739.—Silence m. Robert Keith 1763.

2. Nathan (s. of Samuel 1.) m. Susanna D. of Richard Field
1746, and had Mary 1753, Daniel 1755, Susanna 1758 ; his wife
d. 1758, and he m. Betty Cushman 1761, and Sarah Bonney of
Pembroke 1762, and had Nathan 1765, b. in E.—Mary m. Abner Shirley 1781.—Susanna m. Asa Keith 1780.—Nathan m.
Sally Ripley of Plympton 1789.

3. Jonas (s. of Samuel 1.) and his wife Ruhama had Isaac
1752, Samuel 1755, Jonas 1761, after his father's death ; the wid.
m. Josiah Snell Jr. 1763.—Jonas gra. at Dartmouth 1787 and
settled at Kittery in the ministry 1791.

4. Maj. Daniel (s. of Nathan 2.) m. Mahitabel D. of Jonathan
Copeland 1779, and had Betty 1783, Daniel 1785, Ephraim 1787,
Lentha 1789, Udotia 1791, Polly 1794, Lucy 1796, George 1799.

Daniel m. Irene D. of Zebulun Willis 1717, and had a son
Charles 1818 ; she d. 1818, and he m. Mary Soper 1821.—Lentha m. Daniel Richards 1812.—Polly m. Zeba Richards 1817.

5. Isaac (s. of Jonas 3.) m. Abihail D. of Maj. Daniel Lathrop 1775, and had Isaac, Jonas, Ruhama, John.

Ruhama m. David Harvey 1821.—John m. Lucinda D. of Nathan Howard 1801.—Hannah m. Alfred Howard 1799.—Isaac
m. Melinda Manly 1809.—Jonas m. Sally D. of Nehemiah Howard 1820.

Experience m. Jonathan Leach Jr. 1768.—Martha m. Joshua
Packard Jr. 1756.

HARVEY.—1. Elizabeth D. of Dea. John Willis m. a Harvey, and the following were probably her children or grand
children, viz. : Joseph, Nathaniel 1705 ; Jenny, Mary, Elizabeth, and Mehitabel.—Jenny m. Seth Leach 1732.—Mary m.
Charles Cushman 1739.—Elizabeth m. Jonathan Whitman 1747.
Mehitabel m. Caleb Orcutt 1738.

2. Joseph (see Elizabeth 1.) and his w. Mary, had Joseph 1730.

3. Nathaniel (see Elizabeth 1.) m. Margaret D. of John Willis
1733, and had David 1735, Nathaniel 1744.—Nathaniel Harvey
d. 1801, æ. 96.

4. Joseph Jr. m. Keziah Washburn 1749, and had Zerviah 1750,
Seth 1754, Joseph 1756.—Keziah Harvey m. Nathan Keith 1773.

5. Joseph 3d. m. Betty (wid. of Israel Keith perhaps : her
maiden name Chandler, D. perhaps of Jonathan Chandler,) 1749,

and had Abthiar 1755, Jonathan 1761.—Abthiah m. Nathan Williams of R. 1781.

6. David (s. of Nathaniel 3.) m. Content D. of Nicholas Byram 1756, and had Nathan 1757, Mary 1759, Martha 1761, Olive 1763, Hannah 1765, Oliver 1768, David 1770, Content 1773, Byram 1775, Susanna 1777.—Mary m. Edmund Harvey of Woodstock Ct. 1782.—Martha m. Daniel Ripley 1783.—Content m. Josiah Winslow 1798.—Susanna m. Isaiah Macomber 1799.

7. Nathaniel (s. of Nathaniel 3.) m. Bethiah D. of John Hayward perhaps 1766, and had Daniel, Bezer.—Bezer m. Ruth Carver 1795.

8. Nathan (s. of David 6.) m. Mehitabel Harvey 1788, and had Otis 1789, Galen 1791, Seth B. 1794, Betty H. 1796, Content R. 1799, Nathan 1803, Mehitabel A. 1810.—Nathan, the father d. 1815.—Otis m. Eunice D. of Benj. Leach 1819.—Galen m. Anna Leach 1817.

9. Oliver (s. of David 6.) m. Desire (or Keziah) D. of George Turner 1793, and had Oliver 1794, Abiezer T. 1798.

10. David (s. of David 6.) m. Olive D. of Jesse Dunbar 1803, (David Harvey m. Phebe D. of Thaxter Dunbar,) and had Thaxter 1811, David 1815, Lorenzo D. 1817, Oliver B. 1820 ; she d. 1720, and he m. Ruhama D. of Isaac Hartwell 1821.

11. Byram (s. of David 6.) m. Parnel D. of Calvin Keith 1800, and had Charles Miller 1801, James Keith 1804, Calvin 1806, Patty Alger 1809, Sally 1811, Willard 1815.

12. Daniel (s. of Nathaniel 7.) m. Mehitabel D. of Simeon Ames 1795, and had Experience 1795, Barzillai 1798, Lydia 1800. He d. and the wid. m. Parmenas Ames 1804.

Bethiah m. John Hayward 1759.—Keziah m. Nathan Keith 1773.—Mary m. Edmund Williams of R. 1781.—Betsy m. William Clark 1781.—Marshall m. Orphah Edson 1785.—Chloe of Freetown m. Robert Robinson 1807.—Sophia m. Levi Osbourne of R. 1797.—Experience m. Elisha Hayward 1708.—Mary m. Nathaniel Hayward 1716.—Abigail Harvey of T. m. James Latham 1739.—Wm. Harvey at T. 1744.—Thomas Harvey at T. 1726 æ. 84, s. of William below probably.

William and Joan Harvey of Boston had Abigail 1640, Thomas 1641, Experience 1644, Joseph 1645.—William and Martha had William 1651, Thomas 1652, John 1654.

HATCH.—1. David Hatch (from Marshfield) m. Mary Turner and lived in E. B. and had David, Mary 1734, John 1737, Mercy 1740.—Mary m. Thomas Phillips Jr. 1755.—Mercy m. Joseph Noyes 1766.—David, father or son, m. Jemima Norton 1754.—David m. Lydia D. of John Allen.

2. John (s. of David 1.) m. Deborah D. of John Allen, and had Walter, Mary, Deborah, Allen, Elizabeth, Louisa, Lurana, and Thirza.—Walter m. Eunice D. of Capt. David Kingman 1780, and went to Belfast.—Mary m. Ichabod Howland 1780, and then Capt. Levi Washburn.—Deborah m. Joseph Joslyn Jr. 1785.—Allen m. Sarah Standish 1787, and lived in Hal., and had

a family and d. 1831 æ. 67.—Louisa m. John Willet 1799.—Lurana m. a Jones.—Thirza m. Seth Beal 1799.

3. Luther (s. of Isaac of Hanover) m. Molly D. of Benjamin Whitman 1790, and settled in E. B., and had Mary 1791, Priscilla 1794, Luther 1796, Isaac 1798 ; she d. 1830, æ. 67.—Luther was killed by lightning 1819, æ. 23.—Isaac m. a Chandler.

Lucy of Hingham m. Micah White 1771.—Roxana, D. of Allen probably, m. Calvin Harden 1813.—James m. Mary Townsend of A. 1819.

HATHAWAY.—Ebenezer Hathaway (s. of Josiah of Halifax,) settled in E. B. a. 1807, and had Ebenezer, Seabury Child, Cushman, John Hooper ; he d. 1830, æ. 62.—Seabury C. m. Sarah Porter of H. 1818.—Cushman m. Mary F. Trask of P. 1820, she d. 1826, æ. 25.

Josiah Hathaway Jr. of Halifax m. Hannah D. of Joseph Latham 1766.—Josiah Hathaway m. Sibil Pettingill 1788.—Zephaniah Hathaway of T. m. Silence Alden of M. 1792.—Chloe Hathaway m. Jonah Benson Jr. 1819.—Olive Hathaway of M. m. Samuel White 1792.—Deborah m. Jonathan Pratt 1817.—Lazarus m. Olive Pratt 1774.

HAYDEN.—1. Jonathan Hayden m. Hannah Cushman of Halifax 1754, and had Sarah 1755, Hannah 1757, Betty 1762, Jonathan 1764, Mary 1767, Moses Cushman 1770, Levinia 1773. —Sarah m. Francis Drake 1775.

Lydia Hayden m. Samuel Lathrop 1751.—Jonathan Hayden of Grafton m. wid Joanna Packard 1807.

2. Col. Josiah, (s. of Benjamin of Braintree) came to N. B. in youth : m. Silence D. of Daniel Howard Esq. 1763: was major in the Revolutionary war : had Charles 1764, Josiah, Daniel, Silence, Mehitabel, Demaris, Elizabeth, Mary.—He removed to Winslow Me. and d. 1814 æ. 84.—Silence m. a Clark, and afterwards Jonathan Cary 1808.

Samuel Hayden was in N. B. 1763, Polly Hayden of Braintree m. Elijah Hayward 4th 1792.—Lewis Hayden of St. m. Abigail Tirrell 1815.

3. Abner Nathaniel Hayden and his wife Sarah, had Abner Wales 1827, Isaac Keith 1829, Edwin 1830.

HAYWARD.—1. Thomas Hayward came from England in the same vessel with John Ames and settled in Duxbury before 1638 : was made a freeman 1646 : was an original proprietor, and among the earliest and eldest of the settlers, of Bridgewater : he d. 1681 : his will dated 1678 : no wife living.—He had Thomas, Nathaniel, John, Joseph, Elisha : Mary w. of Edward Mitchell, and Martha, w. of John Howard : his son Thomas was a witness to his will, and probably wrote it.

2. Thomas Esq. (s. of Thomas 1.) was also one of the first settlers of Bridgewater, and by far the most honored and distinguished man in the place : was one of the first military officers: appointed Lieutenant 1667 and Captain 1692 : was a Magistrate and one of the Governor's Assistants, first chosen 1690, and

Justice of C. C. P., and Sessions 1692: his death was occasioned
by a fall from his horse, 15 Aug. 1698; he left a wid. Sarah, but
no children: he lived near where Daniel Hayward now lives.
3 Nathaniel (s. of Thomas 1.) m. Hannah D. of Dea. John
Willis, and had Nathaniel 1664, John, Thomas, Samuel, Benjamin, Elisha, Patience, and perhaps other Ds.—Patience m. Israel
Alger.
4. John (s. of Thomas 1.) commonly called JOHN OF THE PLAIN,
to distinguish him from John Haward (both being pronounced
alike, Howard): he m. Sarah D. of Experience Mitchell; and
had Sarah 1663, John 1667, Joseph 1669, Mary 1672, Thomas
1674, Benjamin 1677, Susanna 1680, Elizabeth 1683, Benoni
1686, Mercy 1687.—His estate settled 1710.—Sarah m. Nathaniel Brett 1683.—Mary m. William Ames 1698.—Susanna m.
Thomas Hayward 1702.—Elizabeth m. Edmund Rawson 1717.
Benoni m. Hannah Gould 1717, and Hannah Page 1743: qu. if
she did not m. Ephraim Cleveland 1747.—He lived on the Plain
between the late old Mr. Jonathan Copeland's and the old Powder House, where his son-in-law Nath'l Brett lived after him and
where young Jonathan Copeland lives now.
5. Dea. Joseph (s. of Thomas 1.) m. first Alice D. of Elder
William Brett and had Joseph 1673; he had 3 wives, and had a
D. Alice 1683: his 3d. wife was Hannah, D. of Experience
Mitchell, by whom he had Mary 1685, Thomas 1687, Edward
1689, Hannah 1691, Susanna 1695, Peter 1699, Abigail 1702.—
His will 1718.—Alice m. Israel Alger.—Mary m. Thomas Ames
1706.—Hannah m. Capt. Ebenezer Byram 1714.—Susanna m.
Jonathan Packard probably 1719.—Abigail m. Zechariah Snell
1731.—Dea. Joseph, and his father Thomas, lived probably near
where the Rev. Dr. Reed lived.
6. Elisha (s. of Thomas 1.) was never m.: he lived in E. B.,
(at Joppa), and his brother-in-law, Edward Mitchell, lived with
him and had most of his estate, which was considerable: his
will, dated 1703, mentions his nephews, Thomas, s. of Joseph,
Thomas, s. of John, Thomas, s. of Nathaniel.
7. Nathaniel (s. of Nathaniel 3.) lived in E. B. (at Joppa): his
wife Elizabeth, had Josiah 1688, Nathaniel 1690, Isaac 1691,
Hannah 1694, Sarah 1696, Elizabeth 1698, Timothy 1700, Mercy
1702, Mary 1705, Susanna 1707, Bethiah 1711: his will 1734.
Sarah m. Joseph Latham 1717.—Elizabeth m. Samuel Reed
1737.—Mercy m. Elisha Dunbar 1727.—Mary m. Capt. David
Kingman 1732.—Susanna m. David Whitman 1738.—Bethiah
m. Jonathan Perkins 1738.—Col. Edward Mitchell finally owned
the estates of both Samuel and Nathaniel, and there is now no
house where either of them lived.
8. John (s. of Nathaniel 3.) m. Sarah, D. of Nathaniel Willis,
1707, and had John 1707, Ebenezer 1710. Ebenezer m. Elizabeth Hanmer 1750.
9. Thomas (s. of Nathaniel 3.) lived and was the first settler
at the Center, so called; m. Susanna, D. of John Hayward, (m.
23

at Scituate) 1702, and had Elizabeth 1706, d. 1772; Thomas
1708, Susanna 1711, John 1713, Jacob 1717, Jemima 1721.—
The father and mother both d. 1746.—Susanna m. David Dunbar
1738.

10. Samuel (s. of Nathaniel 3.) lived awhile in E. B. near his
brother Nathaniel; his wife Elizabeth ; had Experience 1701,
Patience 1704, Samuel 1706. Experience m. James Dunbar
1722.—Patience m. John Willis 1724.—Samuel Hayward m.
Abigail Torrey of Scituate 1725, and had James 1729.—Samuel
Hayward m. Hannah Hill 1732, perhaps wid. of Nathaniel.

11. Benjamin (s. of Nathaniel 3.) lived in S. B. near Hayward's Bridge, so called, and m. Sarah, D. probably of John Aldrich a. 1700, and had Benjamin 1701, Sarah 1705, Hezekiah
1707, Jacob 1712 : his will 1732 : he d. 1733, æ. 56.—Sarah m.
David Conant 1723.

12. Elisha (s. of Nathaniel 3.) had the homestead of his father,
and lived where his s. Ezra afterwards lived on the south side of
the river : m. Experience Harvey 1708 ; had Elisha and Experience 1710, Hannah 1711, Tabitha and Abner 1714 : he m. Bethiah, D. of William Snow, 1721 ; had Bethiah 1722, Naomi
1726, Ezra 1729. Experience m. Benjamin Curtis 1732.—Hannah m. John Snow 1731.—Tabitha m. Jacob Hayward 1742.—
Bethiah m. Thomas Willis probably 1743.—Naomi m. Joseph
Alger 1747.

13. John (s. of John 4.) m. Susanna, D. of Samuel Edson, and
had Susanna 1699, Sarah 1703: he d. 1705, and the widow m.
Elihu Brett Jr. 1706.—Susanna m. Joshua Howard 1724.—Sarah
m. Josiah Winslow of Freetown 1721.

14. Dea. Thomas (s. of John 4.) m. Bethiah, D. of William
Brett 1706 : he lived on the southerly side of Matfield River,
within the bounds of E. B., where his father-in-law, Brett, lived
before him. There is no house there now. Had Alice 1707,
Bethiah 1715, Mary 1719, Seth 1721, Phebe 1725. He d. 1741,
she 1745. Alice had a son, Thomas Cushman, and m. Joseph
Pratt 2d. 1749.—Bethiah m. Arthur Harris 1741, and afterwards
Robert Latham.—Mary m. Samuel Dunbar 1745.—Phebe m.
Josiah Washburn 1753.

15. Joseph (s. of John 4.) m. Mehitabel, D. of Daniel Dunham, 1700 : he lived where his uncle Thomas Esq. lived, with
whom he was brought up, near where his grandson Daniel now
lives : he had Mehitabel 1701, Thomas 1702, Joanna 1704, Melatiah 1706, Hannah 1708, Sarah 1710, Joseph 1713, d. 1738;
Daniel 1715, d. 1749; Benjamin 1717. He d. 1758; his will
dated 1751 Mehitabel m. Samuel Edson 1738.—Joanna m.
David Snow 1731.—Melatiah m. Samuel Dunbar.—Hannah d.
single 1785.—Sarah never m.

16. Joseph (s. of Dea. Joseph 5.) m. Sarah Crossman 1703,
lived in or near Raynham probably, and had William 1704, Eleazar 1705, Alice 1707, Lydia 1708, Jemima 1711, Sarah 1713,
Mary 1718, Joseph 1725. Alice m. Joseph Drake 1727.—Lydia

m. James Perigo 1728.—This may be the man who was called Joseph Hayward of the neck 1727.—Joseph Hayward of R. m. Mary Cohoon 1744.

17. Thomas (s. of Dea. Joseph 5.) m. Bethiah Waldo, and lived where Dr. Reed lived, and had Edmund and Jane 1720, Eiljah 1722, Hannah 1723, Bethiah 1725, Rebecca 1727. Jane m. Benjamin Pierce Jr. of Scituate 1750.—Hannah m. Oliver Cheney of Pomfret 1744.—Bethiah m. Zephaniah Willis 1754.— Rebecca m. Isaac Willis 1759.

18. Edward Esq. (s. of Dea. Joseph 5.) lived in Easton and m. Keziah White a. 1749. Edward Hayward m. Zilphah Leach 1760.—Capt. Edward Hayward m. Betty Powers 1802.—Edward Hayward 3d m. Parnel Howard 1805.—Edward Hayward Jr. m. wid. Sally Keith 1820.

19. Peter (s. of Dea. Joseph 5.) m. Abigail Williams 1732, and had Jonathan 1734, Hannah 1748. The father d. a. 1765. Hannah m. Samuel Kinsley 1772.—Jonathan m. Mary, D. of Maj. Isaac Johnson 1769 ; had Abigail, 1770, Jonathan, Jerathmael 1776, Polly 1777, Hannah 1778, Martin, Barzillai, Daniel and Betsy twins.—Abigail m. Jonah Willis 1788.—Jonathan m. Mary, D. of Timo. Hayward, 1795, and afterwards Celia Wilbor.—Jerathmael m. Rebecca, D. of Nath'l Manly, 1802.—Polly m. John Tilden 1796.—Hannah m. Jonah Willis 1800.—Martin m. Susanna, D. of Daniel Manly, 1808, and had Susanna 1811, Martin 1813, and Phebe Maria 1816.—Barzillai gra. B. U. 1807, and m. Vesta, D. of James Howard 1811, and afterwards Hannah Rathburn of Bellingham 1813, and lived in Northampton, and then in Munson, where he d. and left a family : he was a physician.—Daniel m. Keziah Wilbor of E. 1815.—Betsy m. a Drake of E.

20. Josiah (s. of Nathaniel 7.) m. Sarah, D. of Samuel Kinsley, 1715, and had Josiah 1717, Nathan 1720, Abraham 1722*, Sarah 1724, Martha 1727*. He then m. Sarah, wid. of Theodosius Moore and D. of John Prior, 1738, and had Hannah : he d. 1764. Sarah m. Silas Willis a. 1745.—Hannah m. Eliphaz Prior of Duxbury.

21. Nathaniel (s. of Nathaniel 7.) m. Mary Harvey 1716, and had Nathaniel, Experience 1719, Simeon, Silence, Dorcas, d. 1756, Mary probably, and perhaps Elizabeth.—He d. 1755, she 1756.—Experience m. Jonathan Alden of Greenwich 1743, and d. 1809 æ. 90.—Mary m. Jacob Tomson 1735.—Simeon m. Mary Besse 1757 and left the town.—Elizabeth m. John Bolton Jr. 1751.—Silence m. Benjamin Price 1643.

22 . Isaac (s. of Nathaniel 7.) m. Martha wid. of Nathan Perkins and D. of Solomon Leonard 1728.—Martha Hayward m. Joseph Perkins 1761.—Solomon Hayward m. Martha Burr.

23. Timothy (s. of Nathaniel 7.) m. Mary wid. of Samuel Reed 1730, and had Timothy 1732, Ebenezer 1734, Daniel 1740. He then m. wid. Jael Peterson and had Mary, Ezra 1751, after his father's death.—The wid. then m. Capt. Seth Alden 1758.—

Ebenezer went to Rindge N. H.—Ezra went to Dux. m. Esther
D. of Lemuel Delano : had Ezra, Daniel, Isaac, and Pamela
who m. John Watson.—Mary went to Windsor, and m. there.
24. John (s. of John 8.) and his wife Esther had Zadock 1733,
Sarah 1735, Mary 1736.—Zadock Hayward m. Experience
Bearce 1768.—Sarah Hayward d. 1768.
25. Nathan Hayward and his w. Content had Nathan 1749,
Daniel 1751, Jonathan 1752.
26. Thomas (s. of Thomas 9.) m. Elizabeth, wid. of Nicholas
Byram and D. of Matthew Gannett, 1746, (lived at the Center)
and had Susanna 1747, Mary 1749, Betty and Thomas 1753:
she d. 1812, æ. 94. Susanna m. Jesse Edson 1768.—Mary m.
Benjamin Marshall 1768.—Betty m. Nath'l Manly 1778.
27. Jacob (s. of Thomas 9.) m. Tabitha, D. of Elisha Hayward 1742, and had Jacob 1743, John 1745, Tabitha 1746, Experience 1748*, Silvanus 1750, Cornelius 1752, Jemima 1754,
Hannah 1756. Jacob left no children.—Cornelius d. a bachelor.—
Jemima m. David Snow 1787.—Hannah m. Thomas Hayward
1781.
28. Samuel (s. of Samuel 10.) m. Susanna, D. of Samuel
Edson, 1736, went to Taunton, and there d. Had Samuel, and
one D. who m. a Stacy, and Betty who m. Nath'l Harvey 1766,
and Abigail who m. Beriah Willis 1759.
29. Benjamin (s. of Benjamin 11.)m. Elizabeth D. of William
Conant 1724, and had Sarah, Rebecca 1729, Hannah 1736, Ruth
1741, after her father's death.—Sarah m. Isaac Buck perhaps
1773.—Rebecca m. Thomas Parris.
30. Hezekiah (s. of Benjamin 11.) m. Huldah D. of Capt.
Josiah Edson 1738, and had Elijah 1741, Huldah 1744, Hezekiah
1746, Ziba 1749, Edward 1753.—Huldah m. Calvin Pierce of
Scituate 1767.—Edward m. Jenny D. of Edward Mitchell 1782;
had no children : the father d. 1790, æ. 83, she 1800 æ. 87.
31. Dea. Jacob (s. of Benjamin 11.) lived in S. Bridgewater :
m. Martha D. of Nehemiah Allen 1736, and had Jacob 1738,
Martha 1744, Benjamin 1747.—Martha m. Major James Allen
1761.—Dea. Hayward d. 1778.
32. Elisha (s. of Elisha 12.) m. Elizabeth, D. probably of
James Washburn, 1740, and had Elisha, Jesse 1742, Caleb 1746,
Betty, Molly and Hannah. Elisha Hayward m. Abigail Eddy
1747.—Elisha m. Mercy Whiting of Plymp. 1760.—Elisha m.
Polly Blanchard 1778. Jesse m. Mary, D. of Abraham Harden
of Hanson 1763, and had Jesse who lived awhile in E. B., and
thence removed to Ohio.—Caleb m. a Clark of Plymo., and had
Caleb, Hannah, Rhoda and Lydia: he d. 1811, æ. 65.—Caleb
Hayward m. Persis Hayward 1773.—Hannah m. Col. Jesse
Reed 1800.—Rhoda d. single 1818, æ. 38.—Betty m. John Hayward 1778.—Hannah m. Abraham Hayward 1787.
33. Abner (s. of Elisha 12.) m. Mary, D. of Joseph Alger,
1739; had Susanna 1742*, Nathan 1744*, Abner 1746, Susanna
1754. He d. 1796; his will dated 1788 : left a wid. Grace : she

was a Turner, m. 1784. Susanna m. Capt. Edward Hayward.—
Capt. Abner m. Abigail, D. of Henry Howard 1772.
34. Ezra (s. of Elisha 12.) m. Lydia Lee 1757, and had Be-
thiah 1758, Ezra 1764, Lydia 1767, Charles 1769, Cyrus 1772,
Sarah 1777. He lived where his father and grandfather lived
before him, and d. 1808 ; she 1816. Bethiah m. Philip Bolton
1787.—Lydia m. Samuel Turner 1794.—Cyrus m. Deborah
Ripley 1804.—Sarah m. Ansel Cobb.
35. Seth (s. of Dea. Thomas 14.) lived in S. B. : m. Tabitha
D. of Joseph Pratt Jr. 1748, and had Azariah 1749, Sarah 1752,
Solomon 1754, Bethiah 1757, Charity 1760. Ruth 1764.—
The father d. 1778: the mother 1789.—Sarah m. Noah Whitman 1774.—Charity m. David Benson 1780.—Seth Hayward m.
Sarah Washburn 1792.
36. Thomas (s. of Joseph 15.) lived in Titicut m. Constant
D. of Samuel Keith, and had Amos 1730, John 1732, m. but left
no children, Eliab 1734, Robert 1737, Mehitabel 1740.—He d.
1789, æ. 87, she 1770.—Mehitabel m. Edward Keith 1778.
37. Benjamin (s. of Joseph 15.) m. Sarah D. of Dea. Recompence Cary 1742, and lived by the River in W. B., and had Sarah 1744, Joseph 1746, Mary 1750, Daniel 1752, Benjamin 1754,
Cary 1759.—He d. 1773: she 1776.—Sarah m. Issachar Snell
Esq. 1769.—Mary m. Capt. Zebedee Snell 1777.—Cary m. Mary
D. of Thomas Tompson 1779, and went to Ware.
38. William (s. of Joseph 16.) and his wife Abigail had Abigail 1730, Lois 1732, Sarah 1735, Keziah 1740, Ann 1743.—Sarah m. Levi Edson 1774.
39. Eleazer (s. of Joseph 16.) and his w. Keturah had Abel
1732, Rufus 1734, Reuben 1742.—Rufus Hayward was with
Gen. Winslow 1755 in seizing the Neutral French at Nova Scotia ; he enlisted from Stoughton.
40. Edmund (s. of Thomas 17.) m. Anna D. of Josiah Snell
1751, and had Mary 1753, Isaiah 1755, Waldo 1758, Edmund
1762, Elijah 1763, Anna 1766, Hannah 1770.—His estate settled
1781: she d. 1776.—Mary m. Daniel Howard 1772.—Edmund
went to Sidney Me. and m. Sukey Matthews 1792.—Anna m.
Solomon Shaw 1782.
41. Elijah (s. of Thomas 17.) m. Silence D. of John Snell
1751, and had Silence 1751, Elijah 1752, Rebecca 1754, Luther
1758.—He d. 1800 ; she 1802.—Elijah, the son, left no children.
42. Josiah (s. of Josiah 20.) m. Sarah D. of Thomas Perkins
1742; had Lois, Sarah ; he then m. Mary Dunham 1756 ; had
Hepzibah, Molly, Phinehas, Cyrus, Independence, Otis, Kinsley,
Eliza, Lucy. He m. a Muxam for his 3d. w. ; he d. 1773.—
Lois m. Moses Simmons 1769.—Sarah m. at Wareham and afterwards P. Turner.—Hepzibah m. Lt. Rotheus Mitchell 1783.
Molly m. Robert Edson 1782.—Cyrus m. Silvia Hayward 1809.
Independence m. Hannah Thorn 1799. Otis m. Betsy Parris
1804.—Kinsley m. Hannah Pool of H. 1805.—Eliza m. a Bar-
tholomew of Boston.—Lucy also went to Boston.

43. Nathan (s. of Josiah 20.) m. Susanna D. of Charles Latham
a. 1748; and had Adam 1749*, Beza 1752, Cephas 1754*, Susanna 1757, Sarah 1759*, Eunice 1761*, Nathan 1763, Betsy
1767*.—He d. 1794, æ. 74.—Susanna m. Doct. James Thacher
of Plymouth 1785.
44. Nathaniel (s. of Nathaniel 21.) m. Elizabeth Curtis of Halifax 1742, and had Nathaniel 1743, Enos 1745, Mary 1750, Barzillai 1753, Calvin 1755, Dorcas 1758, Rebecca; his w. d. 1766,
and he m. Hannah Soule of Plympton 1769, and had Philip 1770,
Oliver 1771, Libeus 1772, Rufus 1774, Isaac, and Adam 1777*.
His will 1780.—Mary m. a Dwier.—Dorcas m. a Bryant.—Nathaniel m. Mary Packard 1762, and he, Enos, and Barzillai went
to Wareham.—Oliver m. Anna D. of Solomon Washburn 1797,
and had Oliver, Solomon 1805, Anna 1807, Harriet 1811, Os-
sian 1813.
45. Timothy (s. of Timothy 23.) m. Hannah D. of Solomon
Pratt 1767, and had Timothy 1770, Hannah 1772, and Mary.—
The mother d. 1795 æ. 63.—Hannah m. Nath'l Perkins Jr. 1794.
Mary m. Jonathan Hayward 1795.
46. Daniel (s. of Timothy 23.) m. Abigail D. of Richard Davenport Jr. 1761, and had Jairus : and removed to Greenwich.—He
also had 2 Ds. who m. at Greenwich (now Enfield.)
47. Thomas (s. of Thomas 26.) lives at the Center, and m.
Hannah D. of Jacob Hayward 1781, and had Ansel 1782, Betsy
1784, Hannah 1793, Harriet 1795, Thomas 1798.—Betsy m.
Nath'l Edson 1802.—Hannah m. Thomas Johnson Jr. 1809.—
Harriet m. Francis Cary 1816.—Thomas m. Lucy Foster of K.
48. John (s. of Jacob 27.) m. Betty D. of Elisha Hayward
1778, and had experience 1779, Jacob 1781, Betty 1782.—Experience m. Rufus Crosman 1818.—Jacob m. Abigail D. of Jonah
Willis 1816 he d. and she m. Alfred Whitman 1833.—Betty m.
Ebenezer Colwell Jr. 1804.
49. Silvanus (s. of Jacob 27.) m. Joanna D. of Joseph Snow,
and had Silvanus, Sarah, Hannah Tabitha, and one other not m.
Sarah m. Daniel S. Brett 1807.—Hannah m. John Colwell 1813:
she d. and then Tabitha m. him 1816.
50. Elijah (s. of Hezekiah 30.) m. Mary Tomson of Halifax
1785, and had Elijah, Edson, Erastus, Edward, Bela.—Elijah m.
Betsy (Eliza) D. of David Kingman 1809, and removed to Cincinnati. She d. 1834 ; he was a Lawyer, Judge and Commissioner of the Land Office at Washington.—Erastus m. Mary
P. Torrey 1813.—Bela lived in Weymouth and was Representative there 1839.
51. Hezekiah (s. of Hezekiah 30.) m. Hazadiah King of R.
1791 ; had Hazadiah, an only child, who m. Caleb Keith 1812.
52. Ziba (s. of Hezekiah 30.) m. Lucy, D. of John Conant,
1773 ; had Ziba, Lucy, Calvin, Jeremiah, Huldah : he d. æ. over
80. Ziba m. Sally Bozworth of H. 1806.—Lucy m. Wm. Bozworth of H. 1807.—Calvin m. Mary, D. of Ezra Fobes 1801,
and had Jane Mitchell 1802, Mary Fobes 1805*, Celesta 1806.

53. Jacob (s. of Dea. Jacob 31.) m. Joanna, D. of Daniel Snell, 1759, and had Joanna 1760, and removed from town.

54. Benjamin (s. of Dea. Jacob 31.) m. Mary, D. of Jonathan Benson, 1767, and had Sarah, Mary, Martha. Sarah m. Caleb Alden 1790.—Martha m. Howe Keith 1795.—Mary m. Oliver Washburn 1804.

55. Charles (s. of Ezra 34.) m. Eleanor Howard of Plymouth 1797, and had Charles 1797, Ezra 1800, Hannah 1805, John 1807, Henry 1810, Ellen 1813.—Charles m. Sally Keith 1821, and d. the same year.

56. Azariah (s. of Seth 35.) m. Ann Pratt 1768, and had Azariah and Davis : he and she both d. 1802 ; he æ. 52, she 55.— Davis m. Freelove, D. of Noah Whitman, 1804, and moved to Me.—Milicent d. 1801 æ. 25.

57. Solomon (s. of Seth 35.) m. Zerviah Washburn 1782, and had Solomon 1783, Martin 1784, Joseph 1786, Silas 1788, Nahum 1790, Seth 1792, Betsy 1794, Almarine 1796, Lewis 1798, Lavinia 1800, Luther 1802. Solomon m. Betsy Bates 1807.— Joseph m. Silvia Conant 1814.

58. Amos (s. of Thomas 36.) m. Mary, D. of John Ripley, 1766, and had Walter 1768, Deborah 1769, John Ripley 1771, Mary. He d. 1816, æ. 86.—Mary m. Capt. Joseph Alden 1800.

59. Eliab (s. of Thomas 36.) m. Martha, D. of John Fobes, 1762, and had Wealthy 1763, Lucy 1765, Thomas 1767, Eliab, Amos, and went to Townsend.—Eliab m. Celia, D. of Dea. Daniel Leach, 1803.

60. Robert (s. of Thomas 36.) m. Hannah Keith 1768, and had Olive 1771, Constant, Caleb, Oliver, Hannah. Oliver gra. B. U. 1804, and settled in the ministry at Barnstable, and m. Lucy, D. of David Hooper, 1815, and d. of a consumption.— Hannah m. Timothy Keith 1819.

61. Joseph (s. of Benjamin 37.) m. Olive Manly 1768, and had Asaph 1770, Hannah 1772, Olive 1774, Sarah 1776, Rebecca 1778, Silvia 1780, Manly 1782, Mary 1784. Hannah m. Jacob Dunbar 1794.—Olive m. Hayward Marshall 1794.—Sarah m. Robert Packard 1798.—Rebecca m. Jonas Reynolds 1798.— Silvia m. Solomon Stone of Easton 1817.—Mary m. Gannett Marshall of St. 1810.—Manly m. Mary Monk 1803, and had Joseph 1810, Mary Clapp 1812.

62. Daniel (s. of Benjamin 37.) m. Bethiah, D. of James Howard, 1777, and had Mehitabel 1780, Adin 1782, Ruby 1784, Sarah 1786, Daniel 1788, Pliny 1790. Sarah m. Hayward Manly 1816.—Daniel m. Vesta Manly 1817.—Pliny m. Polly Kingman.

63. Benjamin (s. of Benjamin 37.) m. Abigail, D. of Josiah Perkins, 1777, and had Mehitabel 1779, Abigail 1781, Lucinda 1784, Sarah 1786, Benjamin 1790. He went to Ware.

64. Isaiah (s. of Edmund 40.) m. Sarah, D. of Samuel Bartlett, 1777, and had Barzillai 1778, and moved away.

65. Waldo (s. of Edmund 40.) m. Lucy, D. of Samuel Bartlett, 1781, and had Ira 1782, Abby 1786, Bela 1787, Zina 1789,

Waldo 1794, Otho 1796, Lucinda 1800. Abby m. Isaac Eames 1811,—Waldo m. Polly 1816, and Nancy 1818, both Ds. of Ebenezer Algér.

66. Elijah (s. of Edmund 40.) m. Polly Hayden of Braintree 1792, and had Eli 1793, Betsy F. 1795, Lavinia 1796, Polly 1798, Jane 1801, Susanna 1802, Anne 1805, Elijah Edmund 1807. He left town.—Betsy F. m. Oliver Bonney of Hadley 1814.

67. Luther (s. of Elijah 41.) m. Betty, D. of Nathan Willis, 1785, and had Luther 1787, Eliza 1789, Nahum 1790, Nathan 1792: his wife d. and he m. Urania White of Marshfield 1794: he d. 1832. Luther m. Clarissa R. Inglee 1812, and had Betsy Willis 1813, Luther 1814, James Ingells 1816.—Eliza m. John Southworth 1806.—Maj. Nathan m. Rhoda, D. of Howard Cary Esq., 1818.

68. Hon. Beza (s. of Nathan 43.) m. Abigail, D. of Col. Briggs Alden of Duxbury, 1784, and had John Alden 1788*, and Beza*: his w. d. 1800, æ. 45, and he then m. Experience, wid. of Capt. James Russell of Plymouth and D. of Ichabod Shaw, 1801, and bad Charles Latham*, John Shaw, and Susanna 1805. He gra. H. U. 1772, studied divinity and preached, but was never settled; spent the early part of his life in fitting young men for college: was Representative, Senator, and Councilor: removed to Plymouth, and held the office of Register of Probate for many years, and until his death.

69. Dr. Nathan (s. of Nathan 43.) gra. H. U. 1785, lives at Plymouth; was a Surgeon in the army, and is High Sheriff of the Co.: m. Joanna, D. of Pelham Winslow Esq., and had Geo. Washington and John Adams, (twins), both d.*; Mary Winslow, James Thacher, Elizabeth, Pelham Winslow, Charles Latham, George Partridge. Mary W. m. Wm. S. Russell.—James T. m. a D. of Judge Thomas Dawes of Boston.

70. Timothy (s. of Timothy 45.) m. Huldah, D. of Silvanus Ames, 1792, and had Polly 1792, Timothy 1795, Huldah 1797, Sally Willis 1800, Sullivan 1802: his wife d. 1807, and he m. Mary Crooker Stetson 1817, and had Bethiah Stetson 1817, Mercutio 1819, Mary 1822, Nathan Stetson 1824, Hannah Pratt 1827. Polly m. Isaac Fobes 1811, and d. before 1822.—Timothy m. Sarah Billings 1817.—Huldah m. Asa Perkins 1815, his mother was a Morse.—Sally W. m. Simeon Perkins.

71. Ansel (s. of Thomas 47.) m. Huldah, D. of Thos. Johnson, 1807, and had Ansel Alonzo 1808, Harriet Ann 1810, Lorenzo Thomas 1812, John Elbridge 1814, Lucy Maria 1815, and went to Belchertown, and writes his name Howard.

72. Azariah (s. of Azariah 56.) m. Silvia, wid. of Silvanus Conant, and D. of John Conant, 1798, and had Tempe 1799, Anna 1800, Chloe 1803, Marshall 1804, and went to Me.

73. Walter (s. of Amos 58.) m. Ruth, D. of old John Alden of M. 1793, and had Alden 1798, Loisa 1801, Franklin 1802, Thos. Jefferson 1804, Walter 1808: he d. 1838. One s. m. a D. of Thomas Mitchell.

74. John Ripley (s. of Amos 58.) m. Nabby Robinson 1801, and Clarissa Robinson of M. 1802, and had Nabby Robinson 1802, Clarissa Robinson 1803, Emily 1807.

75. Constant (s. of Robert 60.) m. Hannah Snow, wid. of Josiah Keen and D. of Ezra Whitman, 1808, and had Henrietta 1809, Harriet Whitman 1812.

76. Asaph (s. of Joseph 61.) m. Polly Drake of Easton 1791, and had Asaph 1793, Olive 1794, Joseph 1796, Laura 1799, Azel 1801, Edwin and Emmy 1803. This family removed to Waybridge, Vt.

77. Ira (s. of Waldo 65.) m. Sarah, D. of Josiah Edson, 1806, and had Otis 1806, Ambrose 1810, Sumner Augustus 1812, Julia 1814, Sarah Reliance 1818: his wife d. 1819, and he m. wid. Susanna Fish 1820, and removed to Kingston.

78. Edward (see Edward 18.) m. Parnel, D. of James Howard, 1805, and had Eliza 1806, Rhoda 1808, Susanna 1810, Edward 1812, Vesta 1815: his w. d. 1818.

James Hayward Jr. m. Sarah Harris 1751.—Martha m. Joseph Perkins 1761.—Jonathan Hayward, or Howard, of E. m. Sarah, D. of Timothy Leach, 1762.—Olive Hayward m. Jeremiah Leach 1776.—Olive m. Joseph Fobes of E. 1780.—Oliver m. Tabitha Howard, of St., 1786.—Adah m. Jedediah Willis of E. 1802.—Bethiah m. Backus Leach 1804.—Benjamin m. Philibert Leonard of Mid'o. 1807.—Ansel of Boston m. Lucinda Tolman 1812.—Lydia m. Nathan Richards 1813.—Silas m. Mary Thayer 1779.

HEARSEY.—1. William Hearsey (s. of William and Abigail (Tirrell) of Abington born 1719.) settled in East Bridgewater · m. Lydia Gurney of Abington 1745 and had Stephen 1751, William 1753, Lydia 1757, and Deborah 1762.—The father d. 1816, æ. 97.—Lydia m. John Harden 1779.

2. Stephen (s. of William 1.) and his w. Polly, had David, Jacob, Nathaniel, Dorothy, Mehitabel, and Relief.—David m. a Barstow of Hanover.—Jacob m. Polly Drake 1812.—Dorothy m. Thomas R. Alden.—Mehitabel m. Ellis Holmes.—Susanna Hearsey m. Achish Pool 1799.

3. William (s. of William 1.) m. Molly Pratt of Abington 1778, and had John, William.—John m. Sarah Lathrop 1807.—William m. Abigail D. of Nathan Dawes.

David m. Esther Reed 1707.—Alice m. Noah Harden 1816.— Galen m. Polly Johnson 1813.—Obadiah m. Naomi Reed 1777. Solomon Jr. m. Silvia Gurney 1802.—Martha m. Jacob Dawes 1800.—Tho's m. Deborah Pool 1793.—Molly m. David Churchill Jr. 1797.—Joseph Jr. m. Sarah White 1799.

HEIFORD or HAYFORD.—John Heiford (or Hayford) m. Lydia Pierce 1706.—Edward Hayford's w. d. 1779, æ. 22, and he m. Lenity, widow of Nathan Kingman, 1779: she was a Thomas of Marshfield: his 2d w.—John Orcutt m. a Heiford. —Thomas Washburn m. Abigail Heiford 1711.

24

HEGENE.—John Hegene and his wife Elizabeth had John 1744, Mary 1745, Elizabeth 1747.

HENRY.—Thomas Henry m. Ann Miller 1743.—This is one of the Irish Families that settled in N. B. a. 1740.—He had Thomas 1744, James 1746, Jennet 1747, John 1750, Margaret 1752, David 1754, Ann 1756, Samuel William.—James m. Mehitabel Hall 1770, Jennet m. Hosea Dunbar of Halifax, and had three Ds. viz. Betsy Dunbar, who m. William Mitchell 1793, and Jennet Dunbar who m. first Allen Latham 1796, and then Zephaniah Howard 1800, and Nancy who m. Ebenezer Hall 1816.— He and all his family except Jennet moved to Harperfield, N. Y. about 1771, and Thomas and James were killed by the Indians and Tories in 1775 or 1776, and John was taken prisoner and d. in Canada.—Robert Henry m. wid. Mary Wormel.

HEWETT.—James Hewett and his w. Abigail had Abigail 1730, Sarah 1732, Susanna 1733, Bathsheba 1735, Abiah 1739, Abraham 1742.

HIGGINS or HAGEN.—John Higgins and his w. Elizabeth resided in E. B. and had Elizabeth 1747, who d. 1777; he d. before 1760; he owned the Wesley Place, so called.—He was in communion with Mr. Morehead's church in Boston; probably a Scotchman.

HILL.—1. Jonathan Hill and his w. Mary early settled in E. B.; hè was s. probably of John and Frances of Dorchester; he had Nathaniel, Ebenezer, Jonathan, Mary and Bethiah.—Jonathan perhaps went to Mid'o.—Mary m. Elnathan Bassett 1702.— Bethiah was a member of the Church 1724.

2. Nathaniel (s. of Jona. 1.) m. Hannah D. of Nathaniel Conant 1710, (she perhaps afterward m. Sam'l Hayward 1732,) and had David 1712, Abijah 1714, Mary 1717, Ebenezer 1719, Josiah 1722, Hannah 1725.—Mary m. Benaiah Smith of Easton 1738.—Hannah m. William Snow 1743.—Nathaniel sold his homestead to Ebenezer 1718.

3. Ebenezer (s. of Jonathan 1.) m. Susanna D. of Jacob Leonard 1714, and had Ebenezer 1715, Jacob 1717, Israel 1719, Eleazar 1730.—The father d. 1760: the mother 1764.—Ebenezer quits his estate to his brother Eleazar 1760, and d. a. 1767.

4. Ebenezer (it is not certain who this man was; he might have been a brother of Jonathan 1.) m. Ruth D. probably of Guido Bailey, and had Ruth 1685, Ebenezer 1686.—Ebenezer and Sarah his w. sold land to John Irish 1694: he d. 1696.—Ruth m. James Hodges of Taunton 1704.—This family probably went to Taunton; there was a John of Kingston R. I., son of Ebenezer, perhaps of this family.

5. David (s. of Nathaniel 2.) m. Mary D. of Thomas Buck 1733, and had Anna 1747, Eunice 1749, Molly 1751, Jerusha 1753, Tiley (or Silence) 1755.—Anna m. Joseph Vinton 1774.— Eunice m. Abraham Joslyn 1769.—Molly m. Nehemiah Shaw 1775. (see Nathan Beal.)—Jerusha m. William Snow 1776.

6. Abijah (s. of Nathaniel 2.) m. Sarah Lawson 1747, and lived in N. B., and had James 1753, Robert 1756.

7. Ebenezer (s. of Nathaniel 2.) m. Abigail Stoddard (or Stodder) of Hingham 1749: she d. 1775: he had Jonathan, Joseph, Solomon, John.—This family lived in S. Corner, Abington, and N. B. till after 1775.—He m. Bathsheba Rogers of Weymouth 1777, for a 2d. wife, and lived in Weymouth, and there d. æ. 88. Jonathan settled in Abington.—Joseph d. leaving a D. Susanna in Abington.—John went to Boston, no children, and he and his w. d. of small pox 1839.

8. Josiah (s. of Nathaniel 2.) and his w. Mary, had Mary 1747, Huldah, Josiah 1751, Noah 1753, Abigail, Sarah, William 1760, Elizabeth, Prudence, Barnum 1770. This family lived in S. B. : he d. 1805 æ. 83.—Mary m. Nathaniel Ames 1783.—Josiah m. Abigail D. of Jonathan Beal 1779, and removed to Plainfield : had Ds. but no son.—Noah m. Hannah Beal 1780, and had Oliver 1781, Cyrus 1786, Alban 1790.—Sarah m. Samuel Codding of T. 1781.—Barnum m. Mary Ellis of R. 1806.

9. Jacob (s. of Ebenezer 3.) m. Abigail D. of Ebenezer Bonney of Pembroke 1754, and had Hezekiah 1754, Jacob 1756, Susanna 1759, Abigail 1761, Eleazar 1764 ; she d. 1781 æ. 51 : he 1804 æ. 87.—Hezekiah and Eleazer went to Me. and lived on an Island near N. Yarmouth.

10. Israel (s. of Ebenezer 3.) m. Beriah D. of Thomas Latham 1748, and had Thomas 1749, John 1753, Tamor 1755, Keziah 1757, Joseph 1759, Anne 1761, Israel 1763, Deliverance 1764, Ebenezer 1766, Deborah 1768, Beriah Latham 1770.

11. Eleazar (s. of Ebenezer 3.) m. Anna D. of Dr. Daniel Field 1769 : they had no children : he d. 1791 æ. 62.

12. Solomon (s. of Ebenezer 7.) m. Rachel Stowell of Abington and afterwards a Hollis of Braintree : he had a D. Polly 1792 : he went to Plainfield.

13. Joseph (s. of Ebenezer 7.) b. and lived in Abington : m. a Stowell of Hingham and lived there till he d. a. 1832 : he had Nabby, Susan, Joseph, Dama, Hannah, Charles, Daniel.

14. Jacob (s. of Jacob 9.) m. Anne D. of Thomas Tribou 1780. and had Melzar 1783, Jacob 1784, Nanny 1786, Leonard 1788, Bela 1790, Bezer 1792 ; she d. 1823 æ. 65 ; he 1827 æ. 70.—Melzar m. Mary Howland 1813, and had Caleb, Lydia, Benjamin and Mary, and went to Minot.—Jacob gra. Br. U. 1807, and settled in the law at Minot, and m. a Lobdell.—Nanny m. Ephraim Cary 1809, and went to Minot.—Leonard m. Polly D. of Jonah Willis 1817, and had Charles ; he m. a 2d. w. and has a D.— Bela m. an Orr, sister of his brother Bezer's wife.—Bezer m. Hannah D. of Robert Orr 1816, and was killed 1821 by the oversetting of his cart.

15. John Hill was an early settler in Bridgewater, -but soon died or removed, and has left no posterity here.—Jonathan sold land to him in Br. 1694.—Susanna m. John Smith 1777.

16. Samuel Hill of Duxbury m. Phebe D. of Philip Leonard

1694: lived in Duxbury, and had Abigail 1697, Philip 1699, Samuel 1701, Richard 1702, Ebenezer 1705, Ephraim 1707, Joseph and Lydia 1710. There was a Leonard Hill in Pembroke, probably one of this family.

HOBART.—1. Seth Hobart (s. of Col. Aaron of Abington) m. Esther D. of Jona. Allen of Braintree 1782, and settled in E. B., and had Betsy 1783, Jonathan 1786, Polly 1790, Joseph 1796, Esther 1798. She d. 1813: he 1814.—Polly m. David Pratt 1815.—Joseph m. Ruth Sherman of Pembroke 1820.—Esther m. Micah White Jr. 1818.

1. Hon. Aaron Hobart (s. of Aaron Esq. and Grándson of Col. Aaron of Abington) m. Maria D. of Andrew Leach, and lived in Hanover and afterwards settled in E. B., and had Susan, Aaron, George, Maria, Edward, John, Catharine.

Elizabeth m. Willis Harden 1802.—Salome m. Marcus Alden 1807.—Benjamin Hobart Esq. m. Lucy Lazell 1811.—John Hobart m. Mary D. of Matthew Allen 1765: he was father of John Hobart Esq. of Leicester.—Noah Hobart m. Deborah W. Thomas 1789.—Jemima m. Shubael Clark of Rehoboth 1818.

HOLDEN.—William and Hannah Holden had Samuel 1737, William 1739.

HOLLOWAY.—Jona. Holloway m. Elizabeth Brown 1746, and had William 1747, Seth 1751, Jonathan 1756.

HOLMAN.—1. Col. John Holman of Milton sold his farm there to Gov. Jona. Belcher 1727, and came and settled in E. B.: he gra. at H. U. 1700, and m. Ann D. of John Quincy Esq. of Braintree 1705; represented the town of Bridgewater several years, and was much respected; had John, Ann, Peggy, Ruth, and Mary: he had a 2d. wife Sarah, who d. 1740 æ. 60; he d. 1759 æ. 80: his will dated 1757, proved 1759: Dea. Thomas Whitman Exor.—Ann m. Joseph Billings of Stoughton 1730.—Peggy m. John Johnson 1731.—Ruth m. Benjamin Johnson 1732.—Mary m. Ezra Cary 1737.

2. Capt. John (s. of Col. John 1.) m. Anne D. of Isaac Harris 1734, and had Sarah 1736, Anne 1738, William 1740, Abigail 1743, Isaac and Jane: he d. 1755: she 1757 æ. 45.—Sarah m. James Keith 1752.—Anne m. Benjamin Byram 1757.—William d. 1762.—Abigail m. Seth Keith 1764.—Jane m. Ephraim Cary 1771.

HOLMES.—1. John Holmes of Halifax m. Abigail D. of Abijah Thayer 1799, and lived in W. B. and had Anna 1800, Freeman 1803, Vesta 1804, Abigail 1806.

2. Dea. Cornelius Holmes and Elizabeth settled in S. B. and had Cornelius 1781, Ellis 1783, Benjamin 1784, Thomas 1788, Betsy 1791, Charles and Henry 1793, William 1796.—Benjamin m. Waitstill Benson 1807.

3. Cornelius (s. of Dea. Cornelius 2.) m. Mehitabel D. of Ezra Conant 1806, and had Cornelius 1807, George W. 1811, Gaius 1816.

4. Ellis (s. of Dea. Cornelius 2.) m. Lois Holbrook Bartlett,

and settled in E. B., and had Louisa Bartlett 1813, Ellis Wins-
low 1816: his wife d. 1830 æ. 39: and he m. Mehitable D. of
Stephen Hearsey.
Ephraim m. Margaret D. of John Washburn 1741.—Betty of
M. m. Lot Conant 1744.—Sarah m. Jonathan Carver 1746.—
William m. Elizabeth Hamlin 1750.—Experience m. Ebenezer
Perkins 1751.—Eunice of H. m. Benjamin Sprague 1762, and
Solomon Ames 1781.—Hannah of H. m. Barnabas Snell 1781.—
Benjamin of N. m. Mehitabel Howard 1783.—Samuel m. Mary
Bryant 1791.—Lucy m. John Harden 1792.—Samuel m. Mary
Orcutt 1794.—Otis of T. m. Nabby Fobes 1796.—Patience m.
Joseph Bailey of Freeport 1796.—Ellis Jr. m. Patty Conant 1803.
Howland m. Huldah Copeland 1804.—Mary m. Solomon Leach
1806.—Ellis of H. m. Lucy Copeland 1806.—Betsy of H. m.
Alpheus Brett 1807.—Nabby m. Eaton Aldridge 1807.—Ellis of
S. B. m. Content Chipman of H. 1808.—Mary m. Caleb Bassett
Jr. 1811.—Samuel m. Deborah Packard 1813, and d. 1827 æ. 34.
—Abigail m. Samuel Sturtevant 1816.—Melzar of H. m. Abigail
Howe 1818.—Roxana m. Hosea Packard 1818.—Philander m.
Elizabeth F. D. of Parmenas Brett, and had George N. 1828,
and Susan W. 1830.
   HOOPER.—John Hooper and his w. Sarah, D. perhaps of
John Harden, had Nathaniel 1703, Sarah 1705, James 1708, and
perhaps others born before they came to this town. Sarah m.
Stephen Leach 1725, and afterwards Ebenezer Snow perhaps
1737.—His estate was settled 1709, and the wid. Sarah m. Francis
Wood 1710. John, Thomas, and William below, were probably
his ss.; and Elizabeth who m. Enoch Leonard 1707, and Ruth
who m. John Bolton Jr. 1710, might have been his sisters.
   2. John (s. of John 1.) m. Elizabeth, D. of Nathaniel or John
Packard, 1722, and had John 1725, Winslow 1729, Hezekiah
1732, Joseph 1735, Rebecca 1738: his will 1741, her's 1742, and
she made her brother Joseph Packard Exor.—Rebecca m. Dea.
Joseph Copeland 1760.—Winslow with his friend Timothy
Mitchell were both lost at sea in youth.
   3. Thomas (s. probably of John 1.) m. Sarah, D. of Nathaniel,
Sam'l, or John Packard, 1722, and had Sarah 1730, Thomas
1737, John 1739, Jerusha 1743: these were all bap. in E. B.
Thomas m. Deborah Cushman of Halifax 1761, and she afterwards m. Wm. Dunham 1781.—John m. Sarah Pool 1766, and
d. 1807, æ. 67, without children.—Jerusha m. Robert Latham
1778, and afterwards Jacob Mitchell 1791, and d. 1829, æ. 85:
she had no children by either husband.—Sarah m. Stephen
Leach perhaps 1749.
   4. William (s. probably of John 1.) m. Lois Thomas of Mid'o.,
and had William, Thomas 1731, Lois 1733, Elisha 1736, Susanna
1740, David 1743, Luther 1746, Calvin 1749. His estate was
divided among the heirs 1757. Thomas m. a White, and afterwards Ebenezer Ames' widow, but had no children.—Lois m.
Jona. Cary 1754.—Elisha went to Stockbridge.

5. Nathaniel (s. of John 1.) and his w. Elizabeth had Elizabeth 1729, Mary 1731, Patience 1732, Nathaniel 1735, Sarah 1737. Mary m. Zephaniah Keith 1750.—Nathaniel m. Elizabeth Bryant of M. 1762.

6. James (s. of John 1.) m. Mary, D. of Isaac Johnson 1737, and had James, Milicent, Abihail. He d. 1784, æ. 76. Milicent m. Daniel Keith 1766.—Abihail m. Solomon Pratt 1767.

7. John (s. of John 2.) m. Sarah Cowing 1746, and had John 1747, Sarah 1749; his will 1750. Sarah m. Thomas Lawrence 1769, and afterwards Capt. Barney of Taunton.

8. Hezekiah (s. of John 2.) m. Elizabeth, D. of Solomon Leonard, 1758, and had Elizabeth, Winslow, Joseph, Hezekiah: she d. 1799, æ. 62; and he m. Hannah, wid. of Timothy Conant, 1803: she was a Blackman. Elizabeth m. Benjamin Conant 1782.—Hezekiah gra. H. U. 1789, and settled in the ministry at Boylston, and d. single 1795.

9. William (s. of William 4.) m. Susannah, D. of Jonathan Cary, 1759, and had William: the father d. young; the wid. d. 1795, æ. 62.

10. David (s. of William 4.) m. Martha Shaw of M. 1768, and d. 1831, æ. 87. He had Lucy, who m. Oliver Hayward 1815, and perhaps others.

11. Luther, (s. of William 4.) and his w. Phebe, had Lois 1780, Susanna 1782, Lyman 1787, Abigail 1791, Thomas 1793. The father d. 1831, æ. 85. Lois m. Avery Fobes Esq. 1801.—Susanna m. Zephaniah Keith 1807.—Lyman m. Hannah Shaw 1810.—Abigail m. Aberdeen Wilbor 1809.

12. James (s. of James 6.) m. Susanna, D. of Benjamin Washburn, 1772, and had Isaac 1772, Molly 1774, Susanna 1776, Azubah 1783, Parnel 1786, Levi 1790.—Isaac m. Sarah, D. of Capt. Simeon Wood, 1799, and went to Oakham.—Susanna m. Rufus Wood 1799.—Azubah m. Zeph. Caswell 1803.—Levi of Walpole d. here 1790, æ. 20.

13. John (s. of John 7.) m. Hannah, D. of Joseph Cowing, 1777, and had John 1779, Joseph 1780, Hannah 1782. He afterwards m. Ruth, wid. of Ebenezer Whitman of Oakham: she was a Delano.—Joseph m. an Ellis of M.—Hannah went to Me. and m. a Matthews.—John, the father, removed to Oakham.

14. Winslow (s. of Hezekiah 8.) m. Polly, D. of Chilton Latham, 1791, and had Hezekiah, Mary, and Betsy. Hezekiah d. in Boston, æ. a. 20; the father d. 1834, æ. 73.—Mary m. Paschal Bassett 1811.—Betsy m. Benja. Bates.

15. Capt. Joseph (s. of Hezekiah 8.) m. Lucia, D. of Edward Mitchell, and had Joseph 1793, Lucia 1797, Jane 1799, Elizabeth 1801, Saba 1804, Mitchell 1808. Joseph m. Betsy, D. of Joseph Alden, and settled in New Bedford.—Lucia m. Philo Leach Esq.—Jane m. Capt. Tripp of Fairhaven.—Saba m. Edwin Keith.—Mitchell m. wid. Hayward, D. of Thomas Mitchell.

16. William (s. of William 9.) m. Polly Tilson of Halifax 1793, and had William, Cyrus, Thomas, Susan, Mary and Sarah.

William went to the Cape, and then to N. Bedford.—Cyrus m.
Jane, D. of Perez Crocker, and went to N. Bedford.—Thomas
m. Eloisa, D. of Calvin Washburn.
17. John (s. of John 15.) m. Betsy Ellis of M. 1803, and had
Eliza 1803, Sally 1805, Catharine 1807, John Ellis 1809, Isabella
1811.
    Anne m. Robert Wallis of P. 1752.—Sarah m. Nehemiah Lis-
comb of S. 1760.—Ebenezer m. Relief Bartlett 1761.—Zilphah
m. Jabez Warren of M. 1766.—Levi m. Susanna Leach 1767.—
Mary m. James Perkins 1771.—Patience m. Moses Robbins 1777.
Zalmuna m. Hopestill Pool 1787.—Thomas m. Susanna Fobes
1795.—Roxana m. Bernice Leach 1797.—Apollos m. Vodisa
Hall of R. 1799.—Isaac m. Susanna Leach 1805.—Sally m.
Stephen Wilbor Jr. of R. 1809.—Charles m. Patty Learned of
Ox. 1810.
    HORTON.—Barnabas Horton (from Winchester N. H.) m.
Polly Morse and settled in S. B. and had David 1785, Sibil 1788,
Daniel 1793, Polly 1798, Hannah 1802.—Sibil m. Daniel Tom-
son 1813.
    Isaac Horton of N. B. m. Betsy Shaw 1805.—Sally Horton
m. Aden Packard 1806.—Mary m. Galen Packard 1809.—Jeru-
sha m. Zenas Packard Jr. 1820.
    HOW.—Azor How settled in S. B., and m. Lydia Pratt 1787,
and had Marcus 1787, Olive 1790: his wife d. 1790, and he m.
Ruth Cheesman 1791, and had Lydia, Melinda, Salome, Ophir,
Martin, Abigail. Marcus m. Deborah Hatch, D. of Joseph
Joslyn, 1813.—Lydia m. Absalom Osborn 1812.—Melinda m.
Abner Shelly 1812.—Salome m. Libeus Smith 1814.—Ophir m.
Mary T. Reed 1818.—Martin m. Lurana Lindsay 1820.—Abigail m. Melzar Holmes 1818.
    HOWARD.—John Howard, with his brother James, came
from England and settled in Duxbury : he was among those able
to bear arms there in 1643. James, it is said, went to Bermuda,
and John came to W. B., and was one of the proprietors and
original settlers in the town a. 1651 ; was young when he came
over, and it is said, lived in Capt. Miles Standish's family : was
a man of much influence in the new plantation ; one of the first
military officers in Bridgewater ; took the oath of fidelity here
1657 : his descendants still own and live on the place where he
first settled : he always wrote his name Haward, and so did all
his descendants till after 1700, and the early town records are
conformable to this spelling ; but for the last century it has been
invariably written Howard. It is remarkable that the two names
of Hayward and Haward, which have always been known as distinct families, were uniformly pronounced alike, Howard. They
were perhaps the same originally, and both Hayward ; but, in
writing, John omitted the Y. There was supposed to have been
some connection between the families, but perhaps it arose altogether from intermarriage, as John m. Martha, D. of Thomas
Hayward, and was a younger man even than Thomas Hayward

Jr. He d. about 1700. He had John, James, Jonathan, Elizabeth, Sarah, Bethiah, Ephraim. Elizabeth m. Edward Fobes.—Sarah m. Zaccheus Packard.—Bethiah m. Henry Kingman.—He was licensed to keep an Ordinary or Tavern as early as 1670, and it is remarkable that a public house has been kept there by his descendants ever since till within a few years.

2. John (s. of John 1.) m. Sarah, D. of Robert Latham, and lived in E. B., where Dea. Samuel Keen now lives, till a. 1703, when he sold to Edw. Mitchell, his uncle by marriage, and removed to W. B. He was sometimes called John Howard minimus, and sometimes John Howard of John's Bridge, not only to distinguish him from his father, but also from John Hayward, who was an older man, both names being pronounced alike.—He had Susanna, Edward 1697, Robert 1699, Martha, Sarah, Bethiah. He d. before 1727, and his estate was settled and divided 1729. Susanna m. Capt. Nathaniel Ames 1702.—Martha m. David Perkins.—Sarah m. David Turner of Rehoboth, a Clergyman 1721.—Bethiah first m. Jona. Randall 1712, and afterwards John Hays of Providence.—Susanna, the eldest child was probably named for her grandmother Susanna Latham, who was D. of John Winslow, brother of Gov. Edward Winslow, and whose mother, Mary Chilton, is said to have been the first lady who came on shore at the landing of our forefathers at Plymouth in 1620.

3. James (s. of John 1.) m. Elizabeth, D. of John Washburn, and had Elizabeth 1686, Mercy 1688, James 1690. He went into the Canada Expedition 1690, and d. in the service.—Elizabeth m. Thomas Buck 1712.—Mercy d. 1704.—The wid. Elizabeth m. Edward Sealey.

4. Ephraim (s. of John 1.) m. Mary, D. of Rev. James Keith, and had Jane 1689, Susanna 1692, Martha 1695, Ephraim 1697, Daniel 1699, David 1703, Silence 1705, Mary 1707. He d. 1750, she 1760. Jane m. Nehemiah Washburn 1713.—Susanna m. Samuel Jacobs a. 1720.—Martha m. Josiah Williams of T. 1714.—Silence m. John Burr 1722.—Mary m. John Field 1726, and afterwards Elisha Pierce of Scituate.

5. Maj. Jonathan (s. of John 1.) m. Sarah Dean, and had Jonathan 1692, Joshua 1696, Susanna 1698, Ebenezer 1700, Seth 1702, Abiel 1704, Sarah 1707, Henry 1710, Kezia 1712. His estate was settled and divided 1739. Susanna m. Benjamin Williams of Norton, probably 1720.—Sarah m. Ebenezer Ames.—Kezia m. Thomas Ames 1731.

6. Maj. Edward (s. of John 2.) m. Mary, D. of Nicholas Byram 1711, and had Sarah 1714, Mary 1717, Bethiah 1719, Jane 1721, Edward 1724, James 1726. She d. 1767, he 1771. Sarah m. Christopher Ripley 1737.—Mary m. Henry Howard.—Bethiah m. Isaac Lathrop.—Jane m. Nathan Howard Esq. 1746.

7. Capt. Robert (s. of John 2.) m. Abigail, D. of Joseph Keith, 1725, and had John 1726, Martha 1729, Robert 1735, Adam

1737, Betty 1744, Daniel 1750 : he was one of the first settlers
in N. B., and d. 1779, æ. 80. Martha m. Wm. Edson 1754.—
Betty m. Abijah Thayer.—Adam m. Mary, D. of Abiah Keith
1759, and d. 1781, æ. 44, without children.
8. James (s. of James 3.) m. Elizabeth Wallis 1710, and had
Mercy 1714, Huldah 1716.—It is said he went to St. and thence
to Woodstock.
9. Ephraim (s. of Ephraim 4.) m. Abigail Tisdale, and had
George 1722, Theophilus 1724, Ephraim 1731, Abigail 1733, Susanna 1736, Martha 1739, Mary 1741.—The mother d. 1758.—
Abigail m. Edward Lathrop 1752.—Mary m. David Lathrop
1762.—Susanna m. Capt John Ames 1759.—Martha m. Capt.
Zebedee Snell 1761.
10. Daniel Esq. (s. of Ephraim 4.) m. Damaris D. of Tho.'s
Williams of Taunton 1724 ; she was born 1698 ; he was also one
of the first settlers in N. B., and was a man of great respectabil-
ity and represented the town many years, and had Mary 1727,
Barnabas 1730, and Silence.—He d. 1779 æ. 80.—Mary m. Col.
Simeon Cary 1754.—Silence m. Col. Josiah Hayden 1763.
11. David (s. of Ephraim 4.) m. Bethiah D. of Samuel Leonard of Taunton, and had David 1728, Phebe 1730, Simeon 1733,
Bethiah 1735, Eliakim 1739, Mary 1742, Catharine 1744.—She
d. 1746 : he 1751 æ. 47.—Phebe d. 1803.—Mary m. Eliphalet
Phillips 1763, and afterwards Seth Harris, and d. 1816.—Catharine m. Nathaniel Southworth 1762. The w. of Mr. David
Howard dis. from Scituate ch. to W. B. 1749 ; a 2d. w. probably.
12. Jonathan (s. of Jona. 5.) m. Sarah D. of John Field 1719,
and had Nathan 1720, Charity 1721, Susanna 1724, Sarah 1726.
Jonathan 1729, Amy 1734.—Charity m. Benjamin Pierce of Scituate 1742 ; who m. Jane D. of Dea. Thomas Hayward 1750, for
his 2d. wife.—Susanna m. Col. Edward Howard 1745.—Sarah
m. Capt. Adams Bailey 1746.—Amy m. Jeremiah Belcher 1756,
and d. a wid. 1812.
13. Joshua (s. of Jonathan 5.) m. Susanna D. of John Hayward Jr. 1724, and had Anne 1725, Thankful 1728, Martha 1735,
Matilda 1737.—This family lived in or near Easton.
14. Ebenezer (s. of Jonathan 5.) and his wife Catharine. had
Silence 1736, Mehitabel 1746.—He d. 1786 : his will 1784.—Silence m. Eliphalet Leonard of Easton 1755.—Mehitabel m. Libeus Fobes 1775.
15. Seth (s. of Jonathan 5.) m. Mary D. of Thomas Ames
1735, and had Mary 1738, Jesse 1740, Susanna 1742, Betty 1749,
Ebenezer 1752. She d. 1758. Mary m. Capt. Eliakim Howard 1759.—Susanna m. Elijah Snell 1760.—Betty m. Joseph
Ford 1769.
16. Dr. Abiel (s. of Jonathan 5.) gra. H. U. 1729, and m. Silence D. of Nehemiah Washburn, and had Silence 1738, Nehemiah 1740, Jane 1742, John 1743, Daniel 1746, Charity 1748,
Ann 1750, Joshua 1751.—Silence m. Dr. Philip Bryant 1757.—
Jane m. Ebenezer Ames 1763.—Charity not m.—Ann m. Jacob
25

Foster of Me. 1776 —Joshua lived in Easton and m. Priscilla
Capen of Stoughton 1776.

17. Henry (s. of Jonathan 5.) m. Mary D. of Maj. Edward
Howard 1733, and lived in Easton and had Mary 1734, Elijah
Esq., Henry, Abigail, Martha 1759, Susanna.—Mary m. Thomas
Packard perhaps a. 1757.—Henry m. Phebe D. of Ichabod Bry-
ant.—Henry m. Mary D. of Jonathan Kingman.—Abigail m.
Capt. Abner Hayward 1772.—Martha m. Zadock Packard 1779.
—Susanna m. Nathan Howard a. 1770.—Abigail Howard m.
Thomas Mitchell of E. 1783.

18. Col. Edward (s. of Edward 6.) m. Susanna D. of Jonathan Howard 1745, and had Daniel 1749, Susanna 1751, Parnel
1753, Edward 1756, Martin 1769. She d. 1785 ; and he m.
Abigail wid. of Joshua Howard of Braintree and D. of Benj. Beal
1786, and had Benjamin Beal 1788, Charles 1790, Frances 1791.
He d. 1809, æ. 85: she 1821. Susanna m. Oakes Angier Esq.
1774, and afterwards Jesse Fobes 1792.—Parnel m. Scotland
Keith of Easton 1772.—Frances m. Ezra Kingman Jr. 1812.

19. James (s. of Edward 6.) m. Betty D. of Thomas Willis
1749, and had Betty 1749, Mary 1751, James 1753, Bethiah 1755,
Chloe 1757, Charles 1759 : she d. 1760, and he m. wid. Elizabeth Babbit 1765, and had Zephaniah 1766, Azel 1768, Persia
1772: she d. and he m. wid. Keziah, late w. of Jona. Ames 1776,
she was a Tinkham.—Betty m. Nathan Snell 1770.—Mary m.
Chilton Latham 1770.—Bethiah m. Daniel Hayward 1777.—
Persia m. Asa Copeland 1792.—Olive Babbit, his 2d. wife's D.
by her first husband, m. Gamaliel Howard 1775.—Azel removed
to Philadelphia and there m. and d. before 1829.

20. John (s. of Robert 7.) m. Abigail D. of Daniel Hudson
1752, and had Ichabod 1754, Bela 1757, Abigail 1762, John 1764,
Adam 1767, Alfred 1770, Keziah 1774. He d. 1792 æ. 66.—
Abigail m. Jona. Perkins 1785.—Keziah m. Joshua Niles 1796.
—Adam went to Mansfield.—Alfred m. Lavinia Bisbee of St.
1794, and lived there, and had Alfred 1796, Levina 1798, Sarah
1800, Abigail Hudson 1802, John 1805, Patty Snell 1807, William Gray 1810.—Levina m. John Willis 1813.

21. Robert (s. of Robert 7.) m. Abigail D. of Zechariah Snell
1757, and had Zechariah, Robert, Silvia, Hannah, Abigail, Lucinda. He d. 1808 æ. 73. Hannah m. Joseph Silvester Esq.
1786.—Abigail m. Ephraim Sturtevant 1791.—Lucinda m. Noah
Cheesman 1799.

22. Daniel Esq. (s. of Robert 7.) m. Vesta D. of Barnabas
Howard Esq. 1773, and had Darius 1773, Daniel 1775, Ambrose
1776, Ziphion 1779, Vesta 1781, Damaris 1784, Cyrus 1788, Sidney 1790, Polly 1792, Lois 1794. He d. 1821. Daniel gra.
H. U. 1797, m. Susan D. of Capt. Ezra Kingman 1802, she d.
1806 æ. 22, and he m. a 2d. wife, and settled as an Attorney in
Maine, and has a son Sidney K.—Ambrose and Ziphion settled
in Winslow Me., Ziphion m. Amy D. of Joseph Reynolds 1803.
—Vesta m. Robert Swan Holbrook of St. 1805.—Damaris m.

Jabez Woodman of New Gloucester Me. 1810.—Cyrus m. Silvia D. of Col. Caleb Howard 1809, and afterwards Abi D. of Wm. Edson, and she d. 1839.—Sidney m. Sally D. of Samuel Alden 1815, and Sally Littlefield of St. 1820.—Polly m. Amos Whiting 1810.

23. George (s. of Ephraim 9.) m. Abigail D. of Jona. Copeland 1745, and had Hannah 1746, Abigail 1748, Betty 1751, George 1753, Oliver 1755, Job 1758, Caleb 1760, Rachel 1763, Patty 1765, Asaph 1768, Nehemiah 1770, and Polly. She d. 1809: he 1815 æ. 93.—Hannah m. Daniel Lathrop 1764.—Abigail m. Timothy Ames 1778.—Betty m. Edmund Lathrop of Easton 1774.—Rachel m. Israel Alger 1785.—Patty m. Azel Kinsley 1785.—Oliver went to Easton.—Job m. Hannah Capen of Dor. 1781.—Polly m. David Bartlett 1796.

24. Theophilus (s. of Ephraim 9.) m. Susanna D. of John Lathrop 1747, and had Susanna 1748, John 1753, Molly 1755, Theophilus 1758, Sarah 1762, Mark 1764, Abigail and Tisdale 1769.—Susanna m. Josiah Lathrop perhaps 1785.—Molly m. Benjamin Pettingill perhaps of Easton 1773.—Sarah m. Daniel Alger 1781.—Abigail m. Ephraim Howard Jr. perhaps 1786.— Mark m. Martha D. of Daniel Alger 1788.—Tisdale m. Chloe D. of Daniel Alger 1791.—Theophilus m. Bathsheba Keith of Easton 1778.

25. Ephraim (s. of Ephraim 9.) m. Hannah D. of Nathaniel Brett 1753, and had Ann 1753, Sarah 1755, Rebecca 1759, Abigail 1761, Ephraim 1764, Eliab 1765, Nathaniel 1771, Lemuel 1773. Ann m. George Williams 1773.—Sarah m. Abiel Kinsley 1777.—Abigail m. a Randall perhaps 1778.

26. Barnabas Esq. (s. of Daniel 10.) m. Mehitabel D. of Seth Packard 1755, and had Vesta 1755, Damaris 1757, Oliver 1758, Daniel 1759, Jonas 1763, Mehitabel 1765, Gideon 1767, Lois 1769. He d. 1813, æ. 84. Vesta m. Daniel Howard Esq. 1773. —Damaris m. Capt. John French 1779.—Mehitabel m. John Wales 1789.—Lois m. Nathan Keith 1786.

27. David (s. of David 11.) m. Keziah D. of Thomas Ames 1751, and had David 1753, Amasa 1756, Abiel 1760, after his father's death; she m. Jotham Ames 1767, and d. 1768.

28. Simeon S. T. D. and A. A. S. (s. of David 11.) gra. H. U. 1758, and settled in the ministry at Boston 1767, and m. Elizabeth wid. of Dr. Jona. Mayhew 1771; (she was a Clarke) and had a son John Clarke, who gra. H. U. 1790, and settled in Boston, as a physician, and m. a Swan, and had a s. John Clarke gra. H. U. 1825.

29. Capt. Eliakim (s. of David 11.) m. Mary D. of Seth Howard 1759, and had Silvia 1761, Eliakim 1763, Keziah 1765, Molly 1767, Simeon 1770, Martha 1772, Alpheus 1775, Susanna 1776, Sarah 1778, John 1780, Uriel 1781. Silvia m. Ebenezer Bailey 1782.—Keziah m. Dea. Noah Edson 1802.—Molly m. Amasa Howard 1783, and afterwards Jonathan Howard 1798. Martha m. James Newbury 1797.—Sarah m. Galen Howard 1799.

30. Nathan Esq. (s. of Jonathan 12) m. Jane D. of Maj. Edward Howard 1746, and had Nathan 1746, Jonathan 1749, Gamaliel 1751, Bezaliel 1753, Thaddeus 1756, Artemas 1758, Sarah 1760, and Jane. Artemas d. 1809, not m.—Sarah m. Caleb Packard 1782, and afterwards Caleb Loring 1802, and died in 1834, a widow.—Jane m. Luther Burr 1785.

31. Capt. Jonathan (s. of Jonathan 12) m. Phebe D. of Joseph Ames 1756, and had Elizabeth 1756, d. 1812, Phebe 1759, Jona. 1767,Rowena 1771, Galen 1774, Salmon 1777. He d. 1809. Phebe m. Dan'l Manly 1782.—Rowena m. Charles Lathrop 1788.

32. Capt. Jesse (s. of Seth 15.) m. Melatiah D. of Samuel Dunbar 1761, and had Seth 1762, Perez 1765, Calvin 1768, Barnabas 1770, Jesse 1776, Lloyd 1778. She d. 1814. Perez m. Hannah Lincoln of Scituate 1795.—Calvin m. Cloe Fuller of Attleboro' 1790.

33. Ebenezer (s. of Seth 15.) m. Silence D. of Charles Snell 1773, and had Cyrus 1774, Polly 1775, Susanna 1776, Charles 1778, Aden 1780, Sybil 1782, Betsy 1784, Albert 1787, Ebenezer 1790, Silence 1793.—This family lived near Easton.

34. Nehemiah (s. of Dr. Abiel 16.) m. Hannah Dean of Easton 1768, and had Abiel, Dean, Asa, Jepthah, Nathaniel, Hannah. This family lived in or near Easton. Dean m. Polly Perkins 1800.—Jepthah m. Betsy D. of Abijah Knapp 1804.—Hannah m. a Mitchell of E.

35. John (s. of Dr. Abiel 16.) m. Mercy D. of William Fobes 1768, lived in Easton and had a son Roland, and a D. who m. a Guild.—John Jr. m. Silence Burr 1773.

36. Daniel (s. of Dr. Abiel 16.) m. Mary D. of Edmund Hayward 1772, and had Jason 1773, Ambrose 1775, Mary 1778.— He d. and his wid. m. Barnabas Dunbar 1784.—Jason studied law, but d. young at sea in the navy with Commodore Prebble.— Ambrose went to Maine, and was a physician.

37. Judge Daniel (s. of Col. Edward 18.) m. Abigail D. of Capt. Isaac Packard 1776 and had Betsy 1777, Francis 1778, Abigail 1779, Susanna 1781*, Daniel 1783, Mary 1784, Ellen 1787, Sybil Porter 1789*, Lucy* and Lois 1791, John Edward 1793, Jane 1795. She d. 1818 : he 1832 æ. 83. Betsy m. Dr. Moses Baker 1803, and afterwards John Crafts.—Francis gra. B. U. 1797, and lived in Boston, and d. young, and not m.—Daniel d. 1814, not m.—Lois D. single 1838.

38. Edward (s. of Colonel Edward 18.) m. Melly Howard of Braintree 1780, and had Walter 1780, Church*, Warren, Cyrus, Joshua, Edward, and two Ds.,and went to Easton, thence to N. Y., and thence to Michigan.

39. Martin (s. of Col. Edward 18.) m. Vashti, D. of Nathan Willis, 1793, and had Frederick Augustus 1795*, William Henry 1799, Maria Willis 1801, Lucia 1803, and John. He removed to Oakham, and thence to Dorchester : his w. d. 1830. William H. m. a Willet, and lives in S. Boston.—Maria W. m. Geo. C. Thatcher of Boston.—John m. an Adams of Oakham, and lives in Dorchester.

40. Capt. Benjamin B. (s. of Col. Edward 18.) m. Olive, D. of Gamaliel Howard, 1810, and had Lucy 1811, Azel 1815, Benjamin 1819. She d. and he m. a Mitchell of Newton.

41. Charles (s. of Col. Edward 18.) m. Betsy Wade of Hanson 1816, and had Charles Edw. 1820, William, Louisa, George.

42. James (s. of James 19.) m. Abigail, D. of Capt. Josiah Snell, 1775, and had Chloe 1777, Rhoda 1779, Reuel 1781, Marcus 1783, Parnel 1786, Vesta 1791. Marcus m. Jemima Hall 1814.—Parnel m. Edward Hayward 3d 1805.—Vesta m. Barzillai Hayward 1811.

43. Zephaniah (s. of James 19.) m. Jennet, wid. of Allen Latham and D. of Hosea Dunbar of Halifax 1800, and had Charles Volney, Ize Annett 1804. John Jay 1807, Lewis Gibbon 1810, Pliny Babbit 1812.—Charles Volney d. at Perry Co. Illinois, Nov. 28, 1838.

44. Dea. Ichabod (s. of John 20.) m. Molly, D. of Levi Keith, 1794, and had Melinda 1796, Bethiah 1797, Linus 1799, Lysander 1802, Nancy 1804, Maria 1806, Henry 1808, David 1810, Mary Ann Keith 1812.—Melinda m. Ozen Gurney 1820.—Bethiah m. Martin Cary.

45. Bela (s. of John 20.) m. Mehitabel, D. of Col. Simeon Cary, 1782, and had Sibil 1784, who m. Oliver Dike 1810. He d. and she m. Samuel Dike 1793.

46. John (s. of John 20.) m. Polly Gill of St. 1794, and had Eliza Gill 1801, Polly Hudson 1803.

47. Rev. Zechariah (s. of Robert 21.) gra. H. U. 1784, and settled at Canton 1787, and there died: he m. Patty, D. of John S. Crafts, 1787, but left no children.

48. Robert (s. of Robert 21.) m. Susanna, D. of Jona. Perkins, 1788, and had Rhoda 1790, Mira 1792, Lucia 1795, Noble 1797*, Harrison 1801. Rhoda m. Col. Edward Southworth 1815.—Lucia m. Nathan Jones 1820.

49. Darius (s. of Daniel Esq. 22.) m. Sophia, D. of Jonas Howard, 1804, and had Elmina 1804, Sophia and Darius* 1807. She d. 1807, and he m. Huldah, D. of Jonathan Cary, 1808, and had Cary 1809, Aurelia 1813, Frederick 1815, Darius 1817, Abigail 1820.

50. George (s. of George 23.) m. Parnel, D. of Thomas Ames, 1777, and had Polly Brett 1777, Thomas 1781, Deborah 1783, George 1786, Abigail 1788, Sidney 1791, Parnel 1795, Franklin 1797, Betsy 1801, Patty 1803: he d. 1812, she 1819. Deborah m. Asa Whitman 1804.—George m. Sarah, D. of Daniel Manly, 1808.—Abigail m. Solomon Reed 1811.—Sidney m. Sally, D. of Caleb Alden, and he and George went to Lancaster.

51. Col. Caleb (s. of George 23.) m. Silvia, D. of Daniel Alger, and had Hannah 1782, Apollos 1784, Abigail 1786, Silvia 1788, Vesta 1790, Chloe 1793, Nancy 1795, Welcome 1797, Olive 1799, Caleb 1802, Thomas Jefferson 1804. She d. 1819, and he m. Abigail, D. of Issachar Snell Esq. 1820: he d. 1831. Hannah m. Zibeon Crafts 1799.—Abigail m. Daniel Howard 1805.—

Silvia m. Cyrus Howard 1809.—Vesta m. a Torrey.—Nancy m.
Azor Packard 1815.—Olive m. John Wales 1820.—Caleb m.
Polly Tilden.

52. Asaph Esq. (s. of George 23.) m. Phebe, D. of Luke Perkins, 1789, and had Phebe 1791, Polly 1793, Martin 1795, Asaph
1797, Azel 1799, and went to Minot, Me.

53. Nehemiah (s. of George 23.) m. Sally, D. of William
Curtis, 1791, and had Hannah 1792, Sally 1793, Seba 1795, Caleb 1797, Polly 1800, Deborah W. 1803, Roxelana R. 1805, Abigail C. 1809. Hannah m. Ambrose Leach 1815.—Sally m. Jonas
Hartwell 1820.—Polly m. Benjamin Marshall 1820.

54. Oliver (s. of Barnabas Esq. 26.) m. Susanna, D. of Thos.
Reynolds, 1780, and had Parnel 1782, Oliver 1784, Daniel 1785,
Emily 1786, Bernice 1787, Lois 1789, Otis 1792, Mehitabel 1794,
Betsy 1796. The mother d. 1817. Parnel m. James Ford 1800.—
Daniel m. Abigail, D. of Caleb Howard Esq. 1805.—Emily m.
Apollos Howard.—Bernice m. Zophar Field 1811.—Lois m.
Samuel Linfield of Randolph 1812.—Mehitabel m. Chas. Cope-
land 1816.—Betsy m. Robert Packard.—Otis m. Reuma South-
worth 1818.

55. Daniel (s. of Barnabas Esq. 26.) m. Silence, D. of Thos.
Packard, and had Polly, Selina, Relief. Polly m. John Hol-
brook of St. 1801.—Selina m. Robt. Swan Holbrook of St. 1800.
Relief m. Benjamin Capen of St. 1805.

56. Jonas (s. of Barnabas Esq. 26.) m. Abigail, D. of Nathan
Packard 1784, and had Sophia 1785, Rowena 1787, Barnabas
1789, Jonas 1791, Anna 1794, Louisa 1798, Lydia 1800, Edwin
1803, Angelina 1806, Sophia 1810. Sophia m. Darius Howard
1804, and d. 1807.—Rowena m. Simeon Cary 1806.—Anna m.
Charles Littlefield of St. 1821.—Louisa m. Loring H. Thayer of
Randolph.—Lydia m. Darius Littlefield.

57. Capt. Gideon Esq. (s. of Barna. Esq. 26.) m. Molly, D. of
Nathan Willis, 1788, and had Gideon 1789, Austin 1791, Martha
1793, Adeline 1796, Lucy 1798, Albert 1800, Mary 1803, Elijah
1805, Betsy 1807, Francis 1809, Nathan Willis 1812. Gideon
m. Sibil, D. of John Harris of A. 1811.—Austin m. Abig. Crane
of St. 1819.—Martha m. Daniel H. Cary 1812.—Adeline m.
Samuel Harris of A. 1815.—Lucy m. Lot Blanchard of St. 1817.
Mary m. Zion Packard.

58. David (s. of David 27.) m. Molly, D. of Jonathan King-
man, 1778, and had Molly 1781, Keziah 1783, Azubah 1786,
Hannah 1789, Sally 1791*. His wife d. and he m. Rebecca, D.
of Nathan Whitman, 1791, and had David 1792, Huldah 1794,
Algernon Sidney 1796. . He then removed to Tamworth, N. H.,
and had three wives more, viz: wid. Abigail, late wife of Wm.
Snell and D. of Eleazar Alden, Miss Roberts, and another wid.
—Azubah m. Ford Whitman Esq.

59. Capt. Amasa (s. of David 27.) m. Molly, D. of Capt. Eliakim Howard, 1783, and had Katy 1784, Arabella 1787, Adonis
1795, Amasa 1797. He d. and his widow m. Jonathan Howard

1798. Katy m. Mark Lathrop Jr. 1805.—Arabella m. Benjamin Eaton of Boston 1805.—Adonis was a Preacher of the New Jerusalem Ch.

60. Abiel (s. of David 27.) m. Keziah, D. of Samuel Bartlett, 1798, and had Jantha 1799, Lewis 1802.

61. Simeon (s. of Capt. Eliakim 29.) m. Hannah, D. of Sam'l Bartlett, 1794, and had Harrison 1794, Maria 1797, Davis 1800, Ansel 1803. She d. 1805, and he m. Bathsheba, D. of Ephraim Jackson, 1807, and had Hannah Bartlett 1809.

62. Alpheus (s. of Capt. Eliakim 29) m. Sally, D. of Capt. Leavitt Thayer, 1803, and had Nancy 1805, Thomas 1807, Jane 1810, Leavitt T. 1813, Lewis 1816.

63. Uriel (s. of Capt. Eliakim 29.) m. Lucy Barnes 1816, and had James 1816, Lucy 1818.

64. Nathan (s. of Nathan 30.) m. Susanna, D. of Henry Howard of Easton, and had Abiel 1771, Nathan 1772, Alfred 1774, Reuel 1776, Lewis 1778, Lucinda 1780, Jane 1782, Bezaliel 1785, Phebe 1787, Cyril 1789: he d. 1833, æ. 87. Nathan m. Lydia Copeland 1799, and went to Winthrop.—Lucinda m. John Hartwell 1801.

65. Jonathan (s. of Nathan 30.) m. Martha, D. of Nathan Willis, 1774, and had Anne 1777, Edwin 1779, Jennet 1783, Charles 1786, Sarah 1788, Sophia 1790, Jonathan 1805. Anne m. Daniel Crane Esq. 1801.—Sarah m. Ichabod Macomber of Easton 1806.—Sophia m. Nathaniel S. Spooner Esq. of New Bedford 1812.

66. Gamaliel (s. of Nathan 30.) m. Olive Babbit, D. of James Howard's 2d w. by her first husband, 1775, and had Lucy 1786, Olive 1788, Azel 1791 : d. 1813, æ. 22. Lucy m. Nathan Church 1810, and d. 1813.—Olive m. Capt. Benjamin B. Howard 1810.

67. Bezaliel S. T. D. and A. A. S. (s. of Nathan 30.) gra. H. U. 1781, and settled in the ministry at Springfield 1784, and there m. a D.˙ of Jonathan Dwight, and had a D. Lucinda Dwight. His w. d. and he then m. a Williams, and had John and Charles, who m. sisters, Ds. of Col. Thomas Dwight : he d. 1838. Lucinda m. Samuel Orne Esq. and had William Wetmore, who m. Lucy Dwight—Sophia, who m. Charles Chapin of Brattleboro', Vt.

68. Thaddeus (s. of Nathan 30.) m. Keziah, D. of Jonathan Ames, 1785, and had Thaddeus 1786, Bathsheba 1788, Harriot 1794, Keziah 1798, d. 1817; Mary 1801. Keziah, the mother, d. 1811, and he m. Seabury, wid. of Hartwell Keith, 1813 : he d. 1813. Thaddeus m. Silvia Lathrop 1810.—Harriot m. Davis Keith 1820.—Bathsheba m. Spencer Lathrop 1812, and d. 1813.

69. Jonathan (s. of Capt. Jonathan 31.) m. Abigail Packard 1794, and had Ruhamah 1795, Walter 1797.

70. Galen (s. of Capt. Jonathan 31.) m. Sarah, D. of Captain Eliakim Howard, 1799, and had Rowena 1800, Freeman 1803, Harriot 1805, Galen 1806, Jonathan 1808, Hiram 1811, Waldo 1814, William Henry 1816, Elbridge 1820.

71. Salmon (s. of Capt. Jonathan 31.) m. Amelia, D. of Capt. Ephraim Snell, 1799, and had Chelsias 1800, Anna Keith 1803, Ephraim Snell 1805, Asenath 1808, Bathsheba Ann 1810, Martha Fobes 1813, Amelia 1815, Salmon Wilkes 1818.

72. Capt. Seth (s. of Capt. Jesse 32.) m. Desire, D. of Jonathan Bailey, 1782, and had Stillman 1785, Everett Ward 1789, Seth 1792, Roland Bailey 1795, Aurelia 1797, Lucretia 1800.— He went to Me.

73. Jesse (s. of Capt. Jesse 32.) m. Parnel, D. of Dea. Elijah Snell, 1799, and had Elijah Snell 1806, Susanna 1808, Mary Ann 1810.

74. Capt. Lloyd (s. of Capt. Jesse 32.) m. Abigail, D. of Dea. Elijah Snell, 1796, and had Abigail 1797, Caroline 1799, Bezer 1801, Louisa 1803, John Eliot 1805, Lloyd 1807, Rhoda 1810, Samuel Nelson 1813 : he d. 1838.

75. John Edward Esq. (s. of Judge Daniel 37.) gra. B. U. 1815, m. Harriet M. D. of Capt. Asa Pratt 1821, and had Harriet Augusta and John Edward.

76. Thomas (s. of George 50.) m. Hepzibah, D. of Dr. Eleazar Carver, 1810, and had Mary Ann 1815, Elam 1817, and others perhaps ; his D. m. Daniel Crane.

77. Apollos (s. of Col. Caleb 51.) m. Olive, D. of Maj. Daniel Cary, 1802, and afterwards Emily, D. of Oliver Howard, and has a family.

78. Oliver (s. of Oliver 54.) m. Lucy, D. of Ephraim Sturtevant, 1808, and had Abigail 1809, Willard 1811, Rufus Emery 1813, Elizabeth 1816.

79. Alfred (s. of Nathan 64.) m. Hannah, D. of Isaac Hartwell, 1799, and had Orynthia 1801, Rhoda Lathrop 1803, Lucinda 1804, Jane 1807.

80. Edwin Esq. (s. of Jonathan 65.) m. Sally Cole of Scituate 1803, and had Edwin 1804, Jonathan 1806, David 1807, Sarah 1808. She d. 1811, and he m. Betsy Spooner of M. 1812 : he d. 1820.

81. Jonathan (s. of Joshua of Randolph): his mother was Colonel Edward Howard's last wife ; m. Molly, widow of Capt. Amasa Howard and D. of Capt. Eliakim Howard, 1798, and had Amasa 1799, Celestia 1801, Mary Beal 1803, Sidney 1805, Eliakim 1807, Sophia 1810 : he d. 1833. Celestia m. John A. Whiting.—Mary B. m. Stephen Otis Copeland.

82. Asa (s. of Benjamin Howard of Randolph) b. 1776, settled in N. B. 1802, and m. Eunice, D. of Isaac Thayer, and had Ephraim 1798, Samuel 1800, Charles 1803, Isaac Thayer 1805, d. 1822 ; Mary Ann 1808, Asa 1813*, Asa 1815*, Elizabeth 1818, and Martha Jane 1820 : he d. 1828. Ephraim m. Lydia, D. of James Cary, 1821.—Samuel m. Mary Carlton and went to Randolph, but returned again.—Charles m. Lavinia Round.—Mary Ann m. William Faxon.

Mehitabel m. Benjamin Holmes of Norton 1783.—Eunice of Braintree m. Abia Packard 1764.—Theodora of Braintree m.

Seth Edson 1784 —Sarah m. Cyrus Perkins 1787.—Joshua of
Sidney m. Zilphar Reynolds 1805.—Tabitha of St. m. Oliver
Hayward 1786.—James of M. m. Charity Blossom 1802.—Ethan
of E. m. Julia Packard 1814.—Eleanor of Plymouth m. Charles
Hayward 1797.—A Howard of Dart. m. Content, D. of Jona.
Sprague.—Albee m. Abigail, D. of Dea. Nathan Alger, 1814,
and had James Lyman 1816.
HUDSON.—William Hudson (from Lancaster or what is now
probably Leominster) settled in W. B. and m. Experience D. of
John Willis: his will dated 1728: no children: his wife and Dr.
Joseph Byram Ex's: he was a mason, and built Rev. Mr. Keith's
tomb.—William Hudson was made free at Boston 1631, and allowed to keep an ordinary (tavern) there 1640: he was probably
the ancestor of all the Hudsons here.—Daniel Hudson and wife
and two daughters were killed by the Indians at Lancaster 1697.
2. Daniel (brother of William 1.) m. Mary D. of William Orcutt 1697, and settled in S. B., and had Mary 1701, Daniel 1704,
William 1707. He m. Abigail wid. of John Fobes 1739: he d.
1750 æ. 73: she 1762. Mary m. Isaac Lazell 1719.
3. Daniel (s. of Daniel 2.) m. Mary D. of John Fobes, and had
Mary 1727, Abigail 1730, Reliance 1733, Daniel 1738, Nathan
1741, John 1743. The father d. 1775 æ. 71, she 1786 æ. 81.
Mary m. Dea. Nathan Alden 1750.—Abigail m. John Howard of
N. B. 1752—Reliance m. Samuel Billings 1756,—Daniel went
westward.
4. William (s. of Daniel 2.) m. Sarah D. of John Fobes 1737,
and had Sarah 1738, Silence 1740, Barzillai 1741, William 1743,
Edward 1745, Marah 1747, Asa 1749, Eli 1751. She d. 1789;
he 1796 æ.87. Sarah m. John Ward of Middletown Ct. 1768.—
Silence m. Ebenezer Soule of Plympton 1764, and d. 1835, æ.
94, and 8 months.—Marah m. Asaph Soule of Plympton 1767.
—Barzillai went to Hartford Ct. and was a respectable bookseller
and printer there; Prentiss Mellen C. J. of S. J. Court Me. m.
one of his Ds.—Edward went to New Braintree.—Asa removed also.
5. Nathan (s. of Daniel 3.) m. Betty D. of Capt. Joseph Gannett 1767; she d. 1777 æ. 28; and he m. Ann Gibbs of Sandwich 1777, and had Betty 1779, who m. Rev. William Briggs
1799, who settled in the ministry at Kittery but now lives in E.
B.—Ann the mother d. 1831, æ. 81, he d. 1834 æ. 93.
6. John (s. of Daniel 3.) m. Bethiah D. of Dr. Isaac Otis 1769,
and had Mary 1770, Mehitabel 1772, Otis 1774, Hannah 1777,
Daniel 1779, Abigail 1782, Melzar 1784, Susanna 1788, Isaac
1791, Bethiah. He d. 1819 æ. 77: she 1825 æ. 78. Mary m.
John Q. Keith 1792.—Mehitabel m. Jonathan Kingman 1793.—
Otis, a Bachelor.—Hannah m. Cyrus Edson 1797.—Abigail m.
Jonathan Snell 1809.—Melzar m. Lucinda D. of Mark Phillips
1818 and has a family.—Susanna m. Martin Whitman 1815.—
Isaac m. Molly D. of John Wade 1819, and has a family,—Bethiah m. Nicholas Wade 1823.
26

7. William (s. of William 4.) m. Lucy D. of Ebenezer Kingman 1767, and had Lucy 1769, Melzar 1771, Barzillai and others.
He removed from town.—Col. Barzillai lived in Boston.
  8. Eli (s. of William 4.) m. Sarah D. of Thomas Perkins 1774,
and had Thomas 1776, Asa 1778, Ovid 1781, Eli 1783, Sally
1785, William 1787, Selah 1790, Olive 1793.   Asa m. Deborah
Osborn 1803.   He had another s. by the name of Eli, who settled
in Randolph, and whose son m. Hannah D. of Zebulun Willis.
  9. Daniel (s. of John 6.) m. Patty D. of Capt. Ephraim Snell
1806, and had John Otis 1807, Semantha Snell 1810, Sarah Ann
1812, Lucy 1813.   His wife d. and he m. Betsy wid. of David
Waterman and D. of Nathaniel Pratt 1822 ; he d. 1838.
  HYDE.—1. The Rev. Ephraim Hyde of Rehoboth m. Mary
D. of the Rev. John Angier 1767, and had Ephraim, John, Samuel, Ezra, and Mary ; he d. and she with her children returned
to E. B. ; she d. 1788 æ. 48.   John is a physician and he and
Samuel went to Freeport Me.—Mary d. 1790 æ. 15.
  2. Ephraim (s. of the above) m. Mary Dresser of Pomfret Ct.
1794, and settled in E. B. and had Mary 1795, Ledyard 1796*,
Eliza 1798, Augustus 1801, Nathan Dresser 1803, Orinda Carpenter 1805* ; he d. Aug. 28 1834 æ. 65.   Mary d. single 1836
æ. 41.—Eliza m. Wallace Rust Esq.—Augustus was a mariner
and d. at sea 1839.—Nathan D. m. Elizabeth C. D. of Nahum
Mitchell 1833.
  3. Ezra (s. of Ephraim 1.) m. Martha D. of Joseph Ames 1805,
and lived and d. in Boston, and had Mary Angier, William A.
Joseph A., Martha W., Armelia W., Margaret P., and Hannah
S. ; the mother and children returned to S. B.—Mary A. m.
Dr. Samuel Alden.
  INGLEE or INGELL.—James Inglee (from Mido.) m. Ke-
ziah D. of John Richards 1787, and lived in W. B., and had
Clarissa Richards 1788.   He d. 1816.   Clarissa m. Luther Hay-
ward Jr. 1812.
  Jane Inglee m. Nathan Orcutt 1781.   Solomon Inglee of Hal-
ifax m. Bathsheba D. of Hugh Orr 1783 and lived and d. in Ply-
mouth.
  JACKSON.—1. Ephraim Jackson m. Lydia Leach 1736, and
went to Wrentham.
  Joanna Jackson m. David Packard 1764, Priscilla Jackson m.
Isaac Brett 1765.   Hopestill Jackson m. Micah Gurney 1765.
Lydia Jackson m. James Keith 1743.—Mary m. Ebenezer Willis
1753.—Lydia D. of Ephraim m. Nathan Packard 1758.—Some
others of these might be Ds. of Ephraim perhaps.
  2. Ephraim (s. of Ephraim 1.) m Bathsheba D. of John
Trask 1765, and had Asa 1765, Oliver 1767, Caleb 1769, Lydia
1771, Bathsheba 1772, George Washington 1776, Rhoda 1778,
Calvin 1779, Clarissa 1780.   His wife d. and he m. Hannah Delano 1784 and had Barnard, Lucy, Polly.   He d. 1814.   Asa
went westward.—Bathsheba m. Simeon Howard 1807.—Rhoda
m. a Dunston.—Clarissa m. Mayhew Packard 1801.— Lucy m.

Sullivan Packard 1805.—Lydia was also m.—George W. m.
Molly Briggs of Halifax 1804 where he lived.—Barnard m. Bathsheba D. of Jonathan Keith 1808.

3. Capt. Oliver (s. of Ephraim 2.) m. Olive D. of Capt. Zechariah Gurney 1807, and had Benjamin Franklin 1807, Henry 1811, Alpheus Gurney 1813.

4. Caleb (s. of Ephraim 2.) m. Zerviah D. of Jonathan Keith, 1801, and had Mary Keith 1801, Hannah 1804, Adeline 1807, Elizabeth 1809, Jonathan Keith 1812, Thomas 1814, Samuel 1818. He removed to Maine.

5. Calvin (s. of Ephraim 2.) m. Sally Godfrey 1810, and had Nahum Hodges 1812, Ophelia Rosseter 1814, Mary Godfrey 1815, Hector Varnum 1818.

6. Widow Thankful Jackson of Abington m. Seth Keith 1775; she was a Studley of Hanover, and wid. of Michael Jackson of Abington, whom she m. 1759, and by whom she had Henry and Sally. Henry Jackson m. Mehitabel D. of Jonathan Alden 1786.—Sally m. James Willis 1786, and both went to Minot.—The wid. Thankful became a wid. a 2d. time and d. 1815 æ. 78.

Hannah m. Barnabas Keith 1771, Silvia m. Asa Wilbur 1783. John Atwood Jackson m. Keziah Benson 1815.

JACOB.—Samuel Jacob m. Susanna D. of Ephraim Howard, and had Seth 1821.

JAMESON.—1. William Jameson m. Eunice D. of Ebenezer Packard 1780, and had Sarah 1781, Ebenezer 1782 Eunice 1788, William 1790.

2. Robert Jamieson, a Scotchman, lived several years with the Hon. Hugh Orr, but returned to Scotland, and became a very rich merchant.

JENKINS.—Meritt Jenkins (grandson probably of David of Abington who came from Scituate and m. Elizabeth Meritt 1741) m. Lydia D. of John Brown, and settled in E. B., and had John W. 1808, Lydia 1811, Betsy 1813.

David was s. of Edward, and g.s. of Edward, who was in Scituate as early as 1646. Widow Keziah m. Levi French 1805.—Charles m. Joanna Collier of Scituate 1785, and his ss. Wm., and Noble Everett settled in Boston.—Lucy Jenkins m. Sam'l Bartlett 1785.

JENNINGS.—1. Richard Jennings (from Sandwich perhaps) m. Mary Bassett, and settled in S. B., and had Joseph, Samuel 1703 ; Ephraim, Elizabeth, Anne, Mary, and Hannah were also his children probably. He d. 1751, his w. 1734. Joseph d. 1756.—Elizabeth m. Wm. Ames 1721.—Anne m. John Cavener (or Carver) 1718.—Mary m. John Tobey 1710.—Hannah m. Joseph Leonard 1712.

2. Ephraim (s. of Richard) m. Deliverance D. of Thomas Washburn 1719, and had Mary 1720, Ephraim 1722, Sarah 1728.

Richard Jennings, ancestor of the above probably, put himself to Robert Bartlett of Plymo. 1635, as an apprentice for 9 years. —Richard of B. had a legacy in Francis Godfrey's will 1666, and was called "kinsman" by Wm. Bassett Jr. of Sandwich 1694.

JOHNSON.—1. Isaac Johnson Esq. of Hingham m. Abiah, or Abial, or Abihail, wid. of Isaac Lazell and D. of John Leavitt, and had David, Solomon, Daniel, and probably James, Deborah and Rebecca. He then came and settled in W. B. a. 1700, and had Sarah 1702, John 1705, Joseph 1707, d. 1730, Benjamin 1711, Mary 1716. He was a captain, a representative, and a magistrate, and was born 1668 : d. 1735 : she was born 1667, and had Isaac Lazell and Abihail Lazell by her first husband.— James m. Jane D. of Isaac Harris and removed to Middleton Conn. Deborah m. Benjamin Perry of Sandwich 1723.—Rebecca called of Hingham m. Jonathan Washburn 1719.—Sarah m. Solomon Pratt 1719.—Mary m. James Hooper 1737.

2. Capt. David (s. of Isaac 1.) m. Rebeckah D. of John Washburn 1719, and had Isaac 1721, David 1724, Mary 1729, Sarah 1732, Rebecca 1734. Sarah m. Joseph Packard 1748.—Rebecca m. Ezra Edson 1756.

3. Solomon (s. of Isaac 1.) m. Susanna D. of Joseph Edson 1723, and had Susanna 1723, Seth 1733, Josiah 1735, Nathan 1738, Mary 1740 ; he d. 1771 æ. 76, she 1779. Susanna m. Jonathan Lathrop of E. 1747.—Seth went to St.—Mary of St. m. James Lovell 1761.—Jacob Johnson of St m. Mercy Snow 1760.

4. Judge Daniel (s. of Isaac 1.) m. Betty D. of James Latham 1726, and had James 1728, Isaiah 1734, Leavitt 1736.— Perhaps he had a 2d. wife Bethiah D. of John Pryor, and had John Pryor, d. 1741, Betty, and Daniel 1747. James and Leavitt d. Bachelors.—Betty d. single 1782.—Daniel grad. H. U. 1767, and settled in the ministry at Harvard 1769, and d. there Sept. 23, 1777.

5. Maj. John (s. of Isaac 1.) m. Peggy D. of Col. John Holman 1731, and had Sarah 1733, Abial 1735, Lewis 1738, Patience 1744, Joseph 1747, Content 1749, Calvin 1751. She d. 1757, he 1770. He had probably a 2d. w. Esther. Abiel m. John Alger 1754, and afterwards Ebenezer Pratt 1758.—Lewis lived in St.—Content m. Capt. Jacob Thomas of M.—Lewis Johnson m. Betsy Sturtevant 1799.

6. Benjamin (s. of Isaac 1.) m. Ruth D. of Col. John Holman 1732, and had Ruth 1736, Benjamin 1739, Rhoda 1743, William 1753. She d. 1764 æ. 48, he 1768 æ. 58. Ruth m. Stephen Richardson.—Benjamin d. in the army.—Rhoda m. Winslow Richardson 1763.—William m. Jane D. of James Robinson 1779, and had Ruth Holman 1780 and then went to Cummington, and thence to Cincinnati.

7. Maj. Isaac (s. of Capt. David 2.) m. Mary D. of Thomas Willis, and had Huldah 1745, Thomas 1747, Elizabeth 1749, Mary 1751, Isaac 1754, Rebecca 1758. He d. 1807. Huldah m. Silvanus Ames 1768, and afterwards John Willis 1784.—Elizabeth m. Elijah Ames 1769.—Mary m. Jonathan Hayward 1769. Rebecca m. David Ames 1781, and d. 1834.

8. David (s. of Capt. David 2.) m. Susanna D. of John Willis Esq. 1743, and had Willis 1744, Daniel 1746, and Susanna 1748.—

His wife d. 1750, he m. Parnel D. of Joseph Packard 1751.—
He went to Brookfield: his sons to Westmoreland.—Susanna
m. Samuel Cony Jr. of Easton 1770.

9. Josiah (s. of Solomon 3.) m. Azubah D. of Ephraim Cary,
and had Solomon, Josiah, Nathan. He d. 1812 æ. 75, she 1816
æ. 76. Solomon m. Sally D. of Gain Robinson 1788, and moved first to Mendon, and afterwards westward, and finally to
Rhode Island.

10. Isaiah (s. of Judge Daniel 4.) m. Ruth D. of Eliphalet
Leonard of E. 1757 and had James, Daniel, Cyrus, and probably Ruth, and Betty. James m. Sally D. of Eleazar Washburn
1798, and went to Easton and then to Maine.—Daniel m. Mary
Barker of Hanson, and lived in Portland, and finally went to
the city of N. York, and settled there as an attorney.—Cyrus
was a physician, went to Maine, and afterwards to N. Bedford
and m. Henrietta D. of Dea. Isaac Lazell: Isaiah, the father
and his brother Leavitt both d. in Me.

11. Joseph (s. of Maj. John 5.) m. Bethiah D. of Joseph Alger 1771, and had Susanna 1772, Vesta, Alfred 1776, Bethiah,
Joseph 1781, Calvin 1783, Daniel 1786, Peggy, Martin 1791.
Susanna m. Isaac Alger 1788.—The father, Joseph, d. and his
estate was settled by Nathaniel Perkins 1792, and the family removed to Maine.—Alfred m. Naomi D. of Nathaniel Perkins
probably 1801.—Bethiah m. Samuel Lathrop 1799.

12. Thomas (s. of Maj. Isaac 7.) m. Molly D. of Maj. Daniel
Lathrop 1771, and had Polly 1774, Rhoda 1776, Rebecca 1778,
Thomas 1780, Daniel 1783, Huldah 1785. He d. 1834 : æ. 86.
Polly m. Nathan Johnson 1789.—Rhoda m. John Atwood 1797.
—Rebecca m. Rufus Perkins 1797.—Thomas m. Hannah D. of
Thomas Hayward 1809.—Daniel gra. B. U. 1806, and settled in
the ministry at Yarmouth, and m. Maria D. of Simeon Sampson.
Huldah m. Ansel Hayward 1807.

13. Isaac (s. of Maj. Isaac 7.) m. Mary Wright of Marshfield
1786, and had Nahum, Isaac, Polly Lathrop. Polly L. m. Silvanus Walker 1819.—Isaac m. a Porter of Halifax.

14. Josiah (s. of Josiah 9.) m. Eunice D. of Isaac Allen 1784,
and had Polly, Sally, Zebina, Eunice: his wife d. 1792 æ. 26 :
and he m. Olive wid. of Daniel Orcutt, and D. of Benjamin
Whitman 1793, and had Rhoda 1797, Sidney 1799. He d. 1836,
she 1828 æ. 63. Polly m. Galen Hearsey of A. 1813.—Sally m.
Nathaniel Ramsdell 1812.—Rhoda m. Cotton Bates of Weymouth 1817.

15. Nathan (s. of Josiah 9.) m. Polly D. of Thomas Johnson
1789, and had Nathan, Polly, Rebecca Perkins, Josiah, Daniel
1804, Harrison, and Azubah. He d. 1821 æ. 52: she 1824 æ.
50.—Daniel was killed in the cotton factory 1816 æ. 12.—Polly
m. Eliphalet Edson 1810.—Harrison lives in Boston, Azubah m
Chester Cooley 1812.

16. Capt. Zebina (s. of Josiah 14.) m. and has a family.

Major Seth Johnson and family (from Boston; originally from Kingston) lived awhile in E. B. where he d. 1826 æ. 67.—Wm. Johnson of Taunton m. wid. Mary Owen 1782.—Mason Johnson m. Elizabeth Fuller 1790.—Mary Johnson of Kingston m. Capt. Abisha Stetson 1821.

JONES.—Capt. Asa Jones (s. of Nathan Jones of Raynham) settled in North Bridgewater, m. Rachel D. of Jeremiah Beal 1792, and had Nathan, Rosseter, Augustus, Asa, Sally : his wife d. and he m. Charity D. of Mark Perkins 1806. Nathan m. Lucia D. of Robert Howard 1820.—Rosseter m. a Marshall.—Sally m. John Thompson 1819.

Simeon Jones of Pembroke m. Susanna D. of Capt. Levi Washburn 1803, and his sons John and Simeon live in E. B.—Joseph Jones m. Elizabeth Eames 1787.—Nancy Jones m. Elezar Carver 2d. 1787.—Freeman Jones m. Nabby Leach 1792.—Polly Jones m. Isaac Whiting 1804.—Lurana Jones of Pembroke m. Joel Edson, his 2d. wife, 1820.—Samuel Jones m. Nabby Benson 1811.

JOSLYN.—1. Joseph Joslyn of Bridgewater (that part probably which is now Abington) m. Sarah Ford 1702 : his will dated 1726 : his ss. Joseph, Ebenezer 1709, Abraham 1716 : Ds. Hannah, Beatrice, Mary, Sarah 1703.—Joseph was absent and his legacies and bequests were on condition he should return.—Joseph the father d. 1726 : Sarah the mother d. 1734.

2. Ebenezer (s. of Joseph 1.) m. Esther Hearsey 1733, and had Mary 1733, Sarah 1735*, Sarah 1736.

3. Abraham (s. of Joseph 1.) m. Rebecca Tirrell 1741, and had Joseph 1742.

4. Joseph Joslyn settled in East Bridgewater near Hanson and Halifax, and m. Deborah D. of John Hatch 1785, and had Deborah Hatch, Earl, Cyrus.—Deborah H. m. Marcus Howe 1813.—Earl m. Anne Brewster 1814.—Cyrus m. a D. of Micah White Jr.

Rebecca of Pem. m. Bezer Ames 1791.—Eunice of Pem. m. Dea. Joseph Kingman 1791.

KEEN.—1. Lemuel Keen (from Pembroke) lived awhile in E. B.; had Jane, Josiah, Charles, Samuel, and Meribah.—Jane m. Matthew Allen 1786.—Meribah m. Bradford Mitchell, his 2d. w. 1801.

2. Josiah (s. of Lemuel 1.) m. Hannah S. D. of Ezra Whitman 1792, and had Calvin Whitman bap. 1795, and Hannah Shaw bap. 1800 after her father's death ; the wid. m. Constant Hayward 1808.—Calvin W. m. Jane D. of Hugh Orr 1812, and had Mary Bass, Calvin Whitman, and Isabella Orr, and d. 1824 æ. 31.—Hannah S. m. Hugh Orr Jr.

3. Charles (s. of Lemuel 1.) m. Celia D. of Cushing Mitchell 1802, and had Warren, d. 1827 æ. 25, Maria Newton, and Lucretia, and d. 1815, æ. 39.—Maria m. Seth Bryant.—Newton lives in Boston.—Lucretia m. Levi Churchill Jr.

4. Dea. Samuel (s. of Lemuel 1.) m. Margaret O. D. of Anthony W. Clift 1804, and had Samuel, Margaret, Sarah Jane,

Lusanna,Harriet, and Mary. Samuel m. Rhoda D. of Eleazar Churchill.—Margaret m. Isaac Nutter.—Sarah J. m. Arvin Holbrook.

Joseph Keen m. Rhoda D. of Daniel French 1815.—Elizabeth Keen lived in B. 1747 ; she had been a Wid. Turner.

KEITH.—Rev. James Keith, a Scotchman, was the first Minister of Bridgewater : was educated at Aberdeen, in Scotland ; came over 1662, at about 18 years of age ; ordained Feb. 1664 ; m. Susanna, D. of his Deacon, Samuel Edson, and had James, Joseph, Samuel, Timothy, John, Josiah, Margaret, Mary, Susanna. He m. a 2d wife, Mary, wid. of Thomas Williams of Taunton, 1707; d. July 23, 1719, æ. 76. Margaret m. a Hunt.—Mary m. Ephraim Howard.—Susanna m. Maj. Jonathan Howard, and d. young without children. It is said that his first sermon was delivered from a Rock in Mill Pasture, so called, near the River.

2. James (s. of James 1.) and his wife Mary had James 1696, Mary 1698, Gershom 1701, Israel 1703, Faithful 1704, Esther 1707, Jane 1709, Simeon 1712 : his inventory 1741. He removed to Mendon a. 1719. John Keith of Thompson, Conn., who d. 1833, æ. 76, was probably one of his descendants. James and Noah were probably his gr. ss. James had 2 ss., Josiah and Aaron, and another who went to Milford.—Noah had 2 ss., Chapin and Abijah, who both went to Barre, Vt.: Chapin was High Sheriff there.

3. Joseph (s. of James 1.) m. Elizabeth, D. of Dea. Edward Fobes, and had Anna 1695, Susanna 1697, Joseph 1699, Jemima 1701, Eleazar 1703, Abigail 1705, Ephraim 1707, Ichabod 1709, Martha 1711, Mary 1713, Elizabeth 1715 : his will 1730 ; her's 1757 · she made Constant Southworth her ex'or. Anna m. Capt. Ebenezer Alden 1717.—Susanna m. Jonathan Cary 1717, and d. young —Jemima m. Dea. James Packard 1722.—Eleazar m. Keziah, D. of Henry Kingman, 1726, settled in Easton, and had Lemuel, Seth, and perhaps other children.—Abigail m. Robert Howard 1725.—Martha m. Constant Southworth 1734.— Ichabod left a wid. Lydia, but no children.—She m. a Dr. Jones of Abington for her 2d husband.—Mary m. Jonathan Kingman 1732.—Eliz. m. Samuel Lathrop 1731. He was ex'or. of his father's will, and had his homestead, and was Representative 1726.

4. Samuel (s. of James 1.) m. Bethiah, D. of Dea. Edw. Fobes, 1703, and had Constant 1703, Amos 1705, Samuel 1707, Bethiah 1710, Susanna 1714, Ebenezer 1716, Robert 1718, Jane 1720, Benjamin 1723. He lived in S. B., and d. 1750. Constant m. Thomas Hayward of Tit.—Bethiah m. John Washburn 1738.— Susanna m. Solomon Ames 1737.—Jane m Joseph Cowen 1743.

5. Timothy (s. of James 1.) m. Hannah, D. of Dea. Edward Fobes, 1710, and had Timothy 1711, Abiah 1712, Nathan 1714, Hannah 1718. He lived in N. B. She d. 1765; he 1767, æ. 83. Hannah m. Daniel Ames 1742.

6. John (s. of James 1.) m. Hannah, D. of Samuel Washburn,

1711, and had John 1712, James 1716, Israel 1719, Hannah 1721,
Keziah 1723, Daniel 1725, Susanna 1727, Zephaniah 1730, Joseph and Mary. He lived in S. B., and d. 1761; she 1766.—
Hannah m. Benjamin Leach Jr. 1740.—Keziah m. Arthur Bennet of M. 1744.—Mary m. Solomon Pratt 1761.

7. Josiah (s. of James 1.) m. Mary, D. of Samuel Lathrop,
1703, and had Margaret 1704, Josiah 1706, William 1708, Mark
1710, Sarah 1712, Mary 1714, Daniel 1716, Jane, Silence, Phebe.
He, with his family, removed to Easton. Margaret m. a With-
rell of Norton.—Sarah m. William Thayer of Easton.—Mary
m. Timothy Gilbert of Hardwick.—Jane m. Daniel Owen of
Easton.—Silence m. Benjamin Smith, and afterwards Seth Willis, and went to Chesterfield.—Phebe m. Daniel White, and went
to Maine.—Mark m. Mercy Parris, and went to New Milford.

8. Joseph (s. of Joseph 3.) m. Susannah, D. of John Field,
1721, and first lived near Easton, and afterwards settled in E.
B. a. 1731, and had Joseph 1722, Abigail 1725, James 1727,
David 1728, Susanna 1731, Eleazar 1733, John 1736, Seth 1739,
George 1742. He afterwards m. Keziah, wid. of Capt. Israel
Bailey 1763: she was a Perry : he d. 1777, æ. 78 ; she 1796, æ.
90.—Abigail m. Joseph Robinson 1746.—Susanna m. Peter
Whitman 1752.

9. Ephraim Esq. (s. of Joseph 3.) gra. H. U. 1729 ; m. Sarah,
D. of Israel Washburn, 1732, and settled in Titicut, and had
Silvia 1735, Philibert 1737, Ephraim 1739, Timothy 1744, Wil-
liam 1746, Solomon 1749, and Sarah : his will dated 1777,
proved 1781. Philibert m. Francis Perkins 1775.—William m.
Eunice, D. of Benjamin Leach, 1767, and had William, Ephraim,
Cassandana, Bulah, Porcia, Cynthia, Amanda, Eunice, Olive, and
Sarah. William m. a Dickerman.—Cassandana m. Alpheus Leach
1787.—Bulah m. Jonathan Howard.—Porcia m. Mark Dogget.—
Cynthia m. Sullivan Shaw of M. 1797.—Amanda m. Consider
Scott.—Eunice m. Eliab Leach 1802.—Olive m. Bernice Leach
1810.—Sarah, D. of Ephraim Esq., m. Dr. Eleazar Carver,
1776.

10. Amos (s. of Samuel 4.) m. Sarah, D. of Stephen or Ebenezer Robinson of Raynham. He d. 1782: his will dated 1778:
no children : mentions his brother Ebenezer's son Amos. She
d. æ. 94.

11. Samuel (s. of Samuel 4.) m. Hannah, D. of Wm. Ames,
1734, and had Bethiah 1736, Edward 1740, Hannah 1742, Saml.
1745: he d. 1759, she 1770. Bethiah m. Daniel Leach 1760.—
Hannah m. Philip Hall 1760.—(See James 19.)

12. Ebenezer (s. of Samuel 4.) m. Mary Pierce of Scituate
1741, and had Luther 1743, Rachel 1744, Mary 1745, Ebenezer
1747, Amos 1750, Lucy 1751, Susanna 1753, Caleb 1755, Calvin
1757: she d. 1758, and he m. Hepzibah, wid. of Eleazar Carver and D. of Thomas Perkins, 1759, and had Hepzibah 1760,
Alexander 1762, Lavinia 1764: he d. of small-pox 1778 ; she
1800, æ. 80.—Mary m. Benjamin Leach 1764.—Lucy m. Jireh

Swift 1776.—Susanna m. Caleb Fobes 1776.—Hepzibah m.
Abiezer Alger Esq. 1778.—Alexander m. Abigail Dean of Easton
1788, and settled in Easton.

13. Robert (s. of Samuel 4.) m. Tabitha Leach 1741, and had
Robert 1742, Phebe, Hazadiah, Tabitha, Sarah*, Constant 1752,
Wealthy, Sarah, Eliab 1756, Asa 1758. His will dated 1787;
he d. 1796 æ. 77. Phebe m. Jedediah Leach 1765.—Hazadiah
m. James Leach 1765.—Tabitha m. Jona. Caswell 1769.—Constant m Nehemiah Leach 1772.—Asa m. Susanna D. of Nathan
Hartwell 1780.

14. Benjamin (s. of Samuel 4.) m. Abigail D. of Nehemiah
Leach 1749, and had Abigail 1753, Lewis 1755, Ruth 1757, Ben-
jamin, Marshall, Eunice, Bethiah. Benjamin, the father d. 1801
æ. 78: she 1806 æ. 75. Marshall m. Hepzibah D. of Benjamin
Leach 1798.—Eunice m. Ebenezer Leach 1794.—Bethiah m.
Caleb Bassett 1782.

15. Timothy (s. of Timothy 5.) m. Bethiah D. of William
Ames 1737, and had Levi 1738, and d. 1740 æ. 29.

16. Abiah (s. of Timothy 5.) m. Mary D. of Joseph Snell
1737, and had Mary 1738, Anne 1748, Asa 1750, Bathsheba 1752,
Keziah 1754, Shepard 1756. He. d. 1781 æ. 69. Mary m. Adam
Howard 1759.—Bathsheba m. Edward Bass of Braintree 1772.

17. Nathan (s. of Timothy 5.) m. Hannah D. of Joseph Snell
1746, and had Mehitabel 1747, Simeon 1749, Damaris 1751,
Isaac 1753, Jonathan 1754, Hannah 1756*, Martha 1761, Nathan
1764. Nathan, the father, d. 1786 æ. 72: she 1773 æ. 49. Mehitabel m. Theophilus Curtis 1766.—Damaris m. Joseph Allen
of Braintree 1769.—Martha m. Elisha Bisbee 1779.

18. John (s. of John 6.) m. Abigail D. of Jonathan Willis
1734.—Abigail Keith m. Zechariah Watkins 1761.—Mary Keith
m. Solomon Pratt 1761.

19. James (s. of John 6.) m. Lydia Jackson 1743, and James
Keith m. Lydia Perkins 1744, and had Deborah 1744, Dardany
1746, Keziah 1748, Hannah 1750, James 1752. These children
were said to have been by his 3d. wife, if so we have no knowledge of his first. Deborah Keith m. Ebenezer Shaw Jr. of M.
1764: and Deborah Keith m. Zadock Leonard of M. 1765, which
was this man's D. is uncertain.—Dardany m. Zebedee Pratt of
M. 1763.—Keziah m. Jona. Wood 1764.—Hannah m. Robert
Hayward 1768. (see Samuel 11.)

20. Israel (s. of John 6.) m. Betty D. of Jonathan Chandler
probably 1741, and had Chandler 1741, Israel 1744, (He d. and
the wid. Betty probably m. Joseph Harvey 3d. 1749.)—Israel m.
Abigail D. of Nathan Leonard 1767.

21. Daniel (s. of John 6.) m. Elizabeth D. of Nathaniel Conant 1744, and had Isaiah 1745, Daniel 1747, Jeremiah 1749;
she d. and he m. Lydia Keyzer of E., and had Naomi 1754, Seth
1757, Salmon 1760, Betty ; his 2d. w. d. 1762. Naomi m. Miles
Standish Jr. 1774.—Betty m. Thomas Sherman 1781.—Isaiah
27

m. Sarah D. of John Burr 1773; lived in M.; his estate settled by Joseph 3d. 1775.

22. Zephaniah (s. of John 6.) (he lived in Easton and afterwards Vermont.) m. Mary D. of Nathaniel Hooper 1750, and had Israel 1750, Scotland, Cyrus, Ruel, Jonathan, Unite, Alfred, and perhaps others; he lived to great age. Israel gra. H. U. 1771, was Adjutant General in Ms, and afterwards went to Vt., and d. 1819 æ. 69.—Ruel, Unite and Alfred also went to Vt.—Jonathan went to Kennebec.—Scotland m. Parnel D. of Col. Edward Howard 1772, and lived in E.—Cyrus m. Bathsheba Sproat, and lived in M.

23. Joseph (s. of John 6.) m. Chloe D. of Samuel Packard 1759, and had Aberdeen 1760, Lurania 1763, John 1765, Timothy 1767, Joseph 1769, Martin 1771.—This family lived in M.; he settled his brother Isaiah's estate 1775, and was called Joseph Keith 3d.—Aberdeen d. 1778.

24. Josiah (s. of Josiah 7.) m. Ruth Manly 1730, and lived in E., and had Milicent 1730, Josiah 1732, Rebecca 1735, Ruth 1739, David 1747, Mary 1749, d. 1824, James 1751, Martha 1754. Milicent m. Benjamin Parris 1753.—Josiah m. wid. Susanna Williams 1758, (she was a Lathrop); lived in Easton: had several wives; and had Bathsheba 1759, Benjamin, Thomas, Ruel, Lewis, and others perhaps, James of Westmoreland was one.— Rebecca m. Ezra Alden 1756, and John Bisbee 1771.—David m. Sarah D. of Jona. Copeland 1769 and had Francis and Bezer of Easton, and Josiah and Friend of Me. and others perhaps.—

25. William (s. of Josiah 7.) m. Mary D. of Henry Kingman 1738 and settled in E. and had Edward, William, Luke, Japhet. Luke m. Martha Littlefield 1768.—Edward m. Susanna Littlefield 1765.

26. Daniel (s. of Josiah 7.) m. a Manly and lived in E. and had Alexander who went to Greenwich; Nehemiah who had a s. Caleb; Daniel who had a s. Daniel and a s. Allen, in Mansfield, by a 2d. wife, who was an Allen.

27. Capt. Joseph (s. of Joseph 8.) m. Ann Turner 1746, and had William 1748*, Joseph 1750*. He d. 1792 æ. 69: she 1807 æ. 79.

28. James (s. of Joseph 8.) m. Sarah D. of Capt. John Holman 1752, and had James 1753, Sarah 1754, Anne 1756, Isaac 1759, Holman 1761, Susanna 1763, William 1765, John Quincy 1769, Molly 1777, Caleb 1782*. He d. 1803 æ. 76: she 1818 æ. 81. Sarah m. Job Bearce 1780.—Anne m. Capt. Ephraim Snell 1780.—Susanna d. single 1839.—Molly m. Seth Keith 1793. —John Quincy m. Mary D. of John Hudson 1792, and went to Minot Me.

29. David (s. of Joseph 8.) m. Jemima D. of Dea. Thomas Whitman 1754, and had David 1755, d. 1778, Abigail 1758, d. 1778. Levi 1760, Molly 1763, Zenas 1766; his wife d. 1771, and he m. Charity wid. of Uriah Brett and D. of Jonathan Kingman 1772,

and had Calvin 1775, David 1778 ; he d. 1812 æ. 84 ; she 1819 æ. 78.—Molly m. Capt. Daniel Kinsley 1785.

30. Eleazar (s. of Joseph 8.) m. Elizabeth D. of Col. Edward Mitchell 1760, and had Betty 1760, Huldah 1762, Silvia 1764, Lucy 1766, Eleazar 1769, John 1772, Timothy 1774, Celia 1777, Susanna 1780, Martin 1782, Jennet 1785*; Silvanus 1787, George 1790. His wife d. 1790 æ. 48, and he m. Susanna wid. of Asa Keith and D. of Ephraim Cary 1795 ; he d. 1809 æ. 76. Betty m. Isaac Keith 1784.—Huldah m. Levi Keith 1786.—Silvia m. Holman Keith 1785.—Lucy m. Ephraim Copeland 1791.—Celia m. Isaac Lathrop Jr. of Easton 1798.—Susanna m. Galen Latham 1802.—Martin m. Sally D. of Job Bearce 1809, and died 1809 æ. 27.—Silvanus m. Lurania D. of Caleb Copeland 1820 and d. 1825 æ. 38.—George m. Phidelma D. of Anthony Winslow Clift 1815.—Sally, Martin's Wid. m. Edward Hayward Jr. of Easton 1820.

31. John (s. of Joseph 8.) m. Alice D. of Col Edward Mitchell 1763, and had Alice 1764 : his wife d. 1766 æ. 22 : and he m. Ann Belcher 1774 ; she d. and he m. Zerviah D. of Benjamin Willis of Hardwick, and had Joseph, Benjamin, Seth ; he d. 1819 æ. 83 : she 1827 æ.73.—Alice m. Libeus Washburn 1792 and d. in Pomfret Con. 1833.—Joseph is a physician in Minot Me.—Benjamin m. Sally D. of Joseph Edson 1811.—Seth lives in Boston.

32. Seth (s. of Joseph 8.) m. Abigail D. of Capt. John Holman 1764, and had Joseph 1765, Seth 1768 ; his w. d. 1771 æ. 28, and he m. Thankful wid. of Michael Jackson of Abington 1775: she was a Studley of Hanover: and had Ichabod 1777, Bethuel 1779, Abigail 1782. He d. 1785 æ. 45 ; she 1815 æ. 78. Seth m. Molly D. of James Keith 1793, and went to Minot Me. and d. 1833.—Bethuel not m.—Abigail m. Hiram Washburn 1806 and d. 1822 æ. 40.

33. George (s. of Joseph 8.) m. Deborah D. of Nathaniel Clift of Marshfield 1768, and had George 1769 ; his wife d. 1777 æ. 29 : and he m. Elizabeth Ford 1780, and had James, who settled in Marshfield. He d. 1819 æ. 77. George lived and d. in Boston, and left Stephen, Nathaniel, George and perhaps others.

34. Ephraim (s. of Ephraim Esq. 9.) gra. H. U. 1762, m. a Smith, and lived in Taunton : had Marshall, who m. a Cushman, and settled in Boston, Julia, who m. a Cushing, and Amelia, who m. a Crosman.

35. Solomon (s. of Ephraim Esq. 9.) m. Lois D. of Jonathan Cary 1777, and had Clarissa 1778, Mary 1780, Solomon 1783, Jona. Cary 1785, Lois 1787, Sumner 1790, Ichabod 1793. Clarissa m. Calvin Pratt 1798.—Polly m. Solomon Eaton of M. 1796.—Lois m. Consider Scott of Charlemont.—Solomon m. Lucinda D. of Salmon Keith 1807, and had Maria, Vassall, Solomon, Ambrose, Clarissa Lloyd, Bartlett, Fayette, and Sumner.

36. Edward (s. of Samuel 11.) m. Mehitabel D. of Thomas Hayward 1778, and had Bethiah 1781. He m. Betsy King 1791

and had Jairus S. 1792, gra. B. U. 1819, Mehitabel 1794, Hannah 1797. He removed to the Eastward.

37. Samuel (s. of Samuel 11.) m. Zilphah D. of Thomas Conant 1766, and had Keziah 1768, not m. Barzillai 1770, Ruth 1772, Abner 1774, Cyrus 1776, Samuel 1779, David and Jonathan 1782. David m. Ruth Wilbur 1806.—Jonathan m. Polly Gushe 1805.

38. Luther (s. of Ebenezer 12.) m. Sarah Tomson 1767, and had a family and removed to Pelham, and thence to Sangersville.

39. Ebenezer (s. of Ebenezer 12.) m. Hannah D. of James Allen 1773, and had a large family and went away with his brother Luther.

40. Amos (s. of Ebenezer 12.) m. Anna wid. of Jesse Fuller Sturtevant and D. of James Alger 1774, and had Mary, Amos, Sarah, Charles, Anna. Polly m. Abraham Leach 1796.—Amos m. Sally Reed of M. 1801.—Sarah m. Gordon Strobridge 1801. The parents went to Oakham.

41. Caleb (s. of Eben. 12.) m. Susanna D. of Nathan Mitchell Esq. 1777, and had Mitchell, Anna, Carlos, and others, and went to Pelham.

42. Calvin (s. of Ebenezer 12.) m. Martha D. of James Alger 1779, and had Sarah, Parnel, and others and went to Pelham.— Sarah m. Levi Blossom of Woodstock 1801.—Parnel m. Byram Harvey 1800.

43. Robert (s. of Robert 13.) m. Silence D. of Nathan Hartwell 1763 and had Hartwell 1764, Jonathan 1766, Silvanus 1767. This woman was mother of Seth Lathrop of S. Carolina.

Robert Keith m. Hannah Southworth of Raynham 1782.— Jonathan m. Sarah D. of James Leach 1792.

44. Benjamin (s. of Benjamin 14.) m. Olive Eaton of M. 1788, and had Otis 1790, Royal 1792, Benjamin 1795, Olive 1797, Lucinda 1800, Oliver 1810.

45. Levi (s. of Timothy 15) m. Jemima D. of Luke Perkins 1759, and had Bethiah 1760, Benjamin 1763, Jemima 1767. Molly 1771, Levi 1773; he d. 1813 æ. 76. Bethiah m. Nath'l Reynolds Jr. 1777.—Jemima m. Wm. Field 1797.—Molly m. Dea. Ichabod Howard 1794.

46. Asa (s. of Abiah 16.) m. Susanna D. of Ephraim Cary 1774, and had Bethuel 1775, Mehitabel 1778, Asa 1779, Huldah 1781, d. 1808, Alden 1783, Susanna 1785, d. 1813, Sybil 1787, Mary 1789, d. 1809. He d. of small pox and the wid m. Eleazar Keith 1795. The ss. moved away westward.—Mehitabel m. John Keith 1800.

47. Shepard (s. of Abiah 16.) m. Sally Hawes 1795, and had Rowena 1795. Abi 1796, Melina 1798, Olive 1799, Sally 1802, Scepter 1809, Mary 1813.

48. Simeon (s. of Nathan 17.) m. Molly D. of Col. Simeon Cary 1775, and had Hampden 1776, Hannah 1777, Molly 1779, Austin 1781, Sidney 1783, Martha 1785, Pardon 1787, Rhoda

1790, Silvia 1792, Keziah 1794. Hampden m. Sally D. of Joseph
Bassett Esq. 1799.—Hannah m. George Haskell 1795*.—Molly
m. Dr. Issachar Snell 1799.—Martha m. Amos Bond of Augusta
1807.—Austin m. Mehitabel D. of Jona. Copeland 1813.—Sidney
m. Semantha D. of Capt. Ephraim Snell 1806.—Pardon m. Abigail Wild of Braintree 1812.—Rhoda m. Rev. Jonas Perkins
1815.—Silvia m. Josiah Williams 1814.—Keziah m. Peter Talbot of Winslow 1812.—Hampden and Sidney settled in Winslow Me.
49. Isaac (s. of Nathan 17.) m. Hannah D. of Ephraim Cole
1775, and had Timothy 1776, and d. 1776 in the army ; and his
widow m. Capt. Seth Keith 1778.—Timothy m. Lavinia Wilbur
1797, and afterwards Hannah D. of Robert Hayward 1819.
50. Jonathan (s. of Nathan 17.) m. Hannah D. of Charles
Snell 1777, and had Isaac 1778, Zeruiah 1782, Tila (Silence)
1785, Sally 1788, Bathsheba 1790, Abigail 1793, Hannah 1795,
Jonas 1797, Susanna 1799.—Zerviah m. Caleb Jackson 1801.—
Silence m. Silvanus French of St. 1804.—Sally m. Calvin Wild
of Braintree 1810.—Bathsheba m. Barnard Jackson 1808.—Isaac
m. Lydia D. of Wm. French 1801.—Jonas m. Mercy E. Bartlett
of Plymouth 1820.
51. Nathan (s. of Nathan 17.) m. Lois D. of Barnabas Howard Esq. 1786, and had Lois 1788, Nahum Mitchell 1794, and
went to Me. Lois m. Francis Nash of Braintree 1810.
52. Daniel (s. of Daniel 21.) m. Melatiah D. of James Hooper 1766, and had Susanna 1767, Zephaniah 1771, Melatiah 1774,
Howe 1779, Rufus 1783, Melinda 1785, and Daniel. Susanna
m. Benjamin Robbins.—Melatiah m. Daniel Washburn 1795.—
Rufus m. Polly Blossom of Eaton N. H. 1804.—Daniel m. Ruth
D. of Dea. Peter Conant 1800.
53. Jeremiah (s. of Daniel 21.) m. Agatha Bryant of M. 1776,
and had Jeremiah, Bethiah, Naomi, Betsy, Susanna.—Jeremiah
m. Sally Pratt 1801, lived in M. and had a s. Nahum.—Bethiah
m. Josiah Pratt.—Naomi m. Isaac Pratt 1804.—Betsey m. Benjamin Tucker 1800.—Susanna m. Zebulun K. Pratt 1814.
54. Capt. Seth (s. of Daniel 21.) m. Hannah wid of Isaac
Keith and D. of Ephraim Cole 1778, and went to Me., afterwards
returned and d. in Titicut.—He had Ephraim, Hannah, Polly,
Isaac, Aberdeen, Lydia, Philander. Ephraim went to Me.—
Hannah m. Hosea Leach 1807.—Polly m. William Pratt.—Aberdeen m. Susanna Murdock 1806.
55. Salmon (s. of Daniel 21.) m. Chloe Wilbor 1779, and had
Zephaniah 1779, Oliver 1781, Lucinda 1785, Salmon 1789, Chloe
1792.—Zephaniah m. Susanna D. of Luther Hooper 1807.—
Oliver m. Susanna Robbins 1809.—Lucinda m. Solomon Keith
1807.—Salmon m. Abigail Robbins 1813.—Chloe m. Joshua
Fobes 2d. 1809.
56. Maj. James (s. of Josiah 24.) m. Anna D. of Henry Kingman, and had Ambrose 1774, Nancy 1778, Abigail 1780, Submit

1783. Nancy m. Daniel Packard 1796, and went to Pelham.—
Abigail m. Nathan Snell Jr. 1800.
  57. James (s. of James 28.) m. Mary D. of Col. Edward
Mitchell 1780, and had Piam, James, Nahum, Madison, Bela,
Nabby, Tamsin, Sarah. James m. Betsy D. of Noah Whitman
1815.—Nabby m. Cyrus Cary 1802.—Sarah m. Ebenezer Whitman. This family all went westward.
  58. Isaac (s. of James 28.) m. Betty D. of Eleazar Keith 1784,
and had Isaac, Perez, Barzillai, Freedom, Betsy. Capt. Isaac
m. Bathsheba D. of Capt. Simeon Curtis 1815.—Perez m Silvia
D. of Holman Keith.—Barzillai m. Tempe D. of Caleb Copeland 1819.—Freedom went to Me. Isaac the father d. 1822, æ.
64. Betty the mother d. 1838 æ. 78.
  59. Holman (s. of James 28.) m. Silvia D. of Elea. Keith 1785,
and had Caleb, Thaxter, Holman, Silvia, Jane. Silvia the mother d. 1828 æ. 64 ; he d. 1835 æ. 74. Caleb m. Hazadiah D. of
Hezekiah Hayward 1812, and had Hezekiah and Elbridge.—
Silvia m. Perez Keith.—Jane m. Caleb Mitchell 1811.—Thaxter
yet single.—Holman m. a D. of B. Pope Esq.
  60. Dea. William (s. of James 28.) m. Abigail D. of Thomas
Russell 1789, and had Agnes 1789, Parlee 1792, Elbridge G.
1795, Semantha 1802. Dea. Keith d. 1826 æ. 62, his wife 1832
æ. 61. Agnes m. Noah Bonney Jr. of Pembroke 1819, and d.
1821 æ. 31.—Capt. Parlee m. Dulcinea D. of Barnabas Dunbar
1821.—Elbridge G. m. a Smith of Pembroke and d. 1834.—Semantha m. Nathan Whitman.
  61. Levi (s. of David 29.) m. Huldah D. of Eleazar Keith
1786, and had Levi and Heman. Capt. Levi m. Mehitabel D.
of Capt. Isaac Whitman 1811.—Heman m. Silvester D. of Capt.
Simeon Curtis.
  62. Zenas (s. of David 29.) m. Jane D. of Ephraim Cary 1792,
and had Zenas, Scott, Willard, Jane, Margaret Orr, Mary Augusta, Ann Maria, Susan Frances : he d. 1840 æ. 74. Zenas m.
Salome D. of Dyer Robinson 1821.—Scott m. Abigail D. of
Dyer Robinson.—Willard m. Eliza Thomas of Marshfield.—
Jane m. Oliver A. Washburn 1814.—Margaret O. m. Gad Robinson 1821.—Ann Maria m. Charles Robinson.—Susan F. m.
Ellis W. Holmes.
  63. Calvin (s. of David 29.) m. Bethiah D. of Abishai Stetson
1794, and had Zebina, Lewis, Joseph Warren, Nahum. Zebina m. Rebecca Wethrell 1820.—Lewis m. Azubah D. of Levi
Churchill 1719.—Joseph Warren m. Eunice Bowen 1823.—Nahum m. a Holmes.
  64. David (s. of David 29.) m. Lydia D. of Nathan Alden
Esq. 1801, had Julia 1802, Mary Russell 1804, Lydia Alden 1806,
David Noble 1808, Abigail 1810. He d. 1813 æ. 35.
  65. Eleazar (s. of Eleazar 30.) m. Bethiah D. of Jona. Kingman
1793, and had Bethiah 1794 ; his wife d. 1797 æ. 25 : and he m.
Zilphah D. of Maj. Tho's Mitchell, and had Huldah 1801, Lucy
and Lucia 1804, Eleazar 1809. He d. 1822. Bethiah m. George

Mitchell 1820.—Huldah m. Rufus Bates of Hanover 1821.—Lucia m. Jacob A. Rogers.

66. John (s. of Eleazar 30.) m. Mehitabel D. of Asa Keith 1800, and had Jennet 1801, Esta Fanny 1804, Timothy, Asa; his wife d. 1813 æ. 36.—Jennet m. Josiah Reed 1820.

67. Timothy (s. of Eleazar 30.) m. Lydia Wyer of Charlestown, where he lived, and d. 1805 æ. 31, leaving 2 ss. Timothy and William. The wid. m. William Manning, a printer in Boston, who removed to Worcester, and has since returned to Boston and is messenger to the Gov. and Council.—She d. 1838.

68. Joseph (s. of Seth 32.) m. Betty D. of Anthony Sherman 1787, and had Salome 1787. He d. 1789 æ. 24, and she m. Timothy Allen 1791.—Salome m. Daniel Alger 1806.

69. Ichabod (s. of Seth 32.) m. Susannah D. of Benjamin Robinson 1802, and had Edwin, Eleanor, Francis, Ralph Sanger, Joseph Robinson. He d. 1833.

70. Abner (s. of Samuel 37.) m. Eunice D. of David Benson 1803, and had Zilpha 1804, Anna 1806, Eunice 1808, Lurania 1811, Abner 1814, Elvira Benson 1818.

71. Hartwell (s. of Robert 43.) m. Seabury Wilbor, and had Silence 1786, Seabury 1789, Jonas H. 1791, Hartwell 1793, Davis 1795, Gideon 1798, Eliza 1798. He d. 1801 æ. 40, and she m. Thaddeus Howard 1813. Jonas H. m. Susanna D. of Nathaniel Manly 1816.—Hartwell m. Mary D. of Joseph Bassett 1816 and went to Dudley.—Davis m. Harriot D. of Thaddeus Howard 1820.—Eliza m. Perez Lathrop 1818.

72. Benjamin (s. of Levi 45.) m. Patty D. of Col. Simeon Cary 1788, and had Ziba 1789, Arza 1791, Bela 1793, Charles 1794, Polly 1798, Jason 1801. Polly m. Franklin Ames 1821. —Ziba m. Sally D. of Jona. Cary 1813.—Arza m. Marcia D. of Abel Kingman Esq. 1814.—Bela m. Mary D. of Seth Kingman 1821.—Charles m. Mehitabel D. of Josiah Perkins 1817. The father d. 1814.

73. Levi (s. of Levi 45.) m. Abigail Porter 1797, and had Alvan 1799, and Clarissa 1801, and removed to Me.

74. Hampden (s. of Simeon 48.) m. Sarah D. of Joseph Bassett Esq. 1799, and had Hannah 1801, James 1803, and went to Winslow, Me.

75. Ambrose (s. of Maj. James 56.) M. Catharine D. of Nathaniel Southworth 1796, and had Cassander Dodge 1797, Omen Southworth 1799, Clifford 1801. He lived in Halifax. Cassander D. m. Mary Darling of M. 1816.—Clifford m. Arethusa D. probably of Oliver Harris of St. 1820.

76. Isaac of Easton (s. of Josiah 24.) m. Mary Randall, and had Howe, Isaac, and Lusanna. He d. 1773, and she m. Capt. Simeon Wood of S. B. 1774.—Lusanna m. Jacob Tomson of Halifax 1795.

77. Isaac (s. of Isaac 76.) m. Joanna wid. of Adam Besse, and D. of Dea. Seth Pratt 1797, and had Edwin, Philo, Asa, Pamelia, Marietta, and Harriet. Edwin m. Saba D. of Joseph

Hooper.—Philo m. Caroline D. of Maj. Theodore Mitchell.—
Pamelia m. Abram Washburn 2d. 1822.
78. Howe (s. of Jsaac 76.) m. Martha D. of Benjamin Hayward 1795, and had Benjamin Hayward 1795, Alexis 1797, Isaac
1799, Sally 1800, Jacob 1803, Polly 1804, Albertina 1810, Howe
1814. Benjamin Hayward m. Lucia D. of Samuel Harden 1719.
79. Mitchell (s. of Caleb 41.) m. Salome D. of Major Isaac
Lazell 1811, and had Thomas Mitchell 1811, James Drances
1815, d. 1834. The mother d. 1838, and he m. wid. Charlotte
Tisdale sister of his first w. 1840.
80. Jacob (of Easton probably) m. Abigail D. of David
Leach perhaps 1734, and had Abigail 1737, Barnabas 1750.—
Barnabas m. Hannah Jackson 1771, and had a son Barnabas.—
Jacob Keith m. Elizabeth Ripley 1801.
Molly m. Geo. Briggs 1768.—Lemuel m. Abihail Lathrop 1768.
—Azael m. Olive Edson 1767.—Mary of Easton m. John Dun-
bar 1768.—Bathsheba D. of Josiah Jr. of Easton m. Theophilus
Howard Jr. 1778.—Patience m. Japhet Beal 1770.—Phebe of
Easton m. Ebenezer Gilbert 1743.—Keziah m. Moses Eddy
1788.—Francis m. Melinda Holbrook of St. 1800.—Betsy m.
Cyrus Snell 1801.—Isaac 5th m. Anna French 1810.—Lemuel
of E. m. Anne Keith 1810.—Eliab m. Patience Wood 1813.—
Hiram m. wid. Sarah Whitmarsh 1816.—Sally m. Charles Hay-
ward Jr. 1821.

KEYZER.—George Keyzer from Boston and his wife Elizabeth had Hannah 1720, Abigail 1723, Seth 1727. The family
removed to Easton —Mary Keyzer m. Isaiah Fuller 1768.—Lydia of E. m. Daniel Keith a. 1753.—Mary of E. m. Henry Kingman Jr. 1761.—Lydia m. Wm. French 1767.

KIFF.—Thomas Kiff in E. B. m. Mary Bunton 1735, and
had John 1736, Mary 1738, Ann 1740.

KING.—Jabez King m. Mary D. of Timothy Washburn 1753,
and had Elizabeth 1755, Daniel 1757, Mary 1761. Hezekiah
King m. Sarah Reed 1712 —Barzillai of Easton m. Betsy Cheesman 1812.—Josiah King and his wife Ruth had John 1773.—
Joanna of T. m. Robert Snell 1786.—Hazadiah of R, m. Hezekiah Hayward 1791.

KINGMAN.—Henry Kingman of Weymouth made free 1636;
grand juror 1637: representative 1638, and 1652: committee to
lay out highways 1649: his wife Joanna d. 1659: his will proved 1666: he d. æ. a. 74: had Edward, Thomas and John: his Ds.
m. one a Holbrook, one a Davis, and one a Barnard.—Moses
Kingman Jr. m. Eliza Pain of Braintree 1747.
1. John (s. of Henry above) purchased of Michael Bacon Jr,
of Billerica the estate in W. B. formerly belonging to his uncle
Daniel Bacon 1685, it being the place where Caleb Kingman
lived. His w. Elizabeth. They had John 1664, Henry 1668,
Samuel 1670, Elizabeth 1673, Deliverance 1676, Susanna 1679.
He d. 1690. Elizabeth m. Tho's Mitchell, and Deliverance m. Jacob Mitchell, both at the same time 1696.—Susanna m. Capt.

Chilton Latham 1699.—Another D. m. Nath'l Packard probably.
2. John (s. of John 1.) m. Desire D. of Isaac Harris and had
Desire 1690, Mary 1692, Seth 1696, Deliverance 1698 ; she d. and
he m. Bethiah Newcomb 1698, and had Isaac 1699, John 1703,
Abigail 1705, David 1708, Ebenezer 1711, Josiah 1713, Bethiah
1716. He d. 1755 æ. 91. Desire m. John Orcutt 1721.—Deliverance m. Ebenezer Orcutt 1725.—Abigail m. Jacob Allen 1730.
—Bethiah m. James Allen 1736.
3. Henry (s. of John 1.) m. Bethiah D. of John Howard, and
had Bethiah 1693, Elizabeth 1695, Sarah 1697, Martha 1699,
Henry 1701, Keziah 1703, Hannah 1705, Jonathan 1708, Anne
1710, Mary 1713. Bethiah m. Benjamin Washburn 1714.—Sarah m. Benjamin Pratt 1719.—Martha m. Benjamin Washburn
1729.—Keziah m. Eleazar Keith 1726.—Hannah m. John Alden
1727.—Anne m. Gershom Conant 1739.—Mary m. William
Keith 1738.
4. Samuel (s. of John 1.) m. Mary D. of Jacob Mitchell 1696,
at the same time with her two brothers, (see No. 1.) and had
Susanna 1697, John 1699, Joanna 1701, Jane 1704, Mary 1706,
Samuel 1710. His will 1740, proved 1742: left a wid. Hannah
2d. wife probably. Susanna m. Solomon Packard.—Joanna m.
Akerman Pettingill 1723.—Jane m. Isaac Kingman 1730.—Ma-
ry Kingman m. Benjamin Vickery 1739.—Hannah Kingman m.
John Wade 1751.
5. Isaac (s. of John 2.) m. Jane D. of Samuel Kingman 1730,
and had Abigail 1730, Lemuel 1732, Jane 1736, Bethiah 1743,
Isaac 1747 ; his wife d. 1769, and he m. wid. Ruth Loring 1770.
Abigail m. Samuel Dawes Jr. 1755.—Jane m. James Loring 1770.
Bethiah m. Robert Robinson 1772.—Isaac m. Content D. of
James Packard 1769.—Isaac the father lived in N. B. till a. 1743,
when he removed to E. B. and d. 1779 æ. 79.—Perhaps Isaac
Jr. went to the westward with his father-in-law.
6. John (s. of John 2.) m. Rebecca D. of Samuel Allen, and
had Mehitabel 1731, Daniel 1732, Abner 1735, Mercy 1737, Eliab
1739, Rebecca 1741. It is said he had a 2d. wife Elizabeth.—
Wid. Elizabeth Kingman joined the ch. in E. B. 1742.—Mehitabel m. Ebenezer Wade 1759, and d. 1772 æ. 41.—Eliab went to
Hingham.
7. David (s. of John 2.) m. Mary D. of Nathaniel Hayward
1732, lived in E. B. and had David 1733, Hannah 1743. He died
1769 æ. 61, she 1792 æ. 87.—Hannah m. Col. Robert Orr 1766.
8. Ebenezer (s. of John 2.) m. Content Turner of Scituate
1740, and had Caleb 1744, Lucy 1748, Silvia 1754, Marlboro'
1756, Susy 1762. Lucy m. William Hudson Jr. 1767.—All this
family except Caleb removed to Harvard.
9. Josiah (s. of John 2.) m. Mary D. of Josiah Williams 1737
and had Josiah 1740, Molly 1742, Edward 1744, Benjamin 1746,
Martha 1750. He settled in E. B., but removed to Easton, and
d., and his wid. m. Ephraim Cary 1784, and d. 1803 æ. 85.—Damon m. Polly Snell 1814.—Mara m. Wm. Phillips 1795.—Eunice
28

m. George Williams Jr. 1797.—Nancy of Mansfield m. Sprague Snow 1820.

10. Henry (s. of Henry 3.) m. Mary D. of Samuel Allen 1726, and had Mary 1727, Jane 1729, Matthew 1731, Henry 1735 ; his w. d. 1740, and he m. Abigail, wid. of Seth Copeland and D. of Thomas White of Braintree 1742, and had Abigail 1749, Anne 1752, Seth 1757, Benjamin 1760, Submit. He d. 1775 æ. 74. Mary m. Benjamin Pettingill 1747.—Jane m. Elisha Gurney 1760.—Henry m. Mary Keyzer 1761.—Abigail m. Daniel Dunbar 1771.—Anne m. Maj. James Keith.—Benjamin m. Rhoda Shaw 1783, and went to Winchester.—Submit m. Simeon Shurtliff 1781.

11. Jonathan (s. of Henry 3.) m. Mary D. of Joseph Keith 1732, and had Martha 1732, Jonathan 1735, Mary 1738, Charity 1740, Bethiah 1743, Betty 1751.—Martha m. James Alger 1750. Mary (or Bethiah) m. Henry Howard of Easton.—Charity m. Uriah Brett 1760, and David Keith 1772.—Betty m. Robert Dunbar 1771.

12. John (s. of Samuel 4.) m. Sarah D. of Thomas Kingman of Weymouth 1722, and had Sarah 1724, Silence 1726, Alexander 1730, Adam 1733.—Sarah m. William Shurtliff 1745.—Alexander m. Sarah D. of John Lathrop 1755.—Alexander m. Abiah Knapp of Easton 1790.—John Kingman m. wid. Anne Pettingill, D. of Nicholas Byram 1771 ; she d. in S. B. 1802 æ. 90.

13. Samuel (s. of Samuel 4.) m. Phebe Washburn 1737, and had Eunice 1737, Hannah 1740, Phebe 1742.

14. Lemuel (s. of Isaac 5.) m. Deborah D. of Capt. John Loring 1754, and had Ruth 1755, Lucy 1757, John 1758, Loring 1762, Priscilla 1764, and Deborah. Ruth m. Jonathan Mehuren 1774.—John removed to Weston and had a family there.—Loring d. a bachelor 1834.—Deborah m. Thomas Sherman of Plymouth.

15. Daniel (s. of John 6.) m. Abigail D. of Ebenezer Copeland of Braintree, and had Nathan 1760, Abigail 1762.—Nathan m. Chloe Smith of Norton 1785.

16. Abner (s. of John 6.) m. Susanna D. of Josiah Leonard 1761, and had Celia 1762, Josiah 1764, Huldah 1767, Cynthia 1770, Bela. This family went to M. and some of them thence to Providence.—Josiah m. Chloe D. of Eliab Fobes 1781.

17. Capt. David (s. of David 7.) m. Abigail Hall 1752, and had Nathan 1752, Molly 1754, Ezra 1756, Nabby 1758, Eunice 1760, David 1763, Barza 1765 ; she d. 1794 æ. 62 : he 1805 æ. 72. Molly m. Robert Young 1776.—Nabby m. Malachi Delano of Duxbury 1807.—Eunice m. Walter Hatch 1780.

18. Caleb (s. of Ebenezer 8.) m. Freelove Fenno, and had Hannah 1768, who m. Timothy Reed Esq. 1788. He d. 1807 ; she 1815. Reed left one s. Caleb Kingman, who d. 1837.

19. Matthew (s. of Henry 10.) m. Jane D. of David Packard 1755, and had Simeon 1756, Mary 1757, Eunice 1760, Hannah 1761, Harmony 1763, Jane 1764, Martha 1766, Abel 1768, Henry

1770, Eliphalet 1775, Keziah 1777. He d. 1809 æ. 79. Simeon Esq. m. Rebecca Freeman of Eastham 1778, and settled at Orleans on the Cape.—Mary m. Charles Snell.—Eunice m. Perez Southworth.—Hannah m. Jacob Packard of Warwick 1806. —Harmony m. Joel Packard Esq. of Fairhaven 1785.—Martha m. Capt. Thomas Thompson 1792.—Capt Henry m. Anna D. of Dr. Phillip Bryant 1792, and removed to Pelham.—Jane m. Micah Shaw 1793.—Keziah m. Cyrus Packard 1795.

20. Seth (s. of Henry 10.) m. Judith Washburn 1787, and had Ambrose 1789, Martin 1791, Benjamin 1793, Henry 1796, Abiel 1797, Mary 1799, Josiah Washburn 1802, John Washburn 1804, Lucy 1808, Judith Washburn 1809; his w. b. 1765 d. 1809; he m. Jennet D. of William Edson 1811, and had Elbridge 1812. Ambrose m. Esther D. of Josiah Edson 1810; he and Henry settled in Reading.—Martin m. Phebe D. of Levi Packard 1816, and went to Pelham.—Benjamin m. Rebecca D. of Josiah Packard 1817.—Josiah W. m. a Packard.—Abiel m. Mary Cary D. of Micah Shaw 1819.—Mary m. Bela Keith 1821.

21. Jonathan (s. of Jonathan 11.) m. Hannah D. of Jonathan Copeland 1759, and had Molly 1760, Hannah and Joseph 1763, Huldah 1766, Jonathan 1768, Bethiah 1772: he d. 1819. Molly m. David Howard 1778.—Hannah m. Josiah Williams 1785, and then Capt. Ephraim Snell 1792, and afterwards Caleb Snell 1808. —Huldah m. Perez Williams 1788.—Bethiah m. Eleazar Keith 1793.

22. Nathan (s. of Capt. David 17.) m. Lenity Thomas of Marshfield, sister of Japhet Allen's wife, 1773, and had Nabby, and d. and his wid. m. Edward Hayford 1779.—Nabby m. Uriah Brett 1790.

23. Ezra Esq. (s. of Capt. David 17.) m. Susanna D. of Peter Whitman 1782, and had Susanna 1784, Nathan 1785, Hannah 1787, Ezra 1789, Melzar 1791*, Charlotte 1792, Caroline 1794; she d. 1797 æ. 36: he 1831 æ. 74. Susanna m. Daniel Howard Esq. 1802, who settled at New Gloucester Me.—Nathan was killed by a cart wheel 1797.—Hannah m. Simon Greenleaf Esq. of Portland, now professor of law at Cambridge, 1806.—Charlotte m. Rev. Ralph Sanger of Dover 1817.

24. David (s. of Capt. David 17.) m. Elizabeth D. of Col. Calvin Smith of Mendon, and had Sophia, Mary, Eliza, Lucy, Susan, George, Frances: he d. 1812 æ. 49. Sophia m. Simeon Ford Esq. who d. 1839, and Mary m. Lauren Ford Esq. 1816, both of Herkimer N. Y.—Eliza m. Elijah Hayward Esq. 1809, and d. 1834.—Lucy m. Oran Gray Otis Esq. of Herkimer, and d. 1837.

25. Barza (s. of Capt. David 17.) m. Molly D. of Mark Phillips 1791, and had Nathan, David, Adna, Eunice, Clarissa, and Charles. Nathan went westward.—David m. a Ramsdell.—Adna went to Wareham.—Eunice m. Wm. Wildy 1812, and afterwards Orren Parris.—Clarissa m. Thomas Parris 1815.—Charles m. a Raymond.

26. Adam (s. of John 12.) m. Ruth D. of Joseph White of Braintree 1760, and had Samuel 1760, and Joseph.   Adam Kingman m. wid Anne Hollis 1780.

27. Hon. Abel (s. of Matthew 19.) m. Lucy Washburn 1792, and had Jabez 1793, Marcia 1796, Tempe 1798, Arnold 1800, Harmony 1802, Albert 1804, Abel Washburn 1806; his wife d. and he m. Betsy Manly 1807, and had Edwin 1809, Polly 1810, Willard, Jane, Lucia, Betsy.   Jabez m. Phebe D. of William Brett 1818.—Marcia m. Arza Keith 1814.—Abel W. gra. Amherst 1830.

28. Eliphalet Esq. (s. of Matthew 19.) m. Zilpha D. of Josiah Edson 1801, and had Lucius 1803, Matthew 1807, Adeline 1809, Isaac 1811, Davis 1814, Lucy 1816.—Lucius gra. B. U. 1830.

29. Dea. Joseph (s. of Jonathan 21.) m. Eunice Joslyn of Pembroke 1791, and had Polly 1792, Huldah 1795, Joseph 1799, Anne 1802, Elizabeth 1808.   Polly m. Pliny Hayward.—Huldah m. Noah Edson of Hadley 1814.—Joseph m. Huldah K. D. of Perez Williams 1821.—Anne m. Samuel Rider Jr.—Elizabeth m. Lewis Rider.

30. Jonathan (s. of Jonathan 21.) m. Mehitabel D. of John Hudson 1793, and had Galen Otis 1793*, Hannah 1796, Alvah 1798, Jonathan 1800, Bethiah 1804, Mehitabel Bass 1807, Henry 1810, Melzar 1812.   Hannah m. John Richards 1820.

31. Ezra (s. of Ezra Esq. 23.) m. Frances D. of Col. Edward Howard 1812, and had Frances, Frederick, Elizabeth, Ezra, Edward, Hannah, John, George, Susanna, James.   Frances m. a Porter and lives in Waltham.

Lydia Kingman m. John Allen 1733.—Mary had a D. bap. 1834 in W. B.—Mehitabel m. John Ford 1794.

KINSLEY.—Stephen Kinsley, freeman 1640, Representative 1650, and first Ruling Elder at Braintree 1653, afterwards of Dorchester, and Representative of Milton 1666, where he d. 1673, having had a s. Samuel who d. before him leaving a wid. Hannah and a s. Samuel b. 1662.

1. Samuel (the last above named probably) m. Mary, D. of John Washburn 1694, and settled in S. B.: he bought Jeduthun Robbins' place, adjoining Thomas Washburn, and had probably Samuel, John, Nathan, Benjamin, Mary, Sarah, Bethiah, Susanna, and perhaps others.   John m. Thankful, D. of William Washburn, 1746.—Nathan m. Betty, D. of James Dunbar, and settled in Easton, and had a s. Calvin, and removed to Belchertown.—Benjamin m. a wid. Perkins, and had Samuel and Benjamin.—Mary m. Thos. Willis 1716.—Sarah m. Josiah Hayward 1715.—Benjamin or Benjamin Jr. had Silas and Abiel. Bethiah m. William Brett 1732.—Susanna m. Samuel Packard 1729.—Calvin m. Susanna, D. perhaps of Seth Lathrop, 1773.— Abiel m. Sarah, D. of Ephraim Howard, 1777.—Many of this family lived in Easton.

2. Samuel (s. of Samuel 1.) m. Sophia White, and had Sophia 1743, Lydia 1745, Samuel 1749, Nymphas 1750, Caleb 1752,

Martin 1754, Luther 1756, Hannah 1758, Eunice 1761, Cephas
1763, and Apollos.   The father d. at Worcester 1773.—Sophia
d. 1800.—Lydia m. Jona. Burr 1792, and d. at Hampden, Me.—
Samuel m. Hannah, D. of Peter Hayward, 1772, and had Samuel
1775, and went to Charlemont, and d. at Turner, Me., 1824 : his
s. Samuel had no children.—Nymphas m. Molly Richmond of
T. 1800, and d. at Hampden 1822 childless.—Caleb went to
Montague, m. 2 Ds. of Parson Nash, and d. 1827, leaving 4 Ds.—
Martin gra. H. U. 1778, went to Hardwick, and then to Hamp-
den, Me., m. a Bellows, and had an only D. who m. Samuel J.
Gardner Esq. of Roxbury, at whose house he d. 1835, æ. 81.—
Luther d. a bachelor.—Hannah m. Perez Snell 1786.—Eunice
m. Silvanus Leonard 1786.—Cephas m. Zilpha, D. of Samuel
Leonard, 1787, and d. 1800, leaving a s. and a D., the only g. s.
who left children.—Apollos m. Hannah Hall of Wallingford,
Conn., and d. at N. York 1803, leaving a D.
    3. Silas (s. of Benjamin of E.) had Azel, Daniel, Adam, Silas,
Zebina, Rodolphus, Benjamin. His w. d., and he m. Rebeckah,
wid. of Zebulun Packard, 1774 : she was a Richardson, and m.
Packard 1764.—Adam m. a Leonard, and he and Silas went to
Canton.—Benjamin removed also.—Zebina went to West Point,
N. York.
    4. Capt. Azel (s. of Silas 3.) m. Martha, D. of George How-
ard, 1785, and lived in W. B., and had Azel 1785, Hannah 1787,
Patty 1789, Silas 1792, Abigail 1795, Martin 1797, Rebecca 1799;
he then removed to Me.
    5. Capt. Daniel (s. of Silas 3.) m. Polly, D. of David Keith,
1785, and settled in E. B., and had Nabby K., Polly*, Daniel,
and Justin. Nabby K. m. Capt. Cyrus Alden 1808.—Capt. Kinsley and Capt. Alden went to Minot, Me.
    6. Rodolphus (s. of Silas 3.) m. Salome, D. of Ephraim Cary,
1794, and settled in E. B., and had a family, and removed to
Pawtucket, N. Providence, where she d. He d. at Canton : he
had William H. Shepard and others. His s. William Holman
is a minister.
    KNAPP.—Joseph Knapp m. Susanna Packard 1760, and had
Joseph 1763, Matilda 1767, Zibah 1769, Elijah 1772, Rhoda
1775.—Joseph of E. m. Eunice Carver 1784.
    2. Abijah (s. of Jonathan of T.) m. Lydia Austin, and had
Drucilla 1793, Nabby 1794, Abijah 1797, Debby 1799, Betsy, Abi,
Lydia, Polly. He settled in N. B. 1793. Betsy m. a Howard.—
Abi m. Arza Packard 1812.—Lydia m. Ezekiel Meritt 1809.—
Polly m. Azel Gurney 1815.
    Abiah Knapp of R. m. Alexander Kingman 1790.—Zenas of
R. m. Anna Leach 1817.
    KNOWLTON.—Thomas Knowlton and his w. Susanna had
John 1784, Joshua 1785, Susanna 1788, Sarah 1790.
    LANDERS.—Ebenezer Landers (from Sandwich) lived in E.
B. and had Gershom 1727, Ebenezer 1729, and Mehitabel 1731.

LATHAM.—William Latham was at Plymouth 1623; at Duxbury 1637, where he sold house and land to Rev. Ralph Partridge
1639; at Marshfield 1643, where he and Roger Cook had their
house burnt 1648.—Cary Latham and his wife Elizabeth, at Cambridge, had Thomas, and Joseph 1639.

1. Robert Latham was Constable at Marshfield 1643; was at
Cambridge two years in the Rev. Thomas Shepard's family;
was s. probably of William, and Cary might have been his uncle.
He m. Susanna, D. of John Winslow, brother of Gov. Edward,
1649, and had Mercy 1650 (at Plymouth), James, Chilton, Joseph, Elizabeth, Hannah, Sarah: he took the oath of fidelity at
Marshfield 1657; settled at E. B. before 1667: his wife's mother
was the famous Mary Chilton, who is said to have been the first
female who set foot on the Plymouth shore 1620. Her father
James Chilton, and her mother Susanna, both d. the first winter.
Latham named his two first sons, after her grandfather, James
and Chilton.—Mercy m. Isaac Harris.—Joseph was at Providence 1690 and 1703, whose wife Phebe signed a Deed 1688.—
Elizabeth m. Francis Cook 1687.—Hannah m. Joseph Washburn
Jr.—Sarah m. John Howard Jr.

2. James (s. of Robert 1.) and his w. Deliverance had Thomas,
Anne 1693, Susanna, Joseph, Betty, and Lucretia: he d. before
1739. Anne m. Nicholas Wade, and Susanna m. Nathaniel
Harden, both the same day, 1715.—Betty m. Judge Daniel Johnson 1726.

3. Capt. Chilton (s. of Robert 1.) m. Susanna, D. of John
Kingman, 1699, and had Charles 1701, Jane 1703, Arthur 1705,
James 1708, Robert 1711, Joseph 1714, Susanna 1717, Mary
1720. He d. 1751, æ. 80; she 1776, æ. 97. Susanna m. Thos.
Wade 1746.—Mary m. Jonathan Allen of Braintree 1742.—Jo-
seph d. a bachelor 1777, æ. 62.

4. Thomas (s. of James 2.) m. Deborah, D. probably of John
Harden, 1712, and had Joseph, Rotheus 1726, Beriah 1728,
Anne, Deliverance, Jennet and Rhoda: he d. before 1769. Anne
m. Seth Mitchell 1738.—Deliverance m. David Howell 1744.—
Jennet m. a Drinkwater of N. Yarmouth, Me.—Beriah m. Israel
Hill 1748.—Rhoda m. David Conant 1748.—Joseph went east-
ward.—Rotheus went to N. Carolina and had a family there.

5. Joseph (s. of James 2.) m. Sarah, D. of Nathaniel Hayward, 1717, and had James, Betty, Joseph, Thomas, Nathaniel,
all bap. 1732, Sarah 1733, Seth 1738. He enlisted into the Canada
expedition and made his will 1758, and d. 1760: his wife d. 1781,
æ. 85.—Betty d. single 1808, æ. 86.—Sarah d. single 1785, æ. 53.

6. Charles (s. of Capt. Chilton 3.) m. Susanna, D. of Capt.
Nathaniel Woodward, and had Betty 1725, Susanna 1727,
Woodward 1729, Mary 1735, Chilton and Jane 1739: he d. 1788,
æ. 87. Betty m. Capt. Joseph Gannett 1744.—Susanna m. Na-
than Hayward.—Mary m. Benjamin Whitman 1757.—Jane m.
Edward Mitchell 1762.

7. Arthur (s. of Capt. Chilton 3.) m. Alice, D. of Nehemiah

LATHAM. 223

Allen 1733, and had Nehemiah 1735, Jane 1736: he d. 1736, and
his wid. m. Jonathan Allen of Braintree 1739.—Jane m. Jonathan Conant 1759.

8. James (s. of Capt. Chilton 3.) m. Abigail Harvey of T.
1739, and had Abigail 1741, Arthur 1742, Mary 1744, James and
Susanna. Mary m. William Britton of Raynham 1766.—Susanna m. Seth Brett 1769. This family and Brett also went to
Winchester.

9. Robert (s. of Capt. Chilton 3. m. Mary, D. of David
Johnson, 1751. She d. and he m. Bethiah, wid. of Arthur Harris and D. of Dea. Thomas Hayward. She d. 1778, æ. 63, and
he m. Jerusha, D. of Thomas Hooper, 1778. He d. 1788, æ.
77, and his last wife m. Jacob Mitchell 1791, and d. 1829, æ. 85.

10. Joseph (s. of Joseph 5.) m. Mary, D. of Joseph Prior,
1748, and had James 1748, Hannah 1751, Nanny 1763, and
Winslow. James m. Esther Baker of R. 1769.—Hannah m.
Josiah Hathaway 1766, and the whole family went to Oakham
or Pelham.

11. Thomas (s. of Joseph 5.) m. Abigail Hanmer 1752, and
had Nabby 1753, William 1756, Betty 1757, Thomas, Benjamin,
Lucinda, Stephen and Roland. He d. of small-pox 1778, æ. 49;
she d. 1786, æ. 55.—Nabby d. 1785, æ. 32.—Betty d. 1785, æ.
28.—Lucinda m. Joshua Pool 1783.—William and Thomas
served in the revolutionary war and went westward.—Benjamin
went to Providence.—Stephen m. Nabby, D. of Amos Whitman,
and he and Roland went to Me.

12. Nathaniel (s. of Joseph 5.) m. Mercy, D. of Nehemiah
Leach, 1756, and had Nathaniel and Levi, and d. young. Nathaniel d. 1776 at N. York in the army.

13. Seth (s. of Joseph 5.) m. Rachel House of Hanover 1763.
She d. 1797, æ. 53; he m. Wid. Elizabeth Hanks 1800, and d.
childless 1825, æ. 87; she 1825, æ. 75.

14. Woodward (s. of Charles 6.) m. Rebecca Dean of R. 1763,
and had Eliab 1764, Susanna 1766, George 1768, Dean 1771,
Barzillai 1773, Galen 1775. He d. 1802, æ. 71; she 1813, æ. 77.
Eliab m. Lucy, D. of Nehemiah Latham, 1786, and went to
Gray in Me., and was burnt with his house.—Susanna m. Thos.
Blanchard of Abington 1786, and moved to Windsor.—George
went to Gray, Me., m. a Matthews, and had a family.—Dean d.
a bachelor 1835, æ. 64.—Barzillai m. Polly, D. of Benja. Washburn, 1801, and went to Me.

15. Chilton (s. of Charles 6.) m. Mary, D. of James Howard,
1770, and had Chilton 1771, Mary 1772: he d. 1792, æ. 52.—
Mary m. Winslow Hooper 1791.

16. Nehemiah (s. of Arthur 7.) m. Lucy, D. of Arthur Harris,
1757, and had Arthur 1758, Alice 1760, Lucy 1764, Allen
1771. She died 1797, æ. 53, and he m. Hannah, Widow of
Samuel Allen and D. of Joshua Pratt, 1801: he d. 1807, æ. 74;
she 1820, æ. 80.—Arthur went to Lyme.—Alice m. Matthew
Gannett 1783.—Lucy m. Eliab Latham 1786.—Allen m. Jennet,

D. of Hosea Dunbar of Halifax, 1796, and d. 1798, and his Wid.
m. Zephaniah Howard 1800.

17. Arthur (s. of James 8.) m. Margaret, D. of Andrew Bearce,
of Halifax, and had nine Ds., and went to Winchester with his
father.

18. Levi (s. of Nathaniel 12.) m. Hannah, D. of Eleazar Alden,
1782, and had Nathaniel, Cyrus, Susanna Alden, Robert 1793,
Marcus 1795, and then with his mother and family went to Windsor, and there had Lewis and Hannah.—Nathaniel was a Deacon
at Windsor 1816.

19. Galen (s. of Woodward 14.) m. Susanna, D. of Eleazar
Keith, 1802, and had Williams 1803, Galen 1805, Charles Austin
1807, Rowena Williams 1809, Susanna 1812, Eliab 1818.—Williams gra. B. U. 1827, and is settled as an Attorney in S. B.—
Galen m. Esther, D. of Azor Harris Esq.

20. Chilton (s. of Chilton 15.) m. Betsy, D. of Dr. Eleazar
Carver, 1803, and had Charles 1804, Susanna 1806, Nathaniel
Woodward 1810. He d. 1811, æ. 42; she m. Joseph Barrows
1816, and had two children.

21. Robert (s. of Arthur of Lyme: see Nehemiah 16.) and
Polly his wife lived awhile in E. B., and had John Tomson 1805.
He returned to Lyme: he had two brothers, Allen and Bela, who
were educated and read law in E. B., and settled as Attorneys
in the western country: he had also a brother William Harris,
and others.

LATHROP.—Mark Lathrop (probably from Duxbury; perhaps from Weymouth or Braintree) settled in W. B. as early as
1656, but not an original proprietor, nor had he any known connection with any of the name in N. E. He has been supposed
by some to have descended from the Rev. John Lathrop of Scituate, but this cannot be ascertained, nor is it probable. He d. a.
1686, and had Elizabeth, Mark, Samuel, and Edward: no w. is
mentioned.—Elizabeth m. Samuel Packard Jr.—Mark "designed
into the war," made his will 1690, and d. in the Canada expedition.—Edward d. a. 1696 without children.

2. Samuel (s. of Mark 1.) m. Sarah Downer, and had Mary
1683, Samuel 1685, John 1687, Mark 1689, Sarah 1693, Joseph
and Edward 1697: he d. a. 1724. Mary m. Josiah Keith 1703.—
Joseph m. Mary, D. of Joseph Snow, 1718, and d. without issue.—
Sarah m. Solomon Packard 1715, and d. young.

3. Samuel (s. of Samuel 2.) m. Abial, D. of Isaac Lazell, 1710,
and had Samuel 1711, Isaac 1714, Sarah 1717, Daniel 1721,
Abiel 1729. Sarah m. Abiezer Edson 1737.—Abial m. Israel
Alger Jr. 1747.

4. John (s. of Samuel 2.) m. Mary, D. of Joseph Edson, 1716,
and had Mary 1720, Sarah 1724, Susanna 1726. Mary d. single.—
Sarah m. Alexander Kingman 1755.—Susanna m. Theophilus
Howard 1747.

5. Mark (s. of Samuel 2.) m. Hannah, D. of Joseph Alden,
1722, went to E., and had John, Seth, Jonathan, and Joseph: she

LATHROP. 225

d. æ. 81. Jonathan m. Susanna, D. of Solomon Johnson, 1747.—
Seth m. Martha, D. of Thomas Conant, 1755.
6. Edward (s. of Samuel 2.) m. Hannah, D. of Thomas Wade,
and had Seth 1722, Josiah 1726, Edward 1728, David 1735, Mark
1738. David m. Mary, D. of Ephraim Howard, 1762, and d. 1787
without children.
7. Samuel (s. of Samuel 3.) m. Elizabeth, D. of Joseph Keith,
1735; his will 1776; had Nathan 1735, Jonathan 1738, Mark
1746, Samuel Lathrop m. Lydia Hayden 1751.
8. Isaac (s. of Sam'l 3.) m. Bethiah, D. of Maj. Edward Howard. She d., and he m. Patience, D. of Joseph Alger, 1742, and
had Bethiah 1744, Edmund 1746, Isaac 1748, Zephaniah 1750,
Abihail 1752, Nathan 1755, John 1757, Sarah 1763, Keziah 1767 :
he d. 1774. Bethiah m. Samuel Willis 1767.—Edmund m. Betty,
D. of George Howard, 1774, and settled in E. and had Howard,
Isaac, and Cyrus, and probably others.—Isaac m. Sarah, D. of
Adams Bailey, 1775, and settled also in E.—Isaac m. Betty
Hacket 1786.—Abihail m. Lemuel Keith of E. 1768.—John m.
Sarah Cook 1780.—Sarah m. John Cook 1790.—Keziah m. Simeon Lathrop 1785.
9. Maj. Daniel (s. of Samuel 3.) m. Rhoda, D. of Thomas
Willis 1744, and had Daniel 1745, Rhoda 1747, Molly 1755, Abihail 1758.—Rhoda m. Daniel Williams Jr. of E. 1763.—Molly
m. Thomas Johnson 1771.—Abihail m. Isaac Hartwell 1775.
10. Joseph (s. of Mark 5.) m. Content, D. of John Washburn,
1746, and settled in E., and had Seth, Jonathan, Joseph, and
probably others. Susanna Lathrop m. Abiel Lapham 1786.
11. Seth (s. of Edward 6.) m. Lydia, D. of George Packard,
1751, and had Susanna 1754. She d. and he m. Mehitabel Daily
of E., and had Lydia 1758, Mehitabel 1761, Seth 1765 : he d.
1804, she 1770.. Susanna m. Calvin Kinsley of E. 1773.—Mehitabel m. Alpheus Fobes 1781.
12. Josiah (s. of Edward 6.) m. Sarah Church of Scituate,
1749, and had Hannah 1753, Sarah 1755, Josiah 1759, Huldah
1764, Charles 1767 : he d. 1808, she 1815.—Hannah m. Joseph
Bassett Esq. 1776.—Huldah m. Edmund Alger 1786.—Sarah m.
Edward Williams of E. 1772.
13. Edward (s. of Edward 6.) m. Abigail, D. of Ephraim
Howard, 1752, and had Barnabas 1758, Simeon 1760, Hannah
1762, Jane 1764, Ambrose 1768, Molly 1770, Vina 1773. Jane
m. Capt. Daniel Briggs of Milton 1782.—Ambrose lived and d.
in Cohasset.—Vina m. Dr. John H. Perkins 1793.
14. Jonathan (s. of Samuel 7.) m. Chloe Dickerman 1765, and
had Lemuel 1766, Libeus 1769, Sarah 1772, Chloe, and perhaps
others. Libeus m. Charity Wharton 1803, and settled in E.—
Sarah m. David Alger 1790.—Chloe m. Jacob Fisher 1797.
15. Mark (s. of Samuel 7.) m. Elizabeth Dickerman, b. 1758,
and had Elijah 1780, Mark, Spencer, Betsy and Silvia. Elijah
m. Lavinia, D. of Barnabas Dunbar, 1818, and settled in St.—
Mark m. Katy, D. of Capt. Amasa Howard, 1805, and had
29

Samuel 1806, Catharine 1808, Almer 1810, and went to Millbury.
Spencer m. Bathsheba, D. of Thaddeus Howard, 1812 ; she d.
1813, and he m. Eleanor White of Millbury 1817.—Betsy m.
Samuel Dunbar 1811.—Silvia m. Thaddeus Howard Jr. 1810.

16. Zephaniah (s. of Isaac 8.) m. Sarah, D. of Nathan Pack-
ard, 1779, and had Silvia 1779, Oliver 1781, Azel 1783, Zepha-
niah 1787. She d. 1790, and he m. Silvia Manly 1791, and had
Avery 1792, Sally 1794, Bezer 1796, Perez 1797, Raymond 1799,
Rhoda 1801, Olive 1803, Manly 1807. Oliver m. Hannah Curtis
of St. 1803.—Avery m. Hannah, D. of Jacob Dunbar, 1819, and
Joanna Bacon of Randolph 1821.—Sally m. George Alger Jr. of
E. 1814.—Bezer m. Vesta Cobb of Mansfield 1820.—Perez m.
Eliza, D. of Hartwell Keith 1817.

17. Daniel (s. of Maj. Daniel 9.) m. Hannah, D. of George
Howard, 1764, and had George 1765, Daniel 1767, Thomas
1768, Hannah 1771. She d. and he m. Lydia, D. of Samuel
Willis 1775, and had Samuel 1777, Sullivan 1778. His 2d wife
d., and he m. Mary, D. of George Turner, 1785, and had Alson :
he had other Ds.—Daniel m. Sally Whiting of Attleboro 1787.—
Samuel m. Bethiah, D. of Joseph Johnson 1799, and had a son
Daniel who d. 1821. This family all removed to Me.—George
m. Molly, D. of Jeremiah Thayer, 1783, and settled in Leeds,
and d. 1839, æ. 74.—Hannah m Joshua Gilmore 1789.—Daniel
Lathrop m. Wid. Abigail Lathrop 1803.

18. Seth (s. of Seth 11.) m. Abigail, D. of Joseph Bassett, 1784,
and had Barzillai, Cyrus, Betsy. Barzillai d. at sea.—Cyrus m.
Mary, D. of Daniel Willis, 1801, and went to Livermore, Me.,
but returned.—Betsy m. Warren French 1813, and went to Me.

19. Josiah (s. of Josiah 12.) m. Susanna, D. of Theophilus
Howard, 1785, and had Vesta 1795, Susanna 1798, Josiah 1802,
Howard 1804, Edwin 1807, Margaret Nevens 1809. This family
removed to Canada.

20. Charles (s. of Josiah 12.) m. Rowena, D. of Capt. Jonathan Howard 1788, and had Phebe Ames 1789, Galen 1791,
Charles 1793, Edward 1795, Rowena 1796. This family also
went to Canada.

21. Barnabas (s. of Edward 13.) m. Sarah, D. of Jonathan
Bozworth, 1777, and had Stillman, Barnabas, Edward, Tisdale,
Sarah, Betsy : he had a 2d wife Rachel, D. of Samuel Bartlett.
Barnabas m. Rachel Thayer 1813.—Sarah m. John Hearsey
1807.—Betsy m. Bernard Alger of E. 1810.—Edward lives in
Boston.

22. Simeon (s. of Edward 13.) m. Keziah, D. of Isaac Lathrop, 1785, and had Hannah, Keziah. Simeon m. Peggy Nevens
of Salem 1807.—Keziah m. Ezekiel Wilson of Methuen, 1808.

23. Lemuel (s. of Jonathan 14.) m. Sarah Reed of E. 1794,
and had George Watson 1805.

24. Azel (s. of Zephaniah 16.) m. Anna Eaton 1805, and had
Philenia 1806, Sarah 1807, Silvia 1809, John Eaton 1812.

25. Zephaniah (s. of Zephaniah 16.) m. Lydia Ripley of Plympton 1812, and had Almon 1815.

Caleb of E. m. Hannah Ellis 1806.—Celia of E. m. Samuel Short 1806.—Rebecca m. Jno. Snow Jr. 1811.—Hannah R. m. Leonard Alger 1821.—Jacob m. Sarah Snow 1787.—Zenas m. Sally Tower 1788.

LAWRENCE.—Thomas and Desire Lawrence had Hannah, Sarah, Thomas: he d. 1759. Hannah m. Capt. Josiah Edson 1760, and Maj. Eliphalet Cary 1782.—Sarah m. Obadiah Eddy 1750.—Thomas m. Sarah, D. of John Hooper 1769.—Jonathan m. Rachel Smith 1765.

LAWSON.—Shurtliff and Millecent (or Milleson) Lawson had Asa Shurtliff 1794.—Sarah Lawson m. Abijah Hill 1749.

LAZELL.—John Lazell (at Hingham 1647) m. Elizabeth, D. of Stephen Gates, 1649, and had John 1650, Thomas 1653, Joshua 1655, Stephen 1656, Isaac 1660, Mary, Sarah, Hannah 1666, Israel 1671: he d. a. 1695. Mary m. a Burr.—Sarah m. Peter Ripley 1693.—Hannah m. a Turner.—Thomas m. Mary Allen at Duxbury 1685, and settled there, and was afterwards at Plympton, and then at Falmouth, and finally at Windham, Conn. John, Stephen and Israel remained at Hingham.—Joshua d. 1689; his Wid. Mary ; he had Elizabeth, Martha, Joshua and Simon.— Simon at Plymouth and Joshua at Duxbury 1709 : Joshua had lived in Mendon where a Joshua Lazell d. 1832, æ. 81.—Simon went to Mid'o, and many of his descendants lived there and in S. B.—Isaac m. Abial (or Abihail), D. of John Leavitt, and d. at Hingham 1690, leaving a son Isaac and a D. Abial: his Wid. m. Isaac Johnson, who came to W. B. a. 1700, and brought these two ch. of his wife with him.   This name is variously written in the early records, Lazell, Lascelle, Lessell, Hazell, Hazael, Hassell.   There is reason to believe the name was originally French, and written La Hassell, and thence corrupted to Lassel and Lazell.—John Hassell was made free in Mass. 1637.—Richard Hassell made free 1647.

1. Isaac (s. of Isaac and gr. s. of John of Hingham) came to Bridgewater a small boy a. 1700, as above stated. (His sister Abial also came with him and m. Samuel Lathrop 1710.) He m. Mary, D. of Daniel Hudson, 1719, and had Isaac 1725, John 1727, Hannah 1729, Daniel 1734 : he d. before 1766, æ. a. 75.— Hannah m. Nathan Conant 1753.

2. Isaac (s. of Isaac 1.) m. Bethiah, D. of Joseph Alger, 1748, and had Edmund 1750, Silvanus 1752, Mary 1754, Isaac 1756, Nathan 1759, Ebenezer 1761, Joseph 1767.   He removed to Cummington in his old age, and there his wife d. and he m. Abigail, Wid. of Capt. Jacob Allen and D. of Capt. Israel Bailey : he d. æ. over 80.—Mary m. Seth Reed of Abington 1776, and lived and d. at Cummington.

3. John (s. of Isaac 1.) m. Mary, D. of Dr. Joseph Byram, 1750, and had John 1751, Luther 1754, Molly 1757, Eunice 1761, Patty 1766, Byram 1770 : he d. 1816, æ. 89 ; she 1818, æ.

80. John m. Lucinda Stetson 1787, and he æ. 56, and his D. æ. 18, both d. 1806.—Luther settled in Abington, and had Daniel and a D. who m. Libeus Gurney.—Molly m. Eliab Washburn 1777, and moved to Paxton.—Eunice m. a Pool.—Patty d. single 1826.

4. Daniel (s. of Isaac 1.) m. Huldah, D. of Nehemiah Leach, 1761, and had Robert, Calvin, Chloe 1772, and two other Ds. He removed to Ashfield, and d. of small-pox in the revolutionary war 1776.—Chloe returned to E. B., and d. 1832, æ. 60, not m.

5. Capt. Edmund (s. of Isaac 2.) m. Mary, D. of Hezekiah Ford of A. and went to Cummington, and had Edmund and Martin; the latter had a college education, and both d. young. He had also Mary, who m. Col. Trowbridge Ward of Worthington, Huldah, who m. Jonathan Dawes, and Deborah, who m. Benjamin Hobart Esq. of A. He is now (1840) living; she d. 1836. He and Judge Davis of Boston are the only surviving members of the Convention for adopting the U. S. Constitution in 1788.

6. Gen. Silvanus (s. of Isaac 2.) m. Abigail, D. of Joseph Robinson, 1775, and had Nabby 1778, Betsy 1781, Lucy 1785. They both d. of paralysis : she 1825, æ. 69; he 1827, æ. 75. Nabby m. Nahum Mitchell, the writer of this, 1794.—Betsy m. Bartholomew Brown Esq. 1801.—Lucy m. Benjamin Hobart Esq., his first wife, 1811, and d. 1812.

7. Maj. Isaac (s. of Isaac 2.) m. Jenny, D. of Benjamin Byram, 1779, and had Anna 1780, Polly 1782, Jane 1786, Salome 1788, Rachel 1790, Charlotte 1792, Henriette 1795, Irene 1800 : he d. June 20, 1810, æ. 54. Anna m. Dr. Noah Fearing 1799.— Polly m. William Randall Bates of Cummington 1803.—Jane m. Elisha Blanchard of Weymouth 1809.—Salome m. Mitchell Keith 1811, and d. 1839.—Rachel m. William Snelling of Boston 1811.—Charlotte m. Simeon Tisdale Jr. of T. 1815, and Mitchell Keith 1840.—Henriette m. Cyrus Johnson of N. Bedford, s. of Jsaiah of W. B.—Irene m. Dea. Morton Eddy 1822.

8. Nathan Esq. (s. of Isaac 2.) m. Deborah D. of Timothy Conant 1783, and had Hannah, Susan, Sally, Deborah, Nathan, Caroline, Harriet, Julia; he d. 1832. Hannah m. Nathan Nye of Freeport 1818, his 2d wife ; Susan was his first wife, m. 1807. Sally m. Jonathan Cushing of Boston 1809.—Deborah not m. —Caroline m. Paul Revere 1816.—Harriet m. Dr. Paul Lewis Nichols of Kingston 1814.—Julia m. George W. Norwood of Boston.

9. Rev. Ebenezer (s. of Isaac 2.) gra. B. U. 1788, and settled in the Ministry at Attleboro', and there m. a Richardson : he thence removed to Black River N. Y. and d. 1828 leaving a number of children, William was one.

10. Joseph, (s. of Isaac 2.) m. Abigail D. of Capt. John Ames, 1787, and had a D. Bethiah : he went to Charleston S. C. and he and his w. both d. there of the yellow fever Aug. 1799.—Bethiah

returned and m. Asa Mitchell Esq. 1806, and settled at New Gloucester and had a D. Sarah Harris : he d. and she returned again
to E. B. and m. George Young Phillips 1812, and went to Poughkepsie, N. Y.—Sarah H. m. there an Overocker, and d. young.
11. Byram (s. of John 3.) m. Jennet D. of Joseph Wesley
1793, and had Betsy, Marston, Jennet, d. single 1825 æ. 27,
Thomas, Mary, Susan, William, Lucy, George: he d. 1820 æ.
50. Marston m. Christiana D. of Joseph Gannett.
12. Nathan Esq. (s. of Nathan Esq. 8.) m. Ann D. of Abraham Wilkinson of North Providence (Pawtucket) 1821, and
had Nathan*; he d., May 1835, and had another s. Nathan b.
after his death. The widow is now dead.
13. Simon (s. of Joshua of Hingham probably) m. Joanna
Wood 1742, (his 2d. w. perhaps) his will 1745 : he had Joshua,
Jacob, William, Abner, Lydia, (1st wife of old John Alden,) Mary Wood, and Sarah : he first lived at Plymouth, and afterwards
at M. where he d. His first wife perhaps was Margaret D. of
Jacob Cook of Plymouth m. 1716.
14. Joshua (s. of Simon 13.) m. Elizabeth D. of John Prince
and wid. of Seth Ames 1742, and d. a. 1753 : he had Prince,
Elizabeth, Mary. He d. 1749 at M. where he lived ; she was
niece of Rev. Thomas Prince, the chronologist.
15. Jacob (s. of Simon 13.) m. Elizabeth D. of Richard Davenport of S. B.1749 lived in M. and d. 1753, and gave his estate
to his child, if it should be born and live.—Molly Lazell m. William Cole 1774.
16. William (s. of Simon 13.) m. Eunice D. of Richard Davenport Jr. 1759, and lived in S. B. and had Eunice 1759 : he
removed from B. and had Joshua, William, John, Abner, Jacob,
Rufus, Isaac, Levi. William went to Philadelphia.—John was
a physician, and he and Abner went to New Salem.—Jacob went
to New York.—Rufus went to Pennsylvania.
17. Joshua (s. of William 16.) m. a Pratt in S. B. and went
to Ware, thence to Windsor, thence to Pomfret Vt. and had
Levi, Rufus, William, Isaac, John.
18. Isaac Lazell of Wardsbury Vt. and his wife Hannah had
Nathan, Isaac, Mariel, Thomas, Samuel, John, Rachel : he d.
a. 1827. Nathan lived in Carroll, Co. of Chautauge N. Y.—
Isaac lived in Dover, Co. of Windham Vt.—Rachel m. a Taylor.
19. Robert Esq. (s. of Daniel 4.) lived in Buckland, and had
Marshall, Hiram, Alva, Philip, Robert, and 5 Ds. ; he d. 1826
while a member of Gen. Court at Boston.—Marshall went to
Pennsylvania.—Hiram and Philip went to N. York.

LEACH.—Giles Leach (from Weymouth) settled in W. B. be-
fore 1665 ; m. Anne Nokes 1656 ; she lived in Dea. Samuel Bass'
family in Braintree ; he had Sarah 1656, Elizabeth, Samuel 1662,
David, John, Ebenezer, Benjamin and perhaps others.—Sarah m.
John Aldrich.—Elizabeth m. John Emerson 1693.—Sarah and
Samuel b. at Weymouth,

2. Samuel (s. of Giles 1.) m. Mary D. of Nicholas Byram, and had Samuel, Josiah, Seth, Elijah.

3. David (s. of Giles 1.) and his wife Hannah had Mercy 1693, Hannah 1696*, Ephraim 1699, Experience 1702, David 1706, Mehitabel 1711, Abigail 1714; he d. a. 1757. Wid. Hannah m. Ebenezer Edson 1758.—Ephraim m. Ruth D. of John Bolton 1734.—Abigail m. Jacob Keith 1734.—David m. Elizabeth D. of Francis Cook of Kingston 1742, and had Susanna 1743.—David Leach m. wid. Hannah Newcomb 1751.

4. John (s. of Giles 1.) and his wife Alice, had John 1695, Giles 1697, Stephen 1698, Abiel 1700, Ebenezer 1702, Mehitabel 1704, Timothy 1707, Nehemiah 1709, Solomon 1712, Jesse 1714, and he d. 1744.

5. Ebenezer (s. of Giles 1.) m. Prudence Stetson of Scituate 1707.—Lydia Leach m. Ephraim Jackson 1736.

6. Benjamin (s. of Giles 1.) m. Hepzibah Washburn 1702, and had Anne 1703, Joseph 1705, Mary 1708, Sarah 1711, Benjamin 1713, Ichabod 1716*, Jerathmael and Benanuel 1718, Nokes 1720, Susanna 1722, Hannah 1725, Phebe, Nathan, and Eunice. Sarah m. Timothy Leach perhaps 1732.—Susanna m. Ezra Washburn 1742.—Phebe m. Abner Fobes.—Eunice m. William Keith 1767.

7. Samuel (s. of Samuel 2.) and his wife Content had Elijah 1726, and Samuel; he d. a. 1756.

8. Seth (s. of Sam'l 2.) m. Mary D. of Thos. Whitman, and had a son Seth, who had a s. Thomas, who was probably father of Mr. Caleb Leach formerly of Plym., the clock maker and ingenious mechanist. Seth Leach m. Jane D. of Joseph Harvey 1732.

9. Elijah (s. of Samuel 2.) m. Jemima D. of Benjamin Snow 1745, and had Elijah 1746, Jemima 1749; he removed to Westmoreland. Elijah Leach's wife died 1763.—Elijah Leach m. Ruth Prince of Kingston 1764.—Jemima Leach m. James Lovell 1785.

10. John (s. of John 4.) m. Susanna White perhaps 1719, and had Alice, Abiah, Stephen, he was d. in 1744, and before his father.—Alice m. David Perkins 1738.

11. Giles (s. of John 4.) went to Halifax, and had John, Micah, Simeon 1734, Elizabeth, and probably others. John had a son John.—Micah was father of Silvanus.—Elizabeth m. Jona. Shurtliff of M.

12. Stephen (s. of John 4.) m. Sarah D. of John Hooper 1725, and had Anne 1727, Stephen 1730; he d. 1729, and qu. if the wid. did not m. Ebenezer Snow 1737.

13. Ebenezer (s. of John 4.) m. Joanna D. of Josiah Washburn 1734, and had Daniel 1735, Joanna 1738; he m. Lydia Tilson perhaps 1739, and Deborah Sampson perhaps 1751; he d. a. 1753. Ebenezer Leach m. Mary Wilbor 1741.—Deborah Leach m. Nathan Leach 1771.—Eben. Leach d. 1803 very aged.

14. Timothy (s. of John 4.) m. Sarah D. of Benjamin Leach probably 1732, and had Rebecca 1733, Ichabod 1735, Sarah

1739, Jonathan 1741, Levi 1744, Nathan 1746, Anne 1749, Timothy 1751. Rebecca m. Joshua Warren Jr. 1760.—Sarah m. Jona. Hayward of E. probably 1762.—Anne m. James Sturtevant probably 1769.

15. Nehemiah (s. of John 4.) and his wife Mercy Staples, had Abigail 1730, Mercy 1732; (2d. w. a Bryant of Plympton) James 1737, Ruth 1739, Robert 1740, Huldah 1742, Mehitabel 1744, Lydia, Nehemiah, Caleb, Susanna; he d. 1769, she 1775. Abigail m. Benjamin Keith 1749.—Mercy m. Nathaniel Latham 1756.—Ruth m. Benjamin Packard 1762.—Huldah m. Daniel Lazell 1761.—Mehitabel m. Nathan Jones.—Lydia m. John Dickerman of Roxbury 1770.—Susanna m. Dea. Isaac Wilbor.

16. Solomon (s. of John 4.) m. Tabitha D. of Samuel Washburn 1736; she d. 1736: and he m. Jerusha Bryant of Plympton 1739, and had Abisha 1739 ; his 2d. wife d. 1743, and he m. Hannah Leach 1743, D. perhaps of Benjamin 6, and had Jerusha 1746, Solomon 1750, Israel 1752, Hannah 1755, Susanna 1758, Joseph 1760. Jerusha m. Isaac Leach of Westmoreland 1763.—Abisha lived in E. and was father probably of Joshua, Philip, Shepard, and others. Philip was educated and settled as a lawyer in Me.

17. Jesse (s. of John 4.) and his w. Alice had Zadock 1741, Giles, Alice, Calvin; he d. and she m. Daniel Bacon 1772.—Alice m. Silas Leach 1778.

18. James (s. of Ebenezer 5. perhaps) and his wife Elizabeth lived in Kingston, and had Elizabeth 1735, Mercy 1738, and Sarah 1740.

19. Dea. Joseph (s. of Benjamin 6.) m. Anna Harris 1736, and had Benjamin, Jepthah, Isaiah.

20. Benjamin (s. of Benjamin 6.) m. Hannah D. of John Keith 1740, and had Jedediah, Peleg, Benjamin, Eliphalet.—Benjamin Leach m. Joanna Wilbor 1751.—Benjamin Leach m. wid. Abigail Bassett 1763.—Wid. Hannah m. Israel Washburn and afterwards Dea. Hall of R.

21. Benanuel (s. of Benjamin 6.) m. Betty Perkins 1741, and Elizabeth D. of Samuel Edson 1745.—Benanuel Leach m. Mehitabel D. of Benjamin Allen of E. B.

22. Samuel (s. of Samuel 7.) and his wife Phebe had Phebe 1753, Silas 1755, Samuel 1757, Jeshurun 1760; he d. in the army 1760 æ. 33.—Silas m. Alice D. of Jesse Leach 1778.—Samuel went to N. York.

23. Stephen (s. of John 10. perhaps) m. Lydia Flora of Halifax 1745, and had Lemuel 1745, Stephen 1747, Jeremiah 1751. Stephen Leach m. Sarah D. perhaps of Thomas Hooper 1749. Stephen Leach 1756 belonged to the baptist ch. in Swanzey.

24. Capt. Simeon (s. of Giles 11.) settled in St. Corner; m. Elizabeth D. of Theophilus Curtis 1765, and had Lot, Relief and Vashti. He d. 1777 æ. 43. Relief m. Oliver Harris 1789.—Vashti m. William Harris 1796.

25. Dea. Daniel (s. of Eben. 13.) m. Bethiah D. of Samuel
Keith 1760, and had Joanna 1761, Bethiah 1764, Deborah 1766,
Ebenezer 1768, Daniel 1771, Olive 1773, Lydia 1775, Susanna
1778, Celia 1780. Joanna m. Dea. Isaac Wilbor.—Deborah m.
Perez White 1787.—Olive m. Azariah Fobes 1793.—Susanna
m. Isaac Hooper 1805.—Celia m. Eliab Hayward Jr. 1803.
26. Ichabod (s. of Timothy 14.) m. Penelope Cobb 1770, and
had Jerathmael, Ephraim, Backus, Abigail. Jerathmael m. Clarissa Leach 1798, and went to Warren.—Ephraim m. Sarah D.
of Zenas Conant 1805.—Backus m. Bethiah Hayward 1804.—
Abigail m. Freeman Jones 1792.
27. Jonathan called Jr. or 2d. (s. of Timothy 14. or William
43.) m. Experience Hartwell 1768, and had Silence 1768, Olive
1770, Lois and Eunice 1772.—Jonathan Leach m. Abigail Leach
1763.
28. Levi (s. of Timothy 14.) m. Hannah D. of Abner Fobes
1771, and had Levi.
29. Nathan (s. of Timothy 14.) lived in N. B. and m. Deborah, wid. perhaps of Ebenezer or D. of William Leach 1771,
and had Reliance 1772, Thaddeus 1775; on the record of these
births his wife is called Hannah.—Reliance m. Noah Tirrell
1794; he had also Oliver, Sarah, who m. Allen Smith 1815, Libeus, Eliphalet, Nathan. Oliver m. Sally D. of Knight Brown
1803, and a D. of Peleg Stetson 1817, and had Elbridge, who m.
a D. of Eleazar Joslyn, and Oliver and others perhaps.
30. James (s. of Nehemiah 15.) m. Hazadiah D. of Robert
Keith 1765, and had Alpheus, Apollos, Caleb, James, Chloe,
Roxiliana, Mercy, Sarah, Huldah, and Ruth.—James m. Betsy
D. of Nathaniel Leonard of T. 1811.—Chloe m. Col. Salmon
Fobes 1807.—Roxiliana m. Elias Dunbar 1799.—Mercy m. Abraham Gould 1809.—Sarah m. Jonathan Keith 1792.—Huldah m.
George Chipman 1803.—Ruth m. Joseph Bassett 1792.
31. Nehemiah (s. of Nehemiah 15.) m. Constant D. of Robert Keith 1772, and had Eliphalet, Oliver, Lewis, and others.
Eliphalet m. Phebe Caswell 1798.
32. Caleb (s. of Nehemiah 15.) m. Molly Adams 1780, and
had Lydia 1782.
33. Zadock (s. of Jesse 17.) m. Susanna D. of Ezra Washburn
of M. 1763, and had Susanna, Bezer, Abraham, Zebedee, Parnel, Rufus, Zadock. Susanna m. Edward Richmond 1788.—
Parnel m. Apollos Eaton of M. 1795.—Rufus m. Nancy D. of
Ebenezer Perkins 1798, and went to N. Y.
34. Giles (s. of Jesse 17.) m. Mehitabel Wilbor of R. and had
Solomon, Hosea, Giles, Chloe, Alice, Laura, Betsy, Mehitabel,
Abigail; he d. and she m. Luther Hall of R. 1806. Solomon
m. Mary Holmes of K. 1806, and went to Rochester.—Hosea
m. Hannah D. of Capt. Seth Keith 1807.—Chloe m. Zephaniah
Wilbor 1796.—Alice m. Seth Crossman 1804.—Betsy m. a Rich-
mond.—Mehitabel m. Samuel Cheesman 1806.—Abigail m. Elias
Ware of Wrentham 1809.

35. Benjamin (s. of Joseph 19.) m. Mary D. of Ebenezer Keith 1764, and had Joseph, Luke, Silas, Jephthah, Isaiah, Mary, Orphah, Lois, Hepzibah, Dinah. The mother d. 1791, and he m. Anna Short 1792, and had Anna 1793, Eunice 1796, Chloe 1799.—Mary m. Libeus Fobes Jr. 1807.—Orphah m. Jacob Chipman.—Lois m. James Starr Esq. 1797.—Hepzibah m. Marshall Keith 1798.—Dinah m. Fiske Ames 1819.—Anna m. Galen Harvey 1817.—Eunice m. Otis Harvey 1819.

36. Jedediah (s. of Benjamin 20.) m. Phebe, D. of Robert Keith, 1765, and had Wealthy 1767, Bernice 1771 : she d. 1811, he 1813. Wealthy m. Joseph Leach 1788.—Bernice m. Roxana, D. of Nath'l Hooper, 1797.—Bernice m. Olive, D. of William Keith, 1810.

37. Lemuel (s. of Stephen 23.) m. Rebecca, D. of William Washburn, 1767, and had Oliver 1768, and then removed to Hardwick, and then to Wendell, and had eight more children, viz : Lemuel, Stephen, Gardner, Barnabas, Lewis, Artemas, Matilda and Rebecca. Gardner was Representative 1839.

38. Capt. Lot (s. of Capt. Simeon 24.) m. a Keith, and had Simeon and Betsy. Betsy m. Perez Southworth Jr. 1821.

39. Ebenezer (s. of Daniel 25.) m. Eunice, D. of Benjamin Keith 1794. Ebenezer Leach d. 1834.

40. Levi (s. of Levi 28.) m. Betsy, D. of Zenas Conant 1798, and had Deborah Jackson 1799, Giles 1801, Anna 1807, Clarinda 1810, Betsy 1812, Sarah 1816, Levi 1818, George M. 1821. Giles gra. B. U.

41. Alpheus (s. of James 30.) m. Cassandana, D. of William Keith, 1787, and had Anna 1787, Ambrose 1791, Sally 1793, Alpheus 1796, Louisa 1800, Wightman Rathburn 1804, Hepzibah Rathburn 1806, James Keith 1811.—Ambrose m. Hannah, D. of Nehemiah Howard, 1815.—Alpheus m. Eliza, D. of Bradford Mitchell.

42. Apollos (s. of James 30.) m. Chloe, D. of Christopher Dyer, 1796, and had Philo 1797, Sarah 1801, Olive 1803, Daniel 1806, Franklin 1809, Philander 1813. Daniel gra. B. U. 1830, m. Mary Lawton of Newport, and lived in Quincy, and afterwards in Roxbury.—Franklin m. Mary, D. of Isaac Fobes.—Sarah m. Ansel Perkins of N. B.

43. William Leach m. Mary Cohoon 1741, and had Jonathan 1742, Olive 1747, Deborah 1750, Hepzibah 1752, Catharine 1756. Deborah Leach m. Nathan Leach 1771.

44. Zadock (s. of Zadock 33.) m. Polly Frost of West Cambridge and had Jane, Vesta, Betsy, Zadock Washburn.—Jane m. a Hammond of Rochester.

45. Abraham (s. of Zadock 33.) m. Mary D. of Amos Keith 1796, and had Eliza, Libeus, Susanna, Jesse, Eveline. He went to N. York, and there d.—Eliza m. Cyrus Miller of Northfield. —Libeus m. Mary Brooks of West Cambridge.—Susanna m. Wm. Piper of Irvin's Grant.—Jesse settled in N. York, and m. Mary Ann Miller.

30

46. Bezer (s. of Zadock 33.) m. Betsy Shaw of M. 1793, and had Ezra, Isaac, Anne.

47. Joseph (s. of Benjamin 35.) m. Wealthy D. of Jedediah Leach 1788, and had Clarissa, who m. Ezekiel Dyer 1811.

48. Luke (s. of Benjamin 35.) m. Polly Starr 1788, and had Amory, and Harris, and removed to Me. Amory m. Lydia D. of Job Bearce 1817.

49. Silas (s. of Benjamin 35.) m. Lois Leach 1796, and went to Charleston S. C.

50. Thomas (s. or g. s. of Seth 8. perhaps) had Thomas, Ebenezer ,Seth, and several Ds. Sarah m. Dea. John Soule 1807.— Seth m. Mercy Sampson of M. 1819.—Thomas m. Mary Nesbit of Leeds 1809, and Susan Holbrook of Braintree 1814.

51. Eliphalet (s. of Nathan 29.) m. Hannah D. of Asa Shaw 1806, and had Isaac 1807, Nahum 1809, Hannah, Washington 1812, Dexter 1814, Martha 1815.

52. Nathan (s. of Nathan 29.) m. Mehitabel Gloyd, and had Nathan 1805, George Washington 1807, Mehitabel 1809, Eliza 1811, Sally 1814.

53. Peleg Leach m. Sally Gilmore 1802, and had Peleg 1802, Sarah Field 1804, Adeline Cornet 1806, Olive 1807, Elisha Gilmore 1809, William Tirrell 1810, Ebenezer 1813.

54. Philo Esq. (s. of Apollos 42.) m. Lucia D. of Capt. Joseph Hooper, and had James Edward 1825.

Tabitha Leach m. Robert Keith 1741.—Rhoda m. David Alden of M. 1755.—Orpha m. Edward Fobes 1761.—Zilpha m. Edward Hayward of E. 1760.—Dinah m. John Shaw of R. 1761. —Susanna m. Levi Hooper 1767.—Mary m. Ebenezer Washburn 1772.—Olive m. John Jones of M. 1770.—Sarah m. Oliver Wentworth 1779.—Polly m. Ephraim Packard 1789.—Jenny m. Lemuel Wilbor 1799.—Lois m. Baruch Wilbor 1799.—Susanna m. Asa Packard 1811.—Eunice m. Seth Britton of R. 1817.— Anna m. Zenas Knapp of R. 1817.—Minerva m. Jarvis White of R. 1819.—Deborah m. Ziba (or Liba) Conant 1820.—Lois m. Seth Packard Jr. 1764.—William m. Mary Cohoon 1741.— Jonathan m. Frances Cohoon 1741.—Clarissa m. Jerathmael Leach 1798.—Asa of Killingsly m. Eunice Turner 1787.—Libeus m. Peggy Starr 1791 and went to Me.—Eliab m. Eunice D. of William Keith 1802, and went to Charlemont, had 2 ss. in Boston.

Lawrence Leach of Salem, freeman 1631 ; d. 1662 æ. 83 : left a wid. Elizabeth : ss. Clement (in England) John, Richard, and Robert ; perhaps Giles above was also his son or grandson.— Richard d. 1647, and left a son John.—John was at Salem 1637, d. 1659.—Robert at Salem 1637, freeman 1644.

LENDALL.—James Lendall (of Duxbury) was an original proprietor of Bridgewater ; his will 1652 at Dux. : his w. Mary ; both d. about 1652 ; he had Timothy and Abigail ; he gave his share in B. to Timothy ; Constant Southworth appointed to administer and take care of the children. He never came to B.

LEONARD.—1. Solomon Leonard (from Duxbury) an original proprietor, and one of the earliest settlers in Bridgewater.—The name was sometimes written LEONARDSON, LENNERSON, or LENNER, but by the family themselves always written LEONARD. He d. 1686: his widow Mary; his children were Samuel, John, Jacob, Isaac, Solomon, and Mary who m. John Pollard of T. 1673.

2. Philip Leonard's estate was settled at Duxbury 1708 by his son-in-law Samuel Hill, who m. Phebe 1694: this man might have been brother or son of Solomon.

3. Samuel (s. of Solomon 1.) settled his father's estate 1686, the first settlement recorded in Plymouth Probate Court.—Samuel perhaps went to Worcester.

Samuel Leonardson, a boy taken by the Indians at Worcester Mar. 15, 1697, was allowed £12 10s. for escaping from them, and slaying several of them, about 1700.—(Mass. Records.)

4. John (s. of Solomon 1.) and his wife Sarah had John, Enoch, Moses, Josiah, Joseph, and Sarah: he d. 1699.—Sarah m. Thos. Washburn perhaps 1708.

5. Jacob (s. of Solomon 1.); his will 1716, mentions his present wife Susanna; he had Abigail, Susanna, Experience, Mary, Sarah, Solomon, Jacob 1702*: he was warned out 1693: he appeared before in Weymouth and also in Worcester.—Abigail b. at Weymouth 1680, m. Thomas Washburn.—Susanna b. at Wey. 1683, m. Ebenezer Hill 1714.—Sarah b. at B. 1699, m. William Orcutt 1721.—Jacob, Isaac, and Moses all settled in Worcester as early as 1718.—Moses was a selectman and ensign there 1725.

6. Isaac (s. of Solomon 1.) and his wife Deliverance had Hannah 1680, and probably Isaac, Deliverance, Joseph, and others. Isaac m. Mary Randall 1701.—Deliverance m. Samuel Washburn 1701.—Isaac, the father, conveyed his homestead to his son Joseph 1717, and went to Worcester perhaps.

7. Solomon (s. of Solomon 1.), no account of. There was an Ephraim Leonard in S. B. in 1738, who had several actions in court at that date; whose s. he was is not ascertained.—Martha Leonard m. Ebenezer Eddy of Norton 1734.

8. John (s. of John 4.) had Seth, 1733, Orphah 1735: he had a dis. from W. B. ch. to Sutton 1741.

9. Enoch (s. of John 4.) m. Elizabeth (D. probably of John) Hooper 1707, and had Enoch 1707, Elizabeth 1719.—Elizabeth Leonard, the mother perhaps, m. James Washburn 1720.

10. Josiah (s. of John 4.) m. Marjoram Washburn 1699, and had John, Josiah, Ezekiel, Samuel, Nathan, Elizabeth, Mary, Margene: he m. Abigail D. of John Washburn 1717: his will 1743.—Mary m. Daniel Harrington of Marlborough 1733.—Margene m. a Pratt.

11. Joseph (s. of John 4.) m. Hannah D. of Richard Jennings 1712, and had Joseph and Hannah 1713, Moses 1714, Seth 1715, Timothy 1718, Rebecca 1721, Mehitabel 1724, Thankful 1726, Ebenezer 1728.

12. Capt. Solomon (s. of Jacob 5.) m. Elizabeth D. of David Perkins, and had Experience 1732, Solomon 1733, Elizabeth, Susanna. He d. 1761. Experience m. Oliver Alden 1765.—Elizabeth m. Hezekiah Hooper 1758.—Susanna m. Samuel Whitman 1761..

13. Wm. Leonard m. Sarah D. of John Bolton: had Wm. 1710, John 1711, Sarah 1714, James 1716, Samuel 1718, Silas 1721, Mercy 1723, Jonathan 1726. James m. Jemima Heiford perhaps 1737.

14. Josiah (s. of Josiah 10.) m. Jemima D. of Josiah Washburn 1740, and had Susanna 1742, Rebecca 1744, Josiah 1745*, Marah 1748, Seth 1750, Moses 1752. He d. 1760: the wid. made her will 1784.—Susanna m. Abner Kingman of M. 1762. —Rebecca m. Capt Abraham Washburn 1765.—Marah m. Nathaniel Orcutt 1768.—Seth d. 1775.

15. Nathan (s. of Josiah 10.) m. Thankful Besse of Wareham 1744, and had Abigail 1745, Lydia 1747*, Sarah 1748*, Nathan 1750*, Huldah 1752*, Daniel 1754, Sarah 1756, Phebe 1758, Nathan 1760, Thankful. He d. 1765. Abigail m. Israel Keith 1767.—Sarah m. John Miller of M. 1778.—Phebe d. 1779.— Daniel m. Phebe Leonard of R. 1781, and went to Pomfret.— Nathan was a physician, m. Anstress, and had Seth 1789, and went to R. I.—Thankful m. Rufus Conant 1783.—Nathan Leonard was a soldier at Roxbury 1776.

16. Samuel (s. of Josiah 10. or William 13.) m. Lydia Besse and had Lydia 1751, Samuel 1753, Roland 1755, Silvanus 1759, Silas, Eunice, Zilphah, Abigail. Roland m. Lydia Smith of Walpole 1786.—Silvanus m. Eunice D. of Samuel Kinsley 1786, and had a D. Clarissa who m. Leonard Pratt 1818 and went to Me.—Silas m. Nabby Smith 1785.—Zilpha m. Cephas Kinsley 1787.—Abigail of M. m. Jacob Perkins 1788.—This family removed perhaps to Pomfret Vt. Samuel Leonard d. 1792 æ. 71.

17. Joseph (s. of Joseph 11.) m. Mary D. of Nathaniel Packard 1721, and had Joseph, David and Jonathan twins, Dan, Simeon, Seth*, Sarah; Mary, the mother, d. 1770.—Sarah m. Isaac Pool 1743.

18. Seth (s. of John 8. perhaps) m. Silence D. of Nehemiah Packard 1769, and had Nehemiah 1769, Lucy 1772; he d. 1775, and his wid. m. Ebenezer Benson 1777.—Nehemiah m. Phebe Pratt 1792.—Lucy m. Alexander Alden 1792.

19. Capt. Solomon (s. of Solomon 12.) m. Joanna D. of Joseph Washburn 1756, and had Jacob 1757, Mary 1759, Hannah 1761, Enoch 1763, Solomon 1765, Marcus 1768, Ophir.— He and several of his sons removed westward. Capt. Jacob m. Mary D. of Isaac Swift 1788.—Mary m. Jeremiah Conant 1782. Hannah m. Capt. Timothy Mitchell 1783.—Solomon m. Huldah D. of Joseph Orcutt 1786.—Marcus m. Polly Richards 1793.— Enoch m. Abigail Hammond 1788.

20. David (s. of Joseph 17,) was with General Winslow in

seizing the Neutral French at Nova Scotia 1755, m. Mary Hall
of T. 1769, and had David, Zenas L., Mary, Bernard, Caleb F.
Linus, George W., Sarah, Fanny, James, Charles Frederick,
Olive, and Hannah. David gra. B. U. 1792, m. Polly Pierce of
M. 1797.—Zenas L. gra. B. U. 1794, and settled in the ministry at Sturbridge.—Mary m. Daniel Leonard 1791, and afterwards Clifford Carver 1806.—Sarah m. Jona. Bassett 1813.—
Fanny m. Zephaniah Dean of M. 1816.—Olive m. Cephas Tomson of M. 1802.—Bernard d. in the western country 1834.—Caleb
F. Esq. m. Nancy Tomson of M. 1807.—George W. went also
to the west.

21. Jonathan (s. of Joseph 17.) m. Martha D. of Benjamin
Washburn 1758, and had Martha 1759, Jonathan, David, Benjamin. She d. 1804 æ. 73. Martha m. Cornelius Pratt.—Jonathan gra. H. U. 1786, and settled as a physician at Sandwich.
—David m. Abigail Clark 1796.

22. Dan (s. of Joseph 17.) m. Mary D. of James Dunbar
1750, and had Mary 1751, Dan 1752, Experience 1753, Phebe
1755, Ziba 1756, Josiah 1758, Keziah 1760*, Calvin, Sally, Rosamond.—Mary m. Thomas Delano of Fairhaven.—Dan m. Hope
Clapp of M. 1775, and went to Ware.—Experience m. Luther
Reading of M. 1773.—Phebe m. Joseph Delano of Fairhaven.
—Ziba m. Chloe Shaw of M. 1783 and went to Ashfield.—Josiah
went to M.—Calvin went to Holly.—Sally m. Isaac Shepard of
Ashfield.—Rosamond m. Nathan Shaw 1782.

23. Simeon (s. of Joseph 17.) m. Ann Smith of Lexington
1764, and had Rachel 1764, Jonas 1767, Ruth 1768, Anna 1770,
Lois 1773, Oliver 1777, Molly 1779, Nahum and Simeon ; he d.
1793 æ. 56. Rachel m. William Swift 1795.—Anna m. Ithamar
Finney 1799.—Lois m. John Croal Stetson 1795.—Jonas removed to Oakham and there m. Chloe Allen 1804.—Ruth m. Lazell
Dean perhaps of R. 1789.

24. Samuel (s. of Samuel 16.) m. Deborah D. of Nathan
Mitchell Esq. 1777, and had Samuel, Ansel, Rebecca, Mary.—
Col. Samuel m. Mehitabel Bennet of A. and had Samuel LaFay-
ette, 1824.—Ansel m. Deborah D. of John Conant 1807.—Rebecca m Libeus Blossom 1804.—Mary m. Silvanus Sturtevant
1801.

25. Capt. Nahum (s. of Simeon 23.) m. Rhoda D. of Nathan
Snell 1812, and had Jonas 1813, Rhoda 1815, Anna Smith 1818,
Cyrus 1820 : she d. 1821.

26. Simeon (s. of Simeon 23.) m. Boadicea Tomson of M.
1817, and had Boadicea 1818, Rachel Stone 1819, Fanny 1821,
Eliza* and Eloisa* 1823, Sarah Louisa 1824.

27. Barna Leonard (from Taunton) m. Phebe D. of Joseph
Bassett 1780, and had Barna, Ruth. Barna Jr. m. Lydia D. of
Benjamin Sprague 1815.—Ruth m. Ophir Mitchell 1803.

Benjamin Leonard m. Hannah Phillips 1715.—Benjamin m.
Keturah Briggs 1756 ; she d. 1757.—Eliphalet of E. m. Silence
Howard 1755.—Zadock m. Deborah Keith 1765.—Olive of M,

m. Dr. Samuel Shaw 1781.—Lucy of M. m. Benjamin Whitman
Jr. 1796.—Abigail m. Jacob Fuller 1800.—Spencer m. Mary
Wood 1805.—Ann of R. m. Benjamin Mehuren 1798.—Betsy
m. Bradford Harlow 1806.—Lois m. James Capen Jr. of St.
1807.—Philibert of M. m. Benjamin Hayward 1807.—Betsy T.
m. James Leach 1811.—Anna m. Thomas Conant 1812.—Lewis
m. Betsy Leonard 1812.—Polly m. Francis Perkins 1815.—Lucy m. Ira Conant 1818.—Keziah D. of Jonathan of M. m. Simeon W. Mitchell 1819.—Arza m. Louisa Maria White 1820.—
Clarinda m. Henry W. Pratt 1821.—Seth m. Charlotte Dean
1821.—Wid. Ann m. David Pratt 1738.—Lydia m. Joseph Pratt
1712.

James Leonard of Taunton had Thomas, James, and a D.
Hannah born at Braintree 1671 ; he and his brother Henry came
from Pontepool in Wales and settled in Braintree as early as
1652, and thence went to Taunton, and Henry afterwards went
to N. Jersey ; whether connected with Solomon or not is not
ascertained.

LINCOLN.—Nehemiah Lincoln (s. of Ezekiel of Abington)
m. Kezia D. of Dea. James Packard 1748, and lived in N. B.
and d. 1818 æ. 91.

2. Gideon (s. of Ezekiel 2d. of Abington brother of Nehemiah
above) was adopted by his uncle Nehemiah, and had his estate
and settled in N. B. ; m. Martha D. of Luke Perkins 1781, and
had Nehemiah 1782, Mehitabel 1784, Keziah 1785, Ruel 1787,
Charles 1788*, d. 1794, Martha 1789, Content 1791*, Roxana
1792, Triphena 1792, Charles 1795, Luke, Serena.   Capt. Nehemiah m. Martha D. of Simeon Packard 1802.—Mehitabel m.
Japhet Beals of Augusta 1803.—Keziah m. Bela Curtis 1803.—
Martha m. Benjamin Gardner of Augusta 1806.—Serena m. Ziba
Bisbee 1814.—Charles m. Rebecca Wood Porter 1816, and went
to E.—Luke m. a White.

4. Ruel (s. of Gideon 2.) m. Eunice D. of John Willis 1804,
and had Roxana 1805*, Charles 1807, Isaac 1809, Elbridge 1810,
Emeline 1813*, Eliza 1815.   He settled in E. B.

William of T. m. Hannah Wade 1751.—Hannah of Scituate
m. Perez Howard 1795.—Susanna of Hingham m. John Mitchell 1795.—Rufus m. Lucy Ellis 1804.—Deborah of Hingham m.
Artemas Hale Esq. 1815.

LINDSAY.—Thomas Lindsay lived in W. B. and m. Elizabeth D. of William Turner 1745, and had William 1747, Mary
1749, Hannah 1752, James 1755, Thomas 1758.—James m. but
had no children.—Thomas m. Thankful Baily 1786.

Mary m. Nathaniel Ames 1734.—Lurania m. Martin Howe
1820.—Betsy d. 1815.—John m. Abigail, D. perhaps of Samuel
Washburn 1735.—James m. Hannah Turner 1744.

LITTLEFIELD.—Daniel Littlefield m. Rebecca D. of Josiah
Williams 1732, and had Edmund 1733, Mary 1734, Daniel 1737,
Rebecca 1739, Bethiah 1742, Martha 1744*, Seth 1746, Susanna
1747, Martha 1750, Reuben 1753*, Silence 1754, Adam 1758.

Daniel Littlefield and his wife Rachel had Ralph 1760*; she d. 1760; and he m. Catharine D. of Joseph Cole 1762, and had Rachel 1762, Catharine 1764, Josiah 1765, Waldo 1768. Mary m. David Wade 1756.—Susanna m. Edward Keith of Easton 1765.—Martha m. Luke Keith of Easton 1768.

2. Nathaniel (s. of Nathaniel of Braintree) m. Hannah D. of Moses Curtis and lived in St. and had Samuel, Nathaniel, and Hannah, who m. a Niles.

3. Maj. Samuel (s. of Nathaniel 2.) m. a Wentworth, and had Samuel*, John*, Hovenden*, Charles, Cassander, Dorothy, Sally, Abigail, Hannah. Charles m. Ann D. of Jonas Howard 1821.—Dorothy m. John May 1807.—Sally m. Sidney Howard 1820.

4. Nathaniel (s. of Nathaniel 2.) m. a Tucker and had Nathaniel, James, Isaac, Darius, Betsy, Myra. Nathaniel m. a Brown.—James m. a Cary.—Darius m. Lydia D. of Jonas Howard.

Hannah of R. m. Ezekiel Reed 1807.—Esther m. Samuel Soper 1731.

LORING.—Capt John Loring (from Plympton probably) m. Ruth Sturtevant, and lived in E. B. and had Daniel 1754, Silvia 1757; he had James, Nathaniel, Peleg, Deborah, Rebecca, Priscilla, and Mary, before he came here.—Deborah m. Lemuel Kingman 1754.—Rebecca m. Jacob Mitchell 1763; his wid. Ruth perhaps m. Isaac Kingman 1770.—James m. Jane D. of Isaac Kingman 1770, and had John Esq. who m. Jennet D. of Joshua Barrel 1794, and Laban and James.—Priscilla m. Ebenezer Barker, and had 2 Ds. Priscilla, and Deborah; Priscilla m. Tilden Crooker, and Deborah m. David Oldham Esq.—Nathan'l went to Spenser.—Peleg taken by the Algerines.—Daniel m. a Pope in Boston, and lived in Nantasket.—Mary not m.—Silvia m. Job Barstow.

2. James Loring of N. B. m. Jennet D. of Amos Whitman 1809, and had Lucius 1811*, Vashti 1814. He probably first m. Mercy D. of Ezra Warren 1800.

3. Ignatius Esq. (of Plympton) m. Bathsheba D. of Capt. Jonathan Bass 1750, and had Sarah 1751, Ignatius, Jacob, Jane, Calvin and others.—Jane m. Capt Moses Inglee.—One D. m. a Bradford; another, Silvanus Bartlett Jr.—Capt. Ignatius went to Me.—Jacob remained at Plympton.

Molly d. 1776 æ. 47.—Caleb of Plympton m. Sarah wid. of Caleb Packard and D. of Nathan Howard Esq. 1802.—Hannah of Plympton m. Lewis Ames 1815.

LOVELL.—Dr. Shubael Lovell of Barnstable m. Bethiah D. of Dea. James Perkins 1797, and his ss. Shubael, Nehemiah G., and Lorenzo O., live in S. B. The two last gra. B. U. 1833.

James Lovell m. Mary Johnson of St. 1761.—Andrew Lovell m. Lydia D. of Nath'l Conant 1712.—James m. Dorcas Pratt 1754.—James m. Jemima Leach 1785.

LOVERIDGE.—Barnet Loveridge and his wife Mehitabel, had Caleb Leach 1789 or 1809, Robert Lee 1811*.

LOWDEN or LOUDOUN.—Nathaniel Lowden (from Duxbury) m. Experience D. of Joshua Pratt 1762, and lived in E. B. and had Sarah 1762, Susanna 1764, John 1765, Experience 1768, Jacob 1771, and Hannah 1776. The mother d. 1813 æ. 72.—Sarah m. Benjamin Darling 1785.—Susanna m. Oliver Pratt 1787.—John m. Susanna Clark 1793.—Experience m. Josiah Parris 1788, and went to Me., and was mother of Virgil Parris, member of Cong.—Jacob m. Susanna D. of Mark Phillips 1794. —Hannah m. Calvin Reed 1807.—The ss. went to Plainfield. Richard and Mary Loudon of Boston had John 1641, and Jeremy 1643.

MANLY.—Daniel Manly and his wife Rebecca had Daniel 1752, Nathaniel 1755; his wife d. and he m. Sarah Monk 1790, and had Sarah 1791; he d. 1804. Sarah m. George Howard 3d. 1808.

2. Daniel (s. of Daniel 1.) m. Phebe D. of Capt. Jona. Howard 1782, and had Daniel 1784, Susanna 1786, Sabin 1789, Harriet 1792, Galen and Salmon 1794, Linus 1798, Phebe 1803.— Susanna m. Martin Hayward 1808.

3. Nathaniel (s. of Daniel 1.) m. Betty D. of Thomas Hayward 1778, and had Rebecca 1780, Betty 1783, Polly 1784, Hayward 1787, Melinda 1789, Olive 1791, Vesta 1793, Sally 1795, Susanna 1797.—Betty m. Abel Kingman Esq. 1807.—Polly m. Nathan Packard 1815.—Melinda m. Isaac Hartwell 1809.—Olive m. Rowlandson Marshall 1808.—Vesta m. Daniel Hayward 1817. —Sally m. Charles Clapp 1816.—Susanna m. Jonas H. Keith 1816.—Rebecca m. Jerathmael Hayward 1802.

4. Hayward (s. of Nathaniel 3.) m. Sarah D. of Daniel Hayward 1816, and had Sarah Hayward 1818.

Thomas Manly m. Lydia D. of John Field 1701.—David m. Joanna D. of Wm. Turner 1752.—Josiah m. Eliza, D. of Seth Bryant 1789.—Silvia m. Zephaniah Lathrop 1791.—Timo. of E. m. Susanna Packard 1761.—Rowena m. Jacob Niles of Randolph 1801.—Sally of E. m. Seth Crossman 1813.—Olive m. Joseph Hayward 1768.—Mrs. Susanna d. 1834 æ. 98.—William Manly and his Neighbors of the north purchase (Easton) allowed to come to meeting here and to build a bridge over Cutting Cove River 1696.

MAY.—Michael May m. Elizabeth D. of John Bolton, and lived in E. B. in what is called Bolton Corner. She was born 1692, and d. 1770.

2. John May m. Dorothy D. of Samuel Littlefield 1807, and had Clarissa 1810, Hannah 1812; he lived in N. B. or Stoughton Corner.

MARSHALL.—Allen Marshall and his w., sister of Ephraim Groves came from Rochester and lived in E. B. but had no children: he d. 1824 æ. 89: she 1825 æ. 86.

2. Benjamin Marshall m. Mary D. of Thomas Hayward 1768,

and had Hayward 1771, Calvin 1774, Benjamin 1777, Rowland-
son 1780, Gannett, and Ambrose* 1784, Rowlandson m. Olive
Manly 1808.—Gannett m. Mary Hayward 1810.
3. Hayward (s. of Benj. 2.) m. Olive D. of Joseph Hayward
1794, and had Benjamin 1798, Hayward 1800, Perez 1801, Han-
nah 1803. Benjamin m. Polly D. of Nehemiah Howard 1820.
—Abigail m. Waldo Field 1816.
McBRIDE.—John McBride m. Jane D. of Alexander Wilson
1754, and had Alexander 1755, Sarah 1757 : he and Wilson were
Irish and settled in N. B. and removed thence to Harpersfield
N. York.
MEHURIN or McHURON.—1. Hugh Mehurin m. Mary
D. of Amos Snell 1725, and lived in S. B. and had David 1726,
Mary 1730, Martha 1732, Bathsheba 1735, d. 1766, Josiah 1737,
Reliance 1739*, Jonathan 1742. Mary m. Nathan Washburn
1748.
2. Benjamin (brother perhaps of Hugh) m. Lydia D. of Jo-
seph Pratt Jr. perhaps 1731, and had Sarah 1732, Hezekiah
1734, Lucy 1736*, Benjamin 1739, Isaac 1741 ; she d. 1741 æ.
28, and he m. Mehitabel Williams 1749, and had Jonathan 1752,
Silvia 1754 ; he d. 1761, she 1770. Sarah m. John Mitchell
1751—Benjamin m. Mary Wethrell 1771.—Isaac m. Mary D. of
Ebenezer Allen 1781, and had Bethiah 1783, Allen 1785.—Jonathan m. Ruth D. of Samuel Kingman 1774, and had Deborah,
Priscilla and others.
3. Jonathan (brother of Hugh perhaps) m. Mary, wid. of
George Packard, and D. of Samuel Edson perhaps, 1740, and
had Ephraim 1741 ; he d. 1757.
4. David (s. of Hugh 1.) and his w. Anna, had Sarah 1750,
Hannah 1752, David 1755, Anna 1758*, Anna 1759, Jonathan
and Susanna 1762.—Sarah m. Benjamin Orcutt 1773.—Susanna
of E. m. Seth Burr 1781.
5. Hezekiah (s. of Benj. 2.) m. Abigail Dickerman 1760, and
lived in W. B. and had Maria 1761, Amasa 1763, Chloe 1765.—
Abigail Mehurin m. Luther Hall of R. 1781.
6. Josiah (s. of Hugh perhaps) m. Bethiah D. of Benjamin
Pratt perhaps 1769, and had Bethiah 1770, Josiah 1772 ; he also
m. Martha D. of Jeremiah Conant 1779. Benjamin Mehurin
m. Ann Leonard of R. 1798.—Bethiah of Pembroke m. Ezra
Churchill 1799.—Lucy m. Martin Conant Jr. 1806.—Mary m.
William Bassett 1719.—Bathsheba m. Solomon Snow 1723.
MITCHELL.—1. Experience Mitchell was one of the forefathers, (a name usually applied to those, who arrived in the
three first ships) and came over in the third ship, the Ann, in
1623 : he sold his place in Plymouth to Samuel Eddy in 1631
and removed to Duxbury, where he purchased Wm. Paybody's
house and farm 1650: he was an original proprietor of Bridgewater, but sold his share or proprietary right to Thomas Hayward ; he came to Bridgewater late in life, with his son Edward ;
while at Plymouth he lived at Spring Hill, so called, and at Dux-
31

bury he lived at a place called Blue Fish River : at Bridgewater he lived at a place called Joppa, where his descendants still live : he d. 1689 æ. a. 80 ; his will dated 1684 : he was at Leyden with the Pilgrims and left a brother Thomas, who lived and died in Holland : he had a share in the first division of Lots at Plymouth in 1623, and of the live stock in 1627 : it is supposed he m. Jane D. of Francis Cook for his first wife : the wife of his old age was named Mary, but her family name is not ascertained ; he had a sister Constant, who m. John Fobes : the names of his children as appears from his will, deeds, and other written documents, were Thomas, John, Jacob, Edward, Elizabeth, Mary, Sarah and Hannah. Thomas first had land of his father at Dartmouth, but relinquished it again to his father 1669, who the same day conveyed it to Jacob. There is no farther account of Thos. Elizabeth m. John Washburn 1645.—Mary m. James Shaw of M. 1652, who d. 1679, and left a D. Mary.—Sarah m. John Hayward.—Hannah m. Joseph Hayward.

2. John (s. of Experience 1.) m. Mary Bonney 1675, and had Experience 1676 ; she d. 1677, and he m. Mary Lathrop 1679 : she d. 1680, and he m. Mary Prior 1682, and had Mary 1682, Hannah 1683, Joseph 1684, Elizabeth 1685*, Elizabeth 1686, John 1689, Sarah 1690, Esther 1692.—This family lived in Duxbury.—Joseph settled his brother John's estate 1711.—The father sold house and lands in Duxbury to George Williamson 1701.

3. Jacob (s. of Experience 1.) m. Susanna D. of Thomas Pope of Plymouth 1666, and settled at Dartmouth, now Fairhaven, was a carpenter and an Ensign, and in 1675, at the commencement of Phillip's war, was killed and his wife also by the Indians early in the morning as they were going to the garrison, whither they had sent their children the afternoon before ; they both lived to reach the garrison, but d. of their wounds ; their children were Jacob, Thomas, and Mary ; the children came to Bridgewater, and were taken care of and brought up by their uncle Edward.—Mary m. Samuel Kingman 1696.

4. Ensign Edward (s. of Experience 1.) m. Mary D. of Thos. Hayward, and lived with her 40 years without children ; she d. and he then, 1708, m. Alice D. of Maj. John Bradford of Kingston s. of William Jr. and g. s. of Gov. William ; she was b. 1678, and d. 1746 æ. 67 ; he bought Francis West's proprietary right, and settled in E. B. before 1682 ; he had Mary 1709, Alice 1714, Edward 1716 ; he d. 1717, and it is said he was near 70 years of age when his son Edward was born : his wid. m. Dea. Joshua Hearsey of Hingham and removed thither with her children, and Mary m. Joshua, and Alice m. Noah, ss. of Dea. Hearsey, who had also a D. Sarah by his last w., who m. Thomas Loring and d. 1798. Edward sold the family estate at blue fish river in Duxbury to Samuel Sprague 1708, which his father had conveyed to him in 1670.

5. Experience (s. of John 2.) settled in Povidence and had

a family : one of his descendants by the name of Experience d. a few years since in Uxbridge over 100 years of age, and left a s. John in or about Gloucester R. I. : there was also a Capt. Elisha Mitchell and Maj. Thomas and Darius Mitchell in that vicinity, probably of the same family.—Elisha is mentioned in R. I. records in 1700.

6. Joseph (s. of John 2.) m. Bathsheba Pillips probably ; first lived in Plymouth 1711 ; and settled in Kingston about 1719, was a Tanner, and had Sarah 1711*, Hannah 1713, Joseph 1714*, John 1716*, Mary 1718, Sarah 1719, Bathsheba 1721, Alice 1723, Joseph 1726, Benjamin 1728, Martha 1731, Ruth : his w. d. and he m. Hannah Hersey of Abington 1753 : he d. 1755, and his wid. m. John Whitman of E. B. and d. 1788 æ. 85. Mary m. Thomas Phillips Jr. 1743, and d. the same year.—Sarah m. Jonathan Ring.—Bathsheba m. Timothy Briggs of T.—Martha m. Japhet Rickard.—Joseph went to Norton.

7. Jacob (s. of Jacob 3.) m. Deliverance D. of John Kingman 1696, and had Jacob, 1696 : he removed to Kingston, and there had a 2d. wife Rebecca D. of Isaac Cushman probably, he was a blacksmith, and sold his house and lands to Benjamin Sampson 1728, and removed to North Yarmouth Me., and d. a. 1744.

8. Thomas (s. of Jacob 3.) m. Elizabeth D. of John Kingman 1696 : he, his brother, and sister Mary, were all m. at the same time, and all m. Kingmans, who were also brother and sisters : he had Thomas 1696*, Henry 1698*, Timothy 1700, Susanna 1703, Edward 1705*, Elizabeth 1710, Mary 1713, Seth 1715 ; he d. 1727 ; she 1733 ; he lived in S. B. where his g. g. s. William now lives.—Susanna m. Joseph Packard 1724.—Elizabeth and Mary d. young probably.

9. Col. Edward (s. of Edward 4.) m. Elizabeth D. of Elisha Cushing of Hingham 1738, and returned to E. B. and had Edward 1739, Cushing 1740, Elizabeth 1742, Alice 1744, Elisha 1746, John 1748, William 1750, Bradford 1752, Mary 1754, Celia 1757, Sarah 1759, Bela 1761 : she d. 1799 æ. 85 : he 1801 æ. 86. Elizabeth m. Eleazar Keith 1760.—Alice m. John Keith 1763, Mary m. James Keith Jr. 1780.—Celia m. Arthur Harris 1781.—Sarah m. Maj. Benj. Harris 1791, and d. a widow June 29, 1839 æ. 80. *

10. Benjamin (s. of Joseph 6.) m. Mary Phillips of Duxbury 1750, and lived in Kingston, and had Bathsheba 1752, Benjamin 1753, Abigail 1755, Molly 1757, Rebecca 1760, John 1762, Ezra 1764, Sarah 1767, Hannah 1770, Joseph 1773, Thomas 1775*. Isaac R. Mitchell a jeweller in Boston was son of Joseph Mitchell of Kingston.

11. Dea. Jacob (s. of Jacob 7.) m. Mary Howland 1721, and settled in Pembroke, and had Jonathan 1724 ; his wife d. and he m. wid. Rachel Cushing, sister of the Rev. Mr. Lewis, and had David 1728, Rachel 1730, Jacob 1732, Sarah 1736 ; he removed to North Yarmouth.—Rachel m. a Chandler.—Mary m. Judge Lewis.—Sarah m. a Gray.

12. Timothy (s. of Thomas 8.) m. Deborah D. of Nathaniel Packard, and had Thomas, Nathan 1729, Abiel, Deborah, Timothy* ; he d. 1733 : she 1744. Deborah m. a Bliss of Rehoboth 1730.—Timothy was lost at sea with Winslow Hooper, both young.—There was a wid. Mitchell d. in S. B. 1762, perhaps she was Sarah Mehurin, who m. John Mitchell 1751 ; this John is the man perhaps who was under guardianship of Jonathan Howard 1742, and was from Milton.

13. Seth (s. of Thomas 8.) m. Ann D. of Thomas Latham 1738, and had Jacob 1740, Reuben 1741*, Seth 1744, Zenas 1746*, Phineas 1747*, Eliphaz 1749, Timothy 1751*, Rotheus 1753, Ann 1755, Reuben 1757, Betty 1759 ; his wife d. and he m. Mary D. of Nicholas Wade 1760, and had Molly 1761, Nabby 1762, Susanna 1766 ; he d. 1802 æ. 87, she 1809 æ. 83.—Eliphaz d. a bachelor 1820 æ. 70.—Ann m. Solo. Washburn 1773.—Betty and Molly were never m.—Nabby m. James Lincoln of Cohasset 1788.—Susanna m. Asa Forrest 1787 and her D. Susanna m. William Mitchell, an Englishman, 1821.

14. Edward (s. of Col. Edward 9.) m. Jane D. of Charles Latham 1762, and had Jane 1763, Edward 1766, Lucia 1769, Eunice 1773, Theodore, Ophir and Oreb twins.—He d. 1828 in his 90th year ; she 1829 æ. 88.—Jane m. Edward Hayward 1782.—Lucia m. Capt. Joseph Hooper.—Eunice m. Dan'l Mitchell Esq. 1795.—Oreb d. single.

15. Cushing (s. of Col. Edward 9.) m. Jennet D. of Hon. Hugh Orr 1765, and had Alice 1767, Nahum 1769, Jennet 1771 ; his wife d. 1774 æ. 26, and he m. Hannah wid. of Josiah Newton and D. of Anthony Sherman 1780 and had Hannah 1781, Celia 1783, Cushing 1784, Charles 1788, Newton 1789, George 1793. He d. 1820 in his 80th year ; she 1839 in her 90th year. Alice m. Dea. William Harris 1788.—Jennet m. Daniel Bryant 1789.—Hannah m. Hon. Ezekiel Whitman Esq.—Celia m. Charles Keen 1802.—Newton d. at Franconia 1810 æ. 21.—His 2d. wife had one child, Ruhamah, by her first husband and she m. Maj. Theodore Mitchell 1798.

16. Elisha Esq. (s. of Col. Edward 9.) m. Hannah D. of Dea. Barnabas Tomson of Halifax and had an only child Asa 1782; they both d. of a consumption, she 1783 æ. 35 ; he 1790 æ. 44.

17. John (s. of Edward 9.) m. Anna D. of Benjamin Byram 1781, and had John Holman 1783, Caleb 1785, Jenny Byram 1787, Anna 1790, Elisha 1792 ; she d. 1794 æ. 36; and he m. Susan Lincoln of Hingham 1795 ; he d. 1829 æ. 81.—John Holman not m.—Jenny B. d. single.—Anna m. Nahum Washburn 1816.—Elisha m. Joanna D. of Henry Joslyn of Pembroke and removed to New Bedford.

18. William (s. of Col. Edward 9.) settled in Cummington, and m. Elizabeth, D. of William Ward Esq., and had Piam, Cushing, William, Chester, Elisha, Bela, Betsy, Clarissa, Sally, Laura, Polly, Jennet. Piam m. Sally Orcutt, and then a Warner.—Cushing m. in N. Y., and settled in Windsor.—William m.

Clarissa, D. of Elisha Bisbee.—Chester m. a Richards.—Elisha
m. Lucinda Brewster, and then Wid. Shaw, D. of Nathan Gurney Esq. of Abington.—Bela m. a Streeter.—Betsy m. Elijah
Warner.—Clarissa m. Stephen Warner Jr.—Sally m. Roswell
Hubbard of Northampton and d. 1837.—Laura m. Otis Tileston
of Boston.—Polly m. Seth Porter Jr.—Jennet m. Chester Gaylord of Hadley: he d. 1837, æ. 87 ; she d. 1839 : and it is remarkable that he and his father had each 12 children, and all
lived to be m.

19. Bradford (s. of Col. Edward 9.) settled also in Cummington, and m. Persis, D. of Elijah Warner, and had Nahum and
Lucretia : he then returned to Bridgewater, and his w. d. 1799,
æ. 41. He then m. Meribah, D. of Lemuel Keen of Pembroke,
1801, and had Eliza : he then removed to Minot, and had a son
Bradford that d. in infancy. He returned again to Bridgewater,
where his 2d w. d. 1823, æ. 49 : he is still living.—Lucretia m.
Josiah Bassett 1820.—Eliza m. Alpheus Leach Jr.

20. Bela (s. of Col. Edward 9.) settled in Charlestown, and
there m. Nancy, D. of Maj. Calder, and had Nancy and Bela,
and d., and his wid. m. a French.

21. Maj. Thomas (s. of Timothy 12.) m. Keziah Swift of
Plymouth, and had Timothy 1758, William 1760, Lusanna 1762,
Thomas 1765, Calvin 1767, Luther 1769*, Zilphah 1772: he d
1776. Lusanna m. Marlborough Williams of Easton.—Zilphah
m. Eleazar Keith Jr.—Calvin went to Rochester, was m., but left
no children.

22. Hon. Nathan (s. of Timothy 12.) m. Ann, D. of Jonathan
Cary, 1754, and had Deborah 1755, Timothy 1757*, Susanna
1758, Mary 1760*, Nathan 1762, Cary 1765, Daniel 1767. He
d. of the small-pox 1789, æ. 60. Deborah m. Samuel Leonard
Jr. 1777.—Susanna m. Caleb Keith 1777.—Cary d. 1821, without children.

23. Col. Abiel (s. of Timothy 12.) settled in Easton, and m.
a D. of Eliphalet Leonard, and had Thomas, Abiel, Timothy,
Eliphalet, Leonard, Deborah, Ruth, Mary, Sally, Susanna. He
d. æ. 88. Thomas m. Abigail Howard 1783, and he and Abiel
went to Vermont.—Timothy went to Merrimac.—Eliphalet remained in E., and had Albert, Harrison and others probably.—
Leonard went to Mansfield.—Deborah m. Thomas Willis.—Ruth
m. a Simmons.—Sally m. a Williams.—Mary m. a Williams.—
Susanna m. an Edson.

24. Jacob (s. of Seth 13.) m. Rebecca, D. of Capt. John
Loring, 1763, and had Oliver, Silvia, Zenas, Jacob, John Loring,
Peleg, Levi. She d. 1782, æ. 40, and he m. Sarah, wid. of Josiah Whitman, and D. of Caleb Sturtevant of Halifax, 1783, and
had Josiah Whitman. His 2d w. d. 1789, æ. 35, and he m.
Jerusha, wid. of Robert Latham, and D. of Thomas Hooper,
1791 : he d. 1827, æ. 89 ; she 1829, æ. 85. Oliver m. Amelia
Gannet 1791, and had Warren 1792, and then went to Lyme, N.
H.—Silvia m. Hugh Orr 1785.—Zenas m. Nabby Washburn of

Kingston 1796, and had Ichabod Washburn, Rebecca Loring
1801, and then removed to Maine, and there had Nahum, Zenas,
Gilman, Charles, Cushing, Elisha, Persis Turner, Silvia*, Abigail. Jacob went to Farmington, Conn., and had William, Hiram
and John.—John L. d. young at West Point, and left 2 children.
Peleg and Levi went to Maine and had families.
    25. Seth (s. of Seth 13.) m. Lusanna, D. of Capt. Simeon
Wood, and had Simeon Wood 1795, Sarah Weston 1796, Arnot
1798, Timothy 1800, Susanna 1802, George Washington 1804,
Seth Arnold 1806. Seth, the father, d. 1807, æ. 64. Simeon W.
m. Keziah, D. of Jona. Leonard of Mid'o, 1819.—Timothy m.
Melissa Alden Raymond of Plymouth.—Sarah W. m. a Robbins
of Mid'o.—Seth A. m. a Pickins of Rochester.
    26. Rotheus (s. of Seth 13.) was a Lieut. in the Revolutionary
army, m. Hepzibah, D. of Josiah Hayward, 1783, and had Cynthia 1784, Eliphalet 1785, Horatio 1787, Betsy 1791, and then
removed to Lyme, N. H.
    27. Reuben (s. of Seth 13.) m. Ann, D. of James Wade, 1783,
and had Jane 1785, James 1786, and then removed to Windsor.
    28. Edward (s. of Edward 14.) m. Chloe, D. of Capt. Abra-
ham Washburn, 1789, and had Chloe*, Olive, Edward, Melinda,
Emeline. Olive m. Dr. Rufus Walker of Westport 1814, and
afterwards Isaac Fobes.—Melinda m. Oliver Alden 1819, and d.
1838.—Emeline m. John Winslow.—Edward m. Margaret Sea-
ver of T.
    29. Maj. Theodore (s. of Edward 14.) m. Ruhamah, only child
of Josiah Newton of Brookfield, 1798, (her mother Hannah
was 2d wife of Cushing Mitchell), and had Hannah 1799, Winslow 1800, Miriam 1804*, Caroline 1808, Louisa 1813. Hannah
m. George Bassett 1819.—Caroline m. Philo Keith.
    30. Ophir (s. of Edward 14.) m. Ruth, D. of Barna Leon-
ard 1803, and had Leonard, Willard, Oreb and Polly.
    31. Nahum (s. of Cushing 15.) gra. H. U. 1789, and m. Nabby,
D. of Gen. Silvanus Lazell, 1794, and had Harriet 1796, Silvanus Lazell 1798, Mary Orr 1801, Elizabeth Cushing 1807, James
Henry 1812. Harriet m. Nath'l Morton Davis Esq. of Plymouth
1817.—Mary O. m. David Ames Jr. Esq. of Springfield 1827.—
Elizabeth C. m. Nathan Dresser Hyde 1833.—James H. m. Har-
riet Lavinia, D. of John Angier of Belfast, 1833, and had Henry
Hedge 1839.
    32. Maj. Cushing (s. of Cushing 15.) m. Lusanna T., D. of
Capt. Asa Pratt, 1822, and had Lydia*, Sarah Harris*, Lu-
sanna*, and went to Boston.
    33. Charles (s. of Cushing 15.) m. Bethiah O., D. of Anthony
Winslow Clift, 1813, and had Hannah, Asa, Charles Cushing.
Hannah d. 1834, æ. 18; her mother d. 1835.
    34. George (s. of Cushing 15.) m. Bethiah, D. of Eleazar
Keith, 1820 : has no children. He owns the paternal estate.
    35. Asa (s. of Elisha 16.) gra. H. U. 1802; m. Bethiah, D. of
Joseph Lazell, 1806; settled as an Attorney in New Gloucester;

had Sarah Harris 1807, (she was first called Bethiah). He d.
March 18, 1807, and his wid. m. George Y. Phillips 1812, and
went to Poughkepsie, N. Y. Sarah H. m. an Overocker, and
removed to the western part of New York state, and d. 1833.

36. Caleb (s. of John 17.) m. Jane, D. of Holman Keith 1811,
and has Newton and William.

37. Nahum (s. of Bradford 19.) m. a D. of Josiah Deane Esq.
of R., and lived awhile in Minot, Me., and then removed to
Raynham, where his wife d. and he then m. Chloe, wid. of Alvan
Crossman and D. of Nathaniel Pratt.

38. Capt. Timothy (s. of Thomas 21.) m. Hannah, D of Capt.
Solomon Leonard, 1783, and went to Vermont, and had Luther,
Bernard, Leonard Bradley, and others. He m. a Bradley at Vt.
for a 2d w. Leonard B. is editor of a newspaper in the Western States.

39. William (s. of Thomas 21.) m. Betsy, D. of Hosea Dunbar of Halifax, 1793, and had Betsy 1793, William 1795*, Jennet 1800*, Jane 1801*, William 1805*, Caroline 1807*. Betsy
d. single 1834.

40. Thomas (s. of Thomas 21.) m. Mehitabel, D. of Capt.
Joseph Alden, 1797, and went to Greenwich (Enfield) and had
a family. One D. m. a s. of Walter Hayward.

41. Nathan Esq. (s. of Nathan 22.) m. Rachel, D. of Benja-
min Byram, 1793, and had Mary and Nathan. Mary m. Maj.
James Seymore Allen 1816, who d. young, leaving one child
Mary.—Nathan lived awhile in Boston.

42. Daniel Esq. (s. of Nathan 22.) m. Eunice, D. of Edward
Mitchell, 1795, and had Philo 1803, Eunice 1805, Daniel 1807,
Bela 1809, Mary Ann 1815*. Eunice m. William Dunbar.

43. Josiah W. Esq. (s. of Jacob 24.) m. Sally, D. of Oakes
Angier Esq. and settled as an Attorney in Freeport, Me., and
had Susan A., Harriet Lavinia, and Josiah Angier. His w. d.
and he m. Elizabeth, wid. of Elisha P. Cutler Esq., her maiden
name Delano, and had Victor Moreau, Ezekiel Whitman, Frederick, Lucia, and Sarah Elizabeth.

44. Silvanus L. Esq. (s. of Nahum 31.) gra. H. U. 1817, and
m. Lucia, D. of Hon. Ezekiel Whitman of Portland, 1820, and
had Lucia W. 1821*, Helen McLeod 1822, Julia Willis 1826*,
Edward Cushing 1829, Hannah Whitman 1832*, Morton Davis
1834, Alice Bradford 1837*.

There was a John Mitchell in Marshfield 1825, æ. 85, whose
father John came from old York, Me.: his grandfather was killed
by the Indians: "his father told him he was related to the Mitch-
ells in Bridgewater:" he has several children and grand children
in and about Marshfield.

45. William (an Englishman and Iron Founder) came over
within a few years with his wife and had William*, John, Henry; his wife d. and he m. Susanna D. of Asa Forrist 1821, (her
mother was Susanna D. of Seth Mitchell 13,) and has William,
and Hannah Hall.

MONRO.—Alexander Monro with his wife Mary Hutchinson m. 1775, lived many years in East Bridgewater : he was a Scotchman : they had several children, viz : David 1777, Jennet 1779, William 1781, Eunice 1785, Jane 1788; and Mary 1771, and Nancy, both by a former wife : his first wife d. 1774, æ. 40. Matthias Munroe, Rector of Episcopal Ch., d. in S. B. 1836, æ. 51.—Daniel Munroe lived in E. B., and Henry Munroe m. Deborah Delano 1800, lived in S. B.: both from Hanson.— Daniel's wife d. 1832, æ. 70.

MOORE.—Theodosius Moore m. Sarah, D. of John Prior, 1825, and had Thomas 1726, John 1731. He d. and his widow m. Josiah Hayward 1738. Catharine Moore m. James Bradley 1759.—Ann Moore m. Joseph Prior, and afterwards James Allen. 2. Thomas (s. of Theodosius 1.) m. Mary Hamlin 1746, and had Mary 1746, John 1748, Sarah 1750*, Sarah 1751*, Isaac 1753, Thomas 1756, Samuel 1758, Betty 1760*, Theodosius 1763, Betty 1767, Sarah 1769. Both of these families lived in that part of B. that is now in Hanson.—George Moore of Burlington m. Olive Sanger 1815.

MORSE.—Asa Morse m. Sally (or Susanna) McFarling 1815, and had Asa 1816, Susanna 1818, Edwin 1821, Obadiah 1823, James 1825. Sihon Morse of Stoughton m. Polly Ripley 1804.— Abner Morse m. Polly Wood (or Mary Woodwis) 1804.—Baruck Morse of St. m. Rhoda Gurney 1811.

MORTON.—Nathaniel Morton m. Lucy, D. of Nathaniel Washburn, 1757, and had Nathaniel 1758, Tempe 1762, Abram 1765*. His wife d. 1766, and he then m. Rebecca, sister of Nathaniel Morton Esq. of Freetown, and had Lucy 1768. Nath'l was a Physician in Halifax.

Nathaniel Esq. of Freetown m. Mary, D. of Eleazar Cary, 1782, and was father of Judge Marcus Morton, now Governor.— Seth m. Hepzibah Packard 1757.—Hannah of Mid'o m. Abiel Edson 1774.—Patience m. BenjaminRobbins Jr. 1814.

MUXAM, MUXIM, OR MAXIM.—Joseph Muxam m. Anne, D. of Gershom Conant, 1764, and had Anne 1764, Eunice and Lavinia 1768 : he d. 1790, æ. 52. Anne m. Joseph Smith Jr. 1799.—John Muxam m. Silence, D. of Benjamin Pratt, 1748.— Lavinia m. a Christian, and had 2 ss. George and Caleb, and perhaps others.

NASH.—Joseph Nash and Rebecca his wife had Solomon 1808.

NEWBURY.—Lemuel Newbury and his wife Lydia had Samuel 1798.

James Newbury m. Martha, D. of Capt. Eliakim Howard, 1797.

NEWELL.—Joseph Newell m. Hannah Pierce 1732, and had Jonas 1733, Jane 1736; his wife d. and he m. Rachel Sylvester 1734, and had Jane 1736.

NEWHALL.—William Newhall came from Charlestown and lived in E. B. and m. Nabby D. of Samuel Rogers 1807, and had Eliza Wales 1809, Samuel Rogers 1811, William 1813*, Nabby Rogers 1815. He d. 1818 æ. 37. Eliza W. m. Jacob Folsom.

Samuel Pratt Newhall (brother of William above) m. Lydia Singer of Salem 1814, and had Rebecca Turner 1816, and others.

NILES.—Benaiah Niles m. Martha, D. of Isaac Allen, 1770, and had Benaiah 1770, James 1773, Silvia 1777, and went to Tamworth.

Jacob Niles of Randolph m. Rowena Manly 1801.—Freelove Niles m. Salmon Packard 1795.

NORTON.—Thaxter Norton (s. of John Norton of Weymouth) m. Susanna D. of Joseph Chamberlin 1808, and had Susanna Bass 1809, Charles Thaxter 1811, Sarah 1813, William 1815*, Elizabeth Williams 1817 ; he now lives in Boston.

Noah Norton m. Sarah Noyes 1803.—Jemima m. David Hatch 1754.

NOYES.—Ephraim Noyes (s. of Capt. Daniel of A. and g. s. of Samuel of Newbury) settled in N. B. 1800 ; m. Sarah D. of Samuel Dike 1779, and had Daniel, Jacob, Alva, Sarah, and Rebecca ; he d. 1822 æ. 65. Daniel gra. Yale, 1813, m. a Clark, and lives in Boston.—Jacob m. Olive D. of Josiah Edson, and lives in A.—Alva m. Sophronia D. of Perez Southworth.—Sarah m. Noah Norton 1803 and afterwards Seth Snow.—Rebecca m. Josiah Eames.

Samuel m. Millicent Orcutt 1770.—Ebenezer Noyes d. in E. B. 1832 æ. 36 ; he m. 2 Ds. of Joseph Gannet.—Ebenezer m. Betsy wid. of Daniel Ramsdell 1795.—David Noyes m. Lydia Orcutt 1811.

ORCUTT.—Wm. Orcutt (from Scituate) and his wife Martha, settled in S. B., and had John 1669, Martha 1671, Joseph 1672, Mary and Hannah 1674, Thomas 1675, Benjamin 1679, Elizabeth 1682, Deborah 1683, all b. at Scituate ; in his will 1694, his ch. mentioned are, Wm. 1664, Andrew, John, Joseph, Thomas, Benjamin, Martha, Mary, Hannah and Susanna. William and Andrew were probably born at Weymouth or elsewhere before he went to Scituate, and Susanna perhaps in B. Thomas, Benjamin and Susanna were minors. Elizabeth and Deborah, not mentioned, probably not living.—Mary m. Daniel Hudson 1697.—Andrew, and Benjamin we have no account of.—Joseph sold land here 1697, and speaks of himself as formerly of B.—Thomas sold land and a small house near Joseph Alden's 1700.

2. William (s. of William 1.) m. Jane D. of John Washburn and d. 1739 æ. 75 ; he had Moses, Caleb, Joanna, Elizabeth, Jane, Deliverance 1702, and Martha.—Joanna m. Benjamin Edson 1715.—Elizabeth m. Ebenezer French 1717.—Jane m. Joshua Warren 1725.—Deliverance m. Joseph Washburn, and afterwards a Packard and d. 1790 æ. 88.—Martha m. Solomon Washburn 1732.—Caleb m. Mehitabel Harvey 1738.

3. John (s. of William 1) had Hannah 1695, Samuel 1697, John 1700 ; Hannah was called his 2d child.

4. William (perhaps s. of William 2 or John 3.) m. Sarah D. of Jacob Leonard 1721, and had Jacob 1723.

5. Moses (s. of William 2.) m. Mercy D. of Nathaniel Allen perhaps 1739; his will 1781, mentions no children, probably had none.—Mercy Orcutt m. John Waterman of Halifax 1769. There was a Moses Orcutt d. 1748 æ. 35, and his D. Hannah buried in the same grave with him.

6. John (s. of John 3.) m. Desire D. probably of John Kingman 1721, and had John 1726, Hannah 1729*; his wife d. and he m. Mary Webster D. of a Clergyman near Newburyport, and had Susanna 1733, who d. single 1775 æ. 42.—She d. 1772 æ. 68, he 1781 æ. 81.

7. Ichabod (s. perhaps of Joseph and g. s. of William 1.) and his wife Milicent had Joseph 1730, Nathan 1731, Ichabod 1734; she d. and he m. a 2d w. Mary, and had Milicent 1738, Lydia 1739, Mary 1741, Benjamin 1742, Ephraim 1744, Moses 1749; he d. 1769. Milicent m. Samuel Noyes 1770.—Benjamin m. Sarah Mehurin 1773, and had a son Erasmus.

8. David m. Susanna D. of Daniel Packard 1734, and had Daniel 1734, Stephen 1736, David 1739. Ebenezer Orcutt m. Deliverance D. of John Kingman 1725.

9. John (s. of John 6.) m. Mary and had John 1751*; his w. d. and he m. Jerusha Hanmer 1752, and went to Ct.

10. Joseph (s. of Ichabod 7.) m. Deborah D. of David Pratt 1751, and had Joanna 1752, Nathan 1755, Hannah, Huldah.— Joanna m. Abiel Richmond 1773.—Nathan m. Eunice Whitmarsh 1780, and went to Cummington, and had Joseph, Nathan and John.—Hannah m. Salmon Washburn 1785.—Huldah m. Solomon Leonard 1786.—Wid. Deborah Orcutt d. 1805 æ. 72.

11. Nathan (s. of Ichabod 7.) m. Susanna D. of Daniel Snell and had William, Nathan 1758, Daniel 1760, John Snell, Ichabod. The father, William, John, and Ichabod went to Ackworth N. H.

12. Ichabob (s. of Ichabod 7.) m. Susanna D. of Richard Davenport Jr. 1757, and had John 1758, Susanna 1760. John Orcutt m. a Heiford.

13. Dea. Ephraim (s. of Ichabod 7.) and his wife Abiah had Mary 1778*, Moses 1782, Lydia 1784, Sarah 1787, Ephraim 1791, Thomas 1793, Gershom 1795.

14. Jonathan (from Cohasset) m. Experience, D. probably of William Washburn 1759, and had Jonathan 1760, William 1762, Samuel 1764; his wife d. 1766, and he m. Thankful D. of John Cary 1766.

15. Nathaniel m. Mary D. of Josiah Leonard Jr. 1768, and had Leonard 1768, Mary 1772, Nathaniel 1778, Josiah 1781, Hannah 1787. He and his family removed to Me. Hannah m. Jacob Fuller 1786.—Leonard m. Charity D. of Philip Reynolds 1797.—Josiah m. Naomi D. of Samuel Cheesman 1806.

16. Nathan (s. of Nathan 11.) m. Jane Inglee of M. 1781, and had Alpheus 1783, Galen 1785, Martin 1788, Anna 1790. He d.

of a Cancer 1808. Alpheus m. Mercy Pratt 1802, and d. 1834, leaving a family.—Galen m. Nancy D. of Daniel Willis 1809, and had Mary Ann, Edward Stockbridge, John Gorham, and others.

17. Daniel (s. of Nathan 11.) m. Olive D. of Benjamin Whitman 1784, and had Lucy. He d. and his wid. m. Josiah Johnson Jr. 1793, and d. 1828 æ. 63.—Lucy m. James Bates of Weymouth 1805.

18. Moses (s. of Dea. Ephraim 13.) and his wife Deborah had Deborah 1812, Thomas 1814, Julia Ann 1816, Charles 1818, Amanda 1820.

Lydia Orcutt m. David Noyes 1811.—Mary Orcutt m. Samuel Holmes 1793.—Susanna m. John Edson 3d. 1785.

ORR.—Hon. Hugh Orr (s. of Robert Orr of Lochwinioch, Shire of Renfrew, Scotland :) was born 2d Jan. 1715, O. S. Mar's year, Hansel Monday, and came to America 7th June 1740, and settled in E. B. and m. Mary D. of Capt. Jonathan Bass Aug. 24, 1742, and had Robert 1745, Jennet 1748, Mary 1750, Susanna 1752, Jane 1755*, Bethiah 1757, Margaret 1758, Bathsheba 1761, Matilda 1763*, Hugh 1766. He d. Dec. 6, 1798, æ. 82, she July 27, 1804 æ. 80.—Jennet m. Cushing Mitchell 1765.— Mary m. Stephen Whitman 1767.—Susanna m. Doct. Josiah Otis 1772.—Bethiah m. Anthony Winslow Clift 1777.—Bathsheba m. Solomon Inglee of Halifax 1783, and d. 1833.—Margaret d. single 1837 æ. 79.

There was a Hugh Orr came afterwards from Scotland : m. Agnes Corbett 1771, and went to 9 Partners, so called, N. Y.

2. Col. Robert (s. of Hugh 1.) m. Hannah, D. of David Kingman, 1766, and had Susanna* and Jane 1768, Hector 1770, Robert Boyd 1772, Montgomery 1776, Noble 1780. Jane m. John Boyd of N. Y. 1791 : she d. 1833. Montgomery was in a battle on the Lakes, and d. of his wounds at Boston after his return.—Noble settled in Georgia as a Physician, and d. young, leaving one or more children.—Col. Orr and his wife both d. at Springfield, where he was Master Armorer in the U. S. works : he d. 1811, æ 65.

3. Hugh (s. of Hugh 1.) m. Silvia only D. of Jacob Mitchell 1785; and had Thomas, John Love 1787, Isabella 1789, d. 1816 æ. 27, Jane 1792, Robert 1794, Jennet 1796, Hugh 1798, Silvia 1800, Ralph 1802*, Wilson 1804, Melville 1806, Oliver Mitchell 1810. Jane m. Calvin W. Keen 1812.—Jennet m. John Gilson of Lynn.—Silvia m. Hodijah Robinson.—Wilson went to Singsing N. Y. m. and had a D.—Melville m. Sally Tower of R. and had Sarah Jane.—Oliver is m. and lives in E. B.

4. Dr. Hector (s. of Robert 2.) gra. H. U. 1792, and m. Mary D. of Oakes Angier Esq. 1795, and had Mary Ann 1796, Susanna 1798, Hector Oakes Angier 1800, Samuel Angier 1802, and Jane. Mary Ann m. her cousin Boyd of N. Y. 1833.—Jane also m. in the State of N. Y.

5. Robert B. (s. of Robert 2.) went to Tamworth N. H. and there

m. Abigail Gilman : and had Hannah G., Abigail, Robert, Jane ;
he d. and his wid. and children returned to E. B.—Hannah G.
m. Bezer Hill 1816.—Abigail m. Jonathan Kingman Jr.—Jane
m. Bela Hill.—Robert is m. and lives in E. B.

6. Thomas s. of Hugh 3.) went to Needham, and there m.
Rachel Bolene, and thence to Shirley and there died : he had
Thomas, Rachel, Lucinda, Abigail, Alfred.—his wid. m. again.

7. John L. (s. of Hugh 3.) went to Lynn, and thence to Ashburnham N. H. : he m. Mary Wright of Brooklyn N. H. and
had William, Eliza, John, Daniel, Mary, Charles, Sarah Ellen,
Caroline, and two other Ds.

8. Robert (s. of Hugh 3.) went to Boston : m. Melinda Wilbor of Raynham : and has Melinda and Julianne.

9. Hugh (s. of Hugh 3.) m. Hannah Shaw D. of Josiah Keen,
and had Thomas*, Sarah Jane, Hannah Freelove: he d. at
Canton 1839.

10. Dr. Samuel A. (s. of Dr. Hector 4.) m. Elizabeth D. of
Thomas Williams Esq. of Roxbury, and has Elizabeth.

OSBORNE.—Thomas and Levi Osborne ss. of George Os-
borne of Hanson, lived in E. B.—Thomas m. Hannah D. of James
Wade 1784, and had Absalom 1785, Peleg 1787, Mahala 1789,
Martin 1791, Hannah 1793, Clarana 1795, Nabby 1798, Lavonia
1802. Absalom m. Lydia D. of Azor Howe 1812.—Peleg m.
Sally Pool of H. 1812.—Clarana C. m. Josiah Edson 1820.—
Levi m. Sophia Harvey 1797.—Deborah m. Asa Hudson 1803.

OTIS.—Dr. Isaac Otis (from Scituate s. of Dr. Isaac, and g.
s. of Capt. Stephen, and g. g. s. of John, who came from Barnstable, Devonshire, Eng., b. 1620, and settled at Hingham with
his father John 1635) gra. H. U. 1738 : m. Mehitabel D. of Capt.
Jonathan Bass 1746, and setttled in E. B. and had Bethiah 1747,
Josiah 1749, Isaac and Nabby* 1752, Hannah 1755*, Nabby
1757*, Jacobs 1758, Thomas 1761*, Galen 1763 ; he d. 1785 æ.
66 : she 1800 æ. 72. Bethiah m. John Hudson 1769.—Isaac
went to Cumberland R. I. and had a family, and among them
were William and Isaac, who now live in Philadelphia.—Jacobs
went to Providence and m. Sarah Smith Barker and had a family, among them were, Sewall, and Jacobs a Physician.—Galen
was a Physician, m. Joanna D. of Dea. David Tilden of Hanson, afterwards of Boston, and removed to Maine, and has a
family.

2. Dr. Josiah (s. of Isaac 1.) m. Susanna D. of the Hon. Hugh
Orr 1772, and had Thomas*, Melville 1778, Nabby 1781, Bass
1784, Clarissa 1786, Welcome 1790 : he d. Mar. 25, 1808 æ. 59 :
she d. Dec. 20, 1836 æ. 84. Nabby m. Capt. Wm. Vinton 1803,
and d. 1816 æ. 34, and he then m. her sister Clarissa 1817.—
Bass went to Philadelphia, is a portrait painter, and has a family
there.—Welcome not m.

3. Melville (s. of Dr. Josiah 2.) m. Sophia D. of Capt. Isaac
Whitman 1809, and had Cushing ; she d. 1826 æ. 42.—Cushing
is also m. and has a family.

PACKARD.—1. Samuel Packard and his wife and child
came from Windham, near Hingham, in England, in the ship
called "The Diligent of Ipswich, 133 passengers, John Martin
master," and settled in Hingham here 1638: he thence came to
W. B. and d. a. 1684, the date of his will; he was constable
1664, and licensed to keep an ordinary, or tavern, 1670 ; he had
Elizabeth, Samuel, Zacheus, Thomas, John, Nathaniel, Mary,
Hannah, Israel, Jael, Deborah, and Deliverance. Elizabeth m.
Thomas Alger of Easton 1665.—Thomas was here 1673, and
Israel was appointed Trooper 1671, and no farther account of
them.—Mary m. Richard Phillips of Weymouth.—Hannah m.
Thomas Randall.—Jael m. John Smith.—Deborah m. Samuel
Washburn.—Deliverance m. Thomas Washburn.—In the early
records both at Hingham and Bridgewater the name is written
PACKER, and was here formerly invariably pronounced so. The
name on the town Records was also sometimes written Peckar,
Pecker, Peckard, and Peckerd, but by the family has been gen-
erally written Packard.

2. Ensign Samuel (s. of Samuel 1.) m. Elizabeth D. of Mark
Lathrop, and had Samuel, Daniel, Joseph, Elizabeth, Mary, Su-
sanna ; his estate settled 1698. Susanna m. John Snell 1715.—
Mary m. Amos Snell 1700.

3. Zacheus (s. of Samuel 1.) m. Sarah D. of John Howard,
and had Israel 1680, Sarah 1682, Jonathan 1684, David 1687,
Solomon 1689, James 1691, Zacheus 1693, John 1695, Abiel
1699. He d. 1723. Sarah m. Capt. Josiah Edson 1704.

4. John (s. of Samuel 1.) lived at S. B. near the bridge,
which was called, after him, Packard's bridge, 1688, and since
called Pope's bridge : his estate was settled 1741 by his son
Joseph.—Wid. Packard d. 1761 very aged.

5. Nathaniel (s. of Samuel 1.) m. probably a D. of John Kingman, and had Samuel, Zechariah, George, Fearnot, Margaret,
Sarah, Lydia, Faithful, Hannah, Deliverance, Elizabeth, Mary,
Deborah ; his will 1720. Margaret m. John Washburn 1710.—
Lydia m. Jeremy Howell 1718.—Elizabeth m. John Hooper
1722.—Deborah m. Timothy Mitchell.—Sarah m. Thomas Hooper 1722 or Samuel Bliss 1723.—Faithful m. George Vaughn 1719.
—Mary m. Jo. Leonard 1721.—Deliverance Packard d. in S. B.
1776.

6. Samuel (s. of Samuel 2.) m. Elizabeth D. of Samuel Edson 1705, and had Samuel 1707, Bethiah, Paul 1714, Job 1716 :
he and she both d. 1716.—Bethiah m. Wright Bartlett 1731.

7. Daniel (s. of Samuel 2.) m. Mary D. of Isaac Harris 1713,
and had Sarah 1714, Mary 1716, Susanna 1718, Martha 1720,
Daniel 1722, Isaac 1724*, Nehemiah 1727 ; his will 1732. Sarah m. Zechariah Shaw 1733.—Mary m. James Allen 1732.—
Susanna m. David Orcutt 1734.—Martha m. Jeremiah Conant
1739.

8. Joseph (s. of Samuel 2.) m. Mary D. of John Willis 1723,
and had Joseph 1725, Mary 1729, John and others perhaps.—

Joseph m. Sarah D. of Capt. David Johnson 1748, and had Daniel 1749, Anna 1751, Elijah 1753, Abigail 1756, Bethiah 1758, Martha 1760, Job 1761, and was a soldier under Gen. Winslow 1755, and d. in Easton.—John m. Rachel Niles of E. 1762, and had Hannah 1764, Mary 1767, John 1769, Galen and Mercy 1771, Jazael 1774, and went to Chesterfield.—Mary Packard had Jane, bap. in W. B. 1756.—(See Joseph 17.)

9. Israel (s. of Zacheus 3.) and his wife Hannah had Seth 1703, Mehitabel 1705, Sarah 1707, Eliphalet 1708, Hannah 1710, Zerviah 1713, Israel 1717, Robert 1722. Israel Packard m. Susanna D. of Daniel Field 1735, 2d w. probably.—Mehitabel m. John Ames 1725, and Samuel West 1727, and was d. 1752.— Hannah m. a Phillips.—Zerviah m. Benjamin Washburn a. 1743.

10. Jonathan (s. of Zacheus 3.) m. Susanna D. of Joseph Hayward probably 1719, she d. 1722, and he m. a 2d w. Abigail, and had Jonathan 1724*, Susanna 1726, Jacob 1728, Jonathan 1730, Abigail 1735 : he d. a. 1750. Susanna m. Charles Snell 1745.— Abigail m. Jonathan Perkins Jr. 1752.

11. David (s. of Zacheus 3.) m. Hannah D. of John Ames 1712, and had David 1713, William 1715, Hannah 1718, Isaac 1720, Mary 1722, Ebenezer 1724, Abiah 1727, Mehitabel 1730, Jane 1734. He d. 1755 æ. 68; she 1767. Hannah m. Samuel Brett 1737.—Mary m. Daniel Richards 1740.—Mehitabel m. Simeon Brett 1748.—Jane m. Matthew Kingman 1755.

12. Solomon (s. of Zacheus 3.) m. Sarah D. of Samuel Lathrop 1715, who d. and he then m. Susanna D. of Samuel Kingman, and had Sarah 1719, Jacob 1720, Nathan 1722*, Susanna 1724, Joanna 1725, Martha 1727, Solomon 1729, Nathan 1733, Benjamin 1734, Zebulun 1736, Micah 1738; he m. Dorothy wid. of Mark Perkins perhaps 1760.—Sarah m. Isaac Fuller 1737.— Susanna m. Joseph Alden 1742.—Joanna m. Isaac Allen 1745.— Martha m. Isaac Alden Jr. 1755, and Israel Bailey 1760.—Benjamin m. Ruth D. of Nehemiah Leach 1762, and he and Micah went to Me.

13. Dea. James (s. of Zacheus 3.) m. Jemima D. of Joseph Keith 1722, and had James 1724, Keziah 1727, Jemima 1729, Rebecca 1732, Reuben 1737; he d. 1765 æ. 75. Keziah m. Nehemiah Lincoln 1748.—Jemima m. Ichabod Edson 1759.—Rebecca m. Luke Perkins 1749.

14. Zacheus (s. of Zacheus 3.) m. Mercy D. of Isaac Alden 1725, and had Eleazar 1727, Seth 1733, Simeon 1736, and Mercy; he d. 1775 æ. 82.—Mercy m. Ezra Warren a. 1757.

15. John (s. of Zacheus 3.) m. Lydia Tomson of Halifax, and had Lydia 1726, Abel 1729, Abigail 1733, John 1735, Barnabas 1738. He d. 1738 æ. 43. Lydia m. Edward Southworth 1750. —Abigail m. George Packard 1766.

16. Capt. Abiel (s. of Zacheus 3.) m. Sarah D. of John Ames 1723, and had Josiah 1723, Abiel 1728, d. 1759, Joshua 1730, Thomas 1732, Timothy 1735, Sarah 1737, Betty 1739, Daniel 1742, Eliab 1745, Benjamin 1749. He d. 1776 æ. 76. Sarah

m. Ebenezer Snell 1764.—Betty m. Jacob Edson 1759.—Experience, w. of Abiel Packard, d. in S. B. 1790, æ. 83.

17. Joseph (s. of John 4.) m. Susanna D. of Thomas Mitchell 1724, and had John, Joseph, Edward, Susanna, and perhaps Mary, Parnel, Judith and others; she d. 1756, he 1760. John m. Anna D. of Nathaniel Pratt 1760, and he and Joseph went to Brookfield; Joseph had a son Winslow, gra. Dartmouth 1777, and settled in the ministry.—Susanna m. William Allen 1748, and afterwards Isaac Allen and then Dea. Othniel Gilbert of Brookfield.—Mary perhaps m. Nathaniel Hayward Jr. 1762.—Parnel m. David Johnson 1751.—Judith m. Capt. Jona. Willis 1752.—It is difficult to distinguish this family from that of Joseph 8, and there may be some confusion in the accounts here given of them.

18. Samuel (s. of Nathaniel 5.) and his w. Anne, had Anne 1723, Mary 1725, Betty 1727, Samuel, Hepzibah, Caleb, and Joshua 1735, Chloe, Desire. Anne m. Elijah Edson 1741.—Mary m. Abiezer Edson 1744.—Betty m. Seth Dean 1748.—Hepzibah m. Seth Morton 1757.—David m. Martha Hartwell 1756, and had Chloe 1758, Caleb 1760, and he and his brother Caleb went to Pelham. Chloe m. Joseph Keith 1759.—Most of the family went to Pelham.—Desire m. David Clark or Luke Washburn 1763.—She who m. Clark was called of Easton.

19. Zechariah (s. of Nathaniel 5.) m. Abigail, D. of Richard Davenport, 1724, and had Elijah 1726, Abigail 1728, Nathaniel 1730, Nathan 1733. His will 1771.—Abigail m. Daniel Snell probably 1753.

20. George (s. of Nathaniel 5.) m. Mary, D. of Samuel Edson, 1728, and had George, Jonathan, Lydia, Rebecca, and Ichabod. He d.,and she m. Jonathan Mehurin 1740.—Lydia m. Seth Lathrop 1751.—Rebecca m. Jona. Chandler before 1754.

21. Samuel (s. of Samuel 6.) m. Susanna, D. of Samuel Kinsley, 1729, and had Charity 1733, Samuel 1834, Susanna 1736, Abijah 1740. Charity m. Seth Burr 1753.—Samuel went to Easton.—Susanna Packard m. Joseph Knapp 1760.—Susanna Packard m. Timothy Manly 1761.—Susanna Packard m. Seth Rickard also 1757.

22. Paul (s. of Samuel 6.) m. Susanna Joy of Hingham 1744. Paul Packard m. Sarah Bruce 1749, and had Josiah 1751.

23. Job (s. of Samuel 6.) and his w. Rachel had Job 1749*. She d. and he m. Keziah, D. of Thomas Wade, 1751, and he d. 1805.—Job Packard m. wid. Hannah Edson 1790.

24. Daniel (s. of Daniel 7.) m. Hannah Perkins 1765, and Daniel Packard m. Elizabeth Colony of Easton 1773.

25. Nehemiah (s. of Daniel 7.) m. Silence, D. of Samuel Edson, 1747, and had Silence 1750, who m. Seth Leonard 1769.—Wid. Silence m. Josiah Dunbar 1758.

26. Seth (s. of Israel 9.) m. Mercy Bryant, and had Sarah 1728, Lucy 1731, Mehitabel 1733, Mercy 1735, Isaac 1737, Mary 1739, Seth 1743, Joshua 1741, Abigail 1746, Abner 1749, Jona-

than 1751, Jerusha: he d. 1788, æ. 82. Sarah m. Samuel Cole
1752.—Lucy m. Ebenezer Edson 1751.—Mehitabel m. Barnabas
Howard Esq. 1755.—Mercy m. Thomas West 1756.—Mary m.
Simeon Alden 1763.—Abigail and Jerusha m. two brothers at
Dorchester by the name of Leeds.—Isaac went to Petersham.—
Seth m. Lois Leach 1764, and went to Roxbury.—Abner settled
at Conway.

27. Israel (s. of Israel 9.) m. Ruth D. of Richard Field, 1737,
and had 4 ss. and a D. who all d. young, and he d. 1752, and she
m. Joseph Ames 1754.

28. Robert (s. of Israel 9.) m. Lydia Titus 1749, and had Melzar 1751, Freelove 1753. He d. and the wid. m. Jesse Edson
1754.

29. Jacob (s. of Jonathan 10.) and his w. Deborah had Debo-
rah 1750, Anne 1752, Abigail 1754, Gooding 1756, Gamaliel 1758,
Jacob 1761, Jonathan 1764, Polly 1767, Job 1770. Deborah m.
Seth Bailey 1770.—Anne m. Benj. Sampson 1778.—Abigail m.
Joseph Bailey 1771.—Polly m. Calvin Snell 1785.—He m. wid.
Rachel Myrick of Eastham 1781, 2d w.—The family went to
the westward.

30. Jonathan (s. of Jonathan 10.) m. Martha, D. of Josiah
Williams, 1752, and had Althea 1753, Caleb 1759.

31. David (s. of David 11.) m. Mehitabel, D. of Benjamin
Richards 1737, and had Abiezer 1741, David 1741, Abraham
1749, Ephraim 1751. She d. 1767, he 1785, æ. 73. Abraham m.
Freelove Dyer 1774, and had Cyrus 1775, Relief 1777.—Ephraim
m. Sarah, D. of Josiah Packard, 1773, and he and Abraham
went westward.—Abiezer m. Mary Holbrook of Braintree 1764,
and had Mehitabel 1765, Mary 1767, Lydia 1769, Hannah 1772,
and went to St.

32. William (s. of David 11.) m. Sarah, D. of Benj. Richards,
1740, and had Amy 1741, Hannah 1743, William 1745, Lemuel
1747, Sarah 1750, Silvanus 1752, Keziah 1754, Matilda : he d.
1805, æ. 90. Amy m. Levi French 1760.—Hannah m. Philip
Reynolds 1765, and afterwards Enos Thayer 1782.—Sarah m.
Samuel Sturtevant 1769.—Keziah m. a Pierce.—Matilda m.
Capt. Zechariah Gurney 1783.—Silvanus m. Elizabeth Marston
1777, and had several Ds.

33. Capt. Isaac (s. of David 11.) m. Abigail, D. of Samuel
Porter of Abington, 1745, and had Isaac 1750, Abigail 1754 :
he d. 1792, æ. 72. Abigail m. Hon. Daniel Howard 1776.

34. Ebenezer (s. of David 11.) m. Sarah, D. of Mark Perkins, 1746, and had Alice 1747, Ebenezer 1749, Eunice 1750,
Jonas 1752, Adin 1754, Matthew 1756, Eliphalet 1758, Robert
1760, Joel 1762, Lot 1763, Noah, Joseph : he d. 1803, æ. 79 ; she
1810.—Alice m. Eliab Packard 1769.—Eunice m. Wm. Jamieson
1780.—Joel Esq. m. Harmony, D. of Matthew Kingman, 1785,
and went to Dartmouth, and had a s. Henry, who m. a Kelly,
and lives in N. Y., and it is said has no children : the father is
living with a 2d w.

35. Abiah (s. of David 11.) m. Phebe Paine 1758, and had
Abiah 1759, Levi 1761. She d. 1763, and he m. Eunice Howard
of Braintree 1764, and had Silas 1765, Phebe and Eunice 1767,
Howard 1768, Betsy, Hannah : he d. 1809, æ. 74. Phebe m.
Amzi Brett 1788.—Eunice m. Uriah Capen of St. 1797.—Betsy
m. Isaiah Packard 1792.—Hannah m. Zadock Perkins 1796, and
William Edson 1812.

36. Jacob (s. of Solomon 12.) m. Dorothy, D. of Mark Per-
kins, 1742, and had Jacob, Mark, Oliver, Asa, Hezekiah,
Rhoda, Dorothy, Phile (or Philibert) : he d. 1777, æ. 57. Asa
gra. H. U. 1783, and settled in the ministry at Marlborough.—
Hezekiah D. D., gra. H. U. 1787, and settled in the ministry at
Chelmsford, and afterwards in Me.—Rhoda m. Abijah Stowell
1771, and Dorothy m. James Richards 1777, both of Newton.—
Phile m. Henry Thayer 1783, and went to Winchester.

37. Solomon (s. of Solomon 12.) m. Hannah, D. of Israel
Bailey, 1760, and had Hannah 1764, Sally, Lucy, Solomon,
Mayhew. She d. 1776, æ. 40, and he m. Sarah, wid. of Abishai
Stetson, 1779, and had Cynthia 1780, Micah 1783, Nahum 1789 :
he d. 1807, æ. 77 ; she 1810, æ. 67.—Hannah m. Joel Edson
1789.—Sally d. 1830, æ. 61.—Lucy d. 1830, æ 57.—Cynthia m.
Levi Churchill 1799, and d. 1832, æ. 53.—Nahum m. Mercy Ford
of Marshfield 1817.

38. Nathan (s. of Solomon 12.) m. Martha, D. of Mark Perkins, and had Marlboro' 1763, Nathan 1767, Benaiah 1769. He
d. 1772, and she m. Thomas Packard 1779. Marlborough and
Benaiah went to Me.

39. Zebulun (s. of Solomon 12.) m. Rebeckah Richardson
1764, and had Susanna 1765, Zebulun 1768 : he d. 1769. The
wid. m. Silas Kinsley of Easton 1774.

40. James (s. of Dea. James 13.) m. Mary, D. of Ephraim
Thayer Jr. of Braintree, and had Content 1747, Eve 1750, Mary
1754, Luke 1756, James 1758, Sarah 1760, Israel 1765, Ephraim
1768. He removed westward.—Content m. Isaac Kingman
1769.—Eve m. Benjamin Robinson 1770.—Mary m. a Prince.—
Ephraim m. Charity, D. of Capt. David Packard 1790, and went
to Grafton.

41. Reuben (s. of Dea. James 13.) m. Anne Perkins 1759, and
had Ichabod 1760, Nehemiah 1762, Susanna 1763, Anne 1765.
He removed to Hebron, Me.—Ichabod m. Rachel, D. of Ephraim
Cole perhaps, 1786.—Reuben m. Jerusha Holbrook of Weymouth 1796.

42. Eleazar (s. of Zaccheus 14.) m. Mercy Richards, and
had Olive 1751, Noah 1752, Eleazar 1756. He went westward.

43. Simeon (s. of Zaccheus 14.) m. Mary, D. of Mark Per-
kins, 1761, and had Simeon 1762, d. in the army, æ. 20 ; Isaiah,
Zenas, Barnabas, Alden, Benjamin, Huldah, Mehitabel, Mary,
Olive, Patty. Huldah m. Howard Cary Esq. 1785.—Mary m.
Noah Packard 1790.—Olive m. David Ford 1794.—Patty m.
Capt. Nehemiah Lincoln 1802.—Barnabas m. Melatiah Packard

33

1794, and he, Alden, and Benjamin went to Me.—There was a Barnabas Packard d. in S. B. 1795, æ. 25.

44. Abel (s. of John 15.) m. Esther Porter 1751, and had Abel 1754, Esther 1756, Adam 1758, Lydia 1760, Mary 1764, Olive 1767, Theophilus 1769. This family went to Cummington.— Theophilus is a settled clergyman at Shelburne.

45. John (s. of John 15.) m. Sarah Hammond 1763, and had Azubah 1764, Sarah 1765, Rebeckah 1769. His w. d. 1773, and he m. a Vinson, and went to Plainfield.

46. Barnabas (s. of John 15.) m. Sarah Ford, and had Barnabas 1764, Molly 1766, Pollycarpus 1768, Bartimeus 1769, Cyrus 1771. The parents went to Cummington, and had 2 sons there, John and Philander.

47. Josiah (s. of Capt. Abiel 16.) m. Sarah, D. of Thomas Ames, 1747, and had Susanna 1749, Sarah 1751, Mary 1753, Josiah, Abiel, Shepard, Edward, Ames, Betsy, Anna. He d. 1793, æ. 70. Susanna m. Samuel Sturtevant, and then John Bicknell —Sarah m. Ephraim Packard 1773.—Mary m. Samuel Brett 1778.—Betsy m. Dea. James Perkins.—Anna m. Seth Snow 1795.—Abiel and Edward went to Hebron, Me.—Abiel Packard m. Hannah Harris 1794.

48. Joshua (s. of Capt. Abiel 16.) m. Mehitabel, D. of Samuel Alden, 1755, and had Caleb 1758, Joshua 1759, Ralph, Lebbeus, Mehitabel. This family all went to Me.

49. Thomas (s. of Capt. Abiel 16.) m. Mary, D. of Henry Howard perhaps, 1756, and had Parmenas 1757, Silence 1760, Mary 1762, Thomas 1764, Zibia 1766, Elijah 1769, Cyrus 1772, Daniel 1776. He m. wid. Martha Packard 1779. Silence m. Daniel Howard.—Mary m. John Robinson 1781.—Zibia m. Jacob Packard 1789.—Elijah m. Nabby Packard 1793.—Cyrus m. Kezia, D. of Matthew Kingman 1795.—Daniel m. Nancy, D. of Maj. James Keith, 1796.—Elijah and Daniel went to Pelham.

50. Timothy (s. of Capt. Abiel 16.) m. Sarah Alden, and had Bethuel 1760, Calvin 1762, Luther 1764, Sarah 1767, Timothy 1769, Perez 1771, Josiah Edson 1776 : he d. 1780, æ. 48. Sarah m. Elisha Eames.—Bethuel m. Rebecca Peterson of Dux. 1783, and went to Me.—Calvin went to Easton : his w. Betsy : they had Sally 1786, Zibeon 1789, Tilson 1792.—Timothy m. Aholibama Curtis 1790, and he, Perez, Luther, and Josiah Edson went westward.—Luther m. Abigail Thomas 1787.—Perez m. Mercy Thomas 1792.

51. Daniel (s. of Captain Abiel 16.) m. Hannah Perkins, 1765, and had Hannah 1766, Abigail 1768, Daniel 1770, Rhoda 1772, and went westward. Daniel m. Zibeah, D. of Gain Robinson perhaps, and went to Pelham.

52. Eliab (s. of Capt. Abiel 16.) m. Alice, D. of Ebenezer Packard 1769, and had Eliab 1770, Alice 1771, and went westward. Eliab m. Hannah Shaw of Abington 1792.

53. Benjamin (s. of Capt. Abiel 16.) m. Lurania, D. of Pela-

tiah Phinney 1775: left no children : gave his estate to Capt. Adin Packard.

54. Edward (s. of Joseph 17.) m. Ruth, D. of Elisha Bonney, of Pembroke, and had Chloe and Leah. His w. d. 1764, and he m. Rebecca, sister of Ichabod Pope of Dartmouth, now Fairhaven, 1766, and had Rebeckah, Edward, Jacob, Elnathan, John, Deborah, Susanna. Chloe and Leah went to Brookfield.— Rebeckah m. Seth Gurney 1788, and all the others with their parents went to Minot, Me.

55. Ichabod (perhaps s. of George 20.) was a soldier with Gen. Winslow 1755, m. Ruth, D. of James Allen, 1757, and had Mary 1758, Nehemiah 1760, Ichabod 1763, Lydia 1766, Isaac 1769: he went to Oakham. Ichabod m. Rachel, D. of Ephraim Cole, 1786.

56. Samuel (s. of Samuel 18.) m. Elizabeth, D. of Joseph Carver, 1757, and had Betty 1758, Silvia 1760. He probably m. Mary Washburn 1761 for his 2d wife.

57. Rev. Elijah (s. of Zechariah 19.) gra. H. U. 1750, and settled in the ministry at Plymouth 1754, and afterwards went to Marlborough : his wife Mary Rider: he had Abigail, Benjamin 1760, Elijah 1762, Mary 1765. Abigail m. Dr. Simeon Dunbar 1781.—Mary m. Jesse Fobes 1795.—Benjamin m. Mehitabel, D. of Eliab Fobes, 1784, and went to Vermont.

58. Nathaniel (s. of Zechariah 19.) m. Sarah, D. of Jonathan Snow, 1753, had Zadock 1755, Ichabod 1757. She d. 1758, and he m. Anna Sloan 1758, and had David 1760, Sarah 1762, Zechariah, Nathaniel, and perhaps others. Ichabod m. Rachel, D. of Job Chamberlin 1780.—David m. Mara Robinson 1785. They all went to Lebanon, N. H.

59. Capt. Nathan (s. of Zechariah 19.) m. Lydia, D. of Ephraim Jackson, 1758, and had Oliver, Elijah, Nathan, Ransom, Perez, Sullivan, Jonas, Sarah, Abigail, Lydia, Olive, Roxana. He d. 1798, æ. 65. Sarah m. Zepheniah Lathrop 1779.—Abigail m. Jonas Howard 1784.—Lydia m. Bernard Clapp 1793.—Olive m. Sam'l Dickerman 1799.—Roxana m. Sam'l Randall of Easton 1805.—Oliver m. Mary, D. of Josiah Dunbar 1785, and Ransom m. Abigail Thrasher 1797, and both went to the State of New York.—Nathan m. Polly Manly 1815.—Perez m. Elizabeth Reynolds 1803.—Sullivan m. Lucy, D. of Ephraim Jackson 1805.

60. George (s. of George 20.) m. Abigail Esty 1760, and had Amasa 1761, Philip 1763. His w. d. 1765, and he m. Abigail, D. of John Packard 1766, and had George 1767, Zadock 1768, Zebedee 1770. Philip m. Patty Edson 1786.

61. Jonathan (s. of Seth 26.) m. Susanna Packard or Alger 1778, and had Israel 1779, Ruel 1780, Othniel 1786, Asa 1791, Albe 1793, Isaac 1796, Betsy 1799.—Ruel and Albe went to Randolph.—Othniel went to N. H.—Isaac went to Mid'o.—Betsy m. a Watson.

62. Abijah (s. of Samuel 21.) m. Ann Fobes of Easton 1767, and had Abijah 1768, Simeon 1770, Charles 1772, Gamaliel 1775,

Abijah went to Dartmouth ; m. Hannah, D. of Henry Smith, and
had Henry S., now Representative of the town, Ann Maria, and
Charles Fobes. Henry m. Mary Pierce, and has William Henry,
Mary Ann, Franklin S., and Charles A.—Ann Maria m. Elihu
Wood.—Charles F. went to Rehoboth, then to Boston, then to
N. Y., and d. there : only one child, a D., now living.—Simeon
m. Hannah, D. of Ezra Edson, 1796, and had Simeon, who went
away, and is probably d.: the mother, a wid., is now living.—
Gamaliel went to Dartmouth ; m. Susan Joy, and had Susan,
Louisa and Amy, all now living single.

63. Caleb (s. of Jonathan 30.) m. Sarah, D. of Nathan Howard Esq. 1782, and had Caleb 1783. He d. 1783, æ. 24, and she
m. Caleb Loring of Plympton 1802 : she d. 1834. Caleb m. Sally,
D. of Josiah Packard 1805.

64. Capt. David (s. of David 31.) m. Joanna, D. of Ephraim
Jackson 1764, and had Charity 1770, Abel, John, Olive, Martha,
Mary. He d. of small-pox 1786, æ. 44. Charity m. Ephraim
Packard 1790.—Olive m. Holmes Tilson 1797.—Patty m. Bar-
zillai Field 1794.—Polly m. a Rice.—Abel and John went west-
ward.—Wid. Joanna m. Jona. Hayden of Grafton 1807.

65. William (s. of William 32.) m. Hannah, D. of Nathaniel
Reynolds 1769, and had Silton 1770, Nancy 1772, Eliphaz, William. She d., and he m. Mary Wales 1784, and had Ambrose,
Cyrus, Charles, Hannah, Polly, Matilda, Sarah. Eliphaz went
to Milton.—William went to St.

66. Lemuel Esq. (s. of William 32.) m. Sarah Hunt of Abington 1774, and had Lemuel 1775, Sally 1777, Micah 1780, John
1782, Arza 1784, David 1787, Silvanus 1789, Martin 1791, Oren
1793, Isaac 1796. He d. 1822, æ. 75 : his w. d. 1825. Lemuel
d. in Boston 1822, æ. 47.—Sally m. Thomas Cary 1798.—Micah
m. Lucinda Hartshorn of Walpole, and had Sarah Ann 1811,
Adeline 1813, Catharine 1814, Harriet 1816.—John Esq. m.
Silence, D. of Parmenas Packard, and had John 1806, David
and Jonathan 1809, Lemuel 1814.—Arza m. Abi, D. of Abijah
Knapp, 1812, and had Arza 1813, Edwin 1816.—David m. Susanna, D. of Mark Perkins 1810.—Silvanus, and Martin who m.
a Powers, went to Boston.—Isaac m. Sally Packard 1821.

67. Isaac (s. of Capt. Isaac 33.) m. Mary Atwood of Eastham
1776, and had Isaac 1778, and d. 1778 ; and his wid. m. Daniel
Cooley Esq. of Amherst 1796. Isaac m. a Cobb of Boston, and
had 2 Ds., and removed to N. York, and both of his Ds. are m.
there. One m. the Hon. Dudley Selden.

68. Dea. Ebenezer (s. of Ebenezer 34.) m. Mary, D. of Nath'l
Reynolds, 1774, and had Mehitabel 1774, Philip 1776, Mary
1778. His wife d., and he m. wid. Content Harlow 1781, and
had Sarah 1781, Ebenezer 1783, Silvester 1785, Rhoda 1788,
Ansel 1789, Charles 1792, Content. Sally m. Matthew Randall
1802, Content m. Benja. Southworth 1819.—Mehitabel m. Walter Ames 1796.—Wid Content m. Japhet Beal 1803.—Ebenezer
m. Zerviah Phinney 1806.

69. Jonas (s. of Ebenezer 34.) m. Mehitabel, D. of Samuel Brett, 1777, and had John, Jonas 1782, Moses 1786, Hannah 1787, Lucinda 1790, David 1792, Sibil 1796, Eunice, Joel, Mehitabel. Lucinda m. Capt. David Ames 1816.—Eunice m. Josiah Brett 1812.—Mehitabel m. a Jamieson.—Jonas removed to Maine.—Joel is d.

70. Adin (s. of Ebenezer 34.) m. Keziah, D. of Pelatiah Phinney, 1780, and had Lucy 1781, Adin, Susanna, Sally. She d. 1839, æ. 86.—Lucy m. Atherton Wild of Braintree 1808.—Susanna m. Ephraim Cole 1808.—Sally m. Isaac Packard 1821.— Capt. Adin m. Sally Horton 1806, and went to Merrimack.

71. Matthew (s. of Ebenezer 34.) m. Keziah, D. of Luke Perkins, 1781, and had Nehemiah, Eliphalet, Matthew, Keziah : he d. 1795, or before. Nehemiah m. Chloe, and Eliphalet m. Abigail, Ds. of Nathan Snell, 1807 and 1814, and both went to Me.

72. Dea. Eliphalet (s. of Ebenezer 34.) m. Lydia, D. of Wm. Barrell 1782, and had Robert 1784, Ruth 1786, Bela 1793, Lydia 1795. He went to Me., and had afterwards two wives, a Reed, and Anna Thayer 1800, wid. of David Thayer: she was a French, and had Betsy, Mary, and Esther.—Ruth m. Dr. Samuel W. Thayer.—Dea. Packard d. 1819, æ. 61.

73. Capt. Robert (s. of Ebenezer 34.) m. Ruth, D. of Wm. Barrell 1782, and Sally Perkins 1788, and had Ruth 1789, Huldah 1791, Patty 1793, Olive 1795. His w. d. and he m. Sarah, D. of Joseph Hayward, 1798. He had also Robert, Isaac, Ebenezer, Sally, Silvia, Almira, Mary.—Ruth m. Martin Southworth 1811.—Huldah m. Adam Capen 1816.—Patty m. Theron Ames 1816.—Olive m. Newton Shaw 1818.—Robert m. Betsy, D. of Oliver Howard.

74. Lot (s. of Ebenezer 34.) m. Mary Nelson of New Bedford 1791, and had Polly Nelson 1793, and went to Me.

75. Noah (s. of Ebenezer 34.) m. Polly, D. of Simeon Packard, 1791, and had Mehitabel 1791, Nancy 1792, Robie 1794, and went to Me.

76. Joseph (s. of Ebenezer 34.) m. Lusanna Bates 1794, and had Harmony 1795, and went to Me.

77. Abiah (s. of Abiah 35.) m. Mary French 1788, and had Chloe 1789, Mary 1791, Anna 1792, Lydia 1795.

78. Levi (s. of Abiah 35.) m. Ruth Snow of Eastham 1789, and had Davis 1790, Levi 1793, Phebe 1795, Heman, Josiah.— Davis m. Sarah, D. of Joseph Ford 1813, and went to New Salem.—Phebe m. Martin Kingman 1816.—Levi gra. B. U. 1821.

79. Silas Esq. (s. of Abiah 35.) m. Chloe, D. of Nathan Willis, 1789, and had Silas, Charles, Chloe, Abigail. Silas m. a Cobb of Boston.—Charles m. Charlotte, D. of Capt. Thomas Thompson 1818.—Chloe m. Thomas Wales Jr. 1811.—Abigail m. David Cobb, and is d.

80. Howard (s. of Abiah 35.) m. Jane Capen of St. 1799, and had Eunice 1799, Jane 1804, Charlotte 1810, Susanna Capen 1810.

81. Jacob (s. of Jacob 36.) m. Rebecca, D. of John French, 1774, and had Abigail 1775, and went to Warwick.—Jacob Packard of Warwick m. Hannah Kingman 1806.—Wid. Rebecca m. Charles Snell 1807.

82. Mark (s. of Jacob 36.) m. Hannah, D. of William Shaw, 1774, and had Samuel 1775, Jennet 1777, Phile 1779, Dan 1781, Thirza, Sophia, Hannah, Mark. He went to Winchester.—Jennet m. Phineas Paul of Quincy 1801.—Dan m. Martha, D. of Abiel Edson 1804.

83. Oliver (s. of Jacob 36.) m. Relief, D. of Ichabod Edson, 1777, and had Vashti 1778, Jacob 1780, Jesse 1783.

84. Mayhew (s. of Solomon 37.) m. Clarissa, D. of Ephraim Jackson, 1801, and had Hannah 1802, Salome 1804.

85. Micah (s. of Solomon 37.) m. Susan (or Sarah) Whitmarsh 1812, and had Abiezer Whitmarsh 1814.

86. James (s. of James 40.) m. Jemima, D. of Ephraim Churchill, 1778, and went to Norway, Me., and had Keziah 1779, who m. a Bump, and lived in Otisfield, Me., Mary 1781, James 1783, Ephraim 1787.

87. Isaiah (s. of Simeon 43.) m. Betsy, D. of Abiah Packard, 1792, and had Hezekiah 1793, Zibeon 1795, Simeon 1797, Lucius 1801, Betsy Howard 1804. Hezekiah m. Matilda, D. of Zechariah Gurney 1820.—Zibeon m. a Bicknell and went to A. Simeon m. a Kingman.

88. Zenas (s. of Simeon 43.) m. Deborah, D. of Ebenezer Thayer of Braintree, 1793, and had Deborah 1795, Charlotte 1796, Zenas 1798, Hosea 1800, Rachel 1803, Benjamin Alden 1806, Mary Perkins 1808, Lorenzo Emerson 1810, Horatio 1813, Lydia Thayer 1815. Deborah m. Samuel Holmes 1813.—Charlotte m. Joseph Wild of Braintree 1817.—Zenas m. Jerusha, D. of Isaac Horton, 1820, and had Jerusha, Betsy French, Benjamin, Ezekiel Reed, and Hermon.—Hosea m. Roxana Holmes 1818, and had Celia, Hosea, Roxana, Ebenezer and Jerome Henry.—Benjamin A. m. Rhoda Packard, and had Benjamin Winslow and Andrew Franklin.—Mary P. m. William Lewis.

89. Josiah (s. of Josiah 47.) m. Rebecca Perkins 1783, and had Luke, Abiel, Sally, Rebecca. Abiel m. Abigail, D. of John Harris, 1815.—Sally m. Caleb Packard 1805.—Rebecca m. Benjamin Kingman 1817.

90. Ames (s. of Josiah 47.) m. Susannah Joy 1797, and had William 1797, Nancy 1799, Susanna 1801, Betsy 1803, Josiah 1805, Bathsheba 1808, Charles 1810. William m. Lucy Quincy Norton of Abington 1820.

91. Capt. Parmenas (s. of Thomas 49.) m. Martha, D. of Thomas Reynolds, 1778, and had Ambrose 1778, Parmenas 1782, Galen 1786, Apollos 1788, Susanna 1790, Silence 1792, Roland 1796, Gideon H. 1798, Royal 1802. Apollos m. Sophia, D. of Amzi Brett 1811.—Susanna m. Barna. Thayer of Braintree 1806. Silence m. Capt. John Packard 1814.—Roland m. a Dyer.

92. Thomas (s. of Thomas 49.) m. Joanna, D. of Ichabod

Edson 1788, and had Azor 1790, Austin 1801. He d. 1814.—
Azor m. Nancy, D. of Col. Caleb Howard, 1815.—Austin gra. B.
U. 1821, and is an Attorney in W. B.

93. Elijah (s. of Rev. Elijah 57.) m. Keziah, D. of Capt.
John Ames, 1783, and had Mary, Abigail, and Susanna. He d., and
she then m. Benjamin Robinson 1798. Mary m. Benjamin Robinson Jr. 1809.—Abigail m. Charles Marcy of Plymouth 1812.—
Susanna m. a Ruggles at the westward, and had a D. Susanna,
who m. Isaac S. Washburn.

94. Zadock (s. of Nathaniel 58.) m. Martha, D. of Henry
Howard probably 1779, and had Selah 1779, who m. Pelham
Bradford 1797 and d., Reuel 1782, Molly 1784, Sarah 1787,
Holder 1789, Preston and Pardon 1792, Zadock 1795, Martha
1796. She d. 1799, æ. 40, and he m. a 2d w. Rebecca, and had
Rebecca 1800, Luther 1802, Selah 1804, Jerusha 1807, William
1811.—Mary (Molly) m. Silvanus Conant perhaps 1808.—Sarah
m. Elkanah Billings perhaps 1809.

95. Elijah (s. of Nathan 59.) m. Susanna, D. of Japhet Beal,
1789, and had Lewis 1789, Libeus 1791, Lydia 1793, Isaac 1795,
Elijah 1797, Clara 1799, Patience 1801, Susanna 1803, Nathan
1806, Sophronia 1808, Damson 1811. Lewis m. Betsy Crane
1808.—Libeus m. Minerva, D. of Daniel Alger, 1812, and had
Eliza Stetson 1812, Maria Pickering 1816.—Lydia m. Samuel
Codding of Mansfield 1814.—Isaac m. Sally, D. of Robert Packard perhaps, 1821.—Clara m. Sam'l Dickerman perhaps 1822.

96. Israel (s. of Jonathan 61.) m. Susanna, D. of Josiah Edson, 1801, and had Josiah 1802, Melvin 1804, Sidney 1806, Liberty 1808, Arvilla 1810, Israel 1813, Alpheus 1815, Henry,
Susanna.

97. Asa (s. of Jonathan 61.) m. Susanna Leach 1811, and had
Abigail 1812, Geo. W. 1814, Eugenia Maria 1815, Lucinda 1819.

98. Sihon (s. of William 65.) m. Abigail Scott of Dedham
1794, and had Joseph, Oren, Sihon, Isaac, Washburn, John,
Nathaniel, David, Betsy, Mary. Oren m. Sally Skinner of
Mansfield 1821.—Isaac m. Laura, D. of Daniel Bryant of E. B.
David lives in Boston.

99. John (s. of Jonas 69.) m. Martha, D. of William French,
1802, and had Josiah 1803, Mary F. 1805, Almira 1806, Philo
F. 1808, Sidney 1811. She d., and he m. Lydia Drake 1817.

100. Samuel (s. of Mark 82.) m. Mehitabel, D. of Abiel Harris, 1799, and had Francis 1800, Harriet 1803, Hiram 1805,
Mary 1808, Hannah 1810, Lucius 1812, Mehitabel 1815.

101. Capt. Luke (s. of Josiah 89.) m. Lucinda, D. of Samuel
Battles, 1806, and had Marcus 1808, Nelson 1810, Eliza Dyer
1813, Josiah 1816.

102. Ambrose (s. of Parmenas 91.) m. Esther White 1805,
and had Lucius Sumner 1808, Esther White 1809, Elbridge
Gerry 1811, Martha 1814, Ambrose 1816.

103. Galen (s. of Capt. Parmenas 91.) m. Mary, D. of Isaac
Horton, 1809, and had Edward 1811*, Willard 1812, Mary 1815.

Anne Packard m. a Sampson.—Betty m. Jonathan Snow 1761.—Rebecca m. James Perkins 1783.—Thomas m. Martha Perkins 1789.—Ephraim m. Polly Leach 1789.—Abigail m. Jonathan Howard 1794.—Sally m. Frederick Reed Jr. of Rehoboth 1797.—Wid. Hannah m. Samuel Kimball of E. 1797.— Salmon m. Freelove Niles 1795.—Melatiah m. Barnabas Packard 1794.—Jemima m. Eben'r Phillips, both of E. 1802.—Mary m. Silvanus Conant 1808.—Julia m. Ethan Howard of E. 1814.— Isaac m. Mary Jones Foster of Hr. 1816.—Susannah m. Albert Remington of A. 1820.—Marcus of E. m. Lucy French of E. B. 1821.—Wid. Deliverance d. in S. B. 1790, æ. 88: she was D. of Wm. Orcutt Jr., and first m. Capt. Joseph Washburn : Barnabas d. in S. B. 1795, æ. 25.—Experience, wife of Abiel Packard, d. in S. B. 1790, æ. 83.—Sarah m. Wm. Pool 1795.—Isaac Porter (s. of Joseph) m. a Packard.—Wid. Susanna Packard d. 1773, æ. 89.

PARRIS.—Thomas Parris of London came to Long Island, N. Y., 1683; thence removed to Newbury, Ms., 1685, and to Pembroke 1697 : his father was John, a dissenting minister of Ugborough, near Plymouth, England, whose father was Thomas, a merchant of London, who had a brother a merchant and planter of great wealth, who d. in Barbadoes 1660. (See Deane's Scituate.) Thomas, first above named, had a s. Thomas born at Pembroke 1701 ; m. Hannah, D. of Matthew Gannett of Scituate, 1724, and had Thomas 1725, Elkanah, Benjamin, Matthew. The father d. 1786. Thomas (last named) m. Rebeckah, D. of Benjamin Hayward Jr., and settled within the borders of E. B., and had Benjamin 1753, Thomas 1758. Thomas, the father, d. 1797, æ. 72 ; she 1806, æ. 77. Thomas, the son, perished in a great snow storm 1777.

2. Benjamin (s. of Thomas 1.) m. Sarah, D. of his uncle Benjamin of Halifax 1774. She d. 1787, æ. 36 : he then m. a 2d w. Lydia, and had Betsy 1789, Thomas 1792, Oren 1796. The father was drowned 1817, æ. 66 ; his w. d. 1824, æ. 69. Thomas m. Clarissa, D. of Barza Kingman, 1815.—Oren m. Eunice, wid. of William Wildy and D. of Barza Kingman, and both live in E. B., and have families.—Betsy m. Otis Hayward 1804.

Elkanah (brother of Thomas 1.) m. Grace Mott of Scituate 1761, and has a large family at Williamstown.

Benjamin (brother of Thomas 1.) married Millescent, D. of Josiah Keith of Easton 1753, and had Samuel 1755, Matthew 1757, Josiah, Martin, Dan, Sarah and others probably. This man lived awhile in the border of Halifax, near his brother Thomas, but d. in Pembroke.—Samuel Esq. m. Sarah Pratt of Mid'o, and settled in Hebron, Me., and is father of Albion Keith Parris, late Governor of Me.—Matthew m. Mercy Tomson of Halifax 1780, and d. in Me., and was father of Alexander Esq. of Boston.—Josiah m. Experience, D. of Nath'l Lowden of E. B. 1788, and settled in Me., and has a son Virgil, an Attorney and Member of Congress.—Martin gra. B. U. 1790, and was a Minister of Marshfield, and d. 1839.—Dan has a family in Halifax.

Thomas and Mary Parris, of Cambridge, had Thomas 1641, Mary 1643.—John Parris, of Charlestown 1645, gave a mortgage of his houses in Barbadoes 1650 to secure £650 to be paid in Lombard street at the Green Dragon, London.—Samuel and Elizabeth Parris had Thos. 1681, Elizabeth 1682, Susanna 1687. Thomas and Mary Parris, of Boston, had Mary 1686*, Mary 1687.—Thomas Parris at Duxbury 1710.

PERKINS.—David Perkins (from Beverly) settled in S. B. before 1688: was the first Representative of the town to the Gen'l Court in Boston after the union of the two colonies in 1692; m. Martha, D. of John Howard, 1699, and had John 1700, Mary 1702, Martha 1704, Elizabeth 1707, Susanna 1709, David 1711, Jonathan 1714, Abraham 1716, and Sarah: his w. d. 1735; he d. 1736, æ. 83. Mary m. Gideon Washburn.—Martha m. Dr. Joseph Byram 1724.—Elizabeth m. Solomon Leonard.—Susanna m. Samuel Allen 1733.—Sarah m. Jabez Carver 1742.—Nathan b. before he came here, and Thomas b. here 1688, were his sons by a former wife probably. He built the first mill at the place where Lazell, Perkins & Co. have now a large manufacturing establishment, 1694. He lived on the Boston road, near where the road turns to go to the works.

2. Nathan (s. of David 1.) m. Martha, D. perhaps of Solomon Leonard, 1709, and had Nathan 1710, Solomon 1712, Timothy 1715, Martha 1717, James 1720, Silence 1723. He d., and the widow m. Isaac Hayward 1728.—Martha m. Samuel Edson 3d 1738.

3. Thomas (s. of David 1.) m. Mary, D. perhaps of James Washburn 1717, and had Mary 1718, Hepzibah 1720, Thomas 1722, Ebenezer 1727, Francis 1729: she d. 1750, he 1761. Mary m. Josiah Hayward 1742, Hepzibah m. Eleazar Carver 1746, and Ebenezer Keith 1759.

4. David (s. of David 1.) m. Alice, D. of John Leach, 1738, and had David 1739, Zephaniah 1742, John 1746, Robert 1750, Asa 1754. Zepheniah m. Mary Ford 1766.

5. Jonathan (s. of David 1.) m. Bethiah, D. of Nath'l Hayward 1738, and settled in E. B. and had Jonathan 1739, Elizabeth 1742, Bethiah 1746. His wife d., and he m. Priscilla Bourne, and had Bourne 1758: the father d. 1796, æ. 82; she 1813, æ. 92. Jonathan was badly burnt in a forge, and became entirely blind: he probably m. Mary Hamlin 1765.—Elizabeth m. Consider Bearce of Halifax 1761. Bourne d. of the small-pox 1778, æ. 20.

6. Abraham (s. of David 1.) m. Mary, D. of Eleazar Carver, 1743, and had Abraham 1750, Mary 1752: he d. 1807, æ. 90.—Mary m. Caleb Cary 1778, and d. 1840.

7. Nathan (s. of Nathan 2.) m. Sarah, wid. of Nathan, or D. of Solomon Pratt, 1752, and had Phebe 1753, Joanna 1755,

Nathan 1758, Lucy 1760, Charles, Deborah. Deborah m. John Conant 1772.—Perhaps Charles and Deborah were children of a former wife.

8. Solomon (s. of Nathan 2.) m. Lydia, D. of Jonathan Sprague, 1733, and had Joseph and Benjamin 1735, Solomon 1737, Lydia 1741, Eliab 1743. Joseph m. Martha Hayward 1761.—Benjamin m. Hepzibah Washburn of Mid'o, 1761.—Solomon was in the French war, 1755, under Gen. Winslow, and m. Sarah Edson 1760.—Lydia m. Abner Sears of Mid'o, 1762.

9. Timothy (s. of Nathan 2.) m. Susanna, D. of Samuel Washburn 1736, and had Nathaniel. Timothy Perkins m. Zipporah, D. of William Washburn 1753.—Nathaniel m. Mary, D. of Joseph Alger, 1775.

10. James (s. of Nathan 2.) m. Bethiah Dunham 1742, and had Martha 1743, James 1746, Barnabas 1752, Ezra 1756, Seth 1762. Martha m. John Porter Jr. 1764.

11. Thomas (s. of Thomas 3.) m. Mary, D. of Solomon Pratt, 1748, and had William 1748, Mary 1750, Sarah 1752, Enoch 1754, Thomas 1756, Theodore 1758, Deborah 1761, Cyrus 1767: his will and d. 1773; she d. 1778. William m. Elizabeth, D. of Eleazar Cary, 1777, and d. 1778, and she m. Solomon Snow 1780.—Mary m. Oliver Carver 1774.—Sarah m. Eli Hudson 1776.—Thomas gra. H. U. 1779, and d. young in Kentucky.— Theodore m. Martha, D. of Nathan Conant 1783, and had Thomas 1785. She afterwards m. Rev. William Conant.— Deborah m. Benjamin Edson 1782.—Cyrus m. Sally Howard 1787, and went to Vt.

12. Ebenezer (s. Thomas 3.) m. Experience Holmes 1751, and had Ebenezer 1752, Mary, Holmes 1757, Hepzibah 1759, Susanna 1764, and Nancy: he d. 1770. Holmes moved away.— Susanna not m.—Nancy m. Rufus Leach 1798.

13. Francis (s. of Thomas 3.) m. Susanna, D. of Dea. Robert Waterman of Halifax, 1762, and had Susanna and Robert. She d. 1770, and he m. Philibert, D. of Ephraim Keith, 1775, and had Jacob, Francis, Philibert. He d. 1783. Susanna m. Enoch Perkins 1783.—Robert d. 1793, æ. 29.—Philibert not m.—Francis m. Polly Leonard 1815, and had Francis and one other son, and both went eastward. He m. a 2d w.

14. Charles (s. of Nathan 7.) m. Abigail, D. of Perez Waterman, 1762, and had Olive, Sene, Charles, Philip, and others perhaps: he removed to the westward. Olive m. Nehemiah Edson 1783.—Sene m. Ezra Edson Jr. 1782.

15. Dea. James (s. of James 10.) m. Mary Hooper 1771, and had Bethiah 1772, Rufus 1774, Levi 1776, Martha Porter and Polly. He d. 1795, æ. 75; she 1803, æ. 80. Bethiah m. Dr. Shubael Lovell of Barnstable 1797.—Levi H. Perkins m. Bethiah Dunbar 1804.—Martha P. m. Phineas Blake of Canton 1804.— Polly m. and went westward.

16. Enoch (s. of Thomas 11.) m. Susanna, D. of Francis Perkins, 1783, and had Humphrey 1786, Moses 1788, Enoch

1791, Susanna 1793, Robert 1796, Sarah 1798, Harry 1800 : he
went to Me.
17. Ebenezer (s. of Ebenezer 12.) m. Mary, D. of Solomon
Pratt, 1782, and had Daniel, Solomon, Thomas, Aaron, a Baptist Minister in N. Y.; Ornan, Ebenezer, Simeon, Ozias, went
to Hanson, Minerva, Mary. Simeon m. Sally W., D. of Timo.
Hayward.—Daniel m. Mehitabel Robinson of Taunton 1809,
and d., and she m. Charles Daniels 1814.—Mary m. in Boston.
Minerva m. Allen Edson 1815.—Thomas m. Betsy Munroe 1819.
Ornan m. Betsy Crooker of P. 1818.
18. Jacob (s. of Francis 13.) m. Mary Thomas of Pem. 1808,
and had Mary, Marcia, Jacob, David gra., B. U. 1834, Sally
Keith, Edith, Ellen, Robert, Nathaniel. Mary m. Calvin Pratt
of Mid'o.—Maria m. Thos. Washburn.—Jacob, Sally Keith, and
Edith all d. 1838.—Mary the mother d. 1839.
19. Rufus (s. of Dea. James 15.) m. Rebecca, D. of Thomas
Johnson, 1797, and had Rebecca J. 1799, Cassandra L. 1802,
Huldah A. 1804, Rufus S. 1807, Maria S. 1809, James T. 1813,
Lucy Ann 1818. He went westward.
20. Solomon (s. of Ebenezer 17.) m. Clarissa, D. of Dyer
Robinson 1813, and had Henry 1814, Charles R. 1816, William
Franklin 1818, George Sproat 1820, Ebenezer 1826, Mary and
Martha 1828, Saba 1829, Alfred Holmes 1830.
21. Rev. Daniel Perkins, born in Topsfield, Essex Co. gra.
H. U. 1717, settled in the ministry in W. B., Oct. 4, 1721, m.
Anne Foster of Charlestown, and had Anne 1724, Richard 1730.
She d., and he m. madam Hancock, mother of the Governor : he
d. Sept. 29, 1782, æ. 86. Anne m. the Rev. Matthew Bridge of
Framingham 1747, and afterwards the Rev. Mr. Harrington of
Lancaster.
22. Dr. Richard (s. of the Rev. Daniel 20.) gra. H. U. 1748,
was a Physician, m. Mary, D. of his mother-in-law, and sister of Governor Hancock, 1760, and had Daniel 1761, Mary
1763, Nancy 1764, Richard 1766, Sarah 1767, John Hancock
1769, Lydia Henchman 1770, Elizabeth 1771, William 1773,
Lucy 1775, Foster 1777, George Washington 1778. She d. 1779,
he then m. Mary Hunt of Watertown 1781 : he d. Oct. 16, 1813,
æ. 83. Mary m. Dr. Simeon Dunbar 1804 : his 2d w.—Nancy
not m.—Richard was a Physician; removed to Whitestown.—
Sarah m. a Hughes of Boston, left no children.—John H. m.
Vina, D. of Edward Lathrop, 1793, was a Physician, had a D.
Mary Lathrop 1797, and removed to Whitestown.—Lydia H. m.
Samuel Spear 1795, and had a son Samuel who gra. H. U. 1817,
and d. at S. Carolina (was drowned) in youth ; she d., and he
m. her sister Lucy 1798.—Elizabeth m. Rev. Eben. Withington
1797.—William went to Boston, m. Nabby Butler Crane 1799, and
had William Foster 1800, Abijah Crane 1802.—Foster d. young.
23. Dr. Daniel (s. of Richard 22.) m. Bathsheba, D. of
Josiah Williams 1783, and had Louisa 1804, Mary, Daniel. She
d. 1836, æ. 73 ; he 1839, æ. 78. Mary m. Dr. Noah Whitman

1812.—Daniel went to Charleston, S. C., m. there, and had a family, and has returned to Boston, where his w. d. 1839.

24. George W. (s. of Dr. Richard 22.) m. Anna, D. of Joseph Ames, 1802, and had George W. 1803, Mary Ann 1805, Eliza Jane 1807, Richard Foster 1809, Lucy 1812, Joseph Ames 1814. He removed to Augusta, Me.

25. Mark Perkins came from Ipswich 1741, and settled in N. B.: his wife was a Whipple (probably Dorothy): he had Josiah, Jonathan, Isaac, Jesse, Dorothy, Sarah, Jemima, Martha, Mary: he d. 1756, æ. 58. Dorothy m. Jacob Packard 1742.—Sarah m. Ebenezer Packard 1746.—Jemima m. Levi Keith 1759.—Martha m. Nathan Packard.—Mary m. Simeon Packard 1761.—Dorothy Perkins, the wid. perhaps, m. Solomon Packard 1760.

26. Josiah (s. of Mark 25.) m. Abigail, D. of Benjamin Edson, 1755, and had Mehitabel 1756, Abigail 1758, Mark 1760, Josiah 1762, Sarah 1766, Benjamin 1768, Silvia 1769, Jacob, Shepard: he d. 1798, æ. 73. Mehitabel m. Daniel Ames 1780.—Abigail m. Benjamin Hayward 1777.—Benjamin m. Hannah, D. of Jeremiah Washburn 1789, and went to Me.—Jacob went to Springfield.

27. Jonathan (s. of Mark 25.) m. Abigail, D. of Jonathan Packard, 1752, and had Abigail 1757, Jonathan 1758, Ruby 1761, George 1763, Daniel, Susanna, Parna: he d. 1802, æ. 74. Abigail m. Jonathan Cary 1784.—Ruby m. Alpheus Cary 1786.— George went to Canada.—Susanna m. Robert Howard 1788.— Jonathan m. Abigail, D. of John Howard, 1785, and had a son Moses Hudson 1791.

28. Isaac (s. of Mark 25.) m. Joanna, D. of Benjamin Edson 1754, and settled in Titicut, and had Abraham 1755, Isaac 1757, Joanna 1761, Jacob 1763. Jacob m. Abigail Leonard of Mid'o. 1788.

29. Capt. Jesse (s. of Mark 25.) m. Susanna, D. of Dr. Daniel Field, 1769, and had Zadock 1771, Rachel 1776. His w. d., and he m. Bliss, D. of Pelatiah Phinney, 1789, and had Jesse 1791. He m. Sally Silvester 1808 for his 3d w.—Rachel m. Shepard Perkins 1797.

30. Mark (s. of Josiah 26.) m. Tabitha, D. of Jeremiah Washburn, 1784, and had Charity 1785, Phebe 1788, Susanna and Sibil 1791,—Sally 1796. Charity m. Capt. Asa Jones 1806.—Phebe m. David Macomber of Easton 1805.—Sibil m. Josiah Dunbar 1807. Susanna m. David Packard 1810.—Sally m. Waldo Field 1820.

31. Josiah (s. of Josiah 26.) m. Anna, D. of Jonas Reynolds, 1790, and had Jonas 1790, Nahum 1792, Mehitabel 1795. Jonas gra. B. U. 1813, m. Rhoda, D. of Simeon Keith, 1815, and settled in the ministry at Braintree.—Nahum m. Vesta, D. of Caleb Copeland, 1820.—Mehitabel m. Charles Keith 1817.

32. Shepard (s. of Josiah 26.) m. Rachel, D. of Capt. Jesse Perkins, 1797, and had Azel, Josiah, Zadock, and Susanna.

33. Zadock (s. of Capt. Jesse 29.) m. Hannah, D. of Abiah Packard, 1796, and had Anselm 1797, Sidney 1799. He d., and

the widow m. William Edson 1812.—Anselm m. Dorothy, D. of
Samuel Battles, 1819.—Sidney m. a Capen.

34. Jesse Esq. (s. of Capt. Jesse 29.) m. Elizabeth, D. of Rev.
Thomas Crafts, 1815, and had Caroline Bliss, Thomas Crafts,
Mary Porter, Frederick and Elizabeth.

35. Luke (nephew to Mark 25.) came from Ipswich, settled
in N. B., m. Rebecca, D. of James Packard, 1749, and had Anne
1750, Jemima 1753, Mary 1754, James 1757, Luke, Keziah,
Susanna, Martha, Phebe : he d. 1776, æ. 51. Anne m. Jonas
Reynolds.—Jemima m. Joseph Reynolds 1772.—Mary m. Capt.
William French.—James m. Betsy, D. of Josiah Packard, and
went to Minot, Me.—Luke m. Mary, D. of Nathan Snell perhaps, 1797, and went to Winthrop, Me.—Keziah m. Matthew
Packard 1781.—Susanna m. Simeon Brett 1777.—Martha m.
Gideon Lincoln 1781.—Phebe m. Asaph Howard Esq. 1789, and
went to Minot.—James m. Rebecca Packard 1783.

Betty m. Benanuel Leach 1741.—Lydia m. James Keith 1744.
Phebe m. James Thurston 1749.—Mary m. Joseph Warren 1756.
Rebecca m. Jona. Washburn 1757.—Anné m. Reuben Packard
1759.—Hannah m. Daniel Packard 1765.—Betty m. Samuel
Snow 1775.—Rebecca m. Josiah Packard Jr. 1782.—Sally m.
Capt. Robt. Packard 1788.—Martha m. Thos. Packard 1789.—
Olive m. Benjamin Pratt 1789.—James m. Rebecca Packard
1783.—Nathaniel Jr. m. Hannah Hayward 1794.—Polly m.
Dean Howard of E. 1800.—Naomi m. Alfred Johnson 1801.—
Jesse m. Sally Silvester 1808.—Asa m. Huldah Hayward 1815.
Susanna m. Otis Alger 1817.—Wid. Hannah m. John Snow 1821.
Dan Shaw m. a Perkins of M.

PERRY.—Dr. Nathan Perry (s. of Nathan of Norton) m. a
Clapp, and settled in N. B., and has William, Julia and Sophia.

PETTINGILL.—Akerman Pettigill m. Joanna, D. of Sam'l
Kingman, 1723, and had Daniel 1726, Nathan 1732, Jacob 1734,
and Hannah. His wife d., and he had a 2d w. Mehitabel, and
had Stephen 1743, Silence 1745.—Akerman Pettingill m. Deborah Colson 1749.

2. Samuel Pettingill m. Martha Jackson of A. 1732, and had
Edm'd 1739, Joseph 1743, Jona. 1748, Martha 1751, Sam'l 1753.

3. Joseph Pettingill m. Mary Edson 1745 ; she d. 1746, and he
m. Lydia Phillips 1746, and had Mary 1747, Esther 1749, Hannah 1750, all b. in A.; Lydia 1752, John 1753, Phebe 1755, Joseph 1757, William 1759, Obadiah and Joanna 1762 : he d. 1777 ;
she 1795.—William m. Lydia Cobb 1784.—Joanna m. William
Turner 1781.

4. Daniel (s. of Akerman 1.) m. Hannah, D. of Samuel Soper,
1750, and had Oliver 1752, Molly 1754, Sarah 1756, Hannah
1759, Silvia 1761, Jacob 1763, Asa 1765, Susanna 1767, Sybil
and Celia 1771 : he d. 1808. Asa m. Elizabeth, D. of Thomas
Carr, 1789.—Sybil m. Josiah Hathaway 1788.

5. Nathan (s. of Akerman 1.) was a soldier with Gen. Winslow 1755 at Nova Scotia, and m. Elizabeth, D. of Thomas Carr,

1760, and had Betty 1760, Akerman 1763, Hugh 1766. His w.
d. 1768, and he m. Margaret Markham 1775, and had Thomas
1775, Anne 1778.—Betty (or Joseph's D. below) m. Ichabod
Shurtleff of Plymo. 1787.

6. Daniel Jr. m. Sarah, D. of Matthew Gannett, 1755, and
had Matthew 1756, Daniel 1758, Molly 1761. Wid. Sarah m.
Amos Ford of Dux. 1766. [See Edmund 11.]

7. Joseph (s. of Samuel 2.) m. Hepzibah Townsel 1764, and
had Betty 1765. She (or Nathan's D. above) m. J. Shurtliff
1787.

8. Stephen (s. of Akerman 1.) m. Abigail, D. of Sam'l Ripley
perhaps, 1764, and had Mehitabel 1766, Abigail 1767, Rhoda
1768, Beza 1771, Ruby 1773, Stephen 1777.

9. John (s. of Joseph 3.) m. Elizabeth, D. of Thos. Thompson, 1784, and had John 1785, Arminta 1786, William 1789, after
his father's death.

10. Hugh (s. of Nathan 5.) and his wife Hannah had Ethan
1786, Holmes 1789, Jennet 1791, Betty 1793, Heman 1795.

11. Edmund and his wife Sarah, D. of Ashley Curtis, m. 1760,
had Mehitabel 1761, Edmund 1762, Josiah 1765. Wid. Sarah
m. Amos Ford of Duxbury 1766. [See Daniel Jr. 6.]

12. Obadiah m. Eleanor Cobb 1792, and had Arcadius 1793,
Obadiah 1795.

Mehitabel m. Jonathan Pitcher of Norwich, Conn., 1733.—
Wid. Martha m. Anthony Pierce 1748.—Widow Anne m. John
Kingman 1771.—Benjamin of E. m. Molly Howard 1773.—Benjamin m. Mary, D. of Henry Kingman, 1747.—Daniel of E. was
a magistrate.—Daniel and Esther, of A., had Joseph 1719, Benjamin 1720, Joanna 1722, Sarah 1725, who m. Joseph Bates
1746 : he d. 1726; she 1735.—Obadiah and Martha, of A., had
Daniel 1732, Joanna 1735, Samuel 1739: he d. 1743.—John d.
1742 ; his wid. Priscilla d. 1772, æ. 88: both at A.

PHILLIPS.—Thomas Phillips (from Marshfield) settled in E.
B., and was probably son of Benjamin, who was s. of John,
whose father John was at Marshfield 1638. Thomas m. the wid.
of John Sherman, D. of Mark Eames and g. D. of Anthony
Eames of Marshfield : Sherman lived in Rochester, and left one
s. Anthony Sherman, who came to E. B.—Phillips came to E.
B. about 1735, and had Abiah, Thomas, Lydia, Mark 1736, Deborah 1739. His w. d., and he m. Hannah, wid. of Micah Allen,
and D. of Timothy or Joseph Edson, 1747 : she d. 1768; he d.
before 1767. Lydia m. Zebulun Cary 1749.—Abiah m. Benjamin Taylor 1761, and d. 1800 æ. 70. Taylor d. 1776, æ. 80.—
It is said one D., perhaps Deborah, m. a Wade. [See William 8.]
John, father of Benj., was killed by lightning at Marshfield 1656.

2. Thomas (s. of Thomas 1.) m. Mary, D. of David Hatch,
1755, and had John 1756, Mary 1758, Thomas 1760, Joseph,
Turner, David : he d. at Spectacle Island in the harbor of Boston, of the small-pox, 1781. Mary m. Joseph Whitman 1780.—
Joseph went to New York, and was father of Willard Phillips

Esq. of Boston, Judge of Probate, &c.—David also went to N.
York.—Wid. Mary Phillips d. 1811, æ. 77.

3. Mark (s. of Thomas 1.) m. Mercy, D. of Blaney Phillips
of Hanson, 1762, and had Chloe 1764, Mark 1768, Molly 1770,
Susanna 1772, Wadsworth 1774, Nabby 1777, d. single 1807;
Barzillai 1779, Lucy 1783, Mercy 1787, d. single 1831 : he d.
1811, æ. 75; she 1816, æ. 71. Chloe m. Isaiah Whitman 1784.—
Molly m. Barza Kingman 1791.—Susanna m. Jacob Lowden
1794.—Lucy m. Smardus Snell 1807.—Wadsworth and Barzillai
went westward.

4. John (s. of Thomas 2.) was serjeant in Gen. Washington's
life guard during the Revolutionary war, and m. Jennet, D. of
John Young, 1784, and had George Y. 1788, Jennet 1790, Mar-
quis La Fayette 1792, Eunice Bass 1797, Robert 1802 : his w. d.
1823, æ. 57. George Y. m. Bethiah, wid. of Asa Mitchell and D.
of Joseph Lazell, 1812, and had Abigail Ames 1813, and Asa
Mitchell 1815, and the family all removed to Poughkepsie, N. Y.

5. Thomas (s. of Thomas 2.) m. Martha, D. of Capt. Simeon
Whitman, 1783, and had Thomas and Joanna Whitman : he d.
1809, æ. 49. Thomas went to Natick.—Joanna m. John Corthrell
of Abington 1811.

6. Turner (s. of Thomas 2.) m. Huldah, D. of Capt. Simeon
Whitman, 1787, and had Electa, Huldah, and others. He d.
1824, æ. 60.—Huldah m. Algernon Sidney Brett.—Electa m.
Jared Reed, his 2d wife.

7. Mark (s. of Mark 3.) m. Celia, D. of Job Chamberlin, 1789,
and had Lucinda 1790, Nathan 1793, Nabby 1798, Wadsworth
1800, Phebe 1804, Celia 1810. Lucinda m. Melzar Hudson
1818.—Nabby m. Jona. Pratt of Halifax 1821.—Phebe m. Benjamin H. Washburn.—Celia m. Nathaniel Porter.

8. William Phillips (from Easton) m. Hannah, D. of John
Pryor, 1718, and d. 1743: he lived in Hanson probably (then
Bridgewater). His D. Lydia m. Joseph Pettingill 1746.—Mary,
who m. Ezra Warren 1752, might have been his D. also.—Caleb
Phillips was also in Bridgewater 1738, perhaps father of Elipha-
let below.—Deborah m. Levi Wade 1766. [See Thomas 1.]

9. Eliphalet Phillips m. Mary, D. of David Howard, 1762,
and had Eliphalet 1765, Mary 1768, Caleb 1770, Hannah 1771 :
he d. 1773, and the wid. m. Seth Harris.

Hannah m. Benjamin Leonard 1715.—Cyrus B. m. Lucretia
Barrett of E. 1819.—Samuel of Norton m. Lydia Bassett 1726.—
Ebenezer of E. m. Jemima Packard 1802.— Diana H. m. Jo. Allen Jr. 1814.—William m. Mara Kingman 1795.—Capt. John m.
Bridget Southworth 1749.—Betty m. Wm Brett 1801.—Rebecca
of Plymo. m. Zadock Packard 1799.—Mary M. m. Jo. Blanchard
1807.—Nancy m. Philip Andrews 1820.—Ezra m. Mehitabel, D.
of Joseph Allen, 1809.—Lewis m. Polly Goodspeed 1795.

PHINNEY or **FINNEY.**—Pelatiah Phinney settled in S. B.,
and m. Mercy, D. of Josiah Washburn, 1738, and had Freelove
1740, Lurania 1741, Onesiphorus 1744, Mary 1745, Zerviah

1748, Esther 1751, Keziah 1753, Bliss 1754, Hannah 1758, John
1760. Pelatiah Phinney m. Mary Randall of E. 1764.—Freelove m. Jacob Tomson of M. 1761.—Lurania m. Benja. Packard
1775.—Zerviah m. Ebenezer Packard 1786.—Esther m. Barna-
bas Curtis 1774.—Keziah m. Adin Packard 1780.—Bliss m.
Capt. Jesse Perkins 1789.
   2. Joseph Phinney and his wife Mary had Amy 1745, Noah
1748, Rebecca 1751 : his w. d. 1760. Joseph Phinney m. Alice
Campbell of T. 1761.—Amy m. Robert Randall of E. 1764.—
Noah m. Betty, D. of Jeremiah Conant, 1769.
   Ithamar Phinney m. Anna, D. of Simeon Leonard 1799.—
Achsah m. James Wood 1764.—Experience Phinney m. William
Slack of T. 1775.—Jonathan of M. m. Deborah Wade 1735.
   PIERCE.—Anthony Pierce and his w. Keturah lived in E.
B., (perhaps now Hanson), joined Mr. Angier's Church 1741,
had Susanna 1733, who m. George Bradley 1753. He m. a 2d
w. Martha, wid. of Obadiah Pettingill of A. 1748, and had An-
thony 1755. Anthony m. Sile Pratt 1778.
   John Pierce of P. m. Susanna Newland 1713.—Wid. Polly
Pierce m. Perez Williams 1798.—Benjamin Pierce m. Jane, D.
of Dea. Thomas Hayward, 1750 : his 2d wife.—Mary m. Eben-
ezer Keith 1741.—Martha m. John Fobes 1738.—Sarah m. Elisha
Pierce 1731.—Mary of Scit. m. Benjamin Pope Esq. 1792.—
Elisha Pierce of Scit. m. Mary, wid. of John Field and D. of
Ephraim Howard.—Lydia m. John Heiford 1706.—Mercy m.
Joseph Truant 1767.—Sarah m. John Pratt 1751.—Hannah m.
Joseph Newell 1732.—Abigail m. Eleazar Alden 1819.—Anna m.
Moses Mandell of Dorchester 1819.—Benjamin of Scit. m. Charity, D. of Jona. Howard 1742.—Calvin of Scit. m. Huldah, D.
of Hezekiah Hayward 1767.—Jacob Pierce m. Lucy Conant
1794.—Polly of M. m. David Leonard 1797.—Lucy m. Andrew
Tucker 1814.
   PINCIN OR PINSON.—William Pincin, b. 1757, (s. of Thos.
of Scituate) m. Elizabeth Beal of Hingham 1777, and settled in
E. B., and had Deborah, Benjamin 1781, Betsy 1785, William
1787 : he d. 1828, æ. 72 ; his mother, wid. Ann Pincin, d. 1808,
æ. 77.—Deborah m. Abel Delano 1795.—Benjamin m. and d. 1830,
æ. 49.—Betty m. Elijah Beal of Hingham 1804.—William m.
Margaret Whiting 1807, and d. 1822, æ. 35.—Mehitabel Pincin
m. Martin Beal of Hingham 1816.
   2. Benjamin, b. 1760, (s. of Thomas of Scituate and brother
of William above) came also to E. B. with his mother and brother, and m. Molly, D. of Abishai Stetson 1787, and had Polly,
who m. Daniel Magoun of P., 1816, and Susanna, who m. Dexter Pratt.
   Thomas Pinson, the ancestor of this family, was at Scituate
before 1636. His g. g. s. Thomas m. Anne Taylor 1755 at Scituate, and had Elizabeth 1756, William (above) 1757, and Benjamin (above) 1760.

This name is variously written in the early records, Pinson, Pincin, and Pinchin, and the last accords with the uniform pronunciation. It is undoubtedly the same name as Pynchon, and Pinson is probably the original and true spelling. Wm. Pinson (so spelt) of Wolverhampton Co., of Stafford, Eng., gave a power of attorney to Richard Brown of N. E. 1658. William Pynchon, of Roxbury 1630, went to England 1652, and d. there 1662. Who else of the name could then have had occasion to give this power? Besides, Brown came over the same year, 1630, and was a ruling Elder and Representative at Watertown.—John Pincin of Chesterfield m. Judith Curtis of Scit. 1788.—Abner Pincin m. Hannah Cowen 1770.—Welcome m. Deborah Crooker of P. 1818.—Rebecca m. Southworth Gammons Jr. of M. 1819.

POOL.—Isaac Pool (from Weymouth probably) and his wife Bethiah lived in S. B.: he d. 1759; she 1766. Isaac Pool (father or son) was in the French war 1755 at Nova Scotia.—Hannah Pool m. John Pain 1738.

2. Isaac Jr. m. Sarah, D. of Joseph Leonard 1743, and had Hannah 1744, Mary 1746, Olive 1748, Isaac 1751, Wealthy 1753, David 1755. Isaac m. Rebeckah, D. of Nathan Washburn 1774. This family went to Halifax.

3. Joseph and his w. Rebecca had John 1754, Sarah 1760, Mary 1762, Hopestill 1765, Benjamin 1767: d. 1813.—Sarah m. Ebenezer Snow Jr. 1783.

4. John (s. of Joseph 3.) m. Hannah, D. of Benjamin Price, 1777, and had John 1777, Betsy 1779, George 1781.

5. John (s. of John 4. probably) m. Susanna, D. of Daniel Willis, 1801, had John 1803, Susanna 1808, Mary 1810, Elizabeth 1812, Daniel Willis 1814, George 1816.

6. William m. Sarah Packard 1795, and had William 1796, Daniel 1797, Sally 1799, Belinda 1801.

7. Samuel m. Ruth Fullerton 1759, and lived in E. B., and had Samuel, John, William, Oliver, Olive, and others, ten in all. He went to Easton, where he d. Dec. 1830, she d. Aug. 3, 1835, æ. 97, and had 344 descendants.

Joshua Pool d. in E. B. 1822, æ. 88. Sarah m. John Hooper 1766.—Noah of A. m. wid. Sally Crane 1819, D. of Joshua Pratt.—Samuel m. Lydia Cox 1820.—Sally m. Peleg Osborn 1812.—James Jr. of Abington m. Sarah Benson 1808.—Noah of Boston m. Polly White 1808.—Mary m. Samuel Cary 1704.—Mercy m. Jacob Washburn 1761.—Joshua m. Lucinda, D. of Thomas Latham, 1783.—Anna m. Jacob Whitmarsh Jr. 1784.—Olive m. Rev. Wm. Reed 1784.—Samuel Jr. m. Abigail Porter 1786.—Jacob Jr. m. Zerviah Whitmarsh 1787.—Debo. m. Thos. Hersey 1793.—Achish m. Susanna Hersey 1799.

POPE.—Ichabod Pope (from Dartmouth, now Fairhaven perhaps) settled in S. B., near the bridge, called after him Pope's Bridge: his w. was a wid. Pope, who had a s. Thomas by her first husband. They had Benjamin, Freeman, Mercy, and perhaps others: he d. 1795. Thomas m. Huldah, D. of Sam'l

35

Edson, 1782, and went to Fairhaven, and his son Henry keeps
the Hotel in Halifax.—Benjamin Esq. m. Mary Pierce of Scit.
1792, and had Benjamin Pierce, Hannah, and Orra. Benjamin
P. m. Experience, D. of Silvanus Pratt.—Hannah m. Holman
Keith.—Orra m. Kenelm Winslow.—Freeman m. Hannah
Thayer 1795, and went to Enfield, and had Ichabod, William,
Solon, Lavinia, and others perhaps ; Lavinia m. Charles Pratt
1821.—Mercy m. Freeman Pope of New Bedford 1797.

2. Joseph (from N. Bedford) lived awhile in S. B., and went
to Ware, and thence to the State of N. York : he had Thankful,
(who m. Cornelius Thayer 1796), and others.—Nabby Pope m.
Isaac Washburn 1807.

PORTER.—Rev. John Porter (s. of Samuel and Mary of
Abington, born 1716, and grandson of John, who m. Deliverance, D. of Nicholas Byram, 1660) gra. H. U. 1736, and settled
in the ministry at N. B. 15th Oct., 1740, m. Olive Johnson of
Canterbury, Conn., and had one D. Olive 1749, and she and her
D. both d. the same year : she æ. 23. He then m. Mary Huntington of Lebanon, Conn. and had John 1752, Olive 1753, Huntington 1755, Jonathan 1756, Eliphalet 1758, Mary 1762, Sibil
1766 : he d. Mar. 12, 1802, æ. 86. John gra. Yale Coll. 1770,
was a major in the Revolutionary war, and afterwards went to
the West Indies, and there died.—Olive m. John Crafts 1790.—
Huntington gra. H. U. 1777, and settled in the ministry at Rye,
N. H., and is now living in Roxbury very aged.—Jonathan gra.
H. U. 1777, went on board a privateer as a Surgeon and was
lost.—Eliphalet, D. D., gra. H. U. 1777, and settled in the ministry at Roxbury, and d. 1833, leaving no children.—Mary m.
Rev. Thomas Crafts 1786, minister at Princeton, and afterwards
Mid.—Sibil d. single, at Princeton, while on a visit to her sister.

2. Samuel (s. of Samuel and Sarah (Joslyn) of A., b. 1727,
m. Hannah Green 1758, and settled in E. B., and had Samuel
1759, Betteris 1761, Abigail 1763. He m. wid. Ruth Reed 1764,
and had Ruth 1766 : he d. 1811, æ. 84. Abigail m. Samuel Pool
Jr. 1786.—Ruth m. James Reed 1784.

3. Joseph, born 1730, (brother of Samuel 2.) m. Elizabeth
Burrill 1753, and settled in St. Corner, and had Elizabeth 1753,
Joseph 1755, Hannah 1758, Robert 1762, Isaac 1765, Content
1767, Mehitabel 1769, Libeus, Cyrus : he d. 1804, æ. 74. Elizabeth m. Samuel Linfield.—Hannah m. Jona. Battles.—Content
m. Wm. Glover.—Mehitabel m. Daniel Brown 1797.—Joseph m.
a Capen and had no ch.—Capt. Robert m. a Gay, and had Robert,
John, Joseph, Betsy, Sally and Fanny. Robert m. a Capen.—
Isaac m. a Packard, and had Rodolphus, Samuel, Reuben, Martin, Galen, Susanna, Sybil and Anna. Susanna m. a Thompson ;
Sybil m. a Noyes.—Lebbeus settled in Wrentham, Mass.—Maj.
Cyrus m. a French, and had Ahirah, Cyrus, Luther, Olive, Rebecca, Mehitabel, and Eliza Ann. Olive m. Caleb Copeland Jr.

4. Ebenezer (brother of the 2 preceding, b. 1731) m. Lydia

Loring of Plympton 1754, and had Sarah 1756, Lydia 1758, Molly 1760, Olive 1763, Susanna 1765.

5. James Porter and his wife Mary had Polly 1778, Abigail 1779 at A., Hannah 1781 and James 1788, both at Plainfield; Sarah 1792 at A. Hannah Porter m. Nathaniel Reynolds Jr. of Sidney, Me. 1811.

6. John 2d (s. of John of Abington) m. Susanna (or Susa) D. of Ephraim Groves, 1790, settled in E. B., and had Allen Marshall, who m. Betsy Beals 1816.

Esther m.Abel Packard 1751.—Jona. Porter m. Mary Chipman of Halifax 1763.—John Jr. m. Martha Perkins 1764.—Hezekiah of Windsor m. Sarah Carver 1757.—Hannah m. Judah Wood 1757.—Adam m. Deborah Gannett 1776, and Sarah Hunt 1806.—Sarah m. Abijah Snow of Abington.—Abigail m. Levi Keith 3d, 1797.—Nathaniel of Halifax m. Celia, D. of Mark Phillips.—Abigail (sister of Rev. John) m. Capt. Isaac Packard 1745, and her sister Hannah m. Dea. Barnabas Tomson of H.— Polly m. William Fullerton 1796.—Mary m. Josiah Sears of H. 1817.—Samuel m. Sally Gill of C. 1817.—Sarah of H. m. Seabury Child Hathaway 1818.—Sarah m. Daniel Whitman 1819.— Lydia of A. m. Edw'd Vinton 1820.—Clifford and Mercy Porter had Bathsheba 1786.—Milicent m. John Battles 1816.—Rebecca Wood Porter m. Charles Lincoln 1816.

POWERS.—Edward Powers m. Phillis Bartlett 1753, and had Edward 1753, Samuel 1755, Bethiah 1757, Keziah 1759, Roland 1760*, Betty 1762, Noah 1764, Silvia 1766*, Daniel 1769. She d. 1771, and he m. Betty Whately 1772, and had Silvia 1773, Roland 1775. Betty m. Capt. Edward Hayward 1802.—Noah m. Rhoda Williams 1787, and had Cyrus 1787, Edward 1789 —Keziah m. Prince Ford 1779.—Mary Powers m. John Burr 1748.—Mary Powers d. 1756.—Katharine Powers d. 1760.

PRATT.—Jo. Pratt (from Weymouth) settled in S. B. a. 1705, having with Richard Davenport bought the farm that was Guido Bailey's, near where Zechariah Whitman afterwards lived in 1702. He sold his share of the mill at Little Comfort, Abington, 1704, and named himself of Weymouth: he lived to be very aged: his will dated 1755; he d. 1765: he left a widow Anna (Richards), m. 1721, a 2d wife: she d. 1766. He had Joseph, Nathaniel, Benjamin, Solomon, David, Samuel, Sarah. Sarah m. Ebenezer Snow a. 1728.—Nathaniel m. Sarah, D. of Benjamin Snow probably, and had Seth 1729, and Anna. His w. d. a. 1743, and he m. Hannah, D. of Lot Conant 1745, and d. 1749.—Anna m. John Packard 1769.—The mother of Nathaniel's wife Sarah above, was Sarah, D. of Samuel Allen, and first m. Jonathan Cary and then Benjamin Snow. (See Benjamin Snow.)

2. Joseph (s. of Joseph 1.) m. Lydia Leonard 1712, and had Joseph, Jonathan, Job, Lydia, Susanna, Hannah, Tabitha, Charity, Deliverance, Abigail. He d. 1753: he left a 2d wife Alice, D. of Dea. Thomas Hayward, m. 1749. She was mother of

Capt. Thomas Cushman : she d. 1803, æ. 96. Lydia m. Benjamin Mehurin 1731.—Susanna m. James Richards 1740.—Hannah's will and d. 1764.—Tabitha m. Seth Hayward 1748.—Charity m. Jeremiah Washburn 1754.—Deliverance m. Amasa Rickard 1759.—Abigail m. Edward Curtis 1759.

3. Benjamin (s. of Joseph 1.) m. Sarah, D. of Henry Kingman, 1719, and had Benjamin, Nathan, John, Bethiah, Susanna, Silence, Ann : his will 1753; d. 1762. Bethiah m. Josiah Mehuren 1769.—Silence m. John Muxam 1748.—Ann m. Azariah Hayward 1768.—Susanna d. 1761. The wid. d. 1767.—Benjamin m. Lydia Harlow 1741.

4. Dea. Solomon (s. of Joseph 1.) m. Sarah, D. of Isaac Johnson, 1719, and had Sarah 1721, Abihail, Mary, Solomon 1729, Ebenezer 1731, Hannah, Isaac 1736, Daniel 1741 : his will and d. 1757. Sarah m. Nathan Perkins perhaps 1752. (See Nathan Perkins 7.)—There was a Sarah who died 1767.—Ebenezer m. Abial, widow of John Alger and D. of John Johnson, 1758: he also m. Bulah, D. of Jonathan Washburn, 1760: he settled in Middleborough.—Hannah m. Timothy Hayward 1767.—Isaac m. Catharine Caswell 1758.—Daniel died (a soldier) 1778, and Hez. Hooper settled his estate 1779.—Abihail m. John Conant 1746.—Daniel's wid. Mary m. Capt. John Shaw of Raynham 1779.—Daniel m. a Patten of Conn.

5. David (s. of Joseph 1.) m. Joanna, D. of Ebenezer Allen, 1722, and settled in E. B., and had Rebeckah 1724, Joanna 1726, Dorcas 1728, David 1729, Deborah 1732, Abner 1734. His wife d., and he m. widow Ann Leonard (she was a Bryant probably) 1738, and had Ruth 1740, Peter 1746, Ann 1747, Thomas 1750: he d. 1790, æ. 91. Rebecca m. Elisha Allen 1745.—Joanna m. Phineas Conant 1749.—Deborah m. Joseph Orcutt 1751.—Ruth m. Obadiah Bates 1762.—Dorcas m. James Lovell 1754.—Thos. m. a Morton, and settled in Titicut.

6. Samuel (s. of Joseph 1.) m. Bethiah, D. of Nicholas Byram, 1729, and settled in E. B., and had Mehitabel, Samuel, Paul, Silas, Bethiah 1747. She d. 1774, æ. 65.—Mehitabel m. David French, and afterwards Benjamin Price 1782.—Bethiah m. Wm. Daniels of Abington 1767.—The family went westward.

7. Jonathan (s. of Joseph 2.) m. Elizabeth, D. of Ebenezer French, 1740, and had Jonathan 1741, Lucy, Cornelius 1748, Elizabeth, who m. Andreas Vinacea 1778, and went to South Brimfield, now Wales; Jeremiah 1753, Ebenezer 1757: he d. 1775, she 1778.—Ebenezer m. Charity Besse 1780.—Jeremiah m. Ann Bolton 1777.

8. Job (s. of Joseph 2.) m. Mary, D. of Josiah Washburn, 1757, and had Sarah 1758, and Lydia, who m. Azor Howe 1787: Wid. Mary d. 1804, æ. 77.—Sarah Pratt m. Barnabas Blossom 1778.

9. Nathan (s. of Benjamin 3.) m. Sarah Harlow 1745, and had Sarah and Abigail, he d. 1750. Abigail m. Benjamin Benson

1770.—Perhaps the wid. m. Nathan Perkins 1752.—(See Dea.
Solomon 4.)

10. John (s. of Benjamin 3) m. Martha, D. of Hugh Mehuren, and had Olive 1751, Levi 1754, Bathsheba 1759, Mary 1760.
Olive m. Lazarus Hathaway 1774.—John Pratt m. Sarah Pierce
1751.

11. Solomon (s. of Solomon 4.) m. Mary, D. of John Keith,
1761, and had Mary 1762: his w. d. 1764, and he m. Abihail,
D. of James Hooper, 1767, and had Nancy, and perhaps others.
—Mary m. Ebenezer Perkins 1782.—Nancy m. Timo. Conant
1788.

12. David (s. of David 5.) m. Abigail, D. of William Bowditch,
1753, and had Mary 1756, Oliver 1757, Jeremiah 1760, Allen
1766. She d. 1783, æ. 51, and he m. widow Phebe Atwood (she
was a Gloyd of Abington) 1784, and had David 1787, Isaac 1790 :
he d. 1810, æ. 81 ; she 1817, æ. 70. Mary m. Joshua Pratt 1783.
Jeremiah removed early.—Allen gra. H. U. 1785, and settled in
the ministry at Westmoreland, N. H.—David m. Mary, D. of
Seth Hobart 1815, and had David, and d. 1817, æ. 30.—Isaac m.
Nancy Pratt of Carver 1813, and had George W. and Oliver.—
David 3d m. Mary Weld of Me.

13. Abner (s. of David 5.) m. Martha, wid. of Henry Cary and
D. of Dr. Joseph Byram, 1764, and had Nathan 1765, Susanna
1768 : he removed to S. B.—Nathan m. Lois Fuller 1786.—Susanna m. James Richards 1798.

14. Peter (s. of David 5.) and his w. Amy had Samuel 1775,
Rebeckah 1777, Molly 1779.

15. Dea. Seth (s. of Nathaniel and g. s. of Joseph 1.) was
ex'or. and residuary legatee of his grandfather's will, m. Hannah, D. of Joseph Washburn, 1752, and had Nathaniel 1754,
Joseph 1756, Nehemiah 1757, Simeon 1759, Seth, Silvanus, Asa,
Chloe, Joanna : he d. 1795, æ. 66. Nehemiah d. 1778, and a D.
d. 1778.—Joseph went westward.—Seth gra. H. U. 1785, and
d. young.—Chloe m. Jeremiah Conant 1793.—Joanna m. Adam
Besse 1791, and Isaac Keith 1797.

16. Oliver (s. of David 12.) m. Susanna, D. of Nathaniel
Lowden, 1787, and had Allen, Susanna 1794. His w. d. 1802,
æ. 36, and he m. Rebecca Ford 1805 : he also afterwards m.
Thankful Ford, sister of his 2d. w. Rebecca : he d. 1832, æ. 75.
Allen was a mariner and master of a vessel.—Susanna d. 1816,
æ. 22.

17. Nathaniel (s. of Dea. Seth 15.) m. Betty, D. of Ezekiel
Washburn, 1778, and had Sally, Hannah, Betsy, Elijah, Alber-
tina, Seth, Chloe, Nathaniel. Sarah m. Isaac Swift 2d, 1797.—
Hannah m. Seth Conant 1801.—Betsy m. David Waterman 1802,
and Daniel Hudson 1822.—Seth m. Lucinda Conant 1816.—
Chloe m. Alvan Crossman 1813, and afterwards Nahum Mitchell
of R., s. of Bradford Mitchell.—Nathaniel m. Lucy Thomas of
Marshfield.

18. Capt. Simeon (s. of Dea. Seth 15.) m. Sarah, D. of Judge

Benj. Willis, 1791, and had Simeon 1795, Charles 1794, Henry
W. 1797, Benjamin W. and Sarah twins.—Simeon m. Alice
Waterman.—Charles m. Lavinia, D. of Freeman Pope, 1821.—
Henry W. m. Clarinda Leonard 1821.—Benj. W. m. Joanna
Lucas.—Sarah m. Jabez Harden.

19. Silvanus (s. of Dea. Seth 15.) m. Experience, D. of Oliver
Alden, 1803, and had Experience, who m. Benjamin P. Pope;
and Mary, who m. Benjamin Crooker.

20. Capt. Asa (s. of Dea. Seth 15.) m. Lydia, D. of Benjamin
Sprague, 1799, and had Harriet M. and Lusanna T.: he d. 1831.
Harriet M. m. John E. Howard Esq. 1821.—Lusanna T. m.
Maj. Cushing Mitchell 1822.

21. Elijah (s. of Nathaniel 17.) m. Naomi, D. of Robert
Wade, 1813, and had Betsy 1813, Susanna 1815, Enoch, Loisa.

22. Joshua Pratt (s. of William of Abington) m. Experience
Nash 1728, and settled in E. B. a. 1740, and had Mary, Sarah
1734, Hannah 1737, all born in A., Experience 1741, Joshua
1743: he d. 1772, æ. 67; she 1773. Mary m. Nathaniel Ramsdell 1753.—Hannah m. Samuel Allen 1758.—Experience m.
Nathaniel Lowden 1762.

23. Joshua (son of Joshua 22.) married Mary, D. of David
Pratt, 1783, and had William 1784, Nabby 1785, Polly 1787,
Sarah 1789, Dexter 1791: he died 1813, æ. 70; she 1828, æ.
72. William m. Celia, D. of Nathan Whitman, 1816.—Nabby
m. Eleazar Whitman Jr. 1812.—Dexter m. Polly, D. of Benjamin Pincin.—Sarah m. Spencer Crane of Canton 1809, and afterwards Noah Pool of Ab. 1819.

24. William Pratt and his w. Polly had Albert 1811, William
1813, Anthony 1815.

25. Robert Pratt and his w. Rebecca had Cotton 1785, Ebenezer 1789.

26. John Pratt settled in N. B. a. 1737, and had Barnabas,
John, Thomas, Consider, Jesse, Margery, Priscilla. Margery
Pratt m. Thomas Tribou 1746.—Priscilla m. a Smith.

27. Barnabas (s. of John 26.) m. Isabel, D. of Walter Downey,
1750, and had Thaddeus, Barnabas, Catharine, Mary, Isabel,
Susanna. Thaddeus m. Rachel, D. of Jabez Churchill, 1777,
and Barnabas m. Ruhama, D. of Levi French, 1787, and both
went to Me.—Catharine m. Jeremy Thayer 1780.—Mary m. Asa
Battles.—Isabel m. Levi Brannock 1790.—Susanna m. Simeon
Davie 1788. He d. 1788, and she went to Hebron, Me., with
her son-in-law Davie, and lived to be 102 years old or more.

28. Thomas (s. of John 26.) m. Mercy Jones, and had Micah
1756, Consider 1759, Thomas 1761, Margery 1764, Lot 1767,
Mercy 1769, Patience 1771, Noah 1774: she d. 1777; he a. 1781.
Consider d. in the army.—Lot m. Polly Aldrich 1787, and he
and Noah went to Vt.—Margery m. John Bolton 1787.—Mercy
m. a Spear.—Patience m. John Crane 1793.

29. Thomas (s. of Thomas 28.) m. Susanna, D. of Seth Thayer,

1788, and had Edward, Asa, Arba, Silvia, Azuba, Rebecca, Henrietta, Susanna, Polly, Emily, Abigail. Asa m. Lydia Humphry 1815.—Azuba m. Simeon Dunbar 2d of H. 1813.
30. Cornelius (s. of Jonathan 7.) m. Martha, D. of Jonathan Leonard, and had Jonathan, Martha, Leonard, Ebenezer, Cornelius, Lucy. Jonathan m. Deborah, D. of Ebenezer Hathaway, 1817.—Martha m. Jabez Vaughn of Md. 1817.—Leonard m. Clarissa, D. of Silvanus Leonard, 1818.—Ebenezer m. a Tomson of Halifax.—Cornelius m. Lusanna Tomson.—Lucy m. Thomas Cushman.

Phineas and Joshua Pratt came over in the 3d ship, Ann, and were among the forefathers at Plymouth, and probably ancestors of most of the name in the Old Colony; and Benaijah Pratt admitted Freeman 1654.—John Pratt was in Bridgewater 1699. Elizabeth Pratt m. Samuel Staples 1704.—Nathaniel m. Sarah, D. of Nehemiah Allen, 1734, Hannah m. Napthali Byram 1744. James of E. m. Martha, D. of John Willis, 1733.—A Pratt m. Margerie, D. of Josiah Leonard.—Joseph and Enoch were soldiers 1775.—Enoch m. Salome Rickard 1784.—Sile m. Anthony Pierce 1778.—Charity of Norton m. John Davenport 1763.—Ebenezer m. Ann Dyer 1717.—Olive m. Josiah Torrey 1782.—Matilda m. Isaac Allen 1796.—Mercy m. Alpheus Orcutt 1802.—Ebenezer of Weymouth m. Waitstill Washburn 1720.— Joseph m. Elizabeth French 1738.—Huldah m. Benjamin Reed of Cummington, 1778.—Huldah m. John Carver Jr. 1795.—Molly of A. m. Wm. Hearsey 1778.—Wid. Hannah m. Sam'l Noyes 1771.—Wid. Hannah m. Ebenezer Campbell 1764. Deborah m. Jonathan Ames 1780.—Zebedee of M. m. Dardana Keith 1763.—Lavinia m. Timothy Willis 1786.—Benjamin m. Olive Perkins 1789.—Phebe m. Nehemiah Leonard 1792.—Hannah m. Dea. Isaac Willis 1732.—Noah m. Desire, D. of Joseph Cole 1777.—Lovicy m. Job Staples Bryant 1793.—William of E. m. Amity Brett 1797.—Elijah m. Sibil Dunbar 1798.—Nehemiah m. Chloe Rickard 1793.—Calvin of M. m. Clarissa Keith 1798.—Sally of M. m. Jeremiah Keith Jr. 1801.—Isaac of M. m. Naomi Keith 1804.—Jona. of H. m. Nabby Phillips 1821.— Lydia m. Charles Wilbor of E. 1813.—Zebulun K. of M. m. Susanna Keith 1814.—Judith B. m. Daniel E. Willis 1815.—Sarah d. 1778 in S. B.—Elizabeth d. in S. B. 1794, æ. 71.—Hannah m. Charles Tomson 1816.—Sarah m. Ephraim Thomas 1739.— Consider of H. m. Mary, D. of David Thayer.—Samuel of St. m. Eleanor Whitman 1764.—Molly m. Amasa Tribou 1780.

PRICE.—Benjamin Price (from Dorchester) was a soldier under Gen. Winslow, 1755, at Nova Scotia, and settled in S. B., and m. Silence, D. of Nathaniel Hayward, 1743, and had Mary 1744, Silence 1746, Sarah 1748, Hannah 1750, Benjamin 1753, Lydia 1755, Betty 1758, Susanna 1761. His wife d., and he m. Mehitabel, wid. of David French and D. of Samuel Pratt, 1782: he d. 1805, æ. 85; she d. 1804, æ. 65.—One D. m. a Palmer.— Sarah m. Ebenezer Colwell 1769.—Hannah m. John Pool of H.

1777.—Betty m. Capt. Nathaniel Soper of Hanson 1782.—Benjamin m. Ruth, wid. of Jacob Washburn, 1805, and had Benjamin, who m. a D. of Timothy Harlow.

PRYOR, or PRIOR.—John Pryor (probably from Duxbury, and s. of Joseph, who d. there 1692) settled early in E. B.; m. Bethiah, D. of Samuel Allen, and had Joseph, Hannah, Sarah, Bethiah, and d. 1742. Hannah m. William Phillips 1718.—Sarah m. Theodosius Moore 1725.

2. Joseph (s. of John above) m. Ann Moore, and had Isaac 1726, Mary 1729, Martha 1736, Sarah 1739 : he d., and his wid. m. James Allen.—Mary m. Joseph Latham 1748.—Martha m. John Hanmer 1760.—Sarah m. Josiah Fobes Jr. 1766, and then John Eaton of M. 1780, and afterwards Joseph Bassett 1796 : and she d. 1839, æ. 100.—Eliphaz Pryor of Dux. m. Hannah, D. of Josiah Howard.

٬They all descended probably from Thomas Pryor of Scit., who d. 1639, leaving Sam'l and Thomas in Eng., and Joseph, Elizabeth, Mary, John and Daniel here.

RAMSDELL.—Nathaniel Ramsdell (from Pembroke) settled in E. B., and m. Mary, D. of Joshua Pratt, 1753, and had Daniel 1754, Matthew 1756, James 1758, Joseph 1761. Daniel m. Elizabeth Buck, and had Betsy 1777, and d. 1779 ; and his w. m. Ebenezer Noyes 1795.—Matthew m. Mary, and James m. Eunice, Ds. of Jonathan Allen of Braintree, and both went to Cummington.—Joseph m. Lydia Gloyd of A. 1787, and had Nathaniel 1789, Nancy 1791, Lydia 1794, Mary 1797, Joseph 1806. Nathaniel m. Sally, D. of Josiah Johnson, 1812.—Nancy and Lydia m. David Brown 1812 and 1818.—Mary m. John P. Reed 1816.

Mary m. William Whiting 1748.—Gideon m. Sarah Farrington 1736 —Samuel had Gershom 1750, Martha 1752, in E. B.—Joseph had Sarah 1749 in E. B.—Simeon's w. d. in E. B. 1781.—John m. Hannah Allen 1784.—Charles m. Betty Tirrell 1783.—Lot m. Lucinda Gannett 1794.—Noah m. Hitty Whitmarsh 1790. Lucy m. James Dorrein 1797.—Levi of Milton m. Amie Dunbar 1801.—Noah m. Betsy Allen 1818.—This name was sometimes written Ramsden on early records.

RATCHFORD.—James Ratchford, or Radsford, was early in E. B., (Hanson now perhaps), and m. Margaret Balls 1738, and had James 1739, Thomas 1741, William 1748, John 1750, Walter 1752.

RATHBURN.—Rev. Valentine Wightman Rathburn settled in W. B. over the Baptist Society : his wife Hepzibah : he had Sukey Lethridge 1801, Samuel Carpenter 1805. Hannah Rathburn of Bellingham m. Barzillai Hayward 1813.

REED, or READ.—Samuel and Mary Reed : she was a Davis ; m. 1705 : had Mary 1706 ; (m. Ebenezer Shaw 1733,) and Samuel 1707. Samuel m. Elizabeth, D. of Nathaniel Hayward, 1737.—The wid. m. Timothy Hayward 1730.

2. Joseph and Mary had Mary 1741.—These two families were

from Abington probably, and Samuel might have lived in Abington, as a great part of it then belonged to Bridgewater.

3. Hezekiah (s. of James) m. Deborah, D. of Isaac Tirrell of A., and had James, Isaac, Jeremiah, Calvin, Joseph, Jared, and Nancy. Jared m. Mehitabel Gardner 1811, and Electa Phillips, 2d w.—Joseph m. Charlotte Stetson 1807.—Calvin m. Hannah Lowden 1807.—Wid. Sarah Reed d. 1811, æ. 75.

4. Ezekiel and his wife Mary had Polly 1769, Zelotes 1771, Ezekiel 1772, Zebulun 1774, Hannah 1776, Olive 1777, Jesse 1778, Charles 1780, Abraham 1782, Briggs 1784. Jesse m. Hannah, D. of Caleb Hayward 1800.

5. Rev. John, D. D. (s. of Rev. Solomon of Titicut) m. Hannah Sampson 1780, and settled in W. B.; ord. 7th June, 1780, and had John 1781, Daniel 1783, Solomon 1788, Hannah 1790, Sally 1793*, Caleb 1797, Sampson 1800. She d. 1815, and he m. again. John gra. B. U. 1803, and m. Olive, D. of Abiezer Alger Esq. 1809, and settled in Yarmouth, Co. of Barnstable, as an Attorney ; now, and for many years past, Member of Congress.— Daniel m. Nancy Foster of Mid. 1812.—Solomon m. Abigail, D. of George Howard, 1811.—Hannah m. Jonathan Copeland 3d 1818.—Caleb and Sampson went to Boston ; both gra. H. U.; Caleb 1817, Sampson 1818.

6. Timothy Esq. (bro. of Rev. John 5.) settled also in W. B., m. Hannah, D. of Caleb Kingman, 1788, and had Caleb Kingman 1789*, d. 1796 ; Caleb Kingman 1799, d. 1837, unmarried : the father, Timothy, d. 1813.

7. Jonathan (s. of Ebenezer of Abington) m. Deborah, D. of John Porter of Abington, and settled in E. B., and had Mary 1789, Jonathan Loring 1791, John Porter 1793, Deborah 1795, Elizabeth 1797, Thaxter 1800, Ebenezer 1801, Clarissa 1805, Almira 1806, David Porter 1808. Jonathan L. m. Charlotte Brown of Abington 1816.—John Porter m. Polly, D. of Joseph Ramsdell 1816.—Deborah m. Jonathan R. Gurney of A. 1816.

8. Ezekiel (s. of Ezekiel 4.) m. Rebecca, D. of Jesse Edson, 1794, and had Emma Corbett 1795, Lydia 1797, Josiah 1799, Joseph Edson 1801, Edwin 1804, Charles Briggs 1806.—Emma C. m. Jacob Tirrell 1813.—Josiah m. Jennet, D. of John Keith 1820.

9. James and his w. Rebecca had Andrew Barton 1798.

10. Isaac (s. of Hezekiah 3.) m. Sally, D. of Peleg Stetson, 1803, and had Sally 1803, Isaac 1805, Nahum 1806, Dexter 1809, James Baxter 1815.

11. John (s. of Simeon) m. Lucy Lucas, and had Zadock 1750 in E. B. Zadock m. Lucy Gardner, and had Olive 1773, Miriam, Rachel, Bela, Rhoda, Simeon, John, Obed, Luther, Anna, Lucy, Polly : he removed to Pembroke.—Olive m. Samuel P. French 1801.—Rachel d. 1782, æ. 26.—Bela m. Polly, D. of Jonathan Beals, 1793 : she d. 1795, æ. 25.

12. Joseph (s. of Hezekiah 3.) m Charlotte, D. of Peleg

Stetson, 1807, and had Lucius 1808, Aaron 1811, Charlotte Tirrell 1814.

13. Joshua Reed, from Abington, lives in E. B.; his children
are Joshua, Daniel N., John, Mehitabel, Deborah.

Mary m. Simeon Gannett 1775.—Ezekiel Reed m. Hannah
Beal 1742.—Samuel P. of A. m. Polly Bates 1816.—Rebecca,
member of ch. E. B. 1743.—Mary T. m. Ophir Howe 1818.—
Oran of A. m. Charlotte Harden 1817.—Lucy m. Pliny Edson
1819.—John Jr. of A. m. Harriet Churchill 1818.—Edwin m.
Farozina Glass 1822.—Elizabeth of Scit. m. Seth Gannett Jr.
1821.—Esther m. David Hearsey 1707.—Abigail m. Nat. Whit-
aker of Rehoboth 1711.—Sarah m. Hezekiah King 1712.—Ste-
phen m. Mary Whitmarsh 1714.—Ruth m. Seth Whitman 1741.
Rebecca m. Nathan Allen 1743.—Wid. Ruth m. Samuel Porter
1764.—Capt. Daniel m. wid. Sarah Dawes 1765.—Obadiah m.
Elizabeth Shaw 1770.—Seth m. Thankful Whitmarsh 1773.—
Rhoda m. Richard Smith 1773.—Seth m. Mary Lazell 1776.—
Naomi m. Obadiah Hearsey 1777.—Ruth m. Adams Bailey 1783.
James m. Ruth Porter 1784.—Polly Reed of Plymouth m. a
Muxam, and afterwards William Bowen, and lives in E. B.—
Frederick Jr. of Ran. m. Sally Packard 1797.—Sarah of E. m.
Lem'l Lathrop 1794.—Rachel of Pem. m. Isaac Snell 1800.—
Sally of M. m. Amos Keith Jr. 1801.—Ezekiel m. Hannah Lit-
tlefield of R. 1807.—Jane m. Daniel Bates 1810.—Abiah m. Jane
Gurney 1814.

REA.—Jeremiah Rea and Mary his wife had Daniel Putnam
and Israel Fuller 1798, John Flavel 1801.

REYNOLDS.—Nath'l Reynolds Esq. (s. of Nath'l of Boston)
settled in N. B.; m. Hannah Hartwell 1739, and had Philip 1740,
Jonas 1742. She d., and he m. Mary Tolman, and had Timothy
1746, Hannah 1750, Mary 1754, Nath'l 1757, David 1759, Silence
1760, Jonathan 1764, Cynthia 1769: he removed to Vassalbo-
rough, Me., with his 5 youngest children. Hannah m. William
Packard 1769.—Mary m. Dea. Ebenezer Packard 1774.—Jona.
m. Anna, D. of Jeremiah Thayer, 1794, and went to Sidney,
Me.—Nath'l m. Bethiah, D. of Levi Keith, 1777.

2. Thomas (brother of Nathaniel above) m. Elizabeth Turner
1748, and had Amy 1749*, Joseph 1751, Amy 1753, Elizabeth
1755, Susanna 1757, Martha 1759, Thomas 1762, Josiah 1766:
he d. 1795, æ. 77. Amy m. Silas Dunbar 1772.—Susanna m.
Oliver Howard 1780.—Martha m. Capt. Parmenas Packard
1778.—Thomas m. Tabitha, D. of Jeremiah Thayer, 1785, and
went to Me.—Josiah m. a Phillips and went to Vermont.

Nathaniel of Boston, father of the two brothers above. m.
Mary, D. of Thomas Snell, and when he d. the wid. came back
with her children, and she m. David Ames 1722.

3. Philip (s. of Nathaniel 1.) m. Hannah, D. of Wm. Packard,
1765, and had William 1767, Hannah 1769, Charity 1771, Philip,
and Polly. He d., and she m. Enos Thayer 1782.—Charity m.
Leonard Orcutt 1797.—Polly m. Oliver Belcher 1798.—William

m. Martha, D. of Capt. Zebedee Snell, 1791, and went to Me.—
Philip went to St.

4. Jonas (s. of Nathaniel 1.) m. Anna, D. of Luke Perkins, a.
1768, and had Anna 1769, Jonas 1772, Isaac 1774, John, David
P., Jonathan, Polly. Anna m. Josiah Perkins Jr. 1790.—Polly
m. Isaac French 1800.—Wid. Anna m. Dea. Elijah Snell 1798.—
John m. Falley Wales of St. 1802.—David P. m. Sarah, D. of
Andrew Bartlett of Plymo., 1818, and settled in E. B.

5. Timothy (s. of Nathaniel 1.) and his w. Rebecca had Hannah 1770, Molly 1775: he then went to Vassalboro', Me.

6. Joseph (s. of Thomas 2.) m. Jemima, D. of Luke Perkins,
1772, and had Ichabod, Joseph, Daniel, Simeon, Azel, Thomas,
Jemima, Olive, Amy, Susanna, Vesta. Capt. Ichabod m, Polly,
D. of Isaac Brett, 1796, and went to Minot, Me.—Azel m. Susanna Nash 1812.—Thomas m. Nancy Pike 1819.—Olive m.
Joseph Macomber 1798.—Amy m. Ziphion Howard 1803.—Susanna m. Capt. Silas Dunbar 1806.—Vesta m. Isaac Clapp 1814.

7. Jonas (s. of Jonas 4.) m. Rebecca, D. of Joseph Hayward,
1798, and had Martin Luther 1799, Orren 1801, Anna 1803,
Mary 1805, Jo. Hayward 1808, Rebecca 1814.

8. Isaac (s. of Jonas 4.) m. Mehitabel Ford 1805, and had
Polly 1806, Edwin 1808, Nahum 1809, Benjamin Franklin 1810,
Sibil 1814.

9. Joseph (s. of Joseph 6.) m. Martha, D. of Silas Dunbar,
1798, and had Olive 1798, Pamela 1800, Sophia 1802, Oliver
1804, Nancy 1808, Daniel 1810, Susanna 1812, Luke 1815.—
Joseph Jr. m. Phebe Whitcomb 1817.

10. Simeon (s. of Joseph 6.) m. Mary, D. of Capt. Zebedee
Snell 1809, and had Simeon Otis 1809.

Nathaniel and Sarah Reynolds of Boston had Sarah 1687.—
Isaac m. Dorothy Seeker of Mid'o., 1707.

Elizabeth m. Perez Packard 1803.—Zilpha m. Joshua Howard 1805.—Nathaniel Jr. of Sidney m. Hannah Porter 1811.

RICHARDS.—Benjamin Richards (from Weymouth) settled
in W. B., and m. Mehitabel, D. of Isaac Alden, 1711, and had
Mehitabel 1712, Joseph 1714, Daniel 1716, James 1718, Sarah
1720. His w. d., and he m. Lydia Faxon, and had John 1723,
Josiah 1724, Seth 1726, Ezra 1728, Lydia 1732, Hannah 1736.
He d. 1741: his will makes no mention of James or Seth. James
Richards m. Susanna Pratt 1740, on Abington records : both of
them there said to be of Br.—Mehitabel m. David Packard Jr.
1737.—Joseph went to St.—Sarah m. Wm. Packard 1740.—Ezra
was a schoolmaster.—Lydia m. Dea. Nathan Alden (his 2d wife)
1757.—Hannah m. Dr. Philip Bryant (his 2d wife) 1779.

2. Daniel (s. of Benjamin 1.) m. Mary, D. of David Packard,
1740, and had Daniel 1741*, William 1741*, and a D. 1742*.

3. John (s. of Benjamin 1.) m. Keziah, D. of Capt. Israel
Bailey, 1751, and had Sarah 1752, Keziah 1755, Benjamin 1758,
Seth 1763, James 1766, Ezra 1768, Tamzin 1770, Lydia 1773,
Jennet 1774: he d. 1812. Sarah m. Joseph Thayer Jr. of St.

1795, and afterwards Dea. Zacheus Thayer.—Keziah m. James Inglee 1787.—James and Ezra went westward.—Tamzin m. Joseph Snow Jr. 1795.

4. Dea. Josiah (s. of Benjamin 1.) m. Anna Robinson of Raynham 1781, and had Josiah 1783, Zeba 1786, Daniel 1788: he d. 1815, æ. 90. Zeba m. Polly, D. of Daniel Hartwell 1817.—Daniel m. Lentha, D. of Daniel Hartwell, 1812.

5. Benjamin (s. of John 3.) m. Polly, D. of Richard Bartlett of N. Scotia, 1782, and had Rhoda 1783, Bartlett 1785, Avery 1788, Polly 1792: he d. 1812, æ. 54. Rhoda m. Samuel G. Alden 1804.—Bartlett was a shipmaster, and d. at sea.—Avery went to Duxbury.

6. Seth (s. of John 3.) m. Mehitabel, D. of Joseph Snow, 1791, and had Betsy 1793, John 1796, Luther 1798, Ward 1801, Ruth 1803: he d. 1837. John m. Hannah, D. of Jonathan Kingman, 1820.—Ward m. Mehitabel, D. of John Brown.

Joseph Richards and Sarah of Weymouth: his will 1695 mentions Joseph, James, Susanna, Sarah, and " all the rest of my sons and daughters" of whom probably Benjamin first above named was one. There was a John and Sarah at Weymouth also who had a s. Benjamin 1786.

There was a family of Richards lived in S. B.—Nathan had Nathan, James, Hannah and Polly twins.—Hannah m. Josiah Edson 1791,—Polly m. Marcus Leonard 1793.—James m. Susanna, D. of Abner Pratt, 1798.—Nathan m. Lydia Hayward 1813.—Isaac m. Esther Holbrook 1817.—Anne m. Edward Benton of Prov. 1816.—James of Newton m. Dorothy Packard 1777.—Sarah m. William Davenport 1730.—Joseph m. Mary Hamlin 1742.—Susanna m. Silas Williams 1760.—Timothy of Ded. m. Sarah, D. of Sam'l Edson, 1778.—Milicent m. Silvanus Washburn 1765.—James m. Susanna Pratt 1740.

RICHARDSON.—Winslow Richardson lived in E. B., m. Rhoda, D. of Benjamin Johnson, 1763, and had Benjamin 1764, Ruth Holman 1765. His w. d., and he m. Elizabeth, D. of Joseph Byram, 1768, and had Susanna 1771, Joseph Byram 1773: he then removed from town.

Stephen Richardson m. Ruth, D. of Benjamin Johnson.—Rebeckah Richardson m. Zebulun Packard 1764, and afterwards Silas Kinsley 1774.—Hannah of Leicester m. Joseph Burr 1792.

RICKARD, or RECORD.—Thomas Record lived in E. B., and had John 1725: he was one of the committee for settling the Rev. John Angier: he lived perhaps in what is now Hanson.

2. Elkanah Rickard lived in S. B., m. Bethiah, D. of Nath'l Conant, 1733, and had Seth 1735, Amasa 1738, Uriah 1740, Keturah 1744: he d. 1777. Seth m. Susanna Packard 1757.—Amasa m. Deliverance, D. of Joseph Pratt 1759.—Uriah m. Zilpha White 1761.

3. Nathaniel lived also in S. B., m. Jerusha, D. of James Dunbar, 1751, and had Daniel 1752, Asher 1754, Elkanah 1759, Ebenezer 1761, Susanna 1763, Rufus 1765.

4. Jacob and Hannah had Salome 1758, Hannah 1760, Bartholomew 1765, d. 1789 : the father d. 1809. Salome m. Enoch Pratt 1784.

5. Salmon Rickard m. Olive, D. of Capt. Elijah Edson 1786, and had Seth 1788, How 1790, Thomas 1794, Calvin 1796, Salmon 1799; and went to Mid'o.—This name was often pronounced Ricket.

Hannah Rickard m. Josiah Byram 1720.—Elizabeth m. John Whitman 1726.—Mehitabel m. Arthur Harris 1730.—Rebecca m. Dea. Seth Allen 1735, and then Dea. Thomas Whitman 1767 : these were all from Plympton.—Joseph of P. m. Lydia Willis 1737.—Samuel m. Mary Bumpus 1749.—Nathan m. Mary Snell 1767.—Elisha Reckords m. Ruth Chamberlin 1775.—Alice m. Joab Willis Jr. 1772.—Sarah m. John Willis 1779.—Betty m. Dea. Noah Edson 1782.—Lucy m. Joshua Washburn 1786.—Chloe m. Nehemiah Pratt 1793.—Hannah m. William Badger 1819.

RIDER.—Samuel Rider lived and d. in S. B., m. Lydia, D. of Benjamin Washburn, 1799, and his s. in law, Benjamin Darling, and his brother Abner Rider, a bachelor, live on the same place.

Captain Samuel Rider (from Plymouth) m. a Dunham, and settled and lives in W. B., and has Samuel, Lewis, William, and others.—Samuel m. Anne and Lewis m. Elizabeth, Ds. of Dea. Joseph Kingman.—William went to N. B.

RIPLEY.—William Ripley and his wife, two ss., Abraham and John, and 2 Ds., came from Hingham, England, and settled here at Hingham 1638 : he probably m. Elizabeth, wid. of Thos. Thaxter, 1654, and d. 1656 : he was ancestor probably of all of the name in this part of the country.—Sarah m. Jeremiah Beal at H. 1654.

1. William Ripley and his w. Mary settled in W. B., and had Margaret, Sarah 1696, John 1698, Martha 1700, William 1702, Samuel 1705, Jonathan 1707, Timothy 1710, Christopher 1712. Sarah m. George Bryant.—Martha m. John Rawson.

2. John (s. of William 1.) m. Deborah, D. of Israel Washburn, and had Mary 1730, Waitstill 1732, Deborah 1734. He d., and the wid. m. Nathaniel Bolton 1740, and d. 1759.—Mary m. Amos Hayward 1766.—Waitstill m. Isaac Lee 1751.

3. Samuel (s. of William 1.) m. Abigail, D. of John Bolton, 1736, and had Robert 1737. Abigail, the mother, or a D., m. Stephen Pettingill 1764.

4. Christopher (s. of William 1.) m. Sarah, D. of Maj. Edward Howard, 1737, and had Solomon 1737, Jane 1743, Bethiah 1745. Bethiah m. Jabez Bolton 1765.

5. Solomon (s. of Christopher 4.) m. Miriam Briggs 1758, and had Christopher 1758, Elizabeth 1761, Daniel 1764, Marlbray 1767, Nathaniel 1771, and Deborah : he d. 1809. Marlbray m. Ruth Whiting 1787.—Deborah m. Cyrus Hayward 1804.

6. Capt. Daniel (s. of Solomon 5.) m. Martha, D. of David

286 ROBBINS—ROBINSON.

Harvey, 1783, and had Mary 1783, Martha 1787, Daniel 1791, Susanna 1792, d. 1822; Orra 1795, David H. 1798, Deborah 1801: he d. 1819. Orra m. Alson Field 1820.

Polly m. Sihon Morse of St. 1804.—Sally of Plympton m. Nathan Hartwell 1789.—Hannah of E. m. Sam'l Edson 3d 1797. Elizabeth m. Jacob Keith 1801.—Lydia of Plympton m. Zephaniah Lathrop Jr. 1812.

ROBBINS.—Nicholas Robbins was one of the original Proprietors of B., but never resided here: was at Duxbury 1640, and d. there a. 1650. He had John, Catharine, Mary, and Hannah: he gave John half his land at the New Plantation, and the other half to his daughters.

2. John settled here, and had Jeduthun 1667: he in some way became helpless, for Goodman Turner (George) was ordered to maintain his brother John Robbins 1668.

3. Jeduthun sold his house and land to Sam'l Kinsley a. 1700, "butting on the S. side Town River adjoining the S. E. side of Thos. Washburn's, where his house stands." Robbins had then removed to Plympton, and d. there a. 1726, and had Jeduthun, John, Lemuel, Persis w. of Jona. Wood, Hannah w. of Barnabas Wood, Elizabeth, Abigail, Mehitabel.

4. Benjamin Robbins and his wife Susanna, D. of Daniel Keith, lived in Titicut, S. B., and had a family, but removed to M., and had Benjamin and Susanna 1789, Abigail 1791. Benjamin m. Patience Morton 1814.—Susanna m. Oliver Keith 1809. Abigail m. Salmon Keith Jr. 1814.

Betsy of Watertown m. Alfred Whitman 1809.—Moses of Mid. m. Patience Hooper 1777.—Polly, sister of Betsy, d. here 1794, æ. 17.

ROBINSON.—Gain Robinson (from Ireland) landed at Plymouth, lived at Braintree, Pembroke, and finally in E. B., had recommendations from churches in Ireland, Braintree and Pembroke: his w. was Margaret Watson, by whom he had Alexander, Joseph, Gain 1724, Increase 1727, Betty 1728, James 1730, John 1732, Margaret 1735, Mary 1738, Martha 1740, Jane 1742, Robert 1746: he also had by a former w. a s. Archibald, and a D. Susanna who m. Christopher Erskins, an Irishman also, who settled in A. He d. 1763, æ. 81; she, his 2d wife, 1777, æ. 77. His 9 youngest children only were born here, or after the incorporation of the parish. Alexander m. Hannah White of A. 1745, and had a D. Abigail 1746, and went to Nova Scotia.—Increase m. Rachel Bates of Hingham 1755, and d. in the French war, a Serjeant, under Gen. Winslow at Nova Scotia, between 1755 and 1757: had no children.—Mary m. Richard Bartlett 1757.—Martha m. Archibald Thompson 1761.—John m. a Studley, and settled in Kingston, and had a family: his D. Martha m. Eliphalet Bailey 1782.

2. Joseph (s. of Gain 1.) m. Abigail, D. of Joseph Keith, 1746, and had Joseph 1747, Benjamin 1748, Edward 1750, Susanna 1753, Abigail 1755. His w. d., and he m. Hannah, D. of

Isaac Snow, 1759, and had Isaac 1760*, Hannah 1763*, Snow 1765*. His estate was settled by his wid. and his brother James 1766.—Joseph d. æ. about 20.—Edward d. 1818, æ. 67, a bachelor.—Susanna m. William Vinton 1774.—Abigail m. Silvanus Lazell 1775.—Isaac lost at sea.—Hannah d. single 1802, æ. 39, burnt in a fit.—Snow d. at West Point in the army 1783, æ. 19.

3. Gain (s. of Gain 1.) m. a Dyer, and had Gain, William, Increase, John, Dyer 1765, Joseph, Ansel, Sally, and Zibeah who m. Daniel Packard and went to Pelham: he d. 1778 of small-pox, æ. 54. Gain m. a Gardner, lived in Hanson or Abington, and had a family.—Sally m. Solomon Johnson 1788.—John m. Molly, D. of Thomas Packard, 1781, and had John, Mary, Daniel, Abiel, Sarah, Zibeah. John, Mary, and Daniel went to Portland.—Abiel and Sarah went to Cambridgeport.—Sarah m. Sam'l Pond.—Zibeah not m.—Daniel afterwards went to Bangor.

4. James (s. of Gain 1.) m. Jerusha, D. of Ebenezer Bartlett of Duxbury, and had James and Bartlett twins, Watson, Abner, Gain, Clark, Jerusha Bartlett 1753, Margaret 1754, Mary, Elizabeth, Jane, Esther, Eleanor, Bethiah, and Martha.—James and Bartlett d. in the revolutionary war.—Watson moved to the westward.—Abner was killed at Saratoga 1777.—The family all moved to Cummington.—Gain was a physician there, and Clark d. there.—Jerusha B. m. Wait Wadsworth of Duxbury.—Margaret m. a Fay, and moved westward.—Mary m. David Orr, and went to the 9 Partners.—Elizabeth m. in Cummington.—Jane m. William Johnson 1779.—Esther, Eleanor and Bethiah m. in Cummington.—The father lived first on Clark's Island, and finally lived and d. in Cummington.—He was here in 1766, and administered on his brother Joseph's estate.

5. Robert (s. of Gain 1.) m. Bethiah, D. of Isaac Kingman, 1772, and had Samuel, James, and others probably, and went to Cummington.

6. Archibald (s. of Gain 1. probably) m. Mercy, D. of Richard Field 1747, and had Robert 1747, John 1749.

7. Benjamin (s. of Joseph 2.) m. Eve, D. of James Packard, 1770, and had Anna 1771, Deborah 1777, Susanna 1781, Benjamin 1784, Kilborn 1787, Polly 1790, Hodijah 1793. His w. d., 1796, æ. 46, and he m. Keziah, wid. of Elijah Packard and D. of Capt. John Ames, 1798, and had Nabby Lazell 1799, Bethiah Ames 1802, Margaret Watson 1806 : he d. 1829, æ. 80; she 1838, æ. 74. Anna m. Uriah Brett 1799.—Deborah m. John Alden 1798.—Susanna m. Ichabod Keith 1802.—Polly m. a Bradbury in Maine, and had a 2d husband Herrick in Boston.—Nabby L. m. Samuel P. Condon 1821, and d. 1832, æ. 33.—Bethiah A. m. Martin Ramsdell.—Margaret W. m. Samuel P. Condon, his 2d wife.—Kilborn not m.

8. William (s. of Gain 3.) m. Hannah, D. of Hezekiah Egerton, 1780, and had William 1784, Abigail 1786*, d. 1804 ; Marcus 1791, Sally 1795, Mary Hitchborn and Maria Dyer 1799 : he d. 1816; she 1832, æ. 72. William m. Abigail Delano of

Dux. 1812.—Marcus m. Charlotte Barstow of Pem. 1820.—Sally m. Henry Gray, and Mary H. m. James Sidall, both Englishmen.

9. Dyer (s. of Gain 3.) m. Abigail, D. of Abishai Stetson, 1787, and settled in S. B., and had Clarissa 1787, Increase 1789, Dyer 1792, Gad 1795, Jacob 1798, Charles, Salome, Abigail, Enoch. Clarissa m. Solomon Perkins 1813.—Increase m. Hannah, D. of Benjamin Edson 1812.—Dyer m. a Standish.—Gad m. Margaret Orr, D. of Zenas Keith 1821.—Jacob m. Rhoda W. Chandler of Hanson, and had Caroline E. 1823, Jacob Harvey, 1826, Lydia Hall 1827.—Charles m. Ann Maria, D. of Zenas Keith.—Salome m. Zenas Keith, Jr. 1821.—Abigail m. Capt. Scott Keith.

10. Capt. Benjamin (s. of Benjamin 7.) m. Mary Packard, D. of his mother-in-law, 1809, and had Benjamia Rosseter, James Lawrence, Elijah Packard 1816, Mary 1818. James L. d. at sea 1835.

11. Hodijah (s. of Benjamin 7.) m. Silvia, D. of Hugh Orr, and had Lucia Watson, Herbert.

Increase Robinson was on a Jury at Plymo. 1683: perhaps the Taunton and Raynham family descended from him. There was an Increase Robinson who was a Captain in the beginning of the Revolutionary war.—Increase Robinson m. Margaret Bonney 1738.—Abigail m. John Fobes 1704.—Abigail m. Thos. Bibby 1776.—Margaret, D. of Gain Robinson Jr., m. Joseph Wesley 1773.—Anna of Raynham m. Dea. Josiah Richards 1781.—Nabby of Mid. m. John Ripley Hayward 1801, and Clarissa of Mid. m. him 1802.—Robert m. Chloe Harvey of Freetown 1807.—Mehitabel m. Daniel Perkins 2d 1809.—Perez m. Margaret Tomson of H. 1819.—Zaccheus H. m. Margaret Fillebrown of Mansfield 1819.

ROGERS.—John Rogers of Duxbury was an original Proprietor of this town, but never lived here. He is the same man who went to Scituate, and finally d. in Weymouth 1661. The family tradition is that he was a descendant of John Rogers the martyr of Smithfield. His ss. were John, Thomas, and Samuel, who settled at Rogers' Brook in Marshfield.

2. Samuel (s. of Thomas of Marshfield) came and settled in East Bridgewater, and m. Betty, D. of Capt. Jacob Allen, (who was killed at Saratoga, near Stillwater, at the capture of Bourgoyne, 1777), 1790, and had Nabby 1790, Charles 1799, Jacob Allen 1804, Thomas Hatch 1806. Nabby m. William Newhall 1807.—Charles m. Sarah Tomson at Halifax 1821.—Jacob A. m. Lucia, D. of Eleazar Keith.—Thomas H. m. Charity Tomson of Halifax 1835, sister of Charles' w., D. of Maj. Nathaniel Tomson. Samuel, the father d. 1838, æ. 72; the mother d. 1831, æ. 63.

Sarah Rogers m. Josiah Churchill 1781.—There was a Thos. Rogers, one of the forefathers, who came in the first ship, the Mayflower, 1620, and d. the first winter, who probably left a s.

Joseph, who is named among those to whom lands were allotted in 1623. Whether he was a relation of John first above named is not ascertained.

RUSSELL.—Thomas Russell (from Scotland) first lived at Weymouth, and there m. Abigail Vinton and afterwards settled in E. B., and had Mary, Betsy, Abigail, and Agnes 1775*.—Mary m. Isaac Alden 1781.—Betsy m. Maj. James Barrell 1785.—Abigail m. Dea. Wm. Keith 1789: he d. 1800, æ. 76; she 1802, æ. 56.

RYON.—Micah (or Michael) Ryon, an Irishman, lived in W. B.: his wife Ruth: he had Nathaniel 1787 (at Scituate), Betsy 1789, William 1791, Isaac 1801. He d. 1811.

SANGER.—The Rev. Zedekiah Sanger, D. D., came from Duxbury, where he had been some time settled in the ministry, and was installed in S. B. as colleague with the Rev. John Shaw, Dec. 17, 1788: he was born in Sherburne, gra. H. U. 1771: his w. Irene Freeman: he had Deborah, Richard, Caroline, Joseph, Olive, Ralph, Samuel, Sarah, Zedekiah, Eliza: he d. Nov. 17, 1820, æ. 73. Deborah m. John Ames Jr. 1799.—Richard gra. H. U. 1800, m. Sally Tisdale of Taunton 1807.—Caroline m. Rev. Samuel Clark 1810.—Joseph m. Hannah, D. of Dr. Marcy of Plymo. 1812.—Olive m. Geo. Moore of Burlington 1815.—Rev. Ralph gra. H. U. 1808, and m. Charlotte, D. of Ezra Kingman Esq. of E. B. 1817, and settled at Dover, Ms.—Sarah m. a Physician of Providence.

2. Samuel (s. of Rev. Zedekiah 1.) m. Susan, D. of Caleb Alden, but has no children: he remains on the family estate : all the rest of the family moved away.

SAWIN.—Dr. Daniel Sawin (s. of Eliphalet) came from Randolph and settled in E. B., m. Hannah, D. of Maj. James Barrell, 1810, and had Eliza Russell 1811, Hannah 1814. His w. d., 1816, and he m. a Cushing of Hanson for his 2d wife. He d. 1822, æ. 36.

SEABURY.—Barnabas Seabury (s. of Samuel Jr. of Duxbury) and his w. Mary settled in E. B., and had Rebecca 1723. His w. d., and he m. again, and soon removed from Town.

SEALY.—Edward Sealy m. Elizabeth, wid. of James Howard, and D. of John Washburn, and settled in W. B., and had Benjamin 1693, John 1697: his will 1698: names his ss. Benjamin of Easton (or North Purchase) and John of Bridgewater. The family all went to E. John of E. m. Sabrina, D. of Jona. Snow Esq. 1818.—The name is now generally written Seele or Selee.

SEARS.—Josiah Sears came from Yarmouth and settled in E. B. about 1711, and m. Mercy, D. of Isaac Harris, and had Jonathan 1714, Mercy 1717, Hannah 1720. His w. d. 1720, and he m. Judith Gilbert 1720, and had Nathaniel 1721, Elizabeth 1725. He removed back to the Cape a. 1725. He lived back of Sam'l B. Allen's, in the old house owned afterwards by Capt. Jona. Bass.—Roland Sears of Ashfield m. Jedidah Conant 1777.

37

Capt. Elkanah Sears lived in S. B.—Desire of H. m. Benjamin Washburn 1762.—Josiah Sears of H. m. Mary Porter 1817. Abner of M. m. Lydia, D. of Solomon Perkins 1762.

SEVER.—Christopher Sever (from Dorchester) settled in E. B., m. Hannah Harden of Hanson 1771, and had Robert 1772, Ruth 1774, Amos, 1778, Bethaniah 1780, Daniel 1782, Calvin 1785, Samuel 1787, Christiana 1790, Amelia 1800, Isabella, Hannah Wendell.

Robert Sever (s. perhaps of Robert) m. Priscilla, D. perhaps of Henry Thornbury Smith, 1818.—Wendell m. Joan Dickerman of E. 1813.

SHAW.—Abraham Shaw (of Dedham) made free 1637 : his will on Boston records without date : inventory taken 1638 by Wm. Allen and others : Nicholas Byram and Joseph Shaw witnesses : sons Joseph and John ; Ds. Mary and Martha : John and Martha infants : no wife named, probably d. The ss. had the estate at Dedham, the rest divided among *all* his children.—Joseph Shaw and Nicholas Byram of Weymouth granted to Robert Mason all their house and grounds in Dedham 1639.— It is supposed Byram m. a D. (Susanna) of Abraham, and that he and Joseph, both then of age, sold their lands in Dedham and the family all removed to Weymouth.—Byram called John Shaw of Weymouth his brother in 1687.

John (probably s. of Abraham) and Alice had John, Elizabeth 1655, Abraham 1657, Mary 1660, Nicholas 1662, Joseph 1664, Alice 1666, Hannah 1668, Benjamin 1670, Abigail 1672, Ebenezer 1674. Joseph, elder brother of John, had also a family at Weymouth, Joseph, John, &c., and d. 1653.

1. Joseph (s. of John above, born 1664) m. Judith, D. of John and Sarah Whitmarsh : she was born 1669 : he came and settled in E. B. before 1698. His children were Elizabeth 1687, Joseph 1691, Judith 1693, Abigail 1695, all born at Weymouth, Ruth 1698, Martha 1700, Sarah 1702, Hannah 1704, Ebenezer 1706, John 1708, Zechariah 1711: he d. 1718, æ. 54 ; she 1760, æ. 91. Elizabeth m. Noah Washburn 1710, and Isaac Harris 1719.—Joseph and Judith were never m.—Abigail m. Daniel Alden 1717 : the late Dr. Ebenezer Alden of Randolph was her grandson.—Ruth m. James Snow a. 1719.—Martha m. Eleazar Alden 1720.—Sarah m. Dea. James Cary 1722.—Hannah m. Isaac Snow 1722, and afterwards John Whitman 1743.

2. Zechariah (s. of Nicholas of Weymouth, who was brother of Joseph 1.) lived and d. in E. B.: his wife Sarah : they both joined the church here 1735: he had Zechariah, Sarah b. here 1735. Zechariah chose his uncle John Shaw of Weymouth for his guardian 1736 ; his father then d. The family perhaps returned to Weymouth.

3. Ebenezer (s. of Joseph 1.) m. Mary, D. of Samuel Reed, 1733, and had Mary 1738, Abigail 1740, Hannah 1742, Susanna 1744, Deborah 1746, Huldah 1747, Ebenezer 1752, Betty 1754, Mehitabel 1756: he d. 1776, æ. 70. Mary joined the Ch. 1758,

and had a dis'n. same year. Abigail m. Silas Harris, and afterwards Jonathan Gannett 1785, and went to Cummington.—Susanna m. Pollycarpus Snell 1766.—Deborah m. a Ford of A. Huldah m. John Bisbee 1779.—Ebenezer went to Cummington. Betty d. single 1832, æ. 78.—Mehitabel m. Ebenezer Bisbee 1778.

4. Rev. John (s. of Joseph 1.) gra. H. U. 1729, ord. in S. B., Nov. 17, 1731, m. Ruth, D. of the Rev. Samuel Angier of Watertown, and sister of the Rev. John Angier of E. B., and had Oakes 1736, Bezaliel 1738, William 1741, Eunice 1743, Ruth 1744, Ezra 1746, John 1748, Samuel 1750: she d. 1768, æ. 63; he d. April 29, 1791, æ. 82. Oakes gra. H. U. 1758, and settled in the ministry at Barnstable 1760, and d. 1807, æ. 71, and was father of the Hon. Lemuel Shaw C. J. of the S. J. C. of Mass., and of an only D. who m. Maj. Blish of Barnstable.—Bezaliel gra. H. U., 1762, and settled in the ministry at Nantucket, and his only child was w. of the late Dr. Craigie of Cambridge.— William, D. D., gra. H. U.1762, and settled in the ministry at Marshfield 1766, and d. 1816, æ. 75, and had Josiah Crocker and Philander, both settled in the ministry.—Ezra d. 1764.—John gra. H. U. 1772, and settled in the ministry at Haverhill; m. a Smith, sister of President Adams' wife, and was father of Wm. S. Shaw, former Clerk of the District Court in Boston, who d. single 1826: he d. 1794: his wid. m. Rev. Mr. Peabody of Atkinson, N. H.: he had also a D. who m. Rev. Joseph Felt.— Eunice d. single 1791, æ. 49.—Ruth m. Gen. Nath'l Goodwin of Plymouth 1782, and was mother of the late Rev. Ezra S. Goodwin of Sandwich, and Anne, w. of Dr. Boutelle.

5. Dea. Zechariah (s. of Joseph 1.) remained on the family estate in E. B., m. Sarah, D. of Daniel Packard 1733, and had Sarah 1734, Ruth 1738, Martha 1740, Daniel 1742, Elizabeth 1744, Judith 1749, Zechariah 1751, Nehemiah 1753: he d. 1790, æ. 79; she 1792, æ. 77. Ruth m. Joseph Snow 1759.—Martha d. 1825 not m.—Elizabeth m. Obadiah Reed 1770.—Judith m. John Edson 1770.—Nehemiah m. Molly Hill (or Beal, qu.) 1775. Sarah Shaw m. Elijah Snow in E. B. 1780.

6. Dr. Samuel (s. of the Rev. John 4.) remained on the family estate, and m. Olive, D. of Zebulun Leonard Esq. of Mid'o. 1781, and had Hannah Whitmarsh, John Angier, Zebulun Leonard, Sarah Miller. Hannah W. m. Joseph Ames Jr. 1812.— John A. gra. H. U. 1811, went to the southward, there m. a White; she d.: he returned again, and m. Mira, D. of Capt. Ephraim Sprague : she first m. John Washburn.—Zebulun L. gra. H. U. 1815, and d. at New Orleans July 22d, 1819, æ. 24.— Sarah M. m. Col. Abram Washburn.

7. Zechariah (s. of Dea. Zechariah 5) m. Hannah, D. of Samuel Bisbee, 1777, and had Joseph, Sarah, Alvan 1785. He d. 1820, æ. 68; she 1832, æ. 82. Sarah d. 1825, æ. 43.—Joseph m. Olive, D. of Samuel Dike 1805.

8. Benjamin (s. of Benjamin and Hannah probably of A., b.

1728) and his wife Susanna had Chloe 1757, John 1760, both
bap. in W. B.
9. William (brother of Benjamin next above b. 1730) settled
in N. B., m. Hannah West 1754, and had Hannah, William 1757,
Dan 1758, Rhoda 1762, Napthali 1764, Betsy 1766, Micah 1768,
and Patience. His w. d., and he m. Dorcas Smith 1773, and had
Abigail 1775 : he d. 1809, æ. 79 ; she 1797, æ. 64.—Hannah m.
Mark Packard 1774.—William m. Deliverance, D. of Ezekiel
Washburn, 1778.—William Jr. m. Pamela Rugg of D. 1791.—
Dan m. a Perkins of M. and went to Lyme, N. H.—Rhoda m.
Benja. Kingman 1783, and went to Winchester.—Napthali gra.
Dart. C. 1790, and m. Polly, D. of Dr. John S. Crafts and set-
tled in the ministry at Kensington, N. H.—Betsy m. Isaac Hor-
ton 1804.—Patience m. Nath'l Southworth 1793.—Abigail m.
Ziba Wood.
10. Micah (s. of William 9.) m. Jane (Jenny), D. of Matthew
Kingman 1793, and had Caroline 1794, Newton 1795, Zibeon
1797, Addison, Marcus, Mary Cary, Hannah, Rhoda.   Newton
m. Olive, D. of Capt. Robert Packard, 1818.—Mary Cary m.
Abiel Kingman 1819.
11. James and his w. Margaret Mora m. 1752, had David 1757,
James 1760. He afterwards had a D. Eunice bap. in E. B. 1777,
and brought a certificate from Milton Church ; and had Margaret 1779.
12. John and his w. Silence lived in E. B., and had Hannah,
Philip 1771, John 1773 : Philip and Hannah bap. in E. B. 1773.
13. Azel Shaw m. a D. of Solomon Alden, and lived in S. B.,
and had Alexander, Soranus, Charles, Azel, and others.
Gideon of Raynham m. Abigail Fobes 1767.—Hannah m. John
Haines 1709.—John of Raynham m. Dinah Leach 1761.—Ebenezer Jr. of Mid'o. m. Deborah Keith 1764.—Martha of Mid'o. m.
David Hooper 1768.—Mary of Raynham m. Ezra Fobes 1776.—
Solomon m. Anna Hayward 1782.—Nathan m. Rosamond Leo-
nard 1782.—Chloe of Mid'o. m. Ziba Leonard 1782.—Hannah
of Ab. m. Eliab Packard Jr. 1792.—Betsy of Mid'o. m. Bezer
Leach 1793.—Silas of Ab. m. Lucy White 1794.—Ruth m. Jacob
Washburn 1797.—William m. Molly Crossman 1797.—Sullivan
of Mid'o. m. Cynthia Keith 1797.—Experience m. Luther Jen-
nison of Conn. 1801.—Alexander m. Sally White of Mid'o. 1801.
Hannah of Ab. m. Eliphalet Leach 1806.—Rev. John of Ab. m.
Susanna Cary 1807.—Charles m. Lucy Tomson of Mid'o. 1810.
Charles m. Lucy Thomas of Mid'o. 1811.—Sarah of Mid'o. m.
Azor Harris Esq. 1813.—Elizabeth m. Ephraim Harlow of
Mid'o. 1815.—Ebenezer of Mid'o. m. Mary Dickerman 1816.—
Zephaniah m. Lucy, D. of Zenas Crooker.—Soranus m. Eliza-
abeth M. Alden 1816.—Susan m. Cyrus Snell 1818.—Hannah
m. Lyman Hooper 1820.—Harriet m. Ford Bearce 1820.—Mary
m. Benjamin Aldrich 1721.—Abigail m. Daniel Copeland 1791.
SHELLY.—Abner Shelly m. Melinda, D. of Azor Howe,

1812, and had Mary Hartwell 1813, Ruth Cheesman 1815, Daniel Hartwel 1817.

SHERMAN.—Anthony Sherman (his father was John and his mother was a D. or g. D. of Anthony Eames of Marshfield) came from Rochester and settled in E. B. a. 1766 : he m. Silence Ford of Marshfield, where they both originally belonged. They had Mary 1747, Hannah Oct. 25, 1749, Jane 1751, Thomas 1754, Lydia 1756, Lois 1758, Ruth, Betty 1768. Mary m. Eleazar Allen of Rochester.—Hannah m. Josiah Newton 1776, and afterwards Cushing Mitchell 1780.—Jane m. Eleazar Barrows 1773. Lydia m. Thomas Whitman 1781.—Lois m. a Blazdell of Tamworth, N. H.—Ruth m. Jareb White of Amherst 1794.—Betty m. Joseph Keith 1787, and afterwards Timothy Allen 1791.

2. Thomas (s. of Anthony 1.) m. Betsy, D. of Daniel Keith, 1781, and had Anthony (at Brookfield) 1783, Daniel 1785, Thomas 1787 (2 last at Bridgewater), Lydia, Naomi, Betsy, Martin, Hannah (5 last at Tamworth, N. H., whither he and his father removed).

SHEPARD.—Calvin Shepard m. Mary, D. of Josiah Byram, 1807, and had Silas Cleaveland 1809, Nathan Thomas 1811, Calvin 1816 : he removed to Pembroke.

SHURTLIFF.—William Shurtliff m. Sarah, D. of John Kingman, 1745, and had Silence 1747, Sarah 1749. She d. 1752, and he m. a 2d wife Rachel, and had Content 1753, Amasa 1760, Barnabas 1761. She d., and he m. a 3d w. Abigail, and had Jonathan 1793: he d., and his wid. Abigail m. Capt. Josiah Dunbar 1798.

Lucy Shurtliff m. Eleazer Cole 1769.—Simeon Shurtleff m. Submit, D. of Henry Kingman, 1781.—Ichabod Shurtleff of Plymouth m. Betty Pettingill 1787.—Jonathan of M. m. Elizabeth Leach.

SILVESTER or SYLVESTER.—Israel Sylvester of Duxbury m. Abigail, D. of Josiah Snell of W. B. 1734, and had Joseph 1735, Israel 1737, Seth 1740, Josiah 1742, Zechariah 1744, Abigail 1747. Joseph and Israel were bap. in W. B. 1739, but the family lived afterwards in Duxbury. All of the name, now numerous, descended probably from Richard Sylvester, who was at Weymouth 1630, and removed to Scituate 1642.—Zechariah above m. Mehitabel, D. of Zechariah Cary of N. B.—Abigail m. Samuel Alden of Duxbury.

2. Joseph (s. of Israel 1.) m. Lucy, D. of Ephraim Sampson of Mid'o., and settled in N. B. 1769, and had Lucy 1772, Ephraim 1774 : he had also Seth, Joseph, Benjamin, and Josiah b. before he came to this town : the father d. 1818, æ. 84.—Seth and Benjamin are d.—Josiah went to Tiverton.

3. Joseph Esq. (s. of Joseph 2.) m. Hannah, D. of Robert Howard, 1786, and had Gustavus 1786, Abigail 1788*, Hannah 1790, Clinthy 1792, Wealthy 1794*, Algernon Sidney 1798.— Gustavus m. Martha, D. of Daniel Field 1811.

Mehitabel, D. of Zechariah Sylvester of Dux. m. Zechariah

Snell 1793.—Sally m. Jesse Perkins 1808.—Rachel m. Joseph Newell 1734.—Tabitha d. in E. B. 1794, æ. 47.

SKINNER.—Jno. Skinner from Boston m. Rebecca M'Clench 1797, and had John 1799, at W. B.: he returned again to Boston.

SMITH.—Pelatiah Smith lived in W. B., and m. Jane, wid. of James Dunbar, and D. of Isaac Harris, and had Jane 1692, Pelatiah 1695, James 1697, Samuel 1699, Desire 1701, Joanna 1703, Ruhamah 1705, Robert 1708, Joseph 1710. He purchased John Bolton's house and land butting on the Town River, and bounded westerly by Joseph Hayward and Nath'l Brett 1701.— The family early removed from town.

2. John Smith (s. of John Smith of Randolph) settled in E. B., and m. Mary, D. of John Hanmer, 1749, and had Elizabeth 1750, William 1753, John 1755, Mary 1757, Daniel 1761, Sarah 1763, Dorcas 1765, Hosea 1768.—This family removed from town.—Mary d. 1778, æ. 29.—John the father d. 1790, æ. 69 : he was with Gen'l Winslow in dispersing the Neutral French 1755, at Nova Scotia.

3. John m. Susanna Hill 1777, and had Paul, and d., and she m. John Dyer 1778. John Smith m. Ruth Cornish 1779 : John Smith's w. d. 1779, and Joseph Cornish 7 days after, æ. 77.

John Smith (s. of John of E. B., and g. s. of John of Randolph) m. Hannah, D. of David Edson, 1805, and lived in N. B., and had Albert, Harrison, Salome, and Rachel.

4. Elijah Smith m. Betty, only child of Abner Harris, and lived in E. B., and had Betty 1758, Celia 1760, Abner. He removed from town. Betty d. unmarried.

5. Joseph Smith and his wife Thankful came from the Cape, and settled in E. B., and had Henry Thornbury, Mary, Rhoda, Joseph (all bap. 1779), Priscilla 1779, John 1781, Rachel 1785 : she d. 1823, æ. 74 ; he d. 1831, æ. 84. Mary m. John Crooker perhaps 1798.—Rhoda m. John Tirrell Jr. 1794.—Priscilla not m.—Joseph m. Eunice Muxam 1799 : she d. 1802. æ. 27.

6. Henry Thornbury (s. of Joseph 5.) m. Priscilla, D. of Knight Brown, 1792, and had Libeus and others, and went into Maine and preached. Libeus m. Salome, D. of Azor How, 1814, and Polly, D. of Christopher Bates, 1817.—His D. Priscilla perhaps m. Robert Sever 1818.

7. Rev. Amasa Smith m. Mary Haskell of Westborough 1815, and had Mary Haskell 1816.

8. William Smith came from Duxbury to E. B. 1832, m. a Tilden, and had William Webster 1832, Andrew Jackson, and others.

John Smith m. Jael, D. of Samuel Packard.—Solomon of E. m. Elizabeth, D. of Joseph Cole, 1761.—Elizabeth m. Josiah Whitman 1747.—Margaret of Milton m. Robert Tomson 1754. Samuel m. Abigail, D. of Ebenezer Allen.—Martha m. John Gilmore 1764.—Anna of Lexington m. Simeon Leonard 1764.— Zephaniah m. Lydia Conant 1773.—Jeremiah m. Mary Farr of Easton 1773.—Richard m. Rhoda Reed 1773.—Dorcas m. Wm.

Shaw 1773.—Abigail of Roxbury m. Joshua Bowen 1782.—
Isaac of Braintree m. Mary Conant 1783.—Chloe of Norton m.
Nathan Kingman 1785.—Lydia of Walpole m. Roland Leonard
1786.—Judith of Pembroke m. Rev. Samuel Angier 1796.—Eli-
jah m. Mary Beal 1802.—Becca m. Daniel T. Dickerman 1803.
John of Canton m. Hannah Edson 1804.—Submit m. William
Curtis 1806.—Nabby m. Silas Leonard 1785.—Rachel m. Nathan
Alger 2d 1809, Priscilla of Mid'o. m. Daniel Allen 1815.—Bath-
sheba of Hanson m. Eleazar Carver Jr. 1821.—Mary m. Benj.
Southworth 1763—Rachel m. Jonathan Lawrence 1765.—Be-
naiah m. Mary Hill 1738.—Allen m. Sally Leach 1815.

SNELL.—Thomas Snell (from England, nephew of Dea.
Samuel Edson) settled in W. B. a. 1665. He was probably the
largest landholder in the town, and some portions of it still bear
his name, as Snell's Plain, Snell's Meadows, &c. He m. Martha, D. of Arthur Harris, and had Thomas 1671, Josiah 1674,
Samuel 1676, Amos 1678, John 1680, Joseph 1683, Ann 1685,
Mary 1689, Martha 1692: his will 1724. Ann m. Nicholas Byram 1708.—Mary m. first Nathaniel Reynolds, and then David
Ames 1722.—Martha m. Ephraim Fobes 1714.

2. Thomas (s. of Thomas 1.) had Thomas 1696, Joseph, Abigail 1703, Betty 1705. He appeared to be in Mansfield 1726.—
He d. 1739.—Betty m. Jonathan Copeland 1723.—Joseph was
living with his grandfather 1721, who called him "the eldest surviving son of his son Thomas:" of course there had been other
ss. who were dead, and also, it would seem, one other at least
was living. No further account of Joseph or Abigail is obtained.

3. Josiah (s. of Thomas 1.) m. Anna, D. of Zechariah Alden
of Duxbury, 1699, and had Josiah 1701, Abigail 1702, Zechariah 1704: he d. 1753; she 1705. Abigail m. Israel Sylvester
of Duxbury 1734.

4. Samuel (s. of Thomas 1.) went to Tiverton, and was in
Newport 1726, called a Tanner. He sold land in E. B. to Joseph Shaw 1705.

5. Amos (s. of Thomas 1.) settled in S. B., m. Mary, D. of
Samuel Packard Jr., 1700, and had Mary 1700, Jemima 1704,
Susanna 1706, Amos 1709, Daniel 1711, Moses 1713, Martha
1716, Charity 1719, Keziah 1727. He d. 1769, æ. 91. Mary m.
Hugh Mehuren 1725.—Jemima m. Benjamin Snow 1722.—Susanna m. Richard Davenport Jr.—Martha m. Jonathan Benson
1740.—Charity m. Silvanus Blossom 1738.—Keziah m. Benjamin Benson 1745.

6. John (s. of Thomas 1.) m. Susanna, D. of Samuel Packard
Jr. 1715, and had John 1715*, Nathan 1718*, Samuel 1720*,
Zebulun 1721*, Samuel 1723*, Susanna 1725, Silence 1728: he
d. 1767. Susanna m. Sam'l Willis 1747.—Silence m. Elijah Hayward 1751.—There was a John Snell (at Francis Wood's in S.
B.) warned out 1735, called of Raynham; perhaps of Thomas's
or Samuel's family.

7. Joseph (s. of Thomas 1.) m. Hannah, D. of Thomas

Williams of Taunton, 1712, (Rev. Mr. Keith m. her mother for his 2d wife) and had Joseph 1713, Mary 1716, Charles 1717, Jonathan 1718, Martha 1719*, Ann 1720*, Nath'l 1721, Solomon 1723*, Hannah 1724, Mehitabel 1727*, Seth 1729*, Seth 1730, Martha 1732. He was a Tanner, and d. 1736; she 1755. Mary m. Abiah Keith 1737.—Hannah m. Nathan Keith 1746.—Martha m. Samuel Bisbee 1751.

8. Thomas (s. of Thomas 2.) m. Hannah Lewis of Mid'o. and settled in E. B., and had Deliverance 1727, Thomas 1730, Eleazar 1732, Joseph 1734*, Hannah 1735, Pollycarpus 1737, William 1740, Barnabas 1741, Lewis 1745*, Seth 1747.: he d. 1772, æ. 76; she 1793, æ. 89. Deliverance m. Nath'l Chamberlin (his 2d w.) 1767.—Thomas m. Bethiah, D. of James Allen, and went to Woolwich, Me., and left a family there.—Eleazar went to N. Y., and had a family there.—Hannah m. Benj. Chamberlin 1756.— Seth went to Warren, R. I., and left a large family.

9. Josiah (s. of Josiah 3.) m. Abigail, D. of John Fobes, 1728, and had Josiah 1730, Anna 1732, Elijah 1734, Mary 1736*, Abigail 1739*, Rhoda 1743, Nathan 1748. Anna m. Edmund Hayward 1751.—Rhoda m. Elijah Copeland 1765.

10. Dea. Zechariah (s. of Josiah 3.) m. Abigail, D. of Dea. Joseph Hayward, 1731, and was one of the early settlers in N. B., and had Issachar 1732, Abigail 1734, Zebedee 1736, Ebenezer 1738, Zechariah 1743*, Hannah 1745* : he d. 1768, æ. 64; she lived to a great age, between 90 and 100. Abigail m. Robert Howard Jr. 1757.

11. Amos (s. of Amos 5.) m. Experience Washburn 1759, 2d wife perhaps, and had Isaiah, David, Isaac, and perhaps others. Isaiah went to Me —David m. Molly Bowcker 1783.—Isaac m. Rachel Reed of Pembroke 1800.—David and Isaac went to Ware.—Amos, by first w., went to Freetown.—Amos the father d. 1791, æ. 81.

12. Dr. Daniel (s. of Amos 5.) m. Joanna Harlow 1732, and had Daniel 1733, Susanna 1735, Joanna 1738, John 1741, Lydia 1743*, Keziah 1745, Lydia 1747, Sarah 1749, Benjamin 1752, William 1754 : she d. 1795, æ. 82; he d. 1776. Susanna m. Nathan Orcutt of E. B. a. 1756.—Joanna m. Jacob Hayward 3d 1759.—Keziah m. Jeremiah Washburn 1777.—Lydia never m.— Sarah m. Jeremiah Collins perhaps of R. I. 1771.

13. Moses (s. of Amos 5.) m. Mary Besse 1736, and had Mary 1737, Charity 1739, Moses 1741, Robert 1743. Mary m. Nathan Rickard 1767.—Charity m. Elisha Washburn of Roxbury 1763. Moses m. Hannah, D. of Nathaniel Washburn, 1763, and had 4 children, who all d. 1778, and Robert and Hannah. Robert m. Joanna King of T. 1786.—Hannah m. Wm. Loring.

14. Joseph (s. of Joseph 7.) gra. H. U. 1735, engaged in no profession, lived in N. B., m. Anna Williams, and had Mary 1747, Joseph 1750, Olive 1753, Gilbert 1755 : he died 1791, æ. 78. Olive m. James Alger 2d 1781.—Gilbert d. a bachelor.

15. Charles (s. of Joseph 7.) m. Susanna, D. of Jonathan

Packard, 1745, and lived in N. B., and had Mehitabel 1745*,
Bathsheba 1747*, Jonathan 1749*, Silence 1750, Charles 1753,
Nathaniel 1755, Susanna 1757, Hannah 1759, Reuben 1761*,
Abigail 1765, Shepard 1770: he d. 1771, æ. 54.   Silence m.
Ebenezer Howard 1773.—Susanna m. Abiel Harris 1774.—
Hannah m. Jonathan Keith 1777.—Abigail m. Capt. Leavit
Thayer 1783.—Nathaniel, a bachelor.
    16. Jonathan (s. of Joseph 7.) m. Martha, D. of Ephraim
Fobes, 1751, and had Jonathan 1752, Martha 1753, Ephraim
1756, Thaddeus 1758, William 1760, Sarah and Ann 1762, Ed-
ward 1764*, Mary 1767, Caleb 1769. Mary m. Martin Burr 1792.
    17. Nathaniel (s. of Joseph 7.) gra. H. U. 1740, but engaged
in no profession, kept school, and d. at Taunton a bachelor.
    18. Pollycarpus (s. of Thomas 8.) m. Susanna, D. of Eben'r
Shaw, 1766, and had Lewis 1767, Stephen 1769, Thos. 1772, Cyrus 1774, Ebenezer 1776, d. 1804 ; Hannah 1779, d. 1808 ; Samuel 1781, Susanna 1785, d. 1809 : he d. 1866, æ. 69 ; she 1817,
æ. 73.   Thomas m. Susanna, D. of Joseph Allen 1792, and he
and Lewis went to Ware.—Cyrus was a Physician and went to
Me.—Samuel m. Phebe Cole 1810, and had Nathan T., Soranus,
d. 1833, æ. 16 ; Elbridge, d. 1834, æ. 15 ; Edwin, Mary Anne*.
Nathan T. m. Harriet Frances, D. of Francis Cary.
    19. William Esq. (s. of Thomas 8.) m. Abigail, D. of Eleazar
Alden, 1774, and had William 1776, Seth 1778, Smyrdus 1780,
Eleazar 1784 : he then removed to Ware, and thence to Tamworth, N. H., and had Alden and Martin.   He was a soldier in
the French war, and suffered much : lost the use of one leg :
kept school, and was called here, master Snell.   Wm. m. Sarah
Blossom.—Smyrdus m. Lucy, D. of Mark Phillips 1807.
    20. Barnabas (s. of Thos. 8.) m. Eunice, D. of Gershom Conant,
1783, and had Anna 1785: she d. 1795, æ. 52 ; he 1816, æ. 75.
    21. Capt. Josiah (s. of Josiah 9.) m. Susanna, D. of John
Ames, 1752, and had Susanna 1754, Barnabas 1757, Abigail 1759.
His wife d., and he m. Ruhamah, wid. of Jonas Hartwell 1763,
and had Melzar 1764, Perez 1767, Ruhamah 1769, Josiah 1771,
Hannah 1774, Lydia 1781 : he d. 1803. Susanna m. Capt. Jedediah Willis 1775.—Barnabas m. Hannah Holmes of H. 1781.—
Abigail m. James Howard Jr. 1775.—Melzar m. Anna True of
N. Y. 1789, and went to Me.—Hannah m. Jona. Upham of Canton 1799.—Lydia m. Henry Withington 1801.
    22. Dea. Elijah (s. of Josiah 9.) m. Susanna, D. of Seth How-
ard, 1760, and had Huldah 1762, Bezer 1764, Calvin 1766, Susanna 1768, Rhoda 1770, Elijah 1772, Mehitabel and Parnel
1774, Abigail 1776, Ann 1778, Polly 1780, John Eliot 1783, Lucinda 1789. She d., and he m. Ann, wid. of Jonas Reynolds and
D. of Luke Perkins.—Huldah m. Daniel Brett 1784.—Bezer
gra. H. U. 1789, went to the south, and d. young.—Rhoda m.
Charles Ames 1789.—Mehitabel m. Ebenezer Copeland Jr. 1798.
Abigail m. Capt. Lloyd Howard 1796.—Parnell m. Jesse Howard Jr. 1799.—The father and rest of the family went to Me.
                        38

23. Nathan (s. of Josiah 9.) m. Betty, D. of James Howard, 1770, and had Betty 1771, Mary 1774, Nathan 1776, Cyrus 1778, Chloe 1781, Luther 1783*, Vashti 1785, Abigail 1788, Rhoda 1791, Lentha 1794 : he d. 1802. Betty m. Salmon Copeland 1799.— Mary m. Luke Perkins 1797.—Chloe m. Nehemiah Packard 1807.—Vashti m. Barzillai Cary 1808.—Abigail m. Eliphalet Packard 1814.—Rhoda m. Capt. Nahum Leonard 1812.

24. Issachar Esq. (s. of Zechariah 10.) m. Sarah, D. of Benjamin Hayward, 1769, and had Issachar, Mehitabel*, Abigail, Sarah, Hannah : he d. 1820, æ. 88. Abigail m. Caleb Howard Esq. 1820 : his 2d wife.—Sarah m. Turner Torrey 1803.—Hannah m. Oakes Tirrell 1805.

25. Capt. Zebedee (s. of Zechariah 10.) m. Martha, D. of Ephraim Howard, 1761, and had Hannah 1762, Zechariah 1764, Oliver 1767, Martha 1769, Molly 1772. His wife d., and he m. Mary, D. of Benja. Hayward, 1777, and had Abigail 1779, Zebedee 1781, Lavinia 1783, Mary 1790.—Hannah m. Daniel Field 1786.—Martha m. William Reynolds 1791.—Molly m. Dr. Elisha Tilson 1792.—Lavinia m. Zibeon Brett 1804.—Mary m. Simeon Reynolds 1809.

26. Ebenezer Esq. (s. of Zechariah 10.) m. Sarah, D. of Capt. Abiel Packard, 1764, and removed to Cummington, and was the father of the Rev. Thomas Snell of N. Brookfield, and of a D. who m. Dr. Peter Bryant, and who was mother of Wm. Cullen Bryant, the Poet.

27. Daniel (s. of Daniel 12.) m. Abigail, D. of Zechariah Packard, 1753, and had Abigail 1754. He m. a 2d w. Mary, and had Joanna 1769, Daniel 1775.

28. John (s. of Daniel 12.) went into the French war and was killed at the Isle-aux-Noix 1760. He was the first inhabitant of the town of Bridgewater known to have been killed in battle. We find in the Rev. Samuel Angier's record of deaths the following entry :—" Sept. 19th, 1777. Capt. Jacob Allen and Abner Robinson were killed in battle near Stillwater, above Albany : before these there was no person of this town ever killed in battle except one John Snell, who was slain in the former war with France."

29. Benjamin (s. of Daniel 12.) m. Rebecca, D. of Lot Conant, 1782, and had Rebecca, Benjamin, Susanna, and Stella. Rebecca m. George Baker of Duxbury 1816.—Susanna m. John Carver a. 1823.—Capt. Benjamin and Stella not m.

30. William (s. of Daniel 12.) m. Eunice, D. of Henry Cary, 1781, and had Sarah, Henry, Robie and Joanna Harlow : he d. 1836. Sarah m. Seth Alden 1800.—Henry m. Sarah, D. of Isaac Swift.—Joanna m. Nathaniel Washburn : all d. but Henry.

31. Joseph (s. of Joseph 14.) m. wid. Hannah Cook of the Cape 1785, and had Anna 1785, Alfred 1788, Joseph Doane 1789, Abigail 1792, Luther 1793*, Hannah 1794, George Washington 1796, Azubah 1800, John Westly 1802 : she died 1817. Anna m. Charles Hunt of Dorchester perhaps 1806.

32. Charles (s. of Charles 15.) m. Mary, D. of Matthew Kingman, 1778, and had Alven 1778, Matthew 1780, Cyrus 1787, Polly 1789*. He m. wid. Rebecca Packard 1807. Alven m. Abigail Bryant 1798.—Cyrus m. Susanna Shaw of Ab. 1819.

33. Shepard (s. of Charles 15.) m. Amy, D. of Jeremiah Thayer, 1794, and had Nancy 1795*, Susanna 1797, Ansel 1800, Royal 1802.—Susanna m. John B. Harris perhaps 1818.

34. Capt. Ephraim (s. of Jonathan 16.) m. Anna, D. of James Keith, 1780, and had Amelia 1780, Jonathan 1782, Patty 1784, Semantha 1786, Bathsheba 1788, Anna 1790. He then m. Hannah, widow of Josiah Williams and D. of Jonathan Kingman, 1792, and had Polly 1794, Hannah 1795, Ephraim 1800. He d., and the wid. then m. Caleb Snell 1808.—Amelia m. Salmon Howard 1799.—Jonathan m. Nabby, D. of John Hudson, 1809. Patty m. Daniel Hudson 1806.—Semantha m. Sidney Keith 1806. Polly m. Damon Kingman 1814.

35. Caleb (s. of Jonathan 16.) m. Sarah, D. of Jonathan Bailey, 1799, and had Sarah and Ann 1800, Edwin 1804, Catharine 1806*. She died 1807, and he m. Hannah, wid. of his brother Ephraim, and previously wid. of Josiah Williams, and D. of Jonathan Kingman 1808.

36. Stephen (s. of Pollycarpus 18.) m. Patty Cole 1796, and had Augustus 1797, Cyrus 1800, Lucius 1801, Edward 1803, Emeline 1805*, Susanna Shaw 1809, Emeline 1811, Laura Anne 1813, Lauren 1818. Augustus m. an Eaton of Mid'o.—Cyrus m. Catharine Conday in Boston, and d. 1826, æ. 26.—Lucius d. 1832, æ. 30.

37. Perez (s. of Josiah 21.) m. Hannah, D. of Samuel Kinsley, 1786, and had Perez 1789, Martin 1792, Apollos 1795.

38. Capt. Josiah (s. of Josiah 21.) and his w. Lucy had John Root 1803, Josiah 1806.

39. Calvin (s. of Dea. Elijah 22.) m. Polly, D. of Jacob Packard, 1785, and had Harrison 1786, Roxana 1788, Rhoda 1791, and went to Maine with his father.

40. Elijah (s. of Dea. Elijah 22.) m. Abby, D. of Ebenezer Copeland, 1796, and had Bezer 1797, Noble 1798, Abby Godfrey 1801, and went to Me. with the rest of the family.

41. Nathan (s. of Nathan 23.) m. Abigail, D. of Maj. James Keith, 1800, and had Luther 1800, Minerva 1803, Edward 1804.

42. Cyrus (s. of Nathan 23.) m. Betsy Keith 1801, and had Nahum 1803, Cyrus 1805. He and his w. both d. 1805.

43. Dr. Issachar (s. of Issachar Esq. 24.) gra. H. U. 1797, m. Mary, D. of Simeon Keith, 1799, and had Camilla 1800, Thomas 1802, Willard 1803. He removed to Winthrop, Me.

44. Zechariah (s. of Capt. Zebedee 25.) m. Mehitabel, D. of Zechariah Sylvester of Duxbury, 1793, and had Samuel 1794, Sidney 1795*, Zechariah 1797*, Elbridge Gerry 1799, Daniel 1801, Mehitabel 1803, Patty Howard 1805, Zechariah 1807, Cephas 1810, David 1812, Susanna 1814: he d. 1819. Samuel m. Ruth Reed of Ab. perhaps 1813.—David J. Snell d. at Carlinville, Illinois, July 17, 1838.

45. Oliver (s. of Capt. Zebedee 25.) m. Hannah, D. of Jeremiah Beal, 1792, and had Oliver 1793, Jeremiah 1796, Hannah 1798, Isaac 1801, Polly Tilson 1804, Rachel 1807, Asa Ford 1810, Patty Howard 1812. Jeremiah m. Sally Holbrook perhaps 1819.—Hannah perhaps m. Gordon Stone of Easton 1821.

46. Zebedee (s. of Capt. Zebedee 25.) m. Hannah, D. of Job Ames, 1804, and had Lavinia Dike 1804, Mary Ames 1806, Silence Perry 1808, Enos Tilson 1812.—Job Ames 1814, Ethan Carver 1815.

47. Matthew (s. of Charles 32.) m. Susanna, wid. of Charles Southworth, and D. of Abiel Harris of A., 1806, and had Nath'l 1807, Jane Whitman 1809, Henry 1812: he d. 1839, æ. 59.

Lucy m. Whitcomb Stetson of Abington 1796.—Lydia m. Jona. Dawes 1772.—John and Philippa Snell of Boston had Susanna 1659, Anna 1661, John 1663, (2d wife Hannah), Simon 1667. His will, 1669, mentions his brother Simon of London.—Hannah Snell b. at Hingham 1689.—George Snell of Portsmouth mariner, and his w. Hannah 1698.

SNOW.—William Snow was "an apprentice to Mr. Richard Derby 1637, and by him brought over out of England, and assigned over to Edward Doten 1638, to serve him seven years" at Plymouth. He was of course 21 years old in 1645, and we find his name among those able to bear arms at Plymouth 1643.—Nicholas Snow was at Plymouth 1623, and went to Eastham 1642.— Anthony Snow was at Plymouth 1638, and afterwards at Marshfield, and both appear to have left families; but it is not ascertained that William had any connection with either of them.— William settled early in Duxbury, but probably was not a householder, or not m. in 1645, when the grant of this *plantation* to Duxbury was made, and therefore his name is not found among the original proprietors; but he became a proprietor, and was among the first settlers of the town, in W. B., and took the oath of fidelity among the first in 1657: his will dated 1699, proved 1708: he d. æ. a. 84, and had been taken care of by his s. William. His wife's name was Rebeckah, but her family name not given: his children were William, James, Joseph, Benjamin, Mary, Lydia, Hannah, and Rebeckah.—James d. in the Canada expedition 1690.—No account of the Ds.

2. William (s. of William 1.) m. Naomi, D. of Thomas Whitman, 1686, and had Bethiah 1688, James 1691, Susanna 1694, William 1697, Eleazar 1701, John 1704: his estate settled 1726. Bethiah m. Elisha Hayward 1721.—Susanna m. Israel Alger 1717.—No further account of James.

3. Joseph (s. of William 1.) and his w. Hopestill had Joseph 1690, Mary 1691, James 1693, Rebeckah 1696, Isaac 1700, Jonathan and David 1703: he d. 1753. Mary m. Joseph Lathrop 1718.—Rebeckah m. Thomas Wade 1722.

4. Benjamin (s. of William 1.) m. Elizabeth, D. of Joseph Alden 1693, and had Rebeckah 1694, Benjamin 1696, Solomon 1698, Ebenezer 1702, Elizabeth 1705. His w. d. 1705, and he

m. Sarah, wid. of Jonathan Cary and D. of Samuel Allen, 1705,
and had Sarah 1706: he d. 1743. Rebeckah m. a Campbell.—
Elizabeth m. Joseph Carver 1725 —Sarah m. Nathaniel Pratt,
and was dead at the date of her father's will 1743, having left a
s. Seth (Dea. Seth Pratt).—Solomon m. Bathsheba Mehurin 1724.

5. William (s. of William 2.) m. Mary Washburn 1722, and
had William 1723, Seth 1725, James 1729, Mary 1731, Susanna
1736. Mary m. Samuel Dunbar 1758.

6. Eleazar (s. of William 2.) m. Mercy King 1728, and had
Betty 1729, Reuben 1731, Eleazar 1734, Mercy 1737, Daniel
1742 : she d. 1789; he d. 1796. Betty m. Nathan Ames 1751,
and then William Tolman 1757, and afterwards Micah White.
Mercy m. Jacob Johnson of St. 1760.

7. John (s. of William 2.) m. Hannah, D. of Elisha Hayward,
1731 : no children : she d. 1750, æ. 45 : he then m. Hannah, wid.
of Stoughton Willis (she was a Harlow) 1756, and had Sarah
1758, John 1762.

8. Joseph (s. of Joseph 3.) and his w. Elizabeth had Joseph
1715, James 1717, Elizabeth 1719, Susanna 1722, Sarah 1725,
Daniel 1727. He went to Easton a. 1730, and afterwards to
Providence ; was called Deacon 1738 in a deed he gave to Caleb
Phillips.—Joseph was a Preacher, and settled in Providence ;
Mr. Wilson afterwards in 1793, was settled as colleague with him.

9. James (s. of Joseph 3.) lived in E. B. and m. Ruth, D. of
Joseph Shaw a. 1719, and had Ruth 1720, Abijah 1722, Mary
1724, Nathan 1725, Abigail 1727, Susanna 1729, Jedediah 1731,
Sarah 1732, John 1736, James 1742, by his 2d wife Hannah
Hovey. Ruth m. Perez Bonney 1739.—Nathan m. Mary Mans-
field perhaps 1748, and went to Abington, and John also moved
away.—No account of Jedediah.—Abigail m. John Egerton
1746, and Jonathan Beal 1780.—Susanna m. Abijah Edson 1747.
Sarah m. Benjamin Harris 1751.—Abijah m. Sarah Porter of
Abington —Nathan Jr. went to Cummington.

10. Isaac (s. of Joseph 3.) m. Hannah, D. of Joseph Shaw,
1722, and lived in E. B., and had Hannah 1723, Isaac 1726,
Martha 1728, Peter 1731, Joseph 1734*, Judith 1736. He d. 1737,
and she m. John Whitman 1743. Hannah m. Joseph Robinson
1759, his 2d w.—Martha m. Capt. Simeon Whitman 1750.—Peter went to Harvard.—Judith m. John Barrell 1756.

11. Jonathan (s. of Joseph 3.) m. Ruth Soule, and afterwards
a 2d w. Sarah, and had Samuel 1729, Jesse 1731, Sarah 1732,
Rebecca 1734, Jonathan 1736, Moses 1737, Aaron 1740. Jonathan m. Betty Packard 1761.—Sarah m. Nath'l Packard 1753.—
This family went to Mid'o.—Sam'l Snow m. Betty Perkins 1775.

12. David (s. of Joseph 3.) m. Joanna, D. of Joseph Hayward,
1731, and had David 1732*, Joseph 1734, Joanna 1735, Mehitabel 1737*, Lydia 1740, Rhoda 1742 : she d. 1794, æ. 90. Joanna
m. Nathaniel Edson 1759.—Lydia m. John Whitman 1764.—
Rhoda m. Ezra Whitman 1768.

13. Benjamin (s. of Benjamin 4.) m. Jemima, D. of Amos

Snell, 1722, and settled in S. Bridg., and had Jemima 1723,
Benja. 1724, Daniel 1726, Elijah 1728, Elizabeth 1730, Charity
1733*, Lucy 1735, Amos 1738, Joseph 1740*, Seth 1743*, Joseph
1746*: he d. 1760, æ. 65. Jemima m. Elijah Leach 1745.

14. Ebenezer (s. of Benjamin 4.) m. Sarah, D. of Joseph Pratt,
a. 1728, and had Ebenezer 1729, Nathaniel 1731, Sarah 1733,
Caleb 1736. She died 1737, and he m. Sarah, wid. of Stephen
Leach and D. of John Hooper, 1737, and had Solomon 1741,
Rebecca 1742, Zebedee 1743, John, Eli, and Mary. He went
to R. a. 1751, and m. a wid. Wilbor for a 3d wife, but had no
children by her. Solomon m. Elizabeth, D. of Eleazar Cary,
1780, and had Elizabeth. Solomon, and William.—Caleb was in
the French war, 1755, with Gen'l Winslow.—Zebedee went to
Scituate, R. I., and had Zebedee, Solomon, and William.

15. Ebenezer (s. of Ebenezer next above) m. Betty Hooper,
and had Sarah 1751, Betty 1753, Lydia 1755, Susanna 1757,
Eunice 1759, and Ebenezer, who m. Sarah, D. of Joseph Pool,
1783. This family lived in R.

16. William (s. of William 5.) m. Hannah, D. of Nathan Hill,
1743, and had Calvin 1749, Salome 1751 he d. 1755. Calvin m.
Hannah, D. of Ephraim Churchill, 1784.—William Snow's wife
d. in S. B. 1774.—Wm. Snow m. Jerusha, D of David Hill, 1776.

17. Seth (s. of William 5.) m. Betty, D. of Jona. Sprague,
and had Simeon 1750, Betty 1752, Seth 1755, Jonathan 1757,
Lydia 1759*. Elizabeth Snow m. Josiah Washburn 1775.

18. James (s. of William 5.) m. Mary, D. of Timothy Edson,
1758, and had Eliab 1759, James 1761, and d. 1762. Eliab m.
Lydia Snow 1782, and Eliab Snow m. Dorcas, D. of Ephraim
Churchill, 1787.—James m. Rebecca Alden of Tit. probably 1789.

19. Reuben (s. of Eleazar 6.) m. Hannah, D. of Stoughton
Willis 1768, and had Rhoda 1769, and went to Easton.

20. Eleazar (s. of Eleazar 6.) m. Mary, D. of John Wood,
1757, and settled in N. B., and had Mary 1757, Eleazar 1759,
Priscilla 1761, Jonathan, Silas, Betsy, Sarah, Zevina, Mercy,
Phebe: he died 1797, æ. 64. Eleazar m. Hannah, D. of Jacob
Dunbar, 1780, and settled in the State of New York.—Mary m.
Seth Snow 1778.—Priscilla m. Simeon Snow 1779.—Sarah m. a
Merritt.—Zevina m. Jonathan Snow of N. Y. 1799.—Mercy m.
Nathaniel Wilmouth 1795.—Phebe m. Moses Crafts 1799.

21. Daniel Esq. (s. of Eleazar 6.) m. Hannah, D. of Samuel
Dunbar, 1764, and had Hannah 1765, Daniel 1767, Silvia 1769*,
Sarah 1771*, Mehitabel 1773*, Nathan 1776, Cyrus 1778, Sarah
1780, Melatiah 1782. His w. d. 1812, and he and all his family
went to Maine. Hannah m. Benjamin Alger of Easton 1785.—
Melatiah m. Abiathar Wethrell of Easton 1807.—Nathan, a
bachelor.—Sarah m. a Hill in Readfield, Me.

22. John (s. of John 7.) m. Mary, D. of James Ames, 1784,
and had David 1785, John 1787, Sarah 1789, Charles 1791,
George 1794, Lucy 1798 : his wife d. 1819.—John m. Rebecca
Lathrop 1811, and had Edward James 1811.—Sarah m. William

Dunbar 1807.—Charles m. Hannah Place 1820.—Lucy m. Benjamin Randall 1819.—He m. a 2d w. Hannah, wid. of Nathaniel Perkins and D. of Edmund Hayward 1821.

23. Isaac (s. of Isaac 10.) m. Elizabeth, D. of William Bowditch, 1748, and had Mary 1749, and went to Haverhill.

24. Joseph (s. of David 12.) m. Ruth, D. of Dea. Zechariah Shaw, 1759, and had Sarah 1759, David 1761, Daniel 1763, Mehitabel 1767, Ruth 1769, Joseph 1772, Moses 1775. This family went to Brookfield. David m. Jemima, D. of Jacob Hayward, 1787, and had Vashti 1790, Experience 1791, David 1793, and then went to Brookfield.—Sarah m. Silvanus Hayward 1781.— Daniel m. Sally Allen at Brookfield 1792.—Mehitabel m. Seth Richards 1791.—Joseph m. Tamzin, D. of John Richards, 1795, and then went to Brookfield.

25. Daniel (s. of Benjamin 13.) m. Abigail, D. of Joshua Fobes, 1753, and had Abigail 1754, Daniel 1756, Hosea 1758, Joseph 1760, Lucy 1762, Barzillai 1765, Azariah 1768, John 1770.

26. Elijah (s. of Benjamin 13.) m. Sarah, D. of Samuel Dunbar 1767, and lived in Titicut, and had Sarah 1770, who m. Jacob Lathrop 1787, and a son Benjamin : his wife died 1779 ; he 1792.

27. Simeon (s. of Seth 17.) m. Priscilla, D. of Eleazar Snow, 1779, and had Simeon 1781*, Betty 1783, Priscilla 1785, Lavinia 1787, Hepzibah 1789, Shepard 1791, Phebe 1793, Zibeon 1795, Roxiliana 1797, and went to Whitestown, N. Y.

28. Seth (s. of Seth 17.) m. Mary, D. of Eleazar Snow, 1778, and had Seth 1780, Barnabas 1782, Polly 1785, Cyrus 1787, Asenath 1789, Elijah 1792, Perez 1795, Zerviah 1796, and went to Whitestown, N. Y.

29. Jonathan (s. of Seth 17.) went to N. Y., and probably m. Zevina, D. of Eleazar Snow, 1799.

30. Jonathan Esq. (s. of Eleazar 20.) m. Huldah Snow, and had Huldah 1786, Jonathan 1788, Salmon 1789*, Caleb 1790*, Susanna 1793, Sprague 1795, Sebrina 1797, Martin 1799, Olive 1800, Thomas Jefferson 1803, Relief 1805. Huldah m. Stillman Willis 1809.—Jonathan m. Sally, D. of Nathan Bryant, 1810.— Susanna m. Jeremiah Hickson of St. 1809.—Sprague m. Nancy Kingman of Mansfield 1820.—Sebrina m. John Sealy of Easton 1818.—Martin m. Ann Wilbor 1821.—Thos. J. gra. B. U. 1823.

31. Silas (s. of Eleazar 20.) m. Hannah, D. of Ephraim Cole, 1800, and had Austin 1802, Linus 1804*, Silence 1808, Mary 1811, Lurin 1814.

32. Daniel (s. of Daniel Esq. 21.) m. Hannah Richmond of Mid'o. 1790, and went to Union, Maine, and had Ansel, Azel, Philip, Oliver, Silvia, Hannah, Harriet, Elizabeth, Sarah. Ansel lives in Appleton.—Azel m. a D. of Thomas Johnson of New Gloucester, and lived in N. York, and now lives in Boston, an Apothecary.—The Ds. are all m. and live in Me.

33. Cyrus (s. of Daniel Esq. 21.) m. Ruth Makepeace of

304 SOPER.—SOREIN.—SOULE.—SOUTHWORTH.

Norton 1801, and had Ruth Makepeace 1802, Angelina 1803, Deborah 1805, Hannah Dunbar 1807. He went to Franklin.
34. Seth (s. of Nath'l of Orleans) settled in N. B. 1783, m. Anna, D. of Josiah Packard, 1795, and had Josiah*, Nathaniel, Sally*, Achsah*, Hannah*, and Mary. His wife d. 1820, and he m. wid. Sarah Norton, D. of Ephraim Noyes.
Hannah m. Benj. Mehuren 1767.—Lydia m. Eliab Snow 1782. Bethiah m. Samuel Warren Jr. of Mid'o. 1770.—Molly m. John Wade 1791.—Sarah m. Daniel Tomson 1794.—Hannah m. Heman Linnel 1797.—Ruth of Eastham m. Levi Packard 1789.— Hannah m. Jonathan Bolton 1794.—James m. Freelove Monk of St. 1794.—Zilpha m. David Bolton 1794.—Eunice m. Alfred Edson 1796.—Mehitabel of Easton m. Asa Bryant 1810.—Betsy m. Asa Bryant 1811.—Elijah Snow of E. B. m. Sarah Shaw 1780.
SOPER.—Samuel-Soper m. Esther Littlefield 1731, and lived in W. B., and had Edmund 1731, Hannah 1733, Asa 1734, Sam'l 1736, Esther 1738, Oliver 1740, Amasa 1742, Salter 1744, Sarah 1745, James 1747, Silence 1750. Esther, mother or D., m. Seth Briggs of Berkley a. 1754.—Hannah m. Daniel Pettingill 1750.
2. Edmund (s. of Samuel 1.) m. Bethiah (or Betty), D. of Ephraim Fobes, 1754, and had Betty 1755. His w. d., and he m. Eunice, D. of Capt. Theophilus Curtis of St. 1756, and had Mehitabel 1757, Edmund 1759, Eunice 1761.
3. Amasa (s. of Samuel 1.) m. Ruth Dwelly 1763, and had Huldah 1764, Olive 1766, Amasa 1768, Martin 1772.
Capt. Nathaniel Soper of Hanson (s. of Alexander) m. Betty Price 1779.—Mary Soper m. Daniel Hartwell Jr. 1821.
SOREIN.—John Sorein and his w. Mary had John in E. B. 1735, and went to Boston.
SOULE.—Dea. John Soule m. Sarah, D. of Thomas Leach, and settled in E. B., and had William Norman 1808, and Elizabeth 1809.
Ebenezer Soule of Plympton m. Silence, D. of William Hudson 1764.—Asaph of Plymp. m. Marah, D. of William Hudson, 1767.—A D. of Ebenezer Whitman of S. B. m. a Soule.—Wm. Soule m. Rachel Dillingham 1791.—Rebecca m. Sampson Washburn 1805.—Nathan Soule, brother of Rebecca, m. Charity, D. of Uriah Brett, 1815.—Wid. Joanna, mother of Nathan and Rebecca, m. Nathan Alden Esq. 1818.
SOUTHWORTH.—Widow Alice Southworth arrived at Plymouth 1623, in the third ship, called the Ann, and soon after was married to Gov. William Bradford: she had two ss. by her first husband, to wit: Constant and Thomas Southworth, who came with her or soon afterwards, and were quite young; Thomas not more than six years old. They both became distinguished men in the colony : Constant settled in Duxbury, and was one of the original proprietors of Bridgewater, and d. 1678, leaving three sons, Edward, Nathaniel, and William; and three married Ds. viz: Mercy, w. of Samuel Freeman, Alice, wife of the famous Capt. Benjamin Church, distinguished in Philip's war, and Mary,

wife of David Alden, and two unmarried Ds., Elizabeth and Priscilla.—Thomas feft an only child Elizabeth, who m. Joseph Howland.—Elizabeth, D. of Constant, afterwards m. William Fobes.—Nathaniel "had land towards Taunton, called Freemen's land," perhaps in Mid'o.—Edward, of Mid'o. perhaps, s. of Nathaniel, had 4 ss., Constant, Edward, Lemuel and Benjamin, who all settled early in N. B.

Sarah Southworth of Mid'o. m. Eleazar Washburn Jr. a. 1771. Sarah Southworth m. Peter Edson 1745.

1. Constant (s. of Edward) m. Martha, D. of Joseph Keith, 1734, and had Betsy 1735, Nathaniel 1737, Ezekiel 1739, Martha* and Mary 1741*, Desire 1742*, Jedediah 1745, Constant 1747*, Sarah 1749, Ichabod 1751*: he d. 1775, æ. 64. Betsy m. Joseph Cole 1757.—Sarah d. single.—Jedediah m. an Atherton, and settled in St., and had Constant and Consider.

2. Edward (s. of Edward) m. Lydia, D. of John Packard, 1750, and had Uriah 1751, Perez 1754, Desire 1756, Edward 1758, Abiah 1760, Bridget 1762, Lydia 1764, Avis 1768, Fear 1770. They all moved to Pelham except Perez.—Uriah m. Patience Goodspeed of Easton 1773.

3. Lemuel (s. of Edward) m. Patience West 1757, and had Mehitabel 1758, Hannah 1760*, Patience 1763. Mehitabel m. John Gurney 1777.

4. Benjamin (s. of Edward) m. Mary Smith 1763, but had no children. He d., and his wid. m. Zechariah Gurney 1800.

5. Nathaniel (s. of Constant 1.) m. Catharine, D. of David Howard, 1762, and had Martha 1764*, Simeon 1766, Nathaniel 1769, David 1773*. His wife d. 1775, and he m. Jennet, D. of Simeon Brett, 1777, and had Catharine : he d. 1788, and his wid. m. Ephraim Groves 1789.—Catharine m. Ambrose Keith 1796.— Nathaniel.m. Patience, D. of William Shaw, 1793, and went to Lyme, N. H.

6. Ezekiel (s. of Constant 1.) m. Mary Newman 1761, and had Molly 1762, Ichabod Keith 1764, Constant 1767, and then went westward.

7. Perez (s. of Edward 2.) m. Eunice, D. of Matthew Kingman, a. 1780, and had Harmony 1781, Hannah 1782, John 1784, Edward 1786, Martin 1788, Azel 1790*, Benjamin 1791, Perez and Eunice 1793, Polly 1796, Sophronia 1798, Lucy 1800. Harmony m. Dea. Seth Alden 1802.—Hannah m. John Ames 1802.— Eunice m. Daniel Alden 1815.—Sophronia m. Alva Noyes.— Lucy m. Ornan Cole.—John m. Eliza, D. of Luther Hayward, 1806, and went to New Bedford.—Col. Edward m. Rhoda, D. of Robert Howard, 1815 —Martin m. Ruth, D. of Capt. Robert Packard, 1811.—Benjamin m. Content, D. of Dea. Eben. Packard, 1819, and went to Winthrop, Me.—Perez m. Betty, D. of Capt. Lot Leach of St. 1821.

8. Simeon (s. of Nathaniel 5.) m. Elizabeth Anderson 1789, and had Alva 1791, Justin 1793, and went to Ward.

39

Charles m. Susanna, D. of Abiel Harris, 1794, and Matthew Snell 1806.—Reuma m. Otis Howard 1818.

SPRAGUE.—Francis Sprague was one of the forefathers, and arrived at Plymouth 1623 in the ship Ann : he settled in Duxbury, and was one of the original proprietors of Bridgewater, but did not, nor did any of his family, come to reside here : he had John, Anna, Mary and Mercy. John m. Ruth Bassett 1655, and had John, William, Samuel, Eliza, Ruth, Desire, and Dorcas. Mercy m. William Tubbs 1637.—William d. at Dux. 1712, leaving a wid. Grace, and ss. Jethro and Terah, and Ds. Ruth and Zerviah. Samuel went to Rochester and d. there 1723, leaving a wid. Elizabeth, and a s. Ephraim, and perhaps others. The Spragues of Fairhaven, and the South Shore generally, descended probably from Francis. There was no known connection between him and the following families.

Ralph, Richard, and William Sprague, were among the first comers and settlers in Massachusetts Colony in 1628. They were brothers, and settled at Charlestown, from whence William, the youngest, removed to Hingham. Hosea Sprague of Hingham, one of the descendants of William, has lately presented the public with such a full and particular genealogy of the Sprague family, that it is necessary here only to give some account of William, from whom the Spragues in this town are descended.

William Sprague of Hingham m. Millesaint, D. of Anthony Eames, and had Anthony 1635, John 1638, Samuel 1640, Elizabeth 1641, Persis 1643, Joanna 1644, Jonathan 1648, William 1650, Mary 1652, Hannah 1655: he d. 1675. Anthony remained at Hingham, and d. 1719.—John went to Mendon, and d. 1690.— Samuel went to Marshfield, and d. 1709; was Secretary of the Colony, and great-grandfather of the Hon. Seth Sprague sen'r of Duxbury.—Jonathan d. at Hingham, and left no posterity.— William m. Deborah Lane 1674, and went to Providence.—Persis m. John Dogget.—Joanna m. Caleb Church.—Mary m. Thos. King.—William of Providence had William, Joanna, Deborah, Jonathan, Abiah, John, Benjamin.

1. Jonathan (s. of William of Providence) m. Lydia Leavit of Hingham, and settled in S. B., and had Lydia 1715, Hannah 1717, Jonathan 1720, Mary 1722, Sarah 1725*, John 1727, Content 1729, Betty 1731, Benjamin 1736: his will 1748. Lydia m. Solomon Perkins 1733.—Hannah m. Solomon Bates.—Jonathan went to Stafford, Conn.—Mary m. Nathan Edson 1738.—Content m. a Howard of Dartmouth.—Betty m. Seth Snow a. 1749.

2. John (s. of Jonathan 1.) m. Susanna Cobb 1746, and had John 1746, and went to Block Island.

3. Benjamin (s. of Jonathan 1.) m. Eunice, D. of Ephraim Holmes, 1762, and had Ephraim 1763, Benjamin, Lydia 1777. He d. 1778, of the small pox, æ. 42, and she m. Solomon Ames 1781, and became a wid. again, and d. 1833, æ. 92. Lydia m. Capt. Asa Pratt 1799.

4. Capt. Ephraim (s. of Benjamin 3.) m. Vina, D. of Ezra
Edson, 1783, and had Holmes 1783, Ephraim 1787, Eunice 1790,
Vina 1799, and d. 1818; Chloe 1804, Mira 1806. Ephraim m.
Jane, D. of Joseph Ames, 1813, and went to Bristol, R. I.—
Eunice m. Calvin Washburn 1809.—Mira m. John Washburn,
and afterwards the Hon. John A. Shaw.

5. Benjamin (s. of Benjamin 3.) m. Priscilla Churchill 1786,
and had Benjamin 1790, Friend 1792*, Lydia 1799, George 1801.
Lydia m. Barna Leonard Jr. 1815.—George went to N. York,
and thence to Florida.

6. Capt. Holmes (s. of Capt. Ephraim 4.) m. Betsy, D. of
Daniel Copeland, 1808, and had Ephraim Holmes 1809, Betsy
Copeland 1812, Edgar 1815, Caleb Cary 1819.—Ephraim H. m.
Lois, D. of Nath'l Washburn.

7. Benjamin (s. of Benjamin 5.) m. Lucy, D. of Joseph Ames,
1818, and had Benjamin and Fisher Ames.—John of Abington
m. Rebecca, D. of John Alden of E. B. 1767.

STANDISH.—Capt. Miles Standish (one of the forefathers),
the renowned soldier, and shield and defence of the pilgrims,
came over in the first ship, the May Flower, in 1620 :, he lived
in Plymouth till 1630, when he removed to Duxbury, and d. there
1656, æ. 72 : he was an original proprietor of Bridgewater, and
a principal member of the committee who purchased the plantation of Massasoit (or Ousamequin), the Indian Sachem, in 1649 :
his w. Rose d. the next spring after their arrival, in 1621, and he
m. a 2d w. Barbara, who survived him : his children were Alexander, Miles, Josiah, Charles, Lora, and John. Lora d. before
him. He lived and died at the foot of the hill named after him
" Captain's Hill."

2. Alexander (s. of Capt. Miles 1.) was made a freeman 1648,
and lived on the paternal estate, at Captain's Hill, in Duxbury :
he m. first Sarah, D. of the Hon. John Alden, and had Miles,
Ebenezer, Lorah, Lydia, Mercy, Sarah, and Elizabeth : his wife
d., and he then m. Desire, wid. of Israel Holmes, (formerly wid.
of William Sherman, her maiden name Doten), and had Thomas,
Ichabod, and Desire born in Marshfield 1689 : he d. in Duxbury
1702 ; she in Marshfield 1723. She named her children thus :
William Sherman, John Holmes, Israel Holmes, Hannah Ring,
Experience [wife of Miles] Standish, Desire Weston, and g. D.
Desire Wermall.—Lorah m. Abraham Sampson.—Lydia m. Isaac
Sampson.—Mercy m. Caleb Sampson.—Sarah m. Benjamin
Soule, and Elizabeth m. Samuel Delano.—There was a David
Standish killed in Duxbury by the fall of a tree in 1689 ; perhaps
a s. of Alexander.

3. Miles (s. of Capt. Miles 1.) m. Sarah, D. of John Winslow,
and went to Boston, where he d. a. 1666; and his wid. m. Tobias
Payne 1669, and afterwards Mr. Richard Middlecot.

4. Ens. Josiah Standish (2d s. of Capt. Miles of Duxbury)
lived in East Bridgewater, and first m. Mary, D. of John Dingley
of Marshfield, a. 1654, who died the same year, and he then m.

Sarah, D. of Sam'l Allen of Braintree and sister of Sam'l Allen
of E. B. He soon removed back to Duxbury, where he became
a Captain, Selectman, Deputy, and one of the council of war:
he removed thence to Norwich, in Conn., probably a. 1686 : he
had Miles, Josiah, and other children perhaps. His descendants
are also in New York, among whom Samuel has been a given
name for several generations. He bought 150 acres of John
Parks of Preston, Conn. 1687.

5. Charles (s. of Capt. Miles 1.) we have no account of: his
name does not appear in the records after his father's will in
1655 : perhaps he d. young.

6. John (son of Capt. Miles 1.) was named in the division of
cattle, on the Colony records, in 1627, and we have obtained no
further account of him. He no doubt d. young, as he was not
named in his father's will in 1655.

7. Miles (s. of Alexander 2.) remained on the paternal estate
at Captain's Hill, and d. there 1739. He m. Experience, D. of
his mother-in-law by one of her first husbands (Sherman or
Holmes), and had Miles, Sarah, Patience, Priscilla and Penelope ;
the two last minors. Miles went to Bridgewater.—Sarah m.
Abner Weston.—Patience m. Caleb Jenny of Dartmouth 1735.—
Priscilla m. Elisha Bisbee perhaps of Pembroke.—Penelope d.
single at Duxbury 1740.—The mother Experience survived her
husband, and was perhaps the last of the family who resided at
Captain's Hill.

8. Ebenezer (s. of Alexander 2.) lived in Plympton, and had
Ebenezer, Zechariah, Moses, Hannah, Zeruiah, Sarah, and
Mercy. He and his s. Ebenezer both died a. 1748.—Zerviah
Standish m. Zebedee Tomson of Halifax 1745.—Ebenezer Jr.
m. a Churchill 1739.—Sarah Standish m. Josiah Cushman Jr.
1749.—Mercy Standish m. Ebenezer Lobdell at Plympton 1736 :
her 2d husband was Benjamin Weston : she d. 1794, æ. 78.

9. Thomas (s. of Alexander 2.) born a. 1687, first settled in
Marshfield, and thence removed to Pembroke, where his name
appears in 1718 : his wife Mary : they had David at Marshfield,
and perhaps Amos ; Thomas at Pembroke 1725, Mary 1733,
William 1737, Betty 1739, recorded by Daniel Lewis in Pem-
broke 1742 as the children of Thomas and Mary Standish.—
David m. Hannah Magoun 1746, and died 1793, leaving David,
Lemuel, and several other children.—Lemuel went to Bath, m.
Rachel Jackson, and had David 1777, and Lemuel, and one other
son, and d. 1824, æ. 78.—Amos Standish, an adult, was bap. at
Marshfield 1742 (or 1746.)—Thomas m. Martha Bisbee 1748.—
Thomas Jr. d. in Pembroke 1780.—There was a Miles Standish
d. in Pembroke a. 1793, whose will is on record.

10. Ichabod (s. of Alexander 2.) m. Phebe Ring of Plymouth
1719 : he was the man probably, a cooper, who died at Halifax
1772, leaving 3 Ds. Mary, Phebe, and Desire who m. David Hatch.

11. Miles Standish (s. of Miles 7.) m. Mehitabel Robbins, probably of Plymouth, 1738, and removed from Duxbury to S. B.,

and had Miles, Experience, Penelope, Hannah, and others perhaps : he d. 1784, æ. 89. Miles m. Naomi, D. of Daniel Keith, 1774, and had Miles, and went to Pennsylvania a. 1780. Experience m. Simeon Ames 1765.—Penelope m. Nathaniel Cobb Jr. of Plymp. 1763.—Hannah m. Daniel Fobes 1769.

12. Zechariah (s. of Ebenezer 8.) had Ebenezer, Hannah, Sarah, Abigail, Peleg, Zechariah. Zechariah Standish died at Plympton a. 1780.—Col. John Standish of Plattsburgh, N. Y., s. of a Doctor Standish, formerly of Plympton, was a descendant of Zechariah.—Abigail Standish m. Samuel Wright 1752 : she was mother of Caleb Leach's wife.—Sarah Standish m. Josiah Cushman Jr. 1749.

13. Moses (s. of Ebenezer 8.) and his wife Rachel had Moses, John, Aaron, Rachel, and Rebecca : he died 1769, æ. 89. John Standish was drowned at Plymouth 1787.—Rebecca Standish m. Zechariah Weston 1751.—Rachel and Hannah Standish were both m. at Plympton a. 1740.

14. Ebenezer (s. of Zechariah 12 perhaps) had Mary, Ebenezer, Averick, and Shadrach. Shadrach d. at New Bedford 1837, æ. 92 : he m. Mary Churchill 1771, and had 3 ss. and 5 Ds., and 141 descendants. The Rev. Mr. Holmes preached a funeral sermon at his death, and therein stated that Capt. Miles Standish, the ancestor, was 54 years old when he arrived at Plymouth and 90 when he died ; but he d. Oct. 3, 1656, æ. about 72, according to the account given of it by the late Samuel Davis Esq. and history assures us he was appointed to command the troops raised to go against the Dutch, at Manhattan, in 1653, only three years before he died, and it is altogether improbable that he could then have been 87 years old : he was probably about 36 when he came over, which is corroborated by " New England's Memorial," wherein it is recorded that he went in his " younger time " into the Low Countries as a soldier, and there becoming acquainted with the Church at Leyden came with them to N. England. He was a distant descendant (not a son as Mr. Holmes supposes) of the Rev. Henry Standish D. D., Bishop of St. Asaph's in the reign of Henry the 8th.

Mrs. Bisbee, living in 1809 at Plympton, very aged, was a Standish b. at Captain's Hill in Duxbury.—Betsy Bisbee Standish d. in E. B. 1792, æ. 41.—Isaiah Standish was in Rochester 1805 —Sarah Standish m. Daniel French of E. B. 1817.—Sam'l Standish of Lebanon, Conn., had a son Israel, and a D. Hannah. Israel had Elisha, Jonas, Amasa, and Nathan. Elisha had a s. Lodowick.—Nathan had two ss., one of them Thomas, living in Lebanon ; and another in Bozrah.—Ezra, a respectable man, and cousin of Lodowick, lived in Bozrah.

STAPLES.—Samuel Staples m. Betty, D. of Noah Washburn, 1765, and had Molly in E. B. 1767.—Jacob Staples of T. m. Lois Edson.

STARR.—John Starr was one of the original Proprietors of Bridgewater, but never came to reside here.

Jasper Starr and wife (from Boston) settled in S. B.: he died 1792, æ. 84 ; she d. 1802, æ. 92 (Mrs. Starr d. 1792, æ. 90). He had James and Benjamin. Benjamin was drowned in a well 1779.—Polly m. Luke Leach 1788.—James Jr. m. Lois, D. of Benjamin Leach, 1797, and Peggy m. Libeus Leach 1797, and all went to Me.—James Jr. was a Magistrate in Maine, and had Harriot B. 1799, Louisa L. 1802, both b. in S. B.

John and Martha Starr of Boston had Benjamin 1667.—Comfort and Mary Starr of Boston had Joseph 1668, and Mary 1671. Benjamin Starr m. Mary Maylam 1713, and Eliza Story 1715. John Starr m. Abigail Day 1706.—[Boston records.]

STETSON.—Abishai Stetson (from Pembroke) m. Sarah Crooker, and settled in E. B., and had Molly 1762, Abishai 1764, d. 1771 ; Abigail 1766, Jonathan 1768, Sarah 1770, Abishai 1773, Bethiah 1776. He died 1777, æ. 39, and his widow m. Solomon Packard 1779. Molly m. Benjamin Pincin 1787.—Abigail m. Dyer Robinson 1787.—Sarah m. Harlow Harden 1795.—Bethiah m. Calvin Keith 1794.—Capt. Isaiah Stetson, brother of the preceding, lived also in his youth in E. B., with Col. Edward Mitchell.

2. Jonathan (s. of Abishai 1.) m. Huldah Magoun 1791, and went to Carver and afterwards settled in Marshfield, and had Abishai, Sumner, and others.

3. Capt. Abishai (s. of Abishai 1.) m. Alice, D. of Ezra Allen, 1796, and had Jennet 1797, died 1820 ; Sarah 1799, d. 1820 ; Ethan 1803, Naomi 1805*, Nahum 1807, Nathan 1810, Alice 1813*, Caleb Strong 1815. His wife d. 1821, and he m. Mary Johnson of Kingston 1821.—Nathan went to Pennsylvania, and there m., and was a Preacher, and has returned to E. B.— Ethan m. a Baker, and d. 1831 æ. 29, leaving a D.

4. Nahum (s. of Capt. Abishai 3.) settled in S. B., and m. Sarah Wilson, D. of Rev. George Barstow of Hanson, and had George Barstow 1813, Sarah Lazell, Nahum, and Wm. Butler.

5. Peleg Stetson (from Abington) settled in E. B., and m. Ruth, D. of Perkins Gurney, 1775, and had Adam, Peleg, Charlotte, Sally, Jane. Adam m. Parna, D. of Capt. Levi Washburn, 1817.—Peleg m. Clarissa Gurney 1818.—Charlotte m. Jo. Reed 1807.—Sally m. Isaac Reed 1803.—Jenny m. John Harden 1803.

6. John Croal Stetson lived in S, B., and afterwards in E. B.; m. Lois, D. of Simeon Leonard, 1795, and had Experience Davy 1797, Louisa Leonard 1799, James Oliver 1803, Mary Ann 1811, and d. in S. B. His son James O. m. and lived in E. B , and then in W. B.—Louisa m. the Rev. Mr. Chace of Carver.— Mary A. m. in Foxborough.

Wid. Elizabeth Stetson d. in E. B. 1800, æ. 77.—Abthiah Stetson m. Moses Wade 1738, and Jonathan Chandler 1745, and d. 1792, æ. 85.—Whitcomb of Abington m. Lucy Snell 1796.— Ruth of Pembroke m. David Snow Whitman 1798.—Delpha m. James H. Gurney of Roxbury 1813.—Mary Crooker Stetson m. Timothy Hayward 1817.—Wid. Experience d. in S. B. 1798, æ. 55.—Content m. Zenas Crooker.—Mary (or Mercy) m. Oliver

Leach 1817.—Abishai Stetson of Kingston m. Elizabeth James
of Hingham (or Cohasset) 1730.

STORRS.—Elijah Storrs came from Connecticut and settled
in S. B., and m. Susanna, D. of Isaac Swift, 1782, and had
Susanna 1783, Martha 1785*, and Mary*, and a son*. Susanna m.
Newell Withington 1808.—Mr. Storrs d. March, 1839, æ. 89.
Mary Ann Storrs of Boston m. Laban Burr 1820.

STURTEVANT.—Samuel m. Sarah, D. of William Packard,
1769, and had Zophar 1770.

2. Samuel m. Abigail Holmes 1816, (both from Plymouth), and
settled in E. B., and had Nahum Mitchell, Sherman Allen, Mary
Jewett, Samuel Windsor, Elizabeth Bradford, Levi*, Silvanus*,
James Henry*, John Tilton, Abigail Holmes, Nathan Dresser,
Sarah Jane.

3. Silas (s. of Cornelius of Plympton) m. a Sampson and lived
in N. B., and had Ephraim, Silas, Molly, and Elizabeth : he d.
1814, æ. 84. Betsy m. Lewis Johnson 1799.

4. Ephraim (s. of Silas above) m. Abigail, D. of Robert Howard, 1791, and had Lucy 1793, who m. Oliver Howard 1808.

Sarah, D. of Caleb of Halifax m. Josiah Whitman 1774, and
afterwards Jacob Mitchell 1791.—Patience, D. of Caleb of Halifax m. Jonathan Ames 1783.—Jesse Fuller Sturtevant m. Anna,
D. of James Alger 1771.—Silvanus m. Polly, D. (perhaps) of
David Leonard, 1801.—Foster Sturtevant died in E. B. 1779. æ.
16.—James of Mid'o. m. Ann Leach 1769.—Deborah m. Isaac
Doten of Hartford, Me., 1820.

SWIFT.—Isaac Swift (from Sandwich) settled in S. B., and
m. Susanna, wid. of Solomon Ames and D. of Samuel Keith,
1749, and had Jireh 1749, William 1752, Susanna 1754, Mary
1759 : he d. 1811 ; she 1836. William m. Rachel, D. of Simeon
Leonard, 1795, but had no children : he died 1839, æ. 87.—Susanna m. Elijah Storrs 1782.—Mary m. Capt. Jacob Leonard
1788.

2. Jireh (s. of Isaac 1.) m. Lucy, D. of Ebenezer Keith, 1776,
and had Isaac, Martin, Sion, Ruel, Lois, and others. Isaac m.
Sarah, D. of Nath'l Pratt, 1797.—Martin m. Sarah, D. of Alex.
Ames, 1809.—Sion m. Susanna, wid. of Macey Hall and D. of
Joshua Washburn, 1818.—Reuel m. Mary Borden of Mid'o.
1821.—Lois m. Walter Keyes 1793, and another D. m. Charles
Brett.

TAYLOR.—Benjamin Taylor and his w. Abiah (a 2d wife a
wid. Peterson) lived in E. B., and had a s. Benjamin who m.
Martha Childs 1787, and had a s. Walter, and others. Benjamin,
the father, d. 1776, æ. a. 80 ; she 1800, æ. 76.

Archippus Taylor m. Hannah Warren 1778.—Benjamin Taylor m. Sarah Torrey 1784.

THAXTER.—Maj. Samuel Thaxter (from Hingham) lived
in E. B , and d. here Aug. 6, 1771. He was in the French war,
and in Fort William Henry when it was surrendered to the
French and Indians 1757, and was one of the few who escaped

the massacre which followed by making his way to Fort Edward.
He was father of Dr. Thomas Thaxter of Hingham, and Dr.
Gridley Thaxter of Ab.: he had also a s. William who d. young.

THAYER.—Richard Thayer arrived in this country from
England a. 1640, and settled in Braintree 1641, with 8 children,
Richard, Zechariah, Nathaniel, Jael, Deborah, Sarah, Hannah,
and Abigail.

Richard, the son, m. Dorothy Pray 1651; they had Dorothy
1653, Richard 1655, Nathaniel 1658, Cornelius 1670, and both d.
1705.

Nathaniel (s. of Richard Jr.) m. Hannah Hayden 1679, and
had Nathaniel 1680, Richard 1683, Hannah 1686, Zechariah
1687, Ruth 1689, Dorothy, Lydia, Daniel, Deborah, and Esther.

1. Richard (s. of Nathaniel) m. Susanna, D. of Sam'l White,
1708, and came to W. B.: he had Susanna 1710, Enos 1716,
Anna 1718, Seth 1721, Micah 1724, Abijah 1726, Jeremiah 1729,
Thankful 1731 : he died 1760; she 1759. Susanna m. Daniel
Field 1733.—Anna m. Benjamin Edson Jr. 1739.—Thankful m.
Jacob Dunbar 1776.—No account of Enos or Micah.—In Thayer's memorial it is said Susanna m. Joseph Lovell of St., and
that Anna m. Ephraim Thompson of W. B., and settled in Halifax.

2. Seth (s. of Richard 1.) m. Hannah Pray, and settled in N.
Bridg. 1744, and had Enos 1744, Hannah 1748, Susanna 1749,
Michael 1753*, Molly 1756, Seth 1760 : he died 1798, æ. 77.—
Hannah m. Daniel Cary 1773.—Mary m. Silas Hayward 1779.

3. Abijah (s. of Richard 1.) m. Betty, D. of Robert Howard,
1779, and had Betty 1780, Abigail 1782 : he d. 1805. Abigail m.
John Holmes of Halifax 1799.

4. Jeremiah (s. of Richard 1.) m. Tabitha Leavit 1756, and
had Jeremiah 1757, Richard 1759, Leavit 1761, Molly 1763, Su-
sanna 1765, Tabitha 1767, Anna 1769, Abijah 1771, Amy 1773,
Solomon 1776*, Betty 1779. Molly m. George Lathrop 1783.—
Susanna m. John Dyer 2d 1783.—Tabitha m. Thomas Reynolds
1785.—Anna m. Jonathan Reynolds 1794.—Abijah m. Sally
Bassett 1802.—Amy m. Shepard Snell 1794.—Betty m. Paul
Bailey 1798.

5. Enos (s. of Seth 2.) m. Rebecca Curtis 1765, and had Susanna 1767, Rebecca 1770. He m. Hannah, wid. of Philip Reynolds and D. of William Packard, 1782, but had no children by
her.

6. Seth (s. of Seth 2.) m. Molly Thayer, and had Enos 1788,
Hannah 1789, Micah 1791, Seth 1793, Eliphalet 1795, Zechariah
1797, Zeba 1799, Samuel 1800, Charles 1802. Enos m. Mary
Damon of Hanson 1821.—Hannah m. Thomas Dunbar 1810.—
Micah and Seth went to Springfield.—Eliphalet m. Lydia Stone
of E. 1819.—Zechariah went to Me.—Zeba m. Prudence Stone
of E. 1820.

7. Jeremiah (s. of Jeremiah 4.) m. Catherine, D. of Barnabas
Pratt, 1780, and had Silvina 1783, Thankful 1785, Daniel 1787,

Solomon 1789, Omar 1791, Barnabas 1794, Friend 1797: he probably had a 2d w. Wealthy, and both d. in Sidney, Me., 1832; both æ. 74.—Silvina m. Timothy Reynolds.—Solomon gra. B. U. 1815.—Omar went to Sidney.—Barnabas and Friend both are d.

8. Richard (s. of Jeremiah 3.) m. Eunice, D. of Dea. Nath'l Edson, 1786, and had Earl 1787, Susanna 1790, Huldah Edson 1795, Richard 1798. Susan m. Isaac Fish of Kingston 1813, and had Richard Henry 1815.—Earl m. Orra, D. of Josiah Williams, 1812, and then Mehitabel, wid. of Charles Copeland and D. of Oliver Howard.

9. Capt. Leavit (s. of Jeremiah 3.) m. Abigail, D. of Charles Snell, 1783, and had Sally who m. Alpheus Howard 1802, and afterwards a Berry or Perry. He d. 1838.

10. John Thayer (s. of John Jr. of Braintree) and his wife Thankful lived in E. B.: he d. 1808, æ. 51; she died 1813, and several of their children d. there. He first m. Elizabeth Hollis 1771, and Eunice West 1781, and had John 1783, and Molly 1784.

11. David Thayer (s. of David probably of Braintree) and his family lived awhile in S. B., and d. there. Some of the family went to Boston, and they all removed. He had Solomon, Cornelius, Ebenezer, Hannah, Susanna, Sarah, Mary, and two other Ds.: one m. a Blanchard, and the other m. a White. Solomon m. Sarah Hobart 1789.—Cornelius m. Thankful, D. of Joseph Pope, 1796.—Ebenezer went to Boston.—Hannah m. Freeman Pope 1795.—Susannah m. Benjamin Clark.—Sarah m. Major Nathaniel Tomson of H. 1785.—Mary m. Consider Pratt of Halifax.

Naomi m. Ezekiel Washburn Jr. 1781.—Henry (s. of Richard of Braintree) m. Philibert, D. of Jacob Packard, 1783, and went to Winchester.—Susanna m. Thomas Pratt 1788.—Alexander of Braintree m. Lucy, D. of Ebenezer Edson, 1788.—Deborah of Braintree m. Zenas Packard 1793.—Joseph of Stoughton m. Sarah, D. of John Richards, 1795.—Anna of Braintree m. Dea. Eliphalet Packard 1800.—Sally m. Alpheus Howard 1802.—Elijah m. Elizabeth Slack 1804.—Thomas of Randolph m. Cynthia, D. of Ebenezer Warren, 1805.—Barnabas of Braintree m. Susanna, D. of Capt. Parmenas Packard, 1806.—Silence m. Thomas Cole 1810.—Deborah of Randolph m. Ebenezer Warren Jr. 1811.—John m. Lydia Brown 1811.—Eunice m. Isaac Brown 1813.—Rachel m. Barnabas Lathrop 1813.—Sally m. Francis Tribou 1816.

THOMAS.—James Thomas of Marshfield m. Priscilla, D. of Anthony Winslow, and had James, Winslow, Priscilla, and Deborah Winslow: he died, and Mr. Winslow, the father-in-law, came and settled in E. B., a. 1770, and brought his D. and these gr. ch. with him. Priscilla m. Samuel Faxon 1783.—Deborah W. m. Noah Hobart 1789, and died 1834 at Foxborough.—Priscilla the wid. d. 1807, æ. 70.

1. James gra. H. U. 1778, followed none of the learned
40

professions, was an agriculturalist and schoolmaster : he also was
Representative of the town, and a Magistrate : he m. late in
life Mary Holbrook 1810, but had no children : she d. 1836, æ.
81; he d. 1828, æ. 72. She was gr. D. of Elisha Pierce of Scit.
who m. Sarah, D. of Capt. Josiah Edson. Pierce's D. Sarah
first m. a Holbrook, father of Mary above, and then a Parks
who d. in E. B. 1826, æ. 93.

2. Winslow m. Polly Cole 1790, and had Nathan, d. 1810, æ.
18; and Mary Winslow who m. Dea. William Harris Jr. 1819 :
he d. 1828, æ. 71.

Levi Thomas of Pem. and Lydia Thomas were m. 1800.—
Mary of Pem. m. Jacob Perkins 1808.—Lucy of Marshfield m.
Nathaniel Pratt.—Lenity m. Nathan Kingman 1770, and after-
wards Edward Hayford 1779.—Betty (sister of Lenity, both from
Marshfield) m. Japhet Allen 1761.

THOMPSON.—Archibald Thompson with his wife and son
Robert, from Ireland, came to America 1724, lived awhile in
Abington, then in S. B., where he d. 1776, æ. 85 : he made the
first spinning foot-wheel, probably, that was made in N. E. He
had Robert, Thomas, Archibald, James, John, Jane, Betsy, Anna.
John died young.—Jane m. Andrew Gamel 1756.—Betsy m. a
Strobridge of Mid'o.—Anna m. a Fulton.—Agnes m. Robert
Fulton 1767, qu. if the same.—Jennet m. William Strobridge
1748 : was she not his D. also ?—Archibald m. Martha, D. of
Gain Robinson 1761, and went to Nova Scotia.

2. Robert (s. of Archibald 1.) m. Margaret Smith of Milton
1754, and had Rachel 1755, Elizabeth 1757, Jennet 1759, Margaret 1761 : he removed to Londonderry, N. H.

3. Thomas (s. of Archibald 1.) m. Elizabeth Strobridge 1754,
and had John 1755, Mary 1758, Anna 1760, Elizabeth 1763,
William 1765, Thomas 1767, Margaret 1769, James : he d. 1810,
æ. 81 ; she d. 1811. Mary m. Cary Hayward 1779.—Anna m. a
Buxton.—Elizabeth m. John Pettengill 1784.—William went to
Me.—Capt. John m. Jennet, D. of Isaac Allen, 1778, and went
to Maine.—James m. Olive, D. of Samuel Cheesman, 1798, and
went to Maine : he had Elizabeth 1799, Olive 1802, and Thomas
1804. Olive m. John Field.

4. James (s. of Archibald 1.) gra. Princeton 1761 : he preached
awhile, and was then a preceptor of an academy in Charleston,
S. C.

5. Capt. Thomas (s. of Thomas 3.) m. Martha, D. of Matthew
Kingman, 1792, and had John 1793*, Charlotte 1796, Sophronia,
Jane, Martha, John. Charlotte m. Charles Packard 1818.—John
m. Sarah, D. of Asa Jones 1819.

6. Thomas m. Jane, D. of John Washburn, 1745, and had
Mary 1746, Abishai 1747, Jane 1749, Margaret 1751, Bethiah
1755.

Jacob of M. m. Freelove Phinney 1761.—Maj. Nathaniel of
Halifax m. Sarah, D. of David Thayer, 1785.—Betty of Halifax
m. Nicholas Wade Jr. 1762.—Sarah m. Luther Keith 1767.—

Jane m. Nath'l Bolton 1777.—Mary of Abington m. Abijah Tirrell 1774.—Hannah, D. of Dea. Barnabas of Halifax, m. Elisha Mitchell Esq. 1781.—Martha m. Jonah Benson 1782.—Mary of Halifax m. Elijah Hayward 1785.—Ephraim of Halifax m. Molly Washburn 1791.—Reuben of Halifax m. Eunice, D. of Nicholas Whitman, 1791.—Rebecca of Halifax m. Lewis Chamberlin 1793.—Daniel m. Sarah Snow 1794.—Jacob of Halifax m. Lucinda Keith 1795.—Molly m. Edmund Alger 1796.—Cephas of Mid'o. m. Olive, D. of David Leonard, 1802.—Nathan of Halifax m. Elizabeth Fobes 1802.—Lucy of Mid'o. m. Charles Shaw 1810.—Daniel m. Sibil Horton 1813.—Ezra m. Polly Bates 1813.—Seth of Halifax m. Bethiah, D. of David Benson, 1815. Wid. Mary m. John Tower 1816.—Charles m. Hannah Pratt 1816.—Boadicea of Mid'o. m. Simeon Leonard 1817.—Eliab Jr. of Halifax m. Levinia Washburn 1819.—Margaret of Halifax m. Perez Robinson 1819.—Sarah, D. of Maj. Nathaniel of Halifax m. Capt. Charles Rogers 1821.—Almira m. Sidney Packard. Charity m. Thomas Rogers 1835, the 3 last are sisters.—James of Halifax m. Abigail, D. of Nathan Allen, 1765.—Margaret d. 1815.—John m. Elizabeth Bisbee of Pem. 1762.—Peleg (s. of Ezra Thompson of Halifax) lives in E. B.

TILDEN.—John Tilden (s. of John Tilden of Canton) settled in N. B., m. Polly Hayward 1796, and had John 1798, Polly 1801, Susanna 1805, Abigail 1807, Lavinia 1810, Hayward 1812. Polly m. Caleb Howard.—John m. a Reynolds.

Betsy of Hanson m. John Garner 1806.—Deborah m. Elias Barrell 1813.—Mary of Hanson m. John Tribou 1810.—Wm. Smith, keeper of the hotel, E. B., (from Duxbury) m. a Tilden. Nathaniel m. Susanna Brett 1755.

TILSON.—Holmes Tilson m. Olive, D. of Capt. David Packard, 1797, and had David 1797, Rhoda 1797, Polly 1800, Emery 1802, Eliza 1804. David lived in Boston, and had a son Asahel Allen. The rest of the family went to Me.

2. Dr. Elisha Tilson (brother of the above) lived in N. B., and m. Molly, D. of Capt. Zebedee Snell, 1792, and had Elisha Snell 1794, who m. Betsy Chandler of Easton 1819.

Polly of Halifax m. William Hooper 1793.—Joseph of Halifax m. Lucinda, D. of Samuel Whitman, 1794, and his son Samuel W. lived in E. B. Rhoda, sister of Dr. Elisha, m. Asahel Allen 1794.—Lydia T. of Halifax m. Ebenezer Leach 1739.

TIRRELL.—Lydia Tirrell, D. of John Harden of Abington, m. Robert Dawes of E. B., 1742, and afterwards Isaac Tirrell of Abington 1755, and d. in E. B., 1798, æ. 76.

2. John Tirrell and his wife came from Abington, and settled in E. B., and had John and Noah. John m. Rhoda, D. of Joseph Smith, 1794, and d. 1809, æ. 44. Noah was drowned 1803, æ. 31.—John, the father, was a soldier and drum-major in the French war with Gen. Winslow at Annapolis Royal 1755, and at Fort Wm. Henry in the time of the massacre 1757, and among

the few who made their escape to Fort Edward, and was famil-
iarly called Major Tirrell : he d. 1806, æ. 70 ; she 1805, æ. 68.
Rhoda, wife of John Jr. d. 1830, æ. 54.

3. Lemuel (s. of Jacob and gr. s. of Thomas of Abington) m.
a Trask, and settled in N. B., and had Jacob, Lemuel, Zibeon,
Abigail, Susanna, Mehitabel, and Mary. Abigail m. Lewis Hayden of St. 1815.—Susanna m. Thomas Nightingale of Quincy
1809 : she is called Experience on the record.

4. Jacob (s. of Lemuel 3.) m. Emma Corbet, D. of Ezekiel
Reed, 1813, lived in E. B., and had Emma Reed 1815*, Rebecca
1816.

Noah m. Reliance Leach 1794.—Lucy m. Nathan Warren
1783.—Oakes of Abington m. Hannah, D. of Issachar Snell Esq.,
1805.—William m. Deborah Hearsey 1709.—Betty m. Charles
Ramsdell 1783.—Alexander m. Lydia Bryant 1788.

TOLMAN.—Thomas Tolman's 2d child, Nathaniel, born in
Bridgewater 1691.

2. William m. Betty, wid. of Nathan Ames and D. of Eleazar Snow, 1757, and had Daniel and Reuben : she afterwards m.
Micah White 1768.

3. Daniel (s. of William 2.) m. Chloe, D. of Jonathan Bozworth, 1784, and lived in W. B., and had Olive 1784, d. 1814 ;
Israel 1787, Lucinda 1789, Daniel 1791, Cyrus 1793, Reuben
1796*, Chloe 1798, James 1804. Olive m. Salter Richmond
1806.—Lucinda m. Ansel Hayward of Boston 1812.—Israel m.
Susanna Packard, D. of Josiah Williams Jr. 1813.

Ebenezer W. Tolman of St. m. Mary A., D. of Capt. William
Vinton, 1820, and lived in E. B. Cynthia of St. m. Ezra Cary
1770.—James of St. m. Sarah, D. of Nathan Alden Esq. 1818.

TOMPKINS.—Samuel Tompkins, from Duxbury, was one of
the original proprietors of the town : he lived in E. B.: his wife
was Lettice Foster of Scituate, m. 1639 ; he had no children : in
his will, dated 1673, he gives all his lands to Francis Cary, who
was brought up by and lived with him : he also mentions his
brother John Tompkins, cousins Mary Foster, Elizabeth White,
and Hannah Dogget : he was 63 years old. His brother John
also lived in Br., and was called " John Tompkins from Salem":
they both probably were from Salem. John died probably, or
removed early : no others of the name have ever resided in the
town. The present Francis Cary lives on the same lands which
Tompkins gave to his gr. gr. grandfather Francis.—John Tompkins had Ruth 1640, John 1642.—[Boston records.]

TORREY.—Thomas Torrey and his w. Ruth lived in E. B.,
and had Thomas 1748*, Ruth 1753*, Josiah 1755, Thomas 1758,
Philip 1760, and Ruth who lived single.

2. Philip (s. of Thomas 1.) m. Mary Dyer of Abing. 1792,
and had John 1793, Havelin 1797. She d., and he m. wid. Rosanda Nash, D. of Ebenezer Porter 1817.

Lewis Torrey of Mid'o. m. Bethiah, D. of Eleazar Washburn,
1809 : she afterwards m. Josephus Freeman 1823.—Mary P. m.

Erastus Hayward 1813.—Turner Torrey m. Sally, D. of Issachar
Snell Esq. 1803, and settled in N. B., and had Almedia 1804.—
Sarah m. Benjamin Taylor 1784.

TRASK.—John Trask and his w. Penelope had William 1729,
Samuel 1731, Sarah 1733, Abigail 1736, Bathsheba 1741, Phebe
1744. Bathsheba m. Ephraim Jackson 1765.

2. William (s. of John 1.) and his w. Bethiah had Betty 1750,
Samuel 1753, Molly 1756, John 1757: the father d. 1811. Betty
m. Abel Edson Jr. 1771.

TRIBOU.—Thomas Tribou (a Frenchman) settled in Bridgewater as early as 1745, m. Margery, D. of John Pratt, 1746, and
had Relief 1747*, Isaac 1748, William 1752, Rhoda 1754, Ann
1757, Amasa 1760, Melzar 1766: he d. 1811. Rhoda m. Daniel
French 1792.—Anna m. Jacob Hill 1780.—Melzar settled in
Mid'o., and had a son Nahum Mitchell.

2. Isaac (s. of Thomas 1.) entered Dartmouth College, but did
not graduate: he m. Molly Lyon of Mid'o. 1780, and lived in
E. B., and had Isaac 1781, Molly 1783, Martin 1785, Cynthia
1787, Hannah 1789, Jenny Pateshal 1792, and removed to the
westward.

3. William (s. of Thomas 1.) m. Amy Belcher 1784, and had
Peter 1786, John 1788, Daniel 1790, William 1793, Francis 1795,
Charles 1797, Walter Spooner 1799, Sally 1802: he died 1815.
Peter m. Martha Hall 1817, and had Martin 1818.—John m.
Mary Tilden of Hanson 1810.—Daniel m. an Ashley, and lives
in E. B.—William m. Polly, D. of Asa Ford, 1816.—Francis m.
Sally Thayer 1816.—Walter S. m. a D. of Howland Holmes of
Halifax.

4. Amasa (s. of Thomas 1.) m. Molly Pratt 1780, and had Alpheus 1782, Relief 1783, Adna 1785, Rhoda 1787, Polly 1789,
Francis 1791, Amasa 1793, Zina 1795. Alpheus m. Hannah
Curtis 1804, and Ruth Clark of Hanson 1809. This family went
to Maine.

Thomas Tribou m. Zervia Randall of Easton 1790.—Francis
Treboo of Boston m. Ann Riscomb 1717, and had Ann 1718,
Francis 1720, and probably others.—Thomas, first above men-
tioned, was probably his son.

TROW.—Bartholomew Trow (s. of Bartholomew of Boston,
formerly assistant messenger to the Governor and Council) settled
in E. B., and m. Molly, D. of Capt. Levi Washburn, 1803, and
had Bartholomew, William Call, Mary, Joanne, George Augustus, Francis, and Frederick. Mary m. Henry Johnson, and lives
in the city of N. Y.—Bartholomew m. Bethiah, D. of William
Eldridge of Chatham: she died 1838.—William C. m. Angelina,
D. of Elisha Gilmore of Taunton, now of Turner, Me.—George
A. m. Thankful, D. of George Torrey of Scituate.

TURNER.—George Turner settled early in W. B., and died
about 1696, at which date it is recorded that "John Turner settled his father George Turner's estate." We find also on record
that Goodman [George] Turner was to maintain his brother

John Robbins 1668.—Thomas Turner was also a town officer
here 1678.

2. John (s. of George 1.) and his wife Hannah had John 1686,
William 1687, Hannah 1689 : he and she both d. 1728.

3. John (s. of John 2.) m. Mary Bicknell of Weymouth 1717,
and had John 1719, George 1722, one 1725*, Sarah 1727 : they
both d. 1753.

4. William (s. of John 2.) m. Eleanor, D. of Abiah Whitman
of Weymouth, 1714 ; she was born 1688 : they had Mary 1715,
Eleanor 1717, Hannah 1719, Margaret and Elizabeth 1722, Joanna 1725, George 1728 : he d. 1747.   Eleanor m. Jacob Macomber 1740.—Hannah m. James Lindsay 1744.—Margaret m.
Joseph Crossman of Easton 1756.—Elizabeth m. Thomas Lindsay 1745.—Joanna m. David Manly 1752.   The following places
are mentioned as being near John and William Turner's houses.
" Cooper's Meadow, Cooper's Dam, the Neck, John's house near
N. Purchase Line, easterly by Joshua Howard's ; Stone House
Plain, Elisha Dunbar's house 1738."

5. John (s. of John 3.) and his wife Elizabeth had Bathsheba
1747, Lemuel 1749.

6. George (s. of William 4. probably) and his w. Desire had
Josiah 1754, Mary 1755.   His w. d. 1756, and he m. a 2d w. Jane,
and had William 1760, Desire 1761, George 1763*, Isaiah 1764*,
Jenny 1766, George and Isaiah 1769, Alpheus 1779.   Mary m.
Daniel Lathrop (his 3d w.) 1785.—Desire (or Keziah) m. Oliver
Harvey 1793.—William m. Joanna, D. of Joseph Pettingill 1781.

7. Samuel (from Mid'o.) m. Lydia, D. of Ezra Hayward, 1794,
and had Betsy 1795, Joseph 1797, Cyrus 1800 : he d. 1821.

Content m. Ebenezer Kingman 1740.—Ann m. Capt. Joseph
Keith 1746.—Elizabeth m. Thomas Reynolds 1748.—Mary m.
Job Bryant 1764.—Jane m. Daniel Alden Jr. 1747.—Eunice m.
Asa Leach of Killingsley 1787.—Rachel m. William Whiting of
Stoughton 1811.—Job of Pembroke m. Nabby, wid. of Nath'l
Clift and D. of Josiah Byram, 1818.—David, Minister of Reho-
both, s. of Thomas and g. g. s. of Humphrey of Scituate, m.
Sarah, D. of John Howard, 1721.—David Turner died in E. B.
1774, æ. 33, had Lucy 1772.—Grace m. Abner Hayward 1784.
Jane Turner of Weymouth m. Samuel Allen 1728.

Job Turner (b. at Scituate) enlisted from Bridgewater into the
French war under Gen. Winslow in 1755, at the dispersing of
the neutral French at Nova Scotia.   Mitchel (or Michael) Turner was also in the same expedition, and from Bridgewater.

VAILS.—Edward Vails m. Mary Orberton 1769, and had
Edward 1774.

VAUGHN.—Jabez Vaughn of Mid'o. m. Martha Pratt 1817,
and had Cornelius Pratt 1822.   George Vaughn m. Faithful, D.
of Nathaniel Packard, 1719.—Mary, D. of George Vaughn of
Mid'o. m. Jonathan Washburn a. 1683.

VICKERY.—Benjamin Vickery lived in E. B., m. Mary, D.
of Josiah Allen, 1737, and Mary, D. of Samuel Kingman 1739,

and had Mary 1740, Elizabeth 1743, Eliab 1745, Benjamin 1749, Olive 1753, Huldah 1759. This family removed early from B.
VINTON.—William Vinton (from Braintree, s. of Thomas) settled in E. B., m. Susanna, D. of Joseph Robinson, 1774, and had William, Joseph 1777*, Edward, and Abigail: he d. 1796, æ. 47; she 1821, æ. 69. Abigail m. Ezra Alden, 1798.
2. Capt. William (s. of William 1.) m. Mary, D. of Nathan Alden Esq., 1797, and had Mary Alden. His w. d. 1799, æ. 23, and he m. Abigail, D. of Dr. Josiah Otis, 1803, and had Clarissa, Nabby, d. 1806; Susanna, Elizabeth. His w. d. 1816, æ. 34, and he m. Clarissa Otis, sister of his last w., 1817, and had William, Josiah, Alice, and Joseph. Mary A. m. Ebenezer W. Tolman 1820.—Clarissa m. Bailey Allen.—Susanna d. single.—Elizabeth m. James S. Dagget, and lives in Calais, Vermont.
3. Edward (s. of William 1.) m. Lydia, D. of Ebenezer Porter of Abington 1820, and had Lydia Loring, Lucia, Abigail, Edward Porter, Caroline Augusta, Susan. Lydia L. m. a Trask, and lives in Quincy.
WADE.—Thomas Wade (s. of Nicholas of Scituate) m. Elizabeth, D. of Thomas Curtis, 1672, and had Jacob 1673, Joseph 1675, Sarah 1678, Thomas 1680, Hannah 1682, Ichabod 1685, Moses 1689, Deborah 1691, Rachel 1692. He settled in B. a. 1680; his youngest children were b. here; his will dated 1726. He purchased a farm of Sam'l Staples, near Nippenicket Pond, 1693. Jacob and Joseph remained probably at Scituate.—Sarah had a son whom she called Cornelius Briggs, alias Wade, who m. and moved to Me.—Hannah m. Edward Lathrop a. 1721.—Deborah m. Jona. Phinney of Mid'o. 1735.—Rachel m. Israel Alger 1731 (his 3d w.).
2. Thomas (s. of Thomas 1.) lived in W. B., m. Rebecca, D. of Joseph Snow 1722, and had Hopestill 1725, Mary 1727, Keziah 1729, David 1732, Rebecca 1734. Hopestill m. Zephaniah Alden 1748.—Keziah m. Job Packard 1751.—Rebecca m. Elisha Dunbar 1757.—Thomas Wade m. Elizabeth Hanmer 1743, and Abigail Ames 1752, she d. a wid. 1779, æ. 84.
3. Ichabod (s. of Thomas 1.) we find his will 1747, in which he mentions his ss. Ichabod, Amos, Ebenezer, and Ds. Malison, Abial, Molly.
4. Moses (s. of Thomas 1.) lived in W. B., m. Abthiah Stetson 1738. We find no further notice of him but the following: "Oct. 19, 1640, baptized Moses Wade on a sick bed at home, many present." "Wid. Abthiah Wade admitted to the Church Jan. 10, 1742."—[Rev. Mr. Perkin's Ch. Rec.]—We conclude they had no children. She probably m. Jonathan Chandler 1745, and d. 1792, æ. 85.
5. David (s. of Thomas 2.) m. Mary, D. of Daniel Littlefield, 1756, and had Rebecca 1757, Rhoda 1759*, Silence 1762, Thomas 1764*, David 1766, Thomas 1769, Keziah 1772, Mary 1775. It is said this family went to Easton.
6. Ebenezer (s. of Ichabod 3.) m. Mehitabel, D. of John

Kingman, 1759, and had Ruth 1761 : his wife d. 1772, æ. 41, in E. B.

None of the descendants of Thomas in the male line live in B. now: there are some perhaps in Raynham and Easton.— Hannah Wade m. William Lincoln of Taunton 1751.

7. Nicholas (nephew of Thomas 1. and s. probably of Nicholas Jr. of Scituate) m. Anne, D. of James Latham, 1715, and settled in E. B., and had John, James, Thomas 1721, Amasa, Samuel, Nicholas 1731, Elizabeth, Mary: his w. d. 1770, æ. 77; he d. before her. Elizabeth m. Samuel Harden 1739.—Mary m. Seth Mitchell 1760, his 2d w.—John m. Hannah Kingman 1751, and went to Penobscot.—Amasa went to Weymouth.—Samuel settled in Hanson, and had Samuel, Isaac, Levi, and others.— Levi m. Deborah Phillips 1766.

8. James (s. of Nicholas 7.) m. Ann Clark of Plym. 1754, and had Abig'l 1755*, Anne 1757, Hannah 1759, James 1761*, Abigail 1762, Rebecca 1766 : he d. 1802, æ. 73. Anne m. Reuben Mitchell 1783.—Hannah m. Thomas Osborn 1784.—Abigail m. Spencer Forest 1784.—Rebecca m. Israel Cowing of Scituate 1786.

9. Thomas (s. of Nicholas 7.) m. Susanna, D. of Capt. Chilton Latham, 1746, and had Susanna 1748, Robert 1750, Molly 1754 : he died 1777 of small-pox; she 1800, æ. 83 : the Ds. not m. Susanna d. 1829, æ. 81.

10. Nicholas (s. of Nicholas 7.) m. Betty Tomson of Halifax 1762, and had John 1763, Betty 1765*, James 1768*, Ruth 1770, d. 1792 ; Betty 1772, d. 1790 ; Hannah 1776 : he d. 1780, æ. 49 ; she 1828, æ. 94. Hannah m. Melvill Holmes of Halifax 1801.

11. Robert (s. of Thomas 9.) m. Molly, D. of Ezra Edson, 1780, and had Celia 1782, Sally 1784, Naomi 1787, Thomas 1792, Calvin 1800*: he d. 1813, æ. 63. Celia m. Comfort Carpenter Dresser (brother of Ephraim Hyde's wife) 1802.—Naomi m. Elijah Pratt 1813.—Thomas m. a Wade.

12. John (s. of Nicholas 10.) m. Molly Snow 1791, and had Nicholas 1793, John 1795, Molly 1737: he died 1813, æ. 63. Nicholas m. Bethiah, D. of John Hudson, 1823.—John m. Caroline Wade of Hanson 1821.—Molly m. Isaac Hudson 1819.

Betsy of Hanover m. Charles Howard 1816.—Lydia of H. m. Sam'l Harden 1819.—Thomas from Hanson d. 1832, æ. 50.

Nicholas Wade (the ancestor) took the oath of fidelity 1638 at Scituate. There was also a Richard Wade at Scituate 1640, and a Jonathan Wade at Malden 1634, and a Jonathan Wade at Ipswich 1634, the same man perhaps.—Richard was at Sandwich 1637, and at Lynn the same year : went from Lynn to Sandwich, and was at Scituate 1640.—Nicholas and Jonathan are said to have been brothers, and probably Richard was their brother also.

WALDO.—There was a Waldo among the first settlers in N. B., from Chelmsford : he soon removed to Pomfret, Conn.: his Ds. Bethiah, Hannah, and Susanna, m. in Bridgewater, viz:— Bethiah m. Thomas Hayward a. 1719, and her D. Jane m. Benj.

Pierce Jr. of Scituate 1750, whose D. Bethiah was mother of Rev. Mr. Z. Willis of Kingston.—Hannah m. Ephraim Cary 1709.—Susanna m. Richard Field 1706, and one D. m. a Weld, father of the Rev. Mr. Weld of Braintree.—Shubael Waldo of Windham, Conn., one of the same family probably, m. Abigail, D. of Sam'l Allen of E. B., 1730: hence the christian name Waldo is found in the familes of Hayward, Field, Pierce, and Allen.

WALES.—Thomas Wales (s. of Dea. Nath'l of St. and gr. s. of Dea. Thomas of Stoughton) settled in N. B., m. a Belcher, and had Hannah and Lydia. His w. d., and he m. Polly, D. of Thomas Hobart of Hanson, and had Thomas, Nathaniel, Mary. Hannah m. James Cary 1803.—Lydia m. a Quin.—Mary m. Nathaniel Collamore of Hanson 1813, she d. at Bangor 1836.— Thomas m. Chloe, D. of Silas Packard Esq. 1811.—Nathaniel m. a Cushing.

2. John (brother of Thomas 1.) m. Mehitabel, D. of Barnabas Howard Esq., 1789, and had Mehitabel and Anna Howard 1791: he then m. Susanna Capen of Stoughton 1791, and had Susanna 1792, Sally*, and John. Mehitabel m. Isaac Curtis 1806.—Anna H. m. William French Jr. 1810.—Susanna m. Eliab Whitman Esq. 1817.—John m. Olive, D. of Col. Caleb Howard, 1820, and had afterwards a 2d wife.

Falley of Stoughton m. John Reynolds 1802.—Joshua m. Polly Briggs 1803.—Nathaniel 2d m. Phebe French 1814.

WARD.—Benja. Ward and his wife Bebee had Joseph 1753.

WARREN.—Joshua Warren of N. B. m. Jane, D. of William Orcutt Jr., 1725, and had Ebenezer 1726, Hannah 1728, Ezra 1730, Mary 1733, Sarah 1736, Joshua 1738. The Ds. never m.

2. Ebenezer (s. of Joshua 1.) m. Mary Nightingale 1747, and had Mary 1748, Jane 1750, Susanna 1752, Sarah 1754, Ebenezer 1757, Simeon 1759*, Jemima 1761, Lydia 1763, Joshua 1766. Mary m. Ebenezer Edson 1790.—Jane m. Seth Wentworth 1776.—Susanna m. Seth Harris Jr. 1776.—Sarah m. Nathan Billings 1778.—Jemima m. a Whiting.—Joshua went to Lyme, N. H.

3. Ezra (s. of Joshua 1.) m. Mary Phillips 1752, and had Hannah 1753, and Eunice 1754, Nathan 1756*: he then m. Mercy, D. of Zacch. Packard, and had Ezra 1758, Phillips 1760, Nathan 1762, Benja. 1764*, Sarah 1767, Benja. 1769, Mercy 1771, Mary 1773, and Artemas : his w. d. 1775. He m. a wid. Tirrell for his 3d w. and had a D. Jennet.—Nathan m. Lucy Tirrell 1783, and all the ss. went to Maine.—Sarah m. Silvanus Burr of Easton 1790.— Mercy m. James Loring 1800.—Hannah m. Archipus Taylor 1778.—Eunice m. Ebenezer Warren 1776.

4. Joshua (s. of Joshua 1.) m. Rebecca, D. of Timothy Leach, 1760, and had Joshua 1761, John 1766, William, and Ruby.

5. Ebenezer (s. of Ebenezer 2.) m. Eunice, D. of Ezra Warren, 1776, and had Lois 1776, Cynthia 1778, Simeon 1781, Adah, 1783*, Ebenezer 1785, Eunice 1788, Cyrus 1790, Seth 1792, Galen 1794, Abiah and Azuba. Cynthia m. Thos. Thayer of R. 1805.

41

Simeon m. Rhoda, D. of Seth Harris, 1802.—Ebenezer m.
Deborah Thayer of Randolph 1811.—Eunice m. Joseph Mann
Jr. of Randolph.—Cyrus m. Olive, D. of John Bisbee, 1814.
Joseph Warren m. Mary Perkins 1756.—Jabez of Mid'o. m.
Zilphah Hooper 1766.—Ichabod of Mid'o. m. Molly Leonard
1776.—Jane m. Judah Peterson 1797.

WASHBURN.—John Washburn was early in Duxbury: he
had an action in Court against Edward Doten 1632: is named
in the assessment of taxes 1633: purchased Edward Bonpasse's
place beyond the creek called Eagle's nest, 1634. He and his
2 ss. John and Philip, were included with those able to bear arms in
the colony 1643, and his name is also among the first freemen of
Duxbury. He and his s. John were original proprietors of Bridg.,
and they and Philip became residents and settlers here in S. B.
as early as 1665: he d. here before 1670. We find no notice of
any other children except these two sons. John Washburn was
the first Secretary of the Council of Plymouth in England, and
was succeeded by William Burgess 1628: whether he had any
connection with the family here is not ascertained. William,
Daniel, and John Washburn were proprietors on Long Island as
early as 1653, and soon disappeared from the records there : who
they were, or whither they went, is not ascertained : we have
always supposed that all of the name in this part of the country
descended from John first above named. The name is variously
written on the early records, Washburne, Washborn, Washborne,
Washburn : the latter is now generally adopted, and has always
been so written by the family here.

2. John (s. of John 1.) m. Elizabeth, D. of Experience Mitchell, 1645, and had John, Thomas, Joseph, Samuel, Jonathan,
Benjamin, Mary 1661, Elizabeth, Jane, James 1672, and Sarah :
his will 1686. We find the following: "I do also wish my cousin
Elizabeth much joy with her D., that God has given to her six
ss.," being an extract of a letter from Thomas Mitchell, dated at
Amsterdam 24th July, 1662, to his uncle Experience Mitchell.
The application of this congratulation to this family cannot be
doubted. He sold his house and lands 1670, at Green's harbour,
Duxbury, which his father had given him. John and Samuel
were exor's to their father's will. He appointed his "kind friend"
John Tomson, and his "brother" Edward Mitchell, Trustees and
Overseers in the execution of it, and in taking care of the chil-
dren. Mary m. Samuel Kinsley 1694, or earlier.—Elizabeth m.
James Howard, and afterwards Edward Sealey.—Jane m. Wm.
Orcutt Jr.—Sarah m. John Ames 1697.

3. Philip (s. of John 1.). We cannot find that he left either
wife or children : his father gave him a farm in Duxbury 1666,
which he sold to Samuel Seabury 1679, and he sold other lands
to Thomas Lazell in 1684: his brother John, in his will, directs
his s. John to take care of "his uncle Philip," implying an in-
capacity in him either of mind or body to take care of himself;
probably the latter, as he had been in possession and manager of

a farm. Joseph Washburn " gave a bond to take care of his uncle Philip 1685," who was living 1700.

4. John (s. of John 2.) m. Rebeckah Lapham 1679, and had Josiah 1680, John 1682, Joseph 1683, William 1686, Abigail 1688, Rebeckah, and perhaps other children. He was living 1719, and was d. 1724. Abigail m. Josiah Leonard 1717.—Rebeckah m. David Johnson 1719.

5. Thomas (s. of John 2.) lived near Lazell and Perkins' works ; had 2 wives, the first Abigail, D. of Jacob Leonard ; the 2d Deliverance, D. of Samuel Packard : no children on town records : his will 1729, whence we collect the names of the following : Nathaniel, Thomas, Timothy, Hepzibah, Patience, Deliverance, Elizabeth.—Hepzibah m. John Hutchinson 1708.— Patience was then dead, having left children : whose wife she was is not ascertained.—Deliverance m. Ephraim Jennings 1719. Elizabeth m. Josiah Conant 1701.—No account of Nathaniel.— He gave David Perkins liberty by deed to join the mill dam to his land 1697.

6. Joseph (s. of John 2.) m. Hannah, D. of Robert Latham, and lived in E. B., and had Joseph, Jonathan, Ebenezer, Miles, Ephraim, Edward, Benjamin, Hannah, and perhaps others. It appears he was afterwards in Plymouth and Plympton by deeds he gave 1707, 1714, and 1720, in which his father Latham is mentioned : perhaps he had also a son John of Plymouth. Hannah probably m. Zechariah Whitmarsh 1730.—Hepzibah Washburn (whose D. not known) m. Benjamin Leach 1702.—Miles Washburn was chosen petty juror in B. 1699.

7. Samuel, (s. of John 2.) called Sergeant, m. Deborah, D. of Samuel Packard, and had Samuel 1678, Noah 1682, Israel 1684, Nehemiah 1686, Benjamin, and Hannah : he d. 1720, æ. 69, and left a will, by which it appears Noah and Israel were then dead. Hannah m. John Keith 1711.

8. Jonathan (s. of John 2.) m. Mary, D. of George Vaughn of Mid'o., about 1683, and had Elizabeth 1684, Josiah 1686, Benjamin 1688, Ebenezer 1690, Martha 1692, Joanna 1693, Nathan 1699, Jonathan 1700, Cornelius 1702. Elizabeth m. John Benson 1710.

9. Benjamin (s. of John 2.) enlisted into the old French war, so called in Phipps' expedition against Canada 1690, and made a nuncupative will, and never returned. The frequent probate of wills, made on the occasion of that war, furnishes abundant proof of its disasters. He left no children.

10. James (s. of John 2.) m. Mary Bowden 1693, and had Mary 1694, Anna 1696, James 1698, Edward 1700, Moses 1702, Gideon 1704, Sarah 1706, Martha 1709, Elizabeth 1710. Mary probably m. Thomas Perkins 1717.—Sarah m. Henry Caswell perhaps 1738.—Martha m. Robert Richmond perhaps 1733.— Elizabeth m. Elisha Hayward Jr. perhaps 1740. There was a Mary Washburn who m. William Snow 1722.

11. Josiah (s. of John 4.) and his w. Mercy had Joanna 1703,

Joseph 1705, Lydia 1707, Jemima 1710, Rebeckah 1712, Josiah 1716, Mercy 1718. He had a 2d w., and a s. Nathan. Joanna m. Ebenezer Leach 1734.—Jemima m. Josiah Leonard Jr. 1740. Rebeckah m, Samuel Alden 1752.—Mercy m. Pelatiah Phinney 1738.—Lydia m. Samuel West 1737.—Josiah Washburn's estate settled by his wid. Sarah and Edward Richmond of T. 1734.

12. John (s. of John 4.) m. Margaret, D. of Nathaniel Packard, 1710, and had John 1711, Nathaniel 1713, Robert 1715, Abraham 1717*, Margaret 1718, Abishai 1720, Jane 1722, Content 1724 : his will 1746. Margaret m. Ephraim Holmes 1741, and was d. 1746.—Jane m. Thomas Thompson 1745.—Content m. Joseph Lathrop 1746.—Abishai went to Salisbury, Conn., and afterwards to Middlebury, Vt., and died there, and left no ss.: he sold land to Wm. Loring 1767, in which he was named of Albany.

13. Joseph (s. of John 4.) we find no certain account of.— There was a Joseph, who went to Nova Scotia ; this may be the man, or he may have been the Joseph who was ancestor of the Leicester family. There is much uncertainty about the two Josephs, ss. of John 4 and of Joseph 6. [See Joseph 17.] Which of them was ancestor of the Leicester family, or whether either, is uncertain.

14. William (s. of John 4.) m. Experience Mann 1715, and had Abigail 1715, Alice 1717*, William 1718, Experience 1719*, Zipporah 1721, Thankful 1723, Philip 1726*, Ezekiel 1728, Job 1733 : he died 1756; his will 1749. Abigail m. John Freelove 1739.—Zipporah m. Timothy Perkins 1753.—Thankful m. John Kinsley 1746.—No account of Job.

15. Thomas (s. of Thomas 5.) and his w. Elizabeth had Mary 1722, and Elizabeth (or Betty) 1724. Mary m. Jabez King 1753. Elizabeth, the mother, m. Joseph Crossman 1752.—Thomas Washburn m. Sarah, D. of John Leonard, 1708, and Abigail Heiford 1711.

16. Timothy (s. of Thomas 5.) and his w. Hannah had Timothy 1721, Hannah 1724, and Mary 1725. Timothy Washburn, a tanner, bought land of Ebenezer Washburn Jr. at Poor Meadow 1720.

17. Joseph (s. of Joseph 6.) we have no account of unless it is the following furnished by Col. Seth Washburn's family genealogy at Leicester :—" Joseph had 5 ss. viz: Elijah, Joseph, Seth, Ebenezer, and one who d. young. Col. Seth, s. of Joseph, had Seth, Joseph, and Asa. Seth died in the revolution, leaving an only son.—Joseph had Ebenezer, a lawyer in Montgomery, Alabama ; Joseph, a merchant in Milledgeville, Georgia; Seth, a Physician in Greenfield, lately d.; and Emory, an Attorney at Leicester, now in Worcester.—Asa lives in Putney, Vt., and had Reuben, a Lawyer in Cavendish ; Seth in Randolph, Jacob in Chelsea, and Asa in Putney ; all in Vermont."

Joseph Washburn lived in E. B. 1716, and so also did Jonathan : these were probably ss. of Joseph 6. Jonathan had Silas 1713, Lemuel 1714, b. in E. B.—Most of the sons of Joseph 6.

went to Kingston and Plympton : Joseph, Miles, Edward, Ephraim, Ebenezer, were there as early as 1728; and Dea. John, Ichabod and Elisha, are also found on the records there about the same time. Most of the name about Plymouth, Kingston and Plympton, descended probably from Joseph 6.—Jona. Washburn m. Rebeckah Johnson of Hingham 1719.—[Boston Records.]

18. Samuel (s. of Samuel 7.) and his wife Abigail had David 1704, Deliverance 1706, Solomon 1708, Samuel 1710, Abigail 1712, Susanna 1714, Tabitha 1716. Deliverance m. Joseph Bolton 1740.—Tabitha m. Solomon Leach 1736.—Susanna m. Timothy Perkins 1736.—Samuel Washburn m. Deliverance, D. of Isaac Leonard, 1701, his first w. perhaps.—Know nothing of David and Samuel.

19. Noah (s. of Samuel 7.) m. Elizabeth, D. of Joseph Shaw and sister of Rev. Mr. John Shaw, 1710, and lived in E. B., and had Eleazer and Noah : he d. 1717, and his wid. m. Isaac Harris 1719.

20. Israel (s. of Samuel 7.) m. Waitstill Sumner 1708, and had Sarah 1709, Deborah 1712, Seth 1714, and Israel. He died, and his wid. m. Ebenezer Pratt 1720 : his estate divided between Israel, Sarah, and Deborah 1730. Eleazar Carver guardian to Sarah and Deborah. Sarah m. Ephraim Keith 1732. Deborah m. John Ripley, and afterwards Nathaniel Bolton 1740, and d. 1759.—No account of Seth.

21. Capt. Nehemiah (s. of Samuel 7.) m. Jane, D. of Ephraim Howard 1713, and had Silence 1713, Jane 1715 : his w. d. 1715. Silence m. Dr. Abiel Howard about 1737.—Jane m. Josiah Deane 1737 : he was a respectable man, employed much by the town, and its Representative 1730 : was guardian to Daniel and Hannah Howell 1728, and agent for Titicut 1749.

22. Capt. Benjamin (s. of Samuel 7.) m. Joanna (or Susanna) Orcutt 1715, and had Benjamin and Jonathan, and others.— Benjamin Washburn d. 1774. (Compare this with the account of Benjamin 24. : they may be in some measure confounded.)— Benjamin Washburn of Mid'o. in 1820 was æ. 67.—Joanna Washburn m. Samuel Hacket of Raynham 1736.

23. Josiah (s. of Jonathan 8.) m. Elizabeth Davenport 1723, and had Josiah and Jonathan.

24. Benjamin (s. of Jonathan 8.) m. Bethiah, D. of Henry Kingman, 1714, and had Isaac, Jonathan, Henry, Benjamin, Ezra, and others perhaps. He settled his father Jonathan's estate in 1725, and his brother Ebenezer's 1728. Benjamin Washburn m. Susanna Battles 1742.—Isaac Washburn went to Dartmouth, was a tanner, and enlisted into the French war under Gen. Winslow 1755.—Bethiah Washburn m. Nehemiah Bryant 1741.

25. Ebenezer (s. of Jonathan 8.) d., and his estate was settled by his brother Benjamin 1728 : he was æ. 29 : no children probably.

26. Nathan (s. of Jonathan 8.) We find no account of this man, and know not if he had any family.

27. Jonathan (s. of Jonathan 8.) m. Thankful Newton 1724: sold his house and lands to his son-in-law Ebenezer Pratt, and wife Bulah, 1763. His D. Bulah m. Pratt 1760: he died 1766; Thankful d. 1770.

28. Cornelius (s. of Jonathan 8.) and his wife Experience had Nathan 1728*, Daniel 1730, Ebenezer*, Robert 1736*, Robert 1737*, Cornelius 1739*, Experience 1745, Joanna 1747, and Cornelius: he d. 1779, æ. 77. Experience m. Jonathan Alden 1766.—Joanna m. Daniel Conant 1767.

29. James (s. of James 10.) m. Elizabeth, D. or wid. of Enoch Leonard, 1720; but we find no account of his family.

30. Edward (s. of James 10.) m. Elizabeth, D. of Amos Snell perhaps, or a Richmond, and went to Mid'o., and had Amos, Edward, and Abiel. Capt. Amos had James, Amos Luther, Joshua, and perhaps others. James gra. H. U. 1789, and was an Attorney, and d. unmarried.—Edward settled his father's estate 1767, and was father of Gen. Abiel Washburn.—Abiel sen'r d. in the French war.—There was an Edward Washburn of Plympton who m. Judith Rickard 1732: he was son probably of Joseph 6.

31. Moses (s. of James 10.) m. Hannah Cushman of Plympton 1727, and had Peter 1728, Moses 1730, Robert 1733, Ira 1735.

32. Gideon (s. of James 10.) m. Mary, D. of David Perkins perhaps, and had Abraham, Isaac, Jacob, Gideon, Luke. He, Abraham and Jacob, went to Paxton. This family lived where Dr. Sanger lived. Abraham had James, and Eliab who m. Molly Lazell 1777, and Luke who m. Desire Packard 1763.

33. Capt. Joseph (s. of Josiah 11.) m. Deliverance, D. of William Orcutt Jr., and had Joseph 1729, Jeremiah 1731, Hannah 1733, Joanna 1736, Silvanus 1738, Eliab 1740, Eliphalet 1742, Martha 1744. He d. 1766, and his wid. m. a Packard of N. B., and d. in S. B. 1790, æ. 88. Hannah m. Dea. Seth Pratt 1752.—Joanna m. Solomon Leonard Jr. 1756.—Martha m. Elijah Edson 1766, and went to New Braintree.—Silvanus m. Milicent Richards, and went to Hardwick.—Eliphalet also went to Hardwick, and left 3 sons, Luther, Calvin, and Rufus. Luther was an Attorney in Pittsfield, and d. 1838.

34. Josiah (s. of Josiah 11.) m. Abigail Curtis 1746, and had Bethuel 1746 who went to Albany, Abigail 1748, Peter 1750 who went to Brookfield. His w. d. 1754, and he m. a 2d w. Huldah, and had Salmon 1757, Ephraim 1760, and Huldah. His w. d. 1772, and he m. Elizabeth Snow 1775: he died 1789, æ. 73.—Ephraim m. Rebecca Dunham 1785.—Abigail m. Jona. Waterman 1768.

35. Lt. John (s. of John 12.) m. Bethiah, D. of Sam'l Keith, 1738, and had Thomas 1738, Sarah 1740: his w. d. 1770; he d.

1797, æ. 85. Thomas died a bachelor 1824, æ. 86.—Sarah died single 1836, æ. 96.

36. Nathaniel (s. of John 12) m. Mary Pratt of Mid'o., and had Lucy 1740, Abraham 1742, Nathaniel*, and Hannah. He d., and his wid. m. Eleazar Cary 1753.—Lucy m. Nathaniel Morton 1757, and was mother of Dr. Morton of Halifax.—Hannah m. Moses Snell 1763.

37. Robert (s. of John 12.) m. Mary, D. of Joshua Fobes, 1740, and had John 1743, Calvin 1745, Luther 1747, Martin 1750, Betty 1752. All but Calvin went to Livingston Manor, N. Y.

38. William (s. of William 14.) m. Rebecca Curtis 1738, and had Experience 1738, Elisha 1741, Philip 1743, Rebecca, Thankful, Eunice, William 1752. Experience m. Jonathan Orcutt 1759.—Rebecca m. Lemuel Leach 1767.—Thankful died 1770.—Eunice m. Benjamin Crane 1769.—One s. d. 1762.

39. Ezekiel (s. of William 14.) m. Experience Curtis, 1749, and lived in N. B., and had Zipporah 1750, Ezekiel 1752, Alice, Betty, Experience 1758, Deliverance: he died 1785. Alice m. William French 1773.—Betty m. Nathaniel Pratt 1778.—Deliverance m. William Shaw Jr. 1778.—Ezekiel m. Naomi Thayer 1781, and d. leaving her a wid.

40. Solomon (s. of Samuel 18.) m. Martha, D., of William Orcutt Jr. 1732, and had Lydia, Solomon 1735, Tabitha 1738.

41. Eleazar (s. of Noah 19.) m. Anna, D. of Capt. Ebenezer Alden, 1738, lived in E. B., and had Susanna 1740, Zenas 1741*, Anne 1742*, Anne 1743, Eleaz. 1746, Asa 1749, Levi 1752, Oliver 1755, Alden 1758, Isaac 1760 : he d. before 1770 ; she 1788, æ. 70. Susanna m. Jephthah Byram 1761.—Anne m. Amos Whitman 1764.—Asa went to New York.—Oliver m. Hannah, D. of Seth Gannett, 1781, and went to N. H.—Alden m. Sarah Harden, and went to Maine or N. H.

42. Noah (s. of Noah 19.) m. Mary Staples 1739, and lived in E. B., and had Elizabeth 1739, Noah 1741, Nehemiah 1743, Stephen 1748, Huldah 1750, Mary 1756. Nehemiah m. Ruth, D. of John Egerton, 1770.—Stephen m. Sarah Faxon 1770, and the whole family removed to Williamsburgh.—Perhaps Elizabeth m. Samuel Staples 1765.

43. Israel (s. of Israel 20.) m. Leah, D. of Joshua Fobes, 1740, settled in Raynham, and had Israel, Nehemiah, Seth, and Oliver. Israel's ss. were Israel, Sidney, Benjamin, Ruel, Elihu, Philander, and Eli.—Nehemiah's ss. were Col. Oliver Cromwell, Nehemiah, Davis, Calvin, Lysander, Isaac, and John Marshall. Dr. Seth's ss. were Philo and Benjamin Franklin.—Oliver's ss. were Otis and Caleb Strong.

44. Josiah (s. of Josiah 23.) m. Phebe, D. of Thomas Hayward, 1753, and had Solomon 1754, Seth 1756*, Thomas 1758, Bethiah 1760, Mary 1762, Hannah and Betty 1766, Jonathan 1768.

45. Benjamin (see Benjamin 24.) m. Martha, D. of Henry Kingman, 1729, and had Mary 1730, Martha 1731, Benjamin

1735: he died 1740. Mary m. Joseph Washburn.—Martha m. Jonathan Leonard 1758.—The wid. d. 1794, æ. 95; was b. 1699. (It is difficult to ascertain whose sons these several Benjamins were.)

46. Benjamin Washburn m. Zerviah, D. of Israel Packard, 1743, and had Hannah 1744, Sarah 1748, Ebenezer 1750. Sarah m. Daniel Bryant perhaps 1767.—Ebenezer Washburn m. Mary Leach 1772.

47. Benjamin (s. of Benjamin 22. perhaps) and his wife Mary had Susanna 1749, Mary, Eunice, Asa 1756, Joshua 1759, Olive, and Keziah. Susanna m. James Hooper Jr. 1772.—Olive not m.—Keziah m. Andrew Conant.—There was a Mary who m. Samuel Packard 1761.

48. Isaac (s. of Gideon 32. perhaps) m. Deborah, D. of Lot Conant 1753, and had Elijah 1753, Nathaniel 1757, Edmund 1759, and Isaac. Elijah went to Hardwick.

49. Jonathan (s. of Josiah 23. perhaps) m. Rebecca Perkins 1756, and had Luther 1757, Zerviah 1760. Luther went westward.—Zerviah m. Solomon Hayward 1782.—Jona. Washburn Jr. of M. m. Hannah, D. of Nathan Conant 1778.

50. Henry (s. of Benjamin 24. perhaps) and his w. Sarah had Henry 1741, Susanna 1742, Noah 1744, Sarah 1746, Hannah 1749, Huldah 1751, Samuel 1754, Ruhamah 1757, Experience 1760, and Sarah. This family moved to the westward.—Henry Jr. m. Susannah Hutchins of Mid. 1768.

51. Ezra (s. of Benjamin 24. perhaps) m. Susanna, D. of Benjamin Leach, 1742, and went to Mid'o. His D. Susanna m. Zadock Leach 1763.

52. Nathan (s. of Josiah 11.) m. Mary, D. of Hugh Mehuren, 1748, and had Rebecca 1748, Hugh 1750, Arthur 1752, Patience 1754, Jemima 1756, Charity 1758*, Robert 1760, Salathiel 1763, Bathsheba 1766. Rebecca m. Isaac Pool of Halifax perhaps 1774. If we are correctly informed this family went to New Salem.

53. Daniel (s. of Cornelius 28.) m. Experience Harlow 1752, and had Cornelius 1753, Daniel 1755, Zilphah 1757, Joanna 1759, Lois 1761, Ebenezer 1764, Eunice 1766, Sally 1768: he d. 1801, æ. 70.—Zilphah m. Noah Whitman 1779.—Joanna m. Phinehas Conant Jr. 1785, and d. 1829.—Eunice m. Jonah Besse 1787.— Sally and Lois not m.—Daniel went to Belchertown, and thence removed again.—Ebenezer m. Abigail Weston of Mid'o. 1787.

54. Cornelius (s. of Cornelius 28.) m. Lois D. of Jona. Benson, and had Daniel and Abigail. Daniel m. Melatiah, D. of Daniel Keith 1795.—Abigail m. Levi Blossom 1797.

55. Gideon (s. of Gideon 32.) m. Ruth, D. of Zechariah Whitman, 1765, and had Ruth, d. 1778; Libeus, Asa. He was killed at sea by a cannon-ball, and his widow m. Dea. Ripley of Plympton. Libeus m. Alice, D. of John Keith, 1792, and went to Pomfret, Conn., where they both d.—Asa learnt a blacksmith's trade with Arthur Harris E. B., and removed from town.

56. Joseph (s. of Capt. Joseph 33.) m. Mary, D. of Benjamin
Washburn, and had Levi 1757, Lavinia 1763, Mary 1764, and
went to Hardwick.

57. Jeremiah (s. of Capt. Joseph 33.) m. Charity, D. of Joseph
Pratt Jr. 1754, and had Lydia 1755, Barnabas 1756, Tabitha
1758, Rufus 1760*, Libeus 1762, Hannah 1767, Jeremiah 1769*.
His w. d. 1775, and he m. Keziah, D. of Daniel Snell, 1777, and
had Jeremiah 1779, Levi 1784. Lydia m. Capt. Simeon Wood
1778, his 3d wife.—Barnabas m. Keturah, D. of Thos. Conant,
1782, and went westward, and so did Libeus.—Tabitha m. Mark
Perkins 1784.—Hannah m. Benjamin Perkins 1789, and went to
Me.—Levi went to the southward, and d. at Washington 1838.—
Barnabas went to Pomfret, Vt.

58. Eliab (s. of Capt. Joseph 33.) m. Anna, D. of Elijah Ed-
son, 1762, and had Marshall 1763*, Lucy 1765*, Lewis 1767,
Joseph 1769, Eliab 1772, Anna 1774, Olive 1777, Marshall 1778*,
Marshall 1780. This family went to Hebron, Me.

59. Salmon (s. of Josiah 34.) m. Hannah, D. of Joseph Orcutt,
1785, and had Joseph Orcutt 1786, Huldah Leonard 1788, Josiah
1790, Lavinia 1795, Lucy 1801, Deborah 1804, and Lewis. Joseph O. went to Me.—Josiah went westward.—Lavinia m. Eliab
Tomson of H. 1819, another D. m. a Soule, and all the Ds. are
now d.—Lewis gra. B. U. 1826, and d. at Weymouth 1834.

60. Capt. Abraham (s. of Nathaniel 36.) m. Rebecca, D. of
Josiah Leonard, 1765, and had Nathaniel 1766, Chloe 1768,
Abraham 1772*, Seth 1776, Abram 1779, Lucy 1781. Chloe m
Edward Mitchell Jr. 1789.—Lucy m. Lawson Lyon of Boston
1813, and afterwards a Whitney of Boston.—Capt. Abram, the
son, m. Mary, D. of Dr. Eleazar Carver 1804.

61. Calvin (s. of Robert 37.) m. Rhoda Hammond of Rochester, and had Mary, Nancy, and Calvin. Mary (Polly) m. Oliver
Conant 1796.

62. Eleazar (s. of Eleazar 41.) m. Huldah, D. of Jonathan
Wood, 1769, and had Eleazar. His w. d. 1770, and he m. Sarah
Southworth of Mid'o. a. 1771, and had Southworth, Zenas, Eliphalet, Hiram, Sally 1780, Sampson 1783, Bethiah and Josiah
twins 1788 : she d. 1820, æ. 72 ; he 1828, æ. 82. Eleazar went
South in youth, and nothing more is known of him.—Southworth
m. Rebecca, D. of John Bisbee, 1794.—Zenas went to Plympton,
m. a Sampson, and had a son Isaac Sampson Washburn who d.
in E. B. 1838.—Eliphalet m. in Boston, and he and Southworth
both went to Me.—Sally m. James Johnson 1798.—Bethiah m.
Lewis Torrey of Mid'o. 1809, and Josephus Freeman 1823 —
Josiah d. 1834 a bachelor.

63. Capt. Levi (s. of Eleazar 41.) m. Mary (Molly), D. of
Isaac Allen, 1774, and had Levi 1775*, Susanna 1777, Mary
1778, Zilphah 1780, d. 1807, Levi 1782, Olive 1785, Oliver Alden
1788, Parna 1791, Harmon 1794, Maria 1796. His w. d. 1800,
æ.'45, and he m. Mary, late wife of Ichabod Howland and D. of
John Hatch, 1801 : he d. 1824, æ. 72. Susanna m. Simeon Jones
42

1803.—Mary m. Bartholomew Trow 1803.—Olive m. Capt. Luther Gannett 1810.—Oliver A. m. Jane, D. of Zenas Keith, 1814, and he and Gannett removed to Belfast, Me.—Parna m. Adam Stetson 1817.—Maria m. a Mendall, and went to Vermont : he is dead.

64. Isaac (s. of Eleazar 41.) m. Huldah, D. of Isaac Allen, 1781, and had Anna 1781, Sophia 1789, Cyrus 1791, and he then went to Me., and had other children : Isaac, now living in E. B., is one.—Anna m. Capt. Branch Byram 1802.

65. Solomon (s. of Josiah 44.) m. Anne, D. of Seth Mitchell, 1773, and had Zenas, Anna, Solomon, Reuben, Thomas 1787, Osier 1795, Lewis 1797, Nahum. This family moved away : part of them went to the westward.—Anna m. Oliver Hayward 1797. Nahum m. Anne, D. of John Mitchell 1816.—Solomon m. Sally, D. of Clifford Carver perhaps, 1801, and had Carver and Thos. Lewis lived in Mid'o.—Zenas m. Lydia, D. of Noah Whitman, 1799, and had Selden, Freelove Whitman, Sarah Whitman, Lysander 1810, Angelina 1813, and Lydia 1816 : he d. 1824, æ. 49.

66. Benjamin (s. of Benjamin 45.) was called the 3d : he m. Desire Sears of Halifax 1762, and had Oliver 1763*, Azel 1765*, Sally 1767*, Lydia 1769, Deborah 1771*, Desire 1773*, Sears 1777, Mary 1780, Huldah 1784, Benjamin 1786*: he d. 1796, æ. 61; she died 1800, æ. 57. Lydia m. Samuel Rider 1799.—Mary m. Barzillai Latham 1801.—Huldah m. an Irish in Me.

67. Joshua (s. of Benja. 47.) m. Lovicea (or Louisa or Lucy) Rickard 1786, and had Susanna 1787, Marsena 1789, Joshua 1791, Benjamin 1796, Isaac 1799. Susanna perhaps m. Macey Hall of R. 1807, and afterwards Sion Swift.—Isaac went to Abington.

68. Jeremiah (s. of Jeremiah 57.) m. Sarah, D. of Ezra Edson, 1801, and had Ezra Edson 1801*, Eliza Hyde 1803, Ezra Edson 1806, Robie Snell 1808, Anna Edson 1810, Emily Howard 1812*: he had another son, Jeremiah, who went to N. York. The parents are both dead.

69. Nathaniel (s. of Capt. Abraham 60.) m. Salome Simmons, D. of Moses, and had Rebecca, Abram, Nathaniel, John, Lois, Sarah Simmons. Rebecca m. John Conant.—Lois m. Ephraim Sprague.

70. Seth Esq. (s. of Capt. Abraham 60.) went to the southward, but returned again, and m. Sarah, wid. of Benjamin Willis and D. of Dr. Eleazar Carver, 1812, and had Sarah 1812, Anna 1814*, Seth 1817, Hosea 1819.

71. Calvin (s. of Calvin 61.) m. Eunice, D. of Capt. Ephraim Sprague 1809, and had Nancy Adams Vinton 1812, Eloisa Rowland 1814, Emily Miller 1816, Vina Sprague 1819, Jane Ames 1821. Nancy A. V. m. Greenough Wood.

72. Hiram (s. of Eleazar 62.) m. Nabby, D. of Seth Keith, a. 1809, and had Eliza Sampson 1810, Cyrus 1812, Mary Briggs 1814. His w. d. 1822, æ. 40, and he m. a Washburn of Mid'o., and is d.

73. Sampson (s. of Eleazar 62.) m. Rebeckah Soul of Mid'o 1805, and has a family.

74. Levi (s. of Capt. Levi 63.) m. Sarah, D. of Arthur Harris, 1807, and has Benjamin Harris, Alden, Allen, and Sarah. His w. d. 1826, æ. 42, and he m. a Barstow. Benjamin H. m. Celia, D. of Mark Phillips.—Alden m. a Jones of Pem. or Hanson.— Sarah m. a Dickerman, and is d.

75. Harmon (s. of Capt. Levi 63.) m. Harriet, D. of William Bonney, 1823, and has Harriet and others.

76. Isaac (s. of Isaac 64.) m. Chloe, D. of Oliver Washburn, and has a family.

77. Isaac Sampson (s. of Zenas of Plympton, and gr. s. of Eleazar 62.) m. Susanna Ruggles, gr. D. of Benjamin Robinson's last wife [see Packard, No. 93.], and had children : he d. 1839.

78. Oliver (s. of Benjamin 66.) m. Martha, D. of Eliab Fobes, 1787, and had Thomas 1787, d. 1824 ; Reuel 1789, Eliab 1792, d. 1820 ; Harriet 1794*, Oliver 1796, Chloe 1799, Willard 1802*. His w. d., and he m. Mary, D. of Benjamin Hayward, 1804, and had Willard 1805, Benjamin Hayward 1806, Azel 1808, Martha Fobes 1810, Marshall 1812, Harriet 1813, Mary 1815, John Benson 1817. Reuel died at N. Y.—Oliver went southward.— Chloe m. Isaac Washburn of E. B.

79. Capt. Sears (s. of Benjamin 66.) is now living a bachelor in S. B.

80. Nathaniel (s. of Nathaniel 69.) m. Joanna Harlow, D. of Willliam Snell, and had Maria Snell 1824, and father, mother, and child are all d.

81. Col. Abram (s. of Nathaniel 69.) m. Pamela, D. of Isaac Keith, 1822, and had Lucia C. 1823, Ann 1827*, Saba. His w. d., and he m. Sarah Miller, D. of Dr. Samuel Shaw.

82. John (s. of Nathaniel 69.) m. Mira, D. of Capt. Ephraim Sprague, and d. immediately after marriage, and his wid. m. the Hon. John A. Shaw.

83. Solomon (s. of Solomon 65.) m. Sarah, D. of Jabez Carver of Raynham, 1801, and had Rotheus, Carver, Nahum, Thomas, Albert, Eli, Nathan, John, Maria.

84. Carver (s. of Solomon 83.) m. Harriet, D. of Samuel Harden, and had Mira and Louisa, 1828.

85. Jacob Washburn, m. Mercy, D. of Isaac Pool probably, 1761, had a son 1764*, Bethiah 1765, Jacob 1767, Caleb 1770, Francis 1772. (This man was called Mr. Jacob Washburn of Mid'o.) Jacob probably m. Ruth Shaw in E. B. 1797 : she afterwards m. Benjamin Price 1805.

86. Caleb Washburn m. Mehitabel, wid. probably of Benjamin Allen in E. B. 1756.

Elisha of Kingston m. Martha Perkins of Plympton 1729 : his estate settled 1734.—Elisha of Roxbury m. Charity Snell 1763. Hannah m. Nathan Bassett 1733.—Phebe m. Samuel Kingman 1737.—Hannah m. Thos. Davis 1737.—Keziah m. Joseph Harvey 2d 1749.—Experience m. Amos Snell 1759.—Reuben m.

Betty Dilly 1749.—Hepzibah of Mid'o. m. Benja. Perkins 1761.
Mary m. Samuel Packard 1761.—Huldah m. Solomon Bartlett
1781.—Mary m. Benjamin Munro of Hal. 1787.—Sarah m. Seth
Hayward 1792.—Lucy m. Abel Kingman 1792.—Wid. Elizabeth
m. James Edson 1796.—Mary m. Job Pratt 1757.—Hannah m.
James Carkis Woodwiss 1770.—Seth of Mid'o. m. Elizabeth, D.
of James Dunbar, 1776.—Eunice m. Asa Richmond 1782.—
Reuben m. Abigail Murry (or Muzzy) 1743.—Jesse m. Silence
Washburn 1748.—Patience m. Nathan Richmond 1754.—Alice
m. Bela Fobes 1805.—Isaac m. Nabby Pope 1807.—Mary (or
Mercy) m. Oliver Leach 1817.—Harvey m. Dolly B. Clark 1822.

Jonathan of Mid'o. (s. of Benjamin) m. Judith, D. of Elnathan Wood, and had Jonathan, Benjamin, Isaac, Salmon, and
perhaps others. Isaac went to Taunton.—Benjamin has a son
Jonathan in S. B.

John Washburn of Plymouth sold land that was his gr. father
Irish's to Samuel Bradford 1708.

Ephraim Washburn of Plympton and his wife Mary had William 1726, Lydia 1728, Elizabeth 1732, Mary 1734, Stephen
1736, Isaac 1738, Phebe 1740, Jemima, Japhet, John : his estate
settled 1758. Lydia m. Samuel Noyes.—Elizabeth m. Consider
Benson : all the rest of the Ds. were then single.—Ebenezer's
estate settled at Kingston by his wid. Lydia 1738; her will 1765 :
they had Ebenezer, Simeon d., and Lydia Davis. Joseph, Miles,
Edward, Barnabas, Dea. John, Ichabod, were also at K. as early
as 1729. Jabez 1731, Philip 1765, Melatiah 1756, were m. there
at these dates. Most of them were sons of Joseph 6. Edward
m. Judith Rickard of Plympton 1732.—Reuben Washburn of
B. went to M., and enlisted into the French war 1755.—Benja.
of M. was 67 yrs. old 1820.—Bezaliel of B. went to Dartmouth,
and enlisted in the French war 1755.

Wid. Washburn d. 1775, quite aged.—Hannah d. of small-pox
1778.—Josiah's w. d. 1772.—Wid. Washburn d. 1778.—Josiah's
wife d. 1778.—Lucy d. 1800, æ. 32.—Martha d. 1803, æ. 40.—
Isaac Washburn d. in North Hadley 21st February, 1839, æ. 90.

Abishai Washburn (s. of John 12.) of the County of Albany,
N. Y., and his wife Hannah, sold to Wm. Loring of Plympton a
farm or plantation in Bridgewater bounded at the N. E. corner
of the homestead which is the N. W. corner of Josiah Washburn's homestead ; by Gershom Conant's land ; by the road from
Conant's to Ichabod Orcutt's ; by the road from said Orcutt's to
the S. Meeting House 1767 ; Hugh Orr Jr. witness, acknowledged June 9, 1777, at Salisbury, before Joshua Porter, Justice
of Peace.

Capt. Abraham Washburn was, some years since, living in
Hinsdale, in the County of Berkshire, æ. 74, whose father, Miles
Washburn, first settled in New Milford, and afterwards in Kent,
in Conn., and finally removed to Hinsdale. Capt. Abraham
thought his grandfather's name was Ebenezer.

The family of Washburn is so numerous, and there are so many of the same christian name, that there may be many mistakes, and some confusion, in the account here given of them.

WATERMAN.—Perez Waterman (s. perhaps of Dea. Robert of Halifax) settled in S. B., and had a son Perez, and d. 1793, æ. 90. He had also a D. Abigail, who m. Charles Perkins 1762.

2. Perez (s. of the above) and his wife Abigail had Stephen 1766, Calvin 1768, Ruth 1770, Bethiah 1772, Lydia 1774, Barnabas 1776. He m. Ruth Nye of Sandwich 1784 ; 2d wife : he removed to Oakham. Stephen led a seafaring life.—Calvin m. Salome Allen of Oakham 1793.

Lucy Waterman m. Newland Sampson of Plympton 1766.— Jonathan m. Abigail Washburn 1768.—John of H. m. Mercy Orcutt 1769.—Rebecca m. Elisha Bartlett of Brookfield 1778.— Wid. Sarah m. Samuel Whitman 1776.—Wid. Betsy, late w. of David Waterman and D. of Nathaniel Pratt, m. Daniel Hudson 1822 : she m. Waterman 1802.—Ruth m. Nathan Hall 1790.— Jabez of Hali. m. Hannah Benson 1805.—Elizabeth of Hali. m. Nathaniel French 1811.—Otis of Kingston m. Betsy Waterman 1820.—Minerva m. Isaac Alden 1821.

WENTWORTH.—Theophilus Wentworth (born at Canton 1773) and his wife Betsy (born 1779 at Randolph) lived in S. B., and had Eliza 1796, Prince Wales 1798, Martin 1801, Darius 1803, Hiram 1807, Soranus 1810, Lewis 1814, Ephraim French 1818*.

Edward of Stoughton m. Sarah Winslow 1746.—Seth m. Jane Warren 1761.—Oliver m. Sarah Leach 1779.

WESLEY.—Joseph Wesley m. Jane Gilmore 1739, and settled in E. B., and had Isaac 1740*, Joseph 1742, John 1745*. Joseph quit-claimed all his estate to his mother 1772, being lately the estate of John Hagens : she d. 1787, æ. 80.

2. Joseph (s. of the above) m. Margaret Robinson, D. of Mary Pratt, D. of Joshua Pratt, 1773, and had Jennet bap. 1777, her mother then a widow : Joseph, the father, d. at New York, in the army, 1776. Jennet m. Byram Lazell 1793.—Mary Pratt m. Nath'l Ramsdell 1753.

WEST.—Samuel West m. Lydia, D. of Josiah Washburn, 1739, and had Ezra 1739, Mehitabel 1741, John 1743.—Samuel West m. Mehitabel, wid. of John Ames and D. of Israel Packard, 1727, perhaps first wife of the above.—Hannah m. William Shaw 1754.—Thomas m. Mercy Packard 1756.—Patience m. Lemuel Southworth a. 1757.—Timothy m. Zibia Edson 1787.— Mercy m. Reading Carr 1795.

WESTON.—Jonathan Weston lived in W. B., and had a D. Mary bap. there 1731.

2. Seth Weston from Mid'o. perhaps, and his wife Lusanna, lived in B., and had Daniel 1780, Asa (in Mid'o.) 1784, Lucy (in Duxbury) 1788, Sally 1801.

Rufus of Mid'o. m. Sarah Whitman 1777.

WHARTON.—Robert Wharton and his wife Mary lived in

B., and had Polly (in Plymo.) 1779, Robert 1781, Charity 1783.
WHITE.—Edward White and his wife Keziah lived in W.
B., and had Huldah 1739, Phebe 1741, Keziah 1744.

2. Micah White lived also in W. B., and m. Betty Tolman
1768 : she was D. of Eleazar Snow, and first m. Nathan Ames
1751, and then Wm. Tolman 1757. He had a D. Betsy who m.
Isaac Richmond.

3. Micah, (s. of Thomas of Abington), lived in E. B.: he was
born 1732; was with Gen. Winslow 1755, at the dispersion of
the neutral French at Nova Scotia ; and had Micah, Thomas,
Mehitabel, Lucy, and others perhaps. Major Micah the s. settled in Abington.—Mehitabel m. Jacob Bicknell Jr. 1803.—Lucy
m. Silas Shaw 1794.—Micah White m. Lucy Hatch of Hingham
1771.

4. Thomas (s. of Micah 3.) m. Nancy Harden 1803, and had
Thomas and Jacob : he m. Isabella D. Harden or Hayden,
1810 ; 2d w. Jacob gra. B. U. 1832.

5. Thomas (bro. of Micah 3.) lived in Abington, m. Hannah
Green 1772, and had Rachel, Oliver, and then d., and Oliver was
called after him Thomas, and now lives in E. B., the wid. Hannah having m. Jonathan Alden 1777.

Cornelius White m. Sarah Howell 1747.—Nathaniel White m.
Susanna Crossman 1745, and settled in Easton.—Keziah (per-
haps widow of Edward) m. Edward Hayward Esq. of Easton
a. 1749.—Urania of Marshfield m. Luther Hayward 1794.—Lydia
C. m. Bela Dyer of A. 1812.—Eleanor of Millbury m. Spencer
Lathrop 1817.—Micah Jr. of A. m. Esther Hobart 1818.—Jarvis
of Raynham m. Minerva Leach 1819.—Louisa Maria m. Arza
Leonard 1820.—Benjamin Jr. m. Mary Chamberlin 1780.—Jareb
of Amherst m. Ruth Sherman 1794.—Sarah m. Joseph Hearsey
Jr. 1799.—Hannah of Abington m. Alexander Robinson 1744.—
Ruth m. Adam Kingman 1760.—Zilphah m. Uriah Rickard 1761.
Perez of Raynham m. Deborah Leach 1787.—Sarah of Marsh-
field m. Ensign Nathan Willis, his 2d wife, 1792.—Nancy m.
Geo. W. Blanchard.

WHITING.—Marlborough Whiting (from Pembroke) settled
in E. B., and m. wid. Abigail French, D. of Joshua Howard of
Braintree, 1796, and had Martin 1797, Sumner 1799, John
Adams 1800, Ephraim Howard 1805, d. 1826 : he d. 1830, æ. 75.

Joseph m. Abigail, D. of Isaac Alden, 1778.—William m.
Sarah Ramsdell 1748.—Ruth m. Marlbray Ripley 1787.—Sally
of Attleboro' m. Daniel Lathrop 1787.—Polly m. Benja. Pincin
Jr. 1798.—Isaac m. Polly Jones 1804.—Sam'l m. Abigail Willis
1805.—Margaret m. William Pincin Jr. 1807.—Ruth m. Levi
Beal of Hingham 1810.—Polly or Patty m. John Stock Jr. 1809.
Amos m. Polly Howard 1810.—William of Stoughton m. Rachel
Turner 1811.—Mercy of Plympton m. Elisha Hayward 1760.

This name in the early records is often written Whiton and
Whitten.—James Whiton (so written) was at Hingham 1647, and

was probably the ancestor of Marlboro', first above mentioned,
and of all the others perhaps.

WHITMAN.—John Whitman was one of the first settlers at
Weymouth ; made free 163S ; a very respectable man ; was the
first Deacon ; the first military officer (an ensign) appointed in
that town ; one of the three persons appointed by the Governor
"to end small controversies" there : he died there 1692, æ. a. 90.
He was ancestor of most of the name in this country.   His wife
was probably Mary, her family name not known: his children
mentioned in his will 1685, proved 1692, then living, were 4 ss.,
Thomas, John, Abiah, Zechariah, and 5 Ds., all m. viz : Sarah
Jones, Mary, w. of John Pratt ; Elizabeth, w. of Josiah Green;
Hannah, w. of Stephen French ; and Judith King. Judge Whitman of Portland has given a very full and interesting memoir of
the ancestor and his descendants, published at Portland 1832 ;
but as it is within the scope and purpose of this publication to
give some account of all the early settlers of this town, we shall
notice those branches that became inhabitants here, referring all,
who are solicitous to know more of this numerous and respectable family, to the Judge's Memoir.

1. Thomas (the eldest s. and only one of the children of John
Whitman of Weymouth, who came to Bridgewater) was born in
Eng. a. 1629, came to this country with his mother, (after his fa-
ther,) a. 1641, and m. Abigail, D. of Nicholas Byram, 1656, and
came with his father-in-law Byram, or soon after, and settled in
E. B. a. 1662 : he had John (at Wey.) 1658, Ebenezer, Nicholas,
Susanna, Mary, Naomi, Hannah : his will 1711, proved 1712 :
he died æ. a. 83.   Susanna m. Benjamin Willis.—Mary m. Seth
Leach.—Naomi m. William Snow 1686.   It is not ascertained
whom Hannah m.

2. John (s. of Thomas 1.) m. Hannah (Pratt probably) 1686 ;
had no children : d. 1727, æ. a. 70 : was executor of his father's
will ; gave his own estate by will principally to David, s. of his
brother Nicholas ; mentions his sisters, Mary Leach and Susanna
Willis, and heirs of his sister Naomi Snow ; but says nothing of
Hannah, who probably was not then living, and had d. without
issue.

3. Ebenezer (s. of Thomas 1.) m. Abigail Burnam 1699, and
settled in S. B., and had Abigail 1702, Zechariah 1704, John
1707*, Hannah 1709, Ebenezer 1713: his estate settled by his
wid. 1713, and she m. Edmund Hobart of Hingham 1714, who
came and resided with her : she was appointed guardian to her
children. One of the Ds. m. a Soule, and the other a Little and
afterwards a Perkins.

4. Nicholas (s. of Thomas 1.) m. Sarah Vining of Weymouth
1700, and had Thomas 1702, John 1704, Josiah 1706*, David
1709, Jonathan 1710, Seth 1713.   His w. d., and he m. Mary,
D. of Francis Cary 1715, and had Eleazar 1716, Benjamin 1719*.
His wife d. and he m. Mary, D. of William Conant, 1719, and
had Mary 1720*, William 1722* Josiah 1724, Sarah 1726,

Abigail 1728*, Nicholas 1731, Susanna 1734*, Ebenezer 1736. He was killed, 1746, by his cart-wheel running over him, æ. 70 ; she d. 1770, æ. 77. Sarah m. Eleazar Alden, and d. æ. 94.

5. Zechariah (s. of Ebenezer 3.) m. Eleanor Bennet of Mid'o., and lived in S. B., and had Samuel 1734, Abiah 1735*, Zechariah 1738, Eleanor 1739, Benjamin 1741, d. 1762 ; Abigail 1743, Ruth 1746, Jonah 1749, Ebenezer and Sarah 1752 : he d. 1773, æ. 69 ; she d. 1777. Eleanor m. Nathaniel Chamberlin Jr. 1767, and was living 1832, æ. 93.—Ruth m. Gideon Washburn Jr. 1765, and then Dea. Ripley of Plympton.

6. Ebenezer (s. of Ebenezer 3.) and his w. Rebeckah lived in S. B., and had Ebenezer 1741*, Noah 1743, Hannah 1745, Lydia 1748: she d. 1778; he 1804, æ. 91. Hannah m. Ebenezer Dean of Plympton 1769.—Lydia m. Daniel Dean of Norton 1770.

7. Dea. Thomas (s. of Nicholas 4) m. Jemima, D. of Isaac Alden, 1727, and had Simeon 1728, Peter 1730, Benjamin 1732, Jemima 1734, Nathan 1736, Amos 1738, William 1740, Isaac 1742*. His w. d., and he m. Rebecca, wid. of Dea. Seth Allen, 1767 : she was a Rickard of Plympton. He owned the mills where the E. B. manufacturing works stand, which were called after him Whitman's Mills : he d. 1788 of a cancer, æ. 86 ; she 1791, æ. 82.—Jemima m. David Keith 1754.

8. John (s. of Nicholas 4.) m. Elizabeth Rickard of Plympton 1726, and she d. 1727, and he m. Elizabeth, D. of James Cary, 1729, and had Samuel 1730, Elizabeth 1732, d. 1765 ; John, March 17th, 1735, O. S.; James 1739, d. 1747. She died 1742, and he m. Hannah, wid. of Isaac Snow and D. of Joseph Shaw, 1743, and had Daniel 1744, Ezra 1747 : his wife d. 1762, æ. 58, and he m. Hannah, widow of Joseph Mitchell of Kingston : she was a Hearsy of Abington : she d. 1788, æ. 85 ; he 1792, æ. 88.

9. David (s. of Nicholas 4.) m. Susanna, D. of Nathaniel Hayward, 1738, and had John 1739*, Isaiah 1741*. Isaiah, while in college at New Haven or Princeton, was drowned : the father d. 1789, æ. 80 ; she 1795, æ. 87.

10. Jonathan (s. of Nicholas 4.) m. Elizabeth Harvey 1747, and had Jonathan 1751, Elizabeth 1752. His w. d., and he m. Bethiah, D. of Dea. Joseph Edson, 1753 : he died 1778, æ. 68 ; she 1805, æ. 91. Elizabeth m. Rev. George Briggs of Norton 1791 : he was settled as a Baptist Preacher in Stoughton Corner. Jonathan m. Ruth Churchill a. 1776, and d. 1777, æ. 29, and had a D. Leah born, after his death, 1778, who m. Silvester Briggs 1797.

11. Seth (s. of Nicholas 4.) m. Ruth, D. of Stephen Reed of Abington, 1741, and had Stephen 1745, Sarah 1751, Seth 1754, Enos 1756, Ruth 1759*, Hannah 1762*: he d. 1778, æ. 65 ; she d. before 1767. Sarah m. Pelatiah Gilbert of Brookfield 1777. Enos d. at Valley Forge in the Revolutionary war 1778.

12. Dea. Eleazar (s. of Nicholas 4.) m. Abigail, D. of Daniel Alden 1742, and had Mary 1743*, Eliab 1745*, Abigail* and Hannah* 1747. Jephthah 1748*, Mary 1751, Joshua 1753,

Eleazar 1755, Ephraim 1757, Asa 1761*, Abigail 1763. He removed to Abington, and there d. over 90 years of age.

13. Josiah (s. of Nicholas 4.) m. Elizabeth, D. of Ezekiel Smith of Hingham, 1747 : her mother was Dinah May of Roxbury, whose mother was Mary Duncan from Scotland : he had his father's dwelling-house, and part of the homestead, and had Levi 1748, Lemuel 1750, Abigail 1751, Josiah 1753; he d. 1754, æ. 29; she 1778, æ. 53. Abigail m. Dea. John Whitman, his 2d wife, 1773.—Lemuel settled in Kinderhook, N. Y., and had Simeon, Josiah, William, Levi, John, Betsy, Mary, Joanna, Sarah, and d. æ. 71.

14. Nicholas (s. of Nicholas 4.) m. Mary House of Hanover a. 1759, and had Isaiah 1760, Elijah 1762, Mary 1705, Eunice 1769 : he d. 1803, æ. 72. Mary m. Thomas Chamberlin 1785.— Eunice m. Reuben Tomson of Halifax 1791.

15. Ebenezer (s. of Nicholas 4.) m. Abigail, D. of John Freelove, 1760, and had Abigail 1763, Ebenezer 1765, Jepthah 1767. He d. 1786, æ. 50 : she within 2 mos. after, æ. 45. Abigail not m. Ebenezer m. Lydia, D. of Dea. John Whitman, 1788, and had James 1791.—Jephthah m. Betty Tinkham of Mid'o. 1789, and had Ebenezer 1791, Isaac 1792, Jephthah 1796, Sally 1797, and he and Ebenezer both removed to Windsor, Mass.

16. Samuel (s. of Zechariah 5.) m. Susanna, D. of Capt. Solomon Leonard, 1761, and had Lucinda, Silvia, Susanna, Freelove, Chloe : he was lost at sea ; she d. 1778. Lucinda m. Joseph Tilson of Halifax 1794.—Silvia m. David Conant 1783, afterwards Azariah Hayward 1798.—Susanna m. Oliver Allen 1790.—Chloe not m.—Freelove was drowned.

17. Zechariah (s. of Zechariah 5.) lived in S. B., m. Abigail Kilborn of Connecticut, and had Kilborn 1765, Benjamin 1768, Cyrus 1773*, Angelina 1777, Cassandra. Angelina m. Curtis Barnes of Hingham 1803.—Cassandra m. Rev. Gaius Conant 1802.—Judge Kilborn gra. H. U. 1785, settled in the ministry at Pembroke, afterwards Counsellor at Law, and C. Justice of the C. C. P.; m. Betsy, D. of Dr. Isaac Winslow of Marshfield, and had Isaac Winslow, gra. H. U. 1808, an Attorney in Nantucket, and there d., Charles Kilborn, Eliza Winslow, John Winslow, gra. H. U. 1827, and lived at S. Boston. Sarah Ann, Caroline, Maria Warren, James Hawley, Frances Gay, William Henry ; Eliza W. m. Samuel K. Williams Esq. of Boston ; Sarah A. m. Benjamin Randall Esq. of Bath, Member of Congress ; James H. an Attorney, m. a D. of Alden Briggs Esq., and lives on the paternal estate at Pembroke.—Benjamin Esq. gra. B. U. 1788, settled as an Attorney first in Pembroke, then in Hanover, and finally in Boston, where he was Representative, and Chief Justice of the Police Court many years. He m. Hannah Gardner, and had Zechariah Gardner, Abigail Kilborn*, Abigail Kilborn, Hannah Eddy, Benjamin, Mary Angelina*, Henry M. Lisle, Caleb Strong, George Henry, and Mary Ann. Zechariah G. gra. H. U. 1807, and was an Attorney, and Clerk and historian

of the Ancient and Honorable Artillery Company ; he m.
Maria, D. of Maj. John Bray of Boston, and had 2 other wives,
and d. 1840, leaving a family.—Abigail K. m. Benjamin Thompson of Boston.—Hannah E. m. John H. Pierson.—Benjamin
graduated Brown University 1815, and is an Attorney.—
Henry M. L. died in B. U. 1820.—Caleb Strong is a Physician,
and gra. M. D. at H. U. 1831.—George H. (first named John
Winslow) gra. H. U. 1827, is an Attorney and Clerk of the A.
and H. Art. Co.—Mary Ann m. Dr. Stebbins of South Boston.—
Benjamin, the father, m. Mrs. Nancy Blake, widow of Joseph
Blake Esq., for his 2d wife : she was a Black of Quincy.

18. Dr. Jonah or Jonas (s. of Zechariah 5.) gra. Y. 1772, settled as a Physician in Barnstable, and had a family. One s. John
gra. H. U. 1805, was an Attorney and d. young. Another Josiah
had a medical degree H. U. 1806, and was appointed a Professor
in one of the Western Colleges.

19. Ebenezer (s. of Zechariah 5.) m. Ruth Delano, and went to
Oakham, and had a family there. He d., she m. John Hooper.

20. Noah (s. of Ebenezer 6.) m. Freelove Manchester : she
d. 1772, and he m. Sarah, D. of Seth Hayward, 1774, and had
Lydia and Freelove. His wife d. 1778, and he m. Zilphah, D. of
Daniel Washburn, 1779, and had Ebenezer, Noah, Daniel, Sarah
and Betsy : he died æ. 82. Lydia m. Zenas Washburn 1799.—
Freelove m. Davis Hayward 1804.—Sarah m. a Brown of Jay,
Me.—Betsy m. James Keith Jr. 1815.—Ebenezer m. Sarah, D.
of James Keith, and had Piam Cushing 1809, Nabby 1812,
Noah 1814, Betsy 1816, .and went to Tamworth, Vt.—Dr. Noah
gr. B. U. 1806, m. Mary, D. of Dr. Daniel Perkins, 1812, and
settled in W. B.—Daniel m. Celia, D. of Arthur Harris 1815,
and d. leaving children.

21. Capt. Simeon (s. of Dea. Thomas 7.) m. Martha, D. of
Isaac Snow, 1750, and had Isaac 1750, Simeon 1753, Thomas
1755, Joseph 1757, Martha 1760, Silvia 1765, Huldah 1769. His
w. d. 1781, æ. 53, and he m. Sarah, wid. of Seth Byram, 1783 :
she was a Vinal of Scituate : he d. 1811, æ. 83. Simeon went
to Roxbury, and died 1830 a bachelor, æ. 77.—Martha m. Thos.
Phillips 1783.—Silvia d. single 1708.—Huldah m. Turner Phillips 1787.

22. Peter (s. of Dea. Thomas 7.) m. Susanna, D. of Joseph
Keith, 1752, and had Susanna 1753*, Molly 1754*, Molly 1756*,
Jemima 1758, Molly 1759*, Susanna 1761. His w. d., and he m.
Sarah Wright of Marshfield 1775, and had Dolly 1776, Nancy
1778, Sally 1779, Asa 1782, Christiana 1785 : he d. 1801, æ. 71 ;
she 1831, æ. 84. Jemima, late in life, m. a Smith of Duxbury,
and had no children. Susanna m. Ezra Kingman Esq. 1782.—
Dolly m. Dea. Jacob Bearce of Pembroke, his 2d w.—Christiana
m. Geo. W. Barton of Bath, Me., 1809 ; the other Ds. not m.—
Asa m. Deborah, D. of George Howard, 1804, and had Asa
1804*, Deborah Howard 1806, Mary Ann 1809*, and went to
Walpole. His w. d. 1812, and he m. again.

23. Benjamin (s. of Dea. Thomas 7.) m. Mary, D. of Charles Latham, 1757, and had Olive, Molly 1766, Priscilla 1768, Benjamin 1771, Jane 1775*: he died 1802, æ. 71 ; she 1831, æ. 94. Olive m. Daniel Orcutt 1784, and Josiah Johnson Jr. 1793.— Molly m. Luther Hatch 1790.—Priscilla d. single 1815.—Benjamin m. Lucy Leonard of Mid'o. 1796, and went to Marlow, Vt.

24. Nathan (s. of Dea. Thos. 7.) m. Betty, only child of Dea. Seth Allen, 1761, and had Seth Allen 1762, Rebecca 1764, Nathan 1766, Celia 1768, Eliab 1770*, Asa 1772*, Betty 1777*. They both died 1784 : he æ. 48 ; she 45. Rebeckah m. David Howard 1791. —Celia m. Timothy Allen 1788, and d. 1789, æ. 21.

25. Amos (s. of Dea. Thomas 7.) m. Anna, D. of Eleazar Washburn, 1763, and had Philibert (Phile) 1766, Zenas 1767, Amos 1768, Barza 1770, Anna Washburn 1772, Oliver 1774*, Jennet 1777*, Nabby 1779, Jennet 1782, Susanna 1784, Betsy 1786 : he died 1791, æ. 48; she 1797, æ. 54. Philibert m. Seth Allen Whitman 1787.—Zenas m. Sally, D. of Isaac Allen, 1791, and went to Minot, Me.—Amos went to Ireland as a Carpenter with Mr. Coxe to build a bridge there, and on his return was missing in a sudden and mysterious manner at Philadelphia, and has never been heard of since : he was of age, but not m.— Barza went to sea, and was lost or died before he was of age.— Anna W. m. Timothy Bailey 1796.—Nabby m. Stephen Latham. Jennet m. James Loring 1809, and lived in N. B.—The other two m. at the eastward, where they all settled except Philibert and Jennet.

26. William (s. of Dea. Thomas 7.) m. Mary Studley 1761, and had Polly 1762, William 1763, Lucy 1767, Oakes [1769], Chloe 1773, Luther 1777. Polly m. Capt. James Allen 1778.— William was one of the last three years' men in the revolutionary war, went to Cumberland, R. I., and afterwards to Pomfret, Conn., was m. and had a family.—Lucy m. Israel Bailey 1789.— Oakes m. Susanna, D. of Joshua Barrell 1790, and had Royal, Melvill, Luther, Olive ; and he, Capt. Allen, and Bailey, went to Maine.—Chloe m. Dea. Jacob Bearce of Hanson, and d. there 1839, æ. 65, whither the parents also removed, and where they d. Luther, first named, was drowned in the mill-pond 1782.

27. Samuel (s. of John 8.) m. Elizabeth, D. of Ebenezer Bonney of Pembroke, 1757, and had James 1760*, David 1762, Samuel 1764, Abel 1766, of Frankfort, Me., and two others who d. before 1770, and Beza 1773. His wife d. 1776, æ. 37, and he m. wid. Sarah Waterman of Halifax 1776, and had Sarah 1778, Mehitabel 1779, Freeman 1780*, Freedom 1782.—David went to Lyme, N. H.—Samuel m. Hannah, D. of John Egerton, 1787, went to Williamsburgh, and had a s. Shepard, and a D. He was killed by the falling of a tree, and she m. again, and removed to the banks of the Susquehanna.—Samuel, the father, and his family, went to Cummington, where he became a baptist, and was plunged at the age of 94, and d. 1825, æ. 95.

28. Dea. John (s. of John 8.) m. Lydia, D. of David Snow,

1764, and had Lydia 1765, Elizabeth 1767, James 1769. His
w. d. 1771, and he m. Abigail, D. of Josiah Whitman, 1773, and
had Catharine 1775, d. 1793; Bathsheba 1777, Josiah 1779, Alfred
1781, Obadiah 1783, Nathaniel 1785, Hosea 1788, John 1790,
Abigail 1793, d. 1818; Barnard 1796, Jason 1799 : his w. d. 1813,
æ. 62. The father is now (April 1840) living, in his 106th year.
Lydia m. Ebenezer Whitman Jr. 1788.—Elizabeth m. Benjamin
Strobridge of Mid'o. 1789.—James removed to Belchertown, and
there m. Catharine Smith, and has a family, and has been Representative of the town.—Bathsheba, not m.; well known as a
popular and useful instructor, and as having done much towards
the education of her brothers.—Josiah settled at Wellfleet : a
Magistrate and Representative there; returned to E. Bridgewater ; m., but has no children.—Alfred lives with his father.—
Obadiah went to N. Gloucester, Me., m. Col. Parsons' D., and
has a family.—Nathaniel gra. H. U. 1809, and settled in the ministry at Billerica, Feb. 2, 1804, and was dis. 1835, m. a Holman,
D. of Gen. Holman of Bolton, and is installed at Wilton, N. H.—
Hosea m. a Hodges of Mansfield, and is concerned in manufacturing business at Waltham.—John m. a Bicknell, and lived in
Belchertown, and d., and left no children. Barnard was educated at H. U., entered 1718, but not a graduate, m. a Crosby, settled in the ministry at Waltham, was much known, and distinguished in his profession, and d. 1834, greatly lamented, leaving
a son Crosby.—Jason gra. H. U. 1825, preached at Saco, and
was afterwards an Agent of the Unitarian Society in Boston, and
is settled in the ministry in Portland, and m. a sister of Gov.
Fairfield.

29. Daniel (s. of John 8.) m. a Doten of Plymouth, and had
John, Mary, Daniel : he died 1777, æ. 33. John lives with his
cousin James at Belchertown, a bachelor.—Mary m. a Symmes
in Plymouth.—Daniel m. and went to Cummington, and thence
to the State of N. Y.

30. Ezra (s. of John 8.) m. Rhoda, D. of David Snow 1768,
and had Ezra 1769, Hannah Snow 1771, David Snow 1774,
Calvin 1777*, Rhoda 1779. His wife d. 1796, æ. 53, and he m.
Thankful Freelove 1796 : he died 1814, æ. 67 ; she 1823, æ. 71.
Ezra m. Eunice, D. of Sam'l Allen, 1795, and had Rhoda Snow at
Wellfleet 1797, Eunice at W. 1799, Luther at Pembroke 1802,
Clarissa 1804, Emily 1807, Melinda 1809, Ezra 1812, and then
moved to Winthrop, Me.—Hannah S. m. Josiah Keen 1792, and
afterwards Constant Hayward 1808.—David S. m. Ruth Stetson
of Pembroke, and went to Me.

31. Stephen (s. of Seth 11.) m. Mary, D. of Hon. Hugh Orr,
1767, and had Bethuel 1768*, Robert 1770*, Matilda 1772, Stephen Reed 1774, Independence 1776, Mary 1778 : he d. 1778,
æ. 33 ; she d. 1778, æ. 28. Matilda m. Capt. Seth Byram 1791.
Stephen R. went to N. H.—Independence went to Albany and
Troy, and d. there a bachelor.—Mary not m.

32. Seth (s. of Seth 11.) m. Eunice, D. of Capt. Jonathan

Bass 1781, and had Seth, who now lives in Pembroke, and m.
Joanna, D. of Capt. Thomas Turner. Seth, the father, d. 1783,
æ. 29; his wid. m. Peter Salmon of Pembroke, and had several
children, and became a wid. again, and d. 1834.

33. Joshua (s. of Dea. Eleazer 12.) m. a Tirrell of Abington,
and had Joshua, and d. 1775, æ. 22, and his wid. m. a Gorham,
of Turner, Me., where Joshua now lives.

34. Dea. Eleazar (s. of Dea. Eleazar 12.) m. Mary, D. of
Woodbridge Brown of Abington, 1778, and lives on the paternal
estate in E. B., and had Eleazar, Daniel, Asa, Hannah, Mary,
Dorothy, died 1816, æ. 29: his wife died 1832, æ. 79.—Eleazar
m. Nabby, D. of Joshua Pratt, 1812.—Daniel gra. B. U. 1809,
and m. Sarah Porter of Abington 1792, she died 1831.—Asa m.
Rachel, D. of Thomas Chamberlin, 1820, and died æ. 26.—
Hannah m. Moses Noyes, who gra. B. U., and lives in Providence,
a preceptor and instructor.—Mary m. Eliab Noyes of Abington
1803.

35. Ephraim (s. of Dea. Eleazar 12.) m. a D. of Sam'l Brown
of Abington, and lived on the paternal estate in Abington, and
died 1838, and had one son, Hon. Jared, (gra. B. U., an Attorney,
County Commissioner, and Senator, m. Abigail, D. of Maj. James
Barrell, 1813, and afterwards wid. Susan Hayden, D. of Aaron
Hobart Esq.) and two Ds. One, Sarah, m. Nathan Gurney Esq.;
and the other, Clarissa, m. Isaac Alden Esq. 1811.

36. Rev. Levi (s. of Josiah 13.) gra. H. U. 1779, and settled
at Wellfleet; m. Sarah, D. of Capt. Ichabod Thomas of Pembroke, and had Levi 1789, Sarah 1790, Charles 1791, Josiah
1793, Ruth 1794, Eliza S. 1797, Hope 1799. He m. a Drew for
his 2d wife, and in his old age lived in Kingston, and d. 1838, æ.
90. Levi gra. H. U. 1808, and is counsellor at law, Norway,
Me.; m. a wid. Farrar, and has a s. Francis Henry.—Sarah m.
Gov. Parris of Me.—Charles is an attorney at Waterford, Me.
Josiah, a merchant in Portland, m. a McLellan.

37. Josiah (s. of Josiah 13.) m. Sarah, D. of Caleb Sturtevant
of H. 1774 (her mother was Patience Cushman of Halifax), and
had Ezekiel 1776, Betsy 1778. He d. 1778, æ. 25; his wid. m.
Jacob Mitchell, 1783 (and was mother of Josiah Whitman
Mitchell, a counsellor at law in Freeport, Me.): she d. 1789, æ.
35.—Hon. Ezekiel gra. B. U. 1795, m. Hannah, D. of Cushing
Mitchell, 1799, and lived first in New Gloucester, and then in
Portland, Me., and is a counsellor at law and Chief Justice of
C. C. Pleas in Me.: he has Harrison, Lucia, and Julia.—Betsy
m. a Hawes at Wellfleet, and is now a wid. in Me.—Lucia, D.
of Ezekiel, m. Silvanus L. Mitchell Esq. 1820.—Julia m. Wm.
Willis Esq. Portland.

38. Isaiah (s. of Nicholas 14.) m. Chloe, D. of Mark Phillips,
1784, and had Sally, Isaiah, Chloe, Mary, Naomi, and went to
Windsor, Ms., where he was a deacon, and d. April 7, 1827, æ. 66.

39. Elijah (s. of Nicholas 14.) m. Mercy Randall 1784, and
had Zilphah, Eunice, Polly, Elijah, Alden, Lucy, Clarissa,

Stockbridge, Josiah, Geo. Whitfield. He first removed to Pembroke, and then to Thompson, Conn. Three of the Ds. m. Robbins', and one m. Nath'l Jenkins of Abington.

40. Capt. Isaac (s. of Capt. Simeon 21.) m. Bathsheba, D. of Jonathan Allen, 1785, and had Sophia 1786, Mehitabel 1788, Allen 1792, Bathsheba 1797, Isaac Snow 1805 : he d. 1828, æ. 78; she (at Boston) 1829, æ. 70. Sophia m. Melvill Otis 1809. Mehitabel m. Capt. Levi Keith 1811.—Allen m. Mary Brown (sister of Bartholomew Esq.) and lived in Boston, and d. there 1838.—Isaac Snow lives in Bangor, Me, and m. there.

41. Thomas (s. of Capt. Simeon 21.) m. Lydia, D. of Anthony Sherman, 1781, and had Ford 1783, Martha 1784, Joanna 1786, Thomas 1790: he then went to Tamworth, N. H., and had Simeon, Lydia, Martin*: they are both d. Ford Esq. m. Anna, D. of David Howard, and removed to Bangor, and m. for a 2d w. Bathsheba, D. of Capt. Isaac Whitman.—Thomas returned to E. B., and m. Lusanna W., D. of Anthony W. Clift, 1818, and had Alice and Simeon*, and d. 1832, æ. 42 : the wid. m. Joseph Chamberlin 1839.

42. Joseph (s. of Capt. Simeon 21.) m. Mary, D. of Thomas Phillips, 1780, and had Snow 1781*, Martin 1785, Snow 1789, d. 1810; Joseph 1794, Calvin 1798, Silvia 1800 : he d. 1807, æ. 49; she is still living. Martin m. Susanna, D. of John Hudson, 1815, and d. 1828, æ. 44.—Joseph d. a bachelor.—Calvin gone westward.—Silvia m. William Bourn of Hanson.

43. Seth Allen (s. of Nathan 24.) m. Philibert, D. of Amos Whitman, 1787, and had Eliab, and Jane, who d. 1808, æ. 15. He lived at N. B. with his son Eliab, who gra. B. U. 1817, and is a counsellor at law: she died 1835, æ. 68; he 1839, æ. 77. Eliab Esq. m. Susanna, D. of John Wales, 1817, and has Sarah, Susan and Samuel A.: his w. d. 1825 ; he is a Representative of N. B.

44. Nathan (s. of Nathan 24.) m. Mercy, D. of Josiah Byram, 1788, and had Gilbert 1788, Celia 1790, Freedom 1792, Nathan 1796, Willard 1803, Marcena Allen and Mercy Lewis 1805: she d. 1824, æ. 54; he 1829, æ. 63. Gilbert m. Serena, D. of Ezra Fobes, 1813, and removed to Maine.—Celia m. William Pratt 1816.—Freedom m. Clarissa (or Clara), D. of Dea. Barzillai Allen, and then her half sister Sarah Bass, and lived awhile in Boston; is now in E. B.—Nathan m. Semantha, D. of Dea. William Keith : he also lived awhile in Boston, but has returned to E. B.—Willard is also m., and has a family.—Marsena A. m. Lucia Anne, D. of Capt. Branch Byram.

45. Alfred (s. of Dea. John 28.) m. Betsy Robbins of Watertown 1808, and had Mary Coolidge and Edmund Burke : his w. d. 1832, æ. 46, and he m. Abigail, wid. of Jacob Hayward and D. of Jonah Willis, 1833.—Edmund B. gra. H. U. 1838, m. a Russell of Plymouth, and went to Gardner, Me.

46. John (from Easton, s. of John, s. of Abiah, s. of John) m. Margaret, D. of Samuel Willis, 1745, and settled in W. B., but had no children.

47. Terah (bro. of John preceding) m. Anne, D. of Samuel Willis, 1746, and settled in W. B., and had Silence 1752*, Anna 1754. Anna m. Thompson Baxter 1797, and d. a wid. 1831. Zechariah (s. of Abiah of Weymouth) lived awhile in W. B., with his brother-in-law, William Turner, and while there was warned out of town 1734.—Eleanor Whitman (of the Easton family probably) m. Samuel Pratt of Stoughton 1764.—Abigail m. Nehemiah Cobb of Mid'o. 1773.—Sarah m. Rufus Weston of Mid'o. 1777.—Francis and Mary Whitman of Boston had William 1667*, and another William 1668.—Ezra Whitman m. Bathsheba Richards 1693, and Ebenezer m. Deborah Richards 1705. [Wey. Records.]—Samuel m. Anna Rean 1766, and Davis Whitman m. Mary Taverner 1770. [Boston records.]

WHITMARSH.—Jacob Whitmarsh of Abington m. Hannah, D. probably of Benjamin Shaw 1751, settled in E. B., and had Thankful 1752, Olive 1755, Sarah 1757, Jacob 1759, Huldah 1762, Asa 1764, Mary 1767, Zerviah 1769. Jacob m. Ann Pool 1784.—Zerviah m. Jacob Pool Jr. 1787.—Thankful m. Seth Reed 1773.—Mary m. Reed Erskine 1784.—Huldah m. George Erskine 1781.—Wid. Whitmarsh d. 1808.

2. Asa (s. of Jacob above) and his wife Sarah had Asa 1793, Oliver Gurney 1796. He d., and she m. Hiram Keith of Winchester 1816.

3. Lot (s. of Ebenezer and nephew of Jacob 1.) m. Susanna Pool and had Lot 1796, Mary 1798, John 1801, Susanna, Olive 1804, Thomas, Ezra 1808, and Ebenezer who d. 1810. Lot m. Merrill Corthrell 1820.—Thomas m. Charlotte, D. of Simeon Gannett, 1811, and had Simeon Gannett 1812: he m. Diana, wid. of Joseph Allen Jr. a 2d wife.—Susanna m. Micah Packard 1812.

Judith of Weymouth m. Joseph Shaw a. 1690.—Jacob of Abington m. Betty Crooker 1817.—Mary B. m. Chandler Ripley 1818.—Eunice m. Nathan Orcutt Jr. 1780.—Mercy m. Andrew Ford 1706.—Richard m. Lydia Ford 1712.—Mary m. Stephen Reed 1714.—Mehitabel m. Noah Ramsdell 1790.—Bathsheba m. Ebenezer Bisbee 1745.—Zechariah Whitmarsh m. Hannah Washburn 1730.—Mary Byram Whitmarsh m. Chandler Bisbee 1818.—Ebenezer Whitmarsh d. in E. B. 1810, æ. 23.

WILBOR.—Lemuel Wilbor and his wife Sarah had Chloe (in Raynham) 1758, Asa 1760, Holden 1762, Tryphena 1764. (2d w. Sarah.) Jeremiah 1772, Lemuel 1775, Caleb 1777, Sarah 1779, Amos 1801. Asa m. Silvia Jackson 1783.—Tryphena m. Jabez Hall 1791.—Amos m. Fidelia Woodward of Taunton 1799.—Asa Wilbor was a soldier at Roxbury 1776.

2. George and his wife Lydia had George (in Raynham) 1757, Isaac (in Raynham) 1759, Gideon 1763, Seabury 1771, Bethana 1771, Barak 1773, Lavinia 1778, Nicholas 1781. Bethana m. Azel Alden 1791.—Lavinia m. Timothy Keith 1797.—Nicholas (a D.) m. Daniel Dunbar 1809.—These two families were probably from Raynham, and settled in S. B.

3. Lemuel (s. of Lemuel 1.) m. Jenny Leach 1799, and had Orin 1799, Melvin 1802, Josephus 1804, Royal 1807, Oliver K. 1809, Asa F. 1812, Emery S. 1815.

4. Isaac (s. of George 2.) and his wife Susanna had Lurania 1781, Ruth 1783, Aberdeen 1785, Lydia 1787. (1st w. d. 1790, 2d w. Joanna.) Susanna 1792, Isaac 1794, Olive 1796, Anna 1800. Lurania m. Zephaniah Fobes 1810.—Ruth m. David Keith 3d, 1806.—Aberdeen m. Abigail Hooper 1809.—Lydia m. George Wilbor 1820.—Anna m. Martin Snow 1821.

5. Gideon (s. of George 2.) and his w. Huldah had Gardener 1786, Deborah 1789, Seth 1799.

6. Baruck (s. of Geo. 2.) m. Lois Leach 1799, and had Baruck 1801, Deborah 1805, Kila 1807, Gideon 1811, Seabury 1816.

Mary m. Ebenezer Leach 1741.—Joseph m. Susanna Harris 1741.—Chloe m. Salmon Keith 1779.—Zephaniah of Raynham m. Chloe Leach 1796.—Stephen Jr. of Raynham m. Sally Hooper 1809.—Charles of Easton m. Lydia Pratt 1813.—Keziah of Easton m. Daniel Hayward 2d 1815.—George Wilbor m. Lydia, D. of Isaac Wilbor, 1820.—Seth Wilbor and his w. Rachel had Jemima 1802, and Seth 1804.

WILLIAMS.—Thomas Williams of Taunton and his wife Mary had Maria 1680, Jonathan 1683, Sarah 1685, Macey 1687*, Hannah 1689, Bethiah 1692, Mehitabel 1695, Damaris 1698. He died, and his wid. Mary m. Rev. James Keith 1707. Some of these Ds. probably came with her to Bridgewater.—Hannah m. Joseph Snell 1712.—Damaris m. Daniel Howard Esq. of N. B.—Mehitabel m. Benjamin Webb, perhaps of Eastham, 1720.

2. Josiah Williams of Taunton m. Martha, D. of Ephraim Howard, 1714, and settled in W. B., and had Rebecca 1715, Mary 1718, George 1721*, Seth 1722, Josiah 1725, Martha 1728, Susanna 1730, Macey 1736: he d. 1770, she 1746. Rebecca m. Daniel Littlefield 1732.—Mary m. Josiah Kingman 1737, and Ephraim Cary 1784, and d. 1803, æ. 85.—Seth m. Susanna, D. of William Fobes perhaps, 1750. and went to Easton, and his wid. had Seth and Asa bap. by Mr. Perkins 1759.—Martha m. Jonathan Packard 1752.—Susanna m. Josiah Keith Jr. 1758.— Macey went to Easton.

3. Josiah (s. of Josiah 2.) m. Hannah, D. of Ephraim Fobes, 1751, and had Martha 1751, George 1753, Macey 1755*, Josiah 1757*, Josiah 1759, Perez 1761, Bathsheba 1763, Hannah 1765, Susanna 1767*, Calvin 1770*, Amelia 1772: he d. 1794, she 1807. Martha m. Joseph Ames Jr. 1770.—Bathsheba m. Dr. Daniel Perkins 1783.

4. George (s. of Josiah 3.) m. Ann, D. of Ephraim Howard, 1774, and had George 1775: she d. 1775.

5. Josiah (s. of Josiah 3.) m. Hannah, D. of Jonathan Kingman, 1785, and had Orra 1785, Susanna Packard 1787, Anna 1789. He d., and she m. Capt. Ephraim Snell 1792, and Caleb Snell 1808. Orra m. Earl Thayer 1812.—Susanna P. m. Israel Tolman 1813.—Anna m. Jesse Edson 1811.

6. Perez (s. of Josiah 3.) m. Huldah, D. of Jonathan King-man, 1788, and had Perez 1789, d. 1806; Josiah 1791. His w. d., and he m. wid. Polly Pierce 1798, and had Samuel Pierce 1799, Huldah Kingman 1801, Lavinia 1804, Hannah Fobes 1807, Mary Lathrop 1812, d. 1814: he d. 1819. Josiah m. Silvia, D. of Simeon Keith, 1814, and died 1822.—Huldah K. m. Joseph Kingman 1821.

7. George (s. of George 4.) m. Eunice Kingman of Easton 1797, and had Anna H. 1798, Nahum 1800, Mary 1801, Calvin 1803, Charles 1805, Patty 1807: he died 1809, she 1811. Anna H. m. Albert Copeland 1819.

Richard Williams was a town officer in Bridgewater 1665.— Mehitabel m. Benjamin Mehuren 1749.—Bathsheba of Taunton m. Judge Benjamin Willis 1742.—Anna m. Joseph Snell about 1742.—Daniel Williams (of Easton perhaps) had a D. Joanna bap. by Mr. Perkins, W. B., 1745.—Daniel Jr. m. Rhoda, D. of Maj. Daniel Lathrop 1763.—Silas m. Susanna Richards 1760.— Josiah of Easton perhaps m. Sarah Ames 1763.—Rhoda m. Noah Powers 1787.—Marlborough of Easton m. Lusanna, D. of Maj. Thomas Mitchell, 1782.—Nathan of Raynham m. Abthiah Har-vey 1781.—Edward of Easton m. Sarah, D. of Josiah Lathrop, 1772.—Sarah of Raynham perhaps m. John Benson 1765.— Calvin m. Betsy Copeland 1799.—Abiah of Raynham m. Wm. Bassett 1800.—Hannah of Raynham m. Joseph Bassett 3d, 1816. Calvin m. Abigail Bryant 1799.—Edmund of Woodstock, Conn., m. Mary Harvey 1781.—Abigail m. Peter Hayward 1732.

WILLIS.—Dea. John Willis was at Duxbury very early : he and his wife Elizabeth are recorded as there in 1637 : he was an original Proprietor, and one of the first settlers of Bridgewater : the first Deacon here: sustained many town offices, both at Dux-bury and here : represented Bridgewater at the old Colony Court 25 years : sold his estate in Duxbury to William Paybody 1657 : was appointed to solemnize marriages and administer oaths to witnesses and others: his wife Elizabeth was wid. of William Palmer Jr.; her maiden name Hodgkins: his will dated 1692, proved 1693 : his children therein mentioned were John, Nath'l, Joseph, Comfort, Benjamin, Hannah, wife of Nath'l Hayward ; Elizabeth, who m. a Harvey ; and Sarah, wife of John Ames. Nathaniel, Executor. He gave to Joseph "land at Farfield as we go to Taunton ;" "to Comfort, 15 acres at the Indian Field ;" " to John, land his house stands on ;" " to Nathaniel, the home-stead ;" and mentions the pond " that divides between me and Benjamin:" also " the Wolf Trap Gutter." He had four bro-thers, Nathaniel, Lawrence, Jonathan, and Francis, which we thus ascertain : Elkanah was appointed to settle his father Na-thaniel's estate 1686, his uncle John to assist him. Elkanah also settled his uncle Lawrence Willis' estate in Boston 1703, and in 1704 he sold land in Boston, which he described as the estate of his uncle Francis Willis deceased. On the 8th day of Janu-ary, 1656, the year Bridgewater was incorporated, the following

44

record, and almost the first in the book of records, appears, viz :
" Be it known unto all men by these presents, that we, Nathaniel
Willis and Lawrence Willis, inhabitants of the town of Bridgewater, do bind ourselves to free the said town of Bridgewater
from any charge or damage that may come upon the said town
by the keeping of our brother Jonathan Willis." The following
also appears on the Court Records : " Jonathan Willis, who is
at Duxbury for cure, shall not be maintained by Duxbury, but
by Sandwich, whence he came." Thus we are assured these
five were brothers. There was a Richard Willis, servant of
John Barnes, transferred by consent to Thomas Prince 1634, m.
Amy Glasse 1639, was at Duxbury 1638, and at Plymouth 1640.
Richard, his s. probably, m. Patience Bonum at Plymouth 1670,
was dead 1678, leaving a D. Ruhamah, and no further notice of
them appears.—Henry Willis offered himself as a soldier to go
with Mr. Prince and Lieut. Holmes to assist Mass. and Conn.
against the Pequot Indians 1637, and we have no further account
of him.—Jeremiah Willis was at Duxbury 1638, a youth, and
was required by the Court to procure himself a master : there
was a Jeremiah Willis, a land holder, at Narraganset 1661 :
there was also a Thomas Willis at Lynn, a Representative there
1634, and afterwards a Proprietor of Sandwich 1637. Whether
any of these were of the same family we are not able to ascertain : they were cotemporaneous, and might be brothers, or otherwise related to them.—Lawrence Willis was among the first
settlers in Bridgewater, but not an original Proprietor. He was
in Sandwich 1643, and was a soldier against the Indians, m.
Mary, D. of Thomas Makepeace of Boston, 1656 ; and finally
removed to Boston, and his estate was settled there 1703 : he
probably had no children, as Elkanah, his nephew, settled his
estate. We have no notice of any descendants of these five
brothers excepting of John and Nathaniel, and of these most are
descended from John.

2. John (s. of John 1.) m. Experience, D. of Nicholas Byram,
and had John, Samuel, Experience, and Mary : he d. a. 1712,
the date of his will. Experience m. William Hudson.—Mary m.
Israel Randall 1701.

3. Nathaniel (s. of John 1.) and his wife Lydia had Nathaniel,
Jonathan, John, Ebenezer, Sarah, and Mary : he d. 1716 : his
estate divided among his heirs 1729. Sarah m. John Hayward
1707.—Mary (whether the above or not uncertain) m. William
Gilmore 1731.

4. Joseph (s. of John 1.) was at Scituate 1689, and admitted
a freeman same year : he had a s. Joseph, who is mentioned in
his grandfather's will, and is there called " the eldest son of my
son Joseph," so that there were other ss., and perhaps daughters.
Joseph was on a committee for running lines in B. 1667.—Joseph
Willis is mentioned as a Proprietor of Taunton 1668, 1673, and
1684, and Joseph Willis of Taunton m. a D. of Thomas Lincoln.
Perhaps he finally settled in Easton, which was then a part of

WILLIS. 347

Taunton.—There are no descendants of his in B., nor any further notice of him on B. records. Sometimes the father and sometimes the son is intended probably in the above notices.

5. Comfort (s. of John 1.) lived near the bridge called Comfort's bridge: his ss. were Samuel, Joshua, Isaac, and he had probably other children. He was a Trooper in Philip's war, and left a manuscript, giving an account of one of the skirmishes of that period, which is now unfortunately lost.—Mercy Willis m. Samuel Hall of Taunton 1718.

6. Benja. (s. of John 1.) m. Susanna, D. of Thomas Whitman, made a nuncupative will 1696, declared in presence of Comfort Willis, John Ames Jr.,.and Nathaniel Ames: no children mentioned, but he had 2 ss. Thomas 1694, and Benjamin 1696; and two Ds.: one, Susanna probably, m. Gen. David Cobb's grandfather of Taunton, and the other, Elizabeth, m. Capt. Nathaniel Woodward 1708: he might have had other children: he died æ. 39, and his wid. settled his estate in 1697: she d. æ. 98.—John Ames Jr. was guardian to Benjamin 1714.

7. John (s. of John 2.) m. Mary, D. of Elihu Brett Esq., and had Mary 1699, John 1701, Margaret 1704, Experience, Martha, Mehitabel: his estate settled among his heirs 1733. Mary m. Joseph Packard 1723.—Margaret m. Nathaniel Harvey 1733.—Experience m. John Randall of E. 1732.—Martha m. James Pratt of E. 1733.—Mehitabel m. James Stacy of E. 1743.

8. Samuel (s. of John 2.) m. Margaret, D. of Elihu Brett Esq., 1706, and had Margaret, Solomon, Anna, Zerviah, all bap. 1736: he d. about 1769, æ. 80. Margaret m. John Whitman of E. 1745.—Solomon, a bachelor.—Anna m. Terah Whitman of E. 1746.—Zerviah m. Abishai Willis 1741.

9. Nathaniel (s. of Nathaniel 3.) m. Ruth Porter of Abington, and had Ruth 1708, Nathaniel 1709, Azariah 1712. No certain account of this family. Ruth Willis (the mother probably) made her will 1739, and gave her estate to her niece Esther Porter, D. of her brother Nicholas Porter of Abington.

10. Jonathan (s. of Nathaniel 3.) m. Abigail Stoughton 1713, and had Jonathan 1714, Abigail 1716, Lydia 1718, Stoughton 1720, Keturah 1722, Sarah 1724, Betty 1726, Hannah 1728: his estate settled 1741. Abigail m. John Keith 1734.—Lydia m. Joseph Rickard of Plympton 1737, and went to Killingsley, Conn.—No account of John (s. of Nathaniel 3.)

11. Ebenezer (s. of Nathaniel 3.) m. a Hinds, and had Keziah, Jonathan, Ebenezer, Beriah. His estate was settled by Stoughton Willis 1741: the children all minors: he lived in Titicut or near to it. Keziah m. Daniel Willis 1756.—Ebenezer Willis sold a "great Lot," and part of "Howel's Saw Mill" to Nath'l Hooper 1731.

12. Judge Samuel (s. of Comfort 5.) removed to Dartmouth, and was Judge of the C. C. P. for the county of Bristol: he had Eliakim 1714, Jireh, Samuel, Ebenezer, Benjamin. Eliakim

gra. H. U. 1735, and settled in the ministry at Malden Oct. 25, 1752 : he first had a call at Hull 1750 : he d. March 14, 1801, æ. 87.—Jireh Willis an Ensign under Gen. Winslow at Annapolis Royal 1755.—Benjamin Willis went to Hardwick and had a D. Zerviah who m. John Keith of E. B.

13. Joshua (s. of Comfort 5.) m. Experience Barbour 1707, and had Joshua, Abishai, Joab 1715, Silas, and other children probably : he d. 1758. Joshua Willis and Joshua Willis Jr. both town officers 1739.

14. Dea, Isaac (s. of Comfort 5.) and his wife Mary had Seth 1729*, Isaac 1731. His w. died, and he m. Hannah Pratt 1732, and had Mary 1733, Hannah 1735, Ruth 1738, Abraham 1740*. Hannah m. William Fobes Jr.—Ruth m. Edmund Alger 1761.— Mary never m.

15. Thomas (s. of Benjamin 6.) m. Mary, D. of Sam'l Kinsley, 1716, and had Susanna 1718, Thomas 1721, Jonah 1723*, Mary 1725, Rhoda 1727, Betty 1731, Zephaniah 1733, Nathan 1738. Susanna m. Ephraim Fobes a. 1738.—Mary m. Maj. Isaac Johnson a. 1744.—Rhoda m. Maj. Daniel Lathrop 1744.—Betty m. James Howard 1749.

16. Benjamin (s. of Benjamin 6.) m. Mary Leonard 1719, and had Benjamin.

17. John Esq. (s. of John 7.) m. Patience, D. of Sam'l Hayward, 1724, and had Susanna 1727, Daniel 1732 : he died 1776. Susanna m. David Johnson Jr. 1743, and d. 1750.

18. Nathaniel (s. of Nathaniel 9.): no knowledge of him, unless the following : " Ruth Willis of Sudbury, wid. of Roger Willis : Ebenezer Hill, David Hill, and Nathaniel Willis, yeoman, all of Bridgewater ; Daniel Fisher of Taunton, Thomas Hill of Attleboro' ; sold land in Dorchester, in 1734, to a Robbins, originally granted to the right of John Hill sen'r of Dorchester, deceased." Ruth was D., all the rest grand children of the deceased. Nathaniel C. Willis a witness. Nor do we find any notice of Azariah and Ruth (s. and D. of Nath'l 9.)—[See Nath'l 46 : the above "yeoman" may have been Nath'l 46.]

19. Capt. Jonathan (s. of Jonathan 10.) m. Judith, D. of Joseph Packard, 1752, and had Azariah 1753. He m. Susanna, D. of James Allen, 1764, a 2d wife, and went to Oakham.— Azariah Willis of Oakham m. Abigail, D. of Samuel Willis probably, 1785.

20. Dr. Stoughton (s. of Jonathan 10.) m. Hannah Harlow of Mid'o., and had Jonathan 1742, Azariah 1744*, Stoughton 1746, Hannah 1748, Abigail 1750 (after her father's death). Stoughton m. Mary Monk of Stoughton 1764, and he and Jonathan both removed to Stoughton.—Hannah m. Reuben Snow 1768—Abigail m. Jesse Allen 1768.—The wid. m. John Snow 1756.

21. Jonathan (s. of Ebenezer 11.) went to Brookfield perhaps, and d. there.

22. Ebenezer (s. of Ebenezer 11.) m. Mary Jackson 1753, moved to Mid'o., and thence to Hardwick, was Deacon there,

and had Ebenezer, John, Joseph, Seth, and Mary. Mary m.
Dea. Noah Edson 1787.

23. Beriah (s. of Ebenezer 11.) m. Abigail, D. of Samuel
Hayward Jr. 1759, and had Hannah 1760. He is said to have
been a preacher. Perhaps Hannah m. Mason Hall of Raynham
1789.—Beriah Willis was a soldier with Gen. Winslow at Annapolis Royal 1755.

24. Samuel (s. of Judge Samuel 12.) m. Susanna, D. of John
Snell 1747, and had Nathan 1750, Susanna 1754, Lydia 1756,
Eliakim 1758, Samuel 1760*, Zebulun 1762, Silence 1765 : he
d. 1778; she a. 1783. Nathan m. Elizabeth Spear 1779, and had
Samuel 1781, and moved away.—Lydia m. Daniel Lathrop Jr.
1775.—Eliakim went to Nantucket.—Silence m. Enoch Monk
1784.

25. Joshua (s. of Joshua 13.) m. Hannah Woodward 1734,
and had James who lived in Mid'o., and had James, Joshua, and
Martha. James Jr. lived in E. B., and m. Sarah Jackson 1786,
and went to Minot, Me.—Martha m. a Cox.—Perhaps Joshua,
the father, had other children. He lived in S. B. where Ziba
Hayward lived and died.

26. Abishai (s. of Joshua 13.) m. Zerviah (D. of Sam'l Willis
8.) 1741, and had Samuel 1748, Abishai 1752, Solomon 1755,
Eliab 1758*, Zerviah 1763. Samuel m. Bethiah, D. of Isaac
Lathrop, 1767, and had a son Oliver 1769.—Abishai, Solomon,
and Zerviah went to Belchertown.—Oliver m. Ann Wales about
1790, and had Otis 1769, and a D. who m. a Paine in Boston.

27. Joab (s. of Joshua 13.) m. Martha, D. of John Bolton Jr.
1745, and had John 1745, Joab 1747, Martha 1749, Hezekiah
1751, Timothy 1753*, Caleb 1755, Ruth 1757, Joshua 1760,
Ezra, and Jacob. John m. Abihail, D. of John Conant, 1774,
and had John 1777, Asa 1779.—Martha and Ruth appear to have
been at Winchester, whither most of the family removed.—Joab
m. Alice Rickard 1772, and went to Pomfret, and to N. Y. State.
Wid. Martha Willis died 1802, æ. 77.—Ezra d. here a bachelor.
Jacob m. a Morse and went to Me.

28. Silas (s. of Joshua 13.) m. Sarah, D. of Josiah Hayward,
and had Sarah 1746, Silas 1748, Adam 1750, Edmund 1753,
Olive 1756, Hannah 1758, Betty 1761, Abraham 1764. This
family all removed from town.

29. Isaac (s. of Dea. Isaac 14.) m. Rebecca, D. of Thomas
Hayward, 1759, and had Isaac 1760*, Isaac 1762, Thomas 1765*.

30. Thomas (s. of Thomas 15.) m. Susanna, D. of Thomas
Ames, 1741, and had Lemuel 1742, Jedediah 1744, Thomas 1746,
Susanna 1754, Asa 1756*, Mary 1758. This family went to
Easton probably.—Lemuel m. an Ames in E., and had 2 ss. and
several Ds.—Capt. Jedediah m. Susanna, D. of Capt. Josiah
Snell, 1775, and had Lucy 1777, Martin 1796, and others per-
haps at Easton.—Thomas m. a Huet, and then a Dean, and
had 2 ss. in Boston, and others,

31. Zephaniah (s. of Thomas 15.) m. Bethiah, D. of Thomas

Hayward, 1754, and had Zephaniah 1757, who gra. H. U. 1778, and settled in the ministry at Kingston, and is still living: m. Hannah, D. of Gen. John Thomas, and has a family.

32. Nathan (s. of Thomas 15.) m. Martha, D. of Ephraim Howard, 1757, and had Martha 1758, Nathan 1760*, Nathan 1763, Betty 1765, Molly 1767, Chloe 1771, Vashti 1773, Abigail 1775, Elijah 1777, Lucy 1779. He m. Sarah White of Marshfield 1792, a 2d wife, and removed to Oakham.—Martha m. Jonathan Howard 1774.—Betty m. Luther Hayward 1785.—Molly m. Gideon Howard Esq. 1788.—Chloe m. Silas Packard Esq. 1789.—Vashti m. Martin Howard 1793.—Abigail m. Increase Matthews and d. at Muskingum.—Lucy m. Cyrus Alger Esq. of Boston 1804.

33. Judge Benjamin (s. of Benjamin 16.) gra. H. U. 1740, C. Justice C. C. P. Plym. Co., m. Bathsheba Williams of Taunton 1742, and had a child 1743*: he then m. wid. Sarah Bradford, sister of Dea. Ephraim Spooner of Plymouth, 1761, and had Mary 1762, Benjamin 1765, Sarah 1768: he died July 13, 1807, æ. 87.—Sarah m. Capt. Simeon Pratt 1791.

34. Daniel (s. of John Esq. 17.) m. Keziah (D. of Ebenezer Willis 11.) 1756, and had Daniel and John 1758, Jonah 1764, Ebenezer 1767: he d. 1814; she 1816.

35. Zebulun (s. of Samuel 24.) m. Susanna Bartlett of Carver 1793, and had Wendell 1794, Irene 1796, Susanna 1799, Hannah 1802, Bartlett 1804*, Salome 1807, Mary*, d. 1813. Wendell went to Sandwich, and then to New York.—Irene m. Daniel Hartwell Jr. 1817, and died 1818.—Susanna m. Charles Dunbar 1817.—Salome m. James O. Stetson.—Hannah m. a son of Eli Hudson of Randolph.

36. Isaac (s. of Isaac 29.) m. Huldah, D. of Capt. John Ames, 1786, and had Ruel 1786, Rebecca 1789, and removed to Me., and d., and his wid. m. again.

37. Gen. Nathan (s. of Nathan 32.) m. Sophia, D. of Col. Benjamin Tupper of Chesterfield, 1787, and had Sophia 1789.* His w. d. 1809, and he m. wid. Lucy Dogget, D. of Noah Fearing Esq. of Mid'o. 1790, and had Sophia Tupper 1791, Noah Fearing 1793, Maria 1795*, Charles 1797, Lucy Fearing 1799, Nathan 1802, William Henry 1804, Maria Antoinette 1806, Elijah 1808, George 1810, Caroline 1812*, Frederick Augustus 1815. He removed to Rochester, and then to Pittsfield: he was Representative, Senator, and Counsellor. George m. Louisa, D. of Silas Packard Jr., and lives in Boston.

38. Elijah Esq. (s. of Nathan 32.) removed to Rochester, m. Sarah, D. of Rev. Jonathan Moore, 1807, and had Susan 1809, Abby 1812, Eliza 1815, Sarah 1818, Elijah 1818*. Susan m. Nathan Willis.—Abby m. a Barstow.—Eliza and Sarah m. two men by the name of Munroe.

39. Benjamin (s. of Benjamin 33.) m. Sarah, D. of Dr. Eleazar Carver 1801, and had Benjamin. He d., and his widow m.

Seth Washburn Esq. 1812.—Benjamin gra. B. U. 1825, and is an Attorney, and has gone South.

40. Daniel (s. of Daniel 34.) m. Zilphah, D. of Sam'l Edson, 1778, and had Keziah 1779, Zilphah 1780*, d. 1800; Susanna 1782, Betsy 1784, Nancy 1787, Polly 1790, Roxana 1792, Daniel E. 1794, Cyrus 1797, Galen 1800 : his w. d. 1821, æ. 61.—Keziah m. James Willis of E. 1799.—Susanna m. John Pool 1801.— Nancy m. Galen Orcutt 1809.—Polly m. Cyrus Lathrop 1811.— Betsy m. Benjamin Palmer 1805, and Isaac Alden 1814.—Daniel went to Hanson.

41. John (s. of Daniel 34.) m. Sarah, D. of Joseph Rickard, 1779, and had Sarah 1782*, d. 1800. His w. d. 1783, and he m. Huldah, wid. of Silvanus Ames and D. of Maj. Isaac Johnson, 1784, and had John 1786, Polly 1787*, Martin 1789 : he d. 1835. John gra. B. U. 1807, and has kept school and lives on the farm with his father : he m. Cynthia Danville in Providence and has had 16 children, many of whom are not living.

42. Jonah (s. of Daniel 34.) m. Abigail, D. of Jonathan Hayward, 1788, and had Abigail 1790, Jonah 1792, Polly Hayward 1795, Lyman 1798. His w. d. 1799, and he m. Hannah, another D. of Jona. Hayward 1800, and had Clement 1801, Henry Williams 1803, died in N. Y.; Nathan 1806, Emeline Frances 1808, Augustus 1811, Benjamin 1815. His 2d wife d. 1816, and he m. Freelove, widow of William Fobes (she was a French) 1816.— Abigail m. Jacob Hayward 1816, and Alfred Whitman 1833.— Jonah m. Abigail A. Foster of Kingston 1817, where he lives.— Polly H. m. Leonard Hill 1817.—Lyman lives in Stoughton.— Clement is in Boston.—Benjamin in Boston.—Augustus is with Lyman.—Nathan went to Taunton, is now in S. B.

43. Ebenezer (s. of Daniel 34.) m. Joanna Atwood 1785, and was drowned in a well at Taunton in a fit : he had Ebenezer, George, Huldah, Olive, and Joanna. Ebenezer lived in Mid'o. George m. a D. of John Drew of Taunton, and left two sons, George and William.—Huldah m. Benja. Warren of Mid'o., and Olive m. Dr. Vaughn of Mid'o.—Joanna not m.—Ebenezer Willis d. in Mid'o. 1840, æ. 49.

44. Mr. Nathaniel Willis (brother of Dea. John 1.) was likewise an original Proprietor, and among the first settlers in Bridgewater. He was a respectable man, and designated on the early records as Mr. Nathaniel Willis, which was as high a title as was given in that day : he is said to have been the first schoolmaster here. He d. before his brother John, and his estate was settled 1686 : his w. survived, but her name is not given : he had Elkanah and Bethiah. There was a Mary b. at Sandwich 1648, probably his D. : he lived there a short time. Bethiah d. 1716.

45. Elkanah (s. of Nathaniel 44.) and his w. Mercy had Nathaniel 1678, Judith 1682 : she d. 1709; he 1711.

46. Nathaniel (s. of Elkanah 45.) m. Hannah, D. of John Titus of Rehoboth 1712, and had Ephraim 1713, Elkanah 1719 : he d. 1747; she 1753.—[See Nathaniel, No. 18.]

47. Ephraim (s. of Nathaniel 46.) and his w. Ann settled in N.
B., and had Ann 1750*. His w. d. 1751, and he m. Elizabeth
Gernsey or Ganza 1758, and had Ephraim 1759, John 1761, Ann,
Betsy: he d. 1790, æ. 76. Ann m. Moses Pike 1790.—Betsy
m. Jarvis Pike 1790, both of Attleboro'.
48. Elkanah (s. of Nathaniel 46.) m. Mary Sables of Stoughton 1744: he had also a w. Sarah, perhaps 2d w., and had Sarah
1749*, Samuel 1751, Nathaniel 1753, Sarah 1755. No further
account of this family.
49. Ephraim (s. of Ephraim 47.), a Baptist preacher, m. Eunice, D. of Hezekiah Egerton 1779, and had Polly 1781, Stillman 1785. He m. a 2d wife Frances Lemote of E. 1787, and
had Ephraim, James N., Milton, David, Frances, Sarah. Polly
m. Jacob Dunbar Jr. 1802.—Stillman m. Huldah, D. of Jona.
Snow Esq. 1809.—Frances m. Thos. Willis Jr. of E. 1812.—
Sarah m. a Hunt.—Ephraim lives in Easton.—James N. m. Rosanda Foster of Abington 1815.—Wid. Frances m. William
Hunt 1817.
50. John (s. of Ephraim 47.) m. Mary, D. of Hezekiah Egerton 1781, and had Isaac, John, Abigail, Eunice, Nancy, Sally,
Elizabeth. Isaac m. a Hubbard.—John m. Lavinia, wid. or D.
of Alfred Howard, 1813.—Abigail m. Samuel Whiting 1805.—
Eunice m. Ruel Lincoln 1804.—Nancy m. Ruel Dunbar 1805.—
Sally m. Oliver Dunbar 1807.—Elizabeth m. Richard Beresford
1817.
Abraham Pierce d. 1673, and it appears that one of his Ds.,
Rebecca, m. a Willis.—Seth Willis m. Silence, wid. of Benja.
Smith and D. of Josiah Keith, and went to Chesterfield: she
was b. a. 1720.—Jeremiah, John, Solomon, and Jonathan Willis
were at Stoughton a. 1760.—Sarah m. Robert Hoar of Mid'o.
1744.—Mary m. Lewis Daily 1782.—Timothy m. Lavinia Pratt
1786.—Jedediah of Easton m. Adah Hayward 1802.—Daniel m.
Judith B. Pratt 1815.—Thomas Willis of T. m. Bethiah, D. of
Elisha Hayward, 1743: she was dis. from W. B. Ch. to T. Ch.
1745. The following from Boston Records, viz: John Willis and
Sarah: he d. 1735.—Stephen Willis and Ann: he d. 1729: had
Stephen, Mary, Martha, and Grace; a brother William, and
friend Jonathan Willis. Stephen Jr.'s widow Martha: he had
Jonathan and Mary: his will 1748; his brothers Jonathan and
Benjamin ex'ors: a D. Phebe Willis, alias Potter, by a former
wife Dorothy.—Benjamin and Ann: he d. 1746.—Nicholas Willis 1648.—Michael Willis and Mildred his wife: his will 1669;
hers 1680: 2 ss. Experience and Michael, and a gr. s. Michael:
several Ds. viz: Abigail Bill, Lydia Nowell, Joanna Ellis, and a
Pollard.—Elizabeth, wid. of Michael, a shipwright, 1712.—Edward Wyllys, merchant, and Ruth his widow: inventory taken
1669.
WILMARTH or WILMOUTH.—David and Susanna Wilmarth had Molly 1757, Jotham 1759.
WINSLOW.—Josiah Winslow (from Freetown) m. Sarah, D.

of John Hayward Jr. 1721, lived awhile in E. B., and afterwards exchanged farms with Joseph Keith, and went up to W. B., near to Easton line. Sarah Winslow m. Edward Wentworth of St. 1746.

Anthony Winslow (s. of Gilbert of Marshfield) born 1707, m. Deborah, D. of William Barker Esq., 1728, and settled the estate of his son-in-law Nathaniel Clift, deceased, 1762.—Clift's children were Anthony Winslow, Nathaniel, and Deborah. He had also a son-in-law James Thomas of Marshfield, who was in the army with Gen. Winslow at Annapolis Royal 1755, where he d. leaving James, Winslow, Priscilla, and Deborah. Mr. Winslow came and settled in E. B. before 1770, and brought all these grand children with him, together with his D. the wid. Priscilla Thomas: his D. Deborah Clift was probably then d. Winslow's w. d. 1773, æ. 63 ; he 1789, æ. 83.—His father Gilbert Winslow was son of Nathaniel, who was son of Kenelm, who was brother of Gov. Edward Winslow, and was in Plymouth before 1633.— Nath'l Winslow removed to Damarascotta 1729, testified at York Court 1742, then 63 years old, and of course born 1679.

John Winslow m. Emeline, D. of Edward Mitchell, a. 1822, and his brother Kenelm Winslow m. Orra, D. of Benja. Pope Esq. about the same time.—Susanna, D. of John Winslow, m. Robert Latham 1649 : her mother was the famous Mary Chilton (D. of James and Susanna Chilton who came over in the May Flower 1620, and both died the first winter) who is said to have been the first English lady who set foot on the N. England shore.

WOOD.—Francis Wood lived in S. B., and m. Sarah, widow of John Hooper and D. perhaps of John Harden, 1710, and had John 1710, Mary 1712, Jonathan 1715, Anna 1717.

2. John (s. of Francis 1.) and his w. Priscilla had Anna 1734*, Mary 1735, William 1737*, Priscilla 1738, John 1740, Sarah 1742, Patience 1745, Abigail 1747, Francis 1750, Silas 1752, Joseph 1756. Mary m. Eleazar Snow 1757.— Sarah perhaps m. John Freelove 1774.—John Wood Jr. of Easton m. Rachel Barrow 1766.

3. Jonathan (s. of Francis 1.) and his wife Betty had Betty 1738, Jonathan 1740, Francis 1742, Sarah 1744, Huldah 1749, Salome 1752, Eunice 1754. Betty m. Ephraim Allen 1758.— Huldah m. Eleazar Washburn 1769.

4. Capt. Simeon Wood (from Mid'o.) m. Rachel, and had Lydia 1753*, Barzillai 1754. She died, and he m. Sarah Weston probably, and had a D. Susanna. His wife d. 1771, and he m. Mary, wid. of Isaac Keith of Easton 1774 (she was a Randall) and had Sarah 1775. His w. died, and he m. Lydia, D. of Jeremiah Washburn, 1778, and had Rufus 1779, Mary 1781, Simeon 1784, Lydia 1786, Philander 1789, Lewis 1791 : he died 1802. Susanna m. Seth Mitchell.—Simeon m. Keziah, D. of Jesse Dunbar 1809, settled in Boston, and died 1822.—Mary m. Spencer Leonard 1805.—Sarah m. Isaac Hooper 1799.—Lydia
45

m. Cyrus Benson 1806.—Philander m. Martha, D. of Jonah Benson 1813.

5. Rufus (s. of Capt. Simeon 4.) m. Susanna, D. of James Hooper 1799, and had Rachel 1800, Willard 1802, Eunice H. 1804, Winslow 1806*, Rufus 1812*. Rachel m. Oliver Allen Jr. 1819.

6. Capt. Jonathan (s. of Jonathan 3 perhaps) m. Keziah, D. of James Keith 1764. James m. Achsah Phinney 1764.—Jona. Wood m. Ann Edson (wid. of Elijah, and D. of Samuel Packard) 1771.

Jonathan Wood m. Persis Robbins, and Barnabas Wood m. Hannah Robbins, Ds. of Jeduthun Robbins before 1726.—Mary, D. of Elnathan, m. Thomas Conant 1745.—Judah m. Hannah Porter 1757.—Ziba m. Abigail, D. of William Shaw, 1796.— William m. Amie Mears 1753.—Rebecca of Halifax m. John Harris of E. B. 1811.—Olive m. Amasa Nash of Weymouth 1813.—Patience m. Eliab Keith 1813.—Eliza m. Eli Blanchard Jr. 1817.—George W. m. Lydia Tucker 1821.—Greenough m. Nancy A. V., D. of Calvin Washburn Jr.—Sarah Atwood m. Samuel Derby 1764.—George Wood lived in E. B. 1775, and his child d. there the same year.

WOODWARD.—Capt. Nathaniel Woodward (from Taunton probably) m. Elizabeth, D. of Benjamin Willis, 1708, and settled in S. B., near the Bridge ever since called " Woodward's Bridge," and had Susanna 1709, Sarah 1712: he died 1741, æ. 71. Susanna m. Charles Latham a. 1724.—There was a Hannah Woodward who m. Joshua Willis 1734.

Nathaniel Woodworth, s. of John, born at Taunton 1679. It may be that the name of Woodworth and Woodward were originally the same, like Southworth and Southard.

WOODWISS.—James Carkis Woodwiss m. Hannah Washburn 1770, and had Sarah 1770, John 1772, Mary 1773. Sarah d. 1816.

WORMAL, WERMAL, or WORMELL.—John Wormell m. Mary Bryant 1729, and had Joseph 1732, Benjamin 1735, John 1738. He removed to Halifax and there d., and his estate was settled 1754, and his wid. m. Robert Henry.

Sarah Wormal m. Nehemiah Allen 1707. This family came from Duxbury to Bridgewater probably, and was originally from Scituate, where James Wermal took the oath of fidelity 1638.

YOUNG.—John Young (a Scotchman, born in the Shire of Renfrew) came to this country quite young: was cousin to the Hon. Hugh Orr, with whom he served an apprenticeship, and m. Eunice, D. of Capt. Jonathan Bass 1752, and settled in E. B., and had Robert 1754, Agnes 1756, Samuel 1760, Bethuel 1763*, Jennet 1765, Thomas 1768, John 1771, Eunice 1775. His wife d. 1780, æ. 43, and he m. Leah Bonney of Pembroke: he d. 1798, æ. 68; she 1800, æ. 63. Agnes d. 1777,—Samuel d. 1777.—John died 1792.—Jennet m. John Phillips 1784, and died 1823.—Eunice m. John Harris 1795, and d. 1811.

2. Robert (s. of John 1.) m. Mary, D. of Capt. David Kingman, 1775, and had Samuel 1777, Agnes 1779*, Parnel 1781,
Robert 1782*, Molly 1784*, a son 1787*, Betsy 1790, Welcome
1792 : his wife d. 1831, æ. 77. Samuel was Purser on board the
Boston Frigate, Capt. Little, and was killed at the capture of
the Burceau 1800,—Parney d. 1800.—Mr. Robert Young died
1839, æ. 85.

3. Capt. Thomas (s. of John 1.) m. Bethiah Cushing, D. of
the Rev. Samuel Baldwin of Hanover 1791, and had John 1792,
Hannah Cushing 1794, Fanny 1798, William Cushing and Bush-
rod Washington 1800, Lucy 1802. He removed to Belfast, Me.,
then to Weymouth, then to Roxbury, and finally to Dorchester,
where he died. John d. of a consumption. The widow lived in
Charlestown with her family, and d. 1837.

4. Welcome Esq. (s. of Robert 2.) gra. B. U. 1814, and is a
Counsellor at Law ; m. Jennet Orr, D. of Dea. Wm. Harris,
1816, and had Mary. His w. d. 1821, æ. 31, and he m. Rolinda,
D. of Josiah Sturtevant of Halifax, and has several other
children.

THE FOLLOWING WERE NOT RESIDENTS IN BRIDGEWATER, BUT
MOST OF THEM WERE ORIGINAL PROPRIETORS, AND OTHERS OF
THEM CONNECTED WITH THE EARLY SETTLERS OF THE TOWN;
OF WHOM AND THEIR FAMILIES IT HAS BEEN THOUGHT NOT
INAPPROPRIATE TO INSERT HERE THESE FEW BRIEF AND LIMITED
NOTICES.

ALLERTON.—BARNES.

ALLERTON.—Mr. Isaac Allerton and his wife Mary were
among the first pilgrims, who came over to Plymouth in the May
Flower 1620, and resided there till 1636 : he was one of the Governor's Assistants ; was also one of Gov. Bradford's 8 associates
who assumed the Company's debts in 1627 ; an Agent to England three times ; m. Fear, D. of William Brewster, for his 2d
wife, she died 1633 : he met with losses and removed to New
York, and d. at New Haven 1659, his will on record there : he
had Isaac, Bartholomew, Remember, Mary, and Sarah. Mary
m. Thomas Cushman : he had also a sister Sarah, who m. God-
bert Godbertson.—Isaac (the son) graduated H. U. 1650; went
to New Haven, and a D. of his m. Capt. Simon Eyres and died
1740, æ. 100 : she was said to have sheltered the regicide judges ;
but she was then only eight years old, and could have been only
a witness of it in the house of her grandmother where, if any
where, it took place : he had also a son John, who had a son
Isaac, born in N. E., and d. in Dutchess Co., N. York, 1806, æ.
80, leaving 3 ss. David, Jonathan, and Reuben, all of whom had
ss. in N. Y. State. David had a son Isaac living at Carmel, N.
Y., March 25, 1825. George D. James of the town of America
in Dutchess Co., N. Y., a connection of the family, is said to be
able to give a more particular account of them. Point Allerton
or Alderton in Boston harbour was so named for Isaac, the worthy ancestor above. Early records speak also of Allerton's Hill in
Duxbury.—See N. E. Memorial and Judge Davis' letter in the
7th vol., 3d series of the Collections of the M. H. Society.

BARNES.—John Barnes was at Plymouth in 1634.—Jonathan Barnes, s. of John probably, d. in Plymouth 1715: his w.
was Elizabeth, D. of Wm. Hedge probably : he had John, William, Jonathan, Hannah, Mary, Elizabeth, Lydia, Esther, and
Sarah. Hannah m. Benjamin Rider.—Mary m. John Carver
1689.—Elizabeth m. Isaac Lothrop 1698.—Lydia m. Abiel
Shurtleff 1695.—Esther m. Elkanah Cushman.—Sarah m. Benj.

Bartlett 1702.—John m. Mary, D. of Joseph Bartlett, and had a family: one D., Lydia, m. Lemuel Barnes.—Jonathan m. Sarah, D. of Wm. Bradford 3d, she d. 1720.

2. William (s. of Jonathan above) m. Alice, D. of William Bradford 3d, and had William 1706, Lemuel 1707, Mercy 1708, Benjamin 1710*, and Benjamin 1717: the father d. 1751, æ. 80, the mother d. 1775, æ. 95. William was drowned.—Lemuel m. Lydia, D. of his uncle John Barnes, and had 5 ss. and 3 Ds.: he d. and his wid. m. Jonathan Sampson: one D. m. Nathaniel Bartlett, one m. a Lemote, and another Ephraim Holmes.— Mercy m. Samuel Cole and afterwards Capt. Barnabas Hedge, grandfather of the present Barnabas Hedge Esq., and her D. Mercy m. Thomas Davis, and was mother of the late Hon. Wm. Davis of Plymouth.—Benjamin had Benjamin, Isaac, Bradford, and Mrs. Battles, and died 1760. There are many descendants still in Plymouth, Hingham, and other parts of the County.

BARTLETT.—Robert Bartlett came over in the 3d ship, the Ann, in 1723; m. Mary, eldest D. of Richard and Elizabeth Warren, 1628: he d. 1676, æ. 73, his w. survived him a few years only: he had Benja., Joseph 1638, Rebecca who m. Wm. Harlow 1649, Mary who m. Richard Foster 1651 and then Jona. Morey 1659, Sarah who m. Sam'l Rider of Yarmo. 1656, Elizabeth who m. Anthony Sprague of Hingham 1661, Mercy who m. John Ivey of Boston 1668, and Lydia who m. James Barnaby and then John Nelson of Mid'o. He was said to have been much " opposed to psalm singing ;" Ainsworth's Psalms and the tunes appended, badly printed and worse sung probably, could but offend both good sense and good ears.

2. Benjamin (s. of the above) m. Sarah, only D. of Love Brewster, 1656, and settled in Duxbury, where he was Selectman and Deputy: he m. a 2d w. Cicely or Cecilia 1678: he d. 1691, and had Benjamin, Samuel, Ichabod, Ebenezer, Rebecca who m. Wm. Bradford 3d 1679, and Sarah who m. her cousin Robert Bartlett 1687. Some of his descendants went to Lebanon, Conn.

3. Joseph (brother of the next above) m. probably Hannah, D. of William Followell, (Gabriel Followell d. 1667) and settled in " Pond's Parish," Plymouth : she b. 1638, d. 1710 ; he died 1712, æ. 73: he had Robert, Joseph, Benjamin, Elnathan, Mary w. of John Barnes, Hannah w. of Joseph Silvester, and Lydia w. of Elisha Holmes.

4. Samuel (s. of Benjamin 2.) m. Hannah Peabody and settled in Plymouth, and was called " sen." and mariner, from whom are Samuel, Ichabod, Judah, William, and others. Samuel Jr. was an officer at Louisburgh, and d. 1750, æ. 59, whose son Samuel, called " Quaker Sam," was father of Capt. Joseph, Amasa, Anselm, and others.—There was an Abigail Bartlett m. Gamaliel Bradford, and named one of her sons Peabody.

5. Robert (s. of Joseph 3.) m. his cousin Sarah Bartlett 1687, and afterwards Sarah, D. of Jacob Cook, 1691, and d. 1718, æ. 55 : he had Thomas, Dea. Joseph, Robert, Ebenezer, and

Lemuel.—James and Isaac Bartlett of Plymouth are descendants of Robert Jr.

6. Joseph (s. of Joseph 3.) m. Lydia Griswold 1692, and d. at 'Pond's" 1703, æ. 38, and had Joseph 1693, Samuel (town clerk) 1697, Lydia 1698, Benjamin 1699, Francis LeBaron 1701, Sarah 1703. Capt. Zaccheus and the late Silvanus Bartlett were descendants of Joseph 6.—Samuel (the town Clerk) m. Elizabeth Lothrop, and afterwards wid. Elizabeth Wethrell, who was also a Lothrop: he d. 1769, æ. 72.

7. Benjamin (s. of Benjamin 2, or of Joseph 3.) called Jr., m. Sarah, D. of Jonathan Barnes, 1762, and died at "Ponds" 1727: his wid. m. Joseph Sturtevant of Kingston: he had Joseph, Benjamin, Nathaniel, Jonathan, Elkanah of Staten Island, Hannah and Sarah. Elsewhere it is recorded that his Ds. were Sarah wife of Israel Bradford, Rebecca relict of John Bradford Jr., Ruth wife of John Murdock Jr., Mercy wife of John Turner, Deborah w. of Josiah Thomas of Marshfield, and Abigail of Duxbury: one of his Ds. also is said to have m. Ephraim Bradford, but query.

Lydia Bartlett m. Dr. Lazarus LeBaron 1720.—Sarah, wid. of John Jenny, d. 1655, and in her will, 1654, mentions her son-in-law Benjamin Bartlett.

The family of Bartlett is very numerous, and the preceding is intended as a brief and very general account only of the ancestor and such of his immediate descendants as have fallen under our notice.

BONNEY.—Thomas Bonney was one of the original proprietors of Bridgewater, and of course lived in Duxbury between 1645 and 1650: m. Dorcas, D. of Henry Sampson.—Mary Bonney of Duxbury m. John Mitchell 1675. The family spread into Pembroke and many of the descendants are still there and in the lower part of the county. Abigail, D. of Ebenezer Bonney of Pembroke, m. Jacob Hill of E. B. 1754, and her sister Elizabeth m. Samuel Whitman of E. B. 1757.—Some of the family removed to Chesterfield.—Leah m. John Young of E. B.

BRADFORD.—Hon. William Bradford the 2d, Governor of old Plymouth Colony, was born at Ansterfield in Yorkshire 1588, and educated under the Rev. Mr. Clifton; m. Dorothy May, and came to Plymouth with the forefathers in the first ship, the May Flower, in 1620, and had a s. John: his w. d. (was drowned in Plymouth harbor before they landed) Dec. 7, 1620: he afterwards in 1623, m. the wid. Alice Southworth, whose maiden or family name was Carpenter; she was b. 1590, and there was said to have been a mutual attachment between them in youth, which, after she lost her husband and he his wife, was revived, and she arrived with her two children, Constant and Thomas Southworth, in the ship Ann in 1623: they had William 1624, Mercy, and Joseph 1630. He d. 1657, æ. 71; she 1670, æ. 80. Mercy m. Benjamin Vermays or Vermage 1648.

2. John (s. of William and Dorothy above) was in Duxbury

between 1645 and 1653, was an original proprietor of Bridge-water, was Representative of Duxbury 1652, and of Marshfield 1653, at the old Colony Court at Plymouth : his father in his will 1657 speaks of him as then living, and the records mention him as living in 1662, and no further account is obtained of him : the tradition is that he was lost at sea on a voyage to or from England : he probably had no family.

3. William (s. of the Governor) was a Major and Deputy Governor ; lived in Kingston, near Duxbury, and was one of the original proprietors of Bridgewater ; m. Alice, D. of Thos. Richards of Weymouth ; she was a very respectable woman, and in an eulogy, after her death, on the colony records, was called "Mrs. Alice Bradford Jr.": they had John 1652, William 1655, Thomas, Samuel 1668, Hannah, and Mercy. His w. died, and he m. a wid. Wiswall, and had a s. Joseph. She died, and he m. Mary, wid. of Rev. John Holmes of Duxbury and D. of Dea. John Wood or Atwood of Plymouth, 1661, and had Israel, David, Ephraim, Hezekiah, Melatiah, Mary, Alice, and Sarah : some of these Ds. might have been born of the 1st or 2d wife : his last w. d. 1671, æ. 44 ; he d. Feb. 20, 1704, æ. 79. Thomas and Joseph went to Conn.—Hannah m. Joshua Ripley of Hing-ham.—Mercy and Melatiah m. men by the name of Steel in Conn. Israel m. Sarah, D. of Benja. Bartlett Jr., and he, Ephraim, and Hezekiah settled on the paternal estate in Kingston.—Mary m. Thomas or Samuel Hunt of Duxbury or Kingston.—Alice m. a Fitch of Norwich, Conn.—Sarah m. Kenelm Baker of Marsh-field, and was mother of the late Wm. Baker, Messenger of the Governor and Council, and of a Mrs. Scollay of Boston.—Rev. Timothy Alden said that the children by the first w. were Israel, Ephraim, Samuel, and John ; by the 2d Joseph ; and by the 3d William, Thomas, David, and Hezekiah, and that he had three Ds.; but query.

4. Joseph (s. of the Governor) m. Jael, D. of the Rev. Peter Hobart of Hingham, and had Elisha, and d. 1715, æ. 84 ; she d. 1730, æ. 88. Elisha m. Hannah, D. of James Cole Jr.: it is also said he m. Bathsheba Le Brock, and had a son Carpenter, who went to Me., and several Ds.: one m. a Waters in Sharon, and her descendants are said to possess Gov. Bradford's Bible, in which is to be found a record of the family.

5. Maj. John (s. of William 3.) m. Mercy, D. of Joseph and Priscilla Warren, 1674 : her mother was Priscilla, D. of Mr. John Faunce, and sister of Elder Thomas Faunce, and niece of the Secretary Nath'l Morton author of the Memorial. Mercy was born 1653, he died 1736, she 1748, in her 94th year (Josiah Cotton's Diary says, æ. 90): they had John 1675, Alice 1677, Abigail 1679, Mercy 1681, Samuel 1683, Priscilla 1686, William 1688. John m. Rebecca, D. of Benjamin Bartlett Jr. of Dux-bury, and d. young, leaving a son, Capt. Robert.—Alice m. Ens. Edward Mitchell of East Bridgewater, his 2d wife 1708, and af-terwards Dea. Joshua Hersey of Hingham.—Abigail m. Gideon

Sampson, but left no children.—Mercy m. Jonathan Freeman 1708, and afterwards Lt. Isaac Cushman Jr.—Priscilla m. Seth Chipman of Kingston.—William m. a D. of Dea. John Foster of Plymouth and d. young, and she then m. George Partridge of Duxbury: some of William's descendants settled in Plainfield, Conn.

6. William (s. of William 3.) m. Rebecca, D. of Benjamin Bartlett of Duxbury, 1679: she died 1775; he 1687: they had Alice 1680, Sarah 1683, and William. Alice m. William Barnes of Plymouth, and was g. grandmother of the late Hon. William Davis, and of Barnabas Hedge Esq. of Plymouth.—Sarah m. Jonathan Barnes and d. 1720.—William, it is said, m. Elizabeth Finney, but qu.

7. Samuel (s. of William 3.) m. Hannah Rogers and died at Duxbury 1714, æ. 46: he had Hannah 1689, Gershom 1691, Perez 1694, Elizabeth 1696, Jerusha 1699, Wealthy 1772, and Gamaliel 1704. Gershom m. Priscilla Wiswall 1716, and lived in Kingston.—Perez gra. H. U. 1713.—Gamaliel m. Abigail Bartlett 1728, and d. 1778, æ. 73, and had Abigail 1728, Samuel 1729, Gamaliel 1731, Seth 1733, Peabody 1734, Deborah 1738, Hannah 1740, Ruth 1743, Peter 1745, and Andrew 1746, gra. H. U. 1771. Jerusha m. Rev. Ebenezer Gay of Hingham D. D., and Hannah m. Nathaniel Gilbert of Taunton 1709.—Col. Gamaliel, son of Gamaliel above, m. Sarah, D. of Samuel Alden, and had Perez, Sophia, Gamaliel, Alden 1765, Jerusha, Sally, Daniel, and Gershom.—Perez lived on the paternal estate.— Gamaliel was a mariner and Captain of a Ship, and afterwards Warden of the State Prison in Charlestown, where he d.: he m. a Hickling, and had a s. Gamaliel gra. H. U. 1814, a Physician, who d. 1840; and another s. Geo. Partridge gra. H. U. 1825.— Hon. Alden gra. H. U. 1786, first settled in the ministry in Me., and was afterwards Secretary of Mass.; m. Margaret Stevenson, and has a family in Boston.

8. David (s. of William 3.) m. Elizabeth Finney 1714, and d. 1730, and had Nathaniel 1715, d. 1751; Jonathan 1717, Lydia 1719, Nathan 1722. Lydia m. Elkanah Cushman 1740, and Lazarus Le Baron 1743, and d. 1756.

9. Samuel (s. of Maj. John 5.) m. Sarah, D. of Edw. Gray of Tiverton, s. of Edward Gray of Plymouth, 1714, and settled in Plympton; he d. 1740, æ. 56; she 1770: they had John 1717, Gideon 1719, William 1720*, Mary 1722, Sarah 1725, William 1728, Mercy 1731, Abigail 1732, Phebe 1735, Samuel 1740. Mary m. Abiel Cook.—Sarah m. Ephraim Paddock.—Abigail m. Caleb Stetson.—Phebe m. Shubael Norton Esq.—John m. Elizabeth Holmes, and had Elizabeth, Molly, John, Priscilla, Perez, Hannah, Lydia, Oliver, Mercy, William, and Sarah. John m. Eunice, D. of Ignatius Loring Esq., and had Polly, Eunice, Olive, John, Nancy, Mercy, Sophia, Susanna, and Jane.

10. Gideon (s. of Samuel 9.) m. Jane Paddock, and d. 1793: they had Levi 1743, Joseph 1745, Sarah 1748, Samuel 1750,

Gideon 1752, Calvin 1754, Jenny 1756. Sarah m. Freeman
Ellis.—Jenny m. Noah Bisbee.
11. Hon. William (s. of Samuel 9.) m. Mary, D. of Dr. Laz-
arus Le Baron of Plymouth 1751, and settled as a Physician in
Bristol, R. I.; was afterwards an Attorney, Lt. Governor, and
Senator in Congress : she d. 1775; he died 1808, æ. 80 : he had
William 1752, Le Baron 1754, John 1758*, Mary 1760, Hannah
1762*, One 1764*, Hannah 1767, John 1768, Nancy, Ezekiel
Hersey, and Lydia. William m. Betsy B. James, and had Wil-
liam and others, and d. 1811.—Le Baron m. Sarah, D. of Thos.
Davis of Plymouth, and had Le Baron 1780, and d. 1793, æ. 39.
Mary m. Henry Goodwin, and d. 1834.—Hannah m. Dr. Gus-
tavus Baylies of Uxbridge, and died 1811.—John m. Jemima
Wardwell, and d. 1833.—Nancy m. James De Wolf, and both d.
1838.—Ez. Hersey m. Abby De Wolf, and then Abby Atwood.—
Lydia m. Charles Collins Esq. of Newport.
12. Samuel (s. of Samuel 9.) m. Lydia Pease, and had Shubael, Sarah, Samuel, Edward Gray, Pardon, and Lydia.
13. Levi (s. of Gideon 10.) m. Elizabeth Lewis 1764 : she b.
1743, d. 1813; he d. 1822 : they had Lewis 1768, Joseph 1770,
Levi 1772, Daniel 1774, Ezra 1776, Elizabeth 1778, and Sarah
1782. Lewis is now living in Plympton, and has an accurate
geneological account of the Bradford family, to which recurrence
may be had for all particulars here omitted. Joseph d. 1810.—
Levi m. Mercy Sampson 1800.—Sarah m. Isaiah Tilson.
14. Perez (s. of John and g. s. of Samuel 9.) m. Sarah Prince,
and had Christopher Prince, Louisa, Elizabeth, Deborah, Sarah*,
Ruth, Lucy Prince, Perez, Hezekiah. His w. died, and he m.
Lydia Cushman, and had Sarah, Joanna, and Salome. Louisa
m. Miles Holmes.—Elizabeth m. Richard Sayward.—Deborah
m. Samuel Bryant.—Ruth m. Jona. Ripley.—Lucy P. m. Theodore Cobb and then Hezekiah Cole.—Perez m. Deborah Davis.
Hezekiah m. Margaret Parsons.—Sarah m. Oliver Churchill Jr.
Salome m. William Bradford.
BREWSTER.—William Brewster, b. 1560, came over in the
first ship, the May Flower, 1620; was a ruling Elder in the
Church at Plymouth: his w. (name unknown) d. between 1623
and 1627; he d. 1644, æ. 84 : he had Jonathan, Love, Wrestling,
Patience, and Fear. (Lucretia, William, and Mary, are also set
down as his children in a note in the N. E. Memorial, p. 221 ; but
this is now considered by the learned and able editor himself as
at least doubtful : probably Lucretia was wife of Jonathan, and
William and Mary were probably his two eldest children.) Patience m. Thomas Prince, the Governor, 1624, and died 1634.—
Fear m. Isaac Allerton 1626, and d. 1633.—Wrestling d. single
in youth.—The venerable Elder was one of the oldest men
among the forefathers, being 60 when he arrived.
2. Jonathan (s. of the preceding) and his wife Lucretia, had
William, Mary, Jonathan, and Benjamin. He removed from
Duxbury to Norwich, Conn., after 1648, with his wife and sons.
46

Mary m. John Turner of Scituate 1645, and was living 1691.—
William and Jonathan Jr. were on the military roll in Duxbury,
1643, the latter then 16 years old, and had an action in Court
1650. William was in the Naragansett war 1645. After these
periods neither of their names appears on the records.—Benjamin
was at New London 1661.

3. Love (s. of William 1.) m. Sarah, D. of William Collier
(she afterwards m. a Parks); he died 1650; and had Sarah, Nathaniel, William, and Wrestling. He lived and died in Duxbury,
and was one of the original proprietors of Bridgewater. Sarah
m. Benjamin Bartlett of Duxbury 1656.—Nathaniel d. 1676, his
family (if he had any) extinct : his name appears on Bridgewater
records as a proprietor (of his father's share probably) 1666.

4. William (s. of Love 3.) was a Deacon in Duxbury, and
had William and Benjamin. William, called Jr. 1722, had
Ichabod, Job, and others.—William of Pembroke 1730, had a
son Ichabod.—Benjamin was in Connecticut 1714.

5. Wrestling (s. of Love 3.) was a carpenter, d. 1696, leaving
a wid. Mary, and had Jonathan, Wrestling, John, Mary, Sarah,
Abigail, Elizabeth, and Hannah. One D. m. in Duxbury, and
four of them in Kingston.—Jonathan went to Windham, Conn.,
after 1728 and m. Mary Partridge in Duxb., who was living 1733.

6. Wrestling (s. of Wrestling next above) was a Deacon in
Kingston, and had Wrestling, Thomas, Isaac, Elisha, Mary, &c.,
and d. 1767.

7. John (brother of the preceding) had Joseph and Job in
Duxbury.

8. Nathaniel Brewster gra. H. U. 1642, a Clergyman, went to
England and returned, and finally settled at Brookhaven, L. I.,
and d. 1690, leaving John, Timothy, and Daniel. This Nathaniel
has been supposed to have been a descendant, perhaps a gr. son,
of William. There are many descendants from the worthy Elder
in Duxbury, Pembroke, Plymouth, Kingston, and elsewhere.

BROWN.—John Brown was one of the original proprietors
of Bridgewater, and of course lived in Duxbury between 1645
and 1650. We have no certain account of him or his family,
but take him to be the man who was chosen Assistant 1636, and
often afterwards one of the Commissioners of the united Colonies from 1644 to 1655, and who died at Winnamoiset near Rehoboth 1662. James Brown, an Assistant also, who lived at
Swansey, was his son, and m. Lydia, D. of John Howland. [See
N. E. Memorial, p. 297, note.] Peter Brown came in the May
Flower 1620, and whether he was father of John, or otherwise
related, is not ascertained; Martha and Mary (wife and D. perhaps) are named 1627.

CARVER.—John Carver, first Governor of Plymouth colony,
d. April 1621, and his wife soon after, and the old Colony records
furnish no further account of his family. When he arrived in
1620 his family appears to have consisted of 8 persons, of whom
John Howland was one, and is supposed to have m. Elizabeth,

one of the Daughters. In the allotments of land in 1623, and in
the division of the cattle in 1627, the name of Carver does not
appear. A family however of this name was in Marshfield ever
after 1638, at which date Robert Carver had a grant of land at
Green's harbor, and died there 1680, æ. 86. John Carver (son
of Robert perhaps) d. in Marshfield 1679, æ. 42, leaving a wid.
Milicent, who was D. of William Ford, and 8 children. William
Carver (eldest s. of John) died at Marshfield 1760, æ. 102, and
is noticed by Gov. Hutchinson and Dr. Belknap, in the biography of Gov. Carver, as the grandson of the Governor; but in
Pemberton's Ms. Journal. in the library of the Mass. Hist. Society, he is called " the nephew of Governor Carver, being his
brother's son." Joshua Carver, late of Marshfield, æ. over 90,
was of the same family. John Carver (s. of John probably)
lived in Plymouth, went from Marshfield 1680, m. Mary, D. of
Jonathan Barnes, and his son, Dea. Josiah, d. in Plymouth 1751,
æ. 63. There was a Richard Carver in Watertown, who died
1638, and in his will mentioned his wife Grace, and Ds. Elizabeth and Susanna. Many of the name are still living in Plymo.
and other parts of the old Colony.—[See Carver, p. 129.]

CHANDLER.—Edmund Chandler was one of the original
proprietors of Bridgewater, an inhabitant of Duxbury of course,
before 1650. We have no particular account of him or his family.
Those bearing the name, and probably his descendants, have
been and still are numerous in the old Colony, and other parts
of the country.—[See Chandler, p. 136.]

CHURCH.—Richard Church came over 1630, then æ. 22:
propounded in Mass., where he first arrived probably, 1630, and
made freeman in Plymouth 1632: lived at Eel River in Plymouth
till 1649, when he sold out and went first to Eastham probably
1649, and then to Hingham, where he had a D. Deborah b. 1657,
and d. at Dedham Dec. 27, 1668; but was buried at Hingham;
his will dated at Hingham 1668; was a Carpenter; a volunteer
against the Pequots 1637, called " Sergeant Church;" made the
gun carriages: he, with John Thompson, built the first meeting
house in Plymouth a. 1637; m. Elizabeth, D. of Richard Warren, a. 1635: she d. a wid. at Hingham 1670: he had Elizabeth,
Benjamin 1639, Richard*, Joseph, Nathaniel, Caleb, Abigail
1648, and Deborah 1657. It is doubtful if he ever lived, or was
really settled, at Eastham or Dedham. Being a Carpenter, and
of some repute in his calling, he was doubtless employed much
abroad, and at these places among others: he had early friends
at Watertown and Charlestown, some of whom perhaps came
over with him. Elizabeth m. Caleb Hobart at Hingham 1657,
and died 1659.—Abigail m. Samuel Thaxter at Hingham 1666,
and d. Dec. 1677.—Deborah m. John Irish Jr. perhaps of Little
Compton.—The father gave Joseph, whom he made Executor of
his will, a double portion on account of the " lameness of his
hand."

2. Col. Benjamin (s. of the above) the famous warrior, was

born in Plymouth ; was of his father's occupation, a Carpenter; m. Alice, D. of Constant Southworth of Duxbury, 1667, where he also settled, and thence removed to Saconet, Little Compton, about 1667, and was a magistrate for Saconet and Pocasset, which places included Little Compton and Tiverton; appeared also among the first freemen of Bristol 1681, and was a Selectman and Deputy from Bristol in 1682, and d. January 7, 1718, æ. 79, and was buried at Little Compton. He had Thomas (editor of his father's life), Constant (a Captain under his father), Benjamin, a bachelor, Edward (whose only s. was Dea. Benja.), Charles, who had a numerous family, and an only D. who m. a Rothbotham of Newport. His historians and descendants have erroneously said he was born at Duxbury ; knowing he went from thence to Saconet, they supposed he was of course born there ; but he was born at Plymouth, and was ten years old before his father with his family removed : his sister Abigail was born in Plymouth nine years after him.

3. Joseph (s. of Richard 1.) lived in Hingham, his wife Mary, they were m. about 1665, and had Mary 1666, John 1668, Alice 1670, Benjamin 1672, Sarah 1673, William 1675, Deborah 1677, all born at Hingham : he then removed to Little Compton, and was made freeman there 1682; was Ensign and Deputy there, and had other children probably : was one of the County Associates for Bristol Co. 1691 ; was also a Carpenter: he and his wife Mary are mentioned on the records there 1686 : she was no doubt from Hingham. His will 1711 mentioned Joseph, John, Eliza Blackman, Mary Wood, Deborah Gray, and Abigail Simmons: some of these were born probably after he left Hingham. It has been erroneously stated by Deane in his history of Scituate, and by others, that Joseph was the father of Col. Benjamin, but this is only another of the traditional errors respecting this family.

4. Nathaniel (s. of Richard 1.) settled at Scituate ; was a Carpenter, which seems to have been the family calling : he m. Sarah Barstow, and had Abigail 1666, Richard 1668, Nathaniel 1670, Alice 1679, Joseph 1681, Charles 1683, Sarah 1686 : he died intestate before 1700. Abigail m. Nathaniel Harlow.— Richard and his wife Mary had Richard and two Ds.: one of them, Hannah, m. Josiah Sturtevant, and was grandmother of the late Josiah Cotton Esq. and Dr. Rosseter Cotton.—Nathaniel had Nathaniel 1698, Joseph 1709, and Caleb 1712 at Scituate. Joseph and Charles settled in Plymouth, and Joseph died there 1707, leaving a D. Judith, wife of Isaac Little. Charles afterwards went to Freetown and died there, called Captain 1729.— Sarah m. John Holmes.—Richard and Joseph were both dead before the estate was finally settled.—Nathaniel 3d m. Jerusha Perry 1719, and had Thomas and Lemuel 1742, and 13 others. Thomas Church m. Huldah, D. of Aaron Soule.—Thomas, son of Thomas, was a revolutionary soldier, and died 1830.—Capt. Cornelius was son of Lemuel.—Caleb m. Sarah Williamson

1735, and lived probably in Marshfield.—Ruth Church m. Consider Howland 1795.

Deane's doubt as to the father of Nathaniel is groundless, as Richard of Hingham and Richard of Plymouth, whom he supposed to be distinct men, were one and the same man.

5. Caleb (s. of Richard 1.) m. Joanna, D. of William Sprague in Hingham, 1667, and had Hannah 1668, and Ruth 1670 : he was named of Dedham 1672, and was living in Watertown 1690. [Farmer in his Register says he had Joseph, Caleb, and Benjamin, but query.]

6. Dea. Benjamin (s. of Edward, and g. s. of Col. Benja. 2.) gra. H. U. 1727, was Deacon of Dr. Mather Byle's Church in Boston, and author of a biography of his grandfather, the Colonel, 1772, in which he erroneously calls the Colonel's father Joseph, and his parents "of Duxbury;" the Deacon's son Benjamin gra. H. U. 1754, and was the famous Dr. Benjamin Church of Revolutionary distinction : another son, Edward, gra. H. U. 1759, was a Consul, and d. abroad ; and a D. Abigail is said to have m. Turner Phillips of Boston.

Col. Peter Church died in Bristol a. 1821, æ. a. 80.—Samuel Church also died there, perhaps the gra. of H. U. 1778.—Rev. Nathan Church was of Bridgton, Me. 1799.—Rev. Aaron Church d. in Hartford, Conn., 1823, æ. 77, b. in Springfield 1744, was in the ministry 41 years.—Capt. Joseph Church died at Fairhaven 1839, æ. 87.—Gamaliel Church Esq. Representative from Westport 1839 and 1840.

Many of this name, descendants no doubt of Richard, still reside in the old Colony, and have spread extensively over New England.

CLARK.—William Clark was one of the original proprietors of Bridgewater, but we have no further account of him or of his family. There are many of this name in various parts of the county, and it is a very common name throughout the country. Richard Clark came over to Plymouth in the May Flower 1620, and d. before spring, and there is no further notice of him, or of any family left by him. Thomas Clark came in the Ann 1623, and m. Susanna, D. of wid. Mary Ring before 1631, and died at Plymouth March 24, 1697, æ. 97, according to the grave-stone and the records of the town, but by his deposition given 1664, stating himself then to be only 59, he was only 92 at his death. It has been supposed he was mate of the May Flower, having gone back to Eng., and returned to Plymouth again in 1623, but this is not certain. He had William, James, Nathaniel (the Secretary), Andrew, and Susanna, who m. Barnabas Lothrop Esq. of Barnstable 1658. Thomas Clark of Plymoth m. wid. Alice Nichols of Boston 1664 : she was D. of Richard Hallet.— William Clark's house (a garrison house) was burnt in Plymouth by the Indians 1676, on the Sabbath, and 11 persons killed.— John (g. s. of Thomas) d. in Plymouth 1712, and had John, Joseph, and James.—Trustum Clark was in Plymouth 1634, and

d. in Duxbury 1661, and had Trustum and Henry.—Isaac, son
of Joseph, went to Hardwick.—Whether William, whose house
was burnt, was the proprietor of Bridgewater, is not known, if
he was he must have lived in Duxbury before 1650.

COLLIER.—William Collier was an original proprietor, a
merchant adventurer, and came over about 1633 : he settled in
Duxbury, and was an Assistant many years, and d. 1670 : he had
Sarah, wife of Love Brewster (she afterwards m. a Parks); Re-
becca, wife of Job Cole ; Mary, 2d wife of Thomas Prince,
Gov. m. 1635 ; and Elizabeth, wife of Constant Southworth.

CUSHING.—Peter Cushing of Hingham, Norfolk, Eng., had
2 ss., Theophilus 1579, and Matthew 1588, both of whom came
to N. England and settled in Hingham.

2. Theophilus came over 1633, then 54 years old, and lived
some years at Gov. Haynes' farm near Boston, and finally settled
in Hingham, where he d. nearly 100 years old, and was blind 25
years : he left no children.

3. Dea. Matthew, with his w., 4 ss., and one D., and his wife's
sister, wid. Frances Riecroft, came over 1638, "in the Diligent
of Ipswich, of 350 tons, John Martin, master," and settled in
Hingham : he m. Nazareth, D. of Henry Pitcher : he d. 1660,
æ. a. 72 ; she 1682, æ. 95 : he had Daniel 1619, Jeremiah 1621,
Matthew 1623, Deborah 1625, John 1627. Deborah m. Matthias
Briggs. All of the Cushings in this vicinity, and in the State
perhaps, descended from Matthew.

4. Daniel Esq. (s. of Matthew) was the 3d Town Clerk of
Hingham, and left manuscripts, from which much information
respecting Hingham and its early settlers has been derived : he
m. Lydia, D. of Edward Gilman (ancestor of all the Gilmans)
June 19th, 1645, and had Peter 1646, Daniel 1648, Deborah
1651, Jeremiah 1654, Theophilus 1657, Matthew 1660. She d.
1689, and he m. Elizabeth, wid. of Capt. John Thaxter and D.
of Nicholas Jacob 1691, and d. 1700 ; she 1725, æ. 94. Deborah
m. Benjamin Woodbridge 1679.

5. Jeremiah (s. of Matthew 3.) of Boston, a mariner, was lost
at sea : his wid. Elizabeth mentioned her D. Elizabeth Condy,
and g. s. Jeremiah Condy, and sister Martha Muzer in Redrif,
near London.

6. Matthew (s. of Matthew 3.) of Hingham, m. Sarah, D. of
Nicholas Jacob, 1653, and died a. 1700, and left no children : in
his will he mentioned his brothers and most of his relatives : she
made her will 1701, and mentioned most of her relatives.

7. Hon. John (s. of Matthew 3.) settled in Scituate, and m.
(according to Deane in his account of Scituate) Sarah, D. of
Nicholas Jacob, 1656 (this or the preceding must be an error :
did not John m. Sarah, D. of Matthew Hawke ?): he was Deputy
and Assistant in the old Colony, and Representative at the General Court in Boston the year after the union 1692 : she d. 1678,
æ. 38 ; he 1708, æ. 81 : he had John 1662, Thomas 1663, Matthew 1665, Jeremiah 1666, James 1668, Joshua 1670, Caleb

1672, Deborah 1674, Mary 1676, Joseph 1677, Benjamin 1679, and Sarah. Deborah m. Thomas Loring of Plymouth 1699.— Mary d. single 1698.—Sarah m. Dea. David Jacob 1689.—Joshua settled in Marshfield, and left no family.

8. Peter (s. of Daniel Esq. 4.) of Hingham m. Hannah, D. of Matthew Hawke, 1685, and d. 1719 ; she d. 1737, æ. 82 : he had Peter 1686, Stephen 1687, Jonathan 1689, Lydia who m. a Marshall, and Hannah who m. a Cushing.

9. Daniel (s. of Daniel Esq. 4.) of Hingham m. Elizabeth, D. of Capt. John Thaxter, 1680, and had Daniel 1681*, Elisha, Daniel, Moses, Elizabeth, Sarah, w. of John Jacob ; Ruth, w. of Samuel Lincoln ; Deborah, w. of Benjamin Loring; Abigail, w. of Richard Kilby of Boston ; and Sarah, who d. young probably. Daniel Cushing and his w. Sarah (he d. 1754) had Daniel, Ebenezer, Sarah Smith : sister Elizabeth, gr. s. Thomas, and gr. ss. Thomas and Obadiah Hersey.—Daniel Cushing and his w. Elizabeth (he d. 1793) had Daniel, Susanna, Elizabeth Jones, Deborah Cushing, gr. s. Daniel, and brother Benjamin Lincoln.

10. Jeremiah (s. of Daniel Esq. 4.) gra. H. U. 1676, m. Hannah, D. of Thomas Loring, 1685, and settled in the ministry at Scituate 1691 : he d. March 22, 1705, and his wid. m. John Barker Esq., an attorney, 1706: he had Hannah 1687, Ignatius 1689, Jeremiah 1695, Ezekiel 1698. Hannah m. Samuel Barker, s. of her father-in-law, 1706.—Ezekiel settled at Cape Elizabeth, and his D. Lucy m. Dr. James Otis and was mother of the late Hon. Dr. Cushing Otis.—Wid. Ann Cushing d. at Boston 1759, and in her will mentioned her s. Jeremiah, and Ds. Mary Wheaton, Susanna, w. of Jona. Goddard ; and Hannah.

11. Theophilus (s. of Daniel Esq. 4.) of Hingham m. Mary, D. of Capt. John Thaxter : his will 1718: he had Nehemiah 1689, Adam 1692, David 1694, Abel, Theophilus, Seth, Deborah, and Lydia. Nehemiah settled in Abington or Pembroke.

12. Capt. Matthew (s. of Daniel Esq. 4.) of Hingham m. Jael, D. of Capt. John Jacob, 1684 : she d. 1708 ; he 1715 : he had David 1685*, David 1687*, Solomon 1692, Job 1694, Moses 1696*, Samuel 1699, Isaac 1701, Obadiah 1703*, Jael 1706. Job gra. H. U. 1714, ord. at Shrewsbury 1723, father of Jacob who gra. H. U. 1748, and who was ord. at Waltham, and whose s. John, gra. H. U. 1764, was minister of Ashburnham, and had a s. John of Boston who m. Julia Keith 1795 and died 1806, and had Julia Ann and Mary Keith.—Jael m. John Lazell of Hingham.

13. Hon. John (s. of John 7.) of Scituate m. Deborah, D. of Thomas Loring of Hull, 1687 : she d. 1713 ; he 1737 : he was Chief Just. of the Inferior Court of Plymouth, Counsellor, and then Justice of the S. J. Court : he had Sarah 1687, Deborah 1693, John 1695, Elijah 1697, Mary 1700*, Nazareth 1703, Benjamin 1706, Nathaniel 1709 : he m. a 2d wife Sarah Holmes (a wid. perhaps, and D. of Capt. John Thaxter) 1714, and had Josiah 1715, and Mary 1716. Deborah m. Capt. John Briggs Jr. 1712, and her D. Deborah m. Thos. Savage Esq. of Boston,

and was grandmother of the Hon. James Savage.—Nazareth m. Benjamin Balch of Boston, and was mother of Nathaniel Balch " of facetious memory."—Nathaniel gra. H. U. 1728, read law in Boston, where he m. Mary Pemberton 1729, and died in one month after.

14. Hon. Thomas (s. of Hon. John 7.) m. Deborah, D. of Capt. John Thaxter, 1687, settled in Boston, and d. 1740 : he had John 1688, Thomas 1693, Jonathan 1701, Hannah 1702, w. of Thomas Hill; Margaret 1696, who m. a Fletcher ; Elizabeth 1691, wife of John Wingate ; Deborah 1699, w. of Jona. Watson; Samuel 1704, and others perhaps. Among the heirs who signed a receipt in the settlement of the estate in 1647 were the names of Jonathan, Jonathan (clerk), Peter, and William. Jona. Cushing's estate was settled in Boston by wid. Margaret Newman 1773.—Thomas Esq. (s. of Thos.) gra. H. U. 1711, lived in Boston, was Speaker of the H. of Rep. 1724, m. Mary Broomfield, and d. 1746, and had 2 ss. Thomas and Edward, and a D. Mary. Edward gra. H. U. 1746, and died 1752, not m. probably.—Hon. Thomas (s. of the last Thomas) of Boston gra. H. U. 1744, was the famous patriot, Member of Congress, Commissary General, and Lieut. Governor : m. Deborah Fletcher 1747, and died 1788 : and had Thomas, Edward, Mary who m. an Avery, Margaret, and Deborah who m. a Newman.

15. Matthew (s. of Hon. John 7.) m. Deborah, D. of Capt. John Jacob probably: he d. 1715 : he had Jacob 1695, Matthew Deborah, Hezekiah, Rachel, Josiah, Sarah, and Noah. Hezekiah Cushing d. 1781, leaving a wife Lydia, and 3 ss. Matthew, Thomas, and Nathaniel. Rachel m. Thomas Croade Esq.— Jacob was probably father of Col. Charles Cushing of Lunenburgh, whose s., the Hon. Edmund Cushing, is father of Luther S. Cushing Esq. Clerk of the House of Representatives.

16. Jeremiah (s. of Hon. John 7.) Deane says " we believe Jeremiah left no family." Jeremiah Cushing m. Judith Parmenter at Boston 1693, and we find also wid. Ann Cushing of Boston made her will 1759, and named her children thus : Jeremiah, Mary Wheaton, Susanna w. of Jonathan Stoddard, and Hannah. How these were connected, or if at all, with Jeremiah first above named, we cannot say.—[See Jeremiah 42.]

17. James (s. of Hon. John 7.) was Town Clerk of Scituate, and had a s. James who m. Sarah House 1710 and Lydia Barrell 1713. James Jr. had a s. James who m. Mary Souther of Cohasset 1739, and a D. Lydia who m. George Cushing, and another D. who m. a Lapham.

18. Rev. Caleb (s. of Hon. John 7.) gra. H. U. 1692, ord. at Salisbury 1697, m. Elizabeth, D. of Rev. John Cotton and wid. of Rev. James Alling of Salisbury, and d. 1752 : he had James, Minister of Plaistow, N. H., gra. H. U. 1725, and John,‑Minister of Boxford. Hon. Caleb, Member of Congress from Essex, is also a descendant.

19. Dea. Joseph (s. of Hon. John 7.) was a magistrate and

respectable man, m. Mary Pickles 1710, and had a s. Joseph who
gra. H. U. 1731, and was a Latin Schoolmaster in Scituate.
20. Benjamin (s. of Hon. John 7.) settled in Boston, and was
a member of the Ancient and Hon. Artillery Company 1700.
Deane says " we have not learnt that he left any family." There
was a Benjamin Cushing who gave a power of attorney dated at
Barbadoes 1702. There was also a Benjamin Cushing died at
Boston 1792, who m. Mary Colesworthy, and left Benj., Thomas,
Henry, Stephen, Josiah, Jonathan, Susanna wife of John Withington and afterwards of Solomon Bryant of Mid'o., and Nancy
w. of Joshua Bowcker of Scituate. Samuel Colesworthy Jr. and
Benjamin, Adm'rs. Benjamin m. Abigail Callender 1799 and
d. leaving two Ds. Betsy and Susanna, and the wid. m. Samuel
Jepson.—Thomas died in Boston leaving Thomas, George W.,
Solomon Bryant, and John.—Henry also died in Boston leaving
Henry W. and others.—Stephen lives in Ashburnham.—Josiah has
no children.—Jonathan of the firm of Cushing & Ames, Boston,
m. Sally, D. of Nathan Lazell Esq. of S. B. 1809, and has a
family.—Benjamin, who d. 1792, had a brother Ebenezer, who d.
after him and left Jonathan, Benjamin, Mary, and Hannah.—
Whether any of these last were descendants of Benjamin, at the
head of them, we cannot say. Perhaps Benjamin and Ebenezer
were ss. of Jonathan, s. of Hon. Thomas 14.
21. Capt. Stephen (s. of Peter 8.) of Hingham m. Catharine
Kilby of Boston 1719, and had Stephen, Catharine who m. a
Nichols, Lydia, Hannah who m. a Nichols, Rebecca, John, and
Peter. John d. 1754 leaving no children.—Peter d. 1784 leav-
ing a w. Silence : he had John, Peter, Christopher, Catharine,
Martin, Samuel, Hannah, Lydia, and Ned.
22. Elisha (s. of Daniel 9.) of Hingham m. Leah, D. of Thos.
Loring (she was b. 1688, and her mother was Leah, D. of Benj.
Buckley), and had Elisha, John, and Elizabeth w. of Col. Edw.
Mitchell of E. B., m. 1738. Elisha, the father, d. 1734, æ. 52,
and his wid. m. Jabez Wilder. Elisha, the son, d. 1786.
23. Moses (s. of Daniel 9.) and his w. Lydia had Lucy 1738,
Catharine 1742, Elizab. and Deborah twins 1743, Deborah d. 1745.
24. Adam Esq. (s. of Theophilus 11.) gra. H. U. 1714, lived
in Weymouth, m. Hannah (Greenwood perhaps) died 1751, and
had Greenwood*, Adam, Thomas, Frederick, Beza, and Alithea
w. of Samuel Pratt. Thomas died 1757 leaving a wid. Tabitha
and 2 ss. Regemelick and Er, and a D. Tabitha perhaps.—Frederick d. 1786 leaving a wid. Grace.
25. David (s. of Theophilus 11.) of Hingham m. Rachel Lewis
1718, and had Rachel, Alice, and Hannah : his will 1723.
26. Abel (s. of Theophilus 11.) of Hingham and his w. Mary
had David, Abel, Laban, Mary, and Abigail. Abel d. 1761.—
Laban d. 1760, no children.—David had David, Jonathan, Ruth
wife of Perez Cushing, Molly, Abel (father of the Hon. Abel
Cushing of Boston), Charles, Hosea, Nancy, Jane, Lucy, Elnathan, Josiah, Jerusha, Mabel, and Lydia.
47

27. Seth (s. of Theophilus 11.) m. Lydia Fearing, and had Seth, Ezekiel, Mary, Margaret, and Deborah 1740 who m. Simeon Sampson.

28. Dea. Solomon (s. of Matthew 12.) of Hingham m. Sarah, D. of Thomas and Leah Loring, 1716 : she d. 1765; he 1769 : he had Mary 1717, Matthew 1720, Solomon 1722*, Benjamin* and Joseph* 1724, Benjamin 1725, Sarah 1727*, Joseph 1728, Isaiah 1730, and Caleb 1732*. Matthew d. at N. York 1779, æ. 58.

29. Samuel (s. of Matthew 12.) and his w. Hannah lived in Cohasset, and had Isaac 1724, Jael 1726 (who m. a Bailey), Samuel 1729, Calvin 1731, Ephraim 1734, Joel 1736, Timothy 1738, Lois 1740, Solomon 1742, Job 1745. Samuel d. 1782, and had Beal, Sarah, Asa, and Samuel. Joel d. in Boston 1796, and his wid. Susanna settled his estate.

30. Hon. John (s. of Hon. John 13.) of Scituate, Judge of the S. J. Court, m. Elizabeth Holmes, D. of his father's 2d w., 1718, and had Deborah 1718, Sarah 1720 never m., John 1722: she d. 1726, and he m. Mary, D. of Josiah Cotton of Plymouth 1729, and had Mary 1730, William, March 1, 1732, Charles 1734, Hannah 1738, Bethiah 1740, Lucy 1745, Abigail 1748 d. single 1824, Rowland 1750 gra. H. U. 1768 an Attorney in Pownalboro and d. 1789 without children. John, the father, d. 1778, æ. 82. Deborah m. David Stockbridge.—Mary m. Rev. Ebenezer Gay of Suffield.—Hannah m. Rev. Samuel Baldwin of Hanover.—Bethiah m. Abraham Burbank Esq. of West Springfield.—Lucy m. Thomas Aylwin Esq. of Boston.

31. Elijah (s. of Hon. John 13.) m. Elizabeth Barker 1724, and settled in Pembroke, and had Elijah, Nathaniel, Joseph, Mary wife of Gen. Benja. Lincoln, Deborah w. of Rev. Daniel Shute of Hingham, Elizabeth w. of Maj. Cushing of Hingham. Elijah had Elijah who died at Natches, Thomas, Isaac, and Edward.—Nathaniel had Nathaniel Esq., Capt. Benjamin, Thos., and Charles Esq.—Joseph was Judge of Probate, and had Horatio Esq. of Hanover.—Nathaniel Jr. Esq. had Dr. Ezekiel D. gra. H. U. 1808, and Elijah.

32. Josiah (s. of John 13.) m. Ruth Thomas, and settled in Pembroke, and was father of Capt. Josiah, Ruth w. of Hawkes Cushing, and others perhaps.

33. Rev. John (s. of Caleb 18.) gra. H. U. 1729, and was ord. in Boxford, m. Elizabeth Martyn at Boston 1740, and had John gra. H. U. 1761, and went to Freeport, Me.; and Rev. James, minister of North Haverhill, whom the Rev. Giles Merrill succeeded, and whose D. he m.; she was mother of James C. Merrill Esq., Justice of the Police Court, Boston.

34. Dea. Joseph (only s. of Dea. Joseph 19.) gra. H. U. 1731, a grammar schoolmaster in Scituate, m. Lydia King 1732, and had Joseph 1733 gra. H. U. 1752*, George 1736, Mercy 1739, Nathan 1742, Pickles 1743, Hawkes 1744, Dr. Lemuel 1746 gra. H. U. 1767, Deborah 1752, Caleb and Alice 1754. George m.

Lydia, D. of James Cushing, and had Hannah w. of Perez Turner, George, Robert late of Hull, Rachel w. of Pickles Cushing Jr., Mary wife of Dea. James Loring of Boston, and Lydia. Nathan, Judge of the Supreme Judicial Court, graduated H. University 1763, m. Abigail, D. of Christopher Tilden Esq. of Boston, 1777, and d. 1812 : he had Abigail w. of the Hon. Dr. Cushing Otis, Christopher Esq. (gra. H. U. 1794, m. Lucy Nichols 1817, and died 1819, and the wid. m. the Hon. Wilkes Wood) and Frances w. of Capt. Lemuel Cushing of Roxbury. Pickles m. Abigail Hatch 1768, and had Joseph, Pickles, Bela, Charles, Martin, Roland, Lucy, Abigail, and Sarah.—Hawkes m. Ruth, D. of Josiah Cushing, 1770, and had Dea. Thomas who d. 1825, Ruth, Maj. Isaac who d. in Boston, Sarah w. of Samuel Waterman, Capt. Lemuel of Roxbury, Nancy wife of George Cushing Jr., Clarissa w. of Dea. Joseph Stevens of Boston, and Charlotte w. of Col. Vose of the U. S. A.—Alice m. Nathaniel Cushing of Hingham, who settled in Scituate, and had Nathaniel who m. Jane D. of Hayward Pierce Esq., Deborah w. of John Nash, Betsy, Warren of New Bedford, Samuel late of Boston, Mary w. of Bela Cushing late of Boston, and Chauncy who d. 1813 æ. 19.

35. John (s. of Hon. John 30.) lived in Scituate, and had John of Berwick, Dea. Francis of Maine, and Nathaniel who died on the paternal estate 1825.

36. Dea. Benjamin (s. of Dea. Solomon 28.) m. Ruth, D. of Thomas Croade Esq. of Halifax, 1753, and lived in Hingham: she d. 1803. æ. 67; he 1812, æ. 87: he had William 1754, Rachel 1755, Benjamin 1758, Solomon 1760, Thomas Croade 1764, Matthew 1768, Charlotte 1771, Caleb 1773 d. at Charleston, S. C., 1795, Joshua 1775, Henry 1777, Jerom 1780. Rachel m. Ezra Lincoln and d. 1797.—Matthew d. at Mid'o. 1821, leaving a family.—Thomas C. d. in Salem 1824, leaving 5 ch.—Joshua d. in Lynn.—Jerom d. in Hingham 1824, leaving 2 or 3 ch.

37. Joseph (s. of Dea. Solomon 28.) m. Sarah Leavitt 1757, and had Sarah 1757, Hannah 1760, Mary 1761, Jael 1764, Lydia 1770. His w. d. 1771, and he then m. Deborah Beal 1779, and had Joseph 1782.

38. Judge William (s. of Hon. John 30.) gra. H. U. 1751, C. Justice of S. J. C. of Mass., and then Judge of the S. C. of the U. S.; m. Hannah Phillip of Middletown, Conn., 1774, and d. 1810, his wife surviving, but no children.

39. Col. Charles (s. of Hon. John 30.) gra. H. U. 1755, Clerk of the Courts in Boston, m. Elizabeth, sister of Gov. Increase Sumner, and d. 1810; his only son Charles Esq. gra. H. U. 1796, went to Portsmouth, and the Ds. m. Charles Paine, Henry Sheafe, Stephen Codman, and Elisha Doane, Esqrs.

40. Benjamin (s. of Dea. Benjamin 36.) m. Lydia, D. of John Beal, 1781, and had Charlotte 1783 at Hingham, Lydia 1790 at Halifax, Benja. 1794 at Hal. Charlotte m. Josiah Sturtevant of Halifax 1804, and had Rolinda 1806 at Pembroke, N. H. (w. of

Welcome Young Esq. of E. B.) and Josiah 1806*: she m. Eben'r
Eastman, a 2d husband, 1816, and had Josiah S. 1817, Charlotte
C. 1820, John B. 1823, Charles C. 1825.—Lydia m. Timothy Gile
1818.—Benjamin m. wid. Elizabeth Furnald 1815, and had John
Beal 1816*, Lydia Beal 1817, Elizabeth Moore 1820: by a 2d w.
he had John Beal, Charlotte Jane, and Mary Gile. The family is
now principally in N. H.

41. Thomas Cushing m. Mercy Bridgham 1712: her will at
Boston 1746 mentions 3 children, Joseph Bridgham, Elizabeth
w. of Samuel Holyoke, and Mercy w. of John Smith.

42. Jeremiah (Jeremiah 16, no doubt) who m. Judith Parmenter at Boston 1793, had Jeremiah 1696, Benjamin 1700, John
1705, Ebenezer 1710. Jeremiah was no doubt the husband of
the wid. Ann there mentioned, as the records furnish a Jeremiah
who m. Ann Coffin in 1715, and a Jeremiah who m. Ann Mor-
temore 1723.—Benjamin m. Elizabeth Roberts 1725, and had
Judith 1726, Benjamin 1729, Nathaniel 1731, Jeremiah 1733.—
John m. Sarah Colesworthy 1727, and had Sarah 1727.—Ebenezer m. Elizabeth Daniel 1732, and had Ebenezer 1735.—Benjamin Cushing m. Susanna Salter 1761, and had Benjamin and
Susanna: he then m. Mary Colesworthy 1770, and had Thomas
1772*, Nancy 1774*, Thomas 1776, Henry 1778, Josiah 1780,
Nancy 1782, Stephen 1784, and Jonathan 1786.—[See Jeremiah
16; and compare this also with Benjamin 20.]

43. Theophilus (s. of Theophilus 11.) of Hingham m. Hannah
Waterman probably 1723, and d. a widower 1778: he had Theophilus, Perez, Pyam dec'd, Emma w. of John Burr, and Tamar
w. of Elisha Cushing of Pembroke dec'd, whose children were
Elisha, Tamar, and Tamsin.

44. Pyam (s. of Theophilus 43.) d. 1776, leaving a wid. Hannah: he had Pyam, Robert, Henry, Seth, Hannah, Deborah,
Tamar, and Tamsin. Pyam Jr. lived with Col. Edward Mitchell
in E. B., and died 1778, and in his will dated Jan. 4th, the same
year, he gave a legacy to Mary, D. of Col. Mitchell, "his intended wife." She afterwards m. James Keith, and is now living
in the State of New York, æ. 86, and has a numerous family.—
[See Keith, p. 214, No. 57.]

45. Jonathan and Bethiah Cushing had Jeremiah 1761, Phebe
1762, Mary 1766, Sarah 1770, Benjamin 1772.

Rev. Jona. Cushing m. Elizabeth Cushing 1717.—Nathaniel
m. Mary Pemberton 1729.—John m. Abigail Holder 1741.—
Benjamin m. Susanna Salter 1761.—Jonathan m. Huldah Edes
1777.—Benjamin m. Betsy Godfrey 1788.—Benjamin Esq., Benjamin Jr., and Ann (single), all of Providence, convey land in
Chelsea 1763.—Thomas m. Sally Newell 1799.

The preceding account contains notices, quite imperfect indeed, of but a part of this very numerous and respectable family.

CUSHMAN.—Robert Cushman was among the Plymouth
pilgrims: he set sail from England in the ship called the Speed-
well in company with the May Flower in 1620, but by reason of

leakage the ship put back, and he came the next year, 1621, in
the ship Fortune : he remained here but about one month, when
he returned to England and d. a. 1625 or 1626 : his family came
after his death, and his descendants are now numerous in the
country. He was author of the primitive lay Sermon.

Thomas (s. of the above) born 1607, lived in Governor Bradford's family, having been left there by his father when he sailed
for Eng.; m. Mary, D. of Isaac Allerton : he d. 1691 ; she 1699 :
he had Thomas, Isaac 1649, Elkanah, Eleazar, Sarah, and Lydia.
Isaac was the first minister of Plympton, and d. 1732.—Sarah
m. a Mr. Hook.—Lydia m. a Mr. Harlow.

DELANO.—Philip Delano came over in the second ship, the
Fortune, 1621, was in Duxbury between 1645 and 1650, and one
of the original proprietors of Bridgewater, and sold his share to
Nicholas Byram. The name on the early records was sometimes
written De la Noye, hence he was supposed to be of French origin, and one of the French protestants, who attached himself to
the pilgrims at Leyden, and came over with them. He m. Hester Dewsberry, and had Samuel, Thomas, and John, and was
probably ancestor of the numerous families of the name still
residing at Duxbury, and other towns both in the counties of
Plymouth and Bristol, as well as in other parts of the country.

EATON.—Samuel Eaton was one of the original proprietors
of Bridgewater, was no doubt son of Francis Eaton, who came
over in the May Flower 1620, whose wife was Christian, and
whose children were in 1627. Samuel and Rachel. Samuel settled probably in Duxbury : he must have been there between
1645 and 1650.—Francis had afterwards other children doubtless, and his descendants are still in Middleborough and various
other towns and sections of the country.

FAUNCE.—John and Manasseh Faunce arrived at Plymouth
in the third ship, the Ann, in 1623. We have met with no further notice of Manasseh.

John Faunce m. Patience, D. of George Morton, and had
Thomas 1646, and Priscilla, and perhaps others. Priscilla m.
Joseph Warren about 1650.—Mary Faunce m. William Harlow
1658.—Mercy Faunce m. Nathaniel Holmes 1662.—These two
might also have been Ds. of John.

Thomas (s. of the above) was the distinguished Elder of Plymouth Church, and d. 1745 very aged : he had Patience 1673,
John 1678, Martha 1680. Many descendants of these respectable ancestors are remaining in different parts of the County.

FORD.—William Ford was one of the original proprietors of
Bridgewater ; was son no doubt of wid. Ford, who arrived in the
Fortune 1621 with three children, viz : William, Martha, and
John ; and it is said she had a son born the day the ship arrived :
how long had she been a widow ? William Ford sen'r, on the
military-roll at Marshfield 1643, d. 1676, æ. 72 ; his wid. Anna :
his children were William, Michael, Margaret, and Milicent ;
one of them wife of John Carver ; his grand children were John,

and William Ford, and John Carver.—Martha, D. of wid. Ford,
m. Wm. Nelson 1640.—William Ford, the proprietor of Bridgewater, whoever he was, must have been in Duxbury between
1645 and 1650. The name is still common in Marshfield, Abington, and other parts of the County.

HALL.—Edward Hall, one of the original proprietors of
Bridgewater, was of course an inhabitant of Duxbury before
1650. We have no particular account of him or his family.—
Joseph Hall of Yarmouth m. wid. Mary Morton, relict of John
Morton : she was a Faunce : Morton died of a grievous wound
1709. The name is still common in the old colony. There was
an Edward Hall at Cambridge 1636.

HOBART.—Edmund Hobart with his wife and son Joshua,
and Ds. Rebeckah and Sarah, and his servant Henry Gibbs,
came from Hingham, Old England, and settled here in Hingham,
New England, 1633 : his ss. Edmund, Thomas, and Rev. Peter,
also soon followed him, the two former the same year, and the
last in 1635 : they first lived in Charlestown ; but when the Rev.
Peter arrived with a number of his church, they soon began to
explore the country, and went up a small river at the bottom of
Boston Bay, now called Hingham Cove, where they found a few
of their friends, whom they immediately joined, being pleased
with the situation, and at once concluded to settle there, and
called the place Hingham, from whence the Hobart family had
all come excepting Thomas, who came from a place called
Windham, near old Hingham : he d. 1646; she 1649 : her name
is not given. One of the Ds. m. a Beal, and a sister of Edmund
sen'r. m. a Gilman (probably Edward). The Rev. Peter in his
church records speaks of his father and mother Hobart, and
David, son of Peter, who continued the records after his father
Peter's death, mentions his great aunt Gilman, and the deaths of
his uncle Edmund and Thomas (and their wives, calling them
also his aunts), whence we are confirmed in the knowledge of
their being sons of Edmund sen'r.

2. Edmund (s. of the above) with his wife Elizabeth arrived
in 1633 : she d. 1675 ; he Feb. 1686, æ. 82 ; his will, dated 1684,
calls himself Weaver : their children were Elizabeth, Sarah 1640,
John 1642, Samuel 1645, Martha 1647, Daniel 1649. Elizabeth
m. John Tucker 1657.—Sarah m. Return Manning 1664, and
had a D. Mary.—John m. Hannah Burr 1674 and died, and his
wife settled his estate 1675 : he had one only child Hannah.—
Samuel m. Hannah Gould 1674, and died 1718, æ. 74, and had
Edmund 1674, Samuel 1677*, Hannah 1679*, Samuel 1681*
drowned in a well, Hannah 1683, Peter 1685.—Martha m. Joseph
Basset of Bridgewater 1677.—Mary Hobart 1638 who m. John
Hugh 1664 might also have been his D.

3. Thomas (s. of Edmund 1.) with his wife Jane and three
children came over 1633, and settled in Hingham : he d. 1689,
æ. 83 ; his w. d. 1690 : he had Caleb 1632, Joshua 1639, Thomas
1649, Mehitabel 1651, Isaac 1653, Hannah 1655, Moses 1656,

Aaron 1661, Nathaniel 1665. Caleb settled his father's estate
(de bonis non) 1690.—Mehitabel m. John Lane 1674.—John
Magoun was his son-in-law.—Hannah m. John Records 1672.—
Moses died in prison at Boston 1686.—Aaron's w. was Rebecca,
and undertook the settlement of her husband's estate in 1705,
and completed it in 1724, and then called herself Rebecca Derby wid. of Edward Derby of Weymouth dec'd, and mentions 2
ss. only, Isaac and Aaron Hobart: Aaron died 1726, æ. 23, unmarried, and Isaac settled his estate 1726.—Thomas, by the consent of his father Thomas, puts himself an apprentice to John
Nash of Boston, cooper, 1670.—Joshua Hobart and his w. Mary
(her former husband was Jona. Rainsford) of Boston, quit her
right to her former husband's estate 1674 : he died in Braintree
1713, no ch.
  4. Rev. Peter (s. of Edmund 1.) with his w. Rebeckah and 4
ch. came over in 1635, and settled in Hingham : he d. 1679, æ.
75 ; she in 1693, æ. 73 : his will 1678, proved 1679 : if this is
correct he was 16 years the eldest : he speaks of his mother
Ibrook's death 1664, it may be therefore that his w. was an Ibrook :
he had Ichabod 1635* at Charlestown, Hannah 1637*, Hannah
1638, Bathsheba 1640, Israel 1642, Jael 1643, Gershom 1645,
Japhet 1647, Nehemiah 1648, David 1651, Rebeckah 1654, Abigail 1656, Lydia 1659, all born here : the 4 children who came
with him were Joshua 1628, Jeremiah 1630, Elizabeth 1632,
Josiah 1633 ; in all 17 ch. Joshua was a Minister of Southhold,
L. Island, and died 1717, æ. 89.—Jeremiah gra. H. U. 1650, was
Minister at Topsfield, Hampstead, and Haddam, Conn., and d.
1717, æ. 87.—Elizabeth m. John Ripley, and d. 1692, æ. 60.—
Josiah bought of Ralph Woodward formerly of the city of Dub-
lin, then of Hingham, land in Ireland 1658, and with his wife
Priscilla sold land to one Gross in 1677, and died on L. Island
1711, æ. 78 : he had John, and Daniel, and perhaps others.—
Hannah m. first John Brown and then John Rogers of Salem,
and d. 1691.—Bathsheba or Bashua, first m. John Leavit 1664,
and then m. Dea. Joseph Turner of Scituate, and d. 1724, æ. 84.
Israel d. in Scituate 1731, æ. 89, his will 1729 : his w. was Sarah,
D. of the Rev. Wm. Wethrell of Scituate, m. 1674, and settled
in Scit. 1676, his house in Hingham having just been burnt by
the Indians : he had Nathaniel 1675, Rebecca 1676 b. at Hingham, Nathan and Abigail 1678, Jael 1680, Israel 1682 : in his
will he also mentions Mary Witherton, Grace Davis, and Bathsheba Bradford, children of " my D. Sarah Brock." Jael was
executrix.—Israel Jr. was a householder in 1723, and had Patience, and Grace.—Jael, D. of Rev. Peter, m. Joseph Bradford
of Kingston, and d. 1730, æ. 88.—Gershom gra. 1667, was Minister at Groton ord. 1679, and died 1707, æ. 62 ; Gershom and
Sarah Hobart had a D. Hepzibah 1675.—Japhet gra. 1667, was
lost at sea, a Surgeon.—Nehemiah was Minister of Newton, and
died 1712, æ. 64 : he m. Sarah, D. of Edward Jackson : he sold
land in Hingham commons to his D. Rebeckah in 1712.—David

first m. Joanna Quincy, and then Sarah Joyce of Boston : his
last w. d. 1729, æ. 65, was then a widow : she mentions his ch.
by his first wife, viz : Judith Crocker whose first husband was a
Leavit, Jael Leavit, Abiel Hobart, Rebeckah Nichols : also her
own ch. by him, viz : Sarah w. of John Humphrey, Lydia, Nehemiah, David, Noah.—Rebeckah m. Daniel Mason 1679.—Abigail d. 1683, æ. 26.—Lydia m. Thomas Lincoln 1690, and died
1732, æ. 73.—The wid. Rebeckah, mother of the above named
children, survived her husband, the Rev. Peter Hobart, and made
her will 1693, David executor, and mentions also Nehemiah,
Rebeckah Mason, Lydia Lincoln, Japhet " if he be still living
and shall come in person to demand the legacy," and names no
other of her children.

5. Capt. Joshua (s. of Edmund 1.) came over with his father,
and m. Ellen Ibrook of Cambridge 1638 : he d. 1682, æ. 68 ; she
about 1700 : he had Hannah 1639, Peter 1642, Sarah 1644,
Deborah 1647, Joshua 1650, Solomon 1652, Enoch 1654 : in his
will 1682 he thus names his children, viz : Joshua, Enoch, and
Edward Cowell and Joshua Lincoln sons-in-law, gave to his Ds.
husbands all his lands at a place called by the Indians " Tuncke."
Hannah m. Joseph Grafton 1657.—Peter made a will at Barbadoes 1665, and gives all his estate to his wife Susannah, but if
she should have a child makes provision for it, and mentions his
brother Jacob Elliot. Sarah m. Edward Cowell 1668.—Deborah
m. Joshua Lincoln 1666, and d. 1684, æ. 37.—Joshua and his w.
Faith sold land to Daniel Cushing in 1684, he was a mariner.—
Solomon was a mariner 1683 : he had 2 ch. b., and d. 1682.—
Enoch Hobart, boatman of Boston 1691 : his w. Hannah, D. of
Thomas Harris, m. 1676, and had Hannah 1677*, Ruth 1678,
Hannah 1680, Thomas 1683, Deborah 1685.—Eleanor, Helen
(or Ellen) the mother d. a. 1700, and her estate was settled by
her grandson Joshua Lincoln.—Hannah, D. of Capt. Joshua the
son perhaps, d. 1731.

6. Daniel (s. of Edmund 2.) was a Weaver : he m. first Elizabeth Warren of Boston 1677, and had Ruth 1678, John 1682*,
Joshua 1683, Jeremiah 1684*, Mary 1686, Solomon 1693 : he m.
a 2d wife Patience, and made his will 1704, and mentions only
Joshua, Solomon, and Mary : "in case his now wife should have
a child" he makes provision for it.—Mary m. Isaac Peterson of
Duxbury : he had a D. Patience also who m. David Garnett
1731.—The wid. Patience m. Ibrook Tower 1714.

7. David (s. of the Rev. Peter 4.) m. Joanna, D. of the Hon.
Edmund Quincy, and had Josiah, Rebeckah, Jael, Judith
1681, Peter 1684*, Abiel 1685. He m. Sarah Joyce at Boston
1695, had Nehemiah 1697, Joseph 1699*, David and Sarah 1702,
Lydia 1704, Noah 1706 : his 2d w. d. 1729, æ. 65 ; he d. 1717,
æ. 67. Rebeckah m. Jazaniah Nichols 1714.—Jael m. Jeremiah
Leavit 1712 and d. 1740, æ. 52.—Judith m. Joseph Leavit 1711,
and afterwards a Crocker.—Noah was Minister at Fairfield, Con.,
ord. 1732 : he m. Priscilla, wid. of Isaac Lothrop and of John

Watson Esq. and D. of Caleb Thomas: she died 1796, æ. 90.
[See David under Rev. Peter 4.]

8. Solomon (s. of Daniel 6.) was a Weaver: his will 1736, d. 1737 by falling into the fire in a fit, æ. 44: gave his brother Joshua £5, his sister Peterson two-thirds, and his sister Garnett one-third of his estate. Isaac Peterson ex'or, James Hobart a witness.

9. Rev. Nehemiah (s. of David 7.) was Minister at Cohasset: he m. Lydia Jacob, and had John Jacob 1725*, Sarah 1727, Jerom 1729*, Justin 1731, Lydia 1733, Hannah 1735, John Jacob 1737*. His w. died 1737, æ. 32, and he m. Elizabeth Pratt 1739, and died 1740, æ. 43: his widow gave a receipt to Wm. Penniman ex'or of the will of her honored mother Ruth Thayer for a legacy given her by her mother's will 1742, and she m. Jona. Merrit of Scituate 1742: Hannah æ. 7, and Lydia æ. 9, were put under guardianship of their uncle Jazaniah Nichols: Justin æ. 11, and Sarah æ. 14, were put under guardianship of John Jacob 1741.

10. Isaac (s. of Aaron and grandson of Thomas 3.) settled in Abington: he m. Mary, D. of John Harden, 1724, and had Aaron 1729, Thomas 1725, John 1738, Mary 1735.

11. Caleb (s. of Thomas 3.) settled his father's estate 1690, and settled in Braintree a. 1697: he d. 1711, æ. 89: his 2d wife was Mary Elliot, m. 1662: his 1st w. was Elizabeth Church, m. 1657, she d. 1659: (he had another w., wid. Elizabeth Faxon, m. 1676: his 2d wife Mary died 1675), he had Mary 1663, Caleb 1665, Elizabeth 1666, Benjamin 1677, Hannah 1668, Josiah 1670. Caleb m. Hannah Sanders 1704, but had no children.—Hannah m. Jona. Hayden 1692.—Old wid. Hobart d. in Braintree 1704.

12. Josiah (s. of Caleb 11.) of Braintree m. Mary Cleverly 1695: his 2d w. was Sarah Savil, m. 1719: he d. 1725; his estate was settled 1725: he had Caleb 1696*, Josiah 1697, Mary 1701, she died æ. 26, John 1704, Susanna 1724. John Copeland 1741 called the 1st w. Mary his deceased sister.

13. Benjamin (s. of Caleb 11.) of Braintree m. Susanna Newcomb 1699: she settled his estate 1718; she died 1725: it was divided among his heirs 1727, who were Benjamin, Caleb, Susanna (or Ann), Peter, Israel, Joshua. Wm. Everett of Dedham was their uncle: inventory taken by Josiah Hobart and others.

14. Nathaniel (s. of Thomas 3.): his will 1734: m. wid. Mary Stowell 1695: she was D. of John Beal: no children are mentioned: he gave lands and £100 in money to his cousin (nephew) Isaac Hobart, to Rev. Mr. Gay one-eighth of his saw-mill; mentioned his gr. daughter-in-law Mary Joy; son-in-law John Stowell, and gr. son-in-law Jedediah Joy, ex'ors. In 1689 he sold land to John Lane: David and Lydia Hobart, witnesses.

15. Edmund (s. of Samuel probably and gr. s. of Edmund 2.) m. Abigail, wid. of Ebenezer Whitman of S. Bridgewater 1714: she was a Burnham: he resided with his wife at Bridgewater: was there 1727.

48

16. Rev. Justin (s. of Rev. Nehemiah 9.) was Minister of Fairfield, Conn.; m. Hannah Fairfield of that place 1772, she was b. 1738: he had Ellen 1764, Mary 1765, Jerom 1768*, Noah 1769, Justin 1772, Lydia 1774, Hannah 1777, John Sloss 1781, d. at New York 1803. His wife d. 1809, æ. 71 ; he died 1789. Ellen m. Hezekiah Gold 1786, and had a D. Debby, and Gold was then drowned at New York, and his wid. m. Dr. Stephen Middlebrook of Stratford 1793.—Lydia m. Stephen Beers 1796. Justin m. Desire Burr (b. 1782) of Huntington 1804, and had Rebecca 1806, Jane 1809.

17. David (s. of David 7.) and his w. Rachel had David 1728, and probably Joseph and others : he d. 1780, æ. 72 ; his wife d. 1734. David d. at Cape Breton 1746.

18. Joseph (s. of David 17 probably) m. Sarah Warrick 1750, and had Sarah 1752, Esther 1754, Anna 1755, Rachel 1757, Joseph 1759, Nehemiah 1761, Jeremiah·1763, George 1768, Sibee (or Zibeah) 1770: his w. d. 1783, æ. 53.

19. James Hobart's will 1744, he was b. 1689: his w. Hannah : he named his children thus : James, John, Lydia Bates, and Susanna Todd. Samuel Hobart a witness: whose son he was, not ascertained.

20. Col. Aaron (s. of Isaac 10.) of Abington m. first Elizabeth, D. of Jacob Pillsbury, and had Seth, Nathaniel, Aaron, Noah, Isaac, Elizabeth w. of David Jones Jr., Sarah who m. a Lewis of N. Yarmouth : Nathaniel gra. H. U. 1784, d. 1830, and left no family : Isaac went to Me. His 2d w. was Thankful, wid. of Elihu Adams of Randolph; she was D. of Joseph White Jr.: they had Benjamin, Salome, Thankful, Mary. Salome m. Marcus Alden.—Thankful m. a Perry.—Mary m. a Brigham.— Benjamin Esq. m. Lucy, D. of Gen. Silvanus Lazell, and then Deborah, D. of Capt. Edmund Lazell, and has a family.

21. Thomas (s. of Isaac 10.) m. Jane Bailey, sister of Col. John Bailey of Hanover, and lived in Pembroke (now Hanson), and had Isaac, Thomas, and several Ds. One, Hannah, m. Andrew Leach.—One, Anna, m. Joseph Gannett.—One, Jane, m. Daniel Perry.—One, Polly, m. Thomas Wales.—One, Rachel, m. Jotham Cushman.—One m. a Sawyer.—Sarah m. Nehemiah Thayer 1785, and d. 1792.—One m. a Sayles.

22. John (s. of Isaac 10.) of Abington m. Mary, D. of Matthew Allen of East Bridgewater, 1765, and had John Esq. who settled in Leicester. He died, and his wid. Mary m. a Bearce.

23. Seth (s. of Col. Aaron 20.) of E. Bridgewater m. Esther, D. of Jonathan Allen of Braintree, 1782, and had Betsy 1783, Jacob 1784*, Jonathan 1786, Seth 1788*, Polly 1790, Eunice 1795*, Joseph 1796, Esther 1798, Allen 1801*: she d. 1813; he 1814.

24. Aaron Esq. (s. of Col. Aaron 20.) of Abington m. Susanna, D. of Peter Adams, and had Aaron, Elihu, Susan, Sally, Abby. Honorable Aaron m. Maria, D. of Andrew Leach, and has Susan, Aaron, George, Maria, Edward, John, Catharine.—Elihu

has also a family.—Susan m. a Hayden, and then Jared Whitman
Esq.—Sally and Abby both m. Dr. Champney.
    25. Noah Esq. (s. of Col. Aaron 20.) of Foxborough m. Deb-
orah W., D. of James Thomas 1789 : she lived with her grand-
father Anthony Winslow in East Bridgewater, her father died
when she was young : he had James T., Nathaniel, Aaron,
Albert, Deborah, Jane. Nathaniel was lost in the steamboat
Lexington 1840.—[See Hobart p. 188.]
    Sarah Cleverly, D. of Capt. John Hobart, d. in Boston 1696.
There was a Solomon Hobart born 1689.—[See Thayer's family
Memorial for a further account of the Hobart family.]
    HOWLAND.—John Howland came over in the 1st ship 1620 :
his wife Elizabeth, D. of Gov. John Carver, and two children,
John and Desire, came afterwards, 1627 : he was one of the
Governor's Assistants many years, and a very respectable and
useful man in the infant Colony : he died 1672 at Rocky Nook,
near Kingston, æ. a. 80, on which occasion it is recorded " that
he was the last of the male survivors of those who came over in
the May Flower in 1620, and whose place of abode was Plymouth." By not attending to the last words of this extract
Farmer in his Appendix, as well as others, have been drawn into
a seeming doubt. Howland was only the last of these pilgrims,
who lived and died in Plymouth. John Alden certainly in Duxbury, and perhaps others of them out of Plymouth, survived
Howland. Alden outlived him 15 years. Howland had John
who m. Mary Lee and settled in Barnstable, Jabez who m.
Bethiah Thacher of Yarmouth and finally settled in Bristol and
who was an early Lieutenant under Capt. Standish, Joseph who
m. Elizabeth only child of Thos. Southworth 1664 and lived in
Plymouth, Isaac who m. Elizabeth D. of George Vaughn and
settled in Mid'o. and d. there 1724, Desire who m. John Gorham
1643 who lived in Plymouth, Marshfield, Barnstable and Swansey where he d. 1675, æ. 54, Hope who m. John Chipman of
Plymouth and then of Barnstable, Elizabeth who m. Ephraim
Hicks of Plymouth and then John Dickerson of Barnstable,
Lydia who m. James Brown of Swansey, Hannah who m. a
Bozworth of Hull or Swansey, and Ruth who m. Thos. Cushman of Plymo. 1664.—Isaac Howland had Isaac, Seth, Nathan,
Priscilla Bennet, Susanna Wood, Jael Southworth, and Elizabeth Tinkham.
    Joseph (s. of John) m. Elizabeth, only child of Thos. South-
worth, 1664, and had Thomas, James, Lydia, Mercy, Eliza,
Nathaniel.
    Thomas (s. of Joseph) m. Joanna, D. of James Cole, 1699,
and had Consider 1700, Experience 1705, Thomas 1707, Elizabeth 1710, Hannah 1712, Joanna 1716, Joseph 1718. Experience
m. Benja. Lothrop.—Hannah m. Charles Dyer, and afterwards
Edward Winslow.—Joanna m. Gideon White 1744 : he d. 1779.
    Nathaniel (s. of Joseph) m. Martha, D. of James Cole, 1697,
and had Joseph 1699, Mary 1702, Nathaniel 1705, Joseph 1708.

Consider (s. of Thomas) m. Ruth Bryant 1725 (born 1704), and had Lucy 1726, Eliza 1728, Ruth 1730, Mary 1732, Thos. Southworth 1734 d. 1779, Consider 1735 d. 1743, Joanna 1737 d. 1799, Martha 1739, Bethiah 1743, Consider 1745 d. 1780, Experience 1748, Joseph 1751 d. 1806, Hannah 1753 d. 1780: he d. 1759, she 1775. Lucy m. Abraham Hammatt 1748.—Ruth m. Benjamin Crandon.—Mary m. Dr. William Thomas, whose 2d w. was a Bridgham.—Martha m. Isaac Le Baron.—Experience m. Samuel West.—Bethiah m. a Delano.

Henry Howland was among the first proprietors of Bridgewater, and of course at Duxbury at that period. It is said he and Arthur Howland of Marshfield, 1643, were distinct families from John of Plymouth, and we have no very particular knowledge of their families: their descendants are however no doubt among those of the name living in the lower towns in the county, and the name is common throughout the old colony. Deborah, D. of Arthur, m. John Smith of Plymouth 1648.—Martha Howland m. John Damon of Scituate, his 2d w. 1659.—A Collins of Lynn m. a Howland.—Consider Howland of Marshfield m. Ruth Church 1795, and removed to Scituate and had a son Luther.

HUNT.—Edmund Hunt was at Duxbury before 1650, and a proprietor of Bridgewater, and sold his right to Samuel Edson. We have no further account of him or of his family. The name remains in the county, but whether his descendants are here or not we are not certain.

IRISH.—John Irish was an original proprietor of Bridgewater, and John and George Irish were both at Duxbury before 1658, and were both among the first planters of Saconet. John Irish of Duxbury, roper, with the consent of his wife Elizabeth, sold his share in the new Plantation of Satucket (Bridgewater) to Guido Bailey 1659, and went to Little Compton. He d. 1677, and his son John Irish m. a sister of the famous Capt. Church: another s. Elias, settled in Taunton.

LORING.—Dea. Thomas Loring was early at Hingham ; had a grant of land there 1635; his house was burnt 1646, d. at Hull 1661, his heirs divided the estate 1672 : his w. Jane died 1672, leaving a will : his children were Thomas, John, Josiah, and Benjamin 1644 : no Ds. mentioned either in the division or her will.

2. Thomas (s. of the above) m. Hannah, D. of Nicholas Jacob, 1657 : she was b. 1639 : he lived in Hull, and had Thomas, Caleb, David, Hannah 1665, and Deborah 1669. He d. 1678, and his widow m. Stephen French : his heirs divided the estate 1702. Hannah m. Jeremiah Cushing 1685.—Thomas m. Deborah, D. of John Cushing Esq. 1699, and lived in Plymouth.—Deborah m. John Cushing Jr. 1687, and d. 1713.

3. John (s. of Dea. Thomas 1.) m. Mary, D. of Nath'l Baker, 1657, lived in Hull, had John 1658, Joseph 1660, Thomas 1662, Sarah 1664, Isaac 1666, Mary 1668, Nathaniel, and Daniel. He m. a 2d w. Rachel, and had Jacob, Israel April 15, 1682, Caleb,

and Sarah: his will 1708, proved 1714. Joseph and Isaac died before him, each leaving 4 children.—Mary m. a Jones and was his only surviving D.—He mentioned Israel "having been brought up to learning," who gra. H. U. 1701, and was ord. at Sudbury 1706, and d. 1772, æ. 90.—Nathaniel lived in Boston.

4. Josiah (s. of Dea. Thomas 1.) m. Elizabeth (perhaps D. of John Otis): his will 1712: had Jane 1663, Josiah 1665, Samuel 1668 d. 1774, Job 1670, Elizabeth 1672, Jonathan ex'or. 1674. Jane m. Samuel Gifford.

5. Benjamin (s. of Dea. Thomas 1.) m. Mary, D. of Matthew Hawke, 1670, lived in Hull probably, and had Mary, Matthew, Benjamin, John, and Samuel: the heirs divided his estate 1716. Mary m. James Gould.—Matthew m. Jane, D. of Lieut. Thos. Collier of Hull, and d. 1722 leaving no children.

6. John (s. of John 3): his w. Jane; his will 1719, mentions his "children and his eldest son" but gives no names: John, supposed to be one, chose his uncle Caleb for his guardian 1728.

7. Joseph (s. of John 3.) m. Hannah, D. of John Leavitt 1683, and had Joseph 1684, Nehemiah 1686, Joshua 1688, Submit Aug. 1691 after her father's death. The wid. m. Joseph Eastabrook 1693, and all the children were put under their guardianship. Hannah Dorr settled the estate of her former husband, Joshua Loring late of Boston, 1723, and his children, Abigail, Hannah, and Joshua, minors, were put under guardianship 1729.

8. Thomas (s. of John 3.) m. Leah, D. of Benjamin Buckley, 1687 (Buckley was killed in the disastrous battle with the Indians near Rehoboth): his will 1737: he had Benjamin, Leah 1688, and Sarah. Leah m. Elisha Cushing and afterwards Jabez Wilder, and her D. Elizabeth Cushing m. Col. Edward Mitchell of E. B. 1738.—Sarah m. Solomon Cushing 1716.

9. Daniel of Boston (s. of John 3.) m. a Mann, and had Daniel, Isaac, Nathaniel, and Priscilla, all under his guardianship 1715, that he might take care of the property that came to them from their grandmother Deborah Mann.

10. David (of Hull): his will 1751: he had David, Solomon, Elizabeth, Mary, Abigail, and Lydia.

11. John (of Hull): his will 1753: he had James, Sarah White, Elizabeth Binney, and Hannah Loring.

12. Jacob (of Hull): his children, Jacob, Israel, and Zechariah, divide his estate 1753: his wid. Hannah: Jacob died 1769 without ch.

13. Caleb (of Hull): his children, Caleb, Mary, Joshua, Israel, Joseph, Susanna Watts, Sarah Lincoln, Rebecca Rooke, Rachel, and Celia, divide his estate 1758.

14. Solomon (his will 1765) and his w. Deborah: he had Solomon, Jabez, Job, Abner, Lydia, and Mary.

15. James (of Hull) died 1777: his wife Mary : he had John, Martha, James, Mary, and Joseph.

16. Israel (of Boston) d. 1778: his wid. Mary : he had Israel, Thomas, Eunice, and Betsy.

17. David (of Hull): his will 1781 : his w. Hannah : he had Jonathan, Joseph, Benjamin, Mary White, Hannah Beals, Anna Sergeant, and Jane Cushing, and gr. ch. David, Sarah, Mary, and Hannah.

18. Thomas (of Hingham): his will 1795 : his wid. Sarah D. of Dea. Joshua Hersey : her mother was Alice, wid. of Edward Mitchell of E. B. and D. of Major John Bradford of Kingston. [See p. 242, No. 4.] He had Jane, Jotham, Thomas, Asa, Rachel, and Christiana : his wid. d. 1798. Jane m. a Thaxter.— Col. Jotham lived in Duxbury.—Thomas was father of the present Thomas Loring Esq. Representative of Hingham.

John Loring and Elizabeth his wife, Samuel Loring and Jane his wife, Caleb Loring Esq. and Rebecca his wife, Benjamin Loring and Elizabeth his wife, David Loring and Hannah his w. sold and conveyed Rainsford Island to William Foye Treasurer of the Commonwealth 1736 : perhaps these were ss. of John 6; but it is not ascertained.

The foregoing is but a sketch and brief notice of a few of the very numerous and respectable familes of this name, now widely extended over the country, and all probably descendants of Dea. Thomas.

MERRICK.—William Merrick was an inhabitant of Duxbury before 1650, and one of the first proprietors of Bridgewater, and we have no further knowledge of him. Some of the name have resided on the Cape.

MORTON.—George Morton arrived at Plymouth 1623 in the third ship, the Ann. He and Experience Mitchell in the first allotment of land in 1623 had eight acres together : his w. Sarah was supposed to be sister of Gov. Bradford : he d. 1624 : his ch. were Nathaniel, John, Patience, Ephraim, and Sarah. Patience m. John Faunce father of Thomas Faunce (the distinguished Elder of Plymouth Church, who d. 1745).—Sarah m. George Bonum or Bonham.

2. Nathaniel (son of George 1.) was the Secretary of the Colony, and the worthy author of New England's Memorial : he m. Lydia Cooper 1635, who d. 1673, and he then m. Ann Templar : he had no son, but had 6 Ds. One, Remember, b. 1637, m. Abraham Jackson 1657 ; one m. a Dunham ; one, Joanna, m. Joseph Prince of Hull ; one, Elizabeth, m. Nathaniel Bozworth of Hull ; one, Lydia, m. George Ellison ; and another m. a Bozworth : he d. June 28, 1685.

3. John (s. of George 1.) went to Middleboro' and was ancestor of a numerous family.

4. Ephraim (s. of George 1.) was a Lieutenant and Deacon : he d. 1693, and left a wid. Mary Harlow : she afterwards m. Hugh Cole 1698 : when last m. she was called wid. of Ephraim Morton Esq.: Morton's children were George, Ephraim, Nathaniel, Josiah, Eleazar, Thomas, Patience who m. John Nelson, and Rebecca who m. a Wood.

5. George (s. of Ephraim 4.) m. Joanna Kempton, and had

Hannah 1668, Manasseh 1669, Ephraim 1670, Joanna 1673, Ruth 1676, George 1678, and Timothy 1682.

6. Ephraim (s. of Ephraim 4.) had Ephraim, John, Joseph, Ebenezer, and one D. Ephraim Jr. was father of Ichabod.— John Morton m. Mary Faunce, and d. of "a grievous wound" 1709, and she then m. Joseph Hall of Yarmouth. Joseph was grandfather of Capt. Ezekiel.

7. Nathaniel (s. of Ephraim 4.) was a Lieutenant and d. 1709: he had a s. Nathaniel whose s. Nathaniel b. 1752 and d. 1775 was father of Mrs. Rebecca relict of the late Hon. Wm. Davis.

8. Josiah (s. of Ephraim 4.) d. 1694, and had Henry, Josiah, &c. Josiah m. E. Clark, and had Josiah who d. 1739 æ. 86, and who was father of Thomas who d. 1824 æ. 76.

9. Eleazar (s. of Ephraim 4.) had three children.

10. Thomas (s. of Ephraim 4.) had Nathaniel who was father of Lemuel.

The preceding is but a sketch or outline of this numerous and respectable family, of whom the present Governor, Marcus Morton, is one, as was also the Hon. Perez Morton, late Attorney General of the Commonwealth.

NASH.—Samuel Nash of Duxbury was one of the original proprietors of Bridgewater, and one of the Commissioners appointed by Court to purchase the new Plantation of the Indians. He was Sheriff or Chief Marshal of the Colony, a Lieutenant under Capt. Standish, and also Representative from Duxbury to the old Colony Court at Weymouth: one of his Ds. m. Abraham Sampson. We have no further knowledge of him or his family, and know not if he had any connection with James a cotemporary at Weymouth. He lived in his old age with his son-in-law Clarke. There are many of the name still living in Weymouth, Abington, and the vicinity. James Nash of Duxbury m. Sarah Simmons as early as 1660 or 1670, he may have been son of Samuel, and the same man who was at Weymouth, and Joseph, and others of Scituate may have been his descendants.

PARTRIDGE.—George Partridge and the Rev. Ralph Partridge both of Duxbury were both original proprietors of Bridgewater. The latter was the first Minister of that place, and came over 1636, and George was there the same year: his D. Sarah m. Samuel Allen of Bridgewater about 1658, she was born 1639. Whether they were brothers or in any way connected we know not. The Rev. Mr. Partridge's share in Bridgewater was finally owned by Jonathan Hill of Bridgewater. The late Hon. George Partridge of Duxbury, High Sheriff of Plymouth County, &c., was a descendant of the first George. There are not many of the name now in the County.—Mary Partridge m. Jonathan Brewster, and was living in Conn. 1733.

PAYBODY or PEABODY.—John and William Paybody were both early settlers in Duxbury, and both original proprietors of Bridgewater, and were probably brothers. Of John we have met with no notices. William was Representative of

Duxbury, and m. Elizabeth, D. of John Alden, 1644, she was b.
in Plymouth 1624 : he sold his place in Duxbury to Experience
Mitchell 1650, and removed to Little Compton, R. I.: she died
there 1717, æ. 92, and at her death it was said " her grand D.
Bradford was a grandmother." Her D. Priscilla m. Rev. Mr.
Ichabod Wiswall, and Priscilla Wiswall m. Gershom Bradford.—
Hannah Peabody m. Samuel Bartlett.

PIERCE.—Abraham Pierce, one of the original proprietors
of Bridgewater, was in Plymouth as early as 1627, being named
with others in the division of the cattle, which was made that
year ; but was afterwards before 1650 an inhabitant of Duxbury,
and we have met with no further notice of him.

PRINCE.—Rev. John Prince, rector of East Stafford in
Berkshire, Eng., was 2 or 3 years at the University in Oxford.
His son John came to New England, and settled at Hull, and had
several children : his 4th s., Samuel, was born in Boston 1649.—
Joseph Prince of Hull m. Joanna, D. of the Secretary Nathaniel
Morton of Plymouth.

2. Thomas (s. of John and brother of Samuel) d. in Boston
about 1704, and had Thomas, Benjamin, and Job ; and the wid.
m. Israel Sylvester of Duxbury.—Thomas Prince of Duxbury,
Shipwright, bought a farm of Samuel Sprague sen'r 1713.

3. Samuel (s. of John) settled in Sandwich about 1686, made
free 1690, was twice m.: his last w. Mercy, D. of Gov. Hinckley :
he died 1728, æ. 80 ; she 1736 : he had Samuel, John, Thomas
1687, Joseph, Moses, Nathan, Alice, Martha, Mercy, and Mary.
Samuel had farms at Milford and Coventry, and d. at Rochester
1722, before his father.—John also died at Rochester, and his D.
Elizabeth m. Seth Ames of Bridgewater 1734, who d. at Providence or at sea about 1738.—Thomas (s. of the last w.) gra. H.
U. 1707, and settled in the ministry at the Old South, Boston,
was author of annals and the chronology, and d. Oct. 22, 1758,
æ. 72.—Joseph was a mariner at Strafford, Conn. 1738, but was
afterwards probably at Rochester.—Moses was a mariner at
Boston 1738, and father of Samuel, Jane, and others perhaps.—
Nathan born 1698, gra. H. U. 1718, fellow of the College many
years, died at the West Indies 1748.—Alice m. Samuel Gray of
Little Compton, he died 1733, she was living 1736.—Martha m.
Ezra Bourne Esq. of Sandwich, and her D. Mary Bourne was
wife of the Rev. John Angier, first Minister of East Bridgewater.—Mercy, feeble and infirm, was living single in 1738.—
Mary m. the Rev. Peter Thacher of Mid'o.

4. Governor Thomas Prince (of no known connection with the
preceding families) came over in the 2d ship, the Fortune, in 1621,
lived in Plymouth, his house in High street near Spring Lane : m.
Patience, D. of William Brewster, 1624, the 9th marriage in the
Colony : she d. 1634 : he was chosen Governor 1635, then living
at Duxbury : m. Mary, D. of Wm. Collier, 1635, and removed
to Eastham 1644, and there resided till rechosen Governor in
1658. His wife died at Eastham, and he returned to Plymouth

1663, and lived at "Plain Dealing"; m. Mrs. Mary, widow of
Samuel Freeman, 1662, and d. 1673, æ. 73, his wife surviving at
Yarmouth 1676 : he had a son Thomas who d. before him, and
8 Ds. viz : Rebecca w. of Edmund Freeman Jr. m. 1646, Hannah w. of Nathaniel Mayo m. 1649, Mercy w. of John Freeman
of Eastham m. 1649, Jane w. of Mark Snow of Eastham m. 1660,
Mary w. of John Tracy of Duxbury, Elizabeth w. of Arthur Howland Jr. of Marshfield, Sarah w. of Thos. or Jere'h Howes Jr. of
Yarmouth m. 1650, Judith w. of Isaac Barker of Marshfield and
then of William Tubbs of Pembroke m. 1691 : he had 2 grand
children who d. before 1690 without issue, viz : Lusanna, D. of
his son Thomas, and Theophilus Mayo : he had also a maiden
sister Susanna living at St. Catharine's Gate, near a London
Tower : he called Thomas Clark his brother.

SAMPSON.—Abraham and Henry Sampson of Duxbury were
original proprietors of Bridgewater. Abraham was in Duxbury
as early as 1640, and m. a D. of Sam'l Nash, and had afterwards
a 2d wife : he had Abraham, Isaac, Samuel, and others perhaps:
he was living 1686. Abraham, the s. probably, m. Lorah, D. of
Alexander Standish, and had Abraham, Miles, Ebenezer, Rebecca, Sarah, and Grace.—Samuel was killed in Philip's war
1675 or 1678, leaving a wid. Esther and several young children,
among whom were Samuel and Ichabod.

2. Henry Sampsòn came over to Plymouth 1620 : is named in
the allotments of land in 1623 as one of those who came in the
May Flower in 1620, and yet his name is not inserted among
those who came in the May Flower, nor is it to be found among
those who signed the Compact on board before landing : he was
probably young and included in some of the families : this is the
more probable as he was not made a freeman till 1635, and not
married till 1640 when he m. Ann Plummer : he settled in Duxbury : what his connection with Abraham was is not ascertained :
they may have been brothers. Henry d. 1685 : he had Stephen,
John, Jamés, Caleb, Eliza w. of Robert Sproat, Hannah w. of
Josiah Holmes, another D. w. of John Hammond, Mary w. of
John Simmons, and Dorcas wife of Thomas Bonney. Stephen
and his wife Elizabeth had Benjamin, John, Cornelius, Hannah,
Mary, Elizabeth, Dorcas, and Abigail : he d. 1714.—James settled in Dartmouth.—Caleb m. Mercy, D. of Alexander Standish.

3. Isaac (whose s. uncertain, perhaps s. of Abraham) b. 1660
and d. 1726 ; m. Lydia, D. of Alexander Standish, and had Isaac
1688, Jonathan 1690, Josiah 1692 d. 1731, Lydia 1694, Ephraim
1698, Peleg 1700, Priscilla 1702, Barnabas 1705. Isaac Jr. had a
w. Sarah.—Jonathan had a w. Joanna.—Ephraim had a w. Abigail.—Priscilla m. Jabez Fuller.—Barnabas had a w. Experience.

4. Peleg (s. of Isaac 3.) m. Mary Ring born 1700, and had
Mercy 1731, and Simeon 1736.

5. Simeon (s. of Peleg 4.) m. Deborah, D. of Seth Cushing,
1759, and had Lydia Cushing 1762, Deborah, Mercy, George
W., and Maria : he d. 1789 ; she 1830, æ. 90. Lydia C. m. Wm.

49

Goodwin 1781 and d. 1815.—Deborah m. Rev. Ephraim Briggs
and afterwards William Goodwin for his 2d w.—Mercy m. Levi
Bradford 1800.—Maria m. Rev. Daniel Johnson of Yarmouth.
There was a Gideon Sampson who m. Abigail, D. of Maj.
John Bradford, soon after 1760 : she left no children.
There was a George Sampson who went to Plympton about
1680, and his grand daughter Deborah m. Elijah Bisbee Jr. and
d. 1816, æ. 93; and was mother of Elijah Bisbee Esq. and George
Bisbee.

SIMMONS.—Moses Simmons (sometimes written Symons and
Symonson) of Duxbury was an original proprietor of Bridgewater, and sold his right to Nicholas Byram : he came over in
the ship Fortune 1621 : he had Moses and Thomas, and probably other children. Moses Jr. died in Duxbury 1689, and had
John, Aaron, Mary w. of Joseph Alden, Elizabeth w. of Richard
Dwelly, and Sarah w. of James Nash.—Thomas lived in Scit.,
and had Moses and Aaron, and perhaps others.—Moses and his
w. Patience had Moses 1666 d. in Canada expedition 1690, John
1667, Sarah 1670, Aaron 1672, Job 1674, Patience 1676 after
her father's death. Aaron m. Mary Woodworth 1677, and had
Rebecca 1679, Moses 1680, Mary 1683, Elizabeth 1686, Ebenezer 1689, Lydia 1693 ; Moses m. Rachel Cudworth 1711, and
had Moses 1718, Aaron 1720, Rachel 1723, Leah 1725 ; Ebenezer m. Lydia Kent 1714, and had Abigail 1715, Joshua 1717,
Lydia 1719, Reuben, Peleg, and Ebenezer; Joshua m. Elizabeth Dillingham, and had a son Elisha, father of William, C. J.
of the Police Court, Elisha, Benja., and Franklin all of Boston,
and Ebenezer of Hanover. One of the Ds. of this family m. William Barrell, and she died before 1750 leaving an only child,
Joshua Barrell.—There was a Moses Simmons lived awhile in
S. B. [see page 330, No. 69.], a descendant no doubt of this
family. Joseph Church had a D. Abigail, who m. a Simmons as
early as, and probably before, 1700.

SOULE.—George Soule was one of the first pilgrims and
signers of the political Compact on board the May Flower 1620:
in the general allotment in 1623 he had one acre and afterwards
two more " at the watering place," all of which he sold to Robert
Hicks 1639 ; in 1627 he and his w. Mary and s. Zechariah are
named : he lived at Eel River, N. side the bridge, in 1638, and
then at Powder Point, and removed to Duxbury before 1650 ;
was a Selectman and Deputy there, and one of the original proprietors of Bridgewater : he sold his proprietary right to Nicholas Byram : she d. 1677 ; he 1680 very aged : he had Zechariah,
John, Nathaniel, George, Patience w. of John Haskell, Elizabeth w. of Francis Walker, both of Mid'o., Susanna, and Mary
wife of John Peterson probably of Duxbury, m. before 1672 ;
Mary had been put out to John Winslow 1652 for 7 yrs.; he gave
one-half his Dartmouth lands to Nathaniel 1658, the other half
to George 1668, his Mid'o. lands to Haskell and Walker and
their wives 1668 : Zechariah d. before him, 1663, leaving a wid.

Margaret ; John Soule d. at Duxbury 1707 æ. 75 ; Edm'd Weston and Adam Wright were his ss. in law, John Soule d. at Duxbury 1734 ; Aaron Soule, merchant, d. at Pembroke 1783, who had one s. John and 5 Ds.; one, Leonice, m. a Brewster ; one, Huldah m. Thomas Church; one m. a Dwelly. The descendants of this respectable ancestor are very numerous in the old Colony, and have spread extensively over the country. Dea. John Soule and others in E. B. [see p.304] are doubtless his descendants.

TUBBS.—William Tubbs, of Duxbury, was an original proprietor of Bridgewater: he m. Mercy, D. of Francis Sprague, 1637, and he or his s. or gr. s. William m. Judith, wid. of Isaac Barker and D. of Gov. Thomas Prince, 1691. Some of this name, no doubt his descendants, are still living in the lower towns of the County, but we have no particular knowledge of the family descent.

WADSWORTH.—Christopher Wadsworth of Duxbury was a Representative of that town, and one of the original proprietors of Bridgewater, and Capt. Samuel and Joseph Wadsworth and their representatives retained an interest and shares in Bridgewater longer than any of the non-residents. After 1685 Capt. Samuel's share is entered under the name of wid. Wadsworth ; and in 1686, and after, Timothy Wadsworth's name appears.— This has always been a respectable name in Duxbury and its vicinity. The late Gen. Peleg Wadsworth of Portland gra. H. U. 1769, was of this family.

WEST.—Francis West at Duxbury 1633; m. Margary Reeves 1639 : an orig. proprietor of Bridgewater, sold his share to Edw'd Mitchell, d. 1692 : had Samuel, Peter, Pelatiah, Richard, &c. Samuel m. Tryphosa, D. of George Partridge, and had Samuel : some of his descendants in Martha's Vineyard : Pelatiah went to Conn. Samuel West m. Experience Howland.—The name is common in the old Colony.

WESTON.—Edmund Weston of Duxbury was an original proprietor of Bridgewater, and the name is still common there and in the vicinity ; but if he is the common ancestor, as probably he is, we have no means at hand of tracing the descent.

WINSLOW.—Edward, Gilbert, John, Kenelm, and Josiah Winslow, were brothers and children of Edward Winslow of Droitwich in Worcestershire in England, and all came to New England : they had also 3 sisters, Eleanor, Elizabeth, and Maydelon.

1. Gov. Edward Winslow, b. 1594, came with his w. Elizabeth in 1620 in the 1st ship, the May Flower : she d. the next spring, 1621, and he m. Susanna, wid. of Mr. William White, 1622, the first marriage in N. E., and she was mother of Peregrine White, the first child, and of Josiah Winslow the first Governor, born in N. E. He went as Agent to England and d. at sea 1655 æ. 61 : his residence or seat called Caresrull, was at Marshfield : he had Edward*, John*, Josiah, and Elizabeth who m. Gilbert Brooks and afterwards Capt. George Corwin of Salem.

2. Gilbert arrived also in the first ship 1620. Few notices of
him remain : he soon left the Colony, and, it is said, went to
Portsmouth, and d. before 1660, without issue, as grants of that
date were made to his brothers as his heirs.
3. John, born a. 1596, arrived 1621 in the ship called the Fortune, and m. Mary Chilton before 1627 (she was said to have
been the first lady who came on shore : she was an only child of
James and Susanna Chilton, who both died the first winter): he
had John, Isaac, Benjamin 1653, Edward, Joseph, Susanna,
Mary, and Sarah. Susanna m. Robert Latham a. 1649, who
settled in E. Bridgewater. [See page 222.]—Mary m. Edward
Gray 1650.—Sarah m. Miles Standish Jr. 1660, then Tobias
Payne 1666, and afterwards Richard Middlecot. He and all his
family but the two eldest Ds. finally removed to Boston, where
he d. a. 1674, æ. 78; she died a. 1676. Their posterity became
numerous, of whom the present Isaac Winslow Esq. is one, as
was also the late Gen. John Winslow, both of Boston.
4. Kenelm arrived at Plymouth a. 1629, and m. Eleanor, wid.
of John Adams, 1634, and settled in Marshfield : he d. while on
a visit at Salem 1672 : he had Kenelm, Nathaniel, and Job.
Kenelm went to Yarmouth, and had Kenelm 1668, Josiah 1670,
and Thomas 1672.—Job went to Freetown.—Kenelm Winslow,
a grandson perhaps, m. Ann Taylor 1730.
5. Josiah, b. 1605, arrived with his brother Kenelm a. 1629,
was in Scituate in 1637, and soon after 1643 settled in Marshfield, and m. Margaret, D. of Thomas Bourne, and d. 1674, æ.
69 : he had Elizabeth 1637, Jonathan 1638, Mary 1640, Rebecca
1642, Hannah (or Susanna) 1644, and Margaret. Jonathan d.
1676, leaving a son John born 1664.—One D. m. John Miller.—
One, Rebecca, m. John Thacher, both of Yarmouth.—One m.
William Crow of Plymouth, and another m. John Tracy of
Duxbury, afterwards of Norwich.
6. Gov. Josiah (only surviving s. of Gov. Edw'd 1.) b. a. 1628,
educated at H. U. 1653, but left without taking a degree, as did
many others, on account of the new regulation requiring students
to stay 4 years instead of 3 : he m. Penelope, D. of Herbert Pelham, 1657 : he d. 1680, æ. a. 52 ; she d. 1703, æ. 73 : they had a
D. 1658*, Elizabeth 1664, Edward 1667*, Isaac 1670. Elizabeth
m. Stephen Burton 1684.
7. Nathaniel (s. of Kenelm 4.) resided in Marshfield, and m.
Faith Miller 1664, and had Faith 1665, Nathaniel 1667, James
1669, Eleanor, Gilbert 1673, Kenelm 1675, Josiah 1683. Kenelm
had a son Nathaniel 1709.
8. Col. Isaac (only surviving son of Gov. Josiah 6.) of Marshfield m. Sarah, D. of John Wensley of Boston, 1700 : he d. 1738,
æ. 68 ; she 1753, æ. 80 (her mother was Elizabeth, D. of Dea.
William Paddy whose w. was Alice D. of Edmund Freeman of
Sandwich, m. 1639): he had Josiah 1701, John 1703, Penelope
1704, Elizabeth 1707, Anna 1709*, Edward 1714. Josiah gra.
H. U. 1721, was a Captain, and slain at St. George's River by

the Indians 1724.—Penelope m. Col. James Warren 1725, and died 1737.—Elizabeth m. Col. Benjamin Marston of Salem or Manchester 1729, and died 1760.—The Wensley Portrait among those of the Winslow family in the Mass. Hist. Society's rooms is either Sarah Wensley's (w. of Col. Winslow) or her mother Elizabeth's (D. of Dea. Paddy), and most probably of the latter, as it is understood the family in later times have usually spoken of it " as grandmother Paddy's."

9. Nathaniel (s. of Nathaniel 7.) resided in Marshfield, and m. Lydia, D. of Anthony Snow, 1692, and had Lydia 1693, Thankful 1695, Snow 1698, Oliver 1702, Deborah 1708, Patience 1710, Nathaniel 1712: he then m. a 2d wife, Deborah Bryant of Scituate, 1716, and had Ruth 1718.

10. Gilbert (s. of Nathaniel 7.) of Marshfield m. Mary, D. of Anthony Snow, and had Issachar 1699, Barnabas, Gilbert, and Anthony 1707. Anthony m. Deborah, D. of William Barker Esq., and removed to E. Bridgewater. [See page 353.]

11. Gen. John (s. of Col. Isaac 8.] lived in Marshfield, and m. Mary Little 1726, and had Pelham 1737, and Isaac 1739: he afterwards, late in life, m. a wid. Johnson (whose maiden name was Barker) of Hingham, where he died 1774, æ. 71. He was Captain in the expedition against Cuba 1640, Col. at Louisburgh 1644, and afterwards Maj. Gen'l in the British service.

12. Edward Esq. (youngest son of Col. Isaac 8.) gra. H. U. 1736, m. Hannah, wid. of Charles Dyer and D. of Thos. Howland, 1739, and went to Halifax, N. S., in the revolution, and d. 1786, æ. 72; she survived and d. at Frederickton æ. 82: he had Edward, Penelope, and Sarah. Edward gra. H. U. 1765, was Clerk of the Courts in Plymouth, and went off in the revolution and died at Frederickton 1815, æ. 69, and his son Edward was drowned, and another s., Wentworth, survived.

13. Oliver (s. of Nathaniel 9.) m. Agatha, D. of John Bryant of Scituate, where he also resided, and had Oliver (killed in the French war 1758, æ. 20), John who went to Nobleborough, Me., and Nathaniel. He m. a 2d w. Bethiah Pryor of Hanover 1749, and had Oliver (a revolutionary pensioner) and Joseph* 1753. Oliver had a s. Oliver.

14. Pelham Esq. (s. of Gen. John 11.) gra. H. U. 1753, was an Attorney, and m. Joanna, D. of Capt. Gideon White: he left Plymouth in the revolution, and d. on Long Island, N. Y. 1782, leaving two Ds., Mary who m. Maj. Henry Warren, and Joanna who m. Dr. Nathan Hayward, High Sheriff of Plymouth Co.

15. Dr. Isaac (s. of Gen. John 11.) of Marshfield was a respectable Physician, and m. a D. of Dr. Charles Stockbridge of Scituate, and d. 1819, æ. 80; the w. of his old age was Fanny Gay of Hingham: he had a s. John and 3 Ds. One, Betsy, m. Hon. Kilborn Whitman Esq., one m. a Shaw and then a Dingley, and the other m. a Clapp, an Attorney in Bath, Me.

16. Maj. Nathaniel (s. of Oliver 13.) m. Sarah, D. of Isaac Hatch of Pembroke, 1766, and had Nathaniel 1767, Sarah 1769,

Walter 1772*, Josiah 1774*, Anna 1776, Judith 1780, Lydia 1786, William 1788. Nathaniel died 1830, leaving a family.— Sarah m. Thomas Waterman, and then Ebenezer Copeland.— Anna m. Wm. P. Ripley of Plymouth 1810.—Judith m. Elisha Tolman.—Lydia m. Anthony Collamore of Pembroke.—William remained at Scituate on the paternal estate.

17. John Esq. (s. of Dr. Isaac 15.) gra. B. U. 1795, was an Attorney, and d. at Natchez, whither he went on business 1822, æ. 48, leaving John, Pelham, Isaac, Penelope, Eliza, and Fanny Gay.

Samuel Winslow of Rochester had Samuel and Richard bap. 1679.—Samuel m. Bathsheba Holbrook of Scituate 1700.—Nathaniel (of Freetown) m. Elizabeth Holbrook of Scituate 1701. Josiah of Freetown m. Sarah, D. of John Hayward Jr. of W. Bridgewater, 1721. [See p. 352.]—Oliver, a revolutionary pensioner of Westport, served in the artillery 1777.—Nathaniel Winslow removed to Damarascotta 1729, and testified in Court at old York 1742, then 63 years old.

Isaac Winslow of Boston has a particular geneological account of the Boston branch of this distinguished family.

APPENDIX.

See page 17.—The following extracts from the Records of the General Court, shows that the grant of Titicut was not made till after the grant of Bridgewater plantation was made to Duxbury, and of course was made by the Sachem at Pembroke or Mattakeset, and not by his father Chickatabut of Neponsit :—

"Isaac Wonno appeared to prosecute his claim to three miles of land on each side of Titicut river. Bridgewater agents made it appear that they had purchased of Ossemequin six miles from their centre towards Titicut, and that Chickatabut in his grant to Titicut Indians of three miles doth except any former purchase made by Bridgewater men. We therefore think it necessary that Titicut Indians and the said Wonno have their three miles after the Bridgewater men's three miles be meted out, or to have the remainder if it be not so much."

The foregoing report of the Committee, 1703, was accepted and approved by the General Court on the petition of Edward Fobes, Representative of Bridgewater, Oct. 27, 1708.

See page 19.—The following is the report of a Committee establishing the bounds of the Titicut Purchase :—

" 1729. We the subscribers being a Committee chosen by the Purchasers and Proprietors of the two mile grant on the southerly side of Bridgewater, commonly called Titicut, to establish the bounds of the Divisions of said Titicut lands where they might be found, and to make new bounds where they were wanting as by record may appear, which work we have carefully performed : and we have established the bounds of the northermost parts of said Titicut lands upon the ancient reputed four mile line, as by the return of our work may appear, which line was shown to us

by the Proprietors of Titicut: and we being also a Committee
chosen by the Purchasers and Proprietors of the eight mile
square of Bridgewater as by record may appear to renew the
ancient line between said eight mile and Titicut lands, upon which
said Titicut lots were butted when first laid out, in order to bring
it to record: because the Purchasers' ancient book of records
before it came into our present Clerk's hands was in divers
places defaced, broken and lost, so that the record of said line
cannot be found. Accordingly we did upon the 4th day of February, 1728–9, renew said ancient four mile line as followeth. We
took our departure from a heap of stones at a place called Wolf
Trap Hill where Titicut way parts from Taunton road, which
heap of stones was shewn us by Justice Edson and Dea. Fobes,
being Proprietors on both sides, and avouched to be a station in
the ancient four mile line, or line between said eight mile and
two mile and known by them to be so for more than forty years
past, it being the same line upon which we butted the said Titicut lands as above. From said heap of stones we run West one
degree, South forty-one rods to a great crotched white oak tree
marked and numbered 4: thence West one degree South 100
rods to a maple tree marked and numbered 4: thence West one
degree South 53 rods to a white oak sapling marked and numbered 4, near the little pond: thence West one degree South
one hundred and fifteen rods to a red oak tree marked and
numbered 4 at the head of Leach's land: thence West one
degree South 53 rods to a horn pine tree marked and numbered
4, an ancient marked tree: thence West one degree South 50
rods to a white pine stake standing by a black oak stump standing in Taunton Line marked and numbered 4. Then we began
again at the heap of stones first mentioned and run East one
degree North 85 rods to a maple tree marked and numbered 4:
thence East one degree North 73 rods to a white oak tree standing by the brook in the range of Samuel Leach's land marked
and numbered 4 about a rod below a great rock in the brook;
thence East one degree North 83 rods to a rock between a white
oak and walnut: thence East one degree North to a swamp
white oak tree marked and numbered 4 by Thomas Hayward's
land: thence East one degree North 121 rods to a white oak tree
northward from Benja. Washburn's house marked and numbered

4 : thence East one degree North thrity-six rods to a red oak tree marked and numbered 4 : thence East one degree North 80 rods to a white oak tree marked and numbered 4 : thence East one degree North 50 rods to a maple tree marked and numbered 4 on the South side, being an ancient marked tree : thence East one degree North 120 rods to a maple tree marked and numbered 4 : thence East one degree South 31 rods to a horn pine tree marked and numbered 4, being the corner of the first great Lot in Titicut Division : thence East one degree North 47 rods to a maple tree marked and numbered 4 : thence East one degree North 66 rods to a red oak tree marked and numbered 4 : thence East one degree North 70 rods to a red oak tree marked and numbered 4 standing in the edge of Benjamin Willis's meadow, being an old marked tree : thence East one degree North 47 rods to a poplar sapling marked and numbered 4, being the corner of the first Lot in the last Division of Titicut lands : thence East one degree North 556 rods by a range of old marked trees to a walnut tree marked and numbered 4 standing on the bank of the great river and a little to the North of the mouth of Winnetuxet rive..—Ephraim Fobes, Benj. Leach, and Nath'l Willis."

1737. The above was confirmed 1737 by Sam'l Keith, Jona. Howard and Joshua Willis in behalf of the Eight Mile Proprietors ; and Nathaniel Willis, Benjamin Leach and Ephraim Fobes in behalf of the Two Mile Proprietors.

See page 30.—The following record contains the final laying out of the land on the North and East side of the original four mile grant, on the notherly and easterly part of the town, according to the agreement of the purchasers.

" Pursuant to an Act of the Purchasers of Bridgewater bearing date Feb. 1, A. D., 1710, we the subscribers, who were entrusted and empowered to lay out the undivided lands towards the north-east corner of the Four Mile Grant both upon the East and North side, have bounded out the said lands into seven shares or lots according to the purchasers' agreement in manner and form as followeth :—

" Part of the first lot lyeth westerly from Joseph Shaw's house, beginning at a red oak tree marked on four sides, numbered one : from thence running West to Packard's land, and bounded westerly partly by Packard's land and partly by John Hayward's land, and at the southerly end by the lots that lie upon Matfield River to a white oak tree, which is Joseph Edson's corner bound : from thence running North two hundred rods to the red oak first mentioned, being 100 acres more or less.—The other part of the first lot lieth on the East side of Buck Hill swamp, beginning at a white oak tree near the swamp, numbered one : from thence running East to Joseph Shaw's land by Beaver Brook, and then bounded on the south-east and East by said Shaw's land, and by the lands of Nicholas Byram, and so to the white oak tree standing in the East and West line, which is the southerly bounds of the second lot : from said white oak running West by a range of trees marked to the above said Buck Hill swamp, and so bounded by James Cary's land in Buck Hill swamp to the bounds first mentioned.

" The second lot lieth easterly from Beaver Brook, beginning at a heap of stones upon a flat rock, then running northerly to the four mile line, which is a mile : and from said rock easterly 160 poles to a white oak tree marked on four sides, and then running northerly to the four mile line.

" The third lot beginneth at the white oak last mentioned and runs East 179 poles to a swamp oak, which is marked on four sides : from thence running North 320 poles to the four mile line.

" The fourth lot is bounded westerly by the East side of the third lot, and runs from the above named oak East 160 poles to a stake and heap of stones : thence North to the four mile line.

" The fifth lot lieth on the East side of Weymouth road, bounded northerly by a pine tree marked on two sides standing near to William Dyer's land : from thence to a black oak tree by the road near Lieut. Hersey's field : then bounded by said road to a stake and heap of stones by the way-side : from thence running East to Mr. Moore's land : thence bounded by the river lots to the pine tree first mentioned.

" The sixth lot is bounded northerly by the fifth, beginning at the above stake and heap of stones, and from thence bounded by the way to the Birch swamp to a maple tree, which is the corner bounds of Gannett's land to a white oak tree standing to the northward of the old wolf trap : thence running East to poor meadow lots, and so bounded by lotted lands until it comes to the range of the fifth lot.

" Part of the seventh lot is bounded by the south side of the sixth : the other part of the lot lieth between Theodosius Moore's land and the Major's Purchase, bounded northerly by Mr. Cushing's land and southerly by the Cedar swamp."

See page 34.—The lands on the North side of Titicut River within the township of Bridgewater lying on the South side of the Purchasers' four mile line from the centre, called the Titicut land, is laid out in two divisions of lots, called the great lots and the little lots; there being 64 lots in each division.

" The great lots begin towards the easterly side and run from the four mile line southerly.

The little lots begin on the westerly side of the path left to go down to Titicut wear, and run West for their length, butting on said path, till they come to the river at said wear ; then they begin on the easterly side of the way, and run easterly for their length, butting on the easterly side of the way, till they come to the 63d lot, which buts on a brook, the lot running on both sides of the way. The last lot, James Cary's, No. 64, lies by itself down the river against *Spanyard's* land." Laid out by Edward Mitchell, Sam'l Edson Jr., Sam'l Washburn and John Leonard, May 1685.

See page 43.—Bridgewater's Monitor is the title given to the Rev. Mr. Keith's Sermon, June 14th, 1717, at the dedication of the first meeting-house in the south parish. The following is the preface :—

" The New English Bridgewater has been a town favored of God; yea some favors of Heaven unto it, have indeed been distinguishing.

" It was planted a noble vine.—And may no more of the text from whence this phrase is borrowed, ever be applied unto it! The first planters of it, were a set of people who made religion their main interest ; and it became their glory. There was a time when it stood in a land of unwalled villages, with fierce armies of bloody Indians destroying round about them ; and the dispensations of God our Saviour towards it at this time, were so wonderful, that the short report thereof given, in the Church History of New England, is not unworthy to be here transcribed and repeated.

" ' Remarkable was the fate of Bridgewater, a most praying, and a most pious town, seated in the very midst of the dangers of the war ; that although they were often assaulted by formidable numbers of the enemies, yet in all their sharp assaults they never lost one of their inhabitants, young or old. They were solicited strongly to desert their dwellings, but they resolved, that they would keep their stations. And now on May 8th, 1676, the Indians began to fire the town ; but the inhabitants with notable courage, issued forth from their garrisons, to fight the enemy ; and God from Heaven at the same time fought for them, with a storm of lightning, thunder and rain, whereby a considerable part of their houses were preserved. Thou, Church of Bridgewater !

'O nimium dilecta Deo, cui militat æther.'

O how beloved of Heaven, whom storms defend.

"One that was no Christian, so sang the favors of Heaven to the Emperor Theodosius, and so might the Pagan foe now sing of thy salvations!

"Ever since that memorable day, the town has been proceeding, with the smile of God upon them, and upon the intentions of his gospel among them, until they are now become two bands. They are lovingly and peaceably swarmed into a new assembly, and began to meet in their new edifice on a day of prayer (as it is the manner of New England) when the two sermons were preached, which the affected hearers have here published. God grant, that from the tokens of his gracious presence with them, the place may claim the name of Mahanaim. And may there be still found among them such a number of lively, watchful, fruitful Christians, exemplarily living to God, and by the faith of the Son of God ; may a value for the ordinances of our Saviour, be so preserved in vigor with them, and the success thereof appear in all real and vital godliness quickened among the young as well as the old among them ; and may their brotherly love continue at such a rate, that it may be plainly seen, God is yet among them. Wo to them, if I depart from them, saith the Lord.

"It has been a singular felicity unto this good people, that from the very infancy of their plantation, they have sat under the ministry of that gracious, faithful, humble servant of God, who continues with them to this day. He has been a precious gift of our ascended Lord unto them ; and they have hitherto rejoiced in his light ; and we rejoice with them, that after fifty-four years, his light yet shines with such brightness among them.

" We can make no doubt, but that, as they have grown into such good circumstances under his painful and patient conduct, they will study in all the methods of goodness, to render his old age comfortable to him, and so multiply all the offices and expressions of a grateful people towards him, with an affection and reverence, like what the church of Smyrna paid unto their aged polycarp, that he may anon die, blessing of them, and blessing of God for them. They will certainly find their account in doing so!

" The savoury sermon, which is here extorted for the public from him, we recommend unto the blessing of God, that so the ends of piety, which the good people have proposed in thus exhibiting a lasting memorial of what God has done for them, and a constant remembrancer of their duty, may be answered.

INCREASE MATHER,
COTTON MATHER.

A second edition of it was published and another preface added June 14, 1768, just fifty-one years after, and the Rev. John Angier's sermon, at the ordination of his son, the Rev. Samuel Angier, Dec. 23, 1767, which was the occasion of printing the 2d edition, was bound with some of the copies.

See page 47.—When the South Parish was incorporated in 1716 it was ordered by the General Court, as we have before seen, that the old meeting-house in the West Parish (then called the North Parish) should stand where it was for five years, and then be removed down to the four corners by Isaac Johnson's, in order no doubt to accommodate the easterly part (now East Bridg'r). Before the five years expired however a petition, signed by John Packard and others, was preferred to the General Court, praying that the old house might remain where it was, which was heard by the Court Nov. 9, 1720, and the prayer granted. This was assented to by the East in consideration of a suggestion made by the West, that the East would soon probably be desirous of becoming a separate Parish, and in that case the present house if removed would accommodate neither Parish ; and of a consequent agreement made in parish meeting Nov. 6, 1719, that if the East would contribute towards settling a minister (Mr. Perkins) in the West, whatever they paid (about £65) should be refunded when the East should become a Parish, and thus be called on to build a house and settle a minister for them-selves. When therefore that period occured the East called on the West to refund, but were denied, and no record of any such vote or agreement could be produced. The East then, by Josiah Sears and sixty-three others, applied to the General Court in June, 1726, for some remedy or relief; whereon an order of notice passed, and Nathaniel Brett, Clerk of the old Parish, was summoned to attend, who appeared, and on examination testified that such a vote was passed, which he produced on a loose paper made at the time of passing it, and which he confessed "he ought in discharge of his office to have made a record of at that time." This the Court considered sufficient, but referred the petitioners to the judicial courts for a remedy. An action was accordingly commenced at the next September Term of the C. C. Pleas at Plymouth, in which John Read appeared for plaintiffs, and J. Overing for defendants. The East finally recovered, but not till they had expended nearly the whole amount in prosecuting their claim.

July 1, 1730. Jona. Howard, Joseph Keith, Israel Packard, and Ephraim Fobes, a Committee of the West Parish, applied to the General Court, shewing that their meeting-house was much decayed and that it had been voted to build a new one, and that the inhabitants were much divided about the place where it should be erected, and praying therefore for a viewing Committee to determine where it should stand: whereupon Seth Williams Esq., Mr. Thacher and Mr. Lemon were appointed, and reported Dec. 21, 1730, that "having viewed all the places shewn to them by the contending parties they are of opinion that where the old house stands is the proper place," which was accepted.

See pages 54, 55.—To the List of Graduates there should be added Jairus S. Keith of S. B. or Titicut, gra. B. U. 1819, and Lewis Washburn of S. B. gra. B. U. 1826; also Thomas J. Snow of N. B. gra. B. U. 1823, Abel W. Kingman of N. B. gra. Amherst 1830, Austin Cary of N. B. gra. Amherst 1837, Samuel Dike of N. B. gra. B. U. 1838.

See page 71.—The following is the petition referred to in p. 71:
"To the honored Governor (Thomas Hinckley), and Deputy
  Governor and Assistants sitting at Plymouth in New England
  the first Tuesday in June 1685.
  "God by his providence hath placed the bounds of our

habitation in Bridgewater, and on the eastward side of the town, and about two miles some of us, and some three miles from the meeting-house and mill and chief parts of the town ; and though we have lived there many years, some of us have had no way into the town, but what we have had upon sufferance through men's lands that have been laid out and of our own making of bridges to pass over a river that lies between some of us and the town. We have made and kept up a horse bridge over this river, called Matfield river, many years, which has been a great benefit to us that live there, and to many others, and strangers that have occasion to pass that way, especially in times of great floods, it being the best place and most convenient for a bridge in a mile up and down the river, which runs about South and North for the length of it, but the lands being laid out on both sides of it and butting upon this river, our bridge lying over this river on the northerly side of a twenty acre lot, the owner of the land has fenced it in ; and now we have no way to go to the town without going three-quarters of a mile about, and partly upon sufferance too many of us ; we think it is very hard that living in a wilderness, we cannot have convenient room for highways. We have made our case known to the town and can have no help. This lot where our bridge lies is the chief hindrance, and yet there is common land joining to the lower side of it left as we understand by the feoffees for allowance for a highway, but of itself it is altogether incapable of a way. There are many others in the town that desire there might be a sworn jury to lay out such highways as are needful, and to perfect such as are begun. So desiring your help as God shall direct you. Your humble petitioners." [See the names, page 71.]

The preceding history was principally compiled before Bridgewater was divided, and therefore applies to it as if entire and as it formerly stood after the separation of those parts which were incorporated with Abington, and Pembroke(now Hanson). Large as it was it remained without further division for nearly one hundred years. Movements and applications for it were however early and frequently made. In the year 1719, the South, only three years after its incorporation as a parish, applied to the General Court to be made a distinct town, as appears by the petition of Josiah Edson and sixty others, and the North, then including all the rest of the town, agreed to it, and it was granted in the House of Rep. Nov. 24, 1719, but was non-concurred in by the Council. What is now the North also originally petitioned to be a town in 1738, and the town itself consented, and voted also at the same time, as we have already seen, that the South and East should become distinct and separate towns; but the General Court resisted all these applications. Some years before any division was finally effected strong desires for it were manifested, principally from the South and North Parishes, which were the most remote from the centre. But means were adopted to obviate complaints and to prevent separation. The town however at last, having increased in population, and the discontent, never entirely appeased, reviving and no longer to be restrained, was rapidly divided into four distinct towns. The North, though the youngest parish, had become the most populous as well as the most distant from the town house, first applied and was incorporated June 15, 1821, by the name of North Bridgewater.

The West (the old town) was incorporated Feb. 16, 1822, by the name of West Bridgewater.

The East was incorporated June 14, 1823, by the name of East Bridgewater.

The South, with Titicut, remains therefore with the old name, Bridgewater, and the town records which had for 166 years remained principally at the West, were transferred to the South. It is somewhat remarkable that the South, which was the first to move for separation and often the most forward in it, should after all secure its object and retain the original name by remaining quiet. The inhabitants felt a pride in belonging to so large and respectable a town, and were somewhat reluctant to separate, and therefore endured the inconveniences of union much longer than otherwise perhaps they would have done; and we accordingly see each division still fondly retaining the cherished name as far as public convenience will permit. The old proprietors' records still remain in West Bridgewater.

ADDITIONAL CORRECTIONS TO PAGE 8.

—— 1 8 4 4 . ——

Page 8. To the list of Senators in the first paragraph, add Artemas Hale, and Jesse Perkins.

" 88. No. 17. after Eleazar in the parenthesis *for* 6, *read* 9.

" 106. No. 4. *for Rev. Josiah Smith,* read Rev. Thomas Smith.

" 107. No. 3 & 5, dele Capt.—

" 109. Article *Barrett.* After *James* 1738, add Robert 1740 *b.* at N. B.

" 113. In No. 2, after Daniel, insert Jacob, Polly *w.* of Libeus Smith, and Anna, *w.* of Captain Seth Gurney.

" 122. Article *Brown.* for Emily, read Harriet.

" 127. No. 3. for 1643. at the bottom of the page read 1743.—

" 131. No. 4. dele *probably of John Shaw of Weymouth,* and insert, of Ens'n. Josiah Standish.

" 152. No. 8. after *William Orcutt,* for 1755, read 1715.

" 157. Article Egerton. for 1834, read 1734.—

" 167. Article *Gay.* for 1725 and 1728, read 1825 and 1828.

" 170. Article Hanmer No 2., for *Mary,* read Martha.

" 172. In Article 3, for 1820, read 1720.

" 175. No. 10. for 1720, read 1820.

" 182. No. 45. *Hannah* who *m* Perkins was not this woman, but D. of Edmund Hayward No. 40.—

" 188. Article Holman. for *John* Quincy, insert Daniel Quincy.

" 193. No 9. dele *Captain Zebedee Snell* 1761, and insert Nathan Willis 1757. Snell perhaps *m.* Martha, D. of Joshua Howard, No. 113—*m.*1761.

" 195. No. 24. *Susanna* who *m.* Lathrop, was not this woman, but a D. of Capt. Jona. Howard No. 31.

" 199. No. 60. dele David 27, and insert Nathan 64.—

" 220. Under Article *Lydia Kingman*—for 1834, read 1734.

" 224. Article Lathrop, add Mark Lathrop was at Salem in 1643.

" 226. No. 19. dele *Theophilus,* and insert Capt. Jonathan.—

" 235. No. 5. To the children of Jacob there mentioned, add Joseph, Josiah, and Jacob. Joseph *m.* an Orcutt, and had Ephraim, Joseph 1696, and a D. who *m.* a Fisher. Ephraim, (mentioned under No. 7.) had Huldah *w.* of Josiah Washburn, and perhaps Phebe, who *m.* Eliab Byram 1741, and several other children; he removed to N. Jersey.

" 236. No. 16. dele 10 *or William* 13, in the parenthesis, and insert who was *s.* of Jacob 5.—

" " No. 17. dele 11 in the parenthesis and insert, who was *s* of Jacob 5. He had also three other children, viz: Benjamin 1732, Mary 1722*, Mary 1729*.

" 237. No. 23. To the children of Simeon Leonard, add Stillman 1783.

"   No. 26. To the children of Simeon Leonard, add Mary 1726, Simeon 1829*, Herman 1831.

" 267. No. 22. For 20 in the parenthesis, read 21.

" 269. No. 35. dele *James m. Rebecca Packard* 1783.

" 275. Art. Pratt. " On the 14th of Jan. 1765, died at Bridgewater Joseph Pratt, æ. 100 years wanting one month; a man of good character and profession ; he had 20 children by his first wife, but none by his second, who still survives him, being about 90 years old." Boston News Letter, Jan. 31, 1765.

" 307. No. 4 at the bottom, for 2d. in the parenthesis read 3d.

" 308. No. 8. dele the son *Ebenezer*, and also the following. *He and his son Ebenezer both died a.* 1748. *Zerviah Standish m. Zebedee Tomson of Halifax* 1745. *Ebenour Jr. m. a Churchill* 1739. *Sarah Standish m. Josiah Cushman Jr.* 1749.

" 309. In the account of Mrs. Bisbee, dele *Standish b. at Captain's Hill in Duxbury*, and insert—Sampson, and great grand daughter of Alexander Standish.—

" 310. No. 4. for 1813, read 1830.—

" 358. Art. Bradford. 2d. line for *Ansterfield*, read Austerfield, and for 1588, read 1586.

" 359. Lower line, dele *m. Gideon*, and on the next page, *Sampson but left no children*—and insert *d.* 1697.

" 383. Art. Nash. 6th line for *Weymouth*, read Plymouth.

" 387. Third line from bottom, for *Caresrull*, read Careswell.

" 389. No. 12. 2d line, for *Charles*, read William, and for 1739, read 1741.

A B. KIDDER, PRINTER, 7 CORNHILL.

INDEX

In order to find a person in this volume first look for a genealogical article under the appropriate surname and scan it for the person of interest, then use this index to find references to the person which may be buried in the historical text, other genealogies, or the appendices. This index cites all persons whose names are buried in the historical text, the genealogies, and the appendices. It does not cite names in the genealogies which appear under the appropriate headings. Thus, for example, it does not cite the people named Alden who appear in the Alden genealogy, but it does cite all people named Alden who appear anywhere else in the volume, and it does cite all people who appear in the Alden genealogy who do not have the surname Alden. The latter category includes wives and daughters whose maiden or married names, respectively, were not Alden, as well as husbands, sons-in-law, etc.

411

BUSHNELL, Mehitabel 94
BUXTON, Anna 314
BYLE, Mather 365
BYRAM, 28 56 72 Abigail 86
335 Ann 295 Anna 244 330
Anne 188 218 Benjamin 108
188 228 244 247 Bethiah
276 Branch 330 342 Capt 78
83 Content 175 Deliverance
274 Dr 83 Ebenezer 36 77
177 Ebenezer Jr 86 Eliab
54 401 Elizabeth 166 180
284 Experience 346 Hannah
177 279 285 Japhet 94
Jenny 228 Jephthah 327
Joseph 84 119 133 166 201
227 265 277 284 Josiah 80
88 111 114 119 131 137 169
285 293 318 342 Lucia Anne
342 Martha 133 166 265 277
Mary 114 119 129 151 192
227 230 293 Matilda 340
Mehitabel 114 131
Mehitable 94 Mercy 342
Nabby 137 318 Napthali 279
Nicholas 18 30 32 34 39 40
41 49 62 66 67 70 71 94
111 129 151 166 175 180
192 218 230 274 276 290 295
335 346 373 386 394
Nicholas Jr 31 66 151
Nicholas Sr 19 Phebe 401
Rachel 108 247 Rebecca 119
Ruth 88 Sally 143 Sarah 94
169 338 Seth 143 338 340
Susanna 111 151 290 327
Theophilus 114
BYRON, 129

CADY, Alice 121
CALDER, Maj 245 Nancy 245
CALLENDER, Abigail 369
CAMPBELL, Alice 272
Ebenezer 279 Hannah 279
Rebeckah 301 Sarah 96
CAPEN, 269 274 Adam 261
Benjamin 198 Eunice 257
Hannah 195 Huldah 261
James Jr 238 Jane 261 John
110 150 Lois 238 Mary 110
Polly 92 Priscilla 194
Relief 198 Susanna 93 321
Tiley 150 Uriah 257
CARLTON, Mary 200
CARPENTER, Alice 358
CARR, Anna 124 Daniel 153
Elizabeth 269 Martha 153

Mary 127 Mercy 333 Reading
333 Rhoda 164 Thomas 127
269 William 164 William Jr
124
CARVER, Abigail 94 103 Anne
203 Bathsheba 157 295
Bethiah 89 Betsy 224
Clifford 237 330 Eleazar
48 87-90 132 200 208 224
265 325 329 330 350
Eleazar Jr 295 Elezar 2d
206 Elizabeth 259 301 379
Eunice 221 Experience 132
Hepzibah 200 208 265
Huldah 279 Israel 125
Jabez 265 331 John 157 203
298 356 373 379 John Jr
279 Jonathan 189 Joseph
174 259 301 Mary 88 89 237
265 266 329 356 Mehitable
87 Nancy 206 Nathaniel 94
Oliver 266 Ruth 103 175
Sally 330 Sarah 174 189
208 265 275 330 331 350
Susanna 298
CARY, 239 Abigail 93 268
Alpheus 268 Ann 245 Anne
120 Austin 398 Azubah 205
Barzillai 298 Bethiah 197
Betsy 167 Caleb 37 167 265
Cynthia 316 Cyrus 214
Daniel 121 200 312 Daniel
H 198 Eleazar 248 266 302
327 Eliphalet 36 156 227
Elizabeth 120 168 266 302
336 Ephraim 84 86 95 97
187 188 205 211 212 214
217 221 321 344 Eunice 298
Experience 129 Ezra 188
316 Francis 49 71 80 120
152 182 297 316 335 Hannah
88 120 128 156 166 227 312
321 Harriet 182 Harriet
Frances 297 Henry 128 277
298 Howard 147 184 257
Huldah 95 197 257 Ichabod
166 James 32 49 71 88 109
128 200 290 321 336 394
395 Jane 188 214 John 11
26 27 30 34 35 62-65 93 94
120 128 147 168 171 250
John Jr 34 John Sr 19
Jonathan 34 49 71 78 88 94
115 129 176 189 190 197
207 211 215 245 268 275
300 Joseph 65 82 120 Lois
189 211 Lucius 55 Lucy 90

414

418

426

141 Deborah 262 Desire 307
Elisha 357 Elizabeth 170
360 370 Elizabeth F 122
Ellis 142 185 Ellis Jr 141
Ellis W 214 Ephraim 102
306 324 357 Eunice 102 306
Experience 266 308 Hannah
297 320 385 Hitty 141
Howland 142 317 Huldah 142
Israel 307 John 312 359
364 Josiah 385 Lt 346
Louisa 361 Lucy 142 171
Lydia 357 Margaret 324
Mary 112 124 232 251 359
Mehitabel 141 185 200
Melvill 320 Melzar 191
Mercy 373 Miles 361 Nabby
90 Nathaniel 373 Otis 90
161 Patience 108 Patty 141
Philander 122 Rebecca 110
Rev Mr 309 Roxana 262 Ruth
123 Samuel 124 251 262
Sarah 130 364 367 Susan F
214 Waitstill 116 William
170
HOLT, Richard 34
HOLYOKE, Elizabeth 372
 Samuel 372
HOOK, Sarah 373
HOOKER, 57
HOOPER, 28 Abigail 344
 Abihail 277 Apollos 170
 Azubah 134 Betty 139 302
 Cyrus 144 David 183 292
 Ebenezer 109 Elizabeth 235
 236 253 Hannah 140 143 292
 Hezekiah 37 54 139 140 236
 276 Isaac 232 353 James
 134 204 213 277 354 James
 Jr 328 Jane 144 Jerusha
 223 245 John 74 142 143
 227 230 235 253 273 302
 338 353 Joseph 215 216 234
 244 Joseph Jr 89 Levi 234
 Lois 133 162 Lucia 234 244
 Lucy 183 Luther 162 213
 Lyman 292 Martha 292 Mary
 112 204 210 223 266
 Melatiah 213 Nathaniel 82
 210 233 347 Patience 286
 Polly 315 Rebecca 142
 Relief 109 Roxana 233 Ruth
 118 338 Saba 215 216 Sally
 344 Sarah 102 143 170 227
 230 231 253 273 302 353
 Susanna 8 132 162 213 232
 234 328 354 Thomas 36 48

102 162 223 231 245 253
Vodisa 170 William 82 132
133 315 Winslow 112 223
244 Zilphah 322
HORTON, Betsy 292 Daniel
315 Isaac 262 263 292
Jerusha 262 Mary 263 Sally
261 Sibil 315
HOSKINS, Sarah 151
HOUSE, Mary 337 Rachel 223
 Sarah 368
HOVEY, Hannah 301
HOW, Azor 294 Salome 294
HOWARD, 177 184 Abi 156
 Abiel 53 104 110 123 325
 Abigail 92 103 141 181 201
 207 225 245 256 264 268
 281 296-298 311 334 Adam
 209 Albe 92 Alfred 117 174
 352 Alpheus 313 Amasa 225
 Amelia 299 Amy 283 Ann 239
 344 Anna 143 342 Apollas
 132 Asaph 269 Barnabas 164
 213 256 321 Bathsheba 202
 216 226 Bela 133 147
 Bernice 159 Bethiah 134
 183 217 218 225 Betsy 261
 320 Betty 163 225 298 312
 348 Bezaliel 53 Bulah 208
 Caleb 37 91 263 298 315
 321 Calvin 165 Catharine
 305 Charity 118 272
 Charles 320 Chloe 91 165
 Content 306 Cyrus 156 266
 Damaris 164 344 Daniel 23
 36 37 50 55 133 149 176
 181 219 256 258 344 Darius
 134 David 102 173 219 271
 305 339 342 Dean 269
 Deborah 338 Ebenezer 128
 161 297 Edward 106 127 162
 210 220 225 285 Edwin 138
 Eleanor 183 Eliakim 35 108
 155 248 Elizabeth 125 159
 289 322 Ephraim 103 126
 134 158 203 207 220 225
 272 298 325 344 350
 Ephraim Jr 120 Ethan 264
 Eunice 257 Frances 220
 Francis 53 George 92 103
 110 141 221 225 226 281
 338 George Jr 103 George
 3d 240 Gideon 37 134 350
 Hannah 110 120 143 174 226
 233 238 280 293 Harriet M
 278 Harriot 215 Henry 123
 181 218 258 263 Hepzibah

176 Lurania 157 Mary 381
Mehitabel 231 Mercy 278
Nancy 130 Nathan 197 231
Olive 234 Polly 334 Rachel
114 Samuel 116 Sarah 314
Simeon 329 Susanna 329
JORDAN, Hannah 113 Jedediah
165 Sarah 124 165
JOSLYN, Abraham 186 Deborah
175 Eleazar 232 Eunice 186
220 Henry 244 Joanna 244
Joseph 191 Joseph Jr 175
Rebecca 104
JOY, Jedediah 377 Mary 377
Susan 260 Susanna 255
Susannah 262
JOYCE, Sarah 376

KEEN, Calvin W 251 Celia
244 Charles 124 136 244
Hannah S 340 Hannah Shaw
252 Jane 99 251 Joanna 153
Joseph 164 Josiah 185 252
340 Lemuel 99 245 Libeus
153 Lucretia 136 Margaret
137 Maria 124 Meribah 245
Rhoda 136 164 Samuel 56
137 192 Samuel Jr 136
Tabitha 153
KEITH, Abiah 193 296
Abigail 188 192 230 231
236 275 286 288 289 299
347 Abihail 225 Abner 116
Agatha 125 Agnes 119 Alice
243 328 Ambrose 305 Amos
91 233 Amos Jr 282 Ann 115
318 Ann Maria 288 Anna 86
91 164 299 Anne 218 Arza
220 Asa 133 174 Austin 142
Azel 157 Azuba 136
Barnabas 203 Barzillai 143
Bathsheba 144 195 203 Bela
219 Benjamin 102 112 133
156 231 233 Benjamin
Hayward 171 Bethiah 100
112 159 219 232 246 282
310 Betsy 293 299 338
Betty 98 136 174 293 Caleb
182 245 Calvin 91 118 175
310 Caroline 246
Cassandana 233 Catharine
305 Charity 121 218
Charles 268 Charlotte 228
Chloe 162 255 344 Clarissa
279 Constant 181 232
Cynthia 292 Daniel 138 139
190 216 286 293 309 328

Dardana 279 David 121 141
218 221 336 David Jr 89
David 3d 344 Davis 199
Deborah 137 237 292
Dulcinia 150 Ebenezer 92
95 130 161 233 265 272 311
Edward 181 239 Edwin 190
Eleazar 113 133 142 217
219 224 243 246 288
Eleazar Jr 245 Eleazer 113
Eliab 354 Eliza 226
Elizabeth 138 159 163 225
243 286 Ephraim 53 55 130
266 325 Eunice 116 230 233
234 George 137 163 Hampden
112 Hannah 95 100 101 137
159 170 183 203 231 232
274 296 297 323 Harriot
199 Hartwell 113 199 226
Hazadiah 182 232 Heman 144
Hepsibah 92 Hepzibah 130
233 265 Hiram 343 Holman
247 274 Howe 183 Huldah
113 Ichabod 287 Isaac 117
137 144 164 165 277 331
353 Isaiah 126 Israel 45
136 174 236 Jacob 230 286
Jairus S 398 James 11 26
31 34 43 45 75 115 134 151
188 192 202 218 258 269
299 338 344 354 372 James
Jr 243 338 Jane 134 143
247 330 Jemima 159 254 268
336 Jennet 281 Jeremiah
125 Jeremiah Jr 279 Joanna
116 117 277 John 76 81 115
231 243 277 281 323 328
347 348 John Q 201 Jonas H
240 Jonathan 55 164 203
232 297 Joseph 36 75 86 93
98 108 132 158 159 192 218
225 254 255 286 293 305
318 338 353 398 Josiah 87
117 224 264 352 Josiah Jr
344 Julia 367 Keziah 108
151 174 175 217 354
Lavinia 343 Lemuel 225
Levi 159 197 268 282 342
Levi 3d 275 Lewis 136 Lois
133 195 Lucia 171 288
Lucinda 315 Lucy 142 311
Luke 239 Lurany 143 Luther
314 Lydia 89 165 202 216
269 Marcia 220 Margaret
288 Marshall 233 Martha 91
117 133 183 239 305 Martin
115 Mary 112 113 148 190

NOWELL, Increase 18
NOYES, Alva 305 Daniel 55
David 251 Ebenezer 167 280
Eliab 341 Elizabeth 280
Ephraim 105 146 304 Hannah
279 341 Jacob 156 John 121
Joseph 175 Lydia 251 332
Mary 158 341 Mercy 175
Milicent 250 Moses 341
Olive 156 Polly 123
Rebecca 105 Samuel 158 250
279 332 Sarah 146 249 304
Sophronia 305 Susanna 167
Sybil 274 Zibia 121
NUTTER, Holbrook 207
Margaret 207
NYE, Hannah 228 Nathan 228
Ruth 333

OAKES, Charlotte 104 Hannah
105 Nathan 104 Urian 105
OLDHAM, David 239 Deborah
239
ORBERTON, Mary 318
ORCUT, Mercy 94 Moses 94
Sarah 96
ORCUTT, Alpheus 279
Benjamin 241 Caleb 174
Charity 282 Daniel 113 205
339 David 253 Deborah 276
Deliverance 217 264 326
Desire 217 Ebenezer 217
Elizabeth 165 Eunice 343
Experience 327 Galen 351
Goodman 66 Hannah 165 329
Huldah 236 Ichabod 83 332
Ichabod Jr 145 Jane 202
321 322 Jerusha 170 Joanna
152 325 John 185 217 John
Jr 170 Jonathan 132 327
Joseph 236 276 329 Josiah
136 Leonard 282 Lucy 113
Lydia 249 Marah 236 Martha
327 Mary 189 201 Mehitabel
174 Mercy 279 333
Millicent 249 Nancy 351
Naomi 136 Nathan 156 202
296 Nathan Jr 343
Nathaniel 165 236 Olive
205 339 Sally 244 Sarah
170 235 241 Susanna 145
151 154 156 253 296 325
Thankful 132 William 32 34
48 65 75 79 152 165 201
235 401 William Jr 264 321
322 326 327
ORNE, Lucinda 199 Lucy 199

Samuel 199 William Wetmore
199
ORR, 132 Bathsheba 202
Bethiah 137 David 287
Hannah 187 206 217 Hector
37 54 106 Hugh 36 37 58 99
111 129 137 202 203 206
244 245 252 288 340 354
Hugh Jr 206 332 Jane 206
Jennet 244 355 Margaret
288 Mary 106 111 287 340
Mr 59 Robert 187 217
Silvia 245 288 Susanna 252
OSBORN, Absalom 191 Clarana
C 156 Deborah 202 Hannah
320 Lydia 191 Peleg 273
Sally 273 Thomas 320
ORBOURNE, Levi 175 Patience
90 Sophia 175
OSSAMEQUIN (Indian) 12 16
20 22
OSSEMEQUIN (Indian) 391
OTIS, Abigail 319 371
Bethiah 201 Clarissa 319
Cushing 367 371 Deborah
142 Elizabeth 381 Isaac
111 201 James 367 John 381
Josiah 251 319 Lucy 136
367 Mehitabel 111 Melvill
342 Sophia 342 Stephen 142
Susanna 251
OTWAY, William 12
OUSAMEQUIN (Indian) 11 12
307
OVERING, J 398
OVEROCKER, Sarah H 229 247
OWEN, Abigail 165 Daniel
208 Jane 208 Mary 151 206
Terry 151

PACKARD, 28 119 143 274 393
Abel 275 Abi 221 Abia 121
200 Abiah 156 268 Abiah Jr
165 Abiel 50 83 100 255
298 Abigail 107 145 149
196 198 199 254 268 275
298 Abijah 160 Abraham 151
Aden 191 Adin 137 272
Aholibama 144 Almira 315
Amy 164 Anna 275 304 313
Anne 154 160 269 Apollos
121 Arza 221 Asa 55 234
Austin 55 Azor 198
Barnabas 163 Benjamin 162
231 272 Bethiah 109 Betsy
144 198 269 Betty 152 301
Caleb 196 239 Charity 126

438

Charles 314 Charlotte 314
Chloe 210 298 321 350
Clara A 146 Clarissa 202
Content 114 217 305
Cynthia 136 Cyrus 219
Daniel 75 95 139 148 172
214 250 269 287 291 David
50 100 112 121 159 202 218
268 283 315 David Jr 283
Davis 163 Deborah 107 189
244 313 323 Deliverance
249 323 326 Desire 326
Dorothy 112 268 284
Ebenezer 203 268 272 282
305 Edward 169 Eliab Jr
292 Elijah 53 103 114 149
162 287 Eliphalet 109 145
298 313 Elizabeth 91 130
151 189 224 283 Ens 67 72
Ephraim 234 Esther 275
Eunice 121 200 203 Eve 287
Experience 255 Faithful
318 Freelove 151 249 Galen
191 George 136 152 225 241
254 Hannah 100 108 121 153
156 219 268 269 282 292
312 Harmony 219 Hepzibah
248 Hezekiah 55 169 Hosea
189 Huldah 134 Ichabod 95
135 137 Isaac 124 196 275
Israel 62 100 102 156 158
328 333 398 Israel Jr 158
Jacob 107 219 268 299 313
Jacob 3d 164 Jael 294
James 50 79 136 155 207
217 238 269 287 Jane 218
Jemima 136 155 207 271
Jerusha 191 Joanna 96 155
176 202 Job 153 319 Joel
219 John 40 50 66 73 81
147 164 189 275 305 397
Jonas 101 121 Jonathan 50
177 268 296 297 344 Joseph
79 81 82 96 97 189 204 205
243 347 348 Joshua 87
Joshua Jr 174 Josiah 100
117 121 219 269 304 Josiah
Jr 269 Judith 348 Julia
201 Kezia 103 238 Keziah
219 269 272 287 319 Laura
124 Lemuel 132 Levi 55 219
304 Lewis 144 Libeus 92
Lois 234 Louisa 350
Lucinda 101 113 Lucy 155
164 202 203 Luke 113
Lurania 272 Lydia 109 147
154 202 225 305 Marcus 164

Margaret 324 Mark 91 292
Martha 87 108 139 148 155
174 194 238 268 269 282
344 Mary 89 95 141 149 152
154 172 182 191 194 198
236 241 268 282 283 288
295 328 332 347 Matilda
168 169 Matthew 269 Mayhew
202 Mehitabel 87 100 104
121 162 195 283 333 Mercy
86 125 163 321 333 Micah
343 Minerva 92 Molly 121
287 Nahum 163 Nancy 198
214 Nathan 73 146 198 202
226 240 268 Nathaniel 31
71 189 217 236 244 301 318
324 Nehemiah 116 148 152
236 298 Olive 146 163 292
315 Oliver 149 155
Parmenas 282 313 Parnel
205 Patty 103 159 164
Perez 283 Phebe 121 219
Philibert 313 Phillip 155
Polly 162 165 234 240 299
Rachel 135 137 Rebecca 136
164 219 269 271 299 402
Rebeckah 169 221 284
Relief 155 Reuben 269
Robert 103 109 154 183 198
269 292 305 Roland 151
Roxana 189 Ruth 95 102 109
158 231 304 305 Sally 132
191 269 282 Salmon 249
Samuel 30-32 34 35 62 65
82 91 109 126 130 151 154
189 210 220 294 323 328
332 354 Samuel Jr 39 81
224 295 Sarah 100 105 137
152 163 165 183 189 192
196 204 224 226 239 268
273 283 291 298 301 310
311 Seth 89 125 137 155
195 Seth Jr 234 Sidney 315
Silas 321 350 Silas Jr 350
Silence 116 148 152 198
236 Simeon 134 153 163 238
268 Solomon 50 87 96 108
136 156 157 165 217 224
268 310 Solomon Sr 108
Sophia 121 Sullivan 203
Susanna 87 91 96 97 114
117 137 156 158 177 217
220 221 234 240 243 250
268 284 295 296 297 313
316 343 Thomas 155 194 198
269 287 Timothy 105 144
William 164 168 282 283

442

Josiah 213 Judith B 352
Keziah 90 Lavinia 274 352
Leonard 236 Lois 165 Lot
90 Lovicey 124 Lucinda 141
Lucy 135 314 Lusanna 246
Lydia 123 135 191 238 241
306 344 Margene 235
Margery 317 Martha 128 133
237 318 347 Mary 113 119
133 147 173 208 209 266
267 280 313 327 332 333
335 Matilda 96 Mehitabel
164 165 279 Mercy 251
Micah 173 Molly 185 317
Nabby 271 341 Nancy 140
Naomi 213 320 Nathan 116
165 Nathaniel 95 138 140
202 247 255 301 311 314
327 333 Nehemiah 116 285
Noah 137 Olive 176 269
Oliver 163 240 Patience
144 Peddy 89 Phebe 236
Philip 123 Polly 90 188
213 Rebecca 97 163 Ruhama
164 Sally 144 213 273
Salome 285 Samuel 80 127
164 279 343 369 Sarah 95
118 135 171 204 217 264
265 272 301 302 311 350
Seth 54 117 139 141 215
301 326 Sibil 150 Sile 272
Silence 248 Silvanus 89
274 Simeon 171 350 Solomon
140 182 190 204 208 209
265-267 Susanna 213 240
272 283 284 313 Tabitha
181 Thomas 96 119 150 313
Waitstill 325 William 121
213 342 Zebedee 209
Zebulun K 213
PRAY, Dorothy 312 Hannah
312 Rachel 158
PREBBLE, Commodore 196
PRICE, Benjamin 138 164 179
273 276 331 Betty 304
Hannah 273 Mehitabel 164
276 Ruth 331 Sarah 138
Silence 179
PRINCE, 18 Elizabeth 100
229 Joanna 382 John 100
229 Joseph 382 Judith 387
Martha 106 Mary 257 366
Patience 361 Ruth 230
Samuel 106 Sarah 361
Thomas 229 346 361 366 387
PRIOR, 280 Ann 248 Eliphaz
179 Hannah 179 John 179

248 Joseph 112 170 223 248
Mary 145 170 223 242
Nathaniel 145 Sarah 112
179 248
PROCTOR, Bathsheba 157
PRYOR, Ann 96 Bethiah 94
204 389 Hannah 271 John 94
204 271 Joseph 96 160
Sarah 160
PYNCHON, Edward 104 Susan
104 William 273

QUIN, Lydia 321
QUINCY, Ann 188 Daniel 401
Edmund 46 376 Joanna 376
John 48 188 401

RADSFORD, 280
RAINSFORD, Harriet Amanda
97 Jonathan 375 Mary 375
RAMSDELL, 95 219 Amy 149
Bethiah A 287 Betsey 99
Betsy 249 Betty 316
Charles 316 Daniel 249
Eliza 99 Hannah 99 John 99
Joseph 123 281 Levi 149
Lot 167 Lucinda 167 Lydia
123 Martin 99 287 Mary 278
Mary Pratt 333 Mehitabel
343 Nabby 123 Nathaniel
205 278 333 Noah 99 343
Polly 281 Sally 205 Sarah
334
RAMSDEN, 280
RANDALL, 146 Abigail 96 195
Amy 272 Apollos 148 150
Asa 137 Benjamin 303 337
Bethiah 148 150 192
Cynthia 112 Experience 347
Hannah 137 149 253 Israel
346 Jemima 96 John 347
Jonathan 96 192 Joseph Jr
146 Lucy 129 303 Mary 107
156 215 235 272 346 353
Matthew 260 Mercy 119 341
Phebe 129 Polly 228
Rebecca 139 Robert 139 272
Roxana 259 Sabina 146
Sally 260 Samuel 259 Sarah
A 337 Silence 137 Thomas
68 253 William 228 Zervia
317
RATHBURN, Hannah 179 Mr 51
RAWSON, Edmund 177
Elizabeth 177 John 285
Martha 285
RAYMOND, 219 Rev Mr 52

448

456